MW00414075

PUTIN'S WAR ON UKRAINE

SAMUEL RAMANI

Putin's War on Ukraine

Russia's Campaign for
Global Counter-Revolution

HURST & COMPANY, LONDON

First published in the United Kingdom in 2023 by
C. Hurst & Co. (Publishers) Ltd.,
New Wing, Somerset House, Strand, London, WC2R 1LA
© Samuel Ramani, 2023
All rights reserved.
Printed and bound in Great Britain by Bell and Bain Ltd, Glasgow

Distributed in the United States, Canada and Latin America by
Oxford University Press, 198 Madison Avenue, New York, NY 10016,
United States of America.

The right of Samuel Ramani to be identified as the author of
this publication is asserted by him in accordance with the
Copyright, Designs and Patents Act, 1988.

A Cataloguing-in-Publication data record for this book
is available from the British Library.

ISBN: 9781787388512

This book is printed using paper from registered sustainable
and managed sources.

www.hurstpublishers.com

CONTENTS

1

PUTIN'S WAR ON UKRAINE

AN OPPORTUNISTIC
COUNTER-REVOLUTIONARY GAMBIT

On 24 February 2022, Russian president Vladimir Putin announced the start of a special military operation aimed at the "demilitarisation and denazification" of Ukraine.[1] Putin's speech, which was broadcast at 5.30 am Moscow Time, followed a four-month-long build-up of over 100,000 Russian troops on the Ukrainian border and occurred three days after Russia recognised the Donetsk and Luhansk People's Republics as independent countries. Within minutes of Putin's address, Russia carried out missile and bomb attacks on Kyiv, Kharkiv, Odesa and Donbas, and instigated the most serious European security crisis since the Second World War. Russia initially expected to achieve a rapid victory in Ukraine, which would result in the overthrow of president Volodymyr Zelensky and the installation of a pro-Kremlin puppet regime. However, Russia's grandiose ambitions were thwarted by the Ukrainian military's stoic resilience, a steady influx of Soviet-era and NATO-standard weaponry to Ukraine and a slew of logistical and strategic mishaps. One year after its invasion, Russia's military successes were confined to Luhansk, Mariupol, and parts of Kherson and Zaporizhzhia, and its regime change ambitions in Kyiv were decisively thwarted. Moreover, the imposition of sweeping Western sanctions on Russia had imperilled its great power status aspirations and encouraged Putin to embrace increasingly totalitarian and isolationist tactics to maintain his hold on power.

This book will examine Putin's decision to invade Ukraine and the implications of the Ukraine War for Russia's political future and long-term geopolitical influence. Throughout its duration, it will seek to address three crucial questions: Why did Russia opt for a sweeping regime change mission instead of a far less risky and more eminently achievable Donbas offensive? How did Vladimir Putin's regime survive the combined headwinds of sanctions, military setbacks and war fatigue? And what will Russia's post-Ukraine War political system and foreign policy look like? By proposing answers to these questions, this book will ascertain whether Russia's invasion of Ukraine is a one-off gambit driven by Putin's ambitions, insecurities and world view, or the starting point for an increasingly brazenly revisionist Russian foreign policy. As the Ukraine War has increased the risk of a direct Russia–NATO confrontation and a third world war, examining the sources and implications of Russia's invasion of Ukraine is critically important for academics and policymakers. This chapter will provide a perfunctory layout of this book's principal hypotheses and approaches to its three defining questions, which will provide context for its in-depth examination of the Ukraine War and Russia's future as a great power.

Explaining Russia's Decision to Carry Out a Full-Scale Invasion of Ukraine

Although a full-scale Russian invasion of Ukraine was a scenario that was widely discussed after Russia's February 2014 annexation of Crimea and during the spring 2021 military build-up, it departed markedly from Russia's more restrained approach to military interventions in the post-1991 period. Throughout the 1990s, Russia contributed to the creation of frozen conflicts in Georgia and Moldova and intervened in the disputed Armenia– Azerbaijan border region of Nagorno-Karabakh and Tajikistan under the guise of "peacekeeping missions". The main aim of these missions was not territorial annexation but to prevent the spillover of conflicts in the post-Soviet space.[2] During the 2008 Georgian War, Russia opted for a limited military campaign in the breakaway region of South Ossetia and the Kremlin's antipathy towards Mikheil Saakashvili did not result in a regime change in Tbilisi. Despite significant territorial gains in Crimea and Donbas, Russia did not officially acknowledge its military involvement in Ukraine from 2014–15 and instead used the euphemism "polite people" to describe the soldiers that annexed Crimea. Throughout the first Ukraine invasion and subsequent post-2015 campaign in Syria, Moscow relied heavily on local proxies to advance its aims. By ordering troops into Donbas for "peacekeeping duties" and announcing a "special military operation" rather than a war, Putin continued the Kremlin's longstanding trend of using euphemistic language. However, the scale of Russia's invasion of Ukraine is unprecedented in modern history and, in terms of human costs, is Moscow's largest military intervention in the post-1945 period. Russian foreign minister Sergei Lavrov's claims that Russia would help Ukrainians "liberate themselves from the burden of this absolutely unacceptable regime"[3] constituted Moscow's first overt regime change mission since the 1968 Soviet invasion of Czechoslovakia.

Russia's official justifications for invading Ukraine do not withstand empirical scrutiny and provide little context for the scale of the current war.[4] The official trigger for the war was the Donetsk and Luhansk People's Republics' request for Russian military assistance against Ukraine. This was a legal provision permitted by the 22 February Treaties of Friendship, Cooperation and Mutual Assistance with the Donbas republics and, due to the presence of Russian citizens, was allowable under the self-defence clause in Article 51 of Part 7 of the UN Charter. While Putin ruled out the occupation of Ukraine, he called for its demilitarisation, which was widely interpreted as the destruction of its armed forces, naval and air force capabilities. Despite eight years of war in Donbas, there was no evidence of a humanitarian crisis of the scale to warrant a nationwide invasion. The 14,000-casualty figure oft-cited by Russian officials refers to deaths by all parties over an eight-year time horizon and the UN's International Court of Justice (ICJ) ruled on 16 March that there was no evidence that Ukraine was carrying out genocide against Russian speakers in Donbas.[5] Putin's claims that Ukraine was "anti-Russia", that it had been "placed under full external control, intensively settled by the armed forces of NATO countries and supplied with the most modern weapons", were similarly misleading; Ukraine's NATO membership aspirations stalled after the 2008 Bucharest summit and the most consequential post-2014 arms shipments to Ukraine were suited for territorial self-defence. Putin's claims about the transnational threat of "Ukrainian Nazism," Ukraine's hosting of U.S. biological weapons laboratories and Ukraine's alleged chemical and nuclear weapons programmes were also riddled with disinformation.

Due to the implausibility of Russia's official justifications for war with Ukraine, two alternative explanations have circulated widely in academic, media and think tank publications. The first explanation attributes Russia's aggression to rising insecurity about NATO's expansion towards its borders. This insecurity hypothesis partially aligns with Kremlin discourse but depicts NATO expansion as a long-term risk to Russia's influence and security rather than the imminent threat that Putin invoked to justify the war. University of Chicago Professor John Mearsheimer contends that a succession of events, such as the 2008 Bucharest summit, the U.S.'s December 2017 export of defensive weapons to Ukraine and the July 2021 U.S.-Ukraine naval drills on the Black Sea, made Ukraine a de facto NATO member and encouraged Russia's invasion.[6] Mearsheimer's contentions mirrored his explanation of Russia's 2014 military intervention in Ukraine, which highlighted successive rounds of NATO expansion after 1999, the EU's eastward expansion and support for democracy in Ukraine, and the risk that Crimea would host a NATO naval base.[7] There is evidence that Russia viewed Ukraine's integration with NATO as a threat so profound that it would warrant the use of military force. In October 2021, Putin stated that even if Ukraine did not formally join NATO, the deployment of NATO military infrastructure "really creates a threat to the Russian Federation."[8] In December 2021, Lavrov stated that the emergence of NATO strike missile systems on the Russia–Ukraine border would provoke "serious military risks for all parties involved, up to a large-scale conflict in Europe."[9]

Despite this strident rhetoric, three factors suggest that Russia exaggerated the NATO threat emanating from Ukraine and used it as a pretext for a full-scale invasion. First, there were no discernible indications that Ukraine was moving closer to integration with NATO in the months leading up to the war. In June 2021, U.S. president Joe Biden contradicted Zelensky's assertions that Ukraine was on a definitive path to NATO accession and insisted that Ukraine needed anti-corruption reforms to obtain membership.[10] In February 2022, German chancellor Olaf Scholz stated that "all parties know that Ukraine's NATO membership is not on the agenda."[11] Second, Russia's narratives about Ukrainian NATO membership and NATO's threat to its security had fluctuated considerably over time. Anti-NATO sentiments spiked in 1999 due to the Kosovo War but ebbed con-

siderably in the early 2000s. During a May 2002 press conference with Ukrainian president Leonid Kuchma, Putin said the
following on Ukraine's NATO membership ambitions: "The
decision is to be taken by NATO and Ukraine. It is a matter for
those two partners."[12] It was pro-Western president Viktor
Yushchenko's ascension to power in 2005 that catalysed Russia's
militant opposition to Ukraine's NATO accession; in June 2006,
Russia warned of "very negative consequences" for Russia–
Ukraine relations if Ukraine joined NATO, which was significantly harsher than Lavrov's prior claims it would lead to a
"colossal geopolitical shift."[13] This suggests that Russia tends to
use the NATO threat as a pretext to undermine Ukrainian sovereignty when its relations with the Kyiv authorities become
tense. Third, if Russia failed to occupy Kyiv, historical precedents
suggested that Ukraine's pro-Western pivot would drastically
sharpen. While only a plurality of Ukrainians supported EU
membership and a minority backed NATO membership in early
2014, support for accession to both organisations was consistently in majority territory after Russia's military interventions in
Crimea and Donbas. These surveys translated into votes in the
October 2014 parliamentary elections, and president Petro
Poroshenko claimed that over 75% of voters supported Ukraine's
"Course Towards Europe" in these elections.[14]

The second explanation is Putin-centric, as it links the
Ukraine War to Putin's regime insecurity and power retention
ambitions. In the Western media, Putin's insecurity has often
been attributed to irrationality. Although Central Intelligence
Agency (CIA) Director William Burns has said there is no evidence that Putin is in ill health, speculation that he has a terminal illness or is suffering psychological after-effects from the
COVID-19 pandemic have created a narrative that Putin's para-
noia drove him to war.[15] Academics have focused on Putin's
assessment of his regime's structural vulnerabilities, which are

apparent even though his approval rating has never fallen below 50%. U.S. Military Academy Professor Robert Person, who predicted in an October 2015 article for *The Washington Post* that Russia's end goal in Ukraine was regime change, believes that Putin's authoritarian consolidation ambitions and hostility towards Ukraine's post-Maidan government is driven by his perceived vulnerability.[16] In his 2021 book *Weak Strongman*, Columbia University Professor Timothy Frye contends that Putin's regime has structural weaknesses, as Putin needs to pursue conflicting goals to assuage his inner circle and retain his popularity.[17] The outbreak of mass protests in Belarus over president Alexander Lukashenko's alleged perpetration of voter fraud in the 2020 presidential elections and unrest in Kazakhstan in January 2022 heightened Putin's sensitivity to these weaknesses. As COVID-19 and sluggish economic growth prevented Putin from delivering on the domestic promises that undergirded his re-election to a fourth term in 2018, the Ukraine War could be regarded as a gambit to rally Russians around the flag. The surge in approval ratings that Putin experienced from the Crimea annexation to the 2018 pension reform protests provided a precedent for this contention.

Although Putin has leveraged military interventions to strengthen his hold on power, regime insecurity-premised explanations can be challenged by two factors. First, there was a considerable risk that Russia's invasion of Ukraine would have domestic blowback, as military interventions of this scale have historically been unpopular in Russia. Frye notes that in May 2014, only 31% of Russians supported providing direct military assistance to pro-Russian separatists in Donbas, and the long-term retention of troops in Syria was popular within the security services and firms in import-competing sectors but unpopular amongst the general public.[18] Russian liberals such as dissident oligarch Mikhail Khodorkovsky have viewed a large-scale military conflict as a miscalculation that could lead to Putin's demise.[19] The enduring popularity of the Ukraine War might therefore be an unexpected consequence of effective state propaganda rather than an inevitability that could have been predicted beforehand.

Second, there is little evidence that Putin viewed his regime as especially insecure in early 2022. Despite a Communist Party of the Russian Federation (CPRF) challenge to the Moscow election results and the detention of a hundred protesters against electoral fraud, the September 2021 Russian State Duma elections reaffirmed the dominance of the Putin-aligned United Russia Party. This contrasted with the 2014 annexation of Crimea, which occurred at a time when Putin's popularity had fallen to an all-time low and Viktor Yanukovych, a president with similar kleptocratic ambitions to Putin, had been overthrown by street protests in neighbouring Ukraine. Therefore, there was no imperative for Putin to drastically escalate repression in Russia, and the totalitarian policies implemented after the Ukraine invasion were most likely not necessary for the survival of his regime.

This book's explanation for the Ukraine War departs from these hypotheses and focuses on the aspirational rather than insecurity-premised drivers of the war. The primary motivation for Putin's invasion of Ukraine was to overturn the 2014 Euro-Maidan revolution and its outcomes. Putin's counter-revolutionary agenda stemmed from his desire to reassert Russia's hegemony over Ukraine and promote his brand of illiberalism within the post-Soviet space. These objectives reinforced two key components of Russia's national identity under Vladimir Putin: great power status and Russia's role as a challenger to the U.S.-led liberal international order. The timing of Russia's military intervention can be explained by Putin's overestimation of Russian military capabilities, his underestimation of Ukraine's resistance and ability to procure Western support, and his calculation that the international community would not severely punish Russian aggression. Russia's invasion of Ukraine is an opportunistic counter-revolutionary gambit that has resoundingly failed in its early stages but remains a potential legacy-defining mission for Vladimir Putin.

Russia's Support for Counter-Revolution in Ukraine

After the dissolution of the Soviet Union in December 1991, Russian foreign policy was marred by an acute identity crisis. The academic Peter Duncan contended that this identity crisis revolved around three principal divisions. The first was the centuries-old question of whether Russia is part of the collective West or the East; the second was what the legitimate boundaries of Russia are; and the third was whether Russian nationalism is civic, ethnic and imperial.[20] The lack of consensus around these questions bred factionalism. Associate Professor of National Security at the Monterey Naval Postgraduate School Anne Clunan contended that five "national self-images" emerged in transition-era Russia, which were championed by political rivals.[21] The "Western" self-image valued democracy and free markets; the "statist" self-image valued a centralised governance model with hegemony in the post-Soviet space; the "national restorationist" self-image embraced a restoration of the Soviet Union through coercion and military force; the "Neo-Communist" self-image championed a soft power-driven consolidation of Russia's sphere of influence; and the "Slavophile" self-image highlighted Russia's leadership in the Eastern Slavic world.

During the early 2000s, Vladimir Putin sought to unite these factions under his leadership by creating a centralised power vertical, vigorously pursuing cooperation with the West, suppressing Chechnya's insurgency through force and using co-option to extend Russia's military presence in the post-Soviet space. This strategy, which the academic Andrei Tsygankov calls "pragmatic cooperation," was unsuccessful.[22] The arrest of Mikhail Khodorkovsky and Putin's disdain for U.S. unilateralism alienated pro-Western politicians, and developments such as the expansion of U.S. influence in Central Asia and Ukraine's engagement with the West alienated Russia's remaining factions. The colour revolutions, which caused regime changes in Serbia, Georgia, Ukraine and Kyrgyzstan in the early 2000s and threatened the stability of authoritarian regimes elsewhere in Eurasia, provided Putin with an opportunity to create a new coalition around counter-revolution. Russia's reactionary policy towards popular revolutions underscored its status as an illiberal state that embraced an alternative form of democracy or outright authoritarianism, championed conservative values, built ideational coalitions with non-Western powers, and regarded itself as both a regional hegemon and global great power. This policy resonated across generational, socioeconomic and regional boundaries, and Putin justified his repression of liberals by linking them to revolutions that supported anti-Russian or non-traditional values.

The far-reaching appeal of counter-revolution within Russia stemmed from its historical legitimacy. Russia's framings of popular revolutions and social unrest at home and abroad have been remarkably consistent for two centuries. During Tsar Alexander I's reign from 1801 to 1825, Russia resolutely defended monarchical authoritarianism, Christendom and great power politics in Europe against revolutionary movements, which espoused revanchism, nationalism and secularism, on values-based grounds. Russia's war with Napoleon Bonaparte, who espoused these revolutionary values, saw it align with reactionary monarchies, such as Prussia and Austria, and earned Alexander I the title "the Policeman of Europe." Although the Soviet Union was formed through the 1917 Bolshevik Revolution and championed national liberation movements against European colonialism, it embraced a hardline counter-revolutionary agenda in the Warsaw Pact. The

1953 protests in East Germany, which originated as a construction worker strike and transitioned into a nationwide resistance movement against "Sovietisation," underscored the Soviet Union's commitment to counter-revolution. Nikita Khrushchev's allies within the Communist Party of the Soviet Union (CPSU) delegitimised these protesters as Nazis and stooges of Western imperialism,[23] which resembled Putin's rhetoric ahead of the 2014 and 2022 invasions of Ukraine. Khrushchev used counter-revolution to repress internal dissent, as he painted minister of internal affairs Lavrentiy Beria as willing to surrender East Germany to Western imperialism. This eased the path to Beria's ouster in June 1953 and execution six months later.

The Soviet Union's use of counter-revolution as a tool to limit the sovereignty of satellite states extended to the 1956 Hungarian Revolution and 1968 Prague Spring in Czechoslovakia. The Soviet Union's justification for military interventions in Hungary and Czechoslovakia also closely resembled Putin's case for war with Ukraine. Ahead of its November 1956 military intervention in Hungary, which replaced prime minister Imre Nagy with hardline communist János Kádár, *Pravda* editorials labelled Nagy's supporters as "fascist" and "Hitlerite."[24] The Soviet media framed its military intervention as a noble effort to rescue the Hungarian people from a "revisionist" fringe group around Nagy and claimed that Hungarian workers and peasants would greet invading Soviet forces as liberators.[25] Similarly, General Secretary of the CPSU Leonid Brezhnev framed the 1968 Prague Spring as a transnational contagion that could only be defeated through a Soviet military intervention. This rhetoric echoes in Putin's threat narratives about the colour revolutions. Brezhnev contended that First Secretary of Czechoslovakia Alexander Dubček's rhetoric inspired intellectuals and students in Soviet Ukraine and accused the U.S. and China of supporting the demonstrators. Brezhnev also solicited support from Warsaw Pact allies, such as East Germany's Walter Ulbricht and Poland's Wladyslaw Gomulka, who warned that "hostile elements" in Czechoslovakia were encouraging "saboteurs" in the Eastern Bloc.[26]

Despite Russia's transition to democracy in the early 1990s, the Kremlin's time-tested suspicion of mass protests endured. As the October 1993 constitutional crisis intensified, president Boris Yeltsin accused "communist revanchists and fascist leaders" of staging a pre-planned armed rebellion and prime minister Yegor Gaidar warned that successful unrest would turn Russia into a "huge concentration camp."[27] Although Russia reluctantly acquiesced to the 2000 Bulldozer Revolution in Serbia, which overthrew Slobodan Milošević, and the 2003 Rose Revolution in Georgia, which toppled Eduard Shevardnadze, it stridently opposed the 2004 Orange Revolution in Ukraine. During the mid-2000s, Russia deepened cooperation with authoritarian treaty allies in the Collective Security Treaty Organization (CSTO), such as Belarus and Kazakhstan, and security partners in the Shanghai Cooperation Organization (SCO) against the threat of colour revolutions in Eurasia. Russia embraced a policy of global counter-revolution during the 2011 Arab Spring, which saw it stridently condemn the October 2011 assassination of Libyan dictator Muammar al-Gaddafi and militarily intervene on Syrian president Bashar al-Assad's behalf in September 2015. Russia's 2014 and 2022 invasions of Ukraine firmly align with Putin's counter-revolutionary agenda and add a territorial annexation dimension to other Russian interventions against mass protests, such as the deployment of Wagner Group private military contractors (PMCs) to Sudan in 2018–19 and Belarus in 2020, and the 2022 CSTO intervention in Kazakhstan.

Russia's Invasion of Ukraine: An Opportunistic Gambit for Hegemony?

Since Ukraine became independent in August 1991, Russia has utilised a diverse array of tactics to preserve its hegemony over the country and prevent it from irrevocably pivoting towards the West. Economic coercion has been a central component of Russia's toolkit, as Moscow sought to deter Ukraine's membership in the European Union (EU) and ensure that it would become a core member of the Eurasian Economic Union (EAEU) instead. During the 1990s, Russia used its dominant role as an energy exporter to keep Ukraine in its sphere of influence; Gazprom's strategic sales of discounted Russian gas to Ukrainian oligarchs caused some of Ukraine's wealthiest individuals to support pro-Russian politicians, such as former president Viktor Yanukovych, prime minister Pavel Lazarenko and energy minister Yuriy Boyko.[28] Russia used the tactical suspension of gas exports to Ukraine from 1992 to 1994 and accompanying debt forgiveness offers to secure long-term access to the Black Sea Fleet but Kyiv rejected deals of this nature and blocked privatisations of energy assets that would benefit Russia. The 2005–6 natural gas crisis, which saw Russia cut pipeline supply to Ukraine and disrupt gas exports to Europe, underscored its desire to use rapid gas price increases as a coercive tactic and highlight the economic costs of Ukrainian president Viktor Yushchenko's pro-Western stance. Russia's threats of trade sanctions, which would immediately result in the losses of hundreds of thousands of jobs, convinced Yanukovych to abandon the EU Association Agreement in November 2013.

As economic coercion failed to reorient Ukrainian foreign policy towards Russia, the Kremlin repeatedly undermined Ukrainian sovereignty through political interference and a small-scale military intervention. Initially, Russia relied on soft power to advance its goals, as 81% of eastern Ukrainians identified as Russian speakers and supported closer integration with Moscow.[29] Leonid Kuchma's mobilisation of over 75% of the eastern Ukrainian vote resulted in his victory in the 1994 presidential elections, which eventually resulted in his signing in May 1997 of both a Ukraine–Russia Friendship Treaty and a twenty-year lease of Sevastopol to Russia's Black Sea Fleet. Kuchma's refusal to pursue an unequivocally pro-Russian foreign policy agenda, which was exemplified by his 2002 support for an EU association agreement and participation in the 2003 Iraq War, revealed the limits of relying on soft power. During the 2004 presidential elections, Russia overtly co-opted Yanukovych and tried to delegitimise Yushchenko as U.S. and Poland-backed, and allegedly engaged in malign tactics such as dispatching political technologists, fomenting Galician separatism and participating in Yushchenko's dioxin poisoning.[30]

After the Orange Revolution, Russia continued to assist Yanukovych's political ambitions and Putin's United Russia Party signed a cooperation agreement with Yanukovych's Party of Regions in 2005. While Yanukovych's triumph in the 2010 presidential elections was followed by a succession of compromises to Russia, such as support for Ukraine's neutrality and the extension of Russia's lease of Crimea's Black Sea facilities until 2042, his overthrow left Russia without a partner in Ukraine. Russia subsequently prosecuted a military intervention in Crimea and Donbas in order to create a Georgia-style frozen conflict that would preclude NATO membership. This limited military intervention did not change the course of Ukrainian foreign policy, as Ukraine repealed its neutral non-bloc status in December 2014 and constitutionally enshrined EU and NATO membership as a strategic goal in February 2019. The collapse of Russian soft power in Ukraine, which was illustrated by opinion surveys showing less than 20% of Ukrainians with positive views of Russia[31] and the inability of the pro-Russian Opposition Bloc—Party for Peace and Development to challenge for power, restricted Moscow's non-military options. As a result, Russia's efforts to undermine Ukraine's foreign policy independence pivoted from "deterrence" to "compellence,"[32] and the Kremlin saw a regime change through invasion as a low-cost expedient path to durable influence over Ukraine.

Due to Russia's repeated assurances that it was not planning to invade Ukraine, there is limited open source information on the Kremlin's assumptions about its prospects of success. Historical experience, such as the Soviet Union's protracted post-Second World War struggle against the Ukrainian Insurgent Army and Russia's failure to annex cities like Mariupol, Zaporizhzhia, Dnipropetrovsk and Kharkiv in 2014–15, pointed to a costly protracted Russian invasion of Ukraine. Russian defence minister Anatoly Serdyukov's 2009 military reforms, which restricted the army into brigades and centralised officer training, and Russia's extensive efforts to modernise its air defence, unmanned aerial vehicle (UAV), Black Sea Fleet, fighter jet and hypersonic weapons capabilities increased confidence in the Russian military's strength. Russia's decisive military intervention on Syrian president Bashar al-Assad's behalf contrasted markedly with its attritional struggles in Chechnya and Georgia, and reinforced confidence in the Russian military's modernisation. Pride in Russia's military strength entered the public consciousness—Levada Center surveys conducted after 2015 showed that the armed forces leapfrogged Russian culture and athletic achievements as sources of national pride.[33] This sense of pride fuelled jingoism and unrealistic expectations in the Russian state media. In March 2021, Russian defence news outlet *Avio* claimed that Russia's anti-tank systems were so effective that the Donetsk and Luhansk People's Republics would be able to wipe out 30% of Ukraine's stationed artillery in Donbas in the first hour of a full-scale war.[34] Citing Bulgarian netizens, *Izvestia* boasted in September 2021 that "Russia cannot be pressured by a neighbouring state that will unconditionally surrender within 6–12 hours from the beginning of the invasion."[35]

The belief that the Ukrainian military was a depleted force that lacked unit cohesion further reinforced Russia's confidence in a swift triumph. Vassily Kashin, the director of the Center for Comprehensive European and International Studies at Moscow's Higher School of Economics, predicted that Ukrainian regular forces could be eviscerated in a week at most.[36] Retired Colonel Mikhail Khodaryonok's 3 February *Nezavisimaya Gazeta* article, which cautioned against the belief that Ukraine would be defeated in hours, highlighted three prevailing false assumptions amongst pro-war Russians.[37] The first assumption was that Russia would not need to send regular troops to overrun Ukraine's armed forces, as a single powerful "fire strike" would destroy almost all of its surveillance and communication systems, artillery and tank formations. This assumption belied Russia's limited number of Kalibr cruise missiles, Kinzhal hypersonic missiles, Iskander missiles and Kh-101 air-launched cruise missiles, which could be depleted by the multiple fire strikes that would be required to subdue Ukraine. The second assumption was that Russia's aerial dominance would be the decisive factor in ensuring a swift victory. This contradicted the experiences of the Soviet military in the Afghanistan and Chechen wars where insurgents without air power stymied Russia's goals, or the 2008 Georgian War where anti-air defence systems complicated Russia's offensive operations. The third assumption was that Ukrainians would not mobilise in defence of their unpopular government and that ethnic Russians would greet Russia's occupying forces as liberators. This belief contradicted public opinion surveys from 2016–19, which showed that 65% of residents of separatist-controlled Donetsk and Luhansk wanted to rejoin Ukraine,[38] and Russia's failure to secure large-scale local collaboration in 2014–15.

To compound their skewed assessments of the military balance, Russian officials believed that the Western response would be underwhelming. Sanctions against Russia were expected to be symbolic, an inevitability or potentially more harmful to Europe.

Bogdan Bezpalko, a member of Putin's Council on Inter-Ethnic Relations, quipped that the West would impose "decorative sanctions" on Russia over its recognition of the Donetsk and Luhansk People's Republics, and merely cancel incomplete projects like the Nord Stream 2 pipeline.[39] Sergei Lavrov stated that the West was going to impose sanctions on Russia regardless of its conduct so they would not deter Moscow's policy towards Ukraine.[40] Russian Ambassador to the EU Vladimir Chizhov mocked Europe's "mother of all sanctions warning" as an adaptation of Iraqi dictator Saddam Hussein's rhetoric and stated that "gas consumers in Europe will become victims" of Russian counter-sanctions.[41] Given these assumptions, Russia was confident that its foreign currency reserves, which exceeded $600 billion, and low debt-to-GDP ratio, which stood at 17%, would allow it to weather Western sanctions. Russia was also extremely sceptical of large-scale Western military assistance to Ukraine. Council of Foreign and Defence Policy head Sergei Karaganov's claim that "Article 5 of the NATO Treaty is worthless" underscored Russia's scepticism of its security guarantees.[42] The West's decision not to sanction Russia over its 2008 invasion of Georgia, Europe's unwillingness to divest from Russian energy after the Crimea annexation and the U.S.'s decision not to arm Ukraine in the first Donbas offensive fuelled these assumptions of Western weakness and encouraged Russian aggression.

How Putin Survived Military Setbacks and the Economic Impact of Sanctions

The survival of Vladimir Putin's regime in spite of Russia's dismal failure to achieve its objectives in Ukraine is an intriguing puzzle. Russia's mobilisation of forces on the Ukrainian border resulted in an increase in Putin's approval ratings from 63% in November 2021 to 71% in February 2022. These trends accelerated after the

17

war began, as Putin's approval ratings surged from 68% in February to 80% in May, and remained stable in the succeeding months.[43] The Russian State Duma also experienced a striking increase in public support, as its approval rating soared from 41% in December 2021 to 61% in May 2022.[44] This increase in public support was more durable than during the aftermath of the annexation of Crimea, when support for the Duma briefly spiked to 58% in September 2014 and sharply ebbed in the months that followed. While Putin and the State Duma were the chief political beneficiaries of the Ukraine War, support for other officials, such as foreign minister Sergei Lavrov and prime minister Mikhail Mishustin, received modest upticks. Support for Russian military activities in Ukraine remains comparably high. A July 2022 Levada Center survey revealed that 76% of Russians supported the actions of the armed forces in Ukraine, even as a majority of Russians anticipated that the war would drag on for at least another six months or a year.[45] Generational divides persist on the Ukraine War, as 74% of Russians aged over 55 closely follow developments compared to 36% aged 18–24, and 84% of Russians aged over 55 support the military's activities compared to 57% aged 18–24, but it is undeniable that Putin's prosecution of the Ukraine War commands broad popular support.[46]

The sustainability of the wartime patriotic rally around Putin's regime surprised some Western analysts and policymakers. During the initial stages of the war, optimism in Western countries about political change in Russia reached its highest levels since the 2011–12 Bolotnaya Square protests. On 24 February, political scientist David Rothkopf penned an article for *The Daily Beast* predicting that the Ukraine War would result in mass protests resembling those in Belarus in 2020 and lead to sanctions-inspired oligarch defections that would hasten Putin's demise.[47] An 18 March RAND Corporation briefing contended that "strains in Russia over the war in Ukraine and punishing economic sanctions could spark regime change in Russia" and urged the West to begin considering how to deal with any new government.[48] The detention of 4,888 anti-war protesters in 69 cities by 7 March revealed sizeable groundswells of dissent in Russia, which added fuel to these predictions.[49] One month into the war, however, optimism about revolutionary change in Russia receded markedly. U.S. president Joe Biden's impromptu claim that Putin should not remain in power was deemed so out of touch with U.S. policy that Secretary of State Antony Blinken publicly confirmed that the U.S. had no regime change strategy in Russia.[50] EU High Representative for Foreign Affairs and Security Policy Josep Borrell mirrored Blinken's comments and stated the EU's depiction of Putin as an autocrat did not mean supporting his overthrow.[51] Timothy Frye's widely discussed article "Why Regime Change in Russia Might Not Be a Good Idea" highlighted the reality that merely removing Putin, who is a personalist autocrat, might not fundamentally change Russia's direction.[52]

The unexpected resilience of Putin's regime can be explained by several factors. A key contributor to Putin's survival was the Kremlin's institutionalised repression of anti-war voices. The August 2020 poisoning of Alexei Navalny set into a motion a new wave of repression of Russian opposition voices. After November 2020, the Russian State Duma passed legislation that expanded the reach of the "foreign agents" and "undesirables" laws, further restricted freedom of assembly and online expression, and facilitated the arrest of opposition activists.[53] The December 2021 court-mandated closure of Russia's top human rights organisation Memorial over its alleged support for protests and efforts to disinform the Russian public about Russia's judicial system illustrated the Kremlin's increasingly reactionary outlook.[54] The outbreak of the Ukraine War further intensified Russia's coercion of domestic opposition. The Duma's 4 March legislation, which mandated prison sentences of up to fifteen years for Russians who spread "fake information" about the war, bans on Western social media networks like Meta and Twitter, and the closure of liberal news outlets like *Novaya Gazeta* and *Dozhd* helped silence dissenting voices. The prosecution of prominent dissidents such as Alexei Navalny and Vladimir Kara-Murza and activists such as Alexandra Skochilenko, who was detained on 11 April for replacing supermarket price tags with anti-war messages and faces up to ten years in prison, forced opposition voices into a choice between silence and exile. Aside from rare episodes, such as the anti-war protest at the Kis-Kis concert in St. Petersburg in May 2022, anti-war demonstrations have receded from view and dissidents have emigrated to countries such as Turkey and Georgia.

Expressions of support for the war in public opinion surveys and the absence of a domestic threat to Putin's regime security cannot only be explained by fear of repression, however. Instead, they reflect the popularity of Kremlin messaging about the Ukraine invasion, which has been carefully tailored to align with public opinion in Russia. The notion that Russia and Ukraine shared a common historical destiny features prominently in Putin's wartime rhetoric and the Kremlin has used this contention to justify territorial annexations. In a 3 March address to the Russian Security Council, Putin said that "I will never disavow my conviction that Russians and Ukrainians are one people" and blamed nationalist propaganda for steering Ukrainians away from Russia.[55] This perspective resonated at a popular level, as it was widely accepted as an empirical truth. A 23 February CNN poll showed that 64% of Russians believed that Russians and Ukrainians were "one people," which reflected this narrative's ability to transcend ideological boundaries.[56] Philosopher Alexander Dugin's 1997 claim that "Ukraine as a state has no geopolitical meaning, no particular cultural import or universal significance, no geographic uniqueness, no ethnic exclusive-ness"[57] mirrored statements from hardline nationalists such as Liberal Democratic Party of Russia leader Vladimir Zhirinovsky and Lieutenant General Alexander Lebed. Even though he viewed "imperial chauvinism" as the greatest threat to the interests of the Russian people, Navalny has stated that "I don't see any difference at all between Russians and Ukrainians."[58]

The threats that Putin invoked to justify invading Ukraine, such as the persecution of ethnic Russians in Donbas and NATO's aggressive designs on Russia, also resonated at a popular level. Due to eight years of incessant Russian state media coverage of Ukrainian shelling of civilians in Donetsk and Luhansk, which ignored the military provocations of pro-Russian separatist militias and the human rights abuses of the occupation authorities, the Russian public was overwhelmingly convinced of the existence of a Ukraine-orchestrated humanitarian crisis in Donbas. This did not initially translate into support for the use of military force, as only 43% of Russians wanted a military intervention on the Donbas republics' behalves in a May 2021 Levada Center survey, but rallied support for a change to Donbas's legal status.[59] A March 2022 Levada Center survey revealed that 33% of Russians supported the independence of Donetsk and Luhansk People's Republics, and an additional 25% backed their annexation by Russia.[60] The Kremlin's insistence that military force was the only way to achieve the "liberation" of Donbas and to end a genocide against Russian compatriots ultimately overcame public reticence about a more expansive military intervention in Ukraine. The oft-mentioned homeland security threat posed by NATO received similarly broad acceptance in Russia. A May 2021 survey showed that 48% of Russians believed that the U.S. and NATO were responsible for escalating tensions in eastern Ukraine, and just 4% blamed Russian aggression.[61] Reflecting generational and educational divides, the belief in NATO aggression was especially pervasive amongst state television viewers and less pronounced amongst avid Internet and Telegram users. However, the belief that Ukraine was on the path to join NATO had been crystallised in Russian public opinion since the mid-2000s and the notion that NATO was an unambiguously threatening alliance had endured since the 1999 Kosovo War.

The Kremlin's synthesis of coercion and persuasive rhetoric to stifle dissent has been amplified further by the absence of discernible intra-elite rifts. Since the Ukraine War began, there have been frequent reports that Putin's inner circle of advisors has become increasingly small and overwhelmingly dominated by the *siloviki* ("strongmen") security establishment. Putin's regular consultations with long-standing allies such as Security Council Secretary Nikolay Patrushev and FSB chief Alexander Bortnikov, who have known him since the 1970s, and arms-length relationship with cabinet ministers and oligarchs reflect this trend.[62] The narrowing of Putin's inner circle reflects a series of personnel changes that have occurred since 2016, which broke with his prior preference for leadership continuity and retention of the officials from St. Petersburg who had accompanied him in his rise to power. After dismissing the Baltic Sea Fleet's senior officers in June 2016 and firing a slew of regional personnel in July 2016, Putin dismissed Sergei Ivanov as chief of the presidential administration and replaced him with Anton Vaino. As Vaino was only 44 years old, Putin's personnel shuffle was linked to his calls for "fresh blood" entering the Kremlin through United Russia party primaries and desire to ensure that ambitious younger bureaucrats became loyalists.[63]

The October 2019 dismissal of Sergey Glazyev, a critic of the Russian Central Bank who had served as Putin's advisor since 2012, and February 2020 ouster of long-standing advisor Vladislav Surkov further increased Putin's reliance on the siloviki.

Putin's reliance on informal partners, such as the Wagner Group's financier Yevgeny Prigozhin, allowed him to create an alternative power vertical that consolidated his personal grip on security policy and undermined the Russian ministry of defence. While these measures created an echo chamber inside the Kremlin and contributed to the strategic ineptitude exhibited by the Russian military in the first weeks of the war, they shielded Putin from a palace coup when the war did not proceed according to plan. The encirclement of Putin by a narrow group of loyalists ensured that prominent defections, such as the 23 March resignation of sustainable development advisor Anatoly Chubais and 26 May departure of UN Office diplomat Boris Bondarev, were not followed by a larger exodus. As Putin faces more pressure from maximalists such as Chechnya's leader Ramzan Kadyrov who eschew diplomacy and continue to believe in a Russian occupation of Kyiv, vigorously prosecuting the Ukraine War is more likely to unite elites than sow internal discord.

The Future of Russia's Political System and Foreign Policy

Russia's Political Trajectory: Totalitarianism or Fascism?

In the three decades since the Soviet Union's disintegration, Russia's political system has experienced a series of radical transformations. Although Russia's democratic experiment showed initial promise, president Boris Yeltsin's efforts to expand presidential power and dissolution of the Russian State Duma in September 1993 precipitated a constitutional crisis. Despite the deaths of nearly 150 people in the political violence that ensued, Yeltsin resisted the temptation of authoritarian rule by decree but instead organised a constitutional referendum in December 1993 that created a super-presidential system.[64] The empowerment of anti-democratic forces in the 1993 parliamentary elections, such as the far-right Liberal Democratic Party of Russia (LDPR) and

Communist Party of Russia, and Yeltsin's acceptance of Western interference and perpetration of minor fraud in the 1996 presidential elections sharpened the erosion of Russian democracy.[65] Yeltsin's growing unpredictability which resulted in the dismissal of a succession of prime ministers in the late 1990s, and systemic factors, such as oil dependency, limited economic liberalisation and a weak national legislature, pushed Russia on an authoritarian trajectory.[66] The Russian public's acquiescence to Putin's offer of increased economic growth and security in exchange for the erosion of political freedom ensured that the Kremlin was able to dismantle NGOs, independent media outlets and marginalise opposition political parties with high approval ratings.[67]

As Putin's grip on power strengthened, characterisations of the Russian political system varied. Vladislav Surkov described Russia's political system in 2006 as "sovereign democracy." Surkov's sovereign democracy model emphasised how a dominant political party, United Russia, advanced material welfare and egalitarianism, and shielded Russia from external interference. Sovereign democracy aligned closely with Russian public perceptions of what a democracy constituted, as broad public support for democracy coincided with a disdain for Western-style institutions and backing of an alternative form of democracy that embraced Russia's national character.[68] However, it was criticised as a "non-traditional type of democracy" by future president Dmitry Medvedev and as window dressing for authoritarianism by former prime minister Mikhail Kasyanov. Putin's Russia has also been characterised as an electoral authoritarian regime, which remains stable by manufacturing massive electoral majorities for the ruling party, or as a new form of authoritarianism that rallies public support around illiberal values.[69] The prospects of a devolution into Soviet-style totalitarianism were deemed unlikely, as Putin's selective repression of dissent was more efficient than sweeping Stalinism-inspired purges.[70]

The Ukraine War has overhauled these assumptions and prompted widespread discussions about Russia's pivot towards totalitarianism and fascism. A 2 March editorial in *The Guardian* declared that Putin's Russia had slid into totalitarianism and cited gratuitous acts of repression, such as the detention of schoolchildren and their parents for laying flowers at the Ukrainian embassy, as proof for this designation.[71] Carnegie Moscow Center expert Andrei Kolesnikov contends that the Ukraine War has converted Putin's Russia from an authoritarian state into a "hybrid totalitarian" regime. This system combines totalitarian practices, such as the ostracisation of anti-war voices, the division of society between patriots and traitors and hatred towards everything declared alien, with residual elements of a market economy, political democracy and civic culture.[72]

While there is a consensus around the fact that Russia's political system possesses totalitarian features, it is less certain whether this totalitarian tilt predated the Ukraine invasion. Masha Gessen's 2017 book *The Future is History: How Totalitarianism Reclaimed Russia* contends that Russia's descent into totalitarianism was a gradual process that was inspired by public nostalgia for the Soviet Union in the post-1994 period.[73] Vladimir Putin's efforts to rekindle memories of the Soviet past, retention of popular support through military aggression and mobilisation, and capitalisation on nostalgia for Stalin facilitated the consolidation of a totalitarian regime. The eerie sense of calm as the rouble crashed and police brutality occurred in public view in Pushkin Square underscored how Putin's incremental embrace of totalitarianism had demobilised Russian society.[74] Russian sociologist Lev Gudkov's phrase "recurring totalitarianism," which asserts that Putin's Russia revived totalitarian characteristics that were paused during the Yeltsin era, concurs with Gessen's view that Homo Sovieticus did not perish with the Soviet Union's dissolution.[75] While Gessen and Gudkov's assessments point to a protracted period of totalitarian rule, Kolesnikov's perspective is somewhat more optimistic, as it predicts that totalitarianism's inefficacy and the Russian public's ephemeral taste of civil liberties could eventually cause political change.

While Russia's descent into totalitarianism appears inevitable, it is unclear whether Putin's wartime and potential post-war regime will be a throwback to Soviet-era practices or be reincarnated as a fascist state. Concerns about the rising tide of fascism in Putin's Russia date back to the aftermath of the Crimea annexation. Russian liberal intellectuals, such as Mikhail Iampolski, Yevgeny Ikhlov, Andrei Zubov and Aleksei Shiropaiev, were especially vocal in highlighting Russia's fascist tilt in early 2015. The Kremlin's crackdowns on liberalism and homosexuality, replication of how Italian fascists blended nationalism with clerical support, and creation of a mass Russian consciousness based on imperialism and chauvinistic nationalism provided fertile ground for fascism.[76] While the fascist label for Putin's Russia did not initially receive mainstream acceptance amongst Western academics and media outlets, it has gained popularity since the Ukraine War began. Timothy Snyder justified the depiction of Russia as a fascist state by highlighting Putin's ideological admiration of nationalist philosopher Ivan Ilyin.[77] Francis Fukuyama explicitly compared Putin's Russia to Nazi Germany by stating that its ideology revolves around extreme nationalism and has subordinated institutions to the world view of a single individual Vladimir Putin.[78] Zelensky's popularisation of the phrase "Rashism" to describe Putin's brand of fascism has resonated strongly in Western countries.

Despite these categorisations, scholars such as Stanley Payne and Sheri Berman believe that Putin's dictatorship is reactionary and lacks the revolutionary character of interwar fascist regimes.[79] The influence of fascist ideologues on Putin's regime is also significantly overstated. Putin has only quoted Ivan Ilyin five times in all his public speeches and the Eurasian Economic Union draws greater ideological inspiration from China's harmonious development model than philosopher Alexander Dugin's Eurasianist ideology.[80] If Putin merely embraces tactics of interwar dictators to cling to power, his regime will likely be classified as a totalitarian regime with fascist characteristics. However, if he durably reconstitutes the Russian political order around an ultra-nationalist ideology, future scholars could label Russia as a fascist state.

Russian Foreign Policy in the Age of the Ukraine War

Since invading Ukraine, Russia has grappled with near-complete isolation from the West and a rocky transition to a post-Western foreign policy. Although Lavrov repeatedly argued that Russia's relations with the West were worse than during the Cold War,[81] the total collapse of Russia's Western vector is a seismic shift. Before the Ukraine War, Russia solicited cooperation with Western powers on arms control, regional security issues, aerospace, counterterrorism and climate change, and Europe's reliance on Russian energy created a crisis-proof economic bridge. The flurry of sanctions that followed the Ukraine invasion caused the Kremlin to frame Russia–West relations as passing a point of no return. Russia's suspension from the Council of Europe (COE) and United Nations Human Rights Council (UNHRC) caused tensions to soar to historic heights. On 14 May, Lavrov warned that the collective West had launched a "total hybrid war" of uncertain duration against Russia and insisted that Russia would prevail through the consolidation of partnerships with non-Western powers such as China and India.[82] The decision of erstwhile neutral countries such as Sweden, Finland and Switzerland to punish Russian aggression in Ukraine underscored the unprecedented scale of Russia's isolation from the West and fuelled pessimism about a peace deal leading to sanctions relief.

Although Russia frames itself as a revisionist challenger to the U.S.-led international order and hails its commitment to a multipolar world order, it faces a transitional period characterised by heightened international isolation. Russian treaty allies such as Kyrgyzstan, Armenia, Kazakhstan and Tajikistan did not support the Ukraine invasion. Aside from its military alliance with Belarus, which saw its relations with the West atrophy over Lukashenko's crackdown on election fraud protests in 2020, Russia faces an unprecedented degree of isolation in the post-Soviet space. When the 2 March UN General Assembly Resolution ES-11/1 was proposed, just five countries (Belarus, Russia, Syria, North Korea and Eritrea) overtly backed Russia against allegations of the unlawful use of force. Some of Russia's main non-Western partners including China, Iran, Algeria, Ethiopia and Vietnam opposed its suspension from the UN Human Rights Council, but other key partners such as India, Indonesia, Brazil, Egypt and South Africa facilitated its expulsion by abstaining. Except for discounted energy sales, opposition to sanctions against Russia has not translated into large-scale investments in the Russian economy or new trade deals. China has not provided military assistance to Russia's war effort and aside from Iran's alleged supply of Shahed-class drones and assistance in small arms smuggling, Russia has received no meaningful external support for its military operations in Ukraine. The risk of secondary sanctions, which increased after the expulsion of major Russian banks from SWIFT, could derail critical Russian trade partnerships, especially in the security and technology spheres.

Despite these negative trendlines, Russia still sees opportunities to broaden and deepen its array of partnerships in the Global South. The Kremlin has repeatedly insisted that the Ukraine War eviscerated the unipolar order and accelerated the transition to a multipolar order. Therefore, Russia has sought to undermine the core pillars of U.S. economic and military hegemony that underpin the unipolar order. Russia's efforts to divest from the U.S. dollar intensified after the Crimea annexation, and accelerated in June 2021, as the Kremlin announced cuts to U.S. dollar exposure in its $186 billion National Wealth Fund. Since invading Ukraine, Russia has aggressively championed U.S. dollar divestment to its non-Western partners. Sergey Glazyev boldly proclaimed that an "imminent disintegration of the dollar-based global economic system" was underway and predicted that a consensus-based monetary order based on national currencies would replace it.[83] Due to the long-standing desire of non-Western powers to find alternatives to SWIFT, Russia's SPFS and China's CIPS systems are strengthening their bonds, and the Kremlin hopes that India, which lacks a domestic financial messaging system, will follow suit.[84] Russia's enthusiastic support for the entry of new members such as Iran and Argentina to BRICS builds on its efforts to revive the organisation's relevance during the COVID-19 pandemic. China, Iran and South Africa's promotion of Russia's narratives about NATO expansion underscore Moscow's more ambiguous efforts to create a multipolar security order.

While it remains unclear whether Russia's coalition-building efforts against U.S. unilateralism will be symbolic or substantive, Moscow's great power ambitions in the Middle East, Africa, Latin America and Indo-Pacific region have shown no signs of slowing. Russia's military interventions in Syria, Libya, the Central African Republic (CAR) and Mali have continued in spite of the Wagner Group's recruitment campaign for the Donbas offensive and Russia's manpower shortages in Ukraine. The 2023 Russia–Africa summit provides Moscow with an opportunity to reassert itself as a continent-wide great power. Lavrov's active participation at the 2022 ASEAN summit and the rejection of Zelensky's speaking request by Mercosur Trade Summit members underscores Russia's status as a rising second-tier power in Southeast Asia and Latin America. Russia's soft power in the Global South will be compounded further by the probable relocation of Russian diplomats stationed in Europe to non-Western locations. The dispatch of additional diplomats will likely be complemented by political technologists and intelligence agents, which will compound Russia's growing media presence and social media disinformation campaigns. Therefore, Russia will likely remain a virtual great power on the world stage, as it can engage with a wide array of partners, but lacks the material capabilities to unilaterally exert leverage.

An Overview of This Book

As the causes of Russia's invasion of Ukraine, the reasons why Putin survived its fallout and possible future directions for Russia's political system and foreign policy have been laid out in this opening chapter, the remainder of the book will focus on the path to war, the course of the conflict and its implications for the international order. Chapter 2 examines Russia's policy towards Ukraine in the aftermath of the Euro-Maidan revolution. It assesses Russia's efforts to delegitimise Euro-Maidan to a domestic audience, promote a counter-revolutionary agenda through military intervention, political interference and support for separatism, and leverage the post-Minsk frozen conflict to mitigate the Crimea annexation's backlash. Chapter 3 examines the long build-up to Russia's mobilisations of personnel and military hardware on Ukraine's borders in spring 2021 and autumn 2021/winter 2022. While Russia used brinkmanship and the threat of a limited Donbas intervention to pressure the West into accepting its security guarantees, Russian officials also cryst-allised the narratives that would justify their invasion of Ukraine.

The second section of the book examines how Russia's plans for a blitzkrieg seizure of Kyiv unravelled and Putin weathered this seismic setback. Chapter 4 covers the first phase of the war, which spans from Putin's 24 February "special military operation" speech to Russia's ignominious withdrawals from Kyiv and Chernihiv in early April. Despite humiliating military defeats, heavy casualties and logistical mishaps, Putin's approval rating strengthened as the Kremlin was able to rally the Russian public around the allegedly existential threats of NATO aggression, Western hybrid war and Ukrainian Nazism. Russia's transition from an authoritarian government with superficial characteristics of pluralism to a totalitarian regime began in earnest as patriotic mobilisation around the war and repression of dissent reached post-Cold War highs. Chapter 5 addresses the war's second phase, which saw Russia concentrate its forces in Donbas and achieve modest successes, such as the 20 May conquest of Mariupol and 3 July occupation of Luhansk. The Kremlin used these costly victories to foment public support for the war, as battlefield victories were overtly compared to Second World War battles and benefited from the Russian economy's unexpected resilience in the face of Western sanctions. Chapter 6 covers Ukraine's counter-offensives in Kherson and Zaporizhzhia, the stagnation of Russia's Donetsk campaign and fluctuating tensions in the Black Sea over grain exports and Crimea. It also explores how Russia justified its weaponisation of food and energy to the public, showcased referendum and reconstruction pledges for occupied territories, and sold its narratives on the Ukrainian grain export shutdown and the Zaporizhzhia nuclear plant crisis. Personnel changes, such as the ouster of leading Russian generals and the Wagner Group's rising influence, also provide insights into the state of civil–military relations in Russia. Chapter 7 addresses Ukraine's multi-pronged counter-offensive, which resulted in a resounding Russian defeat in Kharkiv and smaller military setbacks in Kherson, Luhansk and Donetsk, and Russia's pivot towards total war through Putin's declared policy of "partial mobilisation."

The third section of the book examines the implications of Putin's war on Ukraine for Russia's great power status and the broader international order. Chapter 8 examines the extent to which the Ukraine War has transformed Russian foreign policy or expedited long-standing trends. In particular, it explores Russia's growing isolation in its sphere of influence in the post-Soviet space, overt embrace of a post-Western multipolar foreign policy, and efforts to sow internal discord in Western countries as the EU and NATO become increasingly unitary anti-Russian blocs. Chapter 9 provides a deeper examination of Russia's eastward pivot as China, India and Iran's importance as partners continues to grow. The marked deterioration of Russia's relationships with pro-Western states in the Indo-Pacific region such as Japan, South Korea, Taiwan and Australia, and Moscow's courtship of new partnerships in South and Southeast Asia, are also notable trends that deserve in-depth analysis. Chapter 10 examines the sustainability of Russia's standing as a rising power in extra-regional theatres such as the Middle East, Africa and Latin America, as Moscow's traditional partners balance their desire to maintain multi-vector foreign policies with the fear of secondary sanctions. The book concludes with a forward-looking conclusion which examines possible scenarios for the Ukraine War, political change in Russia and the future of Russian foreign policy. By examining the local, domestic and international dimensions of the Ukraine War, this book offers the most comprehensive account of Putin's invasion of Ukraine, its causes and its implications to date, and provides a valuable window into the view from Moscow on the war in Ukraine.

2

RUSSIA TRIES TO OVERTURN THE
EURO-MAIDAN REVOLUTION

On 21 November 2013, mass demonstrations erupted in Maidan Nezalezhnosti or Independence Square in Kyiv. These protests were triggered by Viktor Yanukovych's rejection of an EU association agreement, which had been overwhelmingly approved by the Ukrainian Rada, in favour of closer ties with Russia and membership in the Eurasian Customs Union. As calls for Yanukovych's resignation mounted, mass protests swept across Ukraine's major cities, such as Lviv, Kharkiv, Odesa and Dnipropetrovsk, and extended even to the traditionally Russia-friendly Donbas region. The Ukrainian government's coercive response, which saw Berkut special police units violently repress peaceful protests in Kyiv on 30 November and from 10–12 December, added additional fuel to these protests. Yanukovych's implementation of the 16 January "Dictatorship Laws," which restricted freedom of expression and assembly, converted these demonstrations into a full-blown revolution. From 18–20 February, clashes between the Berkut and demonstrators resulted in a hundred casualties and encouraged

Yanukovych to strike a deal with the Ukrainian opposition on 21 February, which called for the formation of an interim unity government, constitutional reforms and early elections. Despite signing this agreement, Yanukovych fled Kyiv for Moscow hours later and was impeached by the Ukrainian Rada on 22 February. A Ukrainian government led by acting president Oleksandr Turchynov and prime minister Arseniy Yatsenyuk was sworn into office on 27 February.

The overthrow of Yanukovych, which Ukrainians described as the Euro-Maidan Revolution or Revolution of Dignity, was swiftly followed by a Russian military response. Immediately after Yanukovych's overthrow, Vladimir Putin held an all-night meeting with Russia's security chiefs to discuss "returning Crimea to Russia."[1] This crisis meeting was followed by the eruption of pro-Russian demonstrations in Crimea, the intervention of Russian troops in unmarked uniforms and the peninsula's annexation via a widely unrecognised referendum on 18 March. The Russian military subsequently aided separatist militias in Donbas and occupied large swathes of the Donetsk and Luhansk oblasts. While the February 2015 Minsk II accords helped freeze the Ukraine War, Russia continued to delegitimise the post-Maidan government and pursue a policy of destabilisation in Ukraine. This chapter examines Russia's counter-revolutionary policy towards Euro-Maidan, annexation of Crimea, undeclared war on Donbas, freezing of the Ukraine War and efforts to retain its great power status in the face of mounting Western sanctions.

Russia's Reaction to the Euro-Maidan Revolution in Ukraine

From the inception of mass protests in Kyiv, Russia viewed the Euro-Maidan Revolution with extreme hostility and suspicion. On 2 December, Putin declared that "the events in Ukraine no longer resemble a revolution but a pogrom" and claimed that the protesters supported European integration to undermine Yanukovych ahead of the 2015 presidential elections.[2] This mirrored rhetoric from Ukraine's prime minister, Mykola Azarov, who called the Maidan protesters "Nazis and criminals," and described them on Rossiya-1 as "provocateurs" who needed to be suppressed through force.[3] While Putin confined his statements to criticisms of the protests, many of his allies supported more direct political interference and military action. State Duma Deputy Robert Schlegel openly encouraged the anti-Maidan protests, which rallied up to 15,000 people from eastern Ukraine in support of Yanukovych. Sergei Glazyev baselessly accused the U.S. of giving $20 million a week to Ukraine's opposition and supplying arms to Ukrainian rebels, stating that U.S. actions violated the 1994 Budapest Memorandum on Security Assurances, which guaranteed Ukraine's sovereignty and territorial integrity, and contended that Russia could militarily intervene to prevent chaos.[4] After Yanukovych's overthrow, the Kremlin condemned Ukraine's post-Maidan authorities as illegitimate. Dmitry Medvedev stated that "masked and armed people are no partners for dialogue" and condemned Western powers for legitimising a "mutiny" that threatened Russia's security.[5] The Russian foreign ministry derided the Euro-Maidan revolution as an illegal coup d'état and accused its perpetrators of having "nationalist and neo-Nazi moods."[6]

Russia's antipathy towards the Euro-Maidan Revolution was likely not shaped by its loyalty to Yanukovych. Despite his pro-Russian reputation, Yanukovych had supported Ukraine's EU membership and participation in the Iraq War as Leonid Kuchma's prime minister from 2002–4. As Viktor Yushchenko's prime minister from 2006–7, Yanukovych had rejected a NATO Membership Action Plan (MAP) but overseen a strategic airlift agreement with NATO and broadened Ukraine's military exercises with the alliance. Steven Pifer, who served as U.S. Ambassador to Ukraine from 1998–2000, contends that Ukraine's practical cooperation with NATO accelerated markedly during Yanukovych's premiership.[7] Until late 2013, Yanukovych consistently supported a free trade agreement with the EU, resisted Russian pressure to join the Eurasian Customs Union and upheld Ukraine's links with NATO, such as the Sea Breeze exercises.[8] These pro-Western policies continued, even as the EU pressured Yanukovych over his authoritarian leanings and detention of political rival Yulia Tymoshenko in 2011. As Yanukovych's approval ratings slid to 20%, he tried to position himself as the president who had spearheaded Ukraine's integration into the EU to further his re-election prospects. Even after Yanukovych succumbed to Russian pressure over the EU association agreement talks, he left the door open to continued negotiations with Brussels and stated, "As soon as we agree on normal conditions, then we will talk about signing."[9] Moreover, there is considerable anecdotal evidence that Putin viewed Yanukovych with contempt. Due to his botched efforts to invalidate the 2004 presidential election results, Putin reportedly regarded Yanukovych as a "provincial thug" and "serial loser," and an image of Putin grimacing when Yanukovych offered him a sweet in 2004 spread widely.[10] The Russian media similarly mocked Yanukovych's inept response to Euro-Maidan. Political scientist Oleg Bondarenko stated that Yanukovych "really was not aware of what was happening" when the Maidan protests erupted and warned that the Kyiv authorities "flee from all government buildings at the first threat."[11] Yanukovych's inability to create a power vertical, which would silence oligarch dissent, or empower ethnic Russian resistance to Maidan in Donbas, Crimea, Kyiv and Odesa was also roundly criticised.

Given the below-the-surface complications in the Yanukovych–Putin relationship, Russia's opposition to Euro-Maidan can be explained by its desire to subvert Ukraine's foreign policy independence and unite Russians around Putin's counter-revolutionary agenda. Despite past gripes with his foreign policy outlook, Russia viewed Yanukovych's retention of power as its most expedient path to suppressing Ukrainian sovereignty, as he had surrendered Ukraine's EU aspirations due to Russian coercion. Throughout the summer and autumn of 2013, Russian officials combined economic coercion with rhetorical threats to derail Ukraine's EU association agreement. In August 2013, Russia imposed a trade embargo on numerous Ukrainian suppliers of agricultural and manufactured goods, which cost Ukraine's economy an estimated $2.5 billion in revenues. Russian MP Leonid Slutsky explicitly described this trade embargo as the "cost of Ukraine's refusal to accede to Russia's customs union proposal."[12] In September 2013, Sergei Glazyev warned that Russia would not aid Ukraine if EU integration caused it to default on its debts, hinted at new sanctions on Ukraine and accused Yanukovych of violating the Ukraine–Russia friendship treaty. In an ominous premonition of Russia's future military interventions, Glazyev said that "Russia could no longer guarantee Ukraine's status as a state and could possibly intervene if pro-Russian regions of the country appealed directly to Moscow."[13] In October 2013, Putin stated that Ukraine's EU association agreement would preclude integration in a customs union with Belarus, Kazakhstan and Russia. This announcement was expected, as the EU similarly said that Armenia's customs union accession in September 2013 was incompatible with an EU association agreement, but nonetheless undermined Yanukovych's balancing strategy.

Yanukovych initially resisted Russian pressure and supported Ukrainian state energy company Naftogaz's 9 November decision to suspend gas purchases from Russia in favour of commercial deals with Hungary and Slovakia. Nevertheless, Yanukovych acquiesced to Russia's demands and suspended talks on an EU association agreement ahead of the 28–29 November Eastern Partnership summit in Vilnius. In Kyiv, this volte-face was attributed to Russia's successful pressure tactics on Yanukovych. Sergiy Taran, the director of Kyiv's International Democracy Institute, says that Russia threatened to cut off economic relations with eastern Ukraine, which would have destroyed Yanukovych's support base, and blackmailed Yanukovych with new disclosures about his Soviet-era imprisonment on robbery and assault charges.[14] These threats, which were sweetened by Russian financial offers, contributed more to Yanukovych's decision than the EU's linkage on association agreement with Tymoshenko's release.[15] Putin rewarded Yanukovych for his stance by announcing the 17 December Russian–Ukrainian Action Plan, which saw Russia agree to purchase $15 billion in Ukraine-issued Eurobonds and lower its gas export price from over $400 to $268 per cubic metre. On 15 January, Ukraine unveiled a cooperation programme with Eurasian customs union member states that would last until 2020 but refrained from taking official steps towards joining the organisation. The 27 January ouster of Mykola Azarov, who was reviled by the Euro-Maidan protesters for his pro-Russian stance, temporarily froze Russia's Eurobond purchases but Putin's support for Yanukovych was evident from his pledges of deeper cooperation on 8 February in Sochi.

Russia's support for Yanukovych was augmented by its concerns about Euro-Maidan's alleged Western backing and anti-Russian agenda. Euro-Maidan's organisers typically reject these claims. Ukraine's deputy minister of infrastructure Mustafa Nayyem, whose call to action on Meta inspired protesters to congregate on Independence Square, says that Euro-Maidan was not an anti-Russian movement, and noted that Maidan protesters were also frustrated with how EU countries such as Poland, France and Germany had supported Yanukovych's temporary retention of power via a brokered deal.[16] Nevertheless, the Kremlin believed that Yanukovych's likely successor would revive Yushchenko's unfriendly policies. Billionaire businessman Petro Poroshenko, who financed Euro-Maidan protests and supported their agenda via Channel 5, backed Ukraine's NATO membership in 2009 and accepted a role as minister of trade and economic development in 2012 to further Ukraine's EU ambitions. Poroshenko's confectionery company Roshen was adversely impacted by Russia's 2013 trade sanctions against Ukraine, which explained his exceptionally public support for Euro-Maidan by the standards of Ukrainian oligarchs. From the Kremlin's vantage point, Yulia Tymoshenko was a somewhat more palatable prospective Ukrainian president. Although Tymoshenko accused Russia of extortion during the 2006 gas export dispute and blasted the Kremlin's "imperial designs" in 2007, she had criticised Yushchenko's solidarity trip to Tbilisi during the 2008 Georgian War and had cordial meetings with Putin and Medvedev in October 2008.[17] Nevertheless, Tymoshenko's rapprochement with Moscow was eventually regarded as an opportunistic move to undermine Yushchenko's standing rather than a sign of her willingness to make concessions to Moscow.[18]

Russia's opposition to Euro-Maidan also furthered Putin's efforts to unite Russians around his counter-revolutionary agenda. Although the wave of colour revolutions in the post-Soviet space receded after the failed 2006 Jeans Revolution in Belarus, the 2011–12 Russian election protests provided new energy to Putin's efforts to rally Russians in support of counter-revolution. Galvanised by election fraud allegations and government corruption revelations, opposition leaders such as Alexei Navalny, Grigory Yavlinsky and Boris Nemtsov, and a heterogenous coalition of civil society movements ranging from trade unionists to LGBT activists, held opposition rallies in Moscow and St. Petersburg. These demonstrations drew mass crowds, which peaked at 160,000 on 4 February in Moscow, and the last Soviet leader Mikhail Gorbachev called for Putin's resignation. While Western media outlets speculated about the potential for regime change in Russia, Putin saw the protests as an opportunity to rally Russians around his counter-revolutionary vision. On 8 December 2011, Putin accused U.S. Secretary of State Hillary Clinton of fuelling unrest in Russia and warned of a "chaos" scenario resembling the Orange Revolution in Ukraine and 2005 Tulip Revolution in Kyrgyzstan.[19] The United Russia Party organised massive pro-government rallies, such as Putin's 23 February 2012 address to 130,000 at Luzhniki Stadium, and civil society groups such as Nashi and veterans organisations rallied Russians to "Anti-Orange Protests" that sought to thwart an Orange Revolution in Russia. Through ultra-nationalist surrogates such as Alexander Dugin, Channel One commentator Mikhail Leontyev and Essence of Time head Sergei Kurginyan, the Kremlin incited anti-Western counter-revolutionary sentiments. This helped drown out opposition rallies and propel Putin to an irregularity-marred presidential election victory in March 2012.

This counter-revolutionary fervour extended to Syria, where Russia framed Assad's repression of the Arab Spring as a struggle against anti-Christian Islamic extremists, and to opposing Euro-Maidan. The Kremlin's counter-revolutionary policy received broad support, as it tried to thwart Ukraine's decoupling from Russia and hard pivot towards Europe. Although a November 2013 poll showed that 49.7% of Russians saw Ukraine's EU association agreement negotiations as an internal affair, only 37% of Russians saw Ukraine as a foreign country and 3% supported Ukraine's EU membership.[20] Due to the popularity of Putin's counter-revolutionary agenda, Russian opposition figures tepidly supported Euro-Maidan. Navalny confined his backing of Euro-Maidan to retweets of rallies and anti-Yanukovych protests, which dovetailed with the focus of liberal nationalists on the anti-corruption rather than the foreign policy dimensions of Euro-Maidan.[21] Boris Nemtsov's overt support for Ukraine's European integration and participation in Euro-Maidan protests in Kyiv was a rare exception. By contrast, the Kremlin's surrogates were enthusiastic in their support for counter-revolution in Ukraine. Despite concerns about an open rift with the Ukrainian Orthodox Church, which was polarised on Euro-Maidan, Russian Orthodox Church Patriarch Kirill positioned himself as an unambiguous counter-revolutionary champion. In January 2014, he described Euro-Maidan as a "revolutionary situation" that threatened a division of Ukraine, and cited the French Revolution's gateway to Jacobin terror and Napoleon's dictatorship as a historical parallel.[22] Public intellectuals such as nationalist historian Natalia Narochnitskaya linked the Euro-Maidan unrest to Western efforts to expel Russia from the Black Sea and compared these initiatives to Turkey's support for Azerbaijan in the South Caucasus and Britain's historical support for Persia against the Russian Empire.[23]

Due to broad-based opposition to Euro-Maidan, the Russian state media's amplification of counter-revolutionary narratives was highly effective. Initially, the Russian media downplayed the scale of the Euro-Maidan protests. After the toppling of a Vladimir Lenin statue on 8 December, Russia's Channel One reassured viewers that "only a few hundred people" had turned out in the Euro-Maidan protests and that the demonstrations were "dying out."[24] RIA Novosti promoted the conspiracy that Yanukovych had staged the Euro-Maidan protests to illustrate support for European integration, create a pretext for signing the EU association agreement and secure his re-election. Once the protests were undeniably sustained, Russian media pivoted towards framing their participants as extremists or detached from Ukrainian society. RIA Novosti columnist Sergei Petukhov claimed that the Maidan protests represented the interests of a "small creative class" and praised the revolution's opponents as "defenders of traditional family values."[25] Images of nostalgists for the Ukrainian Insurgent Army (UPA)—a Second World War-era nationalist paramilitary organisation led by Nazi collaborator Stepan Bandera—at the Maidan rallies circulated widely. These UPA sympathisers waxed lyrically about using Europe to expel Russian influence from Ukraine and purportedly promoted liberal slogans such as "Better to be Gay in Europe."[26] Once Yanukovych was overthrown, the Russian media framed Euro-Maidan as a violent U.S.-backed coup. RIA Novosti commentator Mikhail Rostovsky asserted that the Ukrainian protesters "do not behave like civilians at all but like fighters armed at the teeth." It also linked the "coup" in Ukraine to U.S.-backed regime changes such as the 1953 reinstatement of Shah Mohammad Reza Pahlavi in Iran and the 1973 overthrow of Salvador Allende in Chile.[27] These counter-revolutionary narratives have endured in Russian media and official discourse since 2014, and Russia has repeatedly described the post-Maidan authorities as unpopular, extremist and illegitimate to justify coercion against Ukraine.

Russia's Annexation of Crimea: A Deniable Landgrab

Although supporters of the Russian military response to Euro-Maidan were initially side-lined, Putin whole-heartedly embraced their demands after Yanukovych's ouster. The first theatre of Russia's military retaliation against Euro-Maidan was Crimea. On 27 February, Russian special forces and local militias seized control over the Supreme Council of Crimea and the Council of Ministers building in Sevastopol. Sergiy Aksyonov, an alleged former lieutenant in the Salem organised criminal gang and chairman of the separatist Russian Unity party, was sworn in as

Crimea's prime minister. Once a pro-Russian regime was installed in Crimea, the Russian military took decisive steps towards annexing the peninsula. Within 48 hours, Russia had occupied several localities in Kherson Oblast's Arabat Spit and separated Crimea from Ukraine by establishing checkpoints on the Isthmus of Perekop and Chonhar Peninsula. After capturing these strategic locations, Russia diverted military personnel from Sevastopol to occupy the rest of Crimea, and besieged Ukraine's Southern Naval Base. Russia's bloodless triumph was followed by Crimea and Sevastopol's Declaration of Independence on 11 March and a referendum on incorporating both regions into Russia on 16 March. Although Yevgeny Bobrov, an official on Putin's Human Rights Council, estimated 50–60% support for joining Russia and opinion polls showed between 23 and 41% support for accession to Russia, the referendum produced an implausible figure of 97% support for uniting with Russia.[28] Ukraine's military withdrawal from the Southern Naval Base on 24 March then cleared the path for Russia to exert de facto control over Crimea.

Russia's annexation of Crimea was enthusiastically welcomed at home but received widespread international condemnation and triggered punitive Western sanctions. Although Crimea was part of Russia for only 168 years of its history, the belief that Khrushchev's 1954 handover of the region to Ukraine was a historical accident inspired support for the Crimea annexation. Putin's 18 March Grand Kremlin Palace address, which exhorted "Crimea has always been an integral part of Russia in the hearts and minds of people," was greeted with thunderous applause, chants of "Russia, Russia" and pro-government demonstrations in Red Square.[29] The Russian interior ministry claimed that 600,000 people congregated in the central squares of major cities to support the Crimea annexation, and these rallies were exceptionally pronounced in Vladivostok and Bryansk where 15,000 people attended.[30] The Russian State Duma voted to annex Crimea by a 445–1 margin. The motion's sole opponent, Ilya Ponomarev, was a branded a "national traitor" on a large billboard in Moscow and was eventually impeached in June 2016. To convert this patriotic rally into support for Putin's regime, Russian officials and state media outlets framed the Crimea annexation as a pivotal event in shaping Russia's national identity. Russian deputy prime minister Dmitry Rogozin described Crimea and Sevastopol's return as "the day of the revival of Russian national identity."[31] Channel One commentator Egor Kholmogorov highlighted how Putin used the word "russkiy" 29 times in his 18 March speech instead of the usual two or three times, and announced that "Putin has de facto announced the birth of a real Russkiy nation-state."[32] These narratives received widespread popular support. A 21–24 March Levada Center poll showed that 88% of Russians supported the Crimea annexation, as 74% believed "Crimea is a Russian land," and Putin's approval ratings soared to 80%.[33]

The resonance of Russian official justifications for military action in Crimea further bolstered popular support for the annexation. The counter-revolutionary rhetoric that Russia avidly promoted during Euro-Maidan extended to Crimea. On 4 March, Russia's UN Ambassador Vitaly Churkin delegitimised Turchynov's interim government by claiming that Yanukovych remained the legitimate president of Ukraine.[34] Churkin invoked Yanukovych's pleas for Russia to "establish legitimacy, peace, law and order, and stability" in Ukraine, and warned that "extremists" and "nationalist armed radicals" who terrorised western Ukraine would migrate to Crimea.[35] Putin similarly warned that "masked militants" were roaming through Kyiv even though the capital was quiet, and described the new Ukrainian authorities as "rats" who followed the U.S.'s agenda of destabilisation.[36] When Putin had asked the Federation Council to authorise Russia's use of force against Ukraine on 1 March, he had warned of a threat to Russian citizens, Russian "compatriots" and military personnel stationed in Crimea.[37] On 2 March, former deputy prime minister of Crimea Andrei Kozenko had argued that Russia had intervened in Crimea to "avoid bloodshed" instigated by the ultranationalist Right Sector or Crimean Tatars and restore equal rights for ethnic Russians.[38]

These narratives were premised on falsehoods like the 20 February "Corsun Pogrom," during which, according to pro-Russian media sources in Crimea, Right Sector affiliates tortured and killed anti-Maidan protesters, but no death records were ever released, and the anti-Maidan activists experienced only minor injuries.[39] Nevertheless, Kremlin propaganda about a threat to ethnic Russians dovetailed with long-standing stereotypes about the situation in Crimea. Moscow State University Professor Sergei Perevezentsev decried thirty years of Ukrainisation of Crimea, accused the Ukrainian government of persistently stoking tensions between Crimean Tatars and ethnic Russians and claimed that his ethnic Russian students often asked him "When will Russia come to save us from Ukraine?"[40] Given these long-standing concerns, Perevezentsev contends that Russia's annexation was a "salvation of Crimea" that prevented a civil war much worse than what subsequently unfolded in Donbas.[41] Due to these oft-repeated conspiracies, only 13% of Russians saw the Crimea annexation as an act of military aggression, and concerns about violence by Ukrainian right-wing radicals and forced Ukrainisation were top reasons for supporting Crimea's reunion with Russia.[42] The deaths of forty-six anti-Maidan activists in the 2 May 2014 Odesa clashes would reinforce myths about the Corsun pogrom, and augment support for the Kremlin's justifications for annexing Crimea.

The international response to Russia's annexation of Crimea was much more critical. In a 27 March vote on United Nations General Assembly (UNGA) Resolution 68/262, which reaffirmed the territorial integrity of Ukraine, only eleven countries (Belarus, Armenia, Syria, North Korea, Sudan, Zimbabwe, Cuba, Nicaragua,

Venezuela and Bolivia, plus Russia itself) accepted the Crimea annexation. U.S. president Barack Obama condemned the annexation of Crimea as an "illegitimate move," a position that was shared by 100 countries at the UNGA, and imposed sanctions on Russian individuals on 17 March.[43] These sanctions targeted key Putin advisors such as Glazyev, Rogozin and Surkov; pro-Kremlin Ukrainian figures such as Yanukovych, Aksyonov and former head of the President's Office Viktor Medvedchuk; and Russian lawmakers who actively supported the Crimea annexation. On 20 March, the U.S. imposed sanctions on fourteen defence companies, financing restrictions on six Russian banks and four energy companies, and barred development financing credits to Russia. These sanctions, which were adopted by the EU, Canada and Japan, triggered the most drastic Russia–West confrontation of the post-Cold War era and were swiftly followed by Russia's suspension from the G8 on 24 March. The Global South's response to the Crimea annexation was much more polarised but even Moscow's core non-Western partners mostly refrained from outright solidarity with Russia. China abstained from UNGA Resolution 68/262 on the grounds that it was supporting diplomacy, while India abstained while acknowledging Russia's legitimate interests in Crimea and refusing to immediately recognise Ukraine's post-Maidan government. The Russian foreign ministry's protestations that Western states used "shameless pressure, up to the point of political blackmail and economic threats" on UNGA member states gained little traction in the international community.[44] Nevertheless, the contradiction between domestic support and international opprobrium of Russia's actions in Ukraine continued, as Moscow embarked on a course of further aggression.

Russia Builds the Case for War in Donbas

Despite Western sanctions and the potential erosion of Russian soft power, the Kremlin doubled down on its aggressive rhetoric and provocative policies towards Ukraine in the spring of 2014. Although Putin denied that he planned to launch a full-scale invasion of Ukraine, his 4 March Channel One interview left the door open for a Russian military intervention in eastern Ukraine "if people ask us for help."[45] The 14 March deaths of pro-Russian youths Artyom Zhudov and Alexei Sharov in clashes with Ukrainian far-right nationalists in Kharkiv encouraged Putin's Press Secretary Dmitry Peskov to state that Russia reserved the right to "protect Ukrainians and Russians" if the situation worsened.[46] These statements encouraged hardliners in Putin's orbit to lobby for sweeping military action in Ukraine. On 24 March, Glazyev warned of "armed violence" and "lynch law" by "neo-fascists" in south-eastern Ukraine, and predicted that the region was heading towards a civil war that would mandate Russia to "protect people."[47] Zhirinovsky concurrently proposed a partition of Ukraine along the lines of the 1939 Nazi–Soviet Pact, which would hand western regions to Poland, Hungary and Romania.[48] Russian officials established a self-defence pretext for further military intervention in Ukraine and primed the Russian public for war in Donbas. On 4 April, Sergei Shoigu baselessly claimed that "extremist organisations" were trying to seize Russian military infrastructure in Crimea. Shoigu's self-defence argument, which alluded to Article 51 of the UN Charter,[49] created an apparent pretext for a more expansive Russian military intervention in Ukraine. On 17 April, Putin admitted that the Russian armed forces had created conditions for Crimea's unification with Russia.[50]

The escalation of Russian aggression towards Ukraine can be explained by two principal factors. First, Russia was emboldened by the apparent weaknesses of the Ukrainian military and the West's limited resolve to counter Moscow's violations of international law. Although Russia's annexation of Crimea was a swift event-driven decision, Ukrainian officials and experts were aware of the risks of a Russian military intervention for a long time. Oleh Rybachuk, who served as Yushchenko's chief of staff in 2005–6, noted that State Duma Deputy Konstantin Zatulin's claims that Crimea and eastern Ukraine would join Russia if Kyiv embraced NATO caused alarm as early as 2003.[51] The pervasiveness of Russian flags, marginalisation of Ukrainian-language media, unprovoked bellicosity of Russia's Black Sea Fleet drills, Russia's alleged interference in the 2006 parliamentary elections in Crimea and Moscow's infiltration of Crimea's security services all signified an invasion loomed.[52] Oleksandr Sushko, the director of the International Renaissance Foundation in Kyiv, contends that Ukrainian resistance to Russia using Crimea as a launchpad for attacks on Georgia in 2008 increased the likelihood of Moscow's annexation of the peninsula.[53] Prior to the 2010 Kharkiv Pact, some Ukrainian experts viewed the 2017 expiration of the Black Sea Fleet lease as the latest possible date for a Russian invasion.[54]

Despite these ominous warnings, the Ukrainian military was woefully unprepared for a Russian invasion. Natalia Galibarenko, who served as deputy foreign minister of Ukraine in 2014–15 and Ukraine's Ambassador to Britain from 2015 to 2020, contends that "Ukraine effectively did not have a working military. It was underfinanced for years and the top-level of our armed forces were infiltrated by Russian spies and FSB agents. After the Euro-Maidan Revolution, these spies fled to Russia."[55] Galibarenko asserts that the process of rebuilding the Ukrainian military only began with the Donbas offensive, as volunteers joined and the army was "reconstructed from scratch."[56] Due to the Ukrainian military's endemic corruption, Russia believed that collaborationists would help it easily annex large swathes of eastern and southern Ukraine. Rinat Akhmetov, the billionaire founder of System Capital Management and former Party of Regions MP, was an especially plausible collaborationist, as he benefited from the decentralisation of Donetsk and was targeted by Euro-Maidan protests as a symbol of Yanukovych-era corruption.[57] Oleksandr Yefremov, who served as Party of Regions faction leader in the Rada from 2010 to 2014, was an expected enabler of Luhansk separatism. Medvedchuk was expected to stoke anti-EU sentiments, as he had previously compared the EU to the Third Reich and reiterated Russian narratives that the EU association agreement would convert Ukraine into an economic vassal of Brussels. Through enlisting local partners and annexing territory, Russia would guarantee a federal system in Ukraine, which would give far-reaching autonomy to Russian-speaking regions and provide it with leverage over Kyiv's strategic decisions, such as pursuing European integration.[58]

Russian officials believed that a more expansive military intervention in Ukraine would strike a devastating blow to the U.S.-led unipolar world order, trigger only mild Western sanctions and bolster Russia's status in the collective non-West. Rogozin's 18 March claim that annexing Crimea caused the "death of the unipolar order" underscored the revisionist intent of Russian aggression in Ukraine. Russia's desire to overhaul the existing international order was not driven by its advancement of a clear set of legal principles.[59] Instead, it was inspired by Russia's desire for respect from Western powers. Sergei Karaganov contends that after the Cold War ended, "Russia's interests and objections were demonstratively disregarded," and as Russia did not see itself as a defeated power, "Weimar syndrome" developed.[60] Russian officials saw a synthesis of diplomacy and hard power in Ukraine as a shortcut to the respect it desired from the West. Lavrov's proposed solution to the Ukraine crisis was distinctly multipolar and consensus-based in character. On 30 March, Lavrov urged Russia, the U.S. and the EU to jointly construct a support group, which would convince Ukraine's post-Maidan authorities to pursue national dialogue and exclude "armed radicals" from the political process.[61] While Lavrov's plan was never seriously debated, Russia believed that more territorial gains would compel the West to recognise Ukraine's place within its sphere of influence and accept a peace settlement on Moscow's terms. Dmitry Suslov, a professor at Moscow's Higher School of Economics, contends that Russia saw its power vis-à-vis the West at its medium-term apex in 2014 and concluded that it was the appropriate time to bolster its force with hard power.[62]

Despite the overt nature of Russia's challenge to the rules-based international order, it did not anticipate the imposition of large-scale sanctions. The U.S.'s swift imposition of the Magnitsky Act sanctions on Russian human rights abusers in December 2012, which occurred in tandem with the repeal of the 1974 Jackson–Vanik Amendment sanctions, created the perception in Moscow that sanctions were inevitable regardless of Russia's actions.[63] Inside the Russian foreign policy expert community, it was widely expected that Germany would block sweeping EU-wide sanctions and that EU member states such as Italy and France could be pried away from the Western consensus on isolating Russia.[64] Russia's nonchalant response to Crimea-related sanctions reflected this lack of concern. On 18 March, Rogozin bombastically declared, "Yesterday's first wave of sanctions is, by and large, a joke. I think that real sanctions will not be announced" and quipped that the "sanctions that have been imposed on us are some kind of kindergarten," as they targeted individuals who lacked U.S. assets.[65] Building on Putin's prior warning that the interconnectedness of the world economy would cause sanctions to incur mutual damage,[66] Russian media focused extensively on their potential blowback on Europe. As France considered abrogating its contract with Russia for Mistral-class helicopter carriers, State Duma Defence Committee Chairman Vladimir Komoyedov predicted windfalls for Russia's ship-building industry, hailed the superiority of Russian naval technology to French "tin can" ships and stated that "if the French refuse, it would be good for Russia."[67]

Despite limited overt international support for the Crimea annexation, Russia saw further aggression in Ukraine as an opportunity to reorient its foreign policy towards the Global South. This recalibration would accelerate trends that began during Yevgeny Primakov's tenure as foreign minister from 1996 to 1998, which saw Russia elevate the strategic importance of relations with China and India, strengthen relations with anti-Western regimes and re-establish Moscow's geopolitical footprints in the Middle East, Africa and Latin America. The growing importance of the non-Western vectors of Russian foreign policy was apparent from Kremlin statements in March 2014. Citing the precedent of Cuba's half-century embargo, Rosneft chief Igor Sechin stated that Russian companies could readily transfer their activities to the Global South, as "Europe and America are no longer the masters" of the global economy.[68] Putin praised China for perceiving the Crimea situation "in all its historical and geopolitical integrity" and extolled India's "restraint and objectivity."[69] Shoigu's claims that Russia was trying to construct bases in Vietnam, Cuba, Venezuela, Nicaragua, the Seychelles, Singapore, Algeria and Cyprus were excessively optimistic but underscored Moscow's ambitions for a more expansive security policy in the Global South.[70] These statements presaged a sweeping array of new Russian trade deals, which were especially pronounced in the energy, mining and defence sectors, and Russia's increasingly assertive support for authoritarian regimes and counter-insurgency missions across the Global South.

Second, Russian officials believed that a more expansive military intervention in Ukraine would bolster their authoritarian consolidation ambitions. The February 2014 Sochi Olympics, which immediately preceded the Crimea annexation, inspired a series of repressive measures from the Russian authorities. Russia's release of Mikhail Khodorkovsky and Pussy Riot rock band members in December 2013 pointed to liberalisation ahead of the games. However, these measures had been preceded by an August 2013 ban on protests around Sochi Olympic sites and a crackdown on promoters of "non-traditional" sexuality and followed by the January 2014 expulsion of former *Wall Street Journal* correspondent David Satter. The Kremlin's pre-Olympic repression was likely triggered by concerns that riots that would expose corruption in the $50 billion budget for the Sochi Olympics and create disorder that could be exploited by Islamic extremists.[71] While the Russian authorities were able to drive dissent underground during the Olympics, Russia's military intervention in Crimea brought liberals back to the streets. The 2 and 15 March "March for Peace" rallies featured a heterogeneous mixture of anti-war activists, Yabloko party members, dissident celebrities and opposition politicians such as Navalny, Nemtsov, PARNAS leader Ilya Yashin and former State Duma Deputy Gennady Gudkov. The 15 March rally brought 20,000 demonstrators to the streets of Moscow, which was the largest congregation of anti-Putin protesters since Bolotnaya Square.

The nationalist euphoria over Crimea marginalised liberal dissent in Russia. Key opposition leaders acquiesced to Crimea's reincorporation into Russia, even if they saw Putin's motivations as self-serving. Ksenia Sobchak, a well-known opposition TV anchor, stated in March 2014 that "if Putin returns Crimea to Russia without blood, he will go down in history as a great and there's nothing you can do about that."[72] Navalny's position was more critical, as he argued that "Putin has cynically raised nationalist fervor to a fever pitch; imperialist annexation is a strategic choice to bolster his regime survival," but subsequently opposed returning Crimea to Ukraine.[73] For Russians who expressed open dissent, the costs were steep. Moscow State

Institute of International Relations (MGIMO) academic Andrey Zubov, who compared Russia's annexation of Crimea to Nazi Germany's 1938 Anschluss union with Austria, was summarily dismissed from his post. Isolated displays of dissent such as holding a "Stop the War" or "Peace to the World" banner became sufficient cause to arrest or fine anti-war activists in Moscow or St. Petersburg.[74] Lone-wolf voices of opposition to the Crimea annexation such as *Nezavisimaya Gazeta* editor-in-chief Konstantin Remchukov and writer Boris Akunin were unable to breach this climate of repression and rally support for the anti-war cause. Due to this near evisceration of dissent, Russia launched an offensive in Donbas to further Putin's totalitarian ambitions and accentuate his grip on power.

Russia's Undeclared War on Donbas

On 7 April, pro-Russian rebels seized a Security Service of Ukraine (SBU) building in Donetsk. These rebels announced the creation of the "Donetsk People's Republic" and unveiled plans to organise a referendum on union with Russia on 11 May. The next day, pro-Russian militias and volunteers from Sevastopol carried out a similar occupation of an SBU building in Luhansk, and announced plans to create a "parliament of the Luhansk Republic."[75] The Ukrainian authorities swiftly tried to delegitimise and quell the pro-Russian insurgency in Donbas. Turchynov claimed that these attacks were the "second wave" of Russia's plan to destabilise Ukraine, pursue regime change and derail Ukraine's presidential elections, and warned that Russia was leveraging Donbas unrest to "dismember" Ukraine.[76] Ukrainian security officials were dispatched to Donetsk, Luhansk and Kharkiv but pro-Russian militias continued their aggressive actions. On 12 April, former FSB colonel Igor Girkin formed a militia consisting of volunteers from Russia, Crimea, Donbas and elsewhere in Ukraine that intended to spearhead a Crimea-style annexation of Donetsk and Luhansk. After pro-Russian militias clashed with local security services in Donetsk's major cities, including Mariupol and Kramatorsk, Turchnyov announced the start of an "anti-terrorism operation" (ATO) in Donbas on 16 April. Citing the risk of a possible civil war, Russia began amassing forces on Ukraine's borders, while Western powers urged Russia to condemn the subversive activities of its Donbas proxies and supported a diplomatic resolution to the crisis via talks with the U.S., EU, Russia and Ukraine.

Efforts to forestall the outbreak of war in Donbas were unsuccessful, as hostilities escalated in Sloviansk and Mariupol. Following the declaration of a "Luhansk People's Republic" by pro-Russian rebels on 27 April, referenda were scheduled on the independence of Donetsk and Luhansk on 11 May. These referenda, which were manifestly unconstitutional and undemocratic, produced 89% support for self-rule in Donetsk and 96% for independence of Luhansk. The Russian foreign ministry urged the EU to respect the results of these referenda, promote dialogue between Kyiv and south-eastern Ukrainian representatives and stop describing the Donbas rebels as "pro-Russian separatists."[77] Russia's legitimisation of these illegal referenda resulted in the creation of a Donetsk People's Republic (DNR) cabinet on 16 May, which was led by far-right ideologue Alexander Borodai and which appointed Girkin as defence minister, and a Luhansk People's Republic (LNR) cabinet on 18 May, which was led by Yefremov-aligned businessman Valery Bolotov. As Ukrainian forces gained ground in separatist-occupied regions, Russia began supplying heavy weaponry such as mortars to DNR and LNR militias and covertly deployed regular forces in larger quantities. The Wagner Group also dispatched 300 PMCs to Donbas, which participated in intelligence gathering and subversive attacks on Ukrainian government institutions and ammunition stocks. The shooting down of an Il-76MD on 16 June, which was orchestrated by LNR militias and resulted in 49 casualties, underscored the improved efficacy of Russian separatist militias in targeting the Ukrainian armed forces.

Although Ukraine recaptured Mariupol on 13 June, Sloviansk in Donetsk on 5 July and Severodonetsk in Luhansk on 22 July, its military advances in Donbas stalled as the summer progressed. The Battle of Ilovaisk, which began on 7 August, was a turning point that convinced Ukraine to abandon its anti-terrorism operation and sue for peace. On 14 August, a column of 23 Russian armoured personnel carriers supported by fuel trucks and logistics vehicles crossed the Russia–Ukraine border. Although Ukrainian forces entered Ilovaisk on 18 August, they were swiftly encircled by Russian troops. Russia's encirclement forced Ukraine's Dnipro Battalion commander Yuriy Bereza to withdraw forces from Ilovaisk and Russian forces inflicted significant casualties on the retreating Ukrainians. Russia's triumph in Ilovaisk encouraged it to expand the scope of its undeclared war on Donbas. By 29 August, DNR prime minister Alexander Zakharchenko was admitting that Russia had deployed 3,000 to 4,000 troops to the frontlines, which coincided with pro-Russian militias opening a new front in south-eastern Ukraine.[78] Russia's offensive was initially successful, as DNR forces seized control of Novoazovsk on 28 August, and advanced in the direction of Mariupol, which would consolidate Moscow's foothold in the Sea of Azov.

As the autumn of 2014 began, the progress of negotiations between Russia and Ukraine accelerated. These talks built on efforts to de-escalate the conflict, which began in the summer but were delayed by provocations from Russia and its separatist allies. After Petro Poroshenko's election victory on 26 May, Lavrov emphasised the need for "mutually respectful dialogue" with the new Ukrainian government and these sentiments were echoed by all major Russian politicians, except Gennady Zuganov, who called the elections an "embarrassment."[79] This tone contrasted markedly with Putin's prior claims that the elections were an "illegitimate political exercise" and State Duma Chairman Sergei Naryshkin's assertions that "punitive conditions" in Donbas precluded free elections.[80] After two phone calls with Putin in mid-June, Poroshenko unveiled a 15-point peace plan, which included promises to decentralise power in Ukraine, hold early local and parliamentary elections, create a 10km buffer zone on the Russia–Ukraine border and a safe corridor for separatist militias to leave the conflict.[81] High-level talks involving Kuchma, Medvedchuk, separatist representatives and the Organization for Security and Co-operation in Europe (OSCE) produced a ceasefire agreement on 23 June. However, Russia's military deployments and the shooting down of Malaysia Airlines Flight 17 (MH17) on 17 July, carried out by the DNR but blamed by Russia on Ukraine, derailed hopes for peace.

The September 2014 Minsk Protocol, devised by representatives of Russia, Ukraine and the OSCE, revived Poroshenko's peace plan and created a narrow window of opportunity for a lasting peace. On 10 September, Poroshenko claimed that 70% of Russia's forces had left Ukraine but recurrent ceasefire violations paved the way for renewed conflict.[82] The November 2014 elections in Donetsk and Luhansk ended this fragile de-escalation. Poroshenko immediately revoked the Minsk Protocol's mandate of special status for Donbas and to pre-empt a Russian offensive, Ukraine deployed additional troops to Mariupol, Berdyansk, Kharkiv, Luhansk and Dnipropetrovsk.[83] The Donbas War's intensity ebbed once again in December 2014, as 1,500 prisoners were swapped in a Minsk Protocol-mandated exchange, but escalated once again in January 2015 as the conflict spread to Donetsk International Airport. The fall of Donetsk Airport on 15 January caused Zakharchenko and LNR separatist leader Igor Plotnitsky to refrain from attending the new round of Minsk talks the next day. Ukrainian forces retaliated by recapturing most of Donetsk Airport over the course of 17–18 January. Russia's deployment of 9,000 troops and artillery reinforcements allowed DNR forces to recapture the airport and advance on Debaltseve, and LNR troops to make advances against Ukraine near the Siverskyi Donets River.

These setbacks encouraged French president François Hollande and German chancellor Angela Merkel to make a last-ditch attempt to revive the Minsk Protocol and deter the U.S. from supplying lethal arms to Ukraine. This Franco–German peace-keeping effort reaped immediate dividends. On 12 February, France, Germany, Russia and Ukraine unveiled the Minsk II accords. This agreement called for a constitutional mandate to decentralise DNR- and LNR-held areas, a ceasefire, a withdrawal of heavy weaponry over a two-week period, the exodus of all foreign troops and illegal armed groups and a general amnesty for POWs.[84] The Minsk II accords suffered an early setback, as DNR forces insisted that the ceasefire did not apply to the active Debaltseve front and on 18 February, Ukrainian troops were forced to exit Debaltseve. After the fall of Debaltseve, progress towards peace accelerated. Although Ukraine ruled out a heavy weaponry withdrawal on 23 February due to rebel attacks, it nonetheless began implementing this dimension of the Minsk accords three days later. On 14 April, German foreign minister Frank-Walter Steinmeier announced that an agreement had been reached to remove heavy weaponry and potentially other catego-ries of weapons from the frontlines.[85] These concessions con-verted the Donbas War into a Nagorno-Karabakh-style frozen conflict, which uneasily persisted until Russia's full-scale invasion of Ukraine in February 2022.

The Minsk II Accords: A Controversial Peace Gambit

Although the Minsk II accords prevented a protracted war, their terms polarised opinion in Kyiv and Moscow. Poroshenko justified Ukraine's acceptance of Minsk II by stating that "Either the situation goes down the road of de-escalation, ceasefire or the situation goes out of control."[86] Ukrainian MP Lesia Vasylenko supported Poroshenko's justification, stating that it stopped "massive bloodshed," as Ukraine received no Western military support and the Ukrainian military had been weakened by Yanukovych's decree that replaced conscription with a contract army.[87] The Ukrainian far-right vocally opposed the Minsk accords. Igor Moseichuk, a former Azov Battalion Deputy Commander who was elected to the Rada, called them an "act of treason" and a "betrayal of national interests," and Right Sector leader Dmytro Yarosh called for continued military operations against pro-Russian separatists.[88] Concerns about structural flaws in the accords permeated across Ukraine's political spectrum. Ukrainian MP Dmytro Natalukha contends that Minsk II was "the first step towards civil war in Ukraine," as Donbas elections would have caused a "radical minority" to enter the Rada with the intention of overturning the majority's agenda. Natalukha believed that this minority would demand specific rights for Donbas, Russian speakers and the Russian Orthodox Church on dubious grounds; counter Ukraine's advance towards the EU and NATO; and polarise Ukrainian society until there was open conflict. Natalukha believes that this scenario was Russia's design in signing Minsk, as the Kremlin wanted to depict Ukraine as a failed state in order to justify future military operations.[89]

While the Minsk II accords did not create comparably overt cleavages in Russia, it constituted a drastic downgrade from the Kremlin's maximalist ambitions in Ukraine. On 17 April, Putin declared that the 1920 handover of regions such as Kharkiv, Luhansk, Donetsk and Odesa to Ukraine was a historical aberration, and called these areas "Novorossiya" or New Russia.[90] Novorossiya was coined after the Russian Empire annexed the Crimean Khanate from the Ottoman Empire in 1764, and due to its imperialist context, Putin's statement was widely interpreted as a call to annex the entirety of south-eastern Ukraine. The geopolitical implications of a Russian takeover of these regions would have been sweeping. Ukraine's population would have declined from 46 to 25 million, and due to the region's industrial potential, two-thirds of Ukraine's GDP would have fallen into Russia's hands.[91] Russia's ceasefire negotiations with Ukraine also provided a veneer of legitimacy to the post-Maidan authorities, which clashed with Moscow's intensified counter-revolutionary propaganda. In June 2014, Glazyev accused Kyiv's "Nazi government" of bombing Ukraine's largest region and said "of course" when asked whether Poroshenko was a Nazi.[92] In October 2014, State Duma Deputy Irina Yarovaya declared that Euro-Maidan was an example of an "Orange Revolution where the state is destroyed with the help of the citizens themselves," and predicted that Ukraine would inevitably slide into a Yugoslavia-style civil war.[93] Russian media outlets described Ukraine as a U.S. puppet regime, as Assistant Secretary of State Victoria Nuland's praise of Yatsenyuk's leadership potential in a leaked February 2014 phone call with U.S. Ambassador to Ukraine Geoffrey Pyatt received obsessive attention.

Why did Russia pause its neo-imperial and counter-revolutionary ambitions in Ukraine by signing Minsk II? Three factors explain this pivot. First, Russia did not view a military solution in Donbas as easily achievable or optimal. Despite intense information warfare against the Ukrainian authorities, grassroots support for Donbas separatist militias was limited and the overwhelming majority of south-eastern Ukrainians believed that Russia was an impediment to peace in Ukraine.[94] Russia's lack of local support prevented it from effectively waging a hybrid war in Ukraine, which mirrored its failures during the 2008 Georgian War. While Russia's undeclared military intervention in Donbas was sufficient to maintain a Chechnya-style war of attrition with inconsistent territorial gains, Ukraine's plans to reform intra-agency coordination, upgrade its weapons arsenals and double its army to 250,000 personnel could have eventually tipped the conflict in Kyiv's favour.[95] Russia's logistical challenges, which were exposed in the 2022 invasion, were already visible, and reinforcements such as the Wagner Group were geared for small-scale operations aimed at disrupting Ukraine's war effort rather than decisive battlefield victories.[96]

Russia could have pre-empted Ukraine's military modernisation by declaring war on Ukraine, but Moscow did not view a Crimea-style annexation of Donbas as being in its economic or strategic interests. Dmitry Suslov contends that Russia wanted to keep Donetsk and Luhansk within Ukraine, as they provided it with leverage over a "new Ukrainian state."[97] Ukrainian officials contend that Russia did not want to annex Donbas because it would be a heavily subsidised region like Chechnya. Given the extensive Russian propaganda about Ukrainian shelling of Donbas, annexation created pressure on Putin to intervene militarily at an inopportune time.[98] Kuchma contended that Russia's aims prior to Minsk II were primarily geared at destabilising south-eastern Ukraine, as keeping a large military presence near the border and financially backing Russian proxies suited its interests.[99] Due to the disadvantages of annexing Donbas, Russian officials saw diplomacy as more beneficial than continued war in securing a durable sphere of influence in eastern Ukraine. Although Minsk II possessed references to laws from Kyiv that were unacceptable for Donbas, *Rossiya Segodnya* commentator Dmitry Kosyrev noted that the accords provided numerous avenues for dialogue between Ukraine, DNR and LNR. Kosyrev conceded that the dialogue provisions were rendered vulnerable by systemic shocks, such as an economic collapse in Ukraine, but left an open door for changes that went beyond a truce in Donbas or the "reorganisation of Ukraine."[100]

Second, the Kremlin believed that a ceasefire in Donbas, which ensconced Russia's territorial gains and incurred significant concessions from Ukraine, would appeal to the broadest base of Russians. During the early stages of the Donbas War, pro-Kremlin ideologues emphasised the necessity of a complete triumph for Novorossiya. Alexander Dugin's support for a large-scale Russian invasion of Ukraine, which mirrored his calls for regime change in Tbilisi in 2008 and the annexation of Crimea in tandem with the Georgian War, was especially striking. Dugin described this cleavage as a conflict between "patriots" and "liberals," and warned that Putin's hesitation would alienate both factions and derail the "Russian Spring."[101] Oleg Tsaryov, a former Party of Regions Deputy, declared that all of Ukraine could become Novorossiya by the spring of 2015 and asserted that Novorossiya's expansion would protect rights for Russian-language speakers and increase salaries and pensions.[102] Girkin, who was actively promoted by Dugin, called for Russian military assistance to secure DNR control over Sloviansk, and Kurginyan regarded Girkin's ultimate surrender of the city as a betrayal of the Novorossiya cause.[103]

Within Putin's inner circle, the Novorossiya project engendered polarised responses. The "Glazyev Tapes," which were released in August 2016, illustrated that key figures, such as Glazyev and Zatulin, tried to finance counter-revolutionary movements in Kharkiv, Odesa and Donbas with the express intention of delegitimising the post-Maidan government in these regions. Surkov was a private voice of restraint on Novorossiya, as he partnered with Akhmetov to rein in the influence of Girkin and Dugin's hardline nationalist approaches.[104] Ultimately, the forces of restraint on Novorossiya prevailed over the more outspoken hardliners. Levada Center surveys reveal that Minsk II was overwhelmingly supported by the Russian public—84% of Russians regarded the ceasefire as a positive development and just

5% of Russians linked the de-escalation to Western sanctions or pro-Western sentiments amongst Russian elites.[105] The intensification of sanctions, which would inevitably occur as the war in Donbas persisted, was also viewed as a potential threat to Putin's regime stability. Appeals from Putin allies such as First Deputy Chief of Staff of the Presidential Administration Vyacheslav Volodin, who claimed that "If there is Putin, there is also a stable Russia, if there is no Putin, there will be no stable Russia," convinced many Russians to support Putin in spite of tightening sanctions. In the long run, the Kremlin feared that sanctions could cause disquiet amongst oligarchs, who saw their businesses get decoupled from Western loans, and divide the ruling elite class.[106]

Third, Russia wanted to portray itself as interested in peace in Donbas, so it would shift the blame for ceasefire violations on Ukraine and the West and create a pretext for a future expansionist war. To further this end, Russia volunteered itself as a supporter of Minsk II's implementation. Due to the undeclared nature of Russia's war in Donbas, Peskov claimed that Russia was "not a party to this conflict" and insisted that it played the role of a "guarantor" of Minsk II.[107] Vasily Likhachev, a member of Russia's delegation to the OSCE, urged an envoy of the UNSC or OSCE to carry out a monitoring mission in Debaltseve, and stated that these measures needed to be taken to prevent Minsk's immediate collapse.[108] Russia claimed that Ukrainian military manoeuvres in Debaltseve were proof that Poroshenko was not serious about Minsk, and that Western officials were enabling Ukrainian aggression. Leonid Kalashnikov, the Deputy Chairman of the State Duma Committee on International Affairs, stated that EU leaders wanted to perpetuate the war in Ukraine as it gave them a convenient excuse for high gas prices and low wages.[109] These accusations crystallised Russia's narratives that Ukraine violated Minsk and was ruled by Western puppets, which eventually justified the February 2022 invasion.

THE EURO-MAIDAN REVOLUTION

Russia Deepens its Embrace of a Multipolar World Order

Despite the Kremlin's strenuous denials of military involvement in Donbas, the Western sanctions regime against Russia inexorably tightened. On 7 April, the Council of Europe voted to suspend Russia from its parliamentary assembly by a 145–21 margin. This ban, which expired at the end of 2014, prompted accusations of Western double standards from Senator Alexei Pushkov, who decried the lack of condemnations of past U.S. aggression against Yugoslavia and Iraq.[110] In the months that followed, the U.S. imposed sanctions on prominent Russian businessmen such as Igor Sechin, bans on transactions on major Russian companies such as Rosneft, Novatek, Gazprombank and Rostec, and Russia's largest bank Sberbank. These sanctions were mirrored by the EU, Japan, Canada, Switzerland and Norway, and disrupted oil extraction cooperation between Russian and Western companies, as well as EU investments in Black Sea oil and gas exploration in Crimea. The sanctions imposed significant costs on the Russian economy. In April 2015, Medvedev estimated that sanctions cost Russia $26.7 billion in 2014 and a further $80 billion in 2015, and the value of Russian foreign trade declined by 30% in the first two months of 2015.[111] The synergistic impact of declining oil prices, which plunged by nearly 50% in the second half of 2014, caused the rouble to lose more than half its value by 2016 and triggered a 3.7% GDP contraction in 2015. Despite initial optimism that they would be lifted by mid-2015, Russian officials were forced to reconcile themselves to the reality of long-term sanctions. The Kremlin's principal economic advisors, such as former finance minister Alexei Kudrin, prepared for Russia's potential cut-off from SWIFT, which could result in an immediate 5% decline in GDP.[112] Glazyev's proposed de-dollarisation measures, such as restricting foreign currency purchases and taxation of currency exchange transactions, underscored the Kremlin's consideration of an autarkic sanctions-proof economy.[113]

Despite these fears, the worst-case scenario for Western sanctions against Russia did not come to pass. Although gas export links to Europe operated at half-supply due to restrictions on Gazprom and pipeline expansion negotiations stalled in January 2015, Europe did not take decisive steps towards divesting from Russian gas and Nord Stream 2 was unveiled in June 2015. In Kyiv, the EU's continued commercial engagement with Russia was viewed as a betrayal. Former Ukrainian Ambassador to Austria Olexander Scherba says he tried to alert EU officials to the "insanity" of Putin's Russia and the prevailing response was that "we have to deal with the insanity," as money can be earned by staying on Russia's good side.[114] Viktor Yushchenko accuses Europe of collaborating directly with Russia and says that European officials did not learn their lesson from the 2008 Georgian War. Yushchenko notes that European officials congregated in Moscow instead of Tbilisi during that conflict and proceeded to expand Nord Stream.[115] To assuage its isolation from the West, Russia strengthened its partnerships with far-right and left-wing populist parties. In November 2014, National Front leader Marine Le Pen admitted that her party borrowed 9 million euros from the Moscow-based First Czech Russian Bank, because, she said, "no one else will give us a cent."[116] Prominent officials in Germany's Alternative für Deutschland (AfD) party, such as Brandenburg's Alexander Gauland, urged Berlin to express "greater understanding" towards Russia's actions in Crimea.[117] Close links between Greece's left-wing Syriza party and Russian ideologues such as Dugin and oligarch Konstantin Malofeev underscored the acceptability of Kremlin narratives in some EU countries.

As sanctions did not result in Russia's complete isolation from the West, the Russian foreign policy community was polarised around the required scale of Moscow's divestment from the West. The siloviki were especially inclined to view the U.S.–Russia rivalry over Ukraine as a zero-sum New Cold War-style confrontation. In October 2014, Patrushev stated that the U.S. wanted to secure access for foreign countries to Russia's natural resources and claimed that the U.S. was using sanctions to contain "the growing power of Russia and other centres of power."[118] The Kremlin's informal advisors on foreign policy issues called for a more moderate approach to Russia's interactions with the West. In July 2014, Primakov urged Russia to refrain from deploying troops to Ukraine, as Moscow would be able to engage with "forces in the West that want to normalise relations with Russia" and prevent a sharp deterioration in relations with Western countries.[119] Karaganov contended that Russia had not definitely embraced anti-Europeanism and urged Moscow's confrontation with the West to be paired with internal reforms.[120]

Nevertheless, there was a broad consensus around the collective non-West's standing as the primary vector of Russian foreign policy. The Kremlin did not explicitly link this transition to Western sanctions but instead framed it as a sign of the international system's inexorable transformation. Vladimir Putin linked Russia's non-Western pivot to the collapse of the unipolar order and claimed that Russia was trying to prevent the "global clashes" that typically accompany world order transitions.[121]

Russia's strategy to preserve its great power status in the face of Western sanctions consisted of three principal planks. The first plank was Russia's reassertion of its hegemony over its self-perceived sphere of influence in the post-Soviet space. Russia's annexation of Crimea and undeclared war in Donbas were not welcomed by its regional partners. Despite its alliance with Russia, Belarus upgraded its relations with Kyiv, as it pledged to supply Ukraine with petroleum products in August 2014 and lifted mutual trade restrictions.[122] While Minsk's overtures towards Ukraine were linked to its mediation role, Belarus's participation in visa negotiations with Brussels and unwillingness to escalate tensions with the Baltic states revealed the limits of its partnership with Moscow.[123] Kazakhstan sympathised with Russia's security concerns and acknowledged widespread support for Crimea's integration with Russia but maintained positive relations with Ukraine, as it viewed Kyiv as a key gateway for commercial ties with Europe.[124] Azerbaijan stridently supported the inviolability of Ukraine's borders and condemned "extremism, radicalism and separatism," which signalled its opposition to Russia's backing of Donbas separatist militias.[125] Uzbekistan's calls for greater Commonwealth of Independent States (CIS) engagement with Poroshenko on the implementation of the Minsk Protocol underscored its desire to pursue a more independent foreign policy course than its Central Asian neighbours.[126] Russia's "alliance and integration" treaty with South Ossetia, which coincided with the first anniversary of the Crimea annexation, was a rare example of enhanced cooperation in the post-Soviet space.

Russia viewed supranational economic integration as the most effective means of reasserting its hegemony in the near abroad. The EAEU, which formed as a result of a treaty between Russia, Belarus and Kazakhstan in May 2014, enhanced Moscow's economic ties with its post-Soviet partners and compartmentalised trade from foreign policy disagreements.

Armenia's 9 October 2014 and Kyrgyzstan's 23 December 2014 signing of treaties to join the EAEU further strengthened the customs union and paved the way for the creation of a single market on 1 January 2015. The Eurasian Economic Commission's structure, which gave EAEU countries equal representation on its governing body and allowed vetoes on decisions that impede the development of smaller states, allowed it to frame itself as a consensus-based rather than a Russian-dominated body.[127]

Despite its initial momentum, the EAEU struggled to achieve its lofty ambitions for regional integration. From 2015–16, intra-regional trade declined by 20% due to falling oil and gas prices, which the EAEU's leadership attributed to "global economic forces."[128] Kazakhstan signed an Enhanced Partnership and Cooperation Agreement with the EU in December 2015, while Belarus's exports struggled to compete with those of its partners in the EAEU bloc. Although the perceived failure of president Emomali Rahmon's multi-vector economic policy led Russia to believe that Tajikistan would inevitably join the EAEU, the bloc did not expand further.[129] Kazakhstan also aggressively resisted Russia's efforts to impose a common currency on the EAEU, which undermined Moscow's efforts to ban dollars and euros in the bloc.[130] These setbacks limited Russia's ability to expand its influence in the post-Soviet space and compensate for the soft power erosion that was triggered by its invasion of Ukraine.

The second plank of Russia's great power reassertion was military modernisation. During the first three years of Putin's third term, Russia's defence budget increased from 2.9 to 4.3% of its GDP. Russia continued modernising its general-purpose armed forces, as it sought to build on its mass fire capabilities that were exhibited in Donbas and achieve its goal of possessing 70% modern equipment by 2020.[131] Russia's Iskander-M missiles, which were paired with conventional warheads and cluster munitions in the 2008 Georgian War, were used in drills by the Eastern and Southern Military Districts, and Kaliningrad. Russia's Black Sea Fleet strengthened markedly, as it procured six new attack submarines and three frigates, and acquired the capability to use Kalibr missiles, which could fire at targets 1,500–2,000 km from its bases in Crimea and Novorossiysk.[132] The Russian Navy also expressed interest in developing new bases on Crimea which were previously used by the Ukrainian military, and potentially reviving the Soviet-era Black Sea Fleet base of Donuzlav.[133]

These policies would reinforce Russia's historical standing as a Black Sea power, which originated with Catherine the Great's 1783 annexation of Crimea from the Ottoman Empire and the Black Sea's standing as a "Soviet Lake" during the Cold War. Russia also tried to establish itself as a twenty-first century military power with global reach. After Shoigu declared in February 2014 that the "Mediterranean Region was the core of all essential dangers to Russia's national interests," Russia devised plans to deploy ten modern warships in the Mediterranean and allow nuclear capable submarines and the aircraft carrier Admiral Kuznetsov to operate in the region.[134] Russia also reorganised the Russian Air Force to increase its operational efficiency, and in August 2015, the Russian Aerospace Forces were formed. The improvements to Russia's conventional capabilities were paired with modernisations of its nuclear arsenal. Rogozin declared that Russia would renew 100% instead of the previously discussed 70% of its strategic nuclear weapons, while Shoigu predicted that advanced missile systems would make up 80% of its arsenal by 2016 and 100% of its arsenal by 2021.[135] These reforms increased Russia's confidence in its military capabilities, which paved the way for its intervention in Syria.

The third plank of Russia's efforts to preserve its great power status was the diversification of its partnerships in the Global South. Russia viewed China as the lynchpin of its pivot to the collective non-West. In May 2014, Gazprom and the China National Petroleum Corporation (CNPC) signed a $400 billion gas supply deal, which created a new pipeline that linked Siberia to China's coastal cities. The magnitude of the Russia–China gas deal could be explained by its $350 per cubic metre cost, which was lower than discounted European contracts of $350–380 and the Asian cost of imported liquefied natural gas, and Beijing's desire for cleaner energy options to advance its "war on pollution."[136] While its benefits for China were manifold, there were concerns about its profitability for Russia. As $55 billion of the $70 billion infrastructure costs would have to be borne by Russia, Gazprom was expected to have only a 9–10% return on its pipeline investments and Russian opposition figures such as Boris Nemtsov decried the deal as a "total loss and robbery."[137] If Russia's "Deal of the Century" would not drastically enrich its flagging economy, it signified Moscow's eastward pivot and the West's inability to isolate Russia through sanctions. Russia's sale of a 10% stake in Rosneft's Vankor oilfields to CNPC in September 2014, pledge to supply China with its S-400 air defence system and series of pacts in 2015 such as a $6 billion Chinese investment in Russia's inner-city rail-line and a non-aggression pact in cyberspace, underscored their partnership's growing strength. In January 2015, RT and Xinhua signed a news exchange and cooperation partnership, which allowed Russia and China to harmonise anti-Western narratives and advance a shared vision for a multipolar order. This narrative harmonisation was especially fruitful, as China's bellicosity in the South China Sea and Russia's aggression in Donbas were being simultaneously criticised in the West.

The consolidation of the Sino-Russian partnership coincided with Russia's diversification of its partnerships in the Global South. The consolidation of Russia–India relations was the cornerstone of Moscow's Indo-Pacific strategy. Vladimir Putin and Indian prime minister Narendra Modi bonded over their shared disdain for Western dominance of global institutions, common nationalist desires to secure hegemony over their respective regions and resistance to liberal values.[138] India's disdain for sanctions against Russia, which dovetailed with its prior resistance to unilateral measures against Iraq and Iran, and Moscow's backing of Indian territorial claims in Kashmir added further heft to this partnership. During their December 2014 meeting, Modi called Russia "India's closest friend," pledged to work with Putin on constructing a new security architecture for Asia, and signed deals with Moscow on atomic energy cooperation, the training of the Indian armed forces by the Russian defence ministry and the joint construction of the Sukhoi Superjet 100.[139] Russia also attempted to strengthen its relations with ASEAN countries but its solidarity with Beijing in the South China Sea dispute and pursuit of a Vietnam-centric strategy in Southeast Asia undermined its influence.[140] The May 2016 Russia–ASEAN summit in Sochi and Moscow's strengthened relations with Thailand's military regime and the Philippines under president Rodrigo Duterte helped overcome these shortfalls.

While the Indo-Pacific region was the foundation of Russia's multipolar foreign policy, Moscow also capitalised on opportunities to assert itself as a rising power in the Middle East, Africa and Latin America. While Russia's support for Bashar al-Assad restricted its prospects for cooperation with Turkey, Saudi Arabia and Qatar, Israel's unwillingness to criticise the Crimea annexation and Egyptian president Abdel Fattah el-Sisi's frictions with the U.S. on human rights created new opportunities for Moscow. Russia's coordination with the West on implementing the Joint Comprehensive Plan of Action (JCPOA) nuclear deal, military cooperation with Iran in Syria and opposition to the March 2015 Saudi-led military intervention in Yemen strengthened the Moscow–Tehran partnership. Russia's arms market dominance and Moscow's solidarity with authoritarian regimes, such as Zimbabwe under president Robert Mugabe and Sudan under president Omar al-Bashir, allowed it to sign nineteen military cooperation agreements in Africa after 2014. Russia's growing security presence in Africa, which would eventually extend to Wagner Group PMC deployments, coincided with an expansion of Moscow's economic presence in the mining and civilian nuclear energy sectors. While Russia's economic footprint in Latin America was historically concentrated in Mexico and Brazil, sympathetic attitudes from left-wing regimes to its policy in Ukraine allowed Moscow to upgrade its partnerships with Cuba, Bolivia, Nicaragua and Venezuela. In response to NATO criticisms of Russia's military intervention in Donbas, the Russian military flew long-range bombers in the Gulf of Mexico, which underscored its desire to militarily push back against the Monroe Doctrine.[141] While Russia's global power projection ambitions had shallow economic foundations, the Ukraine War enabled its efforts to present itself as a "virtual great power" on the world stage. This great power status projection would accelerate in the years leading up to the February 2022 invasion of Ukraine, as relations with the West continued to inexorably deteriorate.

3

BRINKMANSHIP AND THE UNFREEZING
OF THE UKRAINE WAR

On 21 February 2022, Vladimir Putin unfroze Russia's war with Ukraine in a bellicose televised address.[1] During his fifty-five-minute speech, Putin rebuked Soviet leaders such as Lenin, Stalin and Gorbachev for decoupling Ukraine from Russia, and claimed that democratisation and decentralisation had resulted in the "collapse of historical Russia." Putin vowed to correct these historical mistakes, proclaiming that "Ukraine is not just a neighbouring country for us. It is an inalienable part of our own history, culture and spiritual space." Putin also had harsh words for the Ukrainian authorities, as he accused Kyiv of seizing Soviet gold reserves and foreign assets, playing Russia and the West off each other and pursuing weapons of mass destruction. Putin warned that Ukraine could easily create tactical nuclear weapons with foreign support, as it had access to Soviet-era nuclear technology and delivery mechanisms, such as Tochka-U precision tactical missiles with a range greater than 100km. Putin also claimed that Ukraine was deeply embedded within NATO's command-and-control architecture, as NATO used exercises as pretexts to integrate Ukrainian troops into its military bloc and issued orders to the Ukrainian armed forces. Putin attributed Ukraine's pro-Western orientation to elite corruption, as Ukrainian oligarchs concealed billions of dollars in laundered money in Western financial institutions.

While Putin's depiction of Ukraine as a belligerent NATO proxy aligned with years of Kremlin propaganda, his statements on Donbas were a watershed moment in Russia's eight-year conflict with Ukraine. Putin warned that the situation in Donbas had reached an "acute, critical stage" and accused Ukraine of trying to organise a blitzkrieg on the region modelled after the 2014–15 Anti-Terrorism Operation. The imminent threat of a Ukrainian invasion of Donbas compelled Putin to recognise the Donetsk and Luhansk People's Republics as independent countries. In one stroke, Putin declared the Minsk II accords non-existent and ordered Russian troops to enter Donbas for "peace-keeping functions."[2] This military deployment paved the way for Russia's full-scale invasion of Ukraine on 24 February.

This chapter examines the long road to war between Russia and Ukraine. The path to war was hastened by the erosion of Minsk II accords, failed diplomatic efforts to resolve the "Donbas Question" and Moscow's consistent delegitimisation of Ukraine's government through disinformation and coercion. The endurance of Russia's counter-revolutionary foreign policy and marked escalation of the Russia–West systemic confrontation also facilitated Putin's invasion of Ukraine; after carrying out two large-scale mobilisations on the Ukrainian border, the Kremlin redirected its attention from NATO security guarantees to the situation in Donbas and invoked the threat of Ukrainian belligerence as a pretext for war.

An Uneasy Frozen Conflict Between Russia and Ukraine: 2015–18

Despite the Minsk II accords and Ukraine's withdrawal from Debaltseve, a complete de-escalation of the Donbas War proved elusive. In April 2016, the BBC described Donbas as a "frozen war," as the region's bifurcation into hostile pro-Russian and Ukrainian zones triggered periodic ceasefire violations.[3] While the Poroshenko Bloc and former Yanukovych allies in the Opposition Party vied for electoral support in Ukrainian Donbas, the Donetsk and Luhansk People's Republics descended into a state of North Korea-style totalitarianism. Capital punishment was restored, foreigners were largely barred from entering, Ukrainians had to travel 30 hours via Russia to visit relatives in the republic and the region's industrial heartlands atrophied.[4] Despite massive Russian military exercises on the Ukraine border and the outbreak of 1,000 explosions in 24 hours in Donetsk, hostilities in Donbas reached a post-war low in September 2016 and Russia was unable to occupy additional Ukrainian territory in 2016. The 29 January to 4 February 2017 battle of Avdiivka resulted in dozens of casualties, but a modestly successful Ukrainian counterattack and Kyiv's alleged killing of two pro-Russian commanders prevented a major escalation. Russia's retention of 6,000 troops in eastern Ukraine and the consistent mobilisation of 40,000 troops by pro-Russian militias prevented subsequent ceasefires from taking effect.[5] A 27 December prisoner swap of 200 pro-Russian militias for 73 Ukrainian personnel was a rare example of compliance with Minsk II's recommendations.

The persistence of a frozen conflict in Donbas can be explained by the politicisation of Minsk II and Ukraine's increasingly pro-Western orientation, which encouraged Russia to maintain leverage by destabilising and delegitimising Poroshenko's government. The exacerbation of Russia–West tensions and Russia's growing internal confidence in its great power status, which was fuelled by its military successes in Syria, deterred Moscow from pursuing peace with Ukraine. Inside Russia, the Minsk II accords enjoyed superficial elite support. Alexei Chesnakov, the director of the Kremlin-aligned Center for Political Conjuncture, stated that

Minsk II was the only tool to achieve a political settlement and chastised Ukraine for working with Poland on creating new negotiating formats.[6] Due to the impact of Western sanctions and Russia's growing attention to Syria, Surkov began holding regular discussions with Victoria Nuland in January 2016 about the prospect of implementing Minsk II.[7] Calls for an escalation in Ukraine were largely confined to nationalist firebrands with views that departed from mainstream Kremlin thinking. In 2016, Igor Girkin established the Russian National Movement, which supported the unification of Ukraine, Belarus and Russia, and in February 2018, Vladimir Zhirinovsky called for a Russian nuclear decapitation strike aimed at assassinating Poroshenko. Russia's aggressive actions in Ukraine presented a starkly different picture from Moscow's official support for Minsk II. In May 2017, the OSCE Special Monitoring Mission revealed that Russia had instigated 945 explosions compared to 145 initiated by Ukraine, and Russia had blocked access to OSCE personnel 82 times compared to the 54 times they had been obstructed by Ukraine.[8]

Although Russia was the primary violator of Minsk II, it created an alternative reality around the accords that blamed Ukraine for ongoing hostilities in Donbas. The prevailing narrative in Moscow was that Ukraine wanted to recapture full control of Donbas by force and that Germany and France had sanctioned Russia instead of pressuring Ukraine to fulfil its Minsk II obligations.[9] To sustain this narrative at home and abroad, Russian officials stridently criticised Ukraine's alleged non-compliance with Minsk II. In January 2016, Sergei Naryshkin urged the EU to impose sanctions on Ukraine over its "severe violations of the terms and essence of the Minsk Agreements."[10] In September 2017, Leonid Slutsky stated that Ukraine's opposition to Russia's proposal for UN peacekeepers in Donbas was proof that Poroshenko had "deviated from the letter and spirit of the Minsk Agreements."[11] These accusations belied Russia's efforts to dilute the efficacy of Minsk II. To justify actions that acted against the spirit of Minsk II, such as the conviction of Ukrainian pilot Nadezhda Savchenko, the Russian foreign ministry emphasised that it was not a signatory to Minsk II.[12] From 2015 to late 2017, Russia also cited Minsk II to block Ukraine's proposals of EU and UN involvement in the settlement process. Putin's unexpected support for UN peacekeepers in Donbas was possibly aimed at securing international recognition of the legitimacy of Russia's military presence in eastern Ukraine.[13] Therefore, Russia used support for Minsk II as a cudgel to attack Ukraine, while stealthily destroying the accords through illegal military actions and diplomatic ploys.

Russia's non-compliance with Minsk II caused support for the accords to diminish in Ukraine. In November 2017, Ukraine's interior minister Arsen Avakov admitted that "the Minsk Agreements are dead and no longer worth talking about." Avakov justified this statement by saying that Minsk II had temporarily helped reduce Ukrainian military casualties, but Russia's interpretation of the agreements prevented functional peace.[14] Dmytro Kuleba, who served as Ukraine's Permanent Representative to the Council of Europe, called for an alternative framework to Minsk II, as elections in Donbas were an intractable sticking point.[15] Mustafa Nayyem opposed any mention of Minsk II into Ukrainian law, as it had been signed by "terrorists."[16] Although Poroshenko continued to officially support Minsk II, his actions suggested that he was appealing to the agreement's critics. In February 2018, he signed a reintegration law that labelled Russia as an aggressor and Donbas as an illegally occupied territory. Andriy Parubiy, the chairman of Ukraine's Rada, subsequently pushed for a "de-occupation law,"[17] which fuelled speculation that Ukraine could be creating a legal groundwork to forcefully recapture Donbas.

Support for diplomacy with Russia on Minsk II was largely confined to Kremlin-aligned politicians and elder statesmen.

Viktor Medvedchuk urged Ukraine to directly engage with DNR and LNR militias, as he believed that Putin wanted Donbas to remain in Ukrainian hands and that the U.S. and EU would stop Ukraine from recapturing Donbas by force. Medvedchuk argued that Crimea was de facto part of Russia, as the Ukrainian authorities had cut off electricity and water supply to Crimea and pushed its population into Moscow's arms.[18] Former president of Ukraine Leonid Kravchuk believed that a Ukraine–Russia bilateral dialogue could convince Moscow to stop treating Ukraine like a "subordinate client state" and instil respect for Ukrainian sovereignty amongst Russian nationalists who ignored Kyiv's historical influence.[19] Kravchuk argued that Ukraine's dialogue with Russia should focus on recapturing Donbas even if this approach meant accepting the Crimea annexation.[20] This perspective was strenuously rebutted by Poroshenko's political allies. Svitlana Zalishchuk, who served on the Ukrainian Parliament's Foreign Relations Committee, believed that durable diplomacy with an authoritarian Russia was impossible. Zalishchuk argued that Ukraine's commitment to the European development model made a revival of Kuchma-era favour trading with Russia impossible, and created too large a chasm for a genuine reconciliation with Moscow to take place.[21] Poroshenko's re-election ambitions, which precluded dialogue with Donetsk and Luhansk militias, and Russia's refusal to grant him political capital, prevented dialogue from taking place.[22]

Ukraine's increasingly overt pro-Western foreign policy orientation also provided a pretext for Russia's continued destabilising tactics. In December 2014, the Rada voted by a 303–8 margin to suspend Ukraine's non-bloc status. Ukraine's abandonment of neutrality did not necessarily mean universal support for NATO membership. Former Aidar Battalion commander Serhiy Melnychuk believed that Ukraine should cooperate with NATO on counterterrorism but aspire to lead a new collective security system that included all neutral countries.[23] Nevertheless, Poroshenko's decision to rescind non-bloc status coincided with a drastic uptick in Ukrainian public support for NATO membership. A July 2015 poll revealed that 64% of Ukrainians would support NATO membership, and support ranged from 36% in Donbas to 89% in western Ukraine.[24] The EU–Ukraine Association Agreement, which took effect in September 2017, underscored widespread support for EU membership in Ukraine, even though European integration did not lead to a swift improvement in economic conditions.[25] Russia resisted Ukraine's deeper economic engagement with Europe and security cooperation with NATO. In December 2015, the Russian foreign ministry said that it could not prevent Ukraine's "detrimental" engagement with the EU but was within its rights to impose customs duties on Ukraine, which aided the Russian economy.[26] Federation Council International Affairs Committee Chairman Konstantin Kosachev warned that the Euro-Maidan Revolution had ushered in a "treacherously anti-Russian and humiliatingly pro-Western foreign policy,"[27] and scathingly condemned Poroshenko's appointment of former NATO Secretary General Anders Fogh Rasmussen as a special advisor.

Russia's increasingly assertive anti-Western foreign policy also deterred it from seeking a resolution to the Ukraine conflict. Russia's military intervention on Assad's behalf in Syria strained relations with the West, as over 90% of its airstrikes targeted U.S.-aligned moderate Syrian rebels.[28] Russia's insistence on Assad's legitimacy clashed with the U.S.'s calls for his departure, and sharpened tensions with the West. In November 2016, the Russian foreign ministry accused the U.S. of "complicity in international terrorism" in Syria, as Washington allegedly shielded militant "gangs."[29] Unilateral U.S. military actions in Syria, such as the April 2017 and April 2018 strikes over Assad's alleged chemical weapons use, and the February 2018 Battle of

Kamdesh, which killed scores of Wagner Group PMCs, sharp-ened Russia–West tensions even further. Russia's interference in the 2016 U.S. presidential elections exposed it to a fresh round of sanctions, while provocative actions, such as the 2018 Sergei Skripal poisoning and interference on behalf of Eurosceptic populist movements, created new hostilities.

The crisis in Russia–West relations caused Moscow to upgrade its ties with the collective non-West. Through symbolic drills in the Mediterranean, Black and South China Seas, Russia show-cased its increasingly globalised security cooperation with China, and Chinese defence minister Wei Fenghe fired a warning shot to the U.S. about the strength of Sino-Russian military collabo-ration.[30] Russia's "friends with all, enemies of none, allies of none" approach to Middle East diplomacy saw it thaw relations with U.S. partners like Saudi Arabia and Turkey, even as it directly cooperated with Iran in Syria. The Wagner Group's arrival in the Central African Republic underscored Russia's will-ingness to capitalise on Western disengagement in Sub-Saharan Africa. Russia's ability to avoid international isolation together with confidence in its military power convinced it to avoid suing for peace on Western terms in Ukraine, even if doing so would lead to the removal of some Western sanctions.

Renewed Brinkmanship Between Russia and Ukraine: 2018–19

During the final months of Poroshenko's presidency, tensions between Russia and Ukraine escalated over the Russian Orthodox Church and the Sea of Azov. In July 2018, Poroshenko described the Russian Orthodox Church as a national security threat and claimed that "it is absolutely necessary to cut off all tentacles with which the aggressor country operates inside the body of our state."[31] Patriarch Kirill's repetition of Putin's denials of aggres-sion in Ukraine, condemnation of Ukraine's ATO in Donbas as a war waged by Catholics and "schismatics" against Eastern Orthodoxy and December 2017 provision of an award to Sergiy Aksyonov were likely triggers for Poroshenko's comment. These actions reflected the close alignment between Patriarch Kirill and Vladimir Putin, which extended to Russian electoral politics and the war in Syria. Poroshenko's support for the creation of the united Ukrainian Autocephalous Orthodox Church had severe repercussions. In October 2018, the Russian Orthodox Church severed ties with the Ecumenical Patriarch Bartholomew I, the spiritual leader of Orthodox Christians. While this move was not without precedent, as a similar three-month schism occurred in Estonia in 1996, geopolitical frictions between Russia and Ukraine ensured that it was a much more durable rift. Patriarch Kirill described Poroshenko's call for the departure of all Russian Orthodox Church operatives from Ukraine as a campaign to divide global Orthodoxy and claimed that it was "gross and lawless violence" against the beliefs of the majority of Ukrainians.[32] Russian media outlets amplified this rhetoric, which aligned with its prior claims that Kravchuk had instigated an ecclesiastical rift with Russia in the early 1990s to construct a Ukrainian identity.[33]

The Sea of Azov also emerged as a flashpoint for confrontation, as Russia interrupted the freedom of movement of Ukrainian ships. The pretext for Russia's provocative actions was Ukraine's March 2018 seizure of the Russian-flagged Nord fishing boat that operated from Kerch, Crimea, and subsequent announcement of a five-year prison sentence for its captain Vladimir Gorbenko. The construction of the 19km-long Crimean Bridge in May 2018 allowed Russia to retaliate against Ukraine, as it regularly detained Ukrainian ships for three to seven days and violated the spirit of the 2003 Kerch Strait Agreement, which rendered the Sea of Azov shared territorial waters. Ukraine alleged that the Crimean Bridge's construction was illegal, and that Russia's actions were a form of economic warfare.[34] In September 2018, Ukraine moved the Donbas search-and-rescue ship and Korets tugboat from Odesa to Mariupol. Although Ukraine was deploying naval forces to the Sea of Azov for the first time since the Crimea annexation and did not ask Moscow for permission, Russia was surprised by Ukraine's manoeuvre and did not retaliate. Russia's mild-mannered response to Ukraine's transit through the Sea of Azov came to an abrupt end on 25 November, however, as the FSB coast guard captured three Ukrainian vessels that had been moving from the Black Sea to Mariupol. The FSB accused Ukraine of trying to "create a conflict situation in the region," and Poroshenko swiftly imposed martial law in Ukraine as a defensive measure.[35]

The crisis was swiftly defused as Russia reopened the Kerch Strait to commercial shipping on 26 November.[36] Nevertheless, fears of a major escalation between Russia and Ukraine lingered. On 28 November, Poroshenko stated that Russia's border force contingent had "grown dramatically," Russia had tripled the number of its tanks around Ukraine and warned that Ukraine was "under threat of full-scale war with Russia."[37] Poroshenko's precise estimates of the Russian military build-up included 80,000 ground troops, as well as 80 warships and 8 submarines in the Black Sea.[38] Poroshenko also urged NATO warships to be deployed to the Sea of Azov, but this request was denied by Angela Merkel, who opposed a military resolution to the Kerch Strait crisis.[39] For its part, the Kremlin strenuously denied allegations that it planned to carry out military aggression towards Ukraine. Russian MP Dmitry Belik called Poroshenko's allegations about Russia's military build-up a "farce" and claimed he had imposed martial law in Ukraine to secure his re-election.[40] Instead, Russia blamed Ukraine's "unilateral establishment of a state border in the Sea of Azov" for the hostilities and accused Kyiv's Western partners of enabling Ukrainian aggression.[41] These allegations were repeated by Vladimir Putin and Sergei

Lavrov in the months that followed. Despite bellicose rhetoric from both sides, Ukraine's implementation of martial law ended on 26 December and the Kerch Strait crisis did not escalate. Growing hostilities between Russia and Ukraine also did not spill over to the frozen conflict in Donbas. Ukraine's April 2018 reframing of its ATO as a Joint Forces Operation, which implied direct combat with the Russian military, the U.S.'s supply of Javelin anti-tank missiles to Kyiv, and the assassination of Alexander Zakharchenko in August 2018 all increased the risk of hot war in Donbas. However, the Trilateral Contact Group agreed to a new truce on 8 March 2019, which was largely observed by both parties from 10 March.

While a drastic escalation in the military sphere did not transpire, Russia continued to destabilise Ukraine ahead of the 2019 presidential elections. Russia's use of cyberattacks against Ukraine, which included a December 2015 attack on electrical facilities that denied power to over 250,000 Ukrainians and the June 2017 NotPetya virus, accelerated throughout Poroshenko's presidency.[42] In October 2018, Poroshenko vowed to strengthen cybersecurity cooperation with Ukraine's Western partners ahead of the elections, as he wished to avoid a repeat of Russia's 2014 election hack that had falsely showcased Dmytro Yarosh as the winner.[43] This cybersecurity cooperation limited Russia's retaliatory capabilities to spear-phishing and neutralised the Kremlin's ability to use Kaspersky or Yandex for offensive purposes.[44]

While Ukraine was able to hamstring Russia's cyber-capabilities, Kyiv found it harder to constrain the spread of Russian disinformation. Russian media outlets promoted outlandish conspiracies, claiming that Ukrainian children were forced to play with stuffed Adolf Hitler dolls and that Ukraine's national church was a Christian ISIS, which reinforced Kremlin propaganda about the Ukrainian state's Nazi and terrorist character.[45] These brazen attempts to divide Ukrainian society were paired with targeted outreaches to Ukraine's eastern regions. While the horrendous human rights record of pro-Russian officials in Donetsk and Luhansk tarnished Russia's image, stereotypes about Kyiv's infliction of corruption and economic degradation on Donbas, which propelled Yanukovych to power in 2010, still resonated.[46] In Ukrainian-held areas of Donetsk such as Mariupol, a slice of the population harboured romanticised views that Russian occupation improved the quality of life.[47] NewsOne, which Medvedchuk controlled in tandem with pro-Russian lawmakers like Taras Kozak and Yevhen Murayev, aggressively promoted Kremlin propaganda, such as Euro-Maidan being a coup d'état. Despite efforts by Ukraine's Prosecutor-General to try Medvedchuk for treason ahead of the elections, depressed turnout and the Opposition Bloc's appeal to voters over the age of sixty helped it win a plurality of votes in Donetsk and Luhansk in 2019.

Russia–Ukraine Relations Under Volodymyr Zelensky: 2019–21

On 21 April 2019, Volodymyr Zelensky's Servant of the People party achieved a landslide 73.22% to 24.45% victory over Poroshenko's Poroshenko Bloc party in Ukraine's presidential elections. Despite Zelensky's overwhelming popularity, which saw him triumph in every region of Ukraine except Lviv, concerns were expressed about his potentially dovish position towards Russia. As a native Russian speaker from Kryvyi Rih in south-eastern Ukraine and an anti-establishment comedian with no political experience, Zelensky faced widespread criticism from Ukrainian commentators and political rivals. Rutgers University Professor Alexander Motyl's April 2019 *Foreign Policy* article proclaimed that "Ukraine's TV President is Dangerously Pro Russian,"[48] and Poroshenko expressed concern that Zelensky would push Ukraine into Russia's orbit. The Kremlin coolly greeted Zelensky's triumph, as it did not anticipate any significant improvements in Russia–Ukraine relations. Dmitri Medvedev expressed oblique hope for an improvement in bilateral relations but conceded that Zelensky would likely perpetuate his anti-Russian campaign rhetoric.[49] *Sputnik's* post-election assessment warned that "The system of the oligarchic republic as a whole will remain intact. As well as the system of terrorist rule."[50]

Despite these polarised expectations, Zelensky advanced a consistent strategy towards Russia which synthesised Poroshenko's approach with his own vision. Zelensky assiduously supported a peace settlement in Donbas, while deepening Ukraine's security cooperation with the West and cracking down on agents of Russian influence inside Ukraine. Ahead of the July 2019 parliamentary elections, Zelensky suggested meeting with Putin in Minsk to discuss conflict resolution in Donbas. Zelensky's proposed dialogue format included a more expansive array of international leaders than Minsk II, as U.S. president Donald Trump and British prime minister Theresa May would join Angela Merkel and Emmanuel Macron. Zelensky's offer to "discuss who Crimea belongs to and who isn't in the Donbas region" suggested that he wanted to directly challenge Russia over its annexation of Crimea and deployment of military forces in Donbas.[51] Zelensky also spoke directly with Putin about prisoner exchanges; the case of Oleg Sentsov, who Russia had sentenced to 20 years in prison in 2015 for creating a terrorist group in Crimea, was of particular importance for Kyiv. Zelensky's engagement with Russia on Sentsov's release was a watershed moment, as Medvedchuk claimed that all dialogue had ceased after Zakharchenko's assassination.[52]

Despite requests from Ukrainian officials to facilitate a Zelensky–Putin meeting and Alexander Lukashenko's support for a new Minsk summit, Russia greeted Kyiv's overtures tepidly and continued to exacerbate hostilities in Donbas. Zelensky's

June 2019 comment that Ukraine's EU integration would be the "death of the Russian imperial project" and a "powerful blow to Russian authoritarianism" was mocked in Moscow for its striking resemblance to Poroshenko's rhetoric.[53] Days after Zelensky's offer for negotiations with Putin, Russia began issuing passports to Donetsk and Luhansk residents, which built on the Kremlin's April 2019 decree that simplified the Russian citizenship process. The release of twenty-four Ukrainian crew members captured during the Kerch Strait crisis and the resumption of Normandy format talks in September 2019 gave belated momentum to Zelensky's diplomatic efforts. The non-binding Steinmeier formula, which called for Donbas elections under Ukrainian and OSCE legal standards, was a significant breakthrough, signed by Kyiv on 1 October. Russia, the DNR and LNR hailed Zelensky's acceptance of the Steinmeier formula as a step towards peace. Lavrov described it as a "compromise and concession," as it expedited elections in Donbas but was more ambiguous than Minsk II about special status for Donbas.[54] Although the Donbas War was edging closer to a peaceful resolution, Poroshenko rebuked Zelensky's modification of Minsk II and supported the "No to Capitulation Protests!" which intensified by mid-October.

Despite internal resistance to Zelensky's peace-making efforts, the Steinmeier formula achieved early successes. The withdrawal of Ukrainian and LNR forces from Zolote and Petrovske in Luhansk facilitated the 9 December 2019 Normandy format talks. These negotiations called for the release of all POWs by the end of 2019 and elections in Donbas. Although nineteen civilians were killed in March 2020, a full comprehensive ceasefire was agreed on 27 July. This ceasefire was a resounding success, as only three Ukrainian soldiers perished during the first 103 days of its implementation. Nevertheless, Russia's coercive policies towards Ukraine continued. As of August 2020, Russia had distributed nearly 200,000 passports to Donetsk and

Luhansk residents, which contravened Point 4 of the Minsk Protocol, sowed discord in Ukraine over citizenship laws and drained the Donbas of much-needed human capital.[55] Zelensky's opposition to holding elections in Russian-occupied Donbas, which would lead to the legitimisation of Russia's illegal military presence, further increased tensions between Kyiv and Moscow. Lavrov suspended participation in peace talks that were scheduled for September 2020, and Russia backtracked on a 14 September POW release over Kyiv's refusal to hold elections in occupied Donbas.[56] Due to Russian coercion, National Security and Defence Council Secretary Oleksii Danilov claimed in 2022 that Ukraine began preparing for war with Russia in December 2019, and these preparations prevented Russian tanks from entering "Warsaw, Prague, Tallinn and Vilnius."[57]

As diplomatic negotiations on the Donbas War coincided with destabilising Russian conduct, Zelensky continued Ukraine's pro-Western foreign policy course. This policy reflected Ukraine's February 2019 constitutional amendment, which included its aspirations for EU and NATO membership in its Basic Law. In October 2019, Zelensky made his first foreign trip to Brussels where he pitched Ukraine's commitment to modernising the state, anti-corruption reforms and upholding Minsk II to EU and NATO officials.[58] Zelensky's pursuit of EU and NATO membership was not expected to yield swift results, as Poroshenko had set a 2030 target for joining both organisations and the European Commission had previously implied that accession could be as far away as 2040. Due to these constraints, Zelensky pursued a step-by-step approach to EU integration, which initially emphasised the inclusion of Ukraine's markets in the EU, an industrial visa-free agreement with Brussels and a common aviation space.[59] Zelensky's main short-term NATO integration goal was receiving a Membership Action Plan (MAP). Zelensky ultimately had to settle for NATO Enhanced Opportunities Partner status, which was achieved in June 2020, and did not build on Poroshenko's past pledges to hold a referendum on NATO membership. Russian MP Oleg Morozov dismissed this upgrade in Ukraine–NATO cooperation as a "beautiful gesture without any obligations," and said that NATO would not help Kyiv resolve the Donbas War on its terms.[60] Nevertheless, it reinforced Moscow's belief that Ukraine was a silent partner of the Euro-Atlantic community. This perception was reinforced by the arrival of U.S. military instructors at the Yarovsky training ground in Lviv in 2014 and U.S. efforts to construct an operational command centre for the Ukrainian fleet in Ochakiv in 2017.[61]

Zelensky's crackdowns on agents of Russian influence in Ukraine alarmed the Kremlin, as it relied extensively on local surrogates to derail Kyiv's pro-Western course. On 3 February 2021, Zelensky shut down 112, NewsOne and ZIK channels, and imposed a five-year media ban on Taras Kozak. Zelensky justified this bold action by stating that "Ukraine strongly supports freedom of speech. Not propaganda financed by the aggressor country that undermines Ukraine on its way to the EU and Euro–Atlantic integration."[62] Zelensky's assertions were empirically grounded, as these channels routinely denied Russia's military presence in Donbas, accused Ukraine of blocking Minsk II's implementation and allegedly incited hatred against Euro-Maidan and ATO participants.[63] Mikheil Saakashvili praised Zelensky for defying critics who thought "he was not capable of decisive steps," and this opinion was broadly supported by Ukrainian politicians and civil society organisations.[64]

However, Zelensky's move also provoked backlash, as concerns grew that Ukraine was repressing critics of its Euro–Atlantic course in an undemocratic fashion.[65] The Kozak-owned media channels insisted that Zelensky wanted to destroy opposition media in Ukraine, while Dmitry Peskov said these closures "do not meet international norms and standards."[66] Russian commentator Irina Alksnis linked these closures to the "deeply anti-democratic and repressive character of the Ukrainian state," and accused Zelensky of stoking anti-Russian sentiments through repression to boost his 22.1% approval rating.[67]

Despite these criticisms, Zelensky followed up by cracking down on Medvedchuk's pro-Russian influence network. On 20 February, Zelensky signed a degree that imposed sanctions on Medvedchuk and his wife Oksana Marchenko, as well as six individuals and nineteen companies aligned with Medvedchuk. These sanctions enraged Medvedchuk, who decried them as "illegitimate" as they had been imposed without a court ruling, and insisted that he would not flee Ukraine.[68] The U.S. praised Zelensky's decision to sanction Medvedchuk as an action that would strengthen Ukraine's sovereignty, but it was stridently condemned in Russia. Medvedchuk's close personal relationship with Putin, which extended to the Russian president being the godfather of his youngest daughter, likely explained the ferocity of Moscow's opposition to Zelensky's actions. Dmitry Peskov stated that Zelensky's "reactionary line" could be a sign that Ukraine wanted a military solution in Donbas.[69] On 21 February, the Russian defence ministry announced the deployment of 3,000 paratroopers for large-scale exercises, which suggested that Moscow would be using the sanctions on Medvedchuk as a pretext for military escalation against Ukraine.

The Domestic, Regional and External Drivers of Russian Aggression in Ukraine

While Russia's hostile reaction to Zelensky's policies played a critical role in paving the path to war, Moscow's aggressive actions were also triggered by exogenous developments. The 2020–1 Belarusian election protests, which peaked following Lukashenko's fraudulent landslide victory, and the escalation of

Russia–West tensions, which spanned from arms control to human rights, steered Russia towards an aggressive course. Russia's hostile response to popular unrest in Belarus revived its alarmism about colour revolutions and strengthened Moscow's resolve to forcefully reverse Ukraine's Euro-Maidan Revolution. The extent of Putin's commitment to counter-revolution in Belarus was noteworthy, as the Kremlin was uncharacteristically acquiescent to the Armenian Revolution that propelled Nikol Pashinyan to power in May 2018. Despite Pashinyan's triumph, the Kremlin was sceptical of the possibility of an Armenia-style "colour revolution" in Belarus. Before the 2020 election protests, Russian experts believed that the loyalty of Belarus's security services to Lukashenko would stymie regime change but warned that rising nationalist sentiments could pose a long-term "colour revolution" risk.[70] Russia's worst-case scenario unfolded in August 2020, as 200,000 Belarusians rallied in Minsk in support of opposition leader Svitlana Tsikhanouskaya's claims that she had won with 60–70% of the vote.

Russia's response to the popular unrest in Belarus was predictably alarmist and derisive. Although the Belarusian KGB had arrested Wagner Group PMCs for interfering in Belarusian politics in July 2020 and Lukashenko had taunted Russia over its fear of losing Belarus as an ally, as protests endangered his regime in August 2020 Lukashenko pleaded for Russia's assistance.[71] Despite its disdain for Lukashenko's periodic anti-Kremlin rhetoric, Russia responded forcefully to his requests for help and saw an opportunity to subordinate Belarus's foreign policy independence. Russia's rhetorical solidarity with Belarus was aimed as a warning shot at the protesters. In September 2020, Foreign Intelligence Service (SVR) head Sergei Naryshkin warned of a U.S.-organised "colour revolution" and "anti-constitutional coup" against Alexander Lukashenko, which "had nothing to do with the interests of Belarusian citizens."[72] Naryshkin's comments underscored the resonance of Lukashenko's warnings that if a revolution occurred in Belarus, Putin's hold on power in Russia would be jeopardised.[73] Naryshkin also framed Belarus's unrest as a transnational threat, warning in October 2020 that the U.S. was plotting a colour revolution in Moldova, as it disapproved of president Igor Dodon's pro-Russian orientation. As Western countries incrementally recognised Tsikhanouskaya as Belarus's legitimate president and the EU imposed sanctions on Belarus on 2 October, Moscow and Minsk expanded their security cooperation. On 27 August, Putin had announced that Russia had created a "reserve of law enforcement employees," which it would dispatch to Belarus if the "situation got out of control."[74] This contingency was paired with expanded intelligence cooperation between the Belarusian KGB and Russian SVR, which combatted Western destabilisation,[75] and a "large-scale information campaign" aimed at highlighting Tsikhanouskaya's subversive activities from Lithuania.[76]

Russia's solidarity with Belarus was highly effective in preventing Lukashenko's overthrow. Valery Tsepkalo, who served as Belarus's ambassador to the U.S. from 1997 to 2002, contends that it convinced substantial numbers of protesters that the security agencies and armed forces would side with Lukashenko in the event of a major escalation.[77] The manner in which Belarus's popular revolution atrophied had far-reaching implications. Andrei Sannikov, who served as Belarus's deputy foreign minister from 1995–6, believes that the slow pace of EU sanctions against Lukashenko's regime emboldened Russia. Sannikov also argues that a Russian military intervention in Belarus was always out of the question, as Russian propaganda on Belarusians did not depict them as adversaries like Ukrainian nationalists. The West's overestimation of the risk of a Russian military response revealed the efficacy of coercive threats to Putin.[78] Sannikov's assessment is debatable, as Ukrainian intelligence claims that Russia had plans to use the First Tank Army in Belarus,[79] but it nonetheless reveals Putin's mindset that the costs of aggression against non-NATO countries were extremely low. Lukashenko's survival also boosted confidence in Russia that the fortunes of counter-revolutionary forces were on the upswing. Kyrgyzstan's experience with "street riots" and "anarchy," which returned to the fore with mass protests in October 2020, led Russian media to claim that colour revolutions were "discredited."[80] Russian political scientist Kirill Koktysh boasted that Belarus was the third country after Venezuela and Hong Kong to see "colour revolutions" fail to materialise.[81] Russia's confidence that colour revolutions were declining in popularity fuelled the erroneous belief that a counter-revolutionary intervention in Ukraine would receive widespread local support.

The continued deterioration of Russia–West relations was equally significant, as it limited the U.S. and EU's ability to constrain Putin's aggressive instincts through diplomatic means. The U.S.'s August 2019 withdrawal from the Intermediate-Range Nuclear Forces (INF) Treaty was an especially striking signal of the collapse of U.S.–Russia relations. The INF Treaty, which was signed by U.S. president Ronald Reagan and Mikhail Gorbachev in December 1987, banned ballistic missiles, cruise missiles and missile launchers of a 500–5,500km radius. Despite Russia's tests of equipment that violated the INF Treaty's specifications, such as the 3,000km radius SSC-8 cruise missile and the 500–5,500km radius 9M729 cruise missile, the INF Treaty was a key lynchpin of the post-Cold War arms control regime. The Trump administration scrapped the INF Treaty, as China's growing missile arsenal created a new geo-strategic picture and Russia's consistent non-compliance—as it proceeded to develop weapons banned by the treaty, such as hypersonic missiles and nuclear-capable 3M-54 Kalibr systems—rendered the treaty obsolete.[82] China rejected the "multilateralisation of the treaty, while in Russia Trump's INF Treaty withdrawal was lamented. Victor Mizin, a long-time arms control negotiator for the Russian foreign ministry, viewed the INF's collapse as proof of the politicisation of arms control, which began in the late 1990s as the memory of Hiroshima and Nagasaki receded, and reckless threats from both sides became commonplace.[83] The impasse over New START (Strategic Arms Reduction Treaty), which was triggered by the U.S.'s request for a binding declaration on tighter nuclear inspections and China's participation, was resolved in February 2021. Nevertheless, arms control went from being an area of crisis-proof U.S.–Russia cooperation to a competitive theatre of confrontation.

Beyond its contribution to Russia's pivot towards a totalitarian state that could repress anti-war dissent, Navalny's poisoning exacerbated tensions in the Russia–West relationship. Russia's implausible denials that Navalny was poisoned fell on deaf ears in the West, which swiftly proclaimed that the Kremlin was culpable. On 14 October 2020, the EU imposed sanctions on six senior Russian officials, including Alexander Bortnikov and first Deputy Chief of Staff in Putin's administration Sergei Kiriyenko, for their alleged roles in authorising Navalny's poisoning.[84] Peskov claimed that these sanctions harmed EU–Russia relations and Lavrov claimed that the sanctions highlighted the U.S.'s subordination of Europe, seeking to deprive the EU of Russian gas and military products.[85] The election of Joe Biden in November 2020 also sharpened tensions between Washington and Moscow, as the Kremlin feared that the boundary between domestic politics and national security relating to the U.S.'s Russia policy would be further blurred. After Special Counsel Robert Muller's Russia collusion investigation into Trump, Russian experts believed that a Democratic Party triumph in 2020 would prevent a U.S.–Russia normalisation for at least a decade.[86] Russian political consultant Evgeny

Minchenko stated that Biden's efforts to "reconsolidate the West" forced him to frame Russia as an enemy, which contrasted with Trump's economic nationalism and disinterest in "liberal expansionism."[87] Russia's mistrust of the EU and U.S. ensured that diplomatic overtures by Western powers over Ukraine were an uphill struggle.

The First Brinkmanship Crisis on the Russia–Ukraine Border: March to April 2021

In the spring of 2021, Russia gradually expanded its military deployments on the Ukrainian border in response to perceived provocations from Kyiv and NATO. On 30 March, Colonel-General Ruslan Khomchak revealed that Russia had deployed 28 battalion tactical groups (BTGs) in border locations such as Crimea, Rostov, Bryansk and Voronezh, and expressed concerns that Russia's total border force deployment could rise to 53 BTGs.[88] On 31 March, the U.S. European Command raised its awareness level to "potential imminent crisis" amidst fears that Russia had deployed 100,000 forces near Ukraine's border. Amongst units that arrived between 24 March and 9 April, satellite imagery in Pogonovo revealed tank and rifle battalions, multiple launch rocket (MLR) air defence, and short-range ballistic missile (SRBM) batteries. Although Russia had mobilised tens of thousands of troops on the Ukrainian border in August 2016 and had a consistent border presence of 55,000–60,000 troops, the five-week duration of Russia's military exercises was significantly longer than normal and sparked fears of an invasion.[89] By amassing large numbers of troops, Russia would be able to conceal weapons movements to the Donbas and stealthily embark on a major military escalation. Luhansk was viewed as a probable initial target of prospective Russian military operations, as the border force was located 250km north of Ukraine-controlled Luhansk but 400km away from the northern-most tip of LNR.[90]

The spring 2021 brinkmanship crisis had three dimensions. The first facet was the collapse of the fragile ceasefire in Donbas. Pro-Russian militants broke the ceasefire 21 times from 26 February to 1 March, and on 3 March, DNR militias received permission to conduct "warning fire" against Ukraine's military installations.[91] On 26 March, Russia fired mortars on Shumy in Donetsk, which resulted in the deaths of four Ukrainian personnel. As this attack was the largest since the July 2020 ceasefire was signed, it provoked intense backlash in Ukraine. Kuleba urged the international community to condemn Russia for violating the ceasefire, as 23 Ukrainian servicemen died in 2021, but the speaker of Ukraine's Trilateral Contact Group delegation Oleksiy Arestovych expressed optimism that the truce could be preserved.[92] After the Shumy attack, Leonid Kravchuk and the OSCE intervened to prevent a breakdown of the peace process in Donbas. This intervention failed, as pro-Russian forces shot down an OSCE drone and Russia refused to renew the ceasefire on 1 April. Kravchuk's exclusion of an LNR representative from crisis talks that followed the ceasefire's breach further escalated tensions between Moscow and Kyiv over Donbas. In a foreshadowing of Putin's Donbas genocide conspiracy, Duma Speaker Vyacheslav Volodin urged Ukrainian officials to "stop escalating the situation in Donbas if you don't want to end your political career in The Hague."[93] Volodin's comments, which included calls to expel Ukraine from the Council of Europe, were based on unsubstantiated allegations that a Ukrainian drone strike had killed a child in the western suburbs of Russian-occupied Donetsk on 3 April.

The second facet was Ukraine's growing determination to liberate Crimea. Zelensky's March 2021 creation of the Crimean Platform Initiative, which solicited support from Britain, the EU, Canada and Turkey on the de-occupation of Crimea, and Kuleba's claims that Ukraine wished to restore "full sovereignty" over Crimea and Sevastopol, further increased tensions. The Russian foreign ministry warned that Ukraine's attempts to recapture Crimea would be perceived as aggression, while State Duma Deputy Viktor Vodolatsky called the Crimean Platform Initiative a "Russophobic platform."[94] Patrushev warned that the EU, NATO and Ukraine were spreading an "extremist and nationalist ideology" that would lead to terrorist attacks on Crimea,[95] and that the U.S. was emboldening the Ukrainian army to launch military strikes on Crimea, despite Ukraine's poor economic situation. He also claimed that Russia had already thwarted four terrorist attacks on Crimea in 2020. Patrushev's rhetoric was elaborated upon in Russian state media, which provided context for the denazification rhetoric that Russia advanced during the invasion. RIA Novosti commentator Timofey Sergeytsev described Europeanisation as a "Nazi oath" that implied Ukrainian racial superiority and stated that the Ukrainian people who supported this vision were "hostages who became terrorists." Sergeytsev warned that Nazism encouraged Kyiv to pursue territorial annexation campaigns in Donbas, Kuban and other Russian regions.[96] Russia responded to Ukrainian rhetoric about Crimea by carrying out drills that harmonised the Caspian Flotilla and Black Sea Fleet; thrusting FSB-linked ships into a naval confrontation with Ukraine in the Sea of Azov from 14–15 April and closing parts of the Black Sea for foreign warships until October. Russia also staged massive drills on 21 April, which involved 10,000 soldiers and 40 warships, and were personally supervised by Shoigu.

The third facet was the escalation of Russia–NATO tensions over what Moscow saw as provocative NATO exercises. The Defender Europe 2021 drills, which spanned from March to June 2021, inspired particular vitriol in Moscow. Shoigu stated that in response to NATO's "threatening activity," Russia had carried out sudden combat readiness checks of the Southern and

Western Military District force and deployed two armies and three units of the Airborne Forces to its western borders.[97] Germany's defence minister, Annegret Kramp-Karrenbauer, viewed Russia's manoeuvres, which included the deployment of 40,000 troops to Crimea and the Russia–Ukraine border, as an attempt to "provoke a reaction" from NATO.[98] Despite this sabre rattling, tensions between Russia and NATO over Ukraine ultimately ebbed. Shoigu announced on 22 April that the snap readiness check had achieved its goals and that the troops that had participated in the drills would return to their bases on 1 May. Zelensky praised Shoigu's decision, stating that "the reduction of troops on our border proportionately reduces tension" but Putin's insistence that Zelensky engage with Donbas separatist leaders before a meeting remained a sore point between Moscow and Kyiv.[99] Due to these frictions, the Ukrainian defence ministry regarded this brinkmanship crisis as a "trial run for invasion" which was delayed only because the "Minsk II process was not dead yet."[100]

Hot Peace Between Russia and Ukraine: May to December 2021

While the immediate threat of a Russian invasion of Ukraine was forestalled, an atmosphere of brinkmanship persisted. On 5 May, the U.S. Department of Defense expressed concern that only a few thousand troops had been withdrawn, while military equipment remained in place, and an estimated 80,000 troops remained stationed at the Russia–Ukraine border. This retained military infrastructure allowed Russia to escalate its military build-up in November 2021. Ukraine's armed forces chief Valery Zaluzhny estimated that Russia maintained 2,100 troops in occupied Donbas, which included all of the rebel commanding officer positions, and Ukraine's defence ministry estimated that Russia had 90,000 troops stationed at the border.[101] While the

U.S. admitted that it was unaware of Russia's intentions, it raised the spectre of a 2014-style invasion, which the Kremlin strenuously denied. As Russia's force concentration neared 100,000 by mid-November, Kuleba urged France and Germany to prepare for a "military scenario," Ukraine stepped up its diplomatic outreaches to NATO countries and Germany and France published a joint communiqué warning about Russia's mobilisation on the Ukrainian border. The U.S. repeatedly warned Russia against invading Ukraine and began serious negotiations on NATO security guarantees following the 7 December Biden–Putin phone call.

The persistence of a state of hot peace and renewed escalations on the Russia–Ukraine border can be explained by two factors. The first was Russia's perceptions of Western weakness after it opted to de-escalate its brinkmanship tactics on the Ukrainian border. In May 2021, Biden lifted sanctions on Nord Stream 2 and scheduled a summit with Putin in Geneva. Biden's pre-summit comments that "We're not seeking conflict with Russia. We want a stable predictable relationship" with Russia was a drastic climbdown from his March 2021 statement that Putin was a "killer."[102] Despite mounting evidence that Russia had carried out cyberattacks against U.S. pipelines and meat processing companies, the Biden–Putin summit occurred as scheduled on 16 June. The summit's main result, which was strategic stability dialogue in July and September 2021, arrested the downward spiral in U.S.–Russia relations. The completion of Nord Stream 2 in September 2021 and the application of subsequent U.S. sanctions to Russia-linked Transadria Ltd and not to German purchases of gas forestalled a massive escalation between Russia and the West. In Moscow and Kyiv, these actions were regarded as a sign of the West's willingness to appease Vladimir Putin. A 17 June *Nezavisimaya Gazeta* article contended that Putin had benefited from his summit with Biden and the U.S. had chosen to negotiate because it realised that rising commodity prices would neutral-ise the impact of sanctions.[103] Andriy Zagorodnyuk contends that Putin saw Biden's invitation as a "sign of weakness" and a sign that "there was no commitment to defend Ukraine at all costs," which inspired further aggression. Zagorodnyuk saw Nord Stream 2's progress as another catalyst for invading Ukraine, as it secured Europe's dependency on Russian gas during a war that would last through the winter months.[104]

The Belarus–EU migration crisis, which escalated during the autumn of 2021, further convinced Russia of Europe's feckless-ness in a moment of crisis. On 28 May, Lukashenko threatened to flood the EU with human traffickers, drug smugglers and armed migrants, and proceeded to coerce tens of thousands of illegal immigrants, principally from Iraqi Kurdistan, across Belarus's borders with Poland and Lithuania. While Lukashenko's goal of removing sanctions on Belarus, which were imposed after the 2020 elections and the May 2021 Ryanair hijacking, was not achieved, the Western response to the migration crisis was noticeably mild. Poland engaged with NATO in a crisis meeting but struggled to solicit EU support, as disputes between Warsaw and Brussels over the rule of law continued, while Britain's dispatch of a small group of troops for "engineer-ing support" was a symbolic deterrent.[105] As political figures ranging from Antony Blinken to Oleksiy Arestovych believed that the Belarus migration crisis was a mere distraction from the more pressing security threat in Ukraine, the weak response of Western actors was unsurprising. Nevertheless, Andrei Sannikov believes that the migrant crisis was one of the events that instigated the war, as Russia believed that it could weap-onise migration as a hybrid threat alongside an invasion of Ukraine.[106] Valery Tsepkalo concurs that the unwillingness of Western countries to rally behind Poland with "strong sanc-tions" against Russia and Belarus reaffirmed Putin's prior experiences with Western weakness during the 2014–15 Ukraine invasion and encouraged further Russian aggression.[107]

The second factor was Zelensky's de-oligarchisation agenda, which increased his willingness to prosecute political opponents for alleged criminal activities. The arrest of Viktor Medvedchuk in May 2021 and his subsequent 15-year prison sentence increased tensions between Russia and Ukraine. Russian commentator Valery Mikhailov mocked the prosecution's case that Medvedchuk had supplied data on a Ukrainian personnel deployment to Russia. Mikhailov claimed that the U.S. encouraged Ukraine's repression of Medvedchuk much like it had backed the repression of dissent by pro-fascist regimes in Latin America during the Cold War.[108] In response to Kyiv's allegations that Medvedchuk had embezzled Crimea's resources, Crimean Parliament Speaker Vladimir Konstantinov said that Ukraine was "a country of arbitrariness and totalitarianism ruled by a Nazi regime."[109] Russia's strident opposition to Zelensky's prosecution of Medvedchuk came with the risk of unpredictable consequences. Ukrainian academic Volodymyr Dubovyk interpreted Ukraine's actions as a show of leverage over Moscow that could inspire an aggressive Russian response.[110]

While Russia did not opt for military action, it leveraged Medvedchuk's allies in the Rada to sow discord. A notable example was Opposition Platform Deputy Oleg Voloshyn, who used his Parliamentary Assembly to the Council of Europe (PACE) seat to spread Kremlin-stoked conspiracies about Nazism in the Azov Battalion and deprive the regiment of Western military training.[111] The Opposition Platform also highlighted examples of Russian-language discrimination in Ukraine, which aimed to create social conflict that would deter EU support for Kyiv.[112] The efficacy of these acts of internal subversion convinced Russia that it would possess a broad network of local collaborators who would aid a full-scale invasion of Ukraine.

After prosecuting Medvedchuk, Zelensky's attentions pivoted towards Poroshenko. In October 2021, Ukrainian law enforcement officials accused Poroshenko of "facilitating the activities of terrorist organisations" by allowing Medvedchuk to buy coal from mines in Russian-occupied Donbas and use the proceeds to finance separatism. Poroshenko's renamed European Solidarity party strenuously denied these charges as "black PR" and accused Zelensky of ordering his prosecution to distract from the crimes of his own administration.[113] Poroshenko's rising popularity added to speculation that the charges were politically motivated. While a July 2021 poll revealed that Zelensky would trounce Poroshenko by a 31% to 18.6% margin, a December 2021 Razumkov Center survey showed that Poroshenko would triumph 50.1% to 49.9% over Zelensky in a second runoff.[114] Zelensky's consistent push to indict Poroshenko since March 2020 was condemned by Ukraine's Western partners and compared to Tymoshenko's arrest.[115] Despite these criticisms, Poroshenko was indicted on 20 December for allowing the DNR and LNR to sell $54 million in coal to Kyiv, and these treason charges carried up to 15 years in prison. This arrest sharpened frictions between Zelensky and his political rivals, as Arseniy Yatsenyuk warned that Poroshenko's arrest would have "irreparable consequences."

As his rift with Poroshenko intensified, Zelensky faced the threat of a coup. On 26 November, he made a bombshell declaration: "I have received information that a coup d'état will take place in our country on December 1–2."[116] Zelensky backed up this assertion by citing audio recordings obtained by Ukrainian intelligence, which showed Russian and Ukrainian operatives engaging with Rinat Akhmetov's associates on planning a coup. Zelensky warned that Akhmetov was being "dragged into a war with the state of Ukraine" and accused Akhmetov of making a "big mistake" by instigating a conflict with Ukraine's elected president. Akhmetov strenuously denied Zelensky's allegations, stating "I am outraged by the spread of this lie, no matter what the president's motives are" and reaffirmed his commitment to Ukraine's liberation of Donbas and Crimea.[117] On 3 December, Ukraine's Prosecutor General Iryna Venediktova announced 200 criminal investigations into Akhmetov's businesses. Ukraine also suspended $125 million in renewable energy payments to the Akhmetov-owned DTEK company. This fuelled concerns about an intra-elite rift, as Ihor Kolomoisky sided with Zelensky, while Akhmetov amplified Avakov, Poroshenko and other Zelensky critics.[118] The Kremlin quietly capitalised on these internal disagreements and used its media platforms to amplify Opposition Bloc critics, such as Rada Deputy Renat Kuzmin, who called Zelensky "pathetic."[119]

Due to its perceptions of Western weakness and Ukrainian disunity, Russia stepped up its internal propaganda efforts to rally support for an invasion. Putin's July 2021 article titled "On the Historical Unity of Russians and Ukrainians" underscored Russia's delegitimisation of Ukraine's post-Maidan authorities through historical revisionism.[120] Putin described the chasm between Russia and Ukraine as a "great common misfortune and tragedy" and attributed this divergence to centuries of "divide and rule" tactics. Russians, Belarusians and Ukrainians originated as one people bound together by a common Orthodox Christian faith, "Old Russian" language and the historical experience of the Rurik Dynasty. Russia secured control of "Malorossiya" or Little Russia, which included Kyiv and the lands of the left bank of the Dnieper River such as Poltava, Chernihiv and Zaporizhzhia via the 1686 Treaty of Perpetual Peace and Crimea and Novorossiya during the late eighteenth century. To illustrate the historically ordained unity of these regions, Putin quotes Joseph Rutsky from the seventeenth century Uniate Church, who described differences amongst these regions as the equivalent between Rome and Bergamo in Italy, and extols how authors such as Nikolai Gogol and Taras Shevchenko blended the Russian and Ukrainian language. Malorossiya's cultural unity with Russia extended to the Soviet Union, as Khrushchev and Brezhnev had been leaders of Ukrainian heritage who had maintained historical bridges.

Putin contended that successive external forces starting with the Polish–Lithuanian Commonwealth had tried to break the unity that had sprung from this shared history. To justify this foreign interference hypothesis, Putin highlighted Poland's alignment with Malorossiya's nationalist intelligentsia in promoting Ukrainian nationalism; Austria-Hungary's recruitment of the League of Ukrainian Sich Riflemen in the First World War, who had repressed Galicians with Orthodox Christian or pro-Russian sympathies; and Germany's role in creating the Ukrainian People's Republic in 1918. Putin views Ukraine's current authorities as the inheritors of "Polish–Austrian ideologists" who wanted to create an "anti-Moscow Russia," and blasts the post-Maidan government for reframing the shared history of Soviet collectivisation into a genocide of Ukrainians, attacking our "spiritual unity" and glorifying Nazism. While Russia's neo-imperial war in Ukraine is often conflated with Putin's desire to recreate the Soviet Union, he also blames the Soviet leadership for perpetuating this trend, stating "modern Ukraine is entirely a product of the Soviet era," "Russia was robbed indeed" and "the Bolsheviks treated the Russian people as material for their social experiments." Vladimir Lenin's historical mistakes, such as granting Soviet republics a constitutional right to secession, ceding the Russian Empire's western lands to Poland and handing the Donetsk–Krivoy Rog Soviet Republic to Ukraine's SSR, sharpened disunity. Putin explicitly links Lenin's allowance of Polonisation to Ukraine's Second World War collusion with Nazi Germany. Stalin's decision to overrule the desire of Orthodox members of Carpathian Ruthenia to join

Russia and facilitate of the reunification of "Carpathian Ukraine" was another historical mistake from Putin's standpoint. To correct these historical aberrations, which led to Ukraine's de-industrialisation and stagnant economic development, Putin declared that "Kyiv simply does not need Donbas" and called for Minsk II's full implementation.

Zelensky responded derisively to the article, quipping, "I can only say that I'm jealous that the president of such a great country can afford to spend so much time on such a volume of work" and sarcastically suggested it was why Putin did not have time for an in-person meeting with him.[121] Nevertheless, it brought the "Ukrainian Question" back to the forefront of Russia's political debate. It also resonated strongly at a popular level due to its alignment with the Kremlin's post-2014 counter-revolutionary propaganda—in January 2016, Putin had called Lenin's nationality policies a "time bomb" and declared that Stalin had been correct in opposing Lenin's vision of a federal Soviet Union.[122] On 11 October, Medvedev invoked Putin's article in a *Kommersant* counter-revolutionary hit piece titled "Why Contacts with the Current Ukrainian Leadership are Meaningless."[123] Medvedev called Ukraine a "tormented country," accused Zelensky of pandering to a nationalist base of 5–7% of Ukrainians and compared his departure from his Russian roots to the Jewish intelligentsia in Nazi Germany serving in the SS. Medvedev did not explicitly call for war or regime change, but insisted that Russia needed to wait until Ukraine had new leadership to engage in diplomacy. The FSB's December 2021 arrests of neo-Nazi MKU members in 37 of Russia's 80 regions, which the Kremlin linked to Ukraine, and Moscow's politicisation of Ukraine's 17 December vote against a UN resolution condemning Nazism strengthened "Ukrainian threat" narratives ahead of the invasion. Russia paired this alarmism with accusations that Ukraine was about to leave Minsk II, as the Rada had proposed a transitional administration law in August 2021 that would replace the DNR and LNR structures with new authorities after elections in Donbas.[124] The spectre of Ukraine scrapping Minsk II provided Putin with the desired legal pretext to escalate Russia's aggression.

The Final Stage of Brinkmanship from Russia and Ukraine: January to February 2022

In early 2022, Russia continued to take preparatory steps towards an invasion of Ukraine. The U.S. estimated that Russia would assemble a force of 175,000 troops to invade Ukraine, and critical military brigades such as the 41st Combined Arms Army from the Western Military District and the 58th Army in the North Caucasus were moved into Crimea. These brigades were deployed in a strategically ambiguous fashion. They could have been used as a bargaining chip in the Belarus–EU migration crisis or aimed at NATO, as Russia could pair the 41st Combined Arms Army and 11th Army Corps in Kaliningrad against Poland and Lithuania. However, the deployment of the 1st Guards Tank Army in Maslovka near Kharkiv, growing concentration of military equipment in Crimea and the appearance of large numbers of military vehicles in Rostov-on-Don, which also served as a military aviation transit hub, pointed to an invasion of Ukraine.[125] Russia's desire to engage in covert border mobilisations, which contrasted markedly with its public displays in spring 2021, raised concerns about invasion plans.[126] The strikingly close alignment between Russia's bellicose rhetoric and military mobilisations also pointed to an invasion, with Putin's threat to undertake "appropriate military-technical reciprocal measures" in December 2021 standing out.[127]

As February 2022 drew closer, Russia began taking more tangible preparatory steps for war, including mobilising National

Guard forces that would be used to pacify Ukrainian resistance if it occupied large swathes of Ukraine's territory.[128] Russia's deployment of FSB and GRU-aligned mercenaries to Ukraine provoked fears that Russia would carry out an information war, cyberattacks on Ukraine's electricity and gas networks and a military incursion in swift succession.[129] U.S. officials were also alarmed by Russia's movement of medical supplies such as blood to the Ukraine border in late January 2022.[130] Despite these escalations, the scale of Russia's military incursion into Ukraine was unclear. A widely discussed scenario was a limited intervention which would see Russia concentrate military forces in the Donbas to annex the entire region. Joe Biden's controversial claim that a Russian "minor incursion" would invite an uncertain U.S. response added to this speculation. Michael Kofman, the director of the Russia Studies programme at CNA, believed that this outcome was unlikely, as Russia's strategy of leveraging the Donbas had already failed and an offensive of this kind would "worsen its current predicament."[131] Kofman concluded that a regime change in Kyiv was the most advantageous scenario for Russian interests followed by a partition of Ukraine, which would leave Putin to debate whether to cross the Dnieper River.[132]

Russia's inexorable movement towards all-out war with Ukraine was preceded by two critical developments. The first was the January 2022 CSTO mission in Kazakhstan, which reinforced counter-revolution's centrality as a Russian foreign policy goal and underscored the Russian military's efficacy. Although the Kazakh protests which erupted on 2 January were triggered by local factors such as increased gas prices, socioeconomic inequality and clashes between former president Nursultan Nazarbayev's supporters and those loyal to president Kassym-Jomart Tokayev, Russian officials reverted to familiar colour revolution narratives. Dmitry Medvedev stated that the Kazakh protests were "an attempt to implement the usual colour revolution scenario," which was previously applied to Ukraine.[133] To justify the CSTO intervention on 6 January, Russian media outlets repeated Tokayev's unsubstantiated claims of terrorism in Kazakhstan, and framed the protesters as a threat to Kazakh statehood.[134] Russia's paratrooper deployment swiftly stabilised Kazakhstan, which revitalised the CSTO following its failures to intervene in Kyrgyzstan during the 2010 protests or on Armenia's behalf during the autumn 2020 Nagorno-Karabakh War with Azerbaijan.[135] The 67% public approval rating for Russia's "peacekeeping mission" in Kazakhstan, which ended on 19 January, underscored the popularity of swift counter-revolutionary interventions.[136]

The second was the failure of Russia's negotiations with Western countries on NATO security guarantees to achieve a meaningful breakthrough. Russia's 17 December stipulations included the removal of weapons from all countries that had joined NATO in 1997, bans on aircraft and warship deployments that could strike U.S. or Russian territory and a prohibition on intermediate-range missile deployments in Europe.[137] Russia's demand for immediate negotiations on security guarantees was greeted positively by Western countries but Moscow's restrictions on NATO expansion were condemned on sovereignty grounds. The U.S.'s request that Russia withdraw troops from Transnistria, Abkhazia and Crimea further underscored the chasm in perspectives between the two sides.[138] Nevertheless, Emmanuel Macron and Olaf Scholz tried to find common ground with Russia on its security guarantee proposals. Macron's comment "There is no security for Europeans if there is no security for Russia" was criticised as legitimising Russia's revisionism but his opposition to the creation of spheres of influence in Europe countered Moscow's approach to the post-Soviet space.[139] Paris-based security expert Emmanuel Dupuy contends that Macron's outreaches to Russia were a "traditional Gaulliste non-aligned mediating posture," which built on his post-2017 strategy of engaging with Moscow, but were derailed by disagreements within the EU and NATO.[140] Olaf Scholz's 15 February meeting with Putin in Moscow was characterised by similar optimism, as he expressed hope that diplomatic solutions were not exhausted and praised Russia's announced small-scale pullback of forces from the Ukraine border.[141] Scholz's confidence that war had been averted continued until one to two days before the war, as the phrase "freedom chancellor" was widely used by his Social Democratic Party supporters.[142]

Despite Putin's reassurances that he did not want war with Ukraine, Russian state media commentators treated the security guarantee negotiations with derision. RT Editor-in-Chief Margarita Simonyan stated that Russia's security guarantee proposals were not intended to be accepted.[143] On Vladimir Solovyov's 21 February Rossiya-1 show, commentator Karen Shakhnazarov stated that Putin had made the proposals as a pretext to resolve the Donbas question. Macron and Scholz's conciliatory rhetoric did not go far enough to satisfy hardliners in the pro-Kremlin information space. On state TV, academic Dmitry Evstafiev quipped that "decent chancellors of Germany" would have shot themselves if they had repeated Scholz's denial of the Donbas genocide. The steady influx of arms transfers to Ukraine, which included anti-tank weapons deliveries by Britain and the U.S. in January 2022, and repeated warnings of sanctions from Western leaders, further antagonised Russia. The Biden administration's redeployment of 1,000 U.S. troops from Germany to Romania, addition of 2,000 new troops to Germany and Poland in February 2022, and Britain's 17 February trilateral security agreement with Poland and Ukraine further underscored the West's desire to combine deterrence with diplomacy.

Despite these exogenous factors, the security situation in Ukraine remained strikingly stable. Ceasefire violations in Donbas decreased by 70% from December to late January before experiencing an uptick in the month before the war.[144] This stasis fuelled predictions that Russia would instigate a war through false flags. On 17 February, Antony Blinken warned that false flags could consist of a "terrorist" bombing inside Russia, the invented discovery of a mass grave, a staged drone attack on civilians or a chemical weapons attack.[145] While Russia did not stage a false flag attack, it created pretexts for escalation in Ukraine along the lines that Blinken described. Citing fears of a Ukrainian invasion of Donbas, DNR leader Denis Pushilin ordered mass evacuations from Donetsk to Russia on 18 February, which resulted in 50,000 new arrivals in 48 hours. Russian commentator Dmitry Babich stated that these evacuations were necessary to prevent Ukraine's military from crushing the DNR and LNR in a 3- or 4-day offensive, which would result in hundreds of thousands of casualties.[146] Russia had previously sounded the alarm about a potential chemical attack in Ukraine. On 21 December, Shoigu claimed that U.S. mercenaries had delivered an "unidentified chemical substance" to Avdiivka and Lyman, which are part of Ukrainian-controlled Donetsk, "to commit provocations."[147] On 22 December, Pushilin urged Minsk II guarantors and international organisations to prevent Ukraine from using chemical weapons against civilians in Donbas. Pushilin's message included the dire warning that "Ukraine is attempting to stage a man-made humanitarian disaster on our soil, which may trigger unpredictable consequences for the entire world."[148]

The combination of Russian disinformation, counter-revolutionary fervour and erosion of trust with the West culminated in drastic escalations in mid-February. On 17 February, multiple shelling incidents were reported in Donbas, which included an attack from LNR rebels on a kindergarten in Stanytsia Luhanska.[149] Citing significant U.S. intelligence capabilities, Biden stated on 18 February that Putin had already decided to invade Ukraine and Blinken warned that Russia was "on the brink of an invasion." The extension of Russia's military drills with Belarus on 20 February was a final confirmation of Putin's aggressive designs. These exercises, which included up to 30,000 Russian troops and almost the entirety of the Belarusian army, began on 10 February and included the activation of S-400 air defence systems on the Belarus–Ukraine border.[150] On 17 February, Lavrov confirmed that these exercises would end as planned. Belarus's defence minister Viktor Khrenin announced their extension three days later, citing provocations "near our common border."[151] Jingoistic state TV coverage of Ukraine, which included Simonyan's "Where's the champagne?" quip about escalations in Donbas and *Vesti Nedeli* presenter Dmitry Kiselyov's claim that "Russia is forcibly making the world happy by offering a new global system of security. Thanks again to Russian weapons,"[152] set the stage for Putin's recognition of the Donbas republics.

Russia Recognises the Donetsk and Luhansk People's Republics

As negotiations about the European security system stalled, a low-profile campaign in Russia to recognise the Donetsk and Luhansk People's Republics grew in intensity. On 19 January 2022, a delegation of eleven Communist Party Duma Deputies including Gennady Zuganov stated that the recognition of the Donbas republics was "morally justified" because "the actions of the Ukrainian authorities can be compared with the genocide of their own people."[153] This proposal received a frosty welcome in the State Duma. Konstantin Zatulin stated that "I'm not sure that at present this step can be taken without prejudice to the interests of the Russian Federation—strategic and long-term."[154] Zatulin's response, which was shared by the majority of State Duma Deputies, reflected Russia's desire to avoid unilaterally abrogating Minsk II. These concerns about upholding Minsk II disintegrated on 15 February, as Ramzan Kadyrov and Vyacheslav Volodin endorsed Donetsk and Luhansk's independence, which paved the way for Putin to recognise both republics six days later.

On 22 February, Russia signed treaties of friendship, cooperation and mutual assistance with the Donbas republics, which allowed Putin to authorise a military intervention on their territory without the Federation Council's prior approval.[155]

Although the recognition of DNR and LNR was an escalatory move, it was not initially expected to trigger an immediate Russian invasion of Ukraine. Instead, Russian officials and experts framed the recognition as a last-ditch attempt to prevent Ukraine from launching a military campaign in Donbas. Russian political scientist Nikolai Petrov stated that the recognitions were aimed at forcing Zelensky to comply with Minsk II, while Nikolay Patrushev urged the West to put an end to the "slaughter" in two to three days.[156] Dmitri Medvedev made a similar case, as he stated that his decision to recognise South Ossetia and Abkhazia as independent from Georgia saved hundreds of thousands of lives. At the 22 February Security Council meeting, which Putin called ostensibly to hear the opinions of his closest advisors, it was clear that major powerbrokers in the Kremlin viewed independence recognition as a gateway to a Russian annexation. Medvedev stated that Ukraine did not need Donbas and "these are our people," as 800,000 Russian citizens resided in Donetsk and Luhansk.[157] Putin pushed back against Naryshkin's claims that the DNR and LNR should be incorporated into Russia, and in a memorable exchange, he snapped "Speak plainly, Sergei" to cajole the SVR chief into repeating his position on recognition.[158]

Russia's recognition of the DNR and LNR provoked fierce backlash in Kyiv. On 22 February, Zelensky stated that Ukraine would cede none of its territory, and called for emergency meetings of the OSCE, Normandy Format and the UNSC. Ukraine's condemnations of Russia's sovereignty violations were echoed by Western nations, which unveiled a series of sanctions against Russian individuals and institutions. The U.S. imposed sanctions on VEB, which is critical for Russia's ability to raise funds, and PSB, which aids Russia's defence sector, and imposed additional restrictions on Russian sovereign debt.[159] The U.S. also unveiled plans to sanction VTB, Gazprombank and Sberbank if Russia invaded Ukraine. Britain imposed sanctions on five Russian banks, four of which were also sanctioned by the U.S., and three Russian oligarchs: Novatek gas stakeholder Gennady Timchenko, construction magnate Boris Rotenberg and Gazprom Drilling majority stakeholder Igor Rotenberg. The EU imposed sanctions on 351 Duma MPs who recognised Donetsk and Luhansk, while Germany froze Nord Stream 2 and the U.S. imposed sanctions on the pipeline project's operator. Russian experts were initially more hopeful that the DNR and LNR recognitions would be more positively received in the collective non-West. Nikita Mendkovich, the head of the Eurasia Analytical Club, stated that Putin had likely consulted with Xi Jinping on Donbas recognition and predicted that China could eventually recognise the DNR and LNR.[160] These hopes were swiftly dashed, as implicit support was only provided by Belarus, the Central African Republic, Nicaragua and Venezuela. Despite the growing risk of isolation, Russia marched on towards a full-scale invasion of Ukraine.

4

THE "SPECIAL MILITARY OPERATION" BEGINS

On 24 February, a heated exchange broke out on the floor of the UNGA between Ukraine's Ambassador to the UN Sergiy Kyslytsya and his Russian counterpart Vasily Nebenzia. Kyslytsya declared, "There is no purgatory for war criminals. They go straight to hell, ambassador." Nebenzia, who was chairing the session in his capacity as Russia's UN Ambassador, retorted that "We aren't being aggressive against the Ukrainian people, but against the junta that is in power in Kyiv." This exchange encapsulated Ukraine's urgent pleas for peace, as Russia's invasion had followed weeks of reassurances from Zelensky and European officials that war could be averted, and Russia's triumphalist pursuit of regime change in Ukraine. One month later, the tables had turned; Zelensky had maintained power in the face of repeated assassination and coup attempts, while Kyiv was on the verge of liberation. Russia's nationwide military campaign had stalled into a high-cost war of attrition, while Western sanctions threatened its economic future and prided great power status. Russia's withdrawals from Kyiv and Chernihiv and half-hearted pursuit of diplomacy with Ukraine in late March underscored the dramatic climb-down of its short-term ambitions. The narrative that Russia was the world's second strongest military had been eviscerated, while a story of Ukrainian patriotic resilience took its place.

This chapter examines Russia's often-contradictory demilitarisation and denazification objectives, which Putin used to justify invading Ukraine. It will also outline Russia's multiple-axis offensive on Ukrainian territory and why Putin's vision for regime change was swiftly dashed. It concludes by assessing the impact of Western sanctions, the collapse of liberal dissent in Russia and Putin's growing embrace of totalitarianism, trends that continued to worsen through the war's duration.

Russia's Strategy to Demilitarise Ukraine

Vladimir Putin's plan to demilitarise Ukraine sparked confusion within Russia's foreign and security policy community. When asked by the BBC about demilitarisation, Evgeny Buzhinsky, the senior vice president of the PIR Center, conceded, "I don't really understand it myself," and interpreted it as "the destruction of critical elements of the military infrastructure" which had an uncertain boundary.[1] Ivan Safranchuk, an expert at Russia's Council of Foreign and Defence Policy, contends that demilitarisation sought to prevent Ukraine from advancing its goals of political control of Donetsk and Luhansk through military means.[2] Safranchuk's explanation aligned with Russia's flimsy legal rationale for invading Ukraine, which invoked Article 51 without a clear threat from Ukraine to Russia's national security, in support of unrecognised "people's republics" that had seceded from Ukraine, a UN-recognised state.[3] At the time of writing, Russia's Deputy UN Ambassador Dmitry Polyanskiy continues to assert that Ukraine was intending to launch a "pre-emptive attack" on Donbas.[4] This contention to justify demilitarising

Ukraine circulated widely in the early stages of the war. On 8 March, the DNR claimed that it had discovered plans by "Ukrainian radicals" to attack Crimea and Donbas, which Russia would formally investigate.[5]

Beyond neutralising Ukraine's alleged threat to Russia and destroying military hardware, the Kremlin refused to provide a cut-off point for demilitarisation or clarify whether regime change was necessary. Nevertheless, Putin's plea in his 24 February address that Ukrainian forces "lay down their arms and go home" pointed to an expansive campaign. State media and Telegram discourse on demilitarisation pointed to a far-reaching destruction of Ukraine's military potential and dismissed the prospect that Russia was using force as a diplomatic bargaining tactic. Rossiya Segodnya Center for International Journalism and Research head Veronika Krasheninnikova compared demilitarisation through diplomacy with "trying to teach a crocodile to eat cucumbers," as the U.S. would try to attack Russia via Ukraine and would never respect Russia like it had the Soviet Union. Therefore, Krasheninnikova argued that Russia was left with the "less bad" choice of demilitarising Ukraine entirely through force and highlighted her 2014 comments calling for a post-1945 Germany-style demilitarisation of Ukraine.[6] Igor Girkin insisted that Russia had embarked on a "FULL-SCALE WAR" with Ukraine, which would be "neither quick nor easy." Girkin implied that demilitarisation could extend to Poland, as Ukraine would hand over jets to Polish airfields to protect them from Russian airstrikes, and highlighted the Soviet Union's mistaken refusal to extend the war in Afghanistan to Pakistan.[7]

Despite uncertainties about demilitarisation's meaning, Russia framed its progress towards achieving this objective around three criteria. The first was the destruction of Ukraine's military infrastructure, which was exemplified by the Russian ministry of defence's frequent boasts about the destruction of Ukrainian military hardware. By mid-afternoon on 24 February, Russia claimed to have destroyed 74 military ground facilities, which included 11 airfields, 3 command posts and 18 radar stations for anti-aircraft missile systems.[8] By 7 March, Russia claimed to have destroyed 2,396 Ukrainian military infrastructure facilities, including 82 command and communication centres, 119 S-300s, Buk-M1 and Osa air defence systems, and 76 radar stations.[9] These outlandish statistics reflected how Russia viewed the scale of destruction of Ukrainian military equipment as a benchmark for the war's success. The Kremlin also highlighted the purported success of its demilitarisation of Ukraine to justify the cessation of its Kyiv offensive. On 2 April, Dmitry Peskov stated that "Demilitarisation is in full swing indeed. Ukraine's military potential and military infrastructure are largely destroyed in our armed forces' special operation. It is truly one of the goals of this operation, a very important goal."[10]

The second criterion used by Russia to measure the success of demilitarisation was the destruction of Ukraine's growing stock-piles of Western military technology. This objective built on Putin's immediate pre-war rhetoric. On 22 February, Putin called for a "certain degree of demilitarisation of today's Ukraine" as an essential criterion of a Russia–West rapprochement and explicitly linked demilitarisation to Western arms transfers to Ukraine.[11] Putin's demilitarisation calls became more relevant as Western countries rushed to provide military aid to Ukraine after the Russian invasion. During the first month of the war, the U.S. provided $3.8 billion in military aid to Ukraine, including 1,400 Stinger anti-aircraft missile systems, 5,500 Javelin anti-tank missile systems and 16 Mi-17 helicopters; Britain provided $456 million in military aid to Ukraine, including 10,000 short-range missiles and 10,000 anti-tank missiles; and the EU provided $551 million in aid to Ukraine.[12] Despite extensive criticism of their slow arms deliveries, France transferred MILAN anti-tank guided missile systems and CAESAR howitzers to Ukraine, and Germany reversed its historical opposition to conflict zone arms transfers by supplying 1,000 anti-tank weapons and 500 Stinger anti-aircraft defence systems.[13] On 16 March, Putin warned that Ukraine's "Western patrons are simply pushing the Kyiv authorities to continue the bloodshed," and highlighted the dispatch of Western military advisors and mercenaries.[14]

The Kremlin's strategy to neutralise Ukraine's ability to use NATO-class weaponry consisted of the use of nuclear blackmail and threats to interdict arms shipments. On 24 February, Putin urged foreign countries not to interfere in Russia's military efforts, and emphatically warned that "Russia's response will be immediate and will lead you to such consequences that you have never seen in your history." During a 27 February meeting with Shoigu and Gerasimov, Putin ordered the Russian military to place its strategic nuclear forces on a "special mode of combat duty." Russian state media outlets framed Putin's move as a direct response to Britain Foreign Secretary Liz Truss's warnings about the risk of a Russia–NATO conflict.[15] These nuclear threats did not deter NATO countries, as the U.S. decried Putin's nuclear alert threat as an "unacceptable escalation" and expanded arms shipments to Ukraine. On 12 March, Russian deputy foreign minister Sergei Ryabkov warned that Western arms shipments were "legitimate targets," which implied an attack on supply points in eastern Poland and northern Romania.[16] After a British-made Starstreak anti-aircraft missile downed a Mi-28N attack helicopter over Luhansk on 2 April, Russia's ambassador to Britain Andrei Kelin repeated this threat. When these tactics failed to slow the influx of Western arms shipments, the Russian state media claimed that territorial occupation would help demilitarise Ukraine. On 25 March, Russian defence analyst Konstantin Sivkov claimed that "the fate of Ukraine is actually decided" and stated that NATO arms shipments were "additional trophies that will fall into our hands and will be used against their former owners."[17]

The third dimension of demilitarisation was neutralising Ukraine's alleged chemical, nuclear and biological weapons potential. This component of Russia's demilitarisation has fictitious premises. On 11 March, Zelensky asserted that Soviet-era laboratories were involved in scientific research and that Ukraine has no active WMD programmes.[18] Although Russia presented no evidence to counter Zelensky's assertions, it views the destruction of WMD threats in Ukraine as a benchmark for military success. On 20 March, LNR first deputy foreign minister Anna Soroka warned of a "burial of chemically hazardous substances near the Siverskyi Donets River" that Ukrainian forces had prepared for explosion.[19] Colonel-General Mikhail Mizintsev warned that Ukrainian "nationalists" had "mined" ammonia and chlorine storage facilities in Sumykhimprom, which would be aimed at the "mass poisoning of residents in the Sumy region" if Russia sent troops.[20] The 21 March ammonia leak in Sumykhimprom, which occurred two days after Minzintsev's allegations and was likely triggered by Russian shelling, furthered Kremlin propaganda about the need to demilitarise Ukraine and prevent Kyiv from engaging in chemical warfare.

Russia's assertions about neutralising the potential revival of Ukraine's nuclear weapons capabilities were equally dubious. During his 19 February Munich Security Conference speech, Zelensky alarmed the Kremlin with the following quote: "Ukraine has received security guarantees for abandoning the world's third nuclear capability. We don't have that weapon. We also have no security."[21] Zelensky's statement was empirically questionable. Ukraine's early 1990s deterrent was limited by its lack of operational control over its nuclear weapons stocks and the concentration of long-range weapons in Kyiv's possession, which would threaten the Russian Far East rather than major cities. Leonid Kravchuk's arguments for denuclearisation, which included its lack of indigenous warhead production capabilities, the risk that

Russia would invade Ukraine citing a "nuclear threat," and the prospect of a massive Russian retaliation from Nizhny Novgorod, were compelling.[22] Zelensky's "no security" statement was a request for Ukrainian NATO membership rather than a call for Ukraine to rebuild its nuclear arsenal. Oleksii Danilov's December 2021 calls for defensive weapons to be provided to Ukraine as a belated reward for denuclearisation suggests that Zelensky's rhetoric was also a ploy to secure Western arms.[23]

Russian security policy experts were polarised on the plausibility of Ukraine's restoration of its nuclear capabilities. Russian defence analyst Viktor Litovkin contended that "Ukraine is no longer able to produce missiles, and it has never been able to make nuclear weapons and will never be able to do it."[24] This rendered Zelensky's pledge to revise all the terms of the Budapest Memorandum, which included the denuclearisation of Ukraine, a symbolic action. Moscow State University Professor Edward Lozansky asserts that "Ukraine had full scientific knowledge in the field and a material base for the production of nuclear weapons," and noted that Soviet nuclear scientists such as Nobel laureate Lev Landau had been trained at the Kharkiv Physical Technical Institute. Lozansky claims that the Kremlin "had many inside sources that were sending alarming signals on this matter to Moscow."[25] Lozansky's alarmist perspective was more reflective of Kremlin rhetoric. On 2 March, Russian defence ministry spokesman Igor Konashenkov stated that "nuclear weapons and their means of delivery were to appear in the near future" from NATO bases and stated that the Russian military sought to eliminate that homeland security threat.[26] Naryshkin claimed that the U.S. was aiding Ukraine's nuclear weapons programme, as it hoped that "Ukrainian missiles with nuclear warheads would not turn to the West, and [instead] to the east."[27]

Russia's assertions about Ukraine's biological weapons stocks were also rooted in conspiracy. The chairman of Russia's

Investigative Committee Alexander Bastrykin initiated a criminal case, which accused the U.S. of establishing thirty "biological research facilities" in Ukraine at a cost of $200 million.[28] After Victoria Nuland's 8 March admission of the existence of biological research facilities and the need to avoid the transfer of biological materials to Russia, the Russian foreign ministry accused the U.S. of destroying samples of plague, cholera and anthrax after 24 February,[29] and spread the conspiracy that bioweapons had fallen into the "hands of extremists or nationalists—who will provide a guarantee." On 10 March, Konashenkov claimed that U.S. bioweapons labs had carried out experiments with COVID-19 samples. The Kremlin also presented "evidence" that the U.S. planned to construct two additional laboratories in Kyiv and Odesa by late February 2022; these labs had actually been built in 2019 under the Biological Hazard Reduction Program with U.S. support.[30] Alongside supportive clips by FOX News anchor Tucker Carlson and former Hawaii congresswoman Tulsi Gabbard, Russian political scientist Igor Nikulin was the primary messenger of these conspiracies on Russia's state media. Nikulin falsely claimed that the 2005 U.S.–Ukraine agreement on combatting bioterrorism would lead to biological weapons production and stated that "Ukraine has actually been turned into a 'super-range' for developing technologies relating to biological weapons".[31]

On 11 March, Nebenzia raised these conspiracies at the UN Security Council. Citing what Russia described as the UP-4 project, Nebenzia claimed that U.S. biolabs were examining how bats, lice, fleas and migratory birds could spread diseases to humans. This would allow man-made pandemics to appear as if they had occurred naturally. Nebenzia highlighted the deaths of twenty Ukrainian soldiers in Kharkiv in 2016, the 2019 outbreak of plague in Ukraine and a hundred-fold increase in measles as proof of biolab activities.[32] These allegations were immediately dismissed by senior U.S. and UN officials. U.S. Ambassador to the UN Linda Thomas-Greenfield described Nebenzia's assertions as "bizarre conspiracy theories," and the UN's High Representative for Disarmament Izumi Nakamitsu said the UN was not aware of biological weapons activity in Ukraine. Nevertheless, Russia continued to develop these conspiracies and use them to justify invading Ukraine. On 31 March, Russia's Permanent Representative to International Organisations in Geneva Gennady Gatilov stated that Ukraine had transferred 10,000 biological samples to the Lugar Center in Georgia and claimed that other materials had been transferred to Britain and Germany. Gatilov claimed that Germany's Leffler Center was studying the potential for Crimean-Congo hemorrhagic fever to reach Eastern Europe.[33] Leonid Slutsky claimed that dangerous diseases were tested on the "Slavic genotype" and warned that it was Russia's duty "not to let Washington get out of this criminal adventure for the entire Slavic world unpunished again."[34] These assertions rallied anti-Western nationalist sentiments around Russia's crusade to demilitarise Ukraine.

Russia's Plan to Denazify Ukraine: Regime Change or Cultural Genocide?

To justify invading Ukraine, Russian officials and commentators have described the post-Maidan government as a neo-Nazi regime. This categorisation includes direct comparisons to Nazi Germany. Sergei Karaganov opined that Ukraine was becoming something like Germany from 1936–37, which rendered war inevitable.[35] Dmitry Babich characterises Ukraine as a unique totalitarian regime which combines the features of Western ultra-liberalism with crude Ukrainian nationalism that borders on Nazism. Babich contends that Ukraine's regime evolved from seventeenth-century history much like how Nazism's origins in

Germany could be traced to pre-Christian times and the Thirty Years War of 1618–48.[36] Sergiy Aksyonov built on this narrative by stating that "Nazism, paganism, occultism and Satanism have always gone hand in hand—this was the case in the Third Reich, this is happening today in Ukraine."[37] Hawkish pro-war voices highlighted Russia's historical responsibility to destroy Ukrainian Nazism and the grave risks of letting a Nazi regime in Ukraine remain intact. Zuganov declared that "we are finishing the Great Patriotic War there today" and insisted that "everyone understands that Ukraine needs to be cleansed of Nazism and Bandera."[38] Patrushev warned on 24 March that "Nazism must either be 100% eradicated or it will raise its head, and in an even uglier form," and proposed denazification of Ukraine along the lines of the 1945 Potsdam Conference.[39]

Russia's depiction of Ukraine as a Nazi regime confounded much of the international community, as Zelensky was a Jewish president and descendant of Holocaust victims. To reconcile this contradiction, Kremlin-aligned experts and media outlets advanced multiple, often-contradictory conspiracies. A key element was that Zelensky was not the ultimate power broker in Ukraine but a mere puppet of a Nazi-infiltrated Ukrainian military. Crimea Senator Sergei Tsekov stated that "Although Zelensky calls himself president, he does not govern the state. He simply broadcasts from somewhere," and warned that the General Staff, local administrations and the military controlled Ukraine.[40] Vyacheslav Volodin repeatedly asserted that Zelensky had fled from Kyiv to Poland via Lviv and that his wartime videos had been recorded in advance.[41] Russian media also solicited opinions from psychiatrists who warned that Zelensky was a drug addict due to his monotone speech patterns and shifty eye movements.[42] Due to Zelensky's lack of authority, the Kremlin claimed that Nazi battalions had infiltrated the Ukrainian military and freely committed atrocities. State Duma Deputy Mikhail

Sheremet proclaimed that "Today we can say with confidence that Zelensky has completely lost control over the nationalist battalions and militants," and stated that they acted in their own interests, which were monetary rather than patriotic in nature.[43] Moscow-based commentator Mark Sleboda contends that "Russians aren't saying Zelensky is a Nazi. They are reporting the fact that his regime has literally state-armed and funded unequivocal neo-Nazi death squads sent to kill and repress their own people for eight years."[44] A 1 May *Vesti* article describes the entire 44,000-strong army in eastern Ukraine as Nazis and states that in every barrack, there are "swastikas, runes, German posters from the Great Patriotic War, Nazi banners."[45] Bogdan Bezpalko, a member of Putin's Council for Interethnic Relations, similarly called the Ukrainian army "one big national battalion."[46]

To substantiate these conspiracies, Russia greatly exaggerated the presence of neo-Nazis within the Ukrainian military. On 30 March, Polyanskiy briefed the UN on Russia's belief that Nazism was pervasive in Ukrainian military. Polyanskiy highlighted anecdotes such as NATO's removal of a portrait of a Ukrainian soldier with a Nazi chevron from its official page, and admiration for Nazi collaborators like Bandera and UPA military leader Roman Shukhevych.[47] The Azov Regiment, which claimed to have 10,000 fighters in April 2022, earned a central place in Russian conspiracies about Ukrainian Nazism, as the Kremlin had accused it of human rights abuses in Donbas since 2014. Beyond highlighting Nazi ideology, Russian media also fed Putin's "Donbas genocide" conspiracy by accusing Ukraine of carrying out Nazi-style war crimes. Channel 24 presenter Fakhrudin Sharafmal's remark, "Let me quote the words of Adolf Eichmann, who said that in order to destroy a nation, children must be destroyed" was linked to a broader Ukrainian plan to slaughter Russian children.[48] LNR officials accused the Aidar Battalion of creating a base filled with "Glory to the

Nation" posters and swastikas, and of creating a Nazi-style concentration camp to subject Luhansk residents to torture.[49] Russia transposed these policies of nationalist battalions to the Ukrainian government. On Russian Telegram, routine wartime policies such as the imposition of curfew and martial law were cited as proof that the "Kyiv regime" was "allowed to shoot to kill without warning at any citizens" and was "actively getting rid of its citizens."[50] After Russia's 16 March Mariupol theatre airstrike, which killed at least a dozen people, the Russian ministry of defence accused the Azov Battalion of carrying out a "bloody provocation" and Ukrainian Nazis of holding citizens as human shields in Mariupol.[51] This propaganda intensified post-Maidan narratives, such as Slutsky's comparison of the May 2014 Odesa clashes that killed 46 anti-Maidan demonstrators to Nazi crimes.[52]

These accusations are detached from empirical truths about Ukraine's nationalist battalions. Although the Azov Battalion's founder Andriy Biletsky stated in 2010 that Ukraine's goal was to "lead the white races of the world in a final crusade against Semite-led *Untermenschen*" and the battalion's uniform uses the Nazi Wolfsangel symbol, it is misleading to describe the Azov Battalion as a neo-Nazi organisation. Shortly after Biletsky's departure in October 2014, the presence of Nazis within the Azov Battalion was estimated to be 10–20% of its members and the battalion's integration into the Ukrainian military has further diluted its ideological character.[53] While neo-Nazi and illiberal elements within the Azov Regiment remain, the dominance of patriotism over ideology in Ukraine's 2022 resistance to Russia has reined in its extremist impulses. It also belies the presence of neo-Nazi elements within Russia's military apparatus, which include Wagner Group founder Dmitry Utkin, the Rusich unit of the Wagner Group and Lieutenant Colonel Timur Kurilkin, who Pushilin honoured for military heroism.

Russia also sought to redefine the concept of Nazism in ways that blurred the exceptionality of the Holocaust. Sergei Karaganov contends that "Nazis were not only about killing Jews. Nazism is about the supremacy of one nation over another. Nazism is the humiliation of other nations."[54] The case that Ukrainian Russophobia was a form of Nazism undergirded the denazification agenda. The decommunisation of Ukraine was another manifestation of Nazism, as it banned the Soviet anthem but allowed Nazi Germany's anthem and the Nazi Party "Song of Horst Wessel" to be legally played.[55] The destruction of Georgy Zhukov monuments, the phasing out of the Great Patriotic War phrase and banning of the St. George Ribbon on 9 May also added to Russia's denazification case.[56] Russian media also falsely accused Ukraine of banning the Russian language in all areas outside of personal life.[57] The drastic uptick in references to Nazism in the Russian media after 24 February caused these narratives to proliferate. Alexei Miller of St. Petersburg's European University believes that denazification was not a core driver of Russia's decision to invade Ukraine but instead was effective in spoiling the image of Ukrainians, as Russians responded to hours-long state media videos of Azov Battalion torture.[58] However, a sizeable portion of Russians were confused by denazification's meaning and saw it as a denigration of the legacy of the Soviet Union's triumph in the Second World War.[59]

Russian propagandists and lawmakers also created a revisionist history of Ukrainian Nazism to convince the public of its salience as a threat. On 1 April, Grigory Lukyantsev, a senior Russian foreign ministry official responsible for human rights policy, contended that Ukraine's support for Nazi collaborationists as national heroes occurred "long before 2014," stating that "it is erroneous to say that the problems in the corresponding sphere in Ukraine emerged only after the Maidan events."[60] Alexei Denisov claims that the reformatting of Ukraine's consciousness began in the 1920s and 1930s, as violent Ukrainisation occurred in Donbas and Novorossiya. This caused Ukraine to develop an anti-Russian identity, encouraged Nazi collaboration during the Second World War and paved the way for Ukraine's post-1991 efforts to decouple itself from Russia in every possible sphere.[61] Lieutenant-General Yuri Zhdanov attributed Nazism's re-emergence in Ukraine to the May 1947 Decree of the Presidium of the Supreme Soviet of the USSR, which abolished the death penalty and prevented the execution of Nazis like Stepan Bandera for genocide. Zhdanov believes that Khrushchev's 1955 amnesty to Nazi collaborators in the Second World War allowed Banderites to enter the Communist Party's upper echelons and created a "powerful Bandera-nationalist time bomb that will explode in the 90s in the post-Soviet space of Ukraine."[62] After Ukrainian independence, Senator Konstantin Dolgov asserted that Ukraine had few national heroes and had to create "anti-Russian heroes" for identity construction.[63] This impetus led to Bandera's rehabilitation, even though he had not supported Ukrainian independence but had instead wanted Ukraine to become part of the Third Reich.

The contemporary evolution of Ukrainian Nazism began with the Orange Revolution. In April 2022, Vladimir Konstantinov responded to the impending publication of a book in Crimea about the "serious, deadly disease" of Ukrainian Nazism by stating that the Nazification of Ukraine began during Yushchenko's presidency. He argued that Yushchenko "raised the spirit of Bandera from the grave," glorified war criminals and gave space for a small handful of Nazi renegades to take over the government as in Hitler's Germany.[64] Denisov blamed Yushchenko for donating Pavel Shtepa's book *Muskovtsvo* to libraries in Crimea; Shtepa highlighted racial distinctions between Russians and Ukrainians through genetic analysis and viewed Russians as an inferior race.[65] With U.S. support, Nazism became state policy after the Euro-Maidan Revolution. *Rossiya Segodnya* commentator Rostislav Ishchenko contends that without the U.S., Ukrainian Nazism would have been a marginal political force and Ukraine's nationalism would have taken a "moderately Russophobic but outwardly quite civilised" character like that of the Czech Republic. Ishchenko links U.S. support for Ukrainian Nazism to Russophobia, which also manifested itself in Washington's framing of "Nazi totalitarianism" as a democratic alternative to Lukhashenko's rule in Belarus and support for anti-Russian policies in the Baltic states.[66] Irina Yarovaya states that "the regime in power in Ukraine today is a Nazi group methodically rebuilt by the United States," and cites the Pentagon's training of the Azov Battalion in spite of anti-Semitism concerns as evidence.

From a policy standpoint, denazification consisted of the destruction of Nazi battalions, regime change, at least partial occupation and long-term reforms. *Vesti* stated that "denazification is when neo-Nazis from the Azov Regiment rot alive in cold factory basements."[67] On 15 March, Russian commentator Mikhail Demurin rhetorically asked, "What is denazification if not regime change?" and insisted that "there should definitely not be the current Nazi, repressive, hostile regime to Russia."[68] While Dolgov insisted that denazification would not require the occupation of Ukraine, the annexation of Donbas was typically regarded as the minimum required occupation to achieve this goal. A minority view favoured the occupation of the entirety of Ukraine. Former *Kyiv Telegraph* Editor-in-Chief Vladimir Skachko insisted that denazification could only be completed if Russia took control of western Ukraine, as Galicia and Volhynia had been Poland-backed centres of "destructive Ukrainian nationalism" since the early twentieth century. Skachko argues that the dominance of Galician ideology over Ukraine created three pervasive theses: "Away from Moscow," "Ukraine is first of all" and "Ukraine is for

Ukrainians," and the Russian military needed to enter western Ukrainian cities such as Lviv to correct it.[69]

Russia's post-occupation denazification plans called for the complete destruction of Ukraine's political and cultural life. Dmitry Kiselyov called for war crimes trials for nationalist battalion commanders and the elites who enabled them, such as Poroshenko, Avakov, Turchynov and Kolomoisky; the creation of an "anti-fascist" education system that emphasised "common values" with Russia; and bans on nationalist symbols.[70] These retributive actions would be paired with Ukrainian judicial reforms and the restoration of capital punishment.[71] These recommendations were woven into Russian political discourse. Pushilin stated that denazification would take more than one year and would ensure that Nazism would not be revived by future generations of Ukrainians.[72] Volodin proclaimed that "Zelensky and his henchmen are war criminals supporting Nazi ideology" and declared that "they must answer for their actions" such as the torture of civilians that Russia had relayed to European parliaments.[73] Once Ukraine was converted into a "friendly country," Russia would also be open to carrying out further denazification operations in European countries such as Poland and Latvia. Natalia Narochnitskaya argues that as there is "no European ideology," Nazism and "the rehabilitation of Hitler" would likely follow.[74] By effectively claiming that the Second World War never ended, Russia used denazification as a pretext for the occupation of Ukraine and further military aggression in Eastern Europe.

Russia's Military Campaign in Ukraine: Tactical Victories, Strategic Setbacks

Despite jingoistic optimism amongst Russian officials and media outlets, the Russian military failed to achieve its strategic objectives in Ukraine for four reasons. First, the Russian air force was unable to secure uncontested dominance over Ukraine's skies; Zelensky's concerns about the prospect of Russian aerial dominance were evidenced by his persistent calls for a no-fly zone in the early stages of the war, which were only supported by the Baltic states. This development surprised many observers, as Russia made extensive use of VKS fixed-wing jets in Syria but did not replicate that trend in Ukraine, even as ground operations stalled.[75] Justin Bronk, a senior fellow at the Royal United Services Institute (RUSI), discounts popular explanations for this failure, such as the use of VKS jets in reserve in the event of a conflict with NATO, the limited number of VKS jets that can be used for precision munitions and low-risk tolerance in the Russian air force.[76] Instead, Bronk attributes Russia's VKS failings to lack of early warning, coordination capacity and sufficient planning time. These failures, which were augmented by Russia's replication of its use of small formations of jets in Syria and live flying hours for pilots that were only half that of NATO air forces, explain why Russia was unable to subvert a Ukrainian air force that relied on low-altitude flight paths.[77] The U.S.'s swift delivery of anti-aircraft Stingers to Ukraine further eroded Russia's prospects for aerial dominance, as did NATO's intelligence sharing with Ukraine, which allowed it to evacuate airfields ahead of Russian strikes.[78] The losses of 11 planes, 11 helicopters and 2 drones during the first days of the war underscored the vulnerabilities of Russian aircraft, which extended even to its flagship Su-34 jets.[79]

The second factor was the hierarchical rigidity of the Russian military, which restricted its tactical versatility and ability to prosecute an effective hybrid war on Ukraine. Russia's struggles with a multi-directional war reflected the military's bureaucratic nature and culture of risk aversion.[80] The small number of Russian officials who were privy to advanced knowledge about

Russia's invasion plans, such as Bortnikov, Shoigu and Medvedev, exacerbated this problem. In Moscow, it is widely believed that Lavrov's denials of Russia's invasion plans until the war began reflected a lack of consultation and that the opacity of the war effort encouraged Russia to intervene with an inadequate troop concentration.[81] The disappearance of Shoigu and Gerasimov from public view in March exemplified Putin's willingness to personalise control over military operations. Russia's logistical failures in Ukraine, which extended to an absence of cold weather gear and resultant frostbite for military personnel, also reflected a lack of adaptability. Russia's reliance on railway transit was effective in south-eastern Ukraine, as it controlled Melitopol and Kherson, but undermined the Kyiv offensive, as it did not control Chernihiv's railways and was forced to rely on time-consuming truck-based operations.[82] Russia's reliance on a blitzkrieg offensive, which saw a 120-mile push from Crimea to Kherson and a 90-mile Belarus to Kyiv push, strained supply lines and could have been avoided if it had relied on 30–40 mile pushes.[83] When these challenges were apparent, Russia opted not to increase its logistical reinforcements in its BTGs, which meant that just 150–200 out of an average of 900 troops per BTG were supporting combatant forces.

The failure of Russia's conventional tactics was amplified by low morale and failed asymmetric warfare. The marked disparity in morale between Ukrainian and Russian forces was striking from the start of the war. Kremlin disinformation had convinced invading forces that they would be greeted as liberators, which included the claim that they would receive "flowers and cheers, not bullets and bombs," and expectations of a swift victory encouraged Russian forces to pack only two to three days of food supply.[84] The expectation that Russian forces participating in Belarus drills would return home instead of invading Ukraine suppressed morale further. During a 7 March speech by Sergey

Tsivilev, the governor of Kuzbass region in Siberia, an exasperated mother accused Russia of using forces as "cannon fodder" and deceiving them by sending untrained forces to the frontlines.[85] Russia's contradictory policy towards conscription caused further confusion on the frontlines. Although Putin insisted that no conscripts or reservists would be deployed, the Russian ministry of defence admitted on 7 March that conscripts had joined the war effort and had been captured by Ukrainian forces.[86] Despite successful malware attacks against Ukrainian government agencies on 14 January and 23 February, Russia was ultimately unable to pair its offensive operations with its cyberattacks. The EU's cyber rapid response team and Ukraine's 26 February creation of an IT Army blunted the efficacy of Russian cyber-efforts and left Russian media outlets vulnerable to hacks; due to Anonymous's hacks, viewers of St. Petersburg-based Fontanka outlets were warned of "certain death" for Russian troops and censored footage from the frontlines appeared on Russian state TV.[87] Russia's subsequent failures to gain a cyberwarfare advantage was due to poor efficacy rather than restraint, as 4.6 million attacks on Ukraine and Poland were launched on 9 March.

The third factor in Russia's failure to achieve its strategic objectives in Ukraine was the limitations of its diverse array of auxiliary combat units. The Wagner Group was regarded as Russia's most efficient military unit, as it consisted of well-compensated, highly trained veterans from past wars; Wagner Group commanders have much more freedom of action than the vertical nature of the Russian military traditionally would allow and can improvise in the face of changing battlefield conditions.[88] The Wagner Group's efficiency was largely confined to diversionary operations and creation of gaps in the frontlines, which rendered it unable to exert a transformative impact on the battlefield.[89] The Wagner Group's limited manpower in Ukraine, which increased from 300 to a Donbas-centric contingent of 1,000 forces in late March, also restricted its combat potential. The DNR and LNR militias were routinely used as cannon fodder in Russia's Donbas operations and by 22 June, British intelligence estimates showed that 55% of DNR forces had perished. Andriy Zagorodnyuk notes that the quality of DNR and LNR militias degraded from 2017–20, as the Donbas War stabilised as a frozen conflict, and a culture of irresponsibility and alcoholism spread throughout their ranks. Zagorodnyuk also notes that Russia's recruitment of untrained fighters from Donetsk and Luhansk who work in industrial facilities such as petroleum stations and low morale amongst these forces further weakened their efficacy.[90]

The Chechen Kadyrovtsy were the least effective units, as their primary battlefield experience was in suppressing the local population rather than open combat.[91] Although Ramzan Kadyrov boasted that up to 70,000 Chechen fighters would be willing to join the Ukraine War and addressed 12,000 troops in Grozny with a demand to conquer Kyiv, the Kadyrovtsy suffered from poor combat discipline. The reliance of Kadyrovtsy fighters on black uniforms prevented camouflage, while Kadyrov's extensive social media presence and gaffes, which included wearing Prada boots in a combat zone, reinforced this image of unprofessionalism.[92] Kadyrov's political ambitions, which included repairing a reputation tarnished by his January 2022 kidnapping of dissident Zarema Musaeva, encouraged a personalistic administration style. The Ukraine War also revived sharpened internecine divisions amongst Chechnya's paramilitaries, which was exemplified by pro-Ukraine Dzhokhar Dudayev Volunteer Battalion head Adam Osmayev's public condemnations of Kadyrov. The flight of Kadyrovtsy units from Bucha on 27 February created the image of Chechen forces as a "Tiktok Army," diluting the brand of psychological warfare that Kadyrov had relied on in Ukraine.[93]

The fourth factor was Russia's overestimation of the anticipated scale of local collaboration in Ukraine. Based on July 2021 plans for a coup in Ukraine published by the SBU in April, Russia's regime change ambitions relied heavily on grassroots support. Russia's plan required the recruitment of 500 ATO veterans to stage a coup against Zelensky; with the support of villages, district councils and regional councils, the Kremlin planned to create "people's republics" in western Ukraine and a "People's Rada."[94] Russia's collaborator network proved to be significantly smaller than expected, as twelve Opposition Platform deputies fled Ukraine in the days leading up to the war.[95] Ilya Kyva stood alone in supporting the Russian invasion but swiftly fled to Spain and was expelled by the Opposition Platform on 3 March. The Opposition Bloc ultimately called for the swift withdrawal of Russian troops and supported the Ukrainian Territorial Defence Forces in protecting critical infrastructure. Opposition Bloc-affiliated Oleksandr Vikul became the governor of Kryvvi Rih, and former Party of Regions Deputy Mykhailo Dobkin, who was allegedly courted by the FSB to lead a Kharkiv People's Republic, condemned the war. Russia's miscalculations mirrored General Pavel Grachev's belief during the First Chechen War that Russia would prevail within hours due to local support and reflected the Russian military's broader inability to harness lessons from past campaigns.

The Kyiv Offensive: A Failed Regime Change Blitz

Rather than embark on a more costly direct assault on the city, Russia's strategy to achieve a regime change in Kyiv hinged on encircling the capital, fomenting chaos through acts of sabotage, and reinforcing ties with pro-Kremlin politicians who could take power in Ukraine. Russia's cluster of forces on the Chernihiv–Sumy axis of the advance aimed to encircle Kyiv from the east, while its column of combat and logistics vehicles to the north sought to encircle the capital from the west.[96] These ground force clusters were complemented by missile strikes on Kyiv's Boryspil International Airport and airborne assaults which aimed to seize control of Antonov Airport and Vasylkiv Airbase. Russia also seized the Chernobyl nuclear power plant on the first day of the war, which provided a clear path to Kyiv via regional road P02. To aid its eastward encirclement of Kyiv, the Russian ministry of defence announced that it had besieged Chernihiv on 25 February. This siege was followed by airstrikes which damaged much of central Chernihiv, and the extensive use of cluster bombs and mining of exit points from the city, which led to its complete encirclement by 10 March. To aid its western encirclement of Kyiv, Russia seized control of key suburbs like Bucha, Hostomel and half of Irpin.

These military successes did not last. Although Russia struck the Kyiv bridge on 25 May, which isolated Chernihiv, Ukraine's 1st Tank Brigade and accompanying units seized several main roads linking Kyiv to Chernihiv on 31 March, breaking the siege.[97] Kyiv Regional Military Administration head Oleksandr Pavlyuk presented a bleaker picture of the situation in Bucha and Hostomel on 22 March, as he stated that Russia's position was weakening but Ukraine was unable to launch large-scale counter-offensives on either town. Pavlyuk stated that the immediate aim of Ukrainian forces was to prevent Russian troops from crossing the Irpin River and entering Kyiv.[98] Despite this measured assessment, Ukrainian forces ultimately were able to force a Russian withdrawal from Bucha, Irpin and Hostomel in late March.

A key factor in Ukraine's ability to thwart a Russian encirclement in Kyiv was the surprising inefficacy of the 64km Russian convoy of 15,000 troops which entered Ukraine from Belarus on 28 February. It was unclear whether this convoy was supposed to be used to besiege Kyiv or if it was principally a supply line for the Russian forces enveloping the city. The convoy stalled around 25–30km from Kyiv, as Bayraktar TB-2 drones breached its mobile anti-aircraft systems, and a combination of Ukrainian resistance, fuel and food shortages, and mechanical failures delayed its movements.[99] As a stationary target, Ukraine was able to strike the convoy with FGM-148 Javelin anti-tank missiles and create roadblocks to derail its momentum. Ukrainian snipers were able to assassinate Major General Andrey Sukhovetsky, the deputy commander of the 41st Combined Arms Army of the Central Military District, on 3 March. These tactics allowed the Ukrainian army to circumvent Russia's forward deployment of air defence systems such as the S-400s on the Belarus–Ukraine border, which would complicate drone strikes. On 17 March, the U.S. Department of Defense confirmed that the Russian convoy that marched on Kyiv was "stuck and not moving," despite satellite imagery showing some of its forces had entered Hostomel, and Ukraine's control over Brovary in eastern Kyiv further stymied Russia's advance.[100] The convoy disappeared days before Ukrainian forces liberated Kyiv Oblast.

Russia paired its offensive operations with the deployment of saboteurs tasked with assassinating Zelensky. Immediately after the invasion, Zelensky warned that "enemy sabotage groups have entered Kyiv" and the "enemy marked me as the number one target."[101] Zelensky advisor Mykhailo Podolyak similarly warned that Russia wanted to create "maximum panic" and break into Kyiv's government quarter to install a new regime. Initially, the Kremlin tasked Chechen Kadyrovtsy forces with assassinating Zelensky. On 3 February, Putin reportedly ordered Kadyrov to establish a "strike group" in Grozny, and Kadyrov appointed his assistant Danylo Martynov to spearhead this effort. These troops became part of the Roshvardiya forces group, which joined the Eastern Military District units in Belarus and deployed 1,500 elite Chechen units with 250 units of military equipment into Ukraine. On 26 February, an FSB agent tasked with surveillance of the Kadyrovtsy reportedly passed on information to Ukrainian intelligence about their concentration in Hostomel, which led to strikes that killed close Kadyrov ally Magomed Tushayev and neutralised the threat.[102] By late February, 400 Wagner Group PMCs, who had redeployed from African theatres five weeks earlier, were leading Russia's assassination attempt on Zelensky. Despite these mobilisations, Danilov revealed in early March that Zelensky survived three assassination attempts in the space of a week, and by 9 March, Podolyak confirmed that Zelensky had overcome over a dozen such attempts. Putin also called for a military coup in Ukraine, stating, "It seems as if it will be easier for us to agree with you than this gang of drug addicts and neo-Nazis."[103]

Russia also cultivated potential candidates to lead a puppet regime in Kyiv. The U.S. intelligence community viewed Viktor Medvedchuk and Oleg Tsaryov as the most likely candidates to replace Zelensky. On 27 February, Medvedchuk escaped house arrest but remained in Kyiv. Medvedchuk's autumn 2017 prisoner exchange negotiations counted against his installation, as he was accused of advancing Ukrainian interests due to his ties with Poroshenko and not lobbying sufficiently for the release of Novorossiya activists.[104] Medvedchuk's removal as Opposition Bloc co-chair on 8 March further eroded his standing. Tsaryov's support for violent repression of Euro-Maidan protesters and alleged receipt of a death threat from Kolomoisky had bolstered his standing as a counter-revolutionary figure. Tsaryov maintained a large public profile in the early days of the war, as he reportedly provided humanitarian assistance in Russian-occupied Ukraine and proclaimed that Kyiv would be liberated from Nazism. British intelligence had singled out former Opposition Bloc Deputy Yevhen Murayev as a possible president, as he controlled NewsOne's replacement NASH, which was Ukraine's largest pro-Russian media network. Murayev dismissed these rumours, while the Russian foreign ministry responded by urging Britain to "stop spreading nonsense and concentrate on studying the history of the Tatar-Mongol yoke."[105] Ukrainian intelligence officials were concerned that Russia could reinstate Yanukovych, as it would overturn Euro-Maidan, and speculation about his return to power peaked on 2 March when he reportedly arrived in Minsk.[106] Yanukovych's nationwide unpopularity, which extended to Donbas, undermined his case however; Sergei Glazyev's derisive condemnations of how "our boyfriend" Yanukovych tolerated Russophobia in Ukrainian schools underscored hardliner opposition to his legacy.[107] Therefore, Ukrainian officials pivoted their attention towards lesser-known pro-Russian figures who organically capitalised on unrest.[108]

Russia's Slow-Motion Annexation of Southern and Eastern Ukraine

Russia's campaign in southern Ukraine was inextricably linked with its goal of restoring its hegemony over the Black Sea. The integral importance of the Black Sea to Russia's military campaign in Ukraine was apparent from its pre-war efforts to upgrade its Black Sea Fleet's preparedness. In December 2021, the Russian ministry of defence deployed the Georgy Kurbatov minesweeper, Vsevolod Bobrov logistical supply vessel, Krasnodar submarine and Vasily Bekh Rescuer to the Black Sea.[109] On 26 January, at least twenty Russian vessels began naval exercises in the Black Sea, and on 8 February, the Russian defence ministry reported that six large landships were headed to the Black Sea for drills. Russia framed these measures in threat mitigation terms, as it sought to dispel concerns about an impending invasion of Ukraine and stymie NATO's retaliatory build-ups. Russia's partial closure of the Azov-Black Sea area and Kerch Strait for naval drills from 12 to 19 February reflected its desire to prevent U.S. Sixth Fleet ships from providing military aid to

Ukraine and growing concerns about the U.S.'s reinforcement of its military presence in Romania. Russia built on these efforts by annexing Snake Island on 24 February, which is located near Romania and could have served as a logistical station or coastal missile operation base in the event of an amphibious attack on Odesa.[110]

In tandem with its victory in Snake Island, Russia swiftly transited its invading forces from Crimea to Kherson and Melitopol in Zaporizhzhia Oblast. During the first 48 hours of the war, Russia captured the Antonovskiy Bridge in Kherson, which serves as a Dnieper River crossing point to Mykolaiv, and conquered Nova Kakhovka. Despite Ukrainian strike-backs, Russia encircled Kherson on 27 February and advanced from Kherson International Airport to the Kherson–Mykolaiv highway on 1 March. On 2 March, Russia declared victory in Kherson and took initial steps towards establishing an occupation regime, in spite of periodic pro-Ukrainian demonstrations and a rapidly worsening humanitarian crisis. Ukrainian Rada Deputy Roman Hryshchuk attributes Russia's swift victory in Kherson to treasonous local officials and the unexpected nature of Moscow's nationwide offensive.[111] Mykola Bielieskov, a Kyiv-based defence analyst, disputes this narrative, stating that Ukraine pragmatically acknowledged Russia's numerical superiority and chose not to resist strongly, as devoting large numbers of forces to Kherson would have allowed Russia to seize Mykolaiv or Odesa.[112] Russia's occupation of Melitopol on 1 March could be explained by similar factors and gave it the opportunity to advance on Berdyansk and Mariupol. Russia's victory in Melitopol was regarded as a significant strategic success due to its location on the intersection of two critical highways and proximity to Crimea, as it was the primary transit point for passenger trains to the peninsula before the 2014 annexation.

Russia's offensives on Mykolaiv and Odesa were much less successful. Despite an early triumph in Snihurivka, which was subsequently integrated into Kherson, Russian forces were unable to keep Voznesensk and were forced to withdraw to the south-eastern fringes of Mykolaiv Oblast by mid-March. Russia struck military infrastructure in Odesa, including its military airport, at the start of the war and stepped up its cruise missile strikes on the city in late March, which included attacks on its port infrastructure. Russian defence analyst Sergey Marzhetsky anticipated a major campaign in Odesa, as it was where the "remnants of the Ukrainian Navy and warships of the NATO bloc were based" and a gateway to ending the blockade of Transnistria.[113] After the seizure of Kherson, Russian Telegram channels warned that Ukraine was preparing for an amphibious landing on Zatoka,[114] and also highlighted Ukraine's alleged incompetence, such as landmine failures and the explosion of bridges that would isolate ten regions of Odesa in the event of an amphibious landing.[115] Despite this braggadocious rhetoric, Russia was unable to carry out an amphibious landing operation on the city. Volodymyr Dubovyk notes that Russia intended to land on Odesa with speedboats, but Ukrainian artillery shelled Russian ships even prior to the entry of Neptune and Harpoon anti-ship missiles into its arsenal. Volatile weather counted against Russia's offensive operations in Odesa, as did internal discord, as Russian troops were wary about stepping on a mined beach and being exposed to gunfire.[116]

Russia's Donbas offensive concentrated on securing control of Mariupol, which would provide the Russian military with a much-coveted land bridge to Crimea. Russia's advance on Mariupol came through DNR territory and synthesised artillery bombard-ments with an amphibious landing by the Black Sea Fleet on the Sea of Azov. Russia encircled Mariupol on 2 March and, despite the creation of a humanitarian corridor to Zaporizhzhia, Russia continued to shell the city and created a dire humanitarian crisis by leaving 700,000 residents of the city without heat. Russia's offensive on Mariupol included OSCE-designated war crimes, such as the 9 March strike on a maternity hospital and the 16 March Mariupol theatre strike, which resulted in heavy civilian casualties. Russia countered these allegations with an intense disinformation campaign. MGIMO academic Kirill Koktysh described the maternity hospital shelling a "Ukrainian fake" mirroring false flag tactics by the White Helmets in Syria.[117] The Russian defence ministry similarly called it a "staged provocation," as the hospital was demolished through two separate explosions. Russia accused the Azov Regiment of carrying out the Mariupol theatre attack, as media outlets pushed conspiracies that Azov fighters had moved an explosive and detonator to the site prior to the explosion.[118] Mariupol mayor Vadym Boychenko's 28 March warning that Mariupol was in Russia's hands paved the way for the city's eventual surrender. Russia occupied the Azov Regiment's military headquarters and the SBU building in central Mariupol and pivoted its attention towards destroying the final pocket of Ukrainian resistance in the Azovstal steel factory. Russia also carried out military operations in Luhansk, which secured it control over 93% of the oblast except for Severodonetsk and Lysychansk.

The Home Front: Economic Sanctions and Increased Repression

Russia's invasion of Ukraine was swiftly followed by sweeping economic sanctions. The imposition of SWIFT sanctions on Russia were the most significant punitive measure, as the majority of Russian credit institutions relied on SWIFT and Russia had the second largest SWIFT userbase after the U.S. Initially, Biden was pessimistic that the EU would agree to SWIFT sanctions, as Olaf Scholz had expressed concern that they would lead to a disruption of energy supplies to Europe.[119] Nevertheless, French finance minister Bruno Le Maire supported the sanctions, calling them a "financial nuclear weapon," while Germany, Hungary, Italy and Cyprus dropped their objections to the move on 26 February. The SWIFT sanctions did not apply to the entire Russian financial sector, as Sberbank was partially owned by Gazprom and Gazprombank handled energy-related transactions, but extended to seven key Russian banks: Bank Otkritie, Novikombank, Promsvyazbank, Rossiya Bank, Sovcombank, VEB and VTB. The Russian Central Bank was subsequently blocked from accessing $400 billion in assets and the U.S. imposed restrictions on business dealings with the Russian Direct Investment Fund. These financial restrictions were paired with bans by the U.S., EU, Britain and Canada on Russian airlines. The U.S. also imposed personal sanctions on Vladimir Putin. Although Peskov initially claimed that Putin was "indifferent" to Western sanctions as he had no foreign assets, he blasted the West for this measure on 3 April, stating "after the sanctions imposed against our president, it looks like they are capable of doing any stupid thing."[120]

The adverse consequences of sanctions on the Russian economy were immediate. By 1 March, $1 trillion in Russian assets had been frozen, and on 4 March, the U.S. imposed a raft of new sanctions on Russian oligarchs which Britain and the EU mirrored. These sanctions were expected to cause a calamitous economic impact; an Institute of International Finance (IIF) report predicted a 15% contraction of the Russian economy in 2022.[121] On 1 March, the rouble slid to a record low of 117 to the U.S. dollar and as the currency slid further on 7 March, local markets were suspended from trading for two days. The Moscow Stock Exchange plunged by 44% on 24 February even though it was closed the previous day and the Central Bank tried to reassure investors through liquidity offers to Russian banks.[122] Due to the rapid deterioration of Russia's economic conditions, the Kremlin took decisive measures. On 28 February, the Russian

Central Bank increased interest rates from 9.5% to 20% and urged export-focused companies to sell foreign currency reserves in order to shore up the rouble's value.[123] Russia's imposition of capital controls to strengthen the rouble were described as a tit-for-tat retaliation to the freezing of Central Bank assets.[124] The Russian Central Bank also upheld its prohibition on cryptocurrencies, which risked a 1 million rouble fine for non-compliance, in spite of strenuous opposition from the Russian ministry of finance, which wanted banks to issue cryptocurrencies.[125]

The Russian Central Bank's actions coincided with calls for more drastic action to sanction-proof the Russian economy. On 10 March, Medvedev expressed support for the nationalisation of assets of foreign countries that fled Russia due to Western sanctions.[126] These nationalisation measures risked extending to large corporations, such as Apple, McDonald's, IKEA and Toyota. Medvedev's 26 February statements hinted that this was a first step towards a more sweeping nationalisation of properties by U.S., British and European nationals, which would deter the potential arrest of Russian citizens and sanctions on Russian companies based abroad.[127] The Russian Central Bank resisted these economic self-isolation measures, as well as measures proposed by hardliners to restrict gold exports and ban the withdrawal of assets to offshore locations. Russian commentator Konstantin Dvinsky mentioned Central Bank chief Elvira Nabiullina in the same breath as Alexei Kudrin, Anton Siluanov and Anatoly Chubais, and called for a clean-up of the "liberals" that were shaping Russia's economic policy.[128] This outrage did not gain traction; Putin's 23 March decision to grant Nabiullina a five-year term extension after she reportedly threatened to resign signified his efforts to limit the influence of hardliners over economic policy.[129] Putin also retained Kudrin in spite of widespread criticism of his alleged role in ensuring that Western elites viewed Russia as a "junior partner" and his low profile after defending the early 1990s neoliberal economic reforms at the January 2022 Gaidar Forum.[130]

As a result of the Kremlin's policies and avoidance of extreme ideas, the immediate worst-case scenario did not pan out. Russia's GDP might only experience a 3% contraction and the rouble rapidly strengthened, but a steady output decline and brain drain sparked fears of a lost decade for the Russian economy.[131] The U.S.'s 3 March sanctions on Radioavtomatika, which procures foreign items for Russia's defence industry, complicated Russia's ability to replenish cruise missiles, communications systems and electronic warfare complexes that relied heavily on Western electronics.[132] The exact manifestation of Russia's sanctions-induced economic decline is unclear, however. RIAC Director of Programs Ivan Timofeev notes that sanctions have not created an unemployment spiral in Russia, even if inflation remains more volatile, and contends that long-term stagnations of sectors of the Russian economy will not lead to anti-government collective action.[133] Vladimir Inozemtsev contends that the Russian economy can stay afloat for two to three years due to pre-existing stockpiles of sanctioned goods but the heavy reliance of Russian industry on Western equipment and spare parts shortages would be difficult to overcome. Inozemtsev believes that travel restrictions will harden anti-Western sentiments and deepen cleavages between nationalists and Russia's pro-Western minority but will not lead to a long-term patriotic rally for Putin.[134] Russian state media downplayed the long-term economic impact of sanctions, while highlighting the resilience of Putin's regime and their adverse global implications. RIA Novosti commentator Petr Akopov affirmed this view, stating "there is already an understanding that Russia cannot be broken by sanctions alone, as well as the awareness of the futility of hopes for a revolt of the discontented population."[135]

To ensure the stability of his regime in the face of a stagnating war effort and sanctions, Putin mobilised pro-government nationalism around the war effort. The letter Z, which was observable on Russian military vehicles during the pre-war troop build-up, was the symbol of Russia's wartime ultranationalism. The Russian ministry of defence has advanced a variety of explanations for Z's meaning, such as "For Truth," "For Peace" and "For Victory," while the corresponding V symbol meant "Strength is in Truth" and "The Task will be Completed." The use of the letter Z became a public means of displaying loyalty to the war effort; Dmitri Rogozin started using the RogoZin name, while Russian pro-war Telegram channels used the Z as an identifying mark. The Z's proliferation attracted controversy for being in conflict with Putin's denazification agenda, as it resembled the Station Z gas chamber at Sachsenhausen concentration camp. Russia's 4 March blockage of Western social media platforms such as Twitter and Meta further signalled Moscow's pivot towards the creation of a patriotic information space. These social media bans were justified by alleged incitement of "extremism" and violence against Russians, as well as a Western media blockade on RT and Sputnik.[136] The decision of many Russians to lock their Meta accounts and cease discussions about the war on these platforms was a significant victory for the Kremlin's censorship campaign.[137] Displays of anti-war dissent were confined to individual actions, such as Rossiya-1 journalist Marina Ovsyannikova's display of an anti-war banner on state TV.

As the war progressed, Putin's rhetoric grew darker in tone. On 17 March, he stated that "I am convinced that a natural and necessary self-purification of society will only strengthen our country" and claimed that the West was using a "fifth column" of traitorous Russians to sow instability.[138] Putin's phrase "The Russian people will always be able to distinguish true patriots from scum and traitors" was aimed at oligarchs and expatriate Russians. Hardliners in the State Duma such as Gennady Zuganov gleefully supported Putin's comments, warning about an erosion of patriotism that had begun with Yeltsin's takeover in 1991. The 18 March Luzhniki Stadium concert "For a World Without Nazism," which was mandatorily attended by state employees and some students, exemplified this ultra-nationalist spirit. Addressing an audience with Z-shaped St. George Ribbons, Maria Zakharova extolled Russia's support for peace and struggle against evil, while Moscow mayor Sergei Sobyanin hailed Russia's resilient support for Donbas in the face of Western isolation. These jingoistic speeches were paired with songs that appealed to Soviet nostalgia and Russia's historical military victories, such as the Second World War-era Battle for Sevastopol. Vladimir Putin used the Luzhniki rally to make his first public address since the war began, stating, "The country hasn't seen unity like this for a long time."[139] Although an estimated 200,000 people attended the rally, the video cut-off at the end of Putin's speech was widely mocked by the international media.

While this rhetoric about "fifth columns" was not entirely new, as Putin had made similar claims following the Crimea annexation, it nevertheless signified a dramatic totalitarian tilt in Russia. The Russian media and Putin's political surrogates amplified this shift. Vladimir Solovyov shared a Telegram post alleging that anti-war protesters were "urban lunatics and a large number of fooled immature youth, who are ready to shout the pro-Nazi SUGS slogan 'Glory to Ukraine! Glory to the Heroes!'"[140] Dmitry Peskov's defence of Russian anti-war celebrity Ivan Urgant caused intense controversy, which underscored the need for uniformity of thought in Russia. Ramzan Kadyrov condemned Peskov, stating, "It turns out that in order to become a patriot of your country, you need to criticise the actions of Russia and go abroad."[141] Given these demands for conformity, dissent in Putin's Russia rapidly ebbed. Despite public exhortations from Russian liberals such as Andrei Kozyrev for large-scale diplomatic defections,

Russia's climate change envoy Anatoly Chubais was the only senior official to resign over his opposition to the Ukraine War. Chubais's immediate flight from Russia to Turkey, which was followed by media castigation of his pro-Western economic policies, reflected the costs of dissent.[142] Except for Oleg Deripaska's 28 March criticisms of a prolonged war, oligarch dissent was largely silent. Roman Abramovich's mediation efforts and offer to use his £150 million London estate for Ukrainian refugee resettlement, which was not paired with criticisms of Putin, reflected this indirect dissent.

The Istanbul Peace Talks: A Diplomatic Off-Ramp for Vladimir Putin?

Despite its initial confidence in a swift military victory, Russia consistently paired its military campaign with diplomatic outreaches to Ukraine. Belarus hosted the first two rounds of talks on 28 February and 3 March, but the 10 March Antalya Diplomacy Forum negotiations cemented Turkey's role as the primary peace broker between Russia and Ukraine. The 29–30 March peace negotiations in Istanbul were the most serious attempt at a diplomatic solution but no progress was made towards a ceasefire. The rumoured poisonings of Roman Abramovich and Ukrainian MP Rustam Umerov at the Belarusian talks and Ukraine's 7 March shooting of alleged collaborator Denis Kireyev created distractions around the talks. The sole area where negotiations progressed was on humanitarian corridors for civilians in Mariupol. On 3 March, Mykhailo Podolyak announced that both Russia and Ukraine had reached an understanding on the need to create humanitarian corridors and requested OSCE assistance in facilitating a humanitarian solution.[143] Russia responded to Podolyak's assertion by creating corridors from Kyiv to Belarus and Kharkiv to Russia, which Zelensky's spokesperson blasted as "completely immoral" and "using people's suffering to create a television picture."[144] Russia struck a maternity hospital one day before the Antalya negotiations, killing three people, and continued launching airstrikes as talks were underway. Despite subsequent progress towards evacuating civilians from Mariupol, Ukraine was forced to close the corridors on 28 March due to Russian shelling.

The failure to achieve a diplomatic solution to the Ukraine War can be attributed to two factors. The first was the irreconcilability of Russia and Ukraine's negotiating positions. Russia adopted a maximalist negotiating position that included reducing the Ukrainian army to 50,000 troops, denazification, recognising Crimea as part of Russia and the Donbas republics as independent and Ukrainian neutrality. Ukraine's negotiating position emphasised the need for a ceasefire and Russian occupation of its territory. These divergent negotiating positions precluded constructive dialogue until mid-March, as Russia began to compromise on "denazification" and Ukraine considered discussions about neutrality. Vladimir Medinsky, who served as Russia's culture minister from 2012 to 2020, stated on 18 March that Russia and Ukraine were willing to meet each other halfway, even though Kyiv rejected Russian assertions about Nazi formations in the Ukrainian military.[145] Ahead of the Istanbul talks, Zelensky announced plans to compromise on Ukraine's NATO ambitions, stating "Security guarantees and neutrality, non-nuclear status of our state. We are ready to go for it. That is the most important point."[146] Russia was open to dropping denazification and demilitarisation, while also allowing Ukraine to pursue EU membership.[147] Peskov's comments that the EU is "not a military-political bloc" and Russian Ambassador to France Vladimir Meshkov's 15 March dismissal of the prospect of regime change in Ukraine pointed to these shifts in Moscow's bargaining position.

This spirit of compromise ultimately did not carry over to the bargaining table. RIAC Director General Andrei Kortunov stated that Russia had signalled its desire to compromise on the issue of regime change in Istanbul but disagreements over territory had derailed the negotiations.[148] Dmitry Suslov contends that Russia's plans to continue offensive operations in the Odesa and Mykolaiv directions, as well as retain troops in southern and eastern Ukraine until more sweeping negotiations with Kyiv, prevented a breakthrough.[149] Ukraine's counter-proposals on territorial questions were unable to break the impasse. The head of Zelensky's Servant of the People faction and Ukraine's chief negotiator David Arakhamia's proposal for a fifteen-year truce and negotiations on the status of Crimea clashed with Russia's view that Crimea was an inalienable part of Russia. Arakhamia's solicitation of security guarantors for all of Ukraine from the UNSC, Canada, Italy, Poland, Turkey and Israel clashed with Medinsky's claims that Donetsk and Luhansk needed to be exempted.[150] Podolyak's assertion that security guarantees should be adopted through a referendum meant that neutrality was almost certain to fail, as 72% of Ukrainians wanted to join NATO.[151] Peskov's 29 March statement that "denazification" was a core Russian objective in Ukraine epitomised the collapse of the negotiating process, and froze dialogue between Russia and Ukraine.[152] Russia's continued strikes on Chernihiv on 30 March, which coincided with only a partial drawdown from Kyiv and Chernihiv, contradicted the Russian deputy defence minister's pledge to "increase mutual trust" by reducing military activities in both regions.[153]

The second factor in the breakdown of peace negotiations was Russia's selection of hawkish negotiators and pressure from hard-liners to refrain from diplomacy with Ukraine. Vladimir Medinsky's selection as Russia's chief negotiator in particular raised doubts about the seriousness of Moscow's diplomatic overtures. Medinsky positioned himself as a hardline anti-Western conservative, claimed that Russians had an "extra chromosome," and promoted Putin's brand of historical revisionism as head of the Russian Military Historical Society. In February 2022, he extolled Russia's ability to be a modern-day empire which could "unite the peoples of Eurasia around a single economic, political and cultural centre."[154] Although he was born in Smila, Ukraine, Medinsky described Ukraine as a "phantom state" on 22 February and praised the historical nature of Putin's DNR and LNR recognitions.[155] Medinsky's extremist rhetoric continued as the negotiations were underway; on 24 March he warned that the collective West was pursuing Russia's destruction and compared the current period to the 1917 Bolshevik Revolution and Soviet collapse.[156] Other negotiators, such as Russian Ambassador to Belarus Boris Gryzlov—who called for Donbas republic independence in 2020 and enthusiastically supported denazification—and Leonid Slutsky possessed similarly extreme views on Ukraine. Slutsky's 9 March vow that Russia "will not concede on a single negotiating point" underscored the intractability of Putin's negotiating team. These hardline views fuelled provocative demands. Russia's insistence that talks be held in Belovezhskaya Pushcha in Belarus rankled the Ukrainian delegation, as this city is symbolically associated with the dissolution of states.[157]

As Russian and Ukrainian diplomats met in Istanbul, hardliners in Putin's orbit and the state media stepped up their resistance to talks. Their principal argument was that Russia needed to focus on completing its military goals, as diplomacy would be futile. Ramzan Kadyrov was an especially vocal critic of the talks, stating: "There will be no sense in these negotiations. I think we need to finish what we started: to destroy Bandera, Nazis and shaitans. Only then should a decision be made on what to do next."[158] As the talks progressed, the Russian media pushed the narrative that dialogue with Ukraine was a gateway to surrender and reparations. Konstantin Sivkov condemned Medinsky's willingness to entertain a ceasefire in Kyiv, calling him a "fifth column in action."[159] Russian media referred to the Istanbul talks derisively as the "new Khasavyurt,"[160] referring to the August 1996 treaty that ended the First Chechen War by demilitarising Grozny but did not resolve the underlying Chechen separatist issue. These hardline critics ultimately won out as Russia accused Ukraine of bad faith negotiating practices. State Duma Deputy Dmitry Belik, a colleague of Slutsky on the Foreign Affairs Committee, thundered, "Intoxicated by the idea of the triumph of a criminal ideology, the Kyiv regime talks about some victories."[161] Due to the Russian myth that the Istanbul talks were close to a breakthrough but were scuppered by Ukraine, diplomatic interactions dissipated and the hot war continued.

RUSSIA DOWNSIZES ITS GOALS IN UKRAINE

On 9 May, Russia celebrated the 77th anniversary of the Soviet triumph over Nazi Germany with Victory Day celebrations in Red Square. As Russia had few triumphs to celebrate, the Victory Day parade took on a defiant and anti-climactic tone. During his Victory Day address, Putin emphasised the defensive nature of Russia's actions, stating that "NATO countries did not want to listen to us. They had different plans, and we saw it. They were planning an invasion into our historic lands, including Crimea. Russia gave a pre-emptive rebuff to aggression. It was a forced, timely and only right decision."[1] Although Putin carried out provocative gestures such as the laying of flowers at Second World War memorials to Kyiv and Odesa, he did not escalate the "special military operation" into a full-fledged war. The uncharacteristically small amount of military equipment participating in the parade and the cancellation of a scheduled flyover due to adverse weather conditions further added to the subdued atmosphere. Putin's propaganda machinery tried to put a positive spin on an underwhelming event. Vladimir Solovyov extolled the "never ending river" of people attending the parade and praised it as a sweeping mandate for Putin to "crush Nazi scum" in Ukraine. Nevertheless, Putin's refusal to mention any flagship military achievements in his address reflected the uncertainties dogging Russia's military campaign.

This chapter examines the forced pivot of Russia's military strategy in Ukraine from a regime change mission to a Donbas-centric campaign. This transition occurred in tandem with the international community's discovery of extensive Russian war crimes on Kyiv's outskirts, which were compounded by Russia's harrowing human rights abuses in Mariupol. Despite credible allegations of genocide, Russia chose to deny, deflect and intensify its war crimes in Ukraine, and in the process, narrow the prospects for a diplomatic off-ramp. The intensification of Western sanctions against Russia crystallised fears of a "total hybrid war" with NATO, which prompted increased repression of alleged "fifth columns," nuclear brinkmanship and calls for a drastic escalation of the conventional war.

Russia's Pivot Towards a Donbas-Centric Military Campaign in Ukraine

After its ignominious withdrawals from Kyiv and Chernihiv at the end of March, the Russian military scrambled to devise a new set of strategic objectives in Ukraine. Russia's defence community was polarised around whether regime change in Kyiv was a worthy goal or if it should be scrapped entirely. Defence analyst Victor Olevich believes a downsizing of Russia's ambitions would have been futile, as Ukraine would have continued to carry out shellings and sabotage on Donetsk and Luhansk even if Russia stopped the war after liberating the Donbas. Olevich argued that any Russian occupation of territory would be unacceptable to Ukraine and the Western capitals, and Russia had no alternative but to advance deeper into Ukrainian territory.[2] This all-or-nothing vision of the Ukraine War was not universally shared. Vassily Kashin contends that Russia's lack of a decapitation strike on Kyiv underscored that regime change was not a necessary goal of the war. Instead, Kashin argues that Russia sought to damage Ukraine's military assets and economy in a permanent way, which would lay the groundwork for territorial annexation and a diplomatic settlement that would limit Ukraine's sovereignty in international affairs.[3] Russia's announcement of "phase two" of the special military operation, which was unveiled by Lavrov on 19 April and expounded upon by the Russian defence ministry on 22 April, erred closer to a downsized vision of the war effort. Central Military District Acting Commander Rustam Minnekayev emphasised the need for full control of Donbas and southern Ukraine, which would create a land corridor to Crimea, and "influence vital objects of the Ukrainian economy." Through the occupation of Ukraine's southern regions, Russia sought to create a land bridge to Transnistria, which would alleviate the "oppression of the Russian-speaking population" in that region.[4]

The ideal means of executing these goals were widely discussed on Russian pro-war Telegram channels and media outlets. The overarching trend was that Russia needed to prepare for a slow and steady offensive in Donbas rather than a blitzkrieg. Russian military analyst Boris Rozhin viewed artificial deadlines, such as seizing Donbas by Orthodox Easter (24 April) or Victory Day, as an "extremely thankless task" and insisted that Russia's slower-than-expected start to the Donbas offensive aimed to increase war material stocks. Rozhin urged Russia to be cautious about an offensive on Zaporizhzhia, as it was a "fairly powerful fortified area that cannot be taken from a swoop," and urged it to target decision-making centres and create "fire damage" in Mykolaiv and Kharkiv to deplete the Ukrainian army's reserves.[5] Surkov ally Zakhar Prilepin proposed a seven-day takeover of Mariupol, a two-to-three week Donetsk campaign, at least a two-week Odesa campaign and sieges of indeterminate length in Kyiv and Kharkiv. Prilepin, who once claimed that the DNR could ride a white horse into any area of Ukraine, conceded that the fall of Kyiv might not occur, as the Soviet Union had lost 413,000 lives in Kyiv in 1943.[6] Ramzan Kadyrov's calls for a Ukraine-wide phase two campaign, which would prevent weapons from being sold to local residents, "global chaos" and "lawlessness," was an outlier view that gained little traction in Russian decision-making circles.[7]

During the early stages of the Donbas campaign, the Russian military's tactical efficiency noticeably improved. The Pentagon contended that Russia deployed heavy artillery, rotary aviation support and command-and-control enablers ahead of the offensive, which allowed for a more sustainable intervention than in northern Ukraine.[8] Russia initially carried out offensive operations along two axes, southwest of Donetsk and south of Izyum, and combined 75% of its pre-invasion combat power with twelve additional BTGs for the Donbas offensive.[9] Despite these improvements, the Russian military's efforts were swiftly undermined by familiar challenges. Russia's slow mobilisation occurred at a time when Ukrainian forces were entrenched and gaining an influx of NATO weaponry, and heavy casualties within BTGs increased reliance on poorly trained conscripts. The deaths of eight Russian generals by 5 June, which was facilitated by U.S. intelligence support to Ukraine, further undermined the Russian military. The centralisation of Russia's war effort, which saw former commander of Russian forces in Syria Alexander Dvornikov assume leadership on 10 April, perpetuated scorched earth tactics but did not improve efficiency. Russia's limited UAV supply, poor digital communications and lack of medicines allowed Ukraine to spring surprise attacks from well-concealed positions and resulted in heavy casualties amongst Russia's offensive forces. The dearth of drones and uniforms was especially pronounced amongst LNR forces, which caused infantry to advance too early, and mobilised residents from the Donbas republics were forced to retreat from Kharkiv due to a lack of heavy weapons.[10] Rostec's decision to manufacture miniature UAVs was hailed as a positive step but the timing of their entry into the battlefield was uncertain.[11]

The primary focus of Russia's offensive in Donetsk continued to be victory in Mariupol. In mid-April, Russia seized the Vessel Traffic Control Center at Mariupol port and vanquished Ukrainian forces, except for skirmishes in western Primorsky District. These military victories, which resulted in the destruction of 95% of Mariupol, forced Ukrainian forces to retreat into the Azovstal steel factory. Azovstal was a vast complex with networks of tunnels that neutralised Russia's aerial advantage. It swiftly became clear that the resistance, which consisted of 500–800 fighters according to Western estimates and 2,500–2,900 fighters according to Russian estimates, would hold out for some time. On 21 April, Putin ordered Russian forces to blockade rather than storm the Azovstal steel plant and pre-emptively declared victory in Mariupol. Putin justified his decision by emphasising the need to preserve the lives of Russian troops and declared that Russia would seal off Azovstal so that a "fly does not fly through."[12] Russia's plan for a "tunnel war" consisted of sealing off all but one exit route, disrupting ventilation to create unbearable conditions and allowing the pile-up of unexhumed corpses to create unsanitary conditions.[13] This plan did not come to fruition, as Russia launched fifty airstrikes on Azovstal from 27–28 April and proceeded to deploy dumb bombs and thermobaric weapons against the plant. The Azov Regiment reported on 11 April that Russia had used chemical weapons in Azovstal but these claims were not externally verified. By early May, Russia had begun redeploying its twelve BTGs or 8,800–11,000 troops in Mariupol to other areas of Donbas and conducted an almost

entirely air-driven campaign. These airstrikes continued relent-
lessly until 20 May when senior Azov Battalion figures reportedly surrendered to Russia.

Elsewhere on the frontlines, Russia achieved a mixture of successes and failures. On 19 April, Kreminna, Luhansk, which had
had a pro-Russian mayor, Volodymyr Struk, until his 2 March
assassination, fell to Russian forces. This initial military success
was followed by Russia's triumph in Popasna, Luhansk on 7 May.
The Wagner Group—which recruited rural Russian PMCs and
alleged foreign fighters—and Kadyrovtsy featured extensively in
Russia's military operations in Popasna. The humanitarian consequences of Russia's victory were severe, as Popasna transformed
itself from a town of 20,000 people into a virtual ghost town
following Russia's occupation.[14] On 12 May, Russia seized control of Rubizhne, which allowed it to encircle the Luhansk battleground of Severodonetsk. In tandem with these incremental
gains in Luhansk, Russia lost ground in Kharkiv to Ukraine, as
Ukrainian forces launched a counter-offensive in the north and
east of Kharkiv. This counter-offensive, which liberated several
villages from 1–13 May, helped secure the city of Kharkiv from
Russian occupation and limited Russia's strike capacity to an
aborted missile attack on Kharkiv Airport.[15] The sinking of the
Moskva on 14 April dealt a blow to Russia's prestige as a naval
great power and influence in the Black Sea. The Moskva sinking
constituted the first destruction of a Russian flagship since the
1904–5 Russo-Japanese War and dealt a blow to the Russian
navy as it performed crucial operations in Georgia, Crimea and
Syria. While Russia claimed that the Moskva was destroyed in a
fire, Ukraine asserted that its domestically produced Neptune
anti-ship missiles had caused its sinking.[16] The efficacy of
Ukrainian anti-ship weapons, which were bolstered by radar targeting from Bayraktar TB-2 drones, caused Russian Black Sea
Fleet ships to move offshore and left the Russian navy with inad-

equate anti-aircraft cover, as the Moskva was the only Black Sea Fleet ship with S-300s.

Russia Faces War Crimes and Genocide Allegations in Ukraine

Immediately after Russia's withdrawal from Kyiv, evidence of mass civilian casualties in Bucha surfaced. The initial discovery of twenty bodies by the side of a road was followed by the exhumation of a mass grave containing 280 bodies. Bucha mayor Anatoly Fedoruk declared that "All these people were shot," and a torture chamber had been discovered by the Ukrainian military containing civilians shot in the kneecap and the head in systematic fashion.[17] While the scenes in Bucha were the most harrowing, similar atrocities were discovered in other Kyiv suburbs. In Zabuchchya, the Ukrainian Territorial Defence Forces found eighteen mutilated bodies in a summer camp.[18] In Borodyanka, the State Emergency Service of Ukraine discovered forty-one bodies on 7 April, which prompted Zelensky to warn of an even larger massacre than Bucha. While the full scale of these massacres are still being ascertained, 458 civilian bodies have been discovered in Bucha and a total of 1,300 deaths have been documented in Russian-occupied areas of Kyiv Oblast. Ukrainian officials forcefully condemned Russia's alleged perpetration of these atrocities. Zelensky described Russia's actions as proof of genocide, stating that Ukraine's refusal to surrender had caused it to be "destroyed and exterminated," while Kuleba claimed that Russia was "worse than ISIS."[19] Biden described the Bucha Massacre as a "war crime," which was echoed by European Commission president Ursula von der Leyen, who visited Bucha on 8 April.

Russia's atrocities on Kyiv's outskirts were replicated on an even larger scale in Donetsk Oblast. These war crimes included indiscriminate targeting of civilians, extra-judicial executions and acts of cultural genocide, which mirrored tactics that Russia had used in Chechnya, Syria and Crimea. The 8 April Kramatorsk railway station attack, which killed sixty civilians, was an especially egregious example of Russia's attacks on civilian infrastructure. During the final weeks of the Mariupol siege, Russia allegedly killed 20,000 civilians. As this figure was double the casualties inflicted by Nazi Germany during its two-year occupation of the city, Mariupol mayor Vadym Boychenko declared that "Putin is a bigger evil than Hitler and we must stop him."[20] Russia's strikes on civilians extended to humanitarian corridors, as Russian troops fired artillery on the exit zone moments after a corridor was opened near Azovstal.[21] This mirrored Russia's attacks on humanitarian corridors in Syrian cities such as Aleppo and Idlib, which were dubbed "death corridors" by local residents and Russia's shooting of evacuees from Grozny corridors in December 1999. On 27 April, U.S. Ambassador-at-Large for Global Criminal Justice Beth van Schaack accused Russia of executing Ukrainians who were attempting to surrender in Donetsk instead of taking them into custody.[22] Iryna Venediktova accused Russia of the rape of men, women and children as a deliberate strategy to "scare civil society" and force Ukraine to surrender.[23] Zelensky reiterated these allegations on the floor of the UNSC, stating that Russian troops had raped women in front of their children and pulled out victim's tongues "because the aggressor did not hear what they wanted to hear" from them.[24]

Russia's widespread use of filtration camps, which facilitated the deportation of 15,000 to 25,000 eastern Ukrainians per day, fuellled allegations of genocide. On 18 April, Boychenko's advisor Petro Andriushchenko warned that Russia planned the "filtration" of all males in Mariupol, which included vetting for links to Ukraine's Territorial Defence Forces and expressions of Ukrainian nationalist sentiment.[25] Due to the squalid conditions, infectious diseases such as tuberculosis appeared in Mariupol's filtration camps. Ukraine's Human Rights Omdbusman Lyudmila Denisova revealed that Russia's holding facilities for deported Ukrainians had been 100% ready on 21 February, as 36 locations in the North Caucasus, Siberia and Russian Far East had been prepared to hold 33,146 Ukrainians.[26] Russia established a 100-mile evacuation route from occupied Donbas to Rostov-on-Don, which was parallel to a highway from the Sea of Azov's coast to Bezimenne.[27] This would facilitate a two-way exchange, as Russians would be resettled in the Donbas to "Russify" the region and eviscerate Ukraine's cultural identity. These policies built on Russia's extensive use of "filtration points" for illegal detentions during the Chechen Wars, which saw 200,000 Chechens pass through their ranks. An October 2000 Human Rights Watch report describing conditions in Chernokozovo detention centre, Russia's most infamous filtration camp in Chechnya, was titled "Welcome to Hell".

The conduct of Russia's occupation authorities in newly conquered regions of Ukraine was drawn directly from the Crimea playbook. After the annexation, Russian educators in Crimea censored coverage of Holodomor and replaced the term "Kievan Rus" with "Rus," which eviscerated Ukraine's identity.[28] These educational reforms were paired with the creation of youth paramilitary organisations and patriotic indoctrination. Russia's establishment of an occupation administration in Kherson in late April perpetuated these practices. The Kherson administration was administered by former Party of Regions Deputy Vladimir Saldo, Deputy Head Kirill Stremousov and ex-KGB agent Oleksandr Kobets, who served as mayor. Sergiy Aksyonov warned that teachers from newly occupied regions of Ukraine could be trained in Crimea and Vladimir Konstantinov hinted that a "landing force" of volunteer teachers could arrive in Kherson.[29] In Mariupol, the process of re-education began prior to Russia's final victory. A 28 April Rossiya-1 episode proclaimed that "textbooks are being delivered to schools. Importantly, they are Russian, meaning they do not contain lies and falsification of history" and showed how children were so excited to embrace this new education that they were willing to attend summer school.[30] The violent dispersal of pro-Ukrainian rallies, such as the 21 March Freedom Square demonstrations in Kherson, underscored Russia's coercive promotion of its desecration of Ukrainian culture.

Ukraine Investigates and Isolates Russia for its War Crimes

Shortly after the Bucha Massacre, Ukraine initiated a war crimes investigation, which produced compelling evidence of Russian atrocities. Fedorchuk's 7 March comment that "We can't even gather up the bodies because the shelling from heavy weapons doesn't stop day or night. Dogs are pulling apart the bodies on the city streets. It's a nightmare" suggested that Russia began carrying out mass killings shortly after its forces arrived in Bucha.[31] Maxar satellite imagery verifies Fedorchuk's testimony, as eleven "dark objects" resembling human bodies were present on Yablonska Street from 9–11 March, and three bodies were discovered on the same street near bicycles from 20–21 March.[32] These corpses were discovered in identical positions after Russia withdrew from Bucha. Satellite imagery also revealed the existence of a 45-foot-long trench on the grounds of a church in Bucha, which began to be converted into a mass grave on 10 March.[33] Ukrainian intelligence showed that Russia's 64th Separate Guards Motor Rifle Brigade unit 51460, which is affiliated with the Eastern Military District's 35th Army, was responsible for the Bucha Massacre and published lists of Russian soldiers who perpetrated the killings. Eyewitness accounts noted a shift in Russia's occupation force from young soldiers to

Kadyrovtsky and Wagner Group PMCs in Bucha, which suggested that Russian paramilitaries complemented this brigade's efforts.[34] Colonel Ihor Yuschenko testified that Kadyrovtsy had killed two pedestrians in central Bucha on 27 February by firing thirty bullets from a car, and the Kadyrovtsy were also accused of killing heavily injured Russian soldiers in Bucha.[35] The 104th Guards Air Regiment and 234th Guards Air Assault Regiment have also been linked to massacres, as documents belonging to these units were discovered in locations where Ukrainian men were executed.[36]

Ukraine also received Western and ICC assistance in the prosecution of Russian war crimes. Germany's BND intelligence services obtained conversations from Russian soldiers, which included the comment, "First you interrogate soldiers, then shoot them," and produced satellite imagery that illustrated Russia's involvement in Bucha.[37] On 10 April, France became the first NATO country to deploy a forensic team to investigate war crimes. This team was stationed in Lviv and included experts in ballistics, DNA, explosives and fingerprints. France's efforts expounded on earlier actions, such as Britain's Justice Secretary Dominic Raab's 13 March visit to the ICC to offer technical support for potential war crimes trials. On 3 April, Kuleba urged the ICC to send a mission to liberated regions of Kyiv and cooperate with Ukrainian law enforcement on evidence of Russian war crimes.[38] The ICC's chief prosecutor Karim Khan embarked on a war crimes and genocide investigation in Ukraine on 3 March. On 14 April, Khan visited Bucha and called Ukraine a "crime scene", stating that there were "reasonable grounds" that Russia had committed war crimes.[39] The ICC's enforcement power was unclear, however, as Russia and Ukraine are not members of the court. Poroshenko's 2014 and 2015 requests for an ICC investigation into Russian crimes against humanity in Donbas, Crimea and during Euro-Maidan; the ICC's decision to open an investigation into these crimes in April 2014; and a December 2020 ICC assessment which mirrored Khan's views on Bucha were precedents for Kuleba's call for ICC assistance. The EU's 25 April creation of a joint investigative team with the ICC further strengthened these efforts, as did its provision of 7.25 million euros in support of this team on 8 June.[40]

As Western countries supported Ukraine's condemnations of Russian war crimes, Kyiv aggressively pushed for the suspension of Russia's membership from international institutions. This process built on Ukraine's efforts prior to the Bucha Massacre, which saw Russia expelled from the Council of Europe but remain in Interpol and in close cooperation with the Red Cross. On 16 March, Russia was excluded from the Council of Europe, which required its removal from the European Convention on Human Rights on 16 September. This decision was overwhelmingly supported by member states, as only Armenia voted to keep Russia in the Council of Europe and Serbia, Azerbaijan and Turkey declined to vote. On 1 March, Ukraine called for Russia's removal from Interpol, which was enthusiastically supported by British Home Secretary Priti Patel. Interpol agreed to supervise Russia's abuse of "red notices," which allowed it to target dissidents, but kept Russia in the organisation and refrained from aiding in the prosecution of war crimes suspects.[41] After the Red Cross asked Lavrov to open an office in Rostov-on-Don which would facilitate its operations in Russian-occupied Donbas, Ukraine urged the Red Cross to reconsider its plans. On 27 March, Ukrainian Rada Deputy Mykhailo Radutskyi warned that the Red Cross was legitimising Russia's "humanitarian corridors," which facilitated the abduction and forced deportation of Ukrainians.[42] The Red Cross strenuously denied being involved in Russia's "filtration" of Ukrainians and kept its operations to ensure the welfare of POWs.[43]

After the Bucha Massacre, Ukraine took aim at Russia's membership in the OSCE, G20, UN Security Council and UN

Human Rights Council. Kuleba described Russia's actions as a violation of the Helsinki Final Act and stated that "Russia's participation in the OSCE is a threat to security and cooperation in Europe. If OSCE lacks appropriate suspension mechanisms, then set up a procedure and get them out."[44] Russia remained in the OSCE but the Special Monitoring Mission's mandate in Ukraine expired on 31 March, as personnel withdrew from Gurkovo and Donetsk in October 2021, and all of Donbas in early March.[45] Despite U.S. Treasury Secretary Janet Yellen's insistence that the U.S. would not engage with Russia at the G20 and Poland's open calls to replace Russia, no progress was made towards expulsion. On 5 April, Zelensky urged the UN Security Council to expel Russia or "dissolve itself" and attacked the UNSC for being unable to enforce Article 1 of the UN Charter on maintaining peace. Zelensky's call for action included a warning that past atrocities in Syria, Somalia, Afghanistan and Yemen had degraded the UNSC and its stature could only be redeemed by punishing Russia and supporting a Nuremberg-style war crimes tribunal.[46] On 20 April, Sergiy Kyslytsya asked, "Are you ready to relegate the role of the Security Council in addressing the worst security crisis on the European continent since the Second World War to discussions only?" and urged Russia to be expelled, as it was not a legitimate successor state to the Soviet Union.[47]

Although Blinken stated that it was "reasonable" to consider Russia's expulsion from the UNSC and a legal case that Russia had violated Article 4 of the UN Charter could have been advanced, no formal action was taken to remove Russia from the UNSC.[48] Ukraine's efforts to suspend Russia from the UNHRC gained immediate traction, as U.S. Ambassador to the UN Linda Thomas-Greenfield described Russia's participation as a "farce" that "hurts the credibility of the Council and the UN writ large."[49] Despite heavy polarisations between the collective West and non-West, 93 countries voted in favour of

Russia's suspension on 8 April while 58 abstained and 24 voted to keep Russia on the Council. Russia's suspension from the UNHRC was only the second decision of its kind after Libya was removed in 2011 over Muammar al-Gaddafi's repression of Arab Spring demonstrators. Ukraine viewed Russia's suspension as a significant symbolic success. Kyslytsya viewed the suspension as "morally and legally the right thing to do," as it stripped Russia of its impunity. However, he conceded that the growing number of "anti-human rights" members on the UNHRC had eroded its commitment to protecting human rights, especially when compared with the UNGA. Kyslytsya also noted that "Russia still has the right to speak at many meetings of the HRC and suggest via proxies draft decisions or amendments."[50] Russia's decision to completely withdraw from the UNHRC deprived it of its observer-status privileges, and on 10 May, the Czech Republic replaced Russia on the UNHRC with 157 votes in favour and 23 abstentions.[51]

Ukraine has also sought to achieve widespread international recognition of Russia's actions as a genocide. Ukraine's case for genocide was articulated in a 14 April Rada bill. Beyond Putin's well-documented support for de-Ukrainisation, Ukraine's official case for genocide revolved around the commission of premeditated murder and mass atrocities, deliberate destruction of civilian infrastructure and use of physical and psychological violence against Ukrainians.[52] Russian atrocities, such as the blockading of sea routes and destruction of granaries, were also listed as genocidal actions.[53] Ukraine's case has verifiable evidence with accompanying caveats. Ukrainian Rada Deputy Inna Sovsun contends that the strongest case for genocide rests in the extremist rhetoric from Russian officials and Telegram channels, and the theft of Ukrainian children from Donbas, which includes accompanying policies like re-education and easing of adoption laws. Sovsun expressed concern that the Ukrainian Ombudsman's publication of inflated statistics, such as the 300,000 children seized figure, which led to her dismissal, had created challenges but there were an overwhelming number of eyewitness testimonies that would verify these actions. Sovsun also argued that the forced education of the Russian language in Ukrainian schools, which she compared to American children being forced to recite the North Korean anthem, added to the case for cultural genocide. Sovsun conceded that sexual violence was harder to classify as genocide, as boasts of rape came from individual soldiers and there was no evidence that the Russian military endorsed rape as a tactic, even if it did not take measures to stop it. However, Sovsun concluded that the absence of legal documents could create difficulties for a legal case.[54] In September 2022, Ukrainian Rada Deputy Oleksiy Goncharenko conceded that it was debatable whether all five criteria of the Genocide Convention had been met but Ukraine would file a genocide case even if one could not be proven beyond doubt.[55]

Due to ambiguities in the legal case, Western governments are divided on whether to recognise Russia's actions as genocide. Poland, the Czech Republic, Estonia, Latvia, Lithuania, Canada and Ireland have all passed parliamentary resolutions declaring Russia's actions in Ukraine a genocide. A 27 May New Lines Institute and Raoul Wallenberg Centre for Human Rights report, which engaged over thirty international legal scholars, provided academic heft to the case for genocide. The report showed that Russia had already breached two articles of the 1948 Genocide Convention and characterised Russia's indiscriminate attacks on civilians and IDPs, as well as its dehumanising rhetoric towards Ukrainians as proof of genocide.[56] British prime minister Boris Johnson's claims that the Bucha killings were "not far short of genocide" underscored the cautious middle ground that most Western leaders took towards this question.[57] Zelensky praised Biden's 13 April comment that Russia was committing genocide in Ukraine, as it was "trying to wipe out the idea of even being Ukrainian", as "true words of a true leader." However, the White House subsequently reframed Biden's remarks as a personal opinion rather than U.S. official policy.[58] Macron distanced himself from Biden's comments, as he stated that "jurists not politicians" should decide on genocide and cited the fraternal nature of Russians and Ukrainians to support his view.[59] This aligned with Macron's broader avoidance of escalatory rhetoric, such as Biden's description of Putin as a "butcher," which undermined France's diplomatic backchannel to Russia. Genocide expert Waitman Wade Beorn provided intellectual support to Macron's sceptical position, as Russia's extensive targeting of ethnic Russians in Mariupol suggested that its indiscriminate violence and war crimes were not systematically geared at exterminating Ukrainians.[60]

Russia's Disinformation Counter-Offensive Against Ukraine and the West

As allegations of war crimes mounted, the Kremlin combined disinformation with overtly genocidal rhetoric, which appealed to hardline supporters of the war and further narrowed the scope for dissent. Russia's disinformation about the Bucha Massacre and Kramatorsk railway station attack was especially striking. The Russian defence ministry described the Bucha Massacre as "another provocation," and claimed that evidence of killings only surfaced four days after Russian troops had left, when Ukrainian forces and the SBU were present.[61] A 31 March statement from Fedorchuk, which stated that Russian troops had left Bucha, provided "proof" of this assertion. The defence ministry's account ignored Fedorchuk's reports of killings weeks earlier and contradicted reporting from Russian media outlet Zvezda, which showed the Russian defence ministry talking about finishing a "*zachistka*" clean-up operation in Bucha on 1 April. The Russian foreign ministry speculated that Ukraine had released the Bucha footage in order to create a pretext for suspending diplomacy with Russia. Dmitry Polyanskiy concurred with this view by stating that "Ukrainian neo-Nazis are completely faithful to Goebbels' old Nazi school of provocations and are trying to shift the blame to Russia."[62] On 4 April, Russia called for a UN Security Council meeting on Bucha. Britain's attempts to block the UNSC meeting were greeted with derision in Moscow, as Polyanskiy unfavourably contrasted British obstructionism with Russia's willingness to participate in all Ukraine-related meetings.[63] While the implausibility of Kremlin narratives meant that Russia's version of events on Bucha had few international adherents, non-Western UNSC members like China, India and the UAE did not blame Russia specifically, which suggests that the Kremlin was effective in sowing reasonable doubt.

The Kremlin's media surrogates added to the chorus of disinformation about Bucha. Vladimir Solovyov promoted the conspiracy that Russian troops had merely provided food to Bucha residents and there were no reports of atrocities until the Russians left.[64] Solovyov also promoted outlandish conspiracies that implicated Ukraine's Western partners in the fabrication; on 5 April, he accused Britain of staging the Bucha Massacre, as the name of the town sounded a lot like butcher. During his 18 April Rossiya-1 show, Solovyov speculated that Britain had accused Russia of genocide to retaliate for Russia's killing of "British instructors" in Ukraine and justify a pre-emptive nuclear strike on Russia. Other Russian media outlets concentrated their attention on amplifying the staged corpses conspiracy; Channel One claimed that the corpses in Bucha did not have "characteristic cadaveric spots and uncoagulated blood in the wounds," and compared the West's "staging" of the massacre to "staged shootings of Syrian children" and chemical weapons attacks in Aleppo and Douma, which Russia denies.[65] RIA Novosti derisively called Bucha the "new Srebrenica," which refers to Russia's denial of the 1995 genocide of Bosnians, and claimed that "corpses move their arms and remove their limbs so as not to fall under the wheels of military equipment."[66] The presence of white ribbons, which signified civilians who had stayed during the Russian occupation, on the corpses was also cited to absolve Russia. Kremlin propaganda on Bucha contradicted itself, as it also promoted conspiracies that Ukraine was culpable for the massacre. Solovyov amplified the conspiracy that Ukraine's detonation of the Irpin bridge had killed Russian troops in Bucha. Boris Rozhin claimed that the use of 122-mm ZSH1 artillery shells stuffed with metal flechettes provided evidence of Ukrainian involvement, as these shells were used in D-30 howitzers that Ukraine's army had employed in the liberation of Hostomel, Bucha and Irpin.[67]

Russia's disinformation about the 8 April Kramatorsk train station attack was marred by similar contradictions. The Russian defence ministry claimed that the Kramatorsk strike was carried out by a missile division of the Ukrainian armed forces from Dobropolye, which is located 45km southwest of the city. According to defence ministry officials, Ukraine carried out this attack "to disrupt the mass exodus of residents from the city in order to use them as human shields."[68] DNR representative Eduard Basurin elaborated further on this conspiracy in a Channel One interview, noting that Ukraine had requested the evacuations of Kramatorsk, Sloviansk and Kostiantynivka before firing missiles on their congregation point. Ukraine's retraction of its original claim that Russia had used Iskanders in Kramatorsk, which was followed by a confirmation that Tochka-Us were employed instead, gave the Kremlin further ammunition to blame Kyiv. Russian media outlets claimed that the Tochka-U, which had a 120km strike range, had been withdrawn from service in 2019 and noted that Ukraine had allegedly used a Tochka-U to shell central Donetsk in March, killing twenty people.[69] A fake BBC clip showing a missile from the 13th Missile Brigade of the Ukrainian armed forces circulated virally on Russian media, as did the claim that the serial number on the missile matched Ukraine's Tochka-U strikes in Melitopol and Berdyansk.[70]

Beyond its fabrications of evidence, the claims that the Kremlin used to absolve itself from responsibility in Kramatorsk do not stand up to empirical scrutiny. The Russian ministry of defence and pro-war Telegram channels initially confirmed that they had struck the Kramatorsk railway before orchestrating a coordinated take-down of these posts once civilian casualties mounted.[71] In contrast to its claims that Tochka-Us were obsolete, Russia paired these missiles with cluster munitions in northeast Aleppo in March 2021.[72] Channel One reported in November 2021 that LNR militias had six launchers and several dozen Tochka-U missiles, which it refrained from using due to the risk of a retaliatory Ukrainian strike. Russia's 8th Combined Arms Army, stationed in Donbas, was equipped with Tochka-Us.[73] Russia also allegedly struck Chernihiv with Tochka-Us on 6 March and a V tank convoy with Tochka-Us was spotted in Belarus, which still officially operates the system.[74] As Tochka-Us were assembled in Russia, serial numbers were inconclusive and not proof that Ukraine used these missiles. The "For the Children" logo on the Tochka-U missile is circumstantial evidence that Russia was avenging the "Donbas genocide." Due to these factors, the allegation that Russia carried out the Kramatorsk attack holds weight. Justin Bronk contends that Russia was seeking to disrupt Ukraine from using the Kramatorsk railway to reinforce its troops in Donetsk and claimed that it deliberately used Tochka-Us to create a deniability narrative, a tactic that it has used repeatedly in the conflict.[75]

Russia also launched an information war against international human rights institutions and deflected from its atrocities by highlighting Ukrainian war crimes. After Russia's suspension from the UNHRC, Gennady Gatilov lambasted the UNHRC as "being monopolised by one group of states which does not hesitate to use it for its own opportunistic purposes."[76] Dmitry Belik claimed that the UNHRC had "discredited itself" by ignoring the "genocide in Donbas," while Russian media outlets highlighted the symbolic nature of the UNHRC expulsion, as the body has no enforcement power.[77] The structural problems in the UNHRC that necessitated Russia's withdrawal featured in other UN bodies. Polyanskiy emphasised that Russia was not isolated due to a large number of abstentions in the UNGA and accused the West of using economic blackmail to steer countries to vote against Russia.[78] Polyanskiy lamented the West's decision to ignore Russia's arguments in the UNGA and UNSC after 2014, which had paved the way for the special military operation, and expressed frustration with Guterres's "much more verbal blunt" statements on Ukraine than in previous crises.[79] On 13 April, LNR chief Leonid Pasechnik banned the activities of the OSCE Special Monitoring Mission in Luhansk and detained two of its employees for treason. *Izvestia* correspondent Yegor Kildibekov accused the OSCE office in Luhansk of illegally possessing classified information about the LNR's military equipment and its vulnerabilities.[80] This information war against the OSCE escalated, even as Konstantin Kosachev insisted that membership in the OSCE had more value than the Council of Europe.[81]

Russia also deflected from war crimes allegations by highlighting Ukraine's alleged repression of human rights and war crimes. The 12 April arrest of Viktor Medvedchuk in what Zelensky facetiously called a "special operation" fuelled Russian allegations of authoritarianism in Ukraine. Vyacheslav Volodin declared

"Zelensky handcuffed his opponent. These are the political free-
doms in Ukraine" and praised Medvedchuk for supporting an
"independent Ukraine," which clashed with Zelensky's subordination to the U.S. Volodin dubiously described Medvedchuk as
Zelensky's main political rival and warned, "If something happens
to Viktor Medvedchuk, Zelensky will have to answer."[82] Ilya Kiva's
simultaneous defection to Russia, which was framed as an escape
from European repression, added to these narratives. Despite this
rhetoric, Russia refrained from directly aiding Medvedchuk. After
his arrest, Peskov emphasised that Medvedchuk was not a Russian
citizen and denied collusion between the Opposition Bloc and the
Kremlin. After Konstantin Zatulin warned that Ukraine had
arrested Medvedchuk for a prisoner exchange, State Duma hardliners condemned a possible Medvedchuk–Azov Battalion fighter
prisoner swap. On 17 May, Volodin called for a ban on the
exchange of "Nazi criminals" and urged the Supreme Court to
designate Azov a terrorist organisation.[83] Leonid Slutsky concurred, stating that "if their heinous crimes against humanity are
proven, I will once again repeat my proposal to make an exception
from the moratorium on the death penalty."[84]

Immediately after the Bucha Massacre was discovered, the
LNR authorities and the head of Russia's Investigative Committee
Alexander Bastrykin expressed support for a "military tribunal"
to try Zelensky for war crimes in Donbas.[85] In practice, even
Russian lawmakers questioned the efficacy of these tribunals and
the validity of the charges that they would level against
"Ukrainian Nazis." State Duma Deputy Yury Sinelshchikov
emphasised that the glorification of Bandera was not a crime that
affects Russian citizens, noted that Russia's Criminal Procedure
Code had never been effectively used to prosecute crimes against
Russians abroad and conceded that it was difficult to come up
with smoking-gun proof of Ukraine's biological weapons programme.[86] Nevertheless, the spectre of a war crimes tribunal fed

into Russian propaganda about Ukrainian war crimes in Donbas. The narrative that the Azov Battalion wanted to take revenge on the people of Mariupol as they were pro-Russian circulated, as did claims that Azov had obscured the existence of humanitarian corridors for civilians trapped in Azovstal.[87] RIA Novosti alleged that Ukrainian military personnel hid in the yards of residential buildings and shot civilians and claimed that their "blue armbands" were evidence of links to Azov.[88] Although Russian shelling was the primary cause of Ukrainian water supply disruptions, the Kremlin also accused Ukraine of weaponising water against its own citizens: Mikhail Mizintsev accused Ukraine of creating an "epidemiological disaster" in Mykolaiv and State Duma Deputy Alexander Borodai accused Ukraine of shutting off water to Severodonetsk. These preposterous conspiracies, which aligned with Russia's broader accusations that Ukraine was laundering humanitarian aid, helped keep the denazification narrative afloat as the war progressed.

In tandem with the Kremlin's efforts to deny and deflect responsibility from its war crimes in Ukraine, Russian state media commentaries became increasingly forceful in their calls for cultural genocide. This mystifying contradiction was best encapsulated by Timofey Sergeytsev's RIA Novosti article "What Russia Should do with Ukraine," which was published right after the Bucha Massacre was discovered.[89] Sergeytsev's article was striking, as it created a case for collective responsibility for Ukrainian Nazism, calling for the punishment of "passive Nazis" in the majority of Ukraine's population. Sergeytsev argued that pro-Europeanism was the predominant strain of Nazism in Ukraine and hence had much broader support than the "Banderite" elite. He went on to claim that Ukrainian Nazism was a worse threat than Nazi Germany to Russia and stated that the name "Ukraine" had to be scrapped due to its Nazi linkages in favour of creating a collection of people's republics. Sergeytsev's claims that Georgia and the Baltic states could create identities without resorting to Nazism, while Ukraine could not, was indicative of a much more targeted attack on Ukrainians rather than a broader neo-imperial project to reconstruct the Soviet Union. Sergeytsev's calls for the use of forced labour, imprisonment and mass executions to de-Ukrainianise the population provoked allegations of genocide.

Sergeytsev's line of thought was not entirely new. Russian commentator Alexander Zhuchkovsky had previously called for a collective war against the Ukrainian people and claimed "Ukraine, Ukrainian people and Ukrainian language were deliberately and purposefully created by Russia's geopolitical adversaries to fragment the Russian people, and to weaken and dismember Russia."[90] However, Sergeytsev's article converted ideas that were previously confined to neo-fascist organisations, such as the Russian Imperial Movement, into mainstream rhetoric. In an adaptation of Dugin's Dublin to Vladivostok vision, Medvedev called for an open Eurasia from "Lisbon to Vladivostok" and called for the "eradication" of Ukraine as a state through denazification. Patrushev similarly endorsed Sergeytsev's goal of balkanising Ukraine into people's republics, which reflected the integration of ideological extremism with Russia's military objectives.[91] Karaganov argued that the end goal of denazification should be to create a friendly state in the vein of Chechnya.[92] Russian media was also increasingly brazen about brutal punishments against Ukrainian POWs and boasted about filtration. During a 15 April episode of Solovyov's Rossiya-1 show, Margarita Simonyan called POWs "monsters and scumbags" and said they should be used to rebuild Mariupol by "putting up electrical wires, fixing roads, painting fences." To illustrate the rehabilitation potential of Ukrainian POWs, Russian human rights activist Dmitry Agranovsky highlighted the precedent of the Nazis who had helped rebuild Soviet industry for five to seven years before returning to Germany.[93] On a 29 April episode of Olga Skabeeva's Rossiya-1 show, military analyst Viktor Baranets boasted that Russia had one filtration camp that could host up to 100,000 people. This incendiary rhetoric was paired with dehumanising language, such as the depiction of Azov Battalion fighters as "cockroaches."[94] These calls for brutality produced evidence for the very crimes that Russia was denying but nonetheless energised Putin's hardline nationalist base.

The Kremlin Primes the Russian Public for a Total Hybrid War with the West

As evidence of Russian war crimes mounted, the Western sanctions regime against Russia further intensified. On 6 April, the U.S. imposed an investment ban on Americans in Russia and decoupled Sberbank and Alfa-Bank's assets from the U.S. financial system. The U.S. also imposed additional sanctions on Russian oligarchs, while continuing to restrict action against sectors that could cause instability in the global economy. This policy faced criticism but aimed to prevent a repeat of the U.S.'s imposition and retraction of sanctions on Deripaska-linked Rusal, which had destabilised global aluminium markets.[95] The U.S. also carved out an exemption on Russian fertiliser from sanctions to ease food insecurity in the Global South and prevent a disruption to its own supplies, as 6% of potash, 20% of diammonium phosphate and 13% of its urea come from Russia.[96] On 8 April, the EU imposed a coal embargo on Russia, which would deprive the Kremlin of 8 billion euros in revenues after it took effect in August 2022; barred Russian vessels from accessing EU ports; restricted Russian and Belarusian road transit to the EU; and imposed an import ban on Russian cement and luxury goods and an export ban on jet fuel, high-end electronics and advanced semiconductors.[97] The EU's measures built on a ten-point plan advanced by Poland, the Czech Republic and Slovenia, but more extreme measures, such as a common asylum policy for Russian military deserters, the complete cessation of SWIFT, sanctions on all United Russia Party members and a suspension of visas to the EU, were avoided.[98] Britain's sanctions on war crimes violators such as Mikhail Mizintsev and propagandists who condoned these crimes such as RT Managing Director Alexey Nikolov and anchor Sergey Brilev underscored the Bucha Massacre's role in catalysing tighter sanctions.

The EU's efforts to divest from Russian oil and gas also returned to the spotlight, as evidence of Russia's wartime profits surfaced and Russia weaponised gas against Europe. Russia secured $337.5 billion in energy exports in 2022, which was a 38% year-on-year increase.[99] On 31 March, Vladimir Putin signed a decree that foreign buyers must purchase Russian gas in roubles by 1 April or contracts would be halted. Putin claimed that countries that refused to comply with his request would be deemed to have defaulted and defended this policy by stating that "Nobody sells us anything for free and we are not going to do charity either—that is, existing contracts will be stopped."[100] The G7 and EU rejected Russia's rouble payment demand, even though it occurred through a scheme which allowed purchasers to pay in the contracted currency and for Gazprombank to convert this currency into roubles. Nevertheless, Russia doubled down on its demands, as Dmitry Peskov stated that rouble payments could be required for non-energy goods and that Russia wanted to erode global confidence in the U.S. dollar and euro to eventually destroy the Bretton Woods monetary order.[101] After abruptly cutting off gas supply to Poland and Bulgaria, Peskov warned that Russia would impose similar measures on other gas importers and claimed without evidence that four European countries had already agreed to pay in roubles. Despite these pressure tactics, Ursula von der Leyen insisted that rouble payments would violate EU sanctions, and only Hungary expressed overt support for paying for Russian gas in roubles.

Although Russia's rouble payment gambit failed, the EU struggled to coalesce around a comprehensive energy embargo. The EU coal embargo was regarded as a promising first step, as the EU purchased 45% of its coal from Russia, but this solidarity against Russia did not initially extend to oil and gas. While the Baltic states became the first EU countries to suspend Russian gas exports on 3 April, Germany's dependency on Russia for 55% of its gas forestalled a potential gas embargo until 2024. Germany signalled support for an oil embargo by the end of 2022, which received broad support within the EU, but progress was held up by countries that relied on terrestrial oil shipments such as the Czech Republic, Hungary and Slovakia. Hungary was especially outspoken in its support for an EU oil embargo that would apply exclusively to tanker-based transit.[102] After Orbán compared an EU oil embargo on Russia to a "nuclear bomb," von der Leyen travelled to Budapest and Emmanuel Macron called Orbán on 10 May with the intention of striking an oil embargo deal within a week.[103] After twenty-six days of Hungarian obstructionism, the EU passed an oil embargo on Russia, which exempted Hungary on 31 May. European Council president Charles Michel boasted that the oil embargo would halt 90% of Russia's oil exports to the EU, and also prevented the insurance and reinsurance of Russian ships by European companies.[104]

The West's tightening of sanctions on Russia coincided with a significant expansion of NATO arms deliveries to Ukraine. The removal of NATO's informal restrictions on heavy artillery supplies to Ukraine was a significant step forward. The Czech Republic had reportedly supplied tanks to Ukraine by 5 April, which made it the first NATO country to complete these deliveries, and Poland had donated over 240 tanks to Ukraine by 29 April. On 1 April, the U.S. granted Zelensky's request for

Soviet-made T-72 tanks, which would allow Ukraine to conduct long-range artillery strikes on Russian targets in Donbas. On 28 May, Oleksiy Reznikov announced that the U.S. and Denmark were supplying Ukraine with self-propelled howitzers and Harpoon anti-ship missiles, which would allow it to break Russia's Black Sea Fleet blockade.[105] Britain initially hedged on supplying tanks to Ukraine, as Boris Johnson said it "wouldn't be appropriate" for Western allies to approve all of Kyiv's weaponry requests.[106] Nevertheless, the Kramatorsk railway attack encouraged Britain to supply additional Starstreak anti-aircraft missiles to Ukraine and 800 anti-tank missiles, as well as broach transferring tanks to Poland, which would replenish the artillery it had given to Ukraine. Germany's authorisation of the delivery of fifty Gepard anti-aircraft tanks to Ukraine on 26 April was its first heavy weapons transfer to Ukraine. Switzerland's veto on the use of its ammunition in Gepards was a major setback and, despite numerous "ring exchange" proposals to other EU countries, German Leopard and Marder tank deliveries did not occur.[107] France's announcement of Caesar 155mm self-propelled howitzers on 22 April was also followed by an underwhelming weapons supply.

Despite gaps in Western sanctions and weapons deliveries to Ukraine, Russia viewed the combination of economic pressure and military assistance as a hybrid war waged against it by the West. This "total hybrid war narrative" allowed Russia to repress anti-war dissent and dilute the domestic backlash over military setbacks in Ukraine but also energised a highly vocal clique of hardliners, who would eventually steer Putin towards escalating the war. Russia's total hybrid war narrative consisted of three principal dimensions. The first facet was to depict the Ukraine War as a conflict between a "good Russia" and "evil West," which turned Zelensky's narratives about Russian cruelty and Ukrainian heroism on their head. Russia's counterprogramming emphasised its own struggle against Russophobia, and comparative humanity compared to Ukraine and the West. Vladimir Putin accused the West of "trying to cancel a whole 1,000-year culture, our people," which was exemplified by crackdowns on Tchaikovsky, Shostakovich and Rachmaninov and disinvitations of pro-war Russian cultural figures. Putin compared these efforts to censorship of J.K. Rowling over her position on trans issues.[108] Lavrov warned of an absurd degree of "outright racism" in the West towards Russians, which extended to depicting Russia as the primary aggressor in the Second World War.[109] On his 14 May Rossiya-1 show, Solovyov called the "phenomenal Russophobia" in the West a new form of Nazism. Petr Akopov portrayed Russia as a victim in a "civil war" with Ukraine and stated that Anglo-Saxons treat Russians as "second-class people" like Yemenis, Somalis or Afghans.[110] Akopov concluded that Russophobia caused Western countries to frame Russia for war crimes such as the Bucha Massacre.

To justify Russian military failures, Kremlin propagandists also pushed the narrative that Russia was deliberately restraining its military operations to avoid civilian casualties. On Solovyov's 14 April show, Margarita Simonyan declared that Russia was acting slowly because it wanted to avoid a genocide in Ukraine, praised the role of Christian and Islamic values in guiding Russia's policy and warned against labelling opponents of extreme violence as "enemies.[111] During a 20 May Rossiya-1 broadcast, Simonyan claimed that Russia could have overrun Ukraine in a matter of hours if Putin had declared war instead of a "special military operation." Simonyan stated that Putin's restraint was derived from pity for Ukrainians and the recognition that many pro-Russians were being kept as hostages. The Russian ministry of defence regularly highlighted humanitarian aid deliveries to Donbas, which amounted to 23,000 tons by 7 March, and assistance from the Russian Orthodox Church and Maxim Shugaley, a Prigozhin-aligned political technologist, featured in the Russian media.[112] These propaganda gestures resulted in the popular phrase that "the only people who care about Ukrainians are the Russian military."[113] Putin's 12 April statement that the U.S. was willing to "fight Russia to the last Ukrainian" was regularly repeated in the Russian media, as it created a proxy war narrative that villainised the West.[114]

The Russian Orthodox Church played a pivotal role in formulating the Russia–West proxy war in Ukraine as a civilisational clash. On 7 March, Patriarch Kirill framed Russia's invasion of Ukraine as "far more important than politics" and stated that "if humanity accepts that sin is not a violation of God's law, if humanity accepts that sin is a variation of human behaviour, then human civilisation will end here."[115] Patriarch Kirill's depiction of the Ukraine War as a struggle to defend traditional values against alien Western values was exemplified by his passionate defence of the Donbas's resistance to gay pride parades. During his 3 April sermon, he extolled the Russian military for "laying down their lives for their friends" in Ukraine; provided a moral case for de-Ukrainisation; and claimed that the cathedral he was standing in glorified Russia's military might rather than God.[116] On 3 May, he declared that Russia had never launched a war of aggression, stating that "It is amazing when a great and powerful country didn't attack anyone, it only defended its borders."[117] This rhetoric resulted in a concerted push from the EU to sanction Patriarch Kirill. Hungary derailed this sanctions push, as Orbán called freedom of faith a "sacred issue," but Britain and Lithuania ultimately imposed unilateral sanctions on Patriarch Kirill.

The second facet of the hybrid war consisted of reframing the Ukraine War as a direct conflict between Russia and NATO. Although some Kremlin critics, such as Mikhail Khodorkovsky, argue that Putin genuinely believes that he is at war with NATO, this narrative also had compelling propaganda value as it reduced Ukraine to a Western proxy and created an existential threat to Russia. On a 14 April Channel One show, Russian defence commentator Dmitry Drozdenko claimed that Russia was undergoing a "full-scale multi-level war" with the collective West, which would result in as many Russian casualties as possible. On Solovyov's 15 April show, Simonyan justified Russia's slow progress by stating that it was fighting a "huge, armed enemy" in NATO. During her 30 May Rossiya-1 show, Olga Skabeeva proclaimed that "Perhaps the time has come to admit that the special military operation in Ukraine has finished, in the sense that genuine war has begun, what's more it's World War III. We're forced to demilitarise not just Ukraine but all of NATO."[118]

In response to this perceived NATO threat, the Russian state media became increasingly alarmist in its warnings about impending nuclear war. A 28 April Rossiya-1 exchange between Simonyan and Solovyov exemplified this trend. Simonyan declared that "either we lose in Ukraine, or the Third World War starts. Knowing us, knowing our leader Vladimir Vladimirovich Putin, the most incredible outcome that this will end with a nuclear strike seems more probable to me." Solovyov voiced his agreement, stating that "we will go to heaven, they will simply die."[119] Earlier that day on Skabeeva's show, a map was broadcast showing that Russia could nuke Berlin in 106 seconds, Paris in 200 seconds and London in 202 seconds. This nuclear threat-mongering from the Russian state media was not new. Dmitry Kiselyov had warned in March 2014 that Russia was the only country in the world that could turn the U.S. into "radioactive ash", and forecasts of nuclear war on Russian state television were already commonplace in December 2021.[120] However, these nuclear threats caused particular alarm in the West as they coincided with provocative statements from Russian officials and incendiary displays of Russia's nuclear capabilities.

On 28 April, Sergei Lavrov warned that there was a "considerable" risk of nuclear war over Ukraine, which was swiftly dismissed by British armed forces minister James Heappey as "bravado."[121] Under the guise of restating Russia's nuclear doctrine, which allows for first use in response to a homeland security threat, Russian officials such as Peskov and Medvedev raised the spectre of nuclear conflict. The Russian defence ministry's 23 April warnings that the U.S. would use a nuclear, chemical or biological weapons false flag to complete the isolation of Russia added to the alarm. Volodin's narrower interpretation of Russia's nuclear doctrine, which allowed for a nuclear response if the U.S. used nuclear weapons against Russian territory, did little to assuage concerns.[122] On 20 April, Russia tested the RS-28 Sarmat or "Satan II" thermonuclear ICBM from the Plesetsk Cosmodrome in Arkhangelsk Oblast, which Putin claimed in 2018 could breach "any missile defence system."[123] Russian media emphasised the entirely domestic nature of Sarmat's production, amplified the Russian ministry of defence's claims of its unrivalled quality and highlighted Rogozin's assertion that the Sarmat would be the foundation of Russia's nuclear shield for thirty to forty years.[124] While the Kremlin framed the Sarmat as a retaliation for the Prompt Global Strike system and complied with New START, unease about Russia's nuclear brinkmanship permeated through Western capitals.

The third facet of the hybrid war was to highlight the boomerang impact of sanctions, which would weaken European economies to a much greater degree than the Russian economy. These narratives surfaced soon after SWIFT sanctions were imposed, as *Izvestia* warned that rising commodity prices and the collapse of business with Russia could necessitate a bailout of European banks.[125] German economy minister Robert Habeck's statement that a swift suspension of Russian energy would lead to unemployment and poverty, which was justified by Germany's pre-war 55% reliance on Russian gas, 52% reliance on Russian coal and 34% reliance on Russian oil, received widespread attention in the Russian media. A crash test from the German ministry of energy, which predicted a collapse of central heating, massive shortages of medical goods, the death of light industry and animal husbandry due to a "gas famine", and transit sanctions, reinforced Russia's confidence that the West would blink first on sanctions.[126] This resulted in apocalyptic coverage of economic conditions in the West. RIA Novosti commentator Viktoria Nikiforova declared that "the situation is that the inhabitants of the former 'golden billion' including the British are beginning to starve."[127]

This supposedly dire economic outlook allowed Russia to claim that Europe was a mere vassal of the U.S. and that European countries would ultimately refrain from a sweeping energy embargo. State Duma Deputy Mikhail Delyagin, who had previously called for Russia's withdrawal from the IMF due to its "religious influence" on Russian liberals, pushed the narrative that the U.S. was deliberately trying to weaken Europe by forcing it to sanction Russia.[128] Valentina Matviyenko claimed that the U.S. wanted "Europe to pay" for not imposing sanctions on Russia earlier and the EU could concur with U.S. demands, as it had a "complete lack of independence in its relationship with Washington."[129] Andrey Sushentsov warned that the cost of gas would at least double if Europe turned to alternative suppliers and in three years it would be difficult for German politicians to use Ukraine as a justification for these price increases. Sushentsov predicted that electoral pressure would ultimately lead to a "mutually acceptable economic exchange" in the energy sector, and proclaimed that "So far, our colleagues in the West have only proven their willingness to theatrically sacrifice what can be conceded for a short time."[130] This confidence in European weakness caused Russia to use the threat of a complete gas embargo as a bargaining chip rather than a realistic policy scenario.

The Silencing of Russian Liberals and Emergence of
Russia's Hawkish Opposition

Although it was largely grounded in disinformation, the Kremlin's hybrid total war narrative was effective in quashing the remnants of Russia's anti-war opposition. The sentencing of Alexei Navalny to nine years in prison on 22 March, which was followed by an investigation in May that was poised to extend his sentence by an additional fifteen years, and Vladimir Kara-Murza's 12 April arrest for "disobeying police orders", signified the crystallisation of Russia's totalitarian tilt. Although seasoned opposition activists like Oleg Orlov, who had protested against the Soviet war in Afghanistan and in support of Poland's Solidarity movement in the 1980s, refused to leave Russia, the nexus of Russia's liberal opposition was dispersed abroad.[131] Aside from sporadic displays of dissent, such as the 17 April "Time for Change!" online campaign in Sochi and anti-war protests at a 23 May Kis-Kis concert in St. Petersburg, anti-war protests dissipated. Issue-specific dissent, such as petitions from families of soldiers aboard the Moskva for greater transparency from the Kremlin, did not escalate into broader discontent.[132] Although Peskov's admission of "heavy casualties" after the Kyiv withdrawal was an acknowledgement of the war's costs, his refusal to clarify losses on the Moskva continued with impunity. In September 2022, Ilya Matveev lamented a "cognitive dissonance" that impedes outrage over the Bucha Massacre, as the majority of Russians believe it was staged. Matveev contended that Russian allegations that Ukraine shelled the Zaporizhzhia nuclear power plant and used anti-personnel "petal" mines in Donetsk had been effective in steering public scrutiny away from Russian war crimes.[133]

Russian elites were equally reluctant to publicly oppose the war. Cases of alleged house arrest against senior former Russian officials such as Vladislav Surkov, and Pskov senator Andrey Turchak's crackdown on Medvedev advisor Arkady Dvorkovich for criticising Russia's attacks on Ukrainian civilians, underscored this trend. Oleg Tinkov, who founded Tinkoff Bank in 2006, was a rare outspoken critic of the war. On 20 April, Tinkov condemned the "massacre" of Ukrainians and urged the West to help end an "insane war" that 90% of Russians opposed. Tinkov claimed that the 10% of Russians wielding Z symbols were "morons" and declared, "Waking up with a hangover, the generals realised that they have a shit army. And how will the army be good, if everything else in the country is shit and mired in nepotism, sychophancy and servility?"[134] Retribution from the Kremlin was immediate. On 2 May, Tinkov declared that he had been forced to sell his 35% holding in TCS Group to the Putin-supporting oligarch Vladimir Potanin over his anti-war views.[135] Much like Gazprombank vice-president Igor Volobuyev, who had relocated to Ukraine over his anti-war views, Tinkov was forced abroad. On 23 May, Russia's Counsellor at the UN Boris Bondarev resigned over his opposition to the war, stating, "Never have I been so ashamed of my country." Bondarev claims that many Russian diplomats likely oppose the war, even if they do not reveal this publicly, a sentiment that mirrors Volobuyev's belief in silent dissent at Gazprombank.[136]

While anti-war liberals were silenced, Russia's military setbacks created a new hawkish opposition bloc that targeted its animosity at the Russian defence ministry. Andrei Kortunov viewed this development as a realignment of Russian elite politics, as radicals from traditionally opposing ends of the spectrum converged and polarising figures like Kadyrov gained new partners.[137] Igor Girkin was an especially outspoken hardline critic of the war. In late March, Girkin condemned Shoigu as a "Plywood

Marshall," praised the superior organisational capacity of the Ukrainian military and compared the Ukraine War to Stalin's ill-fated Winter War against Finland. Girkin's Telegram posts regularly featured blistering critiques of Russian military strategy in Donbas. On 20 April, Girkin decried the nascent two-pronged Donbas offensive, which hinged on Kramatorsk and Kurakhovo axes, as leading to heavy casualties and slow progress.[138] Due to Russia's inability to encircle Ukrainian forces, Girkin feared that Ukraine would be able to "bleed" Russian power while committing few forces of its own to the defence of Donetsk. Girkin's long-term outlook for Russia's offensive was even more dire. As Ukraine had 200,000–300,000 troops with Western weapons and Russia relied on PMCs, contract soldiers and "alco-Cossacks," Girkin predicted that Russia would replicate Nazi Germany's Second World War defeat in Kursk. Girkin's preferred solution was an "at least partial mobilisation," which would allow for strategic victories and deep offensives rather than the current focus on tactical goals.

Girkin's call for mobilisation received considerable support amongst hawks in Russia. Olga Skabeeva's 14 April Rossiya-1 show featured calls for a declaration of war against Ukraine, which would involve intensified bombing of Kyiv and attacks on railway infrastructure. Alexander Dugin called for a total mobilisation of society in the war against the unipolar order, stating, "We cannot afford to lose this war. Otherwise, the whole world will turn into a big fire."[139] In an allusion to a war economy, Solovyov amplified praise of the early 1930s experience and postwar reconstruction of the Soviet Union as an inspiring precedent for dealing with a "total economic war."[140] Despite a crescendo of state media hype about escalating the war, Peskov ruled out mobilisation ahead of Victory Day on 4 May. Russian state media figures, including Solovyov, responded to the Kremlin's tune. On 7 May, Mikhail Khodaryonok presented his case against mobilisation on Rossiya-1 and stated that Russia's outdated equipment would severely limit the efficacy of mobilisation. RIAC emerged as a crucial expert community voice of restraint. Kortunov warned that "from the pages of newspapers and the TV screens, hawkish pecking is heard much louder than pigeon cooing," and expressed concern that the agitation of Russian society precluded diplomacy even if it was in Russia's interests.[141] Ivan Timofeev warned that even the capture of large swathes of Ukrainian territory would not resolve Russia's fundamental European security concerns and argued that external threats, internal turmoil and poor administrative development were creating a "perfect storm" comparable to 1917–20.[142] These voices of restraint temporarily won out as Russia's slow-motion Donbas offensive continued.

6

RUSSIA'S SUMMER WAR

MINOR VICTORIES AND MANUFACTURED CRISES

On 4 July, Vladimir Putin declared victory over Ukraine in Luhansk. This triumph, which occurred one day after the fall of Lysychansk, was Russia's most significant victory of the Ukraine War. To mark the occasion, Putin urged Russian forces that partook in the Luhansk operation to "rest and increase their combat capabilities," while calling upon units of the East and West groupings of the Russian military to achieve Luhansk-style triumphs elsewhere on the frontlines.[1] Russian state media featured accounts from Lysychansk which urged Russia to "never leave again" and praised the LNR for providing humanitarian aid, as Ukrainian forces had given only expired water bottles to Lysychansk residents.[2] Leonid Pasechnik compared the "new Great Victory Day" to 1945, Cossack and Chechen fighters celebrated in Lysychansk and Russian cosmonauts celebrated the occasion with DNR and LNR flags.[3] Ramzan Kadyrov posted a deepfake video showing Zelensky agreeing to complete "land, sea and air" surrender of Ukraine and agreeing to the "complete denazification" of Ukraine within a month.[4] In Ukraine, the mood was sombre but defiant.

Luhansk governor Serhiy Haidai called the Luhansk defeat "painful" and warned that Russia would proceed to bombard Sloviansk and Bakhmut. In a defiant night-time address, Zelensky warned that Russia's occupation of Luhansk was temporary, as Ukraine would prevail "thanks to our tactics, thanks to the increase in the supply of modern weapons."[5]

After Russia's victory in Luhansk, its battlefield progress ebbed. Russia's offensive in Donetsk was unable to gain momentum, while Ukraine prepared for a multi-directional counter-offensive and exposed the Black Sea Fleet's vulnerabilities. As the military situation deteriorated, Russia threatened large-scale famine in the Global South by blockading Ukraine's Black Sea ports, risked a nuclear disaster by militarising the Zaporizhzhia nuclear power plant (ZNPP) and weaponised energy against Europe through a series of gas supply disruptions. These manufactured crises aimed to raise the stakes of Western support for Ukraine and, with the exception of the increasingly fragile UN-brokered Black Sea grain export deal, proved impossible to resolve. The 20 August assassination of Alexander Dugin's daughter Darya Dugina and the cumulative impact of Russian military failures gave the hardliners in Putin's orbit a crucial upper hand, which paved the way for mobilisation and annexations of occupied Ukrainian territories.

Russia's Pyrrhic Victory in Luhansk and Slow-Motion Donetsk Offensive

After the victory in Mariupol, Luhansk became the primary locus of Russian offensive operations. Severodonetsk, Luhansk's second-largest city with a pre-war population of 101,000, was Russia's first major battleground. Immediately after Russia's withdrawal from Kyiv, the Western Military District's 4th Guards Tank Division launched a ground assault on Severodonetsk. The failure of Russian ground operations caused intensified airstrikes, which began on 18 April, and resulted in the evacuation of the vast majority of civilians from Severodonetsk. Russia's initial plan to capture Severodonetsk hinged on encircling the city. Russia's triumphs in Popasna and Rubizhne advanced this objective, as did its capture of villages on Severodonetsk's southern flank, but stagnant progress around Izyum initially prevented the Russian military from encircling Severodonetsk from the north. By 21 May, Russian pro-war Telegram channels acknowledged a north, south and east encirclement of Severodonetsk and highlighted Russia's efforts to destroy bridges linking Severodonetsk to Lysychansk, which acted as resupply routes for Ukrainian forces.[6] These encirclement efforts failed, which resulted in a costly Russian ground assault on Severodonetsk. To justify this decision, Russian propagandists hailed Severodonetsk as a potentially decisive battle in the struggle for Donbas, which underscores the extensive resources deployed to capturing the city.[7] The Institute of the Study of War (ISW) questions this assumption, as seizing Luhansk provided Russia with few economic or military benefits, and the extensive resource deployments to Severodonetsk derailed Russia's efforts to secure strategically more significant terrain around Izyum.[8]

Russia's ground assault on Severodonetsk gained significant momentum in the final days of May. On 1 June, Haidai conceded that seventy per cent of Severodonetsk was under Russian occupation, all routes for humanitarian assistance had been closed off and that Ukrainian troops were starting to retreat to "advantageous, pre-prepared positions."[9] In early June, Ukraine briefly regained battlefield momentum, as Haidai stated that on 6 June the Ukrainian armed forces had "cleared half of Severodonetsk" and were moving forward.[10] In response to these setbacks, Putin ordered Dvornikov to conquer Severodonetsk or completely encircle Ukrainian forces along the Lysychansk–

Bakhmut axis by 10 June.[11] To satisfy Putin's demands, Dvornikov deployed all three battalions of Russian combat formations to the frontlines and used artillery to carry out a house-by-house destruction of Severodonetsk.[12] Russia also shelled the Azot chemical plant, which was a refuge spot for Severodonetsk civilians, and justified these attacks by falsely claiming that 300–400 militants were sheltering there.[13] Due to Ukraine's dwindling ammunition stocks and mounting casualties, which were estimated at between 100 and 200 per day, Russia's Syria-style tactics resulted in its conquest of eighty per cent of Severodonetsk by mid-June. On 15 June, Ukraine rejected Russia's surrender ultimatum, which called for the evacuation of Azot's inhabitants to Russia-controlled Svatovo.[14] Ukrainian forces mounted a final counterattack on Russia's forces, which involved the use of AHS Krab howitzers and inflicted heavy casualties on the 11th Separate Motorized Rifle Regiment. Ukraine's resistance was unable to hold out, however, and on 24 June, Ukrainian forces retreated to Lysychansk.[15]

While Russia's triumph in Severodonetsk was its largest victory since Mariupol, it was a pyrrhic victory. Heavy personnel losses complicated its ability to reconstitute combat-ready BTGs, and battlefield morale was disrupted by dismissals of senior military figures. Colonel-General Mikhail Teplinsky replaced Commander of Russian Airborne Forces Anatoly Serdyukov, which was a perceived punishment for heavy losses of Russian paratroopers around Kyiv.[16] Serdyukov's ouster was a stunning reversal, as his effective paratrooper leadership role during the January 2022 intervention in Kazakhstan had bolstered his prestige in the Russian military. Dvornikov's dismissal on 25 June reflected Putin's dissatisfaction with the Donbas offensive's slow progress. Dvornikov's preferred tactic was the "integrated forces grouping" strategy, which combined small units of special forces, military advisors and mercenaries with local proxies.

Dvornikov's heavy reliance on poorly trained LNR forces to limit Russian casualties, excessive alcohol consumption and propensity to make major decisions in the middle of the night without intelligence support also undercut his reputation.[17] Despite these setbacks, Putin's allies in the State Duma and state media tried to put a positive spin on the Russian war effort. State Duma Deputy Andrei Gurulyov highlighted heavy casualties amongst Ukraine's most trained military personnel in Severodonetsk, which would not be replaced by "cannon-fodder" from Britain's two-week training course.[18] The surrender of Aidar Battalion fighters in Azot was hailed as a victory for the "denazification" agenda.[19] Hard-line critics of the war effort were less enthused. Due to strategic failures in Donbas, Girkin warned that the Severodonetsk triumph encouraged Western arms transfers in Ukraine, and argued that time was not on Russia's side, as "local successes" prevented much-needed alarmism about a transition to a war economy.[20]

After Severodonetsk's fall, Russian forces targeted Lysychansk, a city of 95,000 people and the last Ukrainian stronghold in Luhansk. Dvornikov's replacement by Colonel-General Gennady Zhidko, a fellow veteran of the Syria campaign, did not appreciably change Russian battlefield tactics. Russia initially aimed to isolate Lysychansk from the south and swiftly established an artillery stronghold at Lysychansk oil refinery. After relentless bombardments, Ukrainian forces withdrew from Lysychansk on 3 July. Oleksiy Arestovych contended that Ukraine's resistance in Lysychansk bought time to secure new Western weapons and strengthen its fortifications elsewhere in Donbas, and by tying Russian forces down, it would open the door for a counter-offensive in other regions. Russian defence commentator Ilya Polonsky mocked Arestovych, quipping that "the liberation of all of Ukraine by the Russian army will be called a great strategic victory" and claimed that substantial numbers of NATO weaponry had been captured as "trophies" by the Russian military.[21] Despite the discovery of atrocities such as Russia's erection of the head of a Ukrainian POW on a pole in Popasna, military activity in Luhansk dissipated after Russia's victory. Ukraine's 14 August HIMARS strike against a Wagner Group Base in Popasna, which had been recently visited by Yevgeny Prigozhin, was the sole notable Ukrainian counter-offensive operation in Luhansk prior to the liberation of Kharkiv.

Russia's offensive operations in Donetsk were significantly less successful than in Luhansk. The Russian military's approach to liberating Donetsk focused on capturing strategically significant small towns and pushing towards a liberation of Donetsk's larger regions, such as Kramatorsk. From 4–16 July, the Kremlin officially declared that the Russian military was on an "operational pause" but offensive operations against Siversk in Donetsk began immediately after Lysychansk fell. The Siversk offensive ended in failure. Russian claims that it occupied parts of Siversk in mid-July were disproven; on 28 July Ukraine's resistance stalled Russian offensive operations and in early September Russia formally withdrew from the outskirts of Siversk. The Siversk offensive's failure impeded Russian offensive operations elsewhere in Donetsk, even though Wagner Group PMCs made marginal territorial gains south of Bakhmut in late July and secured control of the territory of the Vuhledar power plant on 25 July.[22] Russia's efforts to convert these successes into a more expansive offensive on Bakhmut, which began with massive ground attacks on 1 August, ended in failure. By 5 September, British intelligence estimates showed that Russian forces were advancing at a pace of just 1km a week towards Bakhmut.[23] Russia's struggles to capture the depopulated village of Pisky and its eighteen inhabitants encapsulated the dismal failure of offensive operations in Donetsk. Although Russia entered central Pisky on 7 August, it took seventeen days to occupy the town and was forced to use thermobaric artillery shelling to level it. This stagnation prevented Russia from attacking Donetsk's larger regions and ensured that Putin's 15 September deadline to annex Donetsk was not achieved.

Russia's military failures in Donetsk were attributable to manpower shortages, command structure problems and the growing sophistication of Ukraine's military arsenal. On 16 June, British armed forces chief Tony Radakin stated that Russia had "strategically lost" the war, as it had expended 25% of its combat power for small territorial gains and lost 50,000 personnel to deaths and injuries.[24] British intelligence reports confirmed Radakin's dire assessment, as they illustrated that BTGs designed for 600–800 personnel consisted of just 30 personnel. On 9 August, Girkin warned that the attack potential of Russia's infantry units in Donetsk was "practically exhausted" and stated that available forces did not follow for an advance on Avdiivka.[25] A 31 August U.S. intelligence report echoed these concerns, as Russia was increasingly forced to rely on contract soldiers and convicted criminals to plug holes in its frontlines.[26] The Russian defence ministry did not streamline its command structure during its operational pause and instead resorted to an unwieldly "dual command" set-up, which saw two generals implement divergent tactics in a small combat area.[27] Commander of Army Group–South General Sergei Surovikin and Central Military District Chief Colonel-General Alexander Lapin both commanded offensive operations and Shoigu refused to replace Dvornikov with Surovikin. Ukraine's effective use of HIMARS rocket launchers dismantled Russian ammunition caches in Donetsk. The early July strike on Donetsk Kamaz truck centre, which served as an ammunition cache, coinciding with attacks on ammunition dumps throughout Donbas, illustrated Kyiv's newfound precision strike capacity.[28]

Despite Russia's offensive struggles, its war crimes in Donetsk continued to mount. Russia paired the commission of war crimes with conspiracies about Ukrainian culpability, which justified the propaganda that fuelled domestic support for the war and furthered its alleged "denazification" agenda. During the first three months of its invasion of Ukraine, Russia destroyed 43 religious buildings in Donetsk. Russia's 5 June attack on a wooden church in Sviatohirsk Lavra monastery, one of Ukraine's holiest Orthodox Christian sites, accrued particular condemnation. Zelensky accused Russia of "deliberately and systematically destroying Ukrainian culture and its historical heritage" and stated that 113 churches had been destroyed, including churches that had survived the Second World War.[29] Russia denied these allegations and reinflamed historical frictions with Ukraine over religious rights. The Russian Embassy in Britain stated the following: "The church was put on fire by retreating Ukrainian troops namely the 79th Air Assault Brigade. The fact has already been established. It regrettably follows the logic after a bill was introduced in the Verkhovna Rada banning the Russian Orthodox Church which was labelled as the enemy."[30] Alexander Alimov, Russia's Deputy Permanent Representative to the UN Office in Geneva, highlighted repeated Russian warnings that Ukraine would strike churches and claimed that locals had confirmed Ukraine's culpability in the attack.[31]

The 29 July Olenivka Prison Massacre, in which 53 Ukrainian POWs from Azovstal were killed, was an especially egregious war crime. Zelensky deplored Russia's attack on Olenivka as "deliberate mass murder", stating that it proved that Russia was the world's largest source of terrorism.[32] Podolyak stated that Russia had struck Olenivka to disrupt agreements about the exchange of Azov Battalion fighters and conceal the growing extent of Russian war crimes. Podolyak also cited Russia's refusal to allow a UN mission to visit Olenivka and denial of access to Red Cross representatives visiting prisoners as proof of its culpability.[33] In its trademark fashion, Russia denied responsibility for the

Olenivka Massacre and accused Ukraine of perpetrating the killings instead. The Russian defence ministry accused Ukraine of carrying out a HIMARS strike on Olenivka, while the DNR authorities claimed that Ukraine was trying to silence Azov militants who would divulge the criminal orders they had received from the Kyiv authorities.[34] These accusations were swiftly debunked. A HIMARS strike would lead to craters, shattered walls and ceilings, and detonated bodies, which were not observed in Olenivka Massacre footage.[35] Immediately after the Olenivka attacks, Russian officials created post-facto justifications for the killing of Azov Regiment fighters. The Russian Embassy in Britain provided moral justification for the killing of Azov militants, stating, "Azov militants deserve execution but death not by firing squad but by hanging because they're not real soldiers. They deserve a humiliating death."[36] On 2 August, Russia designated the Azov Regiment a terrorist organisation, which Azov interpreted as proof that Russia was looking for "new excuses and explanations for its war crimes."[37] Public Chamber lawyer Ilya Remeslo opined that Azov Regiment fighters would be reclassified from POWs to terrorists, which would give Russia a legitimate right to "use military force and targeted strikes across the world" against them.[38] The terrorism designation also provided a 10–20 year prison sentence for Russian collaborators with Azov.

To counter war crimes allegations in Donetsk, the Kremlin highlighted its commitment to the reconstruction of Mariupol. The image of Chechen Kadyrovtsy celebrating outside a burnt-up building near Azovstal was etched in the minds of international observers, but Russian officials desperately sought to reframe the narrative. On 1 August, Russian deputy prime minister Marat Khusnullin claimed that the first residential buildings would be rebuilt in September 2022 alongside hospitals and an emergencies ministry. Khusnullin also pledged to rebuild Mariupol's historic centre and ensure that its population would reach 350,000 by 2025, which was just shy of its 400,000 pre-war population.[39] This ambitious plan, which had few accompanying details, was panned in Kyiv as unrealistic. Ukrainian estimates show that the reconstruction of Mariupol would cost $14 billion over a 7–10-year period, which would allow for a post-war population of 220,000.[40] Thus far, Russia's reconstruction efforts in Mariupol have been characterised by extensive propaganda. Bread vans in Mariupol had the Z logo emblazoned on them, the Mariupol drama theatre became an aid centre and Russian-built generators featured a giant mobile screen showing Russian state TV. Denis Pushilin pledged to convert Azovstal into a technology park, which extinguished its historical significance for Ukrainians, and stated that Mariupol's reconstruction would convert it into a resort city.[41] Ramzan Kadyrov vowed to reconstruct Mariupol's historic mosque and Orthodox church.[42] The DNR authorities pledged to make Mariupol a model of Donbas's "liberation" and Russia signed a twin-city agreement between Mariupol and St. Petersburg.[43] This added further ammunition to Russia's implausible claims that it would rebuild Mariupol better than before.

Ukraine Prepares for a De-Occupation Counter-Offensive

Despite suffering territorial losses, the Ukrainian military devised plans for a large-scale counter-offensive to liberate Russian-occupied territory. On 2 May, Arestovych predicted that Ukraine would be able to stage a counter-offensive between late May and mid-June due to an influx of NATO-class weaponry.[44] On 25 June, GUR intelligence chief Kirill Budanov declared that "active hostilities will drop to almost zero" by the end of 2022, as Ukraine would return to 1991 borders.[45] These predictions were overly optimistic but Ukraine nonetheless paired predictions of a counter-offensive with requests for additional weaponry. On 10 July, Reznikov stated that Zelensky had ordered the Ukrainian armed forces to recapture occupied southern Ukraine and stated that Ukraine had a well-armed one-million-man fighting force to achieve this goal.[46] On 13 July, Arestovych built on Reznikov's comments by requesting mobile air defence systems and armoured vehicles, which would neutralise Russia's infantry advantage. Arestovych also urged NATO countries to provide multiple launch rocket systems to Ukraine. Arestovych stated that the receipt of 60 MLR systems would stop Russia "dead in its tracks," the receipt of 40 MLR systems would mean a slow Russian advance with heavy casualties and the receipt of 20 MLR systems would mean that Russia would advance with heavier casualties than in Luhansk.[47] In August 2022, Podolyak asked the West for "50, 60, 80 more" MLR systems, which would degrade Russia's supplies and ammunition stocks, and force Russia to revert to the ineffective tactics it had used in the early stages of the war.[48]

Ukraine's Western partners followed through on these requests. The U.S.'s 1 July $820 million military aid package included NASAMS, mid-to-long-range air defence systems and counter-artillery radars. Britain provided Ukraine with 1,600 anti-tank weapons and artillery guns on 21 July, as well as M270 rocket artillery systems in August. Germany delivered the first batch of Gepard anti-aircraft gun systems on 25 July, which was followed by the delivery of eight more systems on 7 August. Despite these arms supplies, Ukraine refrained from starting a full-scale counter-offensive due to its fears that the West would reduce support for Kyiv if its military forays yielded few results. Podolyak's strategy of creating chaos in the Russian armed forces, which differed from Russia's "last century" style one direction offensive, was interpreted as a sign that Ukraine might lack the 2–3 to 1 personnel advantage for a successful counter-offensive.[49] British MI6 chief Richard Moore interpreted Ukraine's restraint as a sign that it planned to wait for Russia to pause operations and then launch a counter-offensive.[50] This restraint was also encouraged by Western officials who feared that Ukraine would launch a counter-offensive too soon, as the Pentagon's available stockpiles to arm Kyiv were diminishing.[51] Boris Johnson's warnings about "Ukraine fatigue" in the West, voiced at the G7 summit, also explained Kyiv's risk-averse approach to its counter-offensive.

Inside Russia's tightly controlled information space, debates about the plausibility of a Ukrainian counter-offensive heated up as the summer war progressed. The prevailing view was that Ukraine's counter-offensive warnings were mere bluster. Podolyak's 9 August admission that Ukraine's rhetoric on counterattacking Kherson was an information and psychological operation aimed at demoralising the Russian army was amplified by Russian media outlets.[52] The Russian Orientalist Telegram channel claimed that the Ukrainian counter-offensive was "not yet visible." It predicted that divisions within NATO between Britain and its hawkish "satellites" such as Poland, Romania and the Baltic states and restrained voices such as Greece and Hungary would undermine Ukraine's cause, as would "growing crisis factors" that slow arms deliveries.[53] Hard-line advocates of mobilisation presented a bleaker picture of Russia's ability to withstand a Ukrainian counter-offensive. Girkin warned that Ukraine would "grope for weaknesses" in the Kherson and Zaporizhzhia directions, and despite its lack of air cover and medium-range air defence capabilities, Ukraine's accrued combat skills and foreign advisors could lead to an "unexpected strike."[54] The Moscow Calling Telegram channel warned that Ukraine's tactical manoeuvres, which facilitated retreats in Kharkiv and Mykolaiv, could be repeated in other combat theatres. In a widely shared post, Moscow Calling predicted that the balance of power would shift in Ukraine's favour in July to August, as Kyiv would be able to inflict "painful cutting blows" on unprotected areas of Kharkiv, Kherson and Zaporizhzhia.[55] Russian policy did not accommodate these alarmist assessments, which gave Kyiv an opening to advance.

While Ukraine waited on launching a full-fledged counter-offensive, it carried out targeted counterattacks that capitalised on Russia's dwindling war materiel stocks. On 27 August, Ukrainian GUR official Vadim Skibitsky asserted that Russia had expended 55% of its pre-war missile stocks, which included 80% of its Iskanders and comparable portions of Kalibrs.[56] As Russia strives to keep a minimum of 30% of its stocks in reserve, it pivoted towards replacing Kalibrs with S-300s and using short-distance Hurricane or Tornado missiles, which fire along a 70–80km radius.[57] This missile shortage was apparent as early as early March. On 9 March, U.S. officials warned that Russia was using "dumb bombs", which are unguided and greatly increase the risk of missing military targets.[58] On 22 March, Russia fired a Kinzhal Kh-47M2 hypersonic missile on an arms depot in western Ukraine. Russia's use of Kh-22 anti-ship missiles, which were designed in 1962 and notorious for their imprecision against civilian targets, became apparent in mid-May. Sanctions restricted Russia's ability to replace missiles and pressured it to lower the cost of its offensives. The $6.5 million cost of Kalibrs and $3 million cost of Iskanders meant that missile barrages like the late June strikes on Kyiv cost the Russian military $150–200 million.[59] Russia's use of Tochka-Us, which cost a paltry $300,000, could be linked to cost-cutting mechanisms. On 31 August, *Ukrainskaya Pravda* published warnings that Russia's depletion of 7 million shells would produce a "tangible shell shortage" by the end of 2022, which would lead to a decrease in Russian artillery usage.[60] In addition to carrying out regular strikes on ammunition depots and supply lines, Ukraine launched limited counterattacks on Snake Island and Kherson, which paved the way for broader counter-offensives.

Ukraine's first major counter-offensive was its 30 June liberation of Snake Island. Ukraine's decision to launch a full-fledged assault on Snake Island polarised Zelensky's inner circle. Budanov stated that whoever controls Snake Island could block civilian vessels in all directions in southern Ukraine, and Russia's occupation of the island threatened Ukrainian grain exports from Odesa port.[61] The symbolic resonance of Snake Island, which was illustrated by Zelensky's vow to defend the island on his 2021 visit and the famous "Russian Warship, Go Fuck Yourself!" exchange at the start of the war, augmented Kyiv's resolve.[62] Arestovych was the main voice of offensive restraint on Snake Island, stating that Russia's occupation was a liability as it left critical military infrastructure transiting through the island vulnerable to Ukrainian strikes.[63] Arestovych called Snake Island "the new Chornobaivka," referring to an air base near Kherson which had hosted Russian equipment destroyed by Ukrainian forces.[64] Despite these divisions, Ukraine escalated its offensive operations on Snake Island in mid-May, as Russia attempted to reinforce its military presence. On 12 May, Ukraine struck Vsevolod Bobrov, one of the newest ships in Russia's Black Sea Fleet that was carrying an air defence system, and forced it to be towed to Sevastopol.[65] Ukraine's 17 June destruction of Russia's Spasatel Vasily Bekh tugboat impeded resupply efforts to Snake Island, while its drone strikes eroded Russia's Pantsir S-1 defence systems. Despite launching Kh-31D missiles on Odesa via Su-35 jets, Russia was unable to derail Ukraine's attacks on its military infrastructure on Snake Island and was forced to withdraw its military presence.[66]

The Russian defence ministry framed its exit from Snake Island as a "gesture of goodwill," which illustrated its unwillingness to impede a humanitarian corridor for grain exports.[67] Hardliners such as Alexander Dugin and State Duma Deputy Chairman Pyotr Tolstoy expressed confidence that Russia would eventually recapture Snake Island, while Tsargrad derisively described it as Zelensky's St. Helena and a potential exile spot for Ukraine's authorities after a Russian victory.[68] Russia's swift exit surprised military observers. Defence expert Dmitry Bolentkov believed that Russia had successfully reinforced its Snake Island presence after the mid-May Ukrainian attacks and wanted to play a "cruel joke" on Ukraine by forcing it to intensely bombard the island in a futile fashion.[69] While the Rybar Telegram channel warned of unauthorised U.S. weapons deliveries on Ukrainian mosquito patrol boats,[70] Gurulyov warned that Ukraine's Snake Island attacks could be a feint and believed in an inevitable Ukrainian defeat.[71] Ultimately, Russia likely viewed retaining control of Snake Island as a "suicide mission" and believed that even if it withdrew, it would be able to strike Ukrainian military infrastructure on the island.[72]

The 27 June Kremenchuk shopping mall attack, which killed 20 civilians, further strengthened Ukraine's counter-offensive resolve. After pro-war Telegram channels spread familiar conspiracies about staged killings and the mall serving as a trojan horse for the Territorial Defence Forces, the Russian defence ministry admitted that it had struck a weapons hangar near the site which had detonated the mall.[73] The dubious nature of Russia's justifications and Moscow's apparent disregard for civilian lives inspired Ukraine to press forward with more counterattacks.

Ukraine's counterattacks on Kherson focused on isolating Russian forces, depriving the Russian military of much-needed supplies and forcing a Kyiv-style retreat. On 1 June, Ukrainian forces struck settlements on the eastern bank of the Inhulets River, which caused Russia to detonate the bridges used in these counterattacks.[74] Russia was able to resist Ukrainian forces in Davydiv Brid and eschewed a large-scale retreat, but by mid-July, Ukraine had liberated settlements that constituted 15% of Kherson's area.[75] Ukraine also systematically destroyed supply routes to the Russian military by using HIMARS to destroy the Antonovskiy Bridge in late July. On 12 August, Ukraine struck the bridge on the Nova Kakhovka dam, 55km northeast of Kherson. These bridge attacks isolated Russian forces and impeded Russia's ability to transit heavy artillery across the Dnieper River. Russia's efforts to overcome Ukrainian attacks, which included failed repairs of the Antonovskiy Bridge and construction of two pontoon crossings to supply its Kherson forces, were unable to rectify these supply problems.[76] Due to this supply-line crisis, Mykolaiv governor Vitaly Kim claimed that Russia's senior command in Kherson had retreated from the west bank of the Dnieper, leaving up to 20,000 Russian troops stranded.[77] By early August, Russia was deploying additional BTGs to Crimea, moving long convoys of equipment from Donbas to the southern front, and shipping equipment from mainland Russia, Berdyansk, Melitopol and Mariupol to Crimea via the Kerch Bridge.[78] These measures underscored Russia's belated efforts to contain Kyiv's momentum in Kherson.

Ukraine's counterattacks were aided by local partisans who resisted Russia's occupation. Local partisans carried out assassination attempts on Russian collaborators, which killed Medvedchuk ally Dmytro Savluchenko and seriously injured the head of Kherson's penitentiary department Yevhen Sobolev.[79] These partisans also aided SBU investigations into alleged local collaborators, such as Kherson City Council member Ilya Karamalikov, who provided supplies to Russian troops and abetted their looting of Kherson.[80] Kirill Stremousov's request for a Russian military base in Kherson, which ignored public opinion, was greeted with $17,000 rewards for his head on posters throughout the city.[81] Although Russia offered 10,000 roubles to accept citizenship and claimed to have granted 10,000 passports to Kherson residents in the month after passport distributions began on 11 June, Kherson residents largely heeded Zelensky's warnings about accepting Russian citizenship.[82] To overcome local resistance, Russian authorities mandated Russian driving licences and Russian passports in order to work in Kherson. House-to-house inspections, which were conducted by 100–150 guardsman and FSB officers, resulted in searches of mobile phones to find "disloyal" Kherson residents.[83] Russia designated Kherson as a rouble zone on 1 May and enforced rouble payments on public sector workers such as teachers and doctors who were brought in from Russia. The rouble transition process would apply first to pensioners, who were disproportionately willing to consider Russian citizenship, and result in a full-fledged integration into rouble zone over four to five months.[84] These repressive measures were unable to stem local resistance in Kherson, even as Russia's occupation authorities marched inexorably towards holding an annexation referendum.

Russia's Weaponisation of Food and the Black Sea Grain Export Deal

During the first five months of the war, Russia impeded the export of Ukrainian agricultural products by blockading Ukraine's Black Sea ports. To enforce its hegemony over Ukrainian ports, the Russian navy bombed at least three civilian ships during the first months of the war, which included one chartered by an agribusiness company. This blockade impeded the export of 20 million tons of Ukrainian grain, which included 6 million tons of wheat or 13% of its 2021 harvest.[85] This blockade caused immense logistical challenges for Ukraine, which relied almost exclusively on ports like Odesa for its annual export of 60 million tons of grain. It also forced Kyiv to establish new water routes like river barges from the Danube River to Romania.[86] Ukraine established railway links to counter the blockade, which passed through Gdansk, Poland and Constanta,

Romania. These railway links allowed 768,300 metric tons of grain to be exported from Ukraine from 1–16 May, which was an uptick from 642,500 metric tons in April and 415,900 metric tons in March. However, this was a mere stop-gap solution, as Ukraine's railway traffic to neighbouring countries was insufficient to cover the entire summer harvest.[87] The EU warned that an end to the war was the only way to resolve the crisis, as "military risks to commercial navigation" drove up insurance and transportation costs for agricultural products.[88] U.S. Deputy Secretary of State Wendy Sherman explicitly blamed Putin for food insecurity emanating from the Ukraine War and the Biden administration complemented EU efforts to resolve this crisis.[89] Biden's plan to establish grain silos on the Poland–Ukraine border to keep grain out of Russian hands was unable to rectify the problem, however. Poland expected that Biden's plan would take three to four months to complete, and Kyiv was not consulted on the specifics of the plan.[90]

The Russian blockade's disruption of Ukrainian grain exports had severe economic implications for Ukraine, which earned $15 billion from grain sales annually. The UN World Food Programme (WFP) was forced to supply emergency food aid to cities facing what it called "medieval tactics of besiegement" such as Kyiv, Kharkiv and Dnipro, but inadequate humanitarian access derailed assistance to Mariupol.[91] The challenges for global food security were even more desperate, as Ukraine contributed 42% of the world's sunflower oil, 16% of its corn and 9% of its wheat.[92] The UN warned on 8 June that hundreds of millions of people in the Global South would be at risk of starvation due to Ukraine War-related food supply disruptions.[93] WFP chief David Beasley accused the Ukraine War of turning the "breadbasket of the world to breadlines," and warned that WFP's budget had been forced to increase by $850 million, which meant that it could distribute food to 4 million fewer people.[94] Beasley highlighted the Yemen food insecurity crisis as an especially dire example, as 8 million people had had their food allotment cut by 50% and "zero rations" were inevitable, but also warned of risks to countries like Egypt and Lebanon, which received 85% and 81% of their grain from Ukraine.[95] The 30–50% increase in global wheat prices had severe spill-over effects, as Sherman highlighted Lebanon, Pakistan, Libya, Tunisia, Yemen and Morocco as countries that were especially vulnerable to Ukraine War-induced food inflation.[96] This exacerbated a trend towards food insecurity, which was triggered by the COVID-19 pandemic, intrastate conflicts and climate change. UN estimates warned prior to the Ukraine War that 44 million people were at risk of famine, while the total number of food insecure people increased by 200 million after COVID-19 to 345 million in 82 countries.[97] The longer-term outlook was even more dire, as the UN warned that "this year's food crisis is about lack of access. Next year's could be about lack of food."[98]

As Russia faced mounting criticism from Western governments and multilateral institutions for exacerbating food insecurity, the Kremlin launched a disinformation counter-offensive. The Kremlin consistently blamed Western sanctions for food insecurity, while the Russian ministry of agriculture cited sanctions as a reason for its March 2022 imposition of grain export restrictions, which ensured adequate supplies in domestic markets. Eduard Zernin, Chairman of the Board of the Union of Grain Exports, claimed that sanctions restricted the export of 10 million tons of grain and insisted that the issue could only be rectified by creating a "separate regional market" with its own clearing currencies.[99] The sanctions narrative was complemented by other often contradictory explanations for the obstruction of grain exports. On 19 May, Vasily Nebenzia stated that the Ukraine War was not a major trigger of food insecurity, as famine of "biblical proportions" was already predicted in 2020. To justify this patently disprovable claim, Nebenzia stated that the "politicisation of energy cooperation" and abrupt transition to green energy had caused food insecurity.[100] On 15 June, Nebenzia insisted that Ukraine's mining of its ports was the primary obstacle to grain exports and a "safe corridor" could only be established through de-mining or circumvention of Ukrainian mines.[101] To illustrate that Russia was part of the solution on the de-mining issue, the Russian defence ministry showcased its assistance to Ukrainian farmers in Kharkiv Oblast, who were struggling to clear farmland with unexploded mines and shells.[102] HSE academic Andrey Suzdaltsev accused Ukraine of not planting new crops, as all of its fuel went to the military, and of re-exporting grain to Europe, as the Kyiv authorities did not care about feeding their own citizens. Suzdaltsev justified these assertions by stating that the Ukrainian government expected its food insecure citizens to flee to Europe and knew that one-third of Ukraine would be guaranteed food as it was under Russian occupation.[103] On her 11 May show, Olga Skabeeva advanced similar conspiracies, as she stated that the U.S. had demanded Ukrainian grain in exchange for Lend-Lease military assistance and was devising plans to smuggle it from Ukraine via Moldova.

In stark contrast to its propaganda, Russia weaponised food in a strikingly flagrant manner and framed it as a retaliation to Western sanctions. On 1 April, Medvedev called for a prioritisation of food supply for Russia's domestic market, the supply of crops in roubles and a cessation of food exports to "unfriendly countries"—"So we'll eat breakfast ourselves. Lunch can be shared with friends. We won't give dinner to our enemies. They will manage."[104] RIA Novosti commentator Sergei Savchuk warned that if Washington, London and Brussels "persist in their Russophobia," rising food prices, shortages and inflation would follow.[105] Savchuk highlighted years of Western investments in Russia's agricultural sector, which had allowed Russia to "chain both individual companies and entire countries to invisible chains" and accused the collective West of pushing Russia into food isolation.[106] Despite diplomatic outreaches from Macron and Scholz, Russia linked its alleviation of the blockade on Ukraine with sanctions relief. On 28 May, the Kremlin released the following statement: "An increase in the supply of Russian fertilisers and agricultural products will also help reduce tensions on the global food market, which, of course, will require the removal of relevant sanctions."[107] This statement was condemned in the West, as U.S. sanctions did not extend to agricultural products writ large but were instead confined to debt financing for the Russian Agricultural Bank and specific sectors such as fish and seafood.[108] The EU's announcement of exemptions on trade with sanctioned Russian banks in the agricultural sector on 20 July complied with these requests but Moscow's ultimate strategy was likely to achieve the removal of SWIFT sanctions.[109]

Russia compounded the food insecurity problem by illegally smuggling grain from occupied regions of Ukraine. During the first six months of the war, Russia smuggled an estimated 4.04 million tons of grain and oilseeds, worth $1.9 billion, from Ukraine.[110] Crimea's record grain harvests, which increased from 1.4 million tons in 2021 to 2.1 million tons in 2022, reflect a small portion of this smuggling.[111] Russia's targeting of Kherson and Zaporizhzhia's grain production was especially pronounced. After Russia had triumphed in Kherson, Kadyrovtsy forces had threatened Albert Cherepakha, the owner of 20,000 hectares of farmland, with beheading unless he forfeited his property to the occupying authorities.[112] The Russian occupation forces demanded that Kherson farmers plant only grain and sunflower and insisted on the seizure of 70% of all production without compensation.[113] Melitopol mayor Ivan Fedorov has produced evidence of Russia smuggling grain from Zaporizhzhia to Crimea on Z-labelled trucks, while trucks with Crimean number plates were spotted removing 1,500 tons of grain from "elevators" in Kherson.[114] Russia's employment of ship-to-ship transfers from Sevastopol, a method also used by Iran and Venezuela to circumvent oil sanctions, prevented countries accepting grain, such as Egypt, from detecting stolen property. Compliance from third party officials, such as Lebanon's facilitation of 10,000 tons of barley and wheat flour that Russia docked in Laodicea, ensured that Russia's smuggling remained undetected.

The extent of Russian state involvement in the smuggling of grain is unknown but circumstantial evidence strongly points to the Kremlin at the very least turning a blind eye to the practice. The SBU has implicated Russian collaborators such as former Party of Regions MP Yevgeny Balytskyi and Berdyansk head Olexander Saulenko of helping Russia loot 650,000 tons of grain worth $200 million on fifteen Syrian-flagged ships.[115] Statements from Kremlin-aligned officials and state media figures also point to the acceptability of smuggling. On 30 May, Stremousov admitted that Kherson had begun exporting grain to Russia. Stremousov stated that agricultural products from Kherson had been shipped to Crimea to "improve the economic well-being" of Kherson and claimed that he was in talks with Russian factories about the production of sunflower oil from Kherson-grown sunflower seeds.[116] Stremousov subsequently complained about the inefficacy of road transit of grain from Kherson to Crimea, which was the sole route due to the alleged mining of the Dnieper–Bug estuary, and asserted that Ochakiv and Mykolaiv needed to be occupied for shipments to continue.[117] A deleted statement from Vladimir Zyryanov, a United Russia Party Agriculture Committee chair in Krasnoyarsk, highlighted plans to transfer southern Ukrainian fertiliser to Siberia. On Solovyov's 1 May show, Dmitry Evstafiev stated, "Ukraine's deal with the Chinese and corn didn't come through. If they need it, we'll supply them with Ukraine's corn."[118]

As Russia's threat to global food security became apparent, NATO countries proposed solutions to the impasse. On 23 May, Lithuania's foreign minister Gabrielius Landsbergis proposed the assembly of a "coalition of the willing" naval escort operation to facilitate grain shipments from Ukraine's ports. Landsbergis's proposal, which was backed by Britain, would not be NATO-mandated but would instead allow food insecure countries such as Egypt to provide necessary protection.[119] This proposal was greeted with alarm in Moscow. Konstantin Sivkov warned that Britain could use a grain export mission as a smokescreen to supply armoured vehicles to Ukraine on ships and facilitate the re-entry of NATO warships into the Black Sea, which was restricted by Turkey's closure of the Bosporus.[120] As military solutions ultimately did not transpire, Turkey played a pivotal diplomatic role in facilitating a resolution to the Black Sea grain impasse. On 14 July, Turkey brokered a deal with Russia, Ukraine and the UN, which would create a joint coordination centre in Istanbul that would guarantee freedom of navigation. The deal allowed Ukraine to supervise the transit of grain across mined ports, implored Russia to accept a truce and created a joint Turkey–UN inspection mechanism, which would allay Russian fears of grain smuggling.[121] The deal did not address Russia's concerns about sanctions and their collateral costs, and the stony-faced images of Russian and Ukrainian negotiators reflected a general sense of unease about its viability. Nevertheless, an interim agreement was upgraded into a formal signing ceremony on 22 July. Less than twenty-four hours later, Russia struck Odesa port with Kalibr cruise missiles, which prompted fears that Moscow would continue weaponising food. Russia denied that its strike on Odesa port was an attempt to sabotage the grain deal, as it stated that it had been targeting a military boat with cruise missiles. Despite calling Russia's strike an act of "barbarism," Zelensky made an unannounced visit to Odesa on 29 July.

On 1 August, the first ship carrying Ukrainian grain left Odesa for Lebanon, and by 7 September, 100 grain shipments had been transited under the deal's framework.

The Zaporizhzhia Nuclear Power Plant Crisis

After Russia triumphed in the Battle of Enerhodar on 4 March, the ZNPP's nuclear and thermal power stations were captured by Russian forces. On 12 March, Rosatom assumed control over ZNPP while Ukrainian technicians operated the plant under Russian supervision.[122] The militarisation of ZNPP created a risk of nuclear disaster, initially revealed by a 4 March fire at the training facility of the plant, which followed clashes involving Ukrainian anti-tank missiles and Russian rocket-propelled grenades. After this brinkmanship episode, the threat of a catastrophe at ZNPP receded but Russia ignited the crisis in June by converting the plant into a military base. A 5 July *Wall Street Journal* report revealed that more than 500 Russian troops had deployed heavy artillery batteries at ZNPP and laid anti-personnel mines on the shores of the reservoir which cools its six reactors.[123] Russia also deployed a Smerch artillery vehicle near the ZNPP's chimneys, which was swiftly joined by rocket launchers, tanks and personnel carriers. This military equipment allowed Russia to shell cities surrounding ZNPP, such as Marhanets, Nikopol and Zaporizhzhia, with impunity. Video footage from 19 August revealed at least five Russian military trucks with the Z symbol in ZNPP, surrounded by tent-like structures that could be used for military purposes.[124] Rosatom established a base in a guarded bunker beneath the plant, which was safe from Ukrainian counterattacks, as Russia believed that Ukraine would not retaliate for strikes launched from ZNPP.[125] This assumption proved correct, as Ukraine's only path to retaking ZNPP would be to liberate its surroundings, encircle the plant and force Russian military personnel to leave.[126]

The crisis at ZNPP was worsened further by regular shelling of the plant. A 9 August International Atomic Energy Agency (IAEA) statement highlighted how persistent shelling damaged the plant's external power supply system, damaged communication cables involved in radiation control, possibly impaired the functioning of three radiation detection sensors and restricted off-site power.[127] While the IAEA refrained from explicitly blaming either side for shelling ZNPP, Ukraine blamed Russia for these attacks. Andriy Yermak, the chief of the Ukrainian presidential staff, claimed that Russia had shelled ZNPP to "force the world to comply with their conditions," and warned that in response Ukraine would "punish them by hard hitting with precision on pain points."[128] Zelensky called Russia's shelling of ZNPP an "audacious act of terror," which inspired Ukrainian officials to accuse Russia of nuclear terrorism and call for sanctions on Rosatom.[129] A GUR intelligence assessment showed that Russia was firing at ash storage sites to create radioactive dust that could spread widely.[130] Russia's continued shelling of the ZNPP increased the risk of a radiological disaster. The U.S. state department expressed frustration with Russia's 28 August decision to block a consensus on the NPT final document and accused Moscow of downplaying the "grave radiological risk" to ZNPP.[131] Ukrainian state-owned nuclear energy operator Energoatom warned that a ZNPP disaster would spread radiation across southern Ukraine and southwestern Russia.[132] Ukraine's Hydrometeorological Institute presented an even more dire picture, which showed radioactive fall-out spreading to thirteen European countries in the event of a Chernobyl-style nuclear disaster at ZNPP.

Russia's harassment of Ukrainian technicians and efforts to reroute electricity towards its occupied territories increased tensions with Ukraine. As 11,000 of Enerhodar's 53,000 pre-war population worked for ZNPP, the nuclear plant was indispensable for the local economy and its operations had ensured that Enerhodar had been among the most prosperous towns in Zaporizhzhia before the war. Russia's occupation of Enerhodar caused the fortunes of local residents to plunge, as ZNPP workers were regularly beaten and threatened with abduction and torture to keep the plant operational.[133] Despite incompatibilities between the Russian and Ukrainian electrical grids and the risk of a nuclear meltdown if power was disrupted for ninety minutes, Russia also sought to redirect power supply from ZNPP towards Crimea. Yevhen Balytskyi denies these allegations by stating that Crimea had supplied power to Zaporizhzhia when the ZNPP was disrupted.[134] This explanation is implausible: Crimea has suffered from chronic blackouts which predate the 2014 annexation and was only partially rectified by the 2018–19 construction of Simferopol and Sevastopol power plants, which each produce 470MW of electricity. The disruption of gas supply from the Boyka Towers on the Black Sea after Ukrainian missile strikes on 20 June undermined the stability of Crimea's electrical grid and moved Russia to seize electricity from ZNPP.[135] Beyond the supply of electricity, Kyslytsya believes that Russia needs to maintain control over ZNPP for "propaganda purposes," as surrendering the plant would symbolise the failure of Putin's campaign to annex southern Ukraine.[136]

To counter accusations of misconduct, Russia rejected Guterres's plea to demilitarise the plant as "unacceptable," as it would make the facility "more vulnerable", and denied using ZNPP as a launchpad for military assaults on Ukraine.[137] A Russian foreign ministry official stated that "We believe a demilitarisation of ZNPP is not necessary, since the plant has never been militarised," and insisted that Russian military personnel were either Russian Guard units, which are like French Gendarmerie or Italian Carabinieri, or "specialists from the radiation, chemical and biological protection (CBRN) troops."[138]

According to the Russian foreign ministry, the Russian Guard troops protected the station and CBRN troops helped overcome the risk of "possible accidents and radiation emergencies" that might result from "continuous Ukrainian shelling."[139] The Russian foreign ministry denied the existence of heavy weapons at ZNPP, as only vehicles to transport Russian Guard personnel, CBRN vehicles and electronic warfare equipment to "neutralise Ukrainian kamikaze-drones" were present.[140] In October 2022, Mikhail Ulyanov, Russia's Permanent Representative for International Organisations in Vienna, declared that the absence of heavy weaponry prevented Russia from being able to shell Nikopol. Ulyanov contended that shelling was taking place because Nikopol was the site from which the ZNPP and Enerhodar had been shelled since May.[141]

Russian propaganda also highlighted alleged biases in international institutions and spread conspiracies about Ukraine's alleged shelling of ZNPP. Russia opposed the Canadian–Polish draft resolution at the IAEA board of governors, as it called for Russia to end its "persistent violent actions against nuclear facilities in Ukraine" but did not mention Ukrainian shelling of ZNPP.[142] A Russian foreign ministry official claimed that Western countries could not answer with specifics on Russia's violent actions towards nuclear facilities, and highlighted that China had voted against the motion, while Burundi, Egypt, India, South Africa, Vietnam, Pakistan and Senegal had abstained.[143] Polyanskiy lamented that the UN had tried to force Russia to suspend operations in ZNPP but had not imposed similar pressure on the U.S. over its seizure of Syrian oil.[144] Sergey Savchuk claimed that Ukraine had struck ZNPP to test the efficacy of Russia's air defence systems guarding the plant, paint Russia as an "uncontrollable bloodthirsty monster" and exact revenge on local residents as Zaporizhzhia would become part of Russia.[145] During a 16 August *Solovyov Live* episode, Russia-aligned Zaporizhzhia governor Vladimir Rogov accused Ukraine of firing projectiles and MLR systems just 10 metres away from a nuclear waste container and claimed that Ukraine was firing heavy weapons at the ZNPP's cooling circuit. Rogov insisted that Ukraine's attacks effectively amounted to the creation of a "dirty bomb" on its territory. Balitsky accused Ukraine of trying to create a panic at ZNPP, which would encourage European countries to provide Kyiv with additional support.[146]

Despite the chasm between Ukrainian and Russian narratives about ZNPP, both countries were ostensibly interested in an IAEA visit to the plant. Before the crisis escalated, Energoatom rejected an IAEA visit to ZNPP, as its delegation would pass through occupied territory, and called the liberation of Zaporizhzhia a precondition for the IAEA's arrival.[147] On 9 August, Kuleba moderated Ukraine's position by writing a letter requesting an IAEA visit, and Kyslytsya insisted that Ukraine had always supported an IAEA visit, which did not occur due to the "destructive Russian position."[148] Ukrainian officials called for the complete "de-occupation" and "demilitarisation" of ZNPP, and expressed support for a permanent IAEA presence at the site. Russia stridently opposed the demilitarisation of ZNPP. Nebenzia warned that demilitarising ZNPP would make the plant vulnerable to "terrorist attacks" and claimed that the UN's security perimeter proposal was ambiguous.[149] Rogov warned that Zelensky's "special operations forces" would occupy a demilitarised ZNPP and use the plant to shell cities. As demilitarisation was an "ousting tactic being employed by the Anglo-Saxons and Zelensky regime," Rogov called for a ceasefire and sanctions for bombardments of the ZNPP.[150] Although a Russian foreign ministry official denied that there was an "impasse in relation to ZNPP,"[151] Ukraine and Russia's irreconcilable positions on resolving the ZNPP crisis complicated the IAEA's visit.

Despite these disagreements, an IAEA delegation led by IAEA director general Rafael Grossi left Vienna for ZNPP on 29 August.

Due to the logistical difficulties associated with travel through exclusively Ukrainian territory, Grossi engaged with both the Russian and Ukrainian sides about safe passage. The safe passage of IAEA inspectors was marred by intense shelling of Enerhodar, paired with Ukrainian precision strikes and attacks from ZNPP by Russian Grad MLRS launchers. Russia also spread disinformation about an imminent Ukrainian attack on ZNPP: on 1 September, the Russian defence ministry claimed that it had spotted sixty Ukrainian assault troops near ZNPP and used its air force to prevent a Ukrainian attack on ZNPP that coincided with IAEA's visit.[152] On 3 September, the Russian defence ministry reiterated these warnings and stated that 250 Ukrainian marines in 20 vessels had been thwarted by Russian helicopters and fighter jets from seizing ZNPP.[153] These reports were undermined by contradictory Russian reports, which ranged from 7 to 40 Ukrainian speedboats being present and the release of a staged video of "dead Ukrainian forces" near ZNPP.[154] A 3 September strike on the Dniprovska power line, which was the last operational 750kV power line in ZNPP, impaired electricity supply, but an agreement was nonetheless reached to leave two of the original six IAEA inspectors at the plant. The IAEA ultimately published a report on 6 September, which accused Russia of violating all "seven pillars" of nuclear safety. The IAEA board of governors passed a resolution, opposed only by Russia and China, urging Russia to leave ZNPP on 15 September.

The IAEA's conclusions about ZNPP faced severe criticism from both the Russian and Ukrainian sides. Nebenzia expressed frustration that the IAEA did not explicitly blame Ukraine for shelling ZNPP and warned that "If provocations by the Kyiv regime continue, there is no guarantee that there won't be serious consequences."[155] While Zelensky was satisfied by the mention of a Russian military occupation of ZNPP in the IAEA report, Ukrainian officials were concerned about the efficacy of the IAEA's inspections. The presence of Russian military and Rosatom employees around IAEA inspectors, the ban on Ukrainian and foreign media representatives during the IAEA delegation's visit and the IAEA's inability to visit the ZNPP's "crisis centre" caused particular consternation in Kyiv.[156] A senior Zaporizhzhia official dismissed the IAEA visit as a "pre-planned and staged show" and expressed concern that Russia had convinced members of the delegation that Ukraine was behind the shelling of ZNPP.[157] As the IAEA visit failed to break the impasse, the U.S.'s recommendation of a "controlled shutdown" of ZNPP gained traction amongst Ukrainian officials. On 11 September, ZNPP's sixth power unit was disconnected, which paved the way for ZNPP's shutdown and transfer to a cold state.

Russia Disrupts Energy Supply to Europe

As the EU deliberated on an energy embargo against Russia, the Kremlin retaliated by slowing the export of natural gas from Nord Stream. By late July, Nord Stream was exporting just 40% of its natural gas capacity, and on 25 July, Gazprom halved gas flows to 33 billion cubic metres. Although Nord Stream was operating at only 20% capacity, Peskov insisted that Russia was not interested in a complete cut-off of gas supplies, as it was a "responsible gas supplier" and largely guarantees Europe's energy security.[158] Nevertheless, Peskov's veiled warning that "If Europe continues on its path of totally reckless imposition of restrictions and sanctions that hit it, then the situation will be different" sparked renewed fears that Russia planned to weaponise gas exports to Europe.[159] These concerns were justified by Russia's dubious claims that turbine repairs were preventing gas exports. From 11–21 July, Nord Stream's operations were sidelined by annual maintenance. Putin warned that only one of two machines that pump gas were functioning, which highlighted Canada's sanctions-induced refusal to return a Siemens Energy turbine to Russia that was undergoing repairs.[160] Putin's claims were greeted with scepticism in Berlin and Kyiv. Germany's Ministry for Economic Affairs and Climate Action insisted that there were "no technical reasons" for Nord Stream's disruptions, as the turbine was sanctions exempt. Ukraine's sanctions envoy Oleksii Makeiev warned that Russia was "using gas supplies as another instrument of pressure on Germany."[161] Canada's 10 July exemption of Russian oil and gas from sanctions, which was fiercely criticised in Kyiv, verifiably contradicted Russia's claims that sanctions were an obstacle. Russia's decision to reject the returned Canadian turbines, citing technical issues and missing documents, provided further evidence to Western sceptics.[162]

As concerns about Russia weaponising gas grew, the EU prepared for a worst-case scenario while continuing to intensify economic pressure on Russia. On 26 July, EU members agreed to voluntarily reduce gas consumption by 15% from August 2022 to March 2023, which would become a mandate if supplies reached "crisis levels."[163] The EU measure passed due to exemptions for non-pipeline dependent countries such as Ireland, Malta and Cyprus, and the Baltic states, which had gas-dependent electricity supply. Germany's 8 July decision to reactivate coal-fired plants, which contradicted economy minister Robert Habeck's environmentalist impulses and Berlin's plans to ban coal by 2030, encapsulated the urgency of the energy supply situation.[164] Norway's replacement of Russia as Europe's largest gas supplier on 24 August and Germany's ability to fill its gas storage tankers to 82.2% by late August, which exceeded its own 75% target, underscored the EU's resilience in the face of Russian gas supply cuts. The EU's July 2022 imposition of sanctions on local Russian officials, such as Moscow Mayor Sergei Sobyanin, Sberbank, companies involved in the smuggling of Ukrainian grain and disinformation actors underscored its maxi-

mum pressure strategy towards Russia.[165] On 31 August, the
EU scrapped the 2007 visa facilitation agreement but Josep
Borrell's comment that a blanket visa ban was "not a good idea"
reflected polarisations amongst EU member states on this issue.
The U.S. extolled the cumulative impact of sanctions on the
Russian economy, which included a 70–90% market capitalisation decline, the suspension of Russian operations by 1,000
multinational companies, 20% inflation and a one-third decline
in the Russian stock market.[166]

On 2 September, the G7 imposed a price cap on Russian oil to
curb inflation and restrict Russia's ability to finance the Ukraine
War. The price cap was not fixed, as it would depend on market
conditions, and mitigation measures were introduced to help G7
countries that were especially dependent on Russian energy. The
G7's main point of leverage was insurance of Russian oil tankers,
since 90% of the insurance market is in the hands of Western
companies.[167] Russian deputy prime minister Alexander Novak
called the G7 price cap a "complete absurdity" and warned that
the costs of the price cap would be levelled on European and
American consumers.[168] Novak also stated that Russia was not
going to work in "non-market conditions," which meant that it
would not sell oil to G7 countries. The Russian state media also
attacked the G7 over its price cap; Sergei Savchuk published an
article entitled "The West has decided that oil prices are not high
enough and is preparing their growth," while RIA Novosti
warned of potential unrest in eastern Germany over the G7 oil
price cap.[169] As Russia's information war against the West intensified, it proceeded to cut off gas supply via Nord Stream on
2 September. Olaf Scholz's defiant response to Russia's retaliation, which included the claim that "Russia is not a reliable
partner in the energy sector",[170] prompted a firestorm of criticism in Moscow. Mikhail Ulyanov stated that "it is not Russia
who started to undermine normal trade and economic relations,

including in the field of energy" and stated it was "absolutely inappropriate" to justify Germany's politically motivated decisions by "questioning the reliability of Russia as a supplier."[171] Medvedev called Germany an "ENEMY of RUSSIA," which declared a hybrid war, and facetiously said "this uncle is surprised that the Germans have some minor problems with gas."[172] This caustic rhetoric paved the way for the Nord Stream leak and its fall-out in late September.

The Darya Dugina Assassination and the Path to Mobilisation

As Ukraine's counterattacks gained momentum and Russia's offensives stalled, Kyiv became increasingly assertive in striking Russian territory including Crimea. Since the first 24 hours of war, which saw Ukraine strike a border checkpoint in Tyotkino in Kursk Oblast and fire a Tochka-U at Millerovo airbase, Kyiv viewed Russian territory as a legitimate target to derail Moscow's offensive operations. On 1 April, Russia accused Ukrainian helicopters of striking a Rosneft-owned fuel depot in Belgorod. While Peskov declared that Kyiv's actions were incompatible with diplomacy, Ukraine denied the attack in an ambiguous fashion. Kuleba stated that he could "neither confirm nor deny Ukraine's involvement," while Danilov facetiously blamed the attack on the People's Republic of Belgorod.[173] On 25 April, Ukraine allegedly struck Bryansk, less than 100 miles northeast of the Ukrainian border, instigating a fire at a civilian facility with 10,000 tons of fuel and a military facility with 5,000 tons of fuel.[174] British armed forces minister James Heappey endorsed Ukraine's attacks on logistics lines, fuel supplies and ammunition depots inside Russia as "completely legitimate," and Russia's warnings to Britain of a "proportional response" did not deter Kyiv.[175] On 3 July, Ukraine allegedly carried out a missile attack on a residential facility in Belgorod which resulted in the deaths of three civilians. This attack was greeted with vitriol from hardline Russian lawmakers. Andrei Gurulyov proposed "razing the office of the President of Ukraine," while Senator Vladimir Dzhabarov warned that "targets will be chosen so that maximum damage is inflicted with minimal losses."[176]

Ukraine also struck Crimea in order to pre-empt Russian attacks on its territory. On 9 August, the Ukrainian air force attacked Saky airbase in Novofedorivka, Crimea, which resulted in the destruction of four Su-30M jets and seven Su-24 jets. While Zelensky acknowledged the attack in his nightly address, Ukraine was cautious about taking responsibility. Podolyak speculated that there could be "numerous scenarios" to explain the attack, while Arestovych attributed it to either Ukrainian long-range weapons or pro-Ukraine guerrillas in Crimea.[177] This attack was followed on 11 August by explosions near the Zyabrovka airfield in south-eastern Belarus, which is located 30km from Ukraine's border and housed Russian aircraft. Podolyak implied that these "technical accidents" were linked, and urged Russia to "forget about Ukraine, take off the uniform and leave."[178] Despite Medvedev's claims that an attack on Crimea would produce World War III or a "Judgement Day" response, Russia downplayed the Saky airbase attack and framed the explosions as an accident. The Ukrainian defence ministry revelled in Russia's meek response, quipping that Russians should "avoid smoking in undesignated areas." Kyiv-based defence expert Mykola Bielieskov believes that the Saky airbase attack was principally a successful act of psychological warfare, as Ukraine's strikes on Crimea did not result in an emphatic Russian retaliation. Bielieskov notes that the timing of the attack coincided with the Crimea Platform summit, which highlighted Zelensky's refrain that the Ukraine War began in Crimea and should end in Crimea.[179] Russia's relocation of Black Sea Fleet assets from Sevastopol to Novorossiyk after the Snake Island defeat compounded this perception, as it undercut Russia's image as a Black Sea power.[180]

The 20 August assassination of Darya Dugina in a car bombing on Mozhayskoye Highway outside Moscow after the "Tradition" annual festival in Moscow, further energised hardliners to escalate the Ukraine War. Dugina's role as chief editor of the Prigozhin-aligned United World International website and promotion of Russian disinformation through her high-profile trip to Azovstal had resulted in her being sanctioned by Britain on 4 July. Dugina's claims that Donbas would be willing to accept a "Eurasian Empire" and castigation of Western materialism mirrored her father's views, and it is unclear whether the assassination attempt aimed to target her, Dugin or both of them. After a swift investigation, the FSB declared on 22 August that "it has been established that the crime was prepared and committed by the Ukrainian special services" and concluded that Dugina had been the principal assassination target.[181] The main suspect was Ukrainian national Natalia Vovk, who had arrived in Russia with her twelve-year-old daughter and had been at the Tradition festival with the Dugins. The FSB claimed that Vovk used a DNR licence plate to enter Russia and a Kazakhstan licence plate in Moscow before switching to a Ukrainian licence plate to cross into Estonia. Vovk was aided by fellow Ukrainian Bogdan Tsyganenko, who helped her assemble the explosive device that carried out the car bombing of Dugina.[182] Russian Telegram accounts amplified the conspiracy that Vovk had served in the Azov Battalion, which was strenuously denied by the Azov Regiment. Ukrainian officials rejected Russia's assertions, with Oleksii Danilov stating that the FSB had carried out the killing to rally support for mobilisation against Ukraine and Podolyak claiming that "Russian propaganda lives in a fictional world."[183] Estonia described Russia's allegations of Vovk's flight as a "provocation" and stated that Russia had not asked Tallinn for assistance in its investigations of Dugina's death. The U.S. stated that it condemned the targeting of civilians after the Dugina assassination, but U.S. intelligence officials privately believed Ukraine was culpable and admonished Kyiv.[184]

The Dugina assassination triggered a coalescence of Russian official and state media rhetoric about hardline narratives, which featured calls for escalation and a mobilisation of Russian society. Zakharova stated that if Ukraine's hand in the assassination was confirmed, "we are talking about a policy of state terrorism carried out by the Kyiv regime."[185] This normalised the Just Russia—For Truth faction head Sergei Mironov's efforts to label Ukraine as a terrorist state and convert the "special military operation" into a counterterrorism operation. Mironov's counterterrorism operation plan would focus on destroying "the leaders of gangs and terrorist organisations" and eliminating the "criminal terrorist regime of Volodymyr Zelensky."[186] Conspiracies about foreign assistance to Ukraine's assassination plan against Dugina also spread widely. Dzhabarov threatened "tough measures against Estonia as a state sheltering a terrorist" for not extraditing Vovk.[187] In a veiled reference to the Skripal assassination, Simonyan predicted that Estonia would not extradite Vovk and that there were people in Russia who "wanted to admire the spires in the vicinity of Tallinn." On a 22 August episode of Skabeeva's Rossiya-1 show, Russian commentator Alexey Anpilogov claimed that Western intelligence agencies had helped Ukraine kill Dugina, as "they always kill valuable people who try to oppose the Western project." Korotchenko attributed the killing to Estonia, Britain and Ukraine working in tandem. Evstafiev claimed that "Britain is starting to play the role of European ISIS" and claimed that the British intelligence agencies and British monarchy had colluded to create instability in Europe. Later that evening, Solovyov declared that the British intelligence agencies viewed anyone who opposed Ukrainian Nazism as a "legitimate target," as their main goal was Russia's destruction. Solovyov's vocal support for these conspiracies was unsurprising, as Russia had detained six neo-Nazis for allegedly trying to assassinate him on 25 April. Putin linked this assassination attempt to Western countries, who also sought to kill Simonyan and Kiselyov.[188]

These conspiracies about Ukrainian terrorism and Western orchestration of Dugina's assassination were paired with calls to escalate the war. The Voenkor Kotenok Telegram channel shared an appeal from a DNR Vostok Battalion fighter urging Russia to declare a full-scale war against Ukraine.[189] Glazyev called for a "quick and decisive mobilisation of all the forces of the Russian world for speedy victory in Ukraine," and highlighted how Dugina's assassination had followed Yermak's comments about making the children and grandchildren of Russians pay for the war.[190] The death of Mikhail Gorbachev on 30 August emboldened Russia's hardliners further, as they denigrated his legacy. While Communist Party stalwarts lamented the Soviet Union's collapse, United Russia State Duma Deputy Vitaly Milonov claimed that Gorbachev's legacy was even worse than Hitler's for Russia.[191] Medvedev used Gorbachev's death to highlight how Russia's unity was more resilient than European colonial empires such as the British and Spanish, and warned that Western countries sought to take Russia back to the chaos of 1991 and oversee Russia's disintegration.[192] While Putin did not immediately take cues from hardliners, their pressure tactics following Dugina's assassination and consolidation after Gorbachev's death paved the way for partial mobilisation.

7

COUNTER-OFFENSIVE AND MOBILISATION

On 14 September, Volodymyr Zelensky made a surprise visit to Izyum and took part in a national flag-raising ceremony. Amidst the rubble, Zelensky announced, "The heroes are here. It means the enemy has gone, ran away" and resolutely declared that "It is definitely impossible to occupy our people, the Ukrainian people."[1] Zelensky's Izyum trip reflected the blistering pace of Ukraine's counter-offensive in Kharkiv Oblast, which saw Kyiv liberate 6,000 square kilometres of Russian-occupied territory in a matter of days. This extraordinarily successful counter-offensive was greeted with euphoria in Ukraine. Mykhailo Podolyak declared, "Just a few kilometres away from the frontline in liberated Izyum, Zelensky indicates specifically why Russia is shamefully and catastrophically losing the war. Has anyone at the 'long table' not understood yet?"[2] Taras Berezovets, a Bogun brigade special forces officer, described Ukraine's Kharkiv triumph as a "turning point for the whole war" and compared it to Nazi Germany's Stalingrad defeat, as it would impede Russia's ability to amount future offensives.[3] Although the Russian defence ministry claimed that it was "regrouping" forces from Kharkiv to

25

5

focus on the liberation of Donbas, criticisms of the war effort from pro-war hardliners intensified. Vladimir Putin responded to these criticisms by announcing the annexation of Donetsk, Luhansk, Zaporizhzhia and Kherson on 20 September, which were formalised by referenda days later, and announcing a policy of "partial mobilisation" in a televised address on 21 September.

This chapter examines Ukraine's multi-pronged counter-offensive, which saw Kyiv advance against Russian forces in Kharkiv, Kherson and Donbas in synchrony, and its contribution to the coalescence of the hardline bloc. It then examines Russia's partial mobilisation fiasco, which was undermined by illegal recruitments and poor training, and the annexation referenda that coincided with another strategic defeat in Lyman. The remainder of the chapter examines Ukraine's increasingly brazen counterattacks on Russian and Russian-occupied territory, which prompted Russia to escalate its assault on Ukrainian civilian infrastructure. It concludes by examining Russia's ongoing weaponisation of food, nuclear energy and natural gas, evidenced by its temporary suspension of the Black Sea grain export deal, continued shelling of ZNPP and response to the Nord Stream pipeline leak, and use of nuclear brinkmanship to present an image of strength at home and encourage de-escalation from Ukraine's NATO partners.

Ukraine's Multi-Directional Multi-Speed Counter-Offensive

On 29 August, Ukraine's Southern Military Command spokesperson Natalia Humeniuk announced the start of "offensive actions in different directions." Zelensky corroborated this statement, urging Russians to "run away, go home" and warning that "the occupiers must know we will chase them to the border."[4] Ukraine's counter-offensive achieved immediate successes in the Kherson direction, as the villages of Novodmytrivka, Arkhangelske,

Tomyna Balka and Pravdyne were swiftly recaptured. Arestovych confirmed that the Ukrainian armed forces had "broken through the frontlines in several sectors" and were shelling ferry crossing points that Russia used for resupply purposes in Kherson.[5] Russian troops reportedly retreated closer to the Dnipro River and were crossing its left bank.[6] Despite these initial break-throughs, Zelensky's closest allies primed the Ukrainian public for a protracted counter-offensive with uncertain outcomes. Arestyovch warned that Ukraine's counter-offensive would be a "slow operation to grind the enemy" and contended that limited funds prevented the swift liberation of cities. Podolyak urged Ukrainian experts, politicians and media personalities to avoid commenting on the counter-offensive before the Ukrainian military released official statements, as Zelensky sought to manage expectations.[7] Ukrainian military personnel prepared for "positional warfare" or an "imitation" counter-offensive, as Russia had an overwhelming advantage in missile capabilities and the efficacy of HIMARS in a full-scale counter-offensive was unclear.[8]

On 7 September, Valery Zaluzhny publicly revealed the scope and objectives of the counter-offensive.[9] He argued that the most significant Russian military threat to Ukraine emanated from the south, as Russia could use advances along this axis to threaten Odesa, Mykolaiv, Kryvyi Rih and eventually central and western Ukraine. Zaluzhny highlighted Russia's control over Crimea, which allowed for nationwide strikes, and strength along the Zaporizhzhia axis via the Gulyai Pole as significant threats. To counter these Russian threats, Zaluzhny proposed assembling 10–20 combined military brigades and neutralising Russia's 2,000km missile strike range through securing equipment such as MGM-140B ATACMS Block 1A surface-to-surface missiles. These NATO-style arms deliveries would be paired with indig-enous Ukrainian weapons development, including the domestic production of long-range missiles. By collapsing the gravitational centre of Russia's military operations and carrying out Saky air-base-style strikes that inflicted pain on Russia, Zaluzhny hoped to achieve decisive breakthroughs in 2023 and prevent Russian long-range missile strikes from creating a years-long war.

Although it initially described Ukraine's counterattacks as increased "kinetic activity" rather than a counter-offensive, the U.S. Department of Defense was increasingly optimistic about Ukraine's prospects. Ukraine's effective force concentrations on the southern flank and Russia's manpower shortages gave it the resources it needed for a counter-offensive, while superior morale and the growing efficacy of Ukrainian air attacks weakened Russia's position further.[10] Due to these advantages, optimistic predictions from U.S. military figures like General Ben Hodges, who predicted that Ukraine could recapture Crimea by mid-2023, began to circulate. U.S. officials also believed that the rate of Ukrainian progress during the first week of the Kherson offensive could lead to its liberation by the end of 2022.[11] Ukraine's decision to downgrade its multi-axis counter-offensive into a southern-focused counterattack was greeted favourably by the Pentagon, which highlighted overextension risks in war games with Kyiv.[12]

Russia denied Ukraine's capacity for effective counterattacks. Immediately after Humeniuk's counter-offensive announcement, the Russian ministry of defence claimed that Ukraine had launched unsuccessful offensives in Mykolaiv and Kherson, which had cost it 560 personnel, 26 tanks and 2 Su-25 jets.[13] On 31 August, Stremousov declared, "The comical counter-offensive, which grew into traffic losses among the people driven into the trenches by the Nazis, ends again before even starting," and vowed that Kherson would become Russian territory.[14] On 5 September, Stremousov repeated this assertion and increased his Ukrainian casualty estimates from 1,000 to 3,000.[15] Russian defence analysts believed that Ukraine's counter-offensive was a symbolic display of Kyiv's ability to strike Russian territory, which built on its attacks on Crimea, shelling of Donetsk and Dugina's murder.[16] Vassily Kashin contended that Ukraine's counter-offensive in Kherson was unlikely to be as effective as its advances on Kharkiv in May and contended that Kyiv was using counterattacks to derail a referendum on joining Russia. Kashin stated that HIMARS were unlikely to be a game-changer for Ukrainian forces in Kherson as they are not particularly effective in striking stationary buildings and contended that Ukraine's extensive use of HIMARS could be due to diminished stocks of domestic Vilkha MLRS systems and Tochka-Us.[17] Igor Girkin was a relative outlier in predicting trouble for the Russian military in Kherson. Girkin highlighted Ukraine's "powerful artillery grouping," showcased the failure of Russian troops to transfer even light military equipment like the Tigr armoured car to Kherson and warned that Ukraine had expanded its bridge-hand on the southern bank of the Inhulets River, which would allow it to advance in the Beryslav direction.[18]

Ukraine's battlefield progress in Kherson was slow but steady. Ukrainian forces broadened the frontlines in Kherson to over 100 miles in width as they tried to prevent Russian troops from concentrating, and escalated sabotage attacks on pro-Russian collaborators.[19] The ultimate aim of Ukraine's southern offensive was to seize control over territories in the north and west of the Dnipro River and liberate the city of Kherson. Ukraine also wanted to secure control of the Nova Kakhovka hydroelectric plant and the North Crimean Canal, which Russia had occupied on the first day of the war, as Russia had destroyed a dam on the canal to divert Dnipro River water to Crimea. The most expedient path for Ukraine to achieve these goals was to avoid a costly urban warfare operation and force a surrender of Russian troops by closing their supply lines.[20] Beyond its sporadic capture of villages, Ukraine made noteworthy progress towards enhancing its battlefield position in Kherson. British intelligence estimates revealed that Ukraine had established three lines of attack on Kherson by 3 September. While the Russian defence ministry denied that Ukraine had established positions on the Kherson–Mykolaiv border, Russian Telegram channels claimed that two of Ukraine's offensive axes were in this region.[21] Russia's late August small-scale offensive in southern Ukraine, which saw it record gains in Mykolaiv's towns of Blahodatne and Vasylky, completely lost momentum. Stremousov's urgent attendance at a "communicative leadership seminar" in Voronezh on 30 August was viewed as a symbolic sign of growing insecurity amongst Russia's occupation authorities.

Despite its apparent commitment to a southern-centric counter-offensive, Ukraine stealthily prepared for a blitzkrieg liberation of Kharkiv. On 6 September, Ukraine began offensive operations in Balakliia, which resulted in the swift capture of twenty settlements 50km into Russian territory and swiftly took over Kupiansk and Izyum. The pace of Ukraine's advance was surprising, as Zaluzhny was unsure whether Ukraine could durably hold Izyum and U.S. chairman of the Joint Chiefs of Staff Mark Milley predicted "steady and deliberate" progress due to Ukraine's limited reserves.[22] Berezovets called the Kherson counter-offensive a "big special disinformation operation," as Ukraine had caught Russian forces by surprise and forced them to flee.[23] Ukrainian forces aggressively targeted pro-Russian collaborators in Kharkiv, who were undercover as Ukrainian civilians, which further limited the Russian military's intelligence capabilities. Due to their swift departure, Russian forces left between ten and eleven T-80 tanks behind in serviceable condition, as Izyum was a key repair hub for armoured vehicles, and a marooned 2S19 Msta self-propelled howitzer.[24] The euphoria in Ukraine about expelling Russia from Kharkiv was tempered by the discovery of mass graves in Izyum on 15 September. These graves contained the bodies of 447 civilians, including 30 with observable signs of torture, men with amputated genitalia and corpses with ropes around their necks, bound hands, broken limbs and gunshot wounds.[25] Zelensky accused Russia of committing genocide in Izyum. This case was strengthened further by the discovery of ten torture chambers on 16 September and Zelensky's 26 September assertion that Ukrainian forces had discovered two more mass graves in Izyum. The Russian media countered these war crimes allegations by highlighting alleged Ukrainian human rights abuses. Colonel Gennady Alekhin claimed that Ukraine was carrying out "filtration" in Kharkiv, while pro-Russian Kharkiv governor Vitaly Ganchev warned, "Repressive actions have already begun, and people need to hide."[26] Ukraine's crackdown on Russian language teachers created a ready-made opening for Russian propagandists to frame the expulsion of Russians from occupied territories as devastating for the local population.

As Ukrainian forces swept through occupied Kharkiv, Russian officials downplayed the scale of their impending defeat. Kupiansk district chief Maxim Gubin claimed on 9 September that "Russian troops are holding positions, the city is in fairly safe conditions" and stated that the local authorities were planning a three to four day civilian evacuation, which would last until the situation stabilised.[27] These unrealistic claims were openly countered on Russian Telegram. The Wagner Group-aligned Reverse Side of the Medal Telegram channel warned that Ukraine could launch a counter-offensive on Balakliia on 30 August and covered Russia's defeat in considerable depth.[28] Russian hardliners responded to the Kharkiv defeat in divergent ways. A Postovo Telegram post spun Ukraine's Kharkiv triumph as a pyrrhic victory, stating: "The enemy, buying into an easy advance on a given sector of the front, drives him into a trap."[29] Kadyrov's tone was defiant, as he vowed to recapture liberated areas of Kharkiv and claimed that "We will reach Odesa in the near future."[30] Other pro-war Telegram channels were overtly critical of the Russian defence ministry. Girkin's tone was especially downcast, as he stated, "The war in Ukraine will continue until the complete defeat of Russia. We have already lost. The rest is just a matter of time," and warned that "If the Kremlin elders do not change their tactics, we will be seeing catastrophic defeats" in the next two to three months.[31]

Girkin's criticisms of the Russian defence ministry and military top brass were echoed on other pro-war Telegram channels. A widely shared Holmogor Talks Telegram post bemoaned Russia's inability to summon the spirit of 1812, which saw its superior resolve defeat Napoleon, and stated that "there is no clear message not to retreat, not to give up, to win."[32] Oleg Tsaryov struck a similar tone, as he stated that Kharkiv residents believed politicians who said that Russia would never abandon them, only to find that "the military did not convince that Russia came forever."[33] Defence analyst Alexander Kots lambasted institutionalised dishonesty within the Russian system, as "bosses don't like bad news" and "subordinates don't like to upset bosses."[34]

Russia's defeat in Kharkiv coincided with military setbacks elsewhere on the frontlines. Russian shelling of Kupiansk, which persisted in the days following the Kharkiv defeat, did not stem the momentum of Ukraine's north-eastern counter-offensive. In Kherson, Putin personally intervened to prevent a military withdrawal, as Ukrainian forces reportedly captured Kyselivka.[35] This built on a 16 May report, which revealed that Putin coordinated with Gerasimov at the level of a "colonel or a brigadier" on tactical wartime decisions, and persistent speculation that the military top brass routinely bypassed Shoigu to consult with Putin.[36] Russia attempted to slow Ukraine's advance by blowing up a dam on the Inhulets River, which flooded parts of the Kherson frontline. On 19 September, Ukraine captured Bilohorivka, a suburb of Lysychansk, which ensured that Russia no longer had complete control of Luhansk. LNR officials deployed "snatch squads" to conscript men from the street and jammed mobile communications to conceal Russian military setbacks.[37] Pasechnik's 15 September admission that Ukrainian forces had achieved "certain successes" and were at the gates of Luhansk underscored unease amongst the LNR leadership. Ukraine's growing assertiveness was evidenced by its 12 September attack on Donetsk International Airport, which was repelled by the DNR's Sparta Battalion.[38] The stagnation of Russia's battle-field progress in Donetsk frustrated hardliners. Girkin openly questioned whether Russia's announced attacks in Bakhmut were taking place and postulated that Russian troops could be preparing for a "withdrawal to more advantageous positions."[39] Zuganov proclaimed that the "issue of victory in Donbas is the issue of our historical survival" and stated that the special military operation had become a full-fledged war.[40] The deteriorating Russian military situation across the frontlines moved Putin to carry out partial mobilisation.

Partial Mobilisation: Putin's High-Stakes Gambit to Forestall Defeat

Although Russia's manpower shortages became increasingly apparent, Putin resisted pressure from hardliners to carry out a general mobilisation. Russian experts explain Putin's restraint along several lines. Alexei Miller noted that pro-war sentiments in urban areas were attributable to the war's limited impact on daily life.[41] Dmitry Suslov believed that Putin resisted pro-mobilisation arguments because he knew that Russian youths were used to "the comforts of Western life" and would be opposed to direct participation in the war.[42] The historical precedent of the 1904–5 Russo-Japanese War, which saw severe public backlash against Tsar Nicholas II's conscription policies, was more relevant than successful mobilisation drives such as during the Napoleonic Wars and the Second World War. While Miller acknowledged massive changes in Russian society due to the Ukraine War, Carnegie Moscow Center expert Alexander Baunov did not see these changes as a reversion to Brezhnev-era norms. Baunov noted that the Russian public was extremely sensitised to state intrusions into private space and was only passively acceptant of ideological justifications for war.[43] Victor Olevich contended that mobilisation would require extensive equipment production for new troops at short notice and conceded it was unclear whether factories could produce what was required. Russian propagandists framed Ukraine's mobilisation as leading to mass casualties, and the Talipo V Telegram channel described it an "insane and thoughtless" policy that Russia should not replicate.[44]

Due to its fear of social backlash and the potential impracticalities of mobilisation, the Kremlin resorted to unconventional measures to increase its troop presence in Ukraine and achieve Putin's stated goal of expanding the Russian armed forces by 137,000 troops from 2023. On 20 May, Russian State Duma Defence Committee chair Andrei Kartapolov removed the 18–40 age limit on Russian soldiers, which allowed the Kremlin to recruit volunteers from 2 million reservists with combat experience.[45] Russia's use of "third battalions," which consist of personnel who handle training and are not typically deployed to a combat zone, gave it an additional 30–40 BTGs. This practice began in mid-May, as Pentagon estimates of Russian BTG deployments in Ukraine increased from 106 to 110 from 16–26 May, even though Russia lost 1–2 BTGs in its abortive crossing of the Siversky Donets River.[46] These third battalion fighters were often saddled with antiquated equipment such as T-62 tanks. As the war progressed, Russia formed volunteer battalions in Novosibirsk, Saratov, Ulyanovsk and Kurgan Oblasts to ease its manpower shortfalls. In late July, the Kremlin announced plans to recruit 30,000 additional volunteer fighters for the war effort and pressured all 85 Russian regions to take part.

Propaganda campaigns such as the Rostov "Military Service on a Contract—the Choice of a Real Man" crusade included the use of colour brochure hand-outs to entice potential recruits.[47] Salaries, which ranged from $2,700 in Rostov to $5,000 per month in Kirov and Perm, greatly exceeded the norm in Russian regions. The excessive costs of these recruitment efforts, which added $2 million to Krasnoyarsk's budget alone and the allowance for only one month of training at Mulino near Nizhny Novgorod, caused these campaigns to be unsustainable and eroded Russia's military efficacy.[48] Russia's creation of the 3rd Army Corps in June 2022, which was overseen by the Western Military District and had a planned strength of 15,000–60,000 forces, was expected to convert these volunteer battalions into a concentrated military force. The 3rd Army Corps was expected to draw manpower from volunteer battalions and recruited forces aged 18–50 with a middle or high school education and prior military experience.[49] Although the 3rd Army Corps possessed more modern equipment, such as T-80BV and T-90M tanks, its reliance on older men and the pervasiveness of alcoholics and drug addicts in its ranks weakened its efficacy.[50] The chaotic retreat of 3rd Army Corps forces from Kharkiv and the failure of these units to stabilise the frontlines on 9 September further eviscerated their effectiveness.

Yevgeny Prigozhin capitalised on these setbacks to enhance his contribution to Russia's war effort and bolster his profile. In mid-July, a billboard was erected in Yekaterinburg stating "The W Orchestra Awaits You," and featured a promotional video of Wagner Group activities in Syria.[51] While this billboard was taken down, the Wagner Group's military exploits were more openly discussed in the Russian media and Putin awarded

Prigozhin a Hero of Russia award. Prigozhin personally travelled to penal colonies such as Tambov, 300 miles outside Moscow, and offered convicts amnesty after six months of service in high-risk conditions.[52] Prisoners were offered a salary of 100,000 roubles a month, but Prigozhin warned that drinking, drug use, looting and desertion in Ukraine would be punishable with execution.[53] The scale of the Wagner Group's recruitment efforts elevated Prigozhin's importance to the war effort. On 19 September, a senior U.S. official revealed that the Wagner Group was planning to recruit 1,500 convicted felons to Russia's war effort. Estimates from prisoners' rights NGO Jailed Russia showed that 11,000 convicts had signed up to the war in Ukraine and the Wagner Group's recruitment drives transported 600 prisoners from Nizhny Novgorod in one sitting.[54] By mid-August, Wagner Group representatives had visited 21 penal colonies in 13 Russian regions and 20% of prisoners requested to serve by Wagner had accepted.[55] As prisoners could only receive a legal military exemption from their sentence if an order was issued from the Russian defence ministry, the Wagner Group's promises of amnesty were disingenuous.

Prigozhin's personal role in recruiting prisoners was confirmed by a 14 September video released by Alexei Navalny's team.[56] The video featured Prigozhin claiming that the Wagner Group fires artillery at a rate two-and-a-half times the pace of the Battle of Stalingrad and boasting about how convicts had stormed the Uhledar heating plant in Donetsk.[57] Prigozhin was candid about the risk of fatalities, as he highlighted the deaths of three prisoners in Uhledar, and asked prisoners to either send themselves or their children to the frontlines. Prigozhin gave prisoners five minutes to decide whether they would accept the Wagner Group's offer to serve in Ukraine. Concord Management and Consulting, the catering company that Prigozhin founded in St. Petersburg in 1995, confirmed the video's authenticity and extolled

Prigozhin's successful support for the "special military opera-tion."[58] Despite numerous lawsuits against media figures linking him to the Wagner Group, Prigozhin admitted his links to the PMC on 26 September. Prigozhin claimed that in 2014, many Russian businessmen had been interested in forming a PMC to stop the Donbas genocide, but "swindlers" and the recruitment of untrained volunteers had derailed these efforts. Prigozhin stated that he had founded the Wagner Group on 1 May 2014 by personally recruiting military specialists, and had enhanced the DNR and LNR's battlefield positions. Prigozhin extolled Wagner Group PMCs as "one of the pillars of the Motherland" for their campaigns in Syria, the Arab world, Latin America and Africa.[59]

These unconventional recruitment measures did not solve Russia's manpower deficit. The Russian military refused to pay some volunteers the promised 8,000 roubles of "combat pay," citing lost banking information, and did not facilitate their trans-portation back from the front. Revelations of the poor treatment of volunteers in the Russian armed forces slowed recruitment, as did reports that police officers without combat experience were leading brigades.[60] The U.S.'s 8 August assessment that Russia had suffered 70,000–80,000 deaths or injuries in the Ukraine War underscored the gravity of the challenges facing Putin. In response to these failures, Kadyrov called for Russian regions to carry out "self-mobilisation" on 15 September.[61] Kadyrov set a 1,000 troops per region target, which would generate 85,000 new personnel for the Russian military, and urged regional governors not to wait for the Kremlin to declare martial law. Peskov declined to endorse Kadyrov's self-mobilisation plan, as he stated that it needed to be assessed by military professionals. Never-theless, Kemerovo Oblast governor Sergei Tsivilev swiftly fol-lowed Kadyrov's lead, while Sergiy Aksyonov announced that Crimea had mobilised 1,200 troops and Kursk governor Roman Starovoit announced that 800 troops had been mobilised.[62]

Girkin viewed Kadyrov's self-mobilisation proposal as insufficient and hyperbolically warned that unless Russia achieved a military victory, it would have to undertake diplomatic negotiations that would lead to Ukraine and NATO forcing it to withdraw from all territories west of the Urals.[63]

Despite escalation pressure, Putin's pursuit of mobilisation was not a foregone conclusion even in the hours leading up to his 21 September address. The Rybar Telegram channel stated that the focus of Putin's speech would likely be on the status of liberated territories, and self-mobilisation and placing the economy on a war footing would likely be as far as Putin would go.[64] Notwithstanding these expectations, Putin ultimately accepted a Russian defence ministry plan for partial mobilisation of reservists with "military skills and relevant experience." Putin highlighted grave threats to Russia's security, and warned that "Today, our armed forces are operating across a frontline that exceeds 1,000km, opposing not only neo-Nazi formations but the entire military machine of the collective West." Shoigu supported Putin's rationales for mobilisation and emphasised that the 300,000 forces requested were only 1% of Russia's available manpower resources.[65] Russian state media and hardliners enthusiastically rallied behind partial mobilisation. Defence analyst Konstantin Sokolov contended that mobilisation was justified, as Ukraine had numerical superiority and units that consisted largely of foreign mercenaries. Sokolov argued that mobilisation would subsume Ukraine, which had only one million men that could be armed, while Russia had 25 million.[66] Kadyrov declared that "Today's appeal to Russians by the Supreme Commander-in-chief Vladimir Putin has put the Kyiv elite and the entire NATO into a hopeless situation."[67] Ukraine responded defiantly to Putin's partial mobilisation order and expressed optimism that it would prevail in spite of Russia's escalation. Zelensky quipped that Russian cadets were "guys who couldn't fight" and stated that Putin wanted to "drown Ukraine in blood, but also in the blood of his own soldiers."[68] Arestovych stated that Russia had declared partial mobilisation to replenish its lost soldiers but 150,000 of the 300,000 troops recruited would likely become casualties.[69]

Russia's Partial Mobilisation Drive Descends into Chaos

Despite initial optimism, Russia's partial mobilisation campaign immediately descended into chaos, as it was significantly more expansive than was officially announced. On 23 September, Meduza reported that 1.2 million Russians were slated for conscription, which included 16,000 from Moscow and 3,200 from St. Petersburg, and sweeping drafts in rural areas due to pro-war sentiments and limited opposition.[70] Minority regions were especially affected. As 3,000 draft papers were handed out in Buryatia, Siberia in the 24 hours after mobilisation began, Free Buryatia Foundation president Alexandra Garmazhapova stated that "It's not a partial mobilisation, it's a 100% mobilisation."[71] Kadyrov insisted that Chechnya would not mobilise citizens as it had surpassed its targets by 254% and commemorated this achievement by holding a pro-war rally in Grozny. This trend was consistent with disproportionate casualties in minority regions, as one-quarter of the fatalities in the first month of the war came from Buryatia, Dagestan and Tuva.[72] Despite allegations of ethnic cleansing, Baunov disputed this categorisation, as financial incentives led to voluntary military participation in Dagestan and informal civil society activism is often conflated with ethnic agitation.[73] Russia also aggressively mobilised Crimean Tatars for war. Police raids in majority Tatar villages followed Putin's speech and 80% of Crimea's draft notices were handed to Tatars even though they constituted 13% of Crimea's population.[74] On 23 September, Zelensky deplored this policy as a "deliberate attempt to destroy the Crimean Tatar people." Tamila Tasheva, Zelensky's Permanent Representative to Crimea, described this policy as the culmination of eight years of illegal mobilisations of Crimean Tatars under the Geneva Convention.[75] As Russia conducted fifteen illegal conscription campaigns in Crimea from 2014–22, drafting 30,000 people, and full mobilisation was announced in DNR and LNR on 19 February, the Kremlin could draw upon a large-scale conscription infrastructure in occupied Ukraine.[76] The recruitment of Russians with medical conditions, such as a 63-year-old man with diabetes and a severe brain injury, and students in Buryatia, underscored the absence of rules governing the process.

Initially, Russian propagandists downplayed the problems associated with partial mobilisation. On her 23 September Rossiya-1 show, Skabeeva claimed that mobilisation would only apply to soldiers and sergeants under age 35, junior officers under age 50 and senior officers under age 55. Skabeeva stated that men in Chechnya and Dagestan were "following their heart" to the enlistment office and stated that 10,000 people had voluntarily mobilised the day after Putin's speech. As the challenges besetting Russia's mobilisation drive became more apparent, they were openly discussed on state TV. On his 26 September Rossiya-1 show, Solovyov said, "We have one million unemployed in Moscow. Why draft the people who have jobs, especially those working for crucial enterprises? If there are sixteen houses in a village and they get five draft notices, what is that for? Why? To turn it into an uninhabited village. Every idiot in those positions who decided to call up a musician, or a person who has minor illnesses or to approach a student despite yesterday's decree explaining exemptions ... Such a person should not be punished, he should be the first to be sent to the frontlines." Solovyov notably absolved Putin of blame for the excesses of mobilisation, as he attacked officials who sought to besmirch the president.

COUNTER-OFFENSIVE AND MOBILISATION

In response to Solovyov's monologue, Margarita Simonyan questioned why "warrior guys" in her network with battlefield experience in Syria and Chechnya were not called up by the Russian defence ministry and said that they were considering voluntary enlistment. Simonyan also offered to assist victims of illegal mobilisation on her Telegram feed and proposed issuing a credit amnesty for mobilised Russians.[77] These concerns were shared by senior Russian officials. Matviyenko claimed that the "harsh reaction we are seeing in society is deserved," while Volodin vowed to correct all wrongful mobilisations.[78] Putin acknowledged these "mistakes" on 29 September and Sobyanin personally oversaw mobilisation in Moscow to reassure critics.

Shortages of military equipment were a further source of humiliation for Russia's mobilisation campaign. A viral video showed a Russian conscript claiming that he had received body armour that lacked bullet resistance. The prices of bullet-proof vests soared 500% to 50,000 roubles each, which was equivalent to a monthly salary in Bryansk.[79] On a 3 October episode of Skabeeva's Rossiya-1 show, Mikhail Khodaryonok proclaimed that "mobilisation is the face of the nation" and claimed that Russia's reputation depended on conscripts possessing proper equipment. These concerns were also embraced by lawmakers, as Andrey Kartapalov and State Duma Anti-Corruption Committee chairman Vasily Piskarev launched an inquiry on 5 October about equipment supply shortages on the frontlines. Peskov admitted that regional budgets were unable to cover the sudden expansion of mobilisation costs but insisted that cooperation with federal authorities would swiftly remedy the crisis.[80]

Due to endemic procedural violations in Russia's mobilisation campaign, popular unrest and mass emigration ensued. During the first five days of mobilisation, over 2,000 Russian demonstrators were arrested and 700 were jailed on 25 September alone. These demonstrators overlapped partially with the anti-war demonstrations in March, as some participants called for an end to the Ukraine War.[81] Alexei Navalny's video message on mobilisation, which included the phrase "It is clear the criminal war is getting worse, deepening and Putin is trying to involve as many people as possible in this," energised anti-war liberals.[82] The Vesna opposition movement called for nationwide protests. Unrest even spread to Chechnya, as an anti-war rally was held in Grozny on 21 September. Kadyrov downplayed these protests as a gathering of 15–20 women who were "paid by European organisations" but the Chechen authorities detained women involved in the unrest and forced their sons to fight on the frontlines.[83]

Chechnya's use of repression and propaganda set the tone for the Kremlin response. The Russian authorities sent anti-mobilisation protesters to the frontlines, punished draft-dodgers with fifteen years in prison and threatened Central Asian migrants with loss of citizenship if they refused to serve.[84] The Russian interior ministry described anti-mobilisation protests which erupted in Moscow, St. Petersburg and Yekaterinburg as "unauthorised actions" that brought together an "extremely small number of participants."[85] Arestovych's incitement of anti-mobilisation protests also gave the Kremlin ammunition to claim that the unrest was Ukrainian-backed.[86] Putin's surrogates also rallied public support for mobilisation. Patriarch Kirill called for "spiritual mobilisation" which would facilitate the complete reconciliation of Russia and Ukraine. Kirill urged Russian Orthodox Christians of true faith not to fear death on the battlefield, stating, "Go bravely to fulfil your military duty. And remember that if you lay down your life for your country, you will be with God in the kingdom, glory and eternal life."[87] Four United Russia State Duma Deputies, Dmitry Khubezov, Vitaly Milonov, Dmitry Sabin and Sergey Sokol, requested to fight on the frontlines. Kadyrov vowed to send three of his teenage sons to the frontlines, while Aksyonov's son immediately joined the war effort.

Dagestan was the most significant long-term epicentre of popular unrest. Babayurt district residents blocked a federal highway on 22 September and protests swiftly diffused to Khasavyurt and Makhachkala. Ethnic tensions between Avars, who primarily staffed the military commissions, and Kumyks, who were sent to fight in the war even if they had just returned from service, intensified in Dagestan.[88] These ethnic hostilities were paired with groundswells of anti-government dissent. A viral video showed a Russian enlistment office employee urging Dagestani men to "fight for the future," which was greeted with the response "Future? We don't even have a present." Another video showed Dagestani women chasing away a lone policeman at an anti-mobilisation protest and included condemnations of Russian aggression towards Ukraine.[89] To mollify popular anger, Dagestan governor Sergei Melikov admitted that "mistakes have been made" during mobilisation. The Russian media accused "pseudo-Dagestanis" of instigating unrest through psychological warfare and claimed that a detained woman was a Ukrainian citizen wearing a hijab.[90] Makhachkala mayor Salman Dadaev accused "destructive anti-state forces" of fuelling opposition rallies. This did not immediately quell unrest in Makhachkala, which has 18% of Dagestan's population, but prevented large-scale protests in rural Dagestan and the region's Sufi and Wahhabi communities.[91] The leaderless grassroots nature of Dagestan's protests, which were driven by underground Telegram networks, forestalled a renewed insurgency and ensured that Melikov could continue large-scale mobilisation.

Immediately after the partial mobilisation decree was announced, lines of cars with conscription-aged men appeared on Russia's eastern, southern and western borders. Finnish border guards reported that traffic from Russia more than doubled in the first 48 hours after mobilisation, while it took 12 hours for Russians to cross the Georgian border.[92] Within a week of Putin's mobilisation speech, over 200,000 Russians had emigrated. Russian commentators responded by either denying the scale of emigration, highlighting the costs of fleeing or condemning Russians fleeing conscription as unpatriotic. Former Kremlin advisor Sergei Markov claimed that only 80,000 Russians had left for the front, as net emigration to Georgia was 16,000 and to Kazakhstan was 30,000.[93] Tsargrad columnist Andrey Perla described "political emigrants" as "real traitors to the Motherland."[94] On her 27 September show, Skabeeva claimed that Russians fleeing mobilisation at the Lars checkpoint near Georgia would be greeted by a "mobile enlistment office." Belarusian commentator Vadim Gigin emphasised that Belarus would deport Russian deserters due to the Union State treaty, while Skabeeva claimed that Kazakhstan would similarly return "wanted" Russians. Girkin warned that draft dodgers created a schism in Russian society between "first-class citizens" with the funds to escape and "cattle" who could not. Girkin urged Russia to consider using deserters for "heavy penal work at the front."[95] Despite these sentiments, Sergei Tsekov's proposal to ban all Russian men of military age from travelling abroad did not gain traction, as the Kremlin shied away from the sweeping implementation of martial law.[96]

Russia Annexes Four Ukrainian Regions Via Pseudo-Referendums

Despite Russia's military struggles in Donbas and southern Ukraine, the Kremlin spoke openly about annexing occupied regions of Ukraine. On 10 April, Viktor Vodolatsky had claimed that 99.9% of residents in Donetsk and Luhansk would vote for unification with Russia if a referendum was held.[97] On 7 September, Andrey Turchak called for referenda in Donetsk, Luhansk and many other Russian cities to be held on 4 November, which is Russia's Day of National Unity, and declared that "the Russian world, now divided by formal borders, will regain its integrity."[98]

While the intention to hold annexation referenda was universally shared amongst Putin's allies, the process of incorporating occupied Ukrainian territory into the Russian Federation was disputed. On 11 May, Stremousov called for Russia's outright annexation of Kherson, as he stated that no Kherson People's Republic would form and there would be no referendum.[99] Turchak appeared to endorse Stremousov's proposal by stating that "Russia is here to stay forever" but Peskov dismissed it, as he stated that a Crimea-style expression of the people's will in Kherson was a necessary precondition for annexation. In late March, Pushilin and Pasechnik insisted that the DNR and LNR would only hold referenda to join Russia after the war was complete.[100] This view was broadly shared within the Russian presidential administration, which feared the annexation of "depressed regions", but Putin overruled these objections as he pushed for a swift annexation timetable.[101] While referenda in Donetsk and Luhansk were initially considered for late April, 14–15 May and mid-July, these votes were repeatedly postponed due to the uncertain security situation.

In the months leading up to the annexation referenda, Russia made numerous preparations for votes. On 7 June, Sergei Kiriyenko visited Kherson to discuss the distribution of Russian passports to local residents and Melitopol to begin preparations for a referendum in Zaporizhzhia.[102] Kiriyenko's trips underscored his leadership role in organising the referenda. He assembled a team to develop "the image of Russia after the war" and burnished Russia's soft power in occupied Ukraine through "patronage" investments overseen by Russian municipal authorities.[103] Under Kiriyenko's "Donbas project," Moscow pledged to oversee the reconstruction of Donetsk and Luhansk, St. Petersburg vowed to rebuild Mariupol, Khabarovsk took responsibility for Debaltseve, and Novosibirsk was accountable for Belovodsky in Luhansk.[104] Kiriyenko also spearheaded a "Leaders of Russia" competition on 29 May which would aid in the selection of long-term occupation authorities.[105] Kiriyenko's proactive role was rumoured to be a bid to succeed Putin and his ability to convince Putin not to postpone the September 2022 gubernatorial elections further bolstered his status.[106] Surkov ally Boris Rapoport and Kiriyenko associate Alexander Kharichev, senior officials in the State Council Affairs Department, appointed political technologists to prepare for referenda in Donbas.[107] The Kremlin also devised plans to replace Pushilin and Pasechnik with Russian officials, as concerns grew that the DNR and LNR chiefs could misuse Russian funds to Donetsk and Luhansk.[108] Russia's long-term aim was to convert occupied Ukrainian territories into a Russian federal district, which would receive considerable financial inflows overseen by Kiriyenko.[109] Ganchev proposed a Russian annexation referendum in Kharkiv on 8 July and deputy head of the Kherson Civilian-Military Administration Ekaterina Gubareva proposed a referendum in occupied Mykolaiv on 8 August. Protests in Snihurivka, Mykolaiv and Russia's occupation of only 20% of Kharkiv prior to Ukraine's counter-offensive derailed these plans.

Ukraine viewed Russia's annexation referenda plans as an illegal action that would derail future peace negotiations. A senior Ukrainian official stated that "the word referendum should not be applied to events in the occupied territories," as referenda cannot be held during war under Ukrainian law and there is no framework in Russian law to hold referenda in occupied Ukraine.[110] The official described the referenda as a "special information operation" and warned that Russian occupiers were harvesting personal data from citizens to compensate for low turnout at polling stations.[111] Partisan resistance, which was complemented by GUR and Ukrainian defence ministry operations, countered

Russia's referendum preparations. On 5 September, the GUR carried out a "special operation" in Kamianets-Dniprovska, Zaporizhzhia, which destroyed a facility storing referendum ballots and inflicted casualties on FSB officers guarding the ballots.[112] To counter Ukraine's delegitimisation of Russia's annexation referenda, the Russian occupation authorities tried to co-opt the local population with economic incentives. In Zaporizhzhia, Russia provided benefits to Melitopol residents in exchange for personal details, gifted 10,000 roubles to parents to send children to Russian schools, used the "We are Together with Russia" headquarters to provide flour and bottled water, and provided electric stoves to compensate for gas shortages.[113] These patronage provisions distracted Zaporizhzhia residents from Russia's shelling of ZNPP, threats of fines and deportations of parents who did not send their children to Russian schools and bans on the import of medical and sanitation products.[114]

Russia's referenda were marred with blatant voting irregularities and produced implausibly high levels of support for annexation. For "safety reasons," Russian occupation authorities encouraged local residents to vote from their homes and only allowed polling station votes on the final day of the referendum.[115] Alexey Koshel, the head of Ukraine's Committee of Voters, described Russia's home voting procedure as follows: "Imagine four armed men walk into your flat. You have to vote to join Russia at gunpoint. If you refuse or vote 'no,' you'll be doing it right in front of them, they can see what you put on the ballot."[116] The questionnaire process did not allow local residents to vote to stay part of Ukraine and due to 2020 legislation in DNR and LNR, voting papers in Donbas were only in the Russian language.[117] The official results for joining Russia were as follows: 99.23% support in Donetsk, 98.42% in Luhansk, 87.0% in Kherson and 93.11% in Zaporizhzhia. On 30 September, Putin announced the annexation of all four regions in an address to both houses of the Russian parliament. The Federation Council ratified Russia's annexations on 4 October, which was followed by the State Duma's announcement on 5 October that Putin had signed four constitutional laws on the accession of territories to Russia. As Russia did not fully control any of the occupied territories, the Kremlin-designated boundaries for the annexed republics were unclear. On 3 October, Peskov stated that Kherson and Zaporizhzhia's borders would be determined by consultations with local residents.[118] Mirroring other hardliners, Tsaryov rejected Peskov's interpretation by claiming that the entire borders of the annexed republics were incorporated into Russia by the State Duma's decree.[119]

Russian media outlets greeted the annexations in a celebratory manner. RIA Novosti interviewed Yulia Sycheva, a woman from Makiivka, Donetsk, living in Voronezh, who made the following proclamation: "Emotions are overflowing, incredible joy! Supreme! I am very happy! We have been waiting for this since 2014."[120] While Putin denied that Russia wished to recreate the Soviet Union in his speech commemorating the annexations, he explicitly condemned the Soviet collapse and Western colonialism. Putin blasted the unintended consequences of the 1991 Belovezh accords, stating that "This tore apart and dismembered our nation, becoming a national catastrophe."[121] In a counterintuitive manner for a celebration of territorial annexation marred by genocide accusations, Putin deplored Western colonial abuses since the Middle Ages and highlighted the West's policy of "deliberately exterminating entire ethnic groups."[122] Mass celebrations were held in Red Square to highlight the unity of the Russian people, including performances from pro-Putin entertainers such as Oleg Gazmanov and Grigory Leps. The chant "We Don't Care About the Price!" was heard in Red Square, as rallygoers vowed to defend annexed Ukraine by any means at Russia's disposal. This message of defending Russia's newest territories at all costs seeped into official and expert discourse. Peskov confirmed that any attack on annexed territory would be deemed equivalent to an attack on Russia.[123] Bureau of Military-Political Analysis expert Pavel Kalymkov believed that the referenda would deter Ukraine from trying to recapture Donetsk and Luhansk but would nonetheless be followed by more intense NATO-backed Ukrainian shelling.[124]

Russia's annexation referenda were largely condemned by the international community. A 12 October UNGA vote saw just Syria, Nicaragua, Belarus and North Korea back Russia's position, as 143 countries condemned Russia's illegal annexations. Guterres described the annexation referenda as a violation of the UN Charter, a position shared by the OSCE, EU and NATO. RIA Novosti downplayed the lack of international support for the annexation referenda, claiming that there had been similar isolation after the Crimea annexation even though proper voting procedures had been employed.[125] The U.S. Treasury Department unveiled sanctions against Nabiullina and Novak, as well as the families of Russian Security Council members and shell companies that aided Russia's defence industry.[126] Ukraine's reaction to the annexation referenda was defiant, as it vowed to continue its counter-offensive and resist pressure to negotiate with Putin. Zelensky declared that "the farce in the occupied territory cannot even be called an imitation of referendums" and vowed to protect the people of annexed regions. Zelensky insisted that Ukraine would only hold negotiations with Russia once Putin was no longer president.[127] Ukraine also announced its formal application for NATO membership in tandem with Putin's annexation speech. Zelensky hailed Ukraine's de facto compatibility with NATO alliance standards and vowed to pursue de jure membership in NATO.[128] Nine NATO member states (Poland, the Czech Republic, Romania, Slovakia, Estonia, Latvia, Lithuania, North Macedonia and Montenegro) immediately supported Ukraine's

NATO membership bid, while Yermak claimed that Canada and Croatia were also supporters. Nevertheless, U.S. National Security Advisor Jake Sullivan poured cold water on Zelensky's NATO accession aspirations by urging Ukraine to take up the issue at a "different time."[129]

Military Setbacks Inspire Russia to Launch a Total War on Ukrainian Civilians

As Putin and his allies celebrated Russia's annexations of Ukrainian land, the Russian armed forces faced an increasingly dire military situation in Lyman. On 27 September, Rybar revealed that Ukrainian forces had gained footholds in the villages of Novoe and Kateryinka, which risked an encirclement of Lyman and the closure of the Svatovo–Lyman supply line.[130] On 30 September, Rybar admitted that Ukraine had gained a military advantage in Yampol and Drobyshevo, which narrowed Russia's defensive line to Lyman's administrative boundaries. Rybar urged the Russian military to take "emergency measures" and transfer reserves to Lyman, and warned that if action was not taken, "nothing will stop Ukrainian forces from developing an offensive deep into Russian territories."[131] Alexander Kots warned that Ukrainian light armoured vehicles were marching on Kreminna with the intention of blocking both Lyman and Torsk.[132] Despite these ominous conditions, the Russian ministry of defence downplayed the dire situation in Lyman. Pushilin warned that Ukrainian forces were sending sabotage and reconnaissance groups but insisted the Svatovo–Lyman supply line was in Russian hands and merely facing Ukrainian fire.[133]

On 1 October, the Kremlin was forced to admit that Lyman was lost, as Ukrainian flags popped up across the city. The Russian defence ministry described the Lyman withdrawal as a regrouping to more advantageous directions and dubiously framed Russia's retreat as a heroic struggle, which saw over 200 Ukrainian servicemen perish.[134] Zelensky hailed Ukraine's victory in Lyman as proof of the irrelevance of the annexation referenda and this optimism was shared by his closest advisors. As Ukraine's battlefield momentum was strengthening, Podolyak requested 100 more 155mm howitzers to counter Russia's mass deployments of military personnel. Podolyak also said that mobilisation had worked to Ukraine's advantage, as untrained conscripts could be exterminated, and mobilisation would show the Russian public that a war was being fought.[135] Arestovych claimed that Putin's refusal to lose face during the annexation ceremony by evacuating Russian military personnel in Lyman cost Russia 1,500 lives. In October 2022, Zagorodnyuk believed that the Lyman defeat showed that Putin's annexation referenda were the "biggest mistake" he had made since the war had begun, as Putin would not be able to preserve his "strongman image" by surrendering Russian territory.[136] Ukraine's euphoria was only tempered by the discovery of a mass grave and a separate burial site with 146 people in Lyman.[137]

Russian hardliners overtly condemned the military leadership for overseeing a disastrous defeat in Lyman. Kadyrov blamed Lapin for the defeat, as he had not provided LNR fighters with ammunition in Lyman and ignored warnings two weeks earlier from the Chechen Akhmat special forces that Lyman was vulnerable. Kadyrov claimed that Gerasimov had reassured him of Lyman's "leadership talent" and did not believe that a retreat from Lyman was possible. Kadyrov blasted Lapin for sitting in Luhansk, which was 150km from the frontlines, and accused Lapin of wrongfully receiving a Hero of Russia award as he was nowhere near Lysychansk's battlefields.[138] Prigozhin implicitly supported Kadyrov's criticisms of Lapin, as Wagner Group Telegram channels ramped up attacks on Shoigu. Gurulyov thundered that "until something completely different appears in the

General Staff, nothing will change" and accused pervasive lying within the Russian defence establishment as contributing to intelligence failures in Lyman.[139] Girkin blamed Gerasimov for the Lyman debacle, as Lapin's units were only sent to the front too late and stated that Shoigu's leadership was "becoming unbearable for everyone who is not keenly interested in defeat in this war."[140] Girkin's condemnations were intriguing, as he regarded Ukraine's Lyman triumph as an "operational-tactical victory" rather than a strategic one, and focused his attention on the absence of a corridor to safely evacuate Russian military personnel.[141]

Russian state TV commentators echoed these pessimistic assessments of Russia's battlefield progress. On his 29 September show, Solovyov expressed frustration that the Russian military had not achieved a major battlefield success to compensate for the Kharkiv reverse and warned, "The whole West is starting to mock us." On a 1 October episode of Andrey Norkin's *Meeting Place* show, commentator Maxim Yusin stated that no country in history had annexed territory without controlling it and expressed doubts that Russia's mobilised forces would be able to subdue 710,000 people in Zaporizhzhia. This despondent mood turned to outrage after a fire broke out on Kerch Bridge on 8 October. The Kerch Bridge attack was carried out by either a truck bomb or a maritime drone, and resulted in the deaths of four people, as well as serious disruption to Russia's military resupply capacity. After meeting with Alexander Bastrykin, Putin described the Kerch Bridge attack as a "terrorist act directed at the destruction of critically important civilian infrastructure of the Russian Federation" and accused the Ukrainian special services of carrying out the strike.[142] Zelensky denied ordering the Kerch Bridge attack, while Podolyak claimed that the explosion showed that the conflict between Russia's military and law enforcement agencies was spiralling out of control.[143] Despite these denials, *Ukrainskaya Pravda* claimed that the Security Service of Ukraine

(SSU) was behind the attack.[144] Podolyak's 17 August claim that the Kerch Bridge was an illegal object that harmed Crimea's ecology and "therefore must be dismantled. Not important how—Voluntary or Not" underscored Ukraine's belief that it was a legitimate military target.

Although the attack was less severe than initially feared, as Russia could rely on rail transit for military equipment and maintained a southern Ukrainian land corridor, the Kerch Bridge's symbolic resonance energised hardliners and fuelled calls for escalation. Solovyov called for sweeping retaliatory strikes which would target Ukraine's "bridges, dams, railways, thermal power plants and other infrastructure."[145] Rybar urged Russia to avoid calling for strikes on decision-making centres, as this did more harm than good, and to pivot its focus towards "destroying the transport supply hubs of the armed forces of Ukraine." Rybar urged Russia to destroy bridges across the Dnipro River and in western Ukraine and argued that Ukraine's shelling of ZNPP legitimised attacks on Ukraine's energy infrastructure. Rybar concluded with a sinister message: "If this is not a reason for really drastic measures, then what is it at all? People demand revenge."[146] The GUR believed that these calls for escalation reflected the Kremlin's covert plans, as the Russian military began preparations for these attacks on 2–3 October and transferred seven Tu-160 strategic bombers with Kh-101 missiles to Olenya airfield on 8 October.[147] Putin responded to cues from Russia's hardliners by appointing Sergei Surovikin as commander of the armed forces in Ukraine on 10 October. Nicknamed "General Armageddon" for his brutal tactics, Surovikin had commanded a unit that killed three anti-coup demonstrators during the 1991 Soviet coup against Gorbachev, led the Eastern Military District from 2013–17 and aided Assad's casualty-heavy military triumph over the Syrian opposition. Surovikin was highly regarded for his efficacy in combat, receiving a Hero of Russia Award in

December 2017 for leading Russian troops in Syria, and was a rumoured successor to Gerasimov after his elevation to the rank of General in 2021. Prigozhin hailed Surovikin as a "legendary person," even though he ironically claimed to be on the side of the anti-coup forces in 1991.[148]

Surovikin's appointment triggered an immediate tactical shift, as Russia began carrying out nationwide missile strikes on 10 October. Russia's strikes on Kyiv were the first of their kind since June and reflected its concerted strategy of targeting Ukraine's electrical infrastructure. These strikes were gleefully celebrated by Russian hardliners. Kadyrov hailed the strikes as retribution for Ukraine's "monstrous oppression" of hundreds of thousands of civilians in Donbas and declared that he was 100% satisfied with how Russia was prosecuting the war.[149] Medvedev praised Russia's actions in similar terms, stating, "The first episode has been played. There will be others" and called for regime change in Ukraine.[150] On Skabeeva's 19 October Rossiya-1 show, Gurulyov called for the systematic destruction of Kyiv's electricity infrastructure to destroy its sewage system and create a man-made epidemic. Gurulyov urged Russia to sharpen its attacks on control centres for railways and banks to disrupt Ukraine's financial system. When co-host Evgeny Popov chided Gurulyov by stating that Russia was striking the Ukrainian military and not civilians, Gurulyov insisted that these strikes were necessary to prevent Ukrainian factories from producing weapons or repairing damaged equipment. Despite Western condemnations and the arrival of an influx of NATO-class air defence systems, which started with Germany's IRIS-Ts, Russia's drone and missile strikes on Ukrainian infrastructure continued. By 1 November, Zelensky admitted that 40% of Ukraine's electricity infrastructure was damaged and Kyiv had developed evacuation plans in the event of a protracted water and electricity supply outage.

COUNTER-OFFENSIVE AND MOBILISATION

The Autumn War: Retreat from Kherson, Stagnation in Donbas

Russia's military outlook in Ukraine remained bleak heading into the winter war. On 19 October, Surovikin admitted that the situation in Kherson was "very difficult" as "the enemy is not abandoning its attempts to attack Russian troop positions."[151] Later that day, Alexander Kots told Skabeeva that Ukrainian forces outnumbered their Russian counterparts by a 4:1 ratio. On 9 November, Stremousov announced that Ukrainian forces had gained a foothold in Snihurivka after intense clashes; Stremousov subsequently died in a reported car crash in Henichesk on the Sea of Azov. Russia's scorched-earth tactics in Kherson also underscored the vulnerability of its occupation. On 21 October, Zelensky warned that Russia was planning to detonate the two-mile Nova Kakhovka dam, which would cause a "large-scale disaster" for Ukrainian cities. Zelensky's dire warnings were likely a reference to the potential destruction of the North Crimean Canal and disruption to ZNPP activities caused by uncontrolled flooding. Ukrainian intelligence officials believed that Russia had begun mining Nova Kakhovka in April but had accelerated these efforts in mid-October, as two military vehicles full of explosives had been placed on the road by the dam.[152] Surovikin's warnings of an imminent Ukrainian attack on Nova Kakhovka, which were followed by reports of power cuts by the Russian authorities and Russian media reports of shelling of the dam, increased the risk of this devastating scenario. Immediately before Stremousov's death, Russia detonated four bridges to slow the Ukrainian advance, including the Dariivka Bridge across the Inhulets River and two bridges in Snihurivka.

Given these negative headwinds, the sustainability of Russia's occupation of Kherson remains uncertain. In late October, Saldo and Stremousov began urging Kherson civilians to exit the west bank of the Dnipro River via boat crossings deeper into Russia's territory. The initial target was to evacuate 60,000 civilians from Kherson; by 22 October, Stremousov claimed that 25,000 civilians had been evacuated. The removal of a Russian flag from a major Kherson administration building, anecdotal reports of the theft of cars, ambulances and tractors, as well as the pilfering of cultural heritage objects like Gregory Potemkin's bones pointed to a Russian departure.[153] Local residents were more sceptical of Russia's departure, as Russian troops had reportedly dressed in civilian clothes and entered abandoned houses in Kherson, and feared a Mariupol-style intense urban war over the winter months.[154] Ukrainian authorities had similarly witnessed Russian forces establishing defensive positions on Kherson's outskirts, meaning that the departures from Chernobaevka and Stepanovka could be a feint.[155] Ukrainian officials framed these evacuations as a guise for forced deportations and the use of civilians as human shields.[156] The continued abduction of children from Kherson, which had seen them not returning from Russian summer schools, reports of forced evacuations to Krasnodar in Siberia and the appearance of 2,000 Kherson residents in camps in Yevpatoria, Crimea, pointed to these practices.[157]

On 9 November, Surovikin and Shoigu opted to retreat from the west bank of the Dnipro River, as resupply capabilities to Kherson had been eviscerated. Russia's decision to evacuate from Kherson received considerable pushback from war hawks and took introspection about the Russian military's failures to new heights. In a remarkable rebuke of Putin's leadership, Alexander Dugin accused Putin of absconding from his responsibilities as an autocrat, which included defending "Russian cities" like Kherson, Belgorod, Kursk, Donetsk and Simferopol. Dugin criticised Russia's nuclear brinkmanship and delayed mobilisation as contributors to its defeat and accused Putin's administration of embracing a fake ideology that was not committed to the "Russian idea."[158] Sergei Markov echoed Dugin's frustrations with Putin's delayed mobilisation and declared that the Kherson defeat was Russia's worst geopolitical setback since the fall of the Soviet Union.[159] Through spotlighting Russia's orderly withdrawal from Kherson and ambiguous pledges that the retreat was temporary, the Kremlin was able to eventually able to stem disquiet and pivot more sharply towards the use of civilian infrastructure strikes.

In Donbas, Russia tried to progress towards the occupation of Donetsk while preventing the collapse of its hold on Luhansk. In Bakhmut, Russia's slow-motion offensive operations continued. On 10 October, British intelligence ascertained that Russian forces had edged closer to Bakhmut, as Russian forces had occupied the villages of Zaitseve and Opytne on its southern outskirts, and on 27 October, Russia recaptured control of the Bakhmut cement plant. Although Bakhmut is a logistical gateway to Sloviansk and Kramatorsk, extensive losses of personnel, especially amongst Wagner Group PMCs and convicts recruited by Prigozhin, suggest that Russia is largely pursuing a symbolic victory that might not advance its strategic goals. On 5 October, Serhiy Haidai announced the official start of the de-occupation of Luhansk, stating that several settlements had already been liberated by the Ukrainian armed forces.[160] On 19 October, Prigozhin announced that a "complex of fortifications" was being built on the contact line in Luhansk, which he dubbed the "Wagner Line." Prigozhin downplayed concerns about the stability of the Luhansk frontlines, as he quipped that the Wagner Group was an "impregnable wall", but his manoevre was widely viewed as a sign that Russia was trying to prevent a Kharkiv-style Ukrainian counter-offensive blitz in Luhansk.[161] Russia also launched offensive operations to recapture Bilohorivka, as it is a gateway to Lysychansk. Ukraine reported heavy casualties amongst Russian forces, including the loss of 500 troops in the Svatovo direction and the deaths of thirty Chechen Akhmat Battalion forces in Lysychansk.[162]

Russia's Asymmetric War: Grain Supply Disruptions, Energy Cut-offs and Nuclear Threats

As Russia's battlefield fortunes suffered numerous setbacks, the Kremlin resorted to its familiar tactics of weaponising food, disrupting energy exports and nuclear brinkmanship. On 7 September, Putin declared that Russia and the Global South had been "cheated" by the Black Sea grain export deal and vowed to revise its terms by limiting the array of countries that could receive grain shipments.[163] This statement built on Russia's prior expressions of frustration that grain exports were not being dispatched to food insecure countries. On 17 August, Mikhail Ulyanov claimed that only one of the twenty-one grain-carrying ships that left Ukrainian ports arrived in Africa and the remainder went to countries not threatened by famine.[164] At the Eastern Economic Forum, Putin declared that "with the exclusion of Turkey as a mediator, practically all the grain exported from Ukraine was sent to the European Union nations instead of the poorest countries."[165] Due to these trade patterns, Putin declared that he would consult with Turkey on restricting grain exports via Ukraine. The Ukrainian Foreign Ministry strongly rejected these claims, stating that two-thirds of Ukraine's grain exports reached Asia, Africa and the Middle East, and warned that Russia was deliberately raising doubts about the deal to "bargain and blackmail" the world.[166] Ukraine provided support for its assertions by pledging 28,000 tons of wheat deliveries to Somalia, which was facing its most acute famine in decades, and dispatching a ship with grain to Djibouti for a WFP relief mission in Ethiopia and Somalia.[167] These actions did not cause the Kremlin to soften its rhetoric. On 20 October, Polyanskiy stated that he was not optimistic about renewing the Black Sea grain export deal, as "The things that were promised to us are not being implemented." Polyanskiy also claimed that sanctions indirectly hindered Russian fertiliser and grain exports due to "overcompliance" from Western companies.[168]

On 29 October, the Kremlin's misgivings with the Black Sea grain export deal's implementation boiled over. The Russian Foreign Ministry announced the indefinite suspension of its participation in the grain deal, as Russia could no longer guarantee the safety of civilian dry cargo ships. Russia justified this assertion by accusing the Ukrainian Armed Forces and British specialists of using UAVs to carry out massive air and sea strikes on the Black Sea Fleet.[169] Russia's decision was hailed by hawkish pro-war commentators, who viewed it as a stepping-stone for more drastic action. Russian political scientist Alexander Dudchak urged Russia to convert its suspension of the Black Sea grain deal into a complete stoppage of participation. Dudchak claimed this action was necessary, as Turkey was not inspecting Odesa-bound ships that carried potential arms shipments to Ukraine and urged Russia to strike Ukrainian ports as legitimate military infrastructure.[170] Political scientist Edward Chesnokov viewed the grain deal suspension as a necessary step to combat British aggression towards Russia, as he claimed that Prime Minister Rishi Sunak's ascension would cause Britain to "play in unison with the Washington saxophonists."[171] This domestic support contrasted markedly with fierce Western criticisms of Russia's grain deal suspension. NATO spokesperson Oana Lungescu accused Russia of weaponising food and called upon it to "renew the deal urgently," while Joe Biden called Russia's move "purely outrageous" and warned that it would increase starvation.[172] To counter these allegations and assuage concerns in the Global South about Russia's unreliability as a food supplier, the Kremlin launched an information counter-offensive. Anatoly Antonov stated that "Washington's reaction to the terrorist attack on the port of Sevastopol was truly outrageous," and claimed that Ukraine's actions triggered the grain deal impasse.[173] Russian media outlets framed its suspension as a pressure tactic to secure the smooth transit of grain and fertiliser from Novorossiyk, which would alleviate food insecurity, and reassured partners that depended on Russian grain, such as Egypt, that exports would proceed according to plan.[174]

To facilitate a swift resolution of the deal, Turkey urged all sides to refrain from provocations and Guterres postponed his arrival at the Arab League summit in Algiers to hold emergency negotiations. These talks bore immediate fruit, as the U.S., Turkey and Ukraine agreed to unblock sixteen grain-carrying ships in Turkish waters, and twelve cargo ships left Ukrainian ports on 31 October. Russia did not militarily resist these grain exports, as it sought to reassure the international community that its refusal to guarantee the safety of ships did not equate to a full-scale Black Sea port blockade.[175] This rhetorical moderation paved the way for Russia's swift return to the grain deal. After receiving "sufficient" guarantees from Ukraine that it would not use the maritime corridor for operations against Russia, the Russian Defence Ministry announced its return to the deal on 2 November.[176] To appease hardliners at home, Putin conceded that Russia could still quit the grain deal again in the future but ruled out blocking grain exports from Ukraine to Turkey.[177] Nevertheless, tangible progress was made in the grain deal's implementation. On 4 November, Erdogan stated that Putin had pledged to provide grain to food insecure African countries, such as Djibouti, Somalia and Sudan, for free.[178] On 18 November, Russia agreed to a four-month extension of the grain deal, and by December 2022, Russia's wheat exports had soared to record highs. This expansion of wheat exports included a resumption of shipments to Iraq after a ten-year pause and record-breaking sales to Saudi Arabia, Algeria, Pakistan, Brazil and Mexico.[179] Nonetheless, Russia's slow inspections of grain-carrying ships have received criticism and by late December 2022, Ukraine alleged that ninety-nine ships remained in place in the Bosporous for months.[180] This underscores Russia's potential for continued obstructionism and an eventual Ukrainian campaign to liberate Crimea could plunge the deal in jeopardy again.

While Russia's weaponisation of food abated as a concern in late 2022, its weaponisation of energy continued to escalate. On 26 September, a series of clandestine bombings and underwater gas leaks occurred on the Nord Stream-1 and 2 pipelines. These leaks coincided with the unveiling of the Baltic Pipe, which supplies North Sea gas from Denmark to Poland, and were swiftly deemed to be acts of sabotage. Despite widespread speculation that Russia triggered the leaks to weaponise gas exports against Europe, the Kremlin turned the tables on the West. Vasily Nebenzia stated that the disruption of gas supply to Europe was beneficial to American suppliers and could not be carried out by "simple terrorists."[181] Nebenzia also declared that "our Western colleagues see this sabotage, no matter who committed it, as a kind of revenge for Russia's actions in Ukraine."[182] Sikorski's controversial deleted tweet, which appeared to blame the U.S. for the sabotage, was also cited by Russian officials as proof of American involvement. In response to Sikorski's tweet, Polyanskiy declared "Thank you Radek Sikorski for making it crystal clear who stands behind this terrorist targeting of civilian infrastructure!"[183] On 29 October, the Russian Defence Ministry accused the same UK Royal Navy experts, who were blamed by the Kremlin for the UAV attack on Sevastopol that suspended the grain deal, of being involved in terrorist activities against Nord Stream.[184] While responsibility for the Nord Stream leaks remains uncertain, in spite of lengthy investigations from Denmark and Sweden, it underscored Russia's growing willingness to use energy as a weapon against Europe. On 5 December, gas exports from Yamal-Europe slid to zero. Alexander Novak left the door open to a restoration of supplies later that month but the EU's push for an oil price cap plunged the future of Russian energy exports into a state of further uncertainty.[185]

Russia's provocative actions towards the Zaporizhzhia nuclear plant and increasingly vocal threats of nuclear weapons use also caused alarm in the West. In a drastic escalation of its long-standing policy of harassing ZNPP staff, a Russian patrol detained ZNPP's director-general Ihor Murashov on 1 October. While Murashov was released three days later due to mounting international pressure, reports of his maltreatment by Russian captors gained widespread attention. A 18 November *Wall Street Journal* investigation revealed that Murashov was hooded and handcuffed on the stone floor of a basement prison, accused by his captors of betraying Russia and coerced into making a canned statement in the lens of a video camera.[186] Murashov revealed that the head of ZNPP's information technology service Oleh Kostyukov was beaten by Russian security forces and Energoatom estimated that over 200 ZNPP staff were detained while dozens were still missing.[187] To compound tensions with Ukraine over ZNPP, Putin decreed that the plant was a Russian federal asset on 5 October and appointed ex-chief engineer of the Balakovo Nuclear Plant Oleg Romanenko to oversee ZNPP.[188] Shelling of the ZNPP continued to threaten a nuclear catastrophe and Russian disinformation about Ukraine's intentions towards the plant impeded a resolution to the crisis. On 8 October, the ZNPP lost its final external power source and was forced to rely on emergency diesel generators. On 16 October, Vladimir Rogov warned that Ukraine was amassing assault groups of around 450 troops around Enerhodar in an attempt to seize control over ZNPP.[189] These escalatory actions, which are paired with resistance from Russian hardliners to a handover of ZNPP, impeded an expeditious resolution to the crisis.

Russia's deteriorating position on the frontlines and annexation of Ukrainian territory was also accompanied with increasingly bellicose threats to use nuclear weapons. During his 21 September speech calling for partial mobilisation, Putin made a veiled but eye-catching threat to use nuclear weapons in defence of the Russian homeland. In a warning shot to NATO, Putin declared "I would like to remind those resorting to such statements against Russia that our country also has various weapons of destruction and some of our components are even more up-to-date than NATO member countries. And when the territorial integrity of our country is threatened, we will obviously use all the means we have at our disposal to protect Russia and our people. This is not a bluff."[190] Kadyrov's call for the potential use of a low-yield nuclear weapon after Russia's defeat in Lyman on 1 October further heightened alarm in Ukraine.[191] To potentially justify a pre-emptive nuclear strike, the Russian Ministry of Defence spread unfounded conspiracies about an imminent dirty bomb detonation in Ukraine. In late October, Shoigu raised the dirty bomb threat in calls with British, Turkish and French defence officials, and spoke twice in three days with Lloyd Austin.

The unusual frequency of communications between Austin and Shoigu was likely attributable to U.S. intelligence showing that Russian officials had privately deliberated about nuclear weapons use.[192] While Shoigu's comments were greeted with derision in Western capitals and regarded as a sign of Russia's military weakness, his warning to his French counterpart Sebastian Lecornu of "uncontrollable escalations" unsettled Western officials.[193] Despite these ominous signs, the threat of a Russian nuclear strike on Ukraine or imminent broadening of the conflict to NATO gradually ebbed. Solovyov's full-throated advocacy for Russia's use of a pre-emptive nuclear strike during a 21 November episode of his show received uncharacteristic pushback from hawkish guests, such as Konstantin Zatulin. Through a mixture of stealth mobilisation and capitalisation on the winter weather, a nuclear catastrophe was temporarily averted after the fall of Kherson.

8

RUSSIA'S ISOLATION FROM THE WEST
AND THE POST-SOVIET SPACE

On 12 October, the UNGA condemned Russia's "illegal so-called referendums" in Ukraine's internationally recognised borders. Every single country in Europe and the collective West, including traditionally sympathetic Hungary and Serbia, condemned Russia's territorial annexations. Aside from Belarus, which refused to condemn Russia but did not recognise Russia's occupation of Ukrainian territory, post-Soviet countries did not side with Moscow. Treaty allies—Armenia, Kazakhstan, Kyrgyzstan and Tajikistan—abstained; Azerbaijan was absent; and post-Soviet republics that experienced or were threatened by Russian aggression—the Baltic states, Georgia and Moldova—condemned Russia's illegal actions. This largely symbolic UNGA vote underscored Russia's failure to create polarisations within the collective West and ensconce a loyal network of satellites in the post-Soviet space. The Kremlin continues to deny these trends, as it tries to present Russia as a great power that is resilient in the face of Western isolation. On 27 October, Putin declared that he was battling Western elites rather than the West

65

as a whole, which underscored his desire to fuel populist angst in Western countries.[1] Russia's proposed creation of a common energy market in the Eurasian Economic Union, as 72% of transactions between its members are paid in roubles, signified its commitment to Eurasian economic integration.[2] Nevertheless, the Ukraine War has severely weakened two of the most significant pillars of Putin's post-2014 foreign policy, and it is unclear whether Russian soft power in the West and post-Soviet space can be rebuilt in the long-term.

This chapter examines how Russia tried to maintain links with friendly left-wing and right-wing populist movements in Western countries. While some of the Kremlin's long-standing surrogates echoed its talking points during the Ukraine War, Russia's ability to interfere in democratic elections and lobby for its interests in Western countries has greatly diminished. This chapter examines Russia's growing isolation in the Black Sea, Baltic Sea, and the post-Soviet space, which has seen it face containment strategies from previously neutral or sympathetic countries. It also explores Russia's attempts to create a second front, especially in Moldova and the Western Balkans, that would divert Western attention from Ukraine, and efforts to prevent a second front from emerging in the South Caucasus and Central Asia.

Russia's Alignment with Populist Movements in Western Democracies

Due to the extensive reach of Western sanctions and limitations on Russian state media access in the U.S. and Europe, Russia's traditional "active measures" tools have been defanged. The threat of sanctions destroyed Russia's network of former Western officials, who lobbied for its state-owned companies. Shortly after the Ukraine War began, former Austrian chancellor Wolfgang Schüssel resigned from Lukoil, former Finnish prime minister Esko Aho stepped aside from Sberbank, former French prime minister François Fillon left Zibur and Zarubezhneft and former Italian prime minister Matteo Renzi exited Delimobil. The European Parliament's 19 May proposal to sanction Europeans with board seats on Russian companies, such as former German chancellor Gerhard Schröder and former Austrian foreign minister Karin Kneissl, deprived Russia of its remaining high-profile lobbyists.[3] Schröder resigned from his Rosneft board seat, which paid him a $1 million annual salary, on 20 May. Schröder continued to defend his position on Russia in spite of EU pressure, claiming that Putin wanted a negotiated settlement after meeting him on 2 August and lobbied for the revival of Nord Stream-2.[4] However, calls for expulsion from the Social Democratic Party (SDP) marginalised Schroder's voice. Kneissl followed Schröder's lead by resigning from Rosneft on 23 May. Although she attended the September 2020 Eastern Economic Forum in Vladivostok, Kneissl emigrated from Austria due to alleged "death threats" and currently resides in Lebanon.[5] The EU's 21 June proposal to ban Russian lobbyists from Gazprom, Lukoil and Rusal from offering their services to EU policymakers further restricted Russia's ability to revive this network.[6]

Russia's invasion of Ukraine also provoked harsh criticisms from establishment politicians who typically supported dialogue with Moscow. Frank-Walter Steinmeier's 5 April admission that Germany's policy towards Russia had "failed on many points" and should have accounted for objections from its Eastern European partners in the post-2014 period was especially striking.[7] Steinmeier's 25 October visit to Kyiv, which featured support for German air defence deliveries to Ukraine and lamentations about the collapse of a "common European home" completed his reincarnation into a Putin critic.[8] Czech president Miloš Zeman's rebuke of the catastrophic consequences of the Ukraine War, which included strong support for arms deliveries and the resettlement of 400,000 Ukrainian refugees in the Czech Republic, broke with his prior support for accepting Crimea as part of Russia.[9] Former Italian prime minister Silvio Berlusconi's claims that he had rekindled his relationship with Putin, who he described as one of his "five real friends," and warnings that Russia sees Italy as being at war with it for arming Ukraine, were rare words of solidarity.[10] Although Berlusconi's centre-right Forza Italia Party is a junior partner in Italian prime minister Giorgia Meloni's conservative coalition, Meloni implicitly rebuked Berlusconi's accusations that Zelensky provoked Putin's invasion and significantly increased Italian air defence equipment shipments to Ukraine.[11] Resignations of officials with pro-Kremlin leanings such as German navy chief Kay-Achim Schönbach, who claimed that Putin deserved respect, in January, or those with alleged Russian links, such as German cybersecurity chief Arne Schoenbaum on 18 October, underscored Moscow's limited reach in Europe's corridors of power.

Russia also struggled to capitalise on its residual soft power in Europe, which restricted its ability to sow discord within the EU. The limited impact of Russian soft power was apparent in the collapse of its traditionally close relationships with Greece and Cyprus. Due to Greece's Orthodox faith and lingering disdain towards the EU's austerity measures, Russia had a groundswell of local support; the Greek public largely supported neutrality towards Ukraine, as only 45% identified with Kyiv and 20% aligned themselves with Russia, while 75% viewed Putin negatively while 60% viewed Zelensky unfavourably.[12] Over 66% of Greeks opposed providing military assistance to Ukraine and the left-wing Syriza Party resisted arms transfers. Despite these sentiments, Greece consistently supplied military equipment to Ukraine, which included participation in a tank supply exchange with Germany and pledge to rebuild the bombed maternity clinic in Mariupol.[13] Although 51% of Cypriots disagreed with the view that Russia had instigated the Ukraine War, Cyprus consistently supported punitive measures against Russia.[14] Cyprus's support for sanctions against Russia reduced its tourism revenues, which amounted to $600 million every year.[15] Russia's resumption of flights to Turkish-occupied northern Cyprus, which were reportedly discussed between Erdogan and Putin in September 2022, underscored Moscow's escalating tensions with Nicosia. The Russian foreign ministry dismissed these claims and reiterated Moscow's support for Cyprus's sovereignty, but Nicosia would no longer lobby to moderate EU sanctions.

Despite its inability to use RT and Sputnik as propaganda tools, Russia's election interference ambitions remained intact. Ahead of the April 2022 French presidential elections, Rossiya-1 linked Putin's decision to blockade instead of bomb Azovstal to engineering Macron's defeat.[16] Evgeny Popov declared that Russia needed to evacuate French personnel from the Azovstal steel factory before the elections to secure Macron's defeat. Colonel Yuri Knutov concurred that "Macron would be forced to resign" if evidence of direct NATO involvement in Mariupol was revealed. Although RT and Sputnik France shared effective propaganda against Macron's COVID-19 policy, the Russian Embassy in Paris's disinformation offensive failed to gain traction during the campaign cycle.[17] Prior to the 8 November U.S. midterm elections, Rossiya-1 stridently criticised Biden and expressed unambiguous support for his Republican rivals; on 29 March, Popov openly called for "regime change" in the U.S. that would reinstall "our partner" Trump before new elections. On 2 September, Rossiya-1 host Igor Kozhevin claimed that "Biden lost the fight for the soul of the nation," lambasted his speech as "scandalous" and played footage from Tucker Carlson's FOX News show that highlighted divisions in America. On 7 November, Prigozhin shelved his past denials of election interference in the U.S., stating, "Gentlemen, we interfered, we interfere, and we will interfere."[18] Prigozhin's comments were widely interpreted as an attempt to highlight the efficacy of his hybrid warfare tactics as the Wagner Group struggled to achieve military breakthroughs in Donetsk.

Due to its modest toolkit, Russia was forced to rely on far-left and far-right surrogate messengers to advance its preferred agenda. Solidarity with Russia was fairly limited even amongst these movements, as only thirteen Members of the European Parliament (MEPs) did not condemn Russia's invasion of Ukraine, although they resisted arms transfers to Ukraine, sanctions against Russia and whitewashed Russian war crimes. Former British Labour Party leader Jeremy Corbyn claimed that arming Ukraine would not bring an end to the war and called for a ceasefire brokered by the UN or international bodies such as the Arab League and African Union.[19] Irish MEP Clare Daly, affiliated with the far-left Independents 4 Change Party, claimed that "nowhere have sanctions ever succeeded in ending a military assault or achieving regime change," and tempered criticisms of Russian conduct by stating "we cannot ignore the role of NATO."[20] Former Italian deputy prime minister Matteo Salvini, leader of the far-right Lega Nord, who signed a cooperation pact with United Russia in 2017, warned that sanctions were "bringing Europe and Italy to their knees."[21] Trump-backed Republicans in Congress such as Arizona congressman Paul Gosar and Georgia congresswoman Marjorie Taylor Greene publicly opposed financial aid to Ukraine. Alternative für Deutschland (AfD) lawmakers questioned Russia's role in the Bucha Massacre and promoted Russian conspiracy theories about biological weapons. Marine Le Pen's stance on Russia moderated ahead of the elections but nonetheless called for France's exit from NATO's Integrated Command and opposed a Russian gas embargo.[22]

Beyond empowering these candidates by weaponising gas exports, the Kremlin amplified and fomented demonstrations against Western sanctions on Russia and military support for Ukraine. Some of these demonstrations were explicitly partisan in nature. On 8 October, the AfD mobilised 10,000 Germans under the "Our Country First" logo to protest against sanctions-induced inflation and AfD co-leader Tino Chrupalla accused Robert Habeck of waging economic war on the German people.[23] Other demonstrations such as the 5 November protests in Italy against arming Ukraine were heterogenous in their political composition, and rallied around former prime minister Giuseppe Conte's call for negotiations.[24] The spontaneous outbreak of dozens of pro-Russian rallies in European cities in April 2022 was linked to Rossotrudnichestvo, which mobilised ethnic Russians to protest against Western support for Ukraine. While the Russian media highlighted the Cologne rally as a "mass uprising" by ethnic Germans against Ukraine, the Russian language was ubiquitous in the protests and right-wing extremist organisations such as the Pro NRW Party leant organisational support.[25] These protests were regularly accompanied by large-scale counter-demonstrations expressing support for Ukraine, and were not indicative of public opinion. An October 2022 poll revealed 73% support for sanctions in Britain, 72% in Denmark, 71% in Sweden and 69% in Spain, while 40–50% of people in France and Germany viewed sanctions against Russia as not strong enough.[26] Nevertheless, polls such as a July 2022 survey which showed that 47% of Germans believed sanctions harmed Germany more than Russia suggested that the Kremlin had populist angst to exploit.[27]

Although Russia's partnerships were largely confined to the fringes of Europe's political spectrum, Viktor Orban's Hungary became an increasingly important obstructionist partner. During his 1 February visit to Moscow, Orban claimed to be visiting

Putin on a "peace mission" and stated that "I have high hopes that for many years, we can work together."[28] Hungary's state M1 channel described Donetsk and Luhansk as "regions between Russia and Ukraine," while Fidesz-aligned Pesti TV accused Ukraine of invading Donbas and of entering Russian territory near Rostov.[29] Ahead of the 3 April elections, Orban announced a Hungary-first approach to the war in Ukraine, which saw him condemn the war but avoid military assistance to Kyiv or targeted criticisms of Russia. On 28 February, Hungarian foreign minister Péter Szijjártó opposed using Hungary as a trans-shipment country for arms to Ukraine, as Russia could threaten its national security and the welfare of Hungarians in Transcarpathia.[30] After the Bucha Massacre, Orban broke with the EU consensus by refusing to condemn Russia and Poland fiercely criticised his comment that "we live in a time of mass manipulation."[31] Tensions between Hungary and Ukraine escalated before the elections. In late March, Zelensky asked Orban to "decide who you are with" and compared the situation in Mariupol to the massacre of Hungarian Jews by local fascists in 1944–5, while Vereshchuk speculated about an Orban–Putin deal to hand Transcarpathia to Hungary.[32] After his victory, Orban retorted by describing Zelensky as an opponent he'd overcome to secure re-election.

Although it reluctantly acceded to the EU's broadening sanctions regime, Hungarian officials highlighted the inefficacy of sanctions and the need for a diplomatic settlement. On 20 September, Szijjártó stated that the EU should not consider new sanctions against Russia, as they would worsen the energy supply crisis and hurt Europe.[33] In August 2022, Hungary deepened its dependency on Russian energy, which broke with the EU consensus. On 15 August, Gazprom began distributing more gas to Hungary via the TurkStream pipeline than was contractually obligated.[34] On 27 August, Hungary issued a permit for Rosatom to construct two new nuclear reactors, which built on a 2014 deal with Russia that aimed to expand the Paks nuclear plant. Zoltán Kovács, serving as Hungary's Secretary of State for Public Diplomacy and Relations, condemned the EU's bans on RT and Sputnik as "not the best way to cope with disinformation," and equated Ukrainian, Russian and Western European disinformation.[35] Orban's defiance of Western sanctions on Russia was popular, as just 32% of Hungarians in October 2022 supported EU sanctions.[36] On 23 July, Orban openly questioned Ukraine's ability to prevail against Russia's superior military and for U.S.–Russia talks to end the war, which would give Moscow the security guarantees it had requested.[37] Hungary offered to host talks on Ukraine, as it brokered the Budapest Memorandum, but placed responsibility for diplomacy on the EU's largest powers.[38]

Russia's Escalation of Tensions with Poland, the Baltic States and Northern Europe

Although Russia framed its invasion of Ukraine as a reaction to NATO encirclement, the war significantly strained its relations with bordering countries and deepened its westward encirclement. The Baltic states were acutely aware of the potential for a Russian victory in Ukraine posing a broader threat to European security. Although Estonian intelligence chief Mikk Marran defused an immediate panic about Russia's intentions by highlighting the border situation's stability on 28 February, Baltic officials warned about the long-term risks associated with the Ukraine War. On 19 February, Landsbergis warned U.S. Secretary of Defense Lloyd Austin that "The battle for Ukraine is a battle for Europe. If Putin is not stopped here, he will go further."[39] On 21 February, Estonian defence minister Kalle Laanet warned of a years-long expanded Russian force presence in Belarus, which would leave 30,000 Russian troops 100km from Vilnius and Warsaw, and urged NATO to strengthen military support to Latvia, Lithuania and Poland.[40] Biden responded to these expressions of concern by deploying additional troops and F-35s to the Baltic states on 22 February. While the U.S. allowed the Baltic states to ship American-made missiles to Ukraine, Germany vetoed Estonia's efforts to ship German-made equipment to Kyiv.[41] Germany's decision reinforced the perception in the Baltic states that the EU viewed their warnings about Russian aggression as alarmist. Former Estonian president Toomas Hendrik Ilves recalled that after pro-Georgian rallies broke out in 2008, Finland mocked Estonia for suffering from "post-Soviet traumatic stress." Ilves noted that NATO had only recognised cyber as a domain of war during the 2016 Warsaw Summit, even though Estonia had grappled with intense Russian cyberattacks since 2007.[42] Ilves also recalled that the Baltic states were aware of the risk of natural gas dependency on Russia, as they had experienced supply cut-offs in 1991–2 as retaliation for declaring independence, but these concerns were dismissed by Germany as it advanced towards Nord Stream-2.[43]

From the start of the war, the Baltic states provided extensive military assistance to Ukraine. Lithuania handed over large quantities of heavy mortar and ammunition, which fuelled concerns about depleted stocks, and spearheaded military training initiatives in April 2022 that allowed Ukraine to use NATO-class weapons.[44] By October 2022, Estonia had delivered over 250 million euros in military aid to Ukraine including howitzers and Javelin anti-tank missiles. Estonia's overall aid to Ukraine stood at 0.83% of its GDP by August 2022 and 37.5% of its military budget by July 2022, while Latvia provided 32.1% of its defence budget to Ukraine. The extensive aid provisions to Ukraine authorised by Baltic leaders and their consistent calls for tighter sanctions inspired fierce backlash in Russia. Latvia's takedown of

Soviet-era monuments and April 2022 decision to downgrade diplomatic relations with Russia, alongside Lithuania, escalated tensions further. Maria Zakharova accused Latvian Deputy Alexander Kirshteins of "Nazism" for criticising Latvian participation in the 9 May celebrations and urged "specialised structures of international organisations to take action."[45] On a 17 August show, Solovyov threatened Russian aggression towards the Baltic states, asking, "Will America be ready to fight for the Baltic Emirates which in their Nazi exaltation are violating the rights of Russian speakers?" The Baltic states have responded to this bellicose rhetoric by banning Russian tourist visas and lobbying the EU to impose mirror bloc-wide restrictions.

Despite these frictions, the restoration of Russian trade with Kaliningrad eased the risks of an immediate confrontation between Moscow and Vilnius. In June 2022, Lithuania banned the transport of Russian iron and steel to Kaliningrad and Landsbergis stated that approximately half of all trade with Kaliningrad would be restricted due to EU sanctions.[46] While the Kaliningrad regional authorities sought to defuse panic buying by announcing a ferry service between the exclave and St. Petersburg, Russia responded ferociously to Lithuania's compliance with EU sanctions. Patrushev warned that "Russia will certainly respond to such hostile actions" in ways that would "have a serious negative impact on the population of Lithuania."[47] Nikolay Mezhevich, president of the Russian Association for Baltic Studies, claimed that Russia could impose a complete trade embargo on Lithuania and solicit support from Belarus and China in isolating Vilnius.[48] Despite these threats, Lithuania expanded the scope of trade restrictions on 11 July and Kaliningrad retaliated by proposing a ban on trade between Russia and the Baltic states. Fearing a broader EU–Russia confrontation, Olaf Scholz spearheaded a sanctions exemption for Kaliningrad on the grounds that "we are dealing with traffic between two parts of Russia."[49] Former Lithuanian foreign minister Linas Linkevičius condemned the decision, as he believed that the EU should be increasing pressure on Russia's war machine, but a crisis was averted.[50]

Poland's strident condemnations of Russian aggression and extensive support for Ukraine escalated Moscow–Warsaw tensions to new heights. President Lech Kaczyński's warning in 2008 that "Today it is Georgia, tomorrow Ukraine, the day after tomorrow the Baltic states and then perhaps my country Poland" encapsulates Polish alarm about Russia's invasion of Ukraine. On 11 May, Polish prime minister Mateusz Morawiecki described the Russkiy Mir ideology as a "cancer" that threatened the whole of Europe and viewed the Kremlin's weaponisation of gas as "drug dealer" behaviour. Due to its security concerns, Poland announced a 3% of GDP defence spending target in 2023, resettled 1.4 million Ukrainian refugees and provided military aid worth $1.7 billion by June 2022. Polish officials have repeatedly warned that the Russian economy has not suffered short-term economic losses and has aggressively lobbied for an energy embargo paired with stringent secondary sanctions on Russia.[51] Poland has persisted with its hawkish stance towards the Ukraine War even though it has not repaired its rift with the EU. Polish MEP Jacek Saryusz-Wolski said that Poland was aggressively countering what it saw as a historical sympathy towards Russia in France and Germany, amplified by agents of influence. However, Wolski lamented that the "EU continues to harass us on internal policy while praising our support for Ukraine" and viewed financing restrictions on Poland as counter-productive to the Ukrainian cause.[52] Radek Sikorski contended that Poland's support for Ukraine strengthened its partnership with the U.S. but Morawiecki's refusal to make minor compromises with the EU in October 2021 continued to haunt Brussels–Warsaw relations.[53]

The Kremlin responded to Poland's position on the Ukraine War by launching a state-led disinformation campaign against Poland and highlighting Poland's tensions with its Western allies to trivialise the risk of a military retaliation. On 21 March, Medvedev accused Polish politicians of sacrificing the interests of their citizens in pursuit of Russophobia and warned that "de-Russification" would drastically weaken the Polish economy. Medvedev concluded that "economic cooperation with our country will only benefit Poles" and highlighted historical exchanges such as Pushkin–Mickiewicz, Tchaikovsky–Chopin and Lomonosov–Copernicus as proof of Poland's anti-historical actions.[54] These generic condemnations were paired with persistent warnings about Poland's neo-imperial designs towards Ukraine. On 28 April, Naryshkin warned that Poland would deploy troops to western Ukraine "under the slogan of protecting the region from Russian aggression" and believed that, much like after the First World War, the U.S. would support Greater Poland's revival.[55] Suzdaltsev claimed that Poland had always seen the Ukrainians as "serfs" and asserted that Ukraine "brought its entire gold and foreign exchange reserves to Poland this winter."[56] Russian media routinely highlighted social discontent emanating from Poland's acceptance of Ukrainian refugees. Exaggerations of small-scale protests with the slogan "Poland is here, not Ukraine" and Medvedev's claims that Poland was resettling Ukrainian refugees with U.S. funds while profiting from its depressed economy exemplify this narrative.[57]

Russia paired this disinformation campaign with calls for military escalation against Poland. Oleg Morozov responded to Morawiecki's comments by stating that "Poland encourages us to put it in first place in the queue for denazification after Ukraine."[58] Mirroring the experience of Chechen fighters in Ukraine, radio commentator Sergey Mardan mused on a 24 August Rossiya-1 show about Russians and Ukrainians storming Warsaw and

Berlin together. These threats extended to postulations about the use of nuclear weapons against Poland. On a 28 October episode of Solovyov's Rossiya-1 show, Institute of Middle East director Yevgeny Satanovsky, who drafted a "kill list" of Western officials, warned that Poland was planning to attack Russia, Ukraine and Belarus. Solovyov responded to Satanovsky's warning by stating, "In that case, there will be a nuclear strike on the territory of Poland." Gurulyov has publicly mused about nuclear strikes on NATO forces in Poland, while Karaganov asked whether the U.S. would be willing to sacrifice Boston for Poznan in the event of a nuclear war.[59] Russia's bellicose rhetoric was matched with real and potential threats to Poland's security. Russian disinformation networks falsified alleged burglaries, assaults and rapes carried out by Ukrainian refugees to sow discord in Polish society.[60] Poland's decision to expel 45 Russian diplomats as suspected spies on 23 March was partially linked to Moscow's subversive conduct. Wolski contended that Poland's visa ban against Russians was aimed at preventing 1,000 Spetsnaz or Wagner Group PMCs in disguise from entering NATO borders and overwhelming a "small European country." Wolski regarded the threat of a ZNPP detonation as the most pressing danger to Poland's security and highlighted Poland's distribution of iodine tablets to mitigate this risk.[61]

Finland and Sweden's anticipated accession to NATO sharpened Russia's isolation in Northern Europe. Although Finnish prime minister Sanna Marin stated on 20 January that NATO membership was "very unlikely" to occur during her term in office, a drastic uptick in Finnish public support for NATO membership to 76% in May 2022 changed Marin's calculus.[62] Former Finnish prime minister Alexander Stubb, an early advocate of NATO membership, believed that Finland's foreign policy synthesis of "realism and idealism" delayed NATO accession. Stubb argued that the Russian military's conventional weaknesses, Finland's belief that its 900,000 reservists and 280,000 mobilised people could deter Russian aggression, and lack of dependence on Russian energy convinced Marin that the risks of NATO membership were limited.[63] Finland's 2 May suspension of a Rosatom nuclear deal with Fennovoima further decreased Russia's leverage in the energy sphere. While Sweden's November 2021 decision to acquire the Patriot missile defence system, which was the first purchase by any non-NATO country, signalled closer ties with NATO, Swedish prime minister Magdalena Andersson's support for NATO membership was a watershed moment. Former Swedish ambasssador to NATO Veronika Wand-Danielsson described Andersson's decision as a "revolution" in Swedish security policy, as Sweden previously believed that military non-alignment was the most effective means of dissuading Russian security threats.[64] Danielsson argued that the Bucha Massacre crystallised Swedish support for NATO but a bloc within the Social Democratic Party, which included climate and environment minister Annika Strandhäll, continued to champion neutrality.[65]

Finland and Sweden's stated intention to join NATO prompted widespread condemnations by Russian officials and defence experts. State Duma Deputy Committee on Security deputy head Anatoly Vyborny castigated "ostentatious anti-Russian activity of NATO," which violated international norms, while Sergei Rybakov warned of heightened instability in Northern Europe.[66] Defence expert Alexey Leonkov warned that NATO could deploy thirty land, sea and air bases in Sweden and Finland, which would host forward-based weapons and shift the balance of forces in northern Europe in its favour.[67] Russian media reacted fiercely to Estonia's claims that Finland's NATO membership turned the Baltic Sea into NATO's "inland sea." Concerns grew that NATO wanted to expel the Russian navy from St. Petersburg, which would be a declaration of war.[68] In response to these perceived threats, Medvedev claimed that Sweden and Finland's NATO membership would end the Baltic region's nuclear-free status, which confusingly ignored the existence of nuclear weapons in Kaliningrad, and called for the deployment of "significant naval forces" in the Gulf of Finland, as well as ground troops and air defence systems.[69] Putin attempted to dial down the hysteria in his official statements. On 29 June, he described Finland and Sweden's NATO membership decision as a sovereign choice and emphasised that Russia did not have Ukraine-style territorial disputes with either country. Nevertheless, Putin warned that Russia would "respond symmetrically" to the deployment of NATO military contingents or military infrastructure to Sweden and Finland.[70] Putin's statements mirrored his July 2016 position on Finland's NATO membership, which called for the reinstatement of Russian personnel that had been placed 1,500km from the Finnish border.

As Finland and Sweden's NATO accession draws closer, Russia has carried out provocations against both countries. Russia's synthesis of airspace violations and cyberattacks mirrored its pre-NATO accession use of hybrid threats. On 8 April, Russia violated Finland's airspace and proceeded to launch cyberattacks on government websites, while Russian hackers launched a DDoS attack on Finland's parliament website on 10 August citing NATO membership. Russian nuclear-capable military violated Swedish airspace in a similar fashion on 31 March and 1 May. In response to Russia's aggression, Britain struck a new security agreement with Sweden and Finland on 11 May, and both countries sought informal security guarantees from NATO to pre-empt Russian threats. Russia's most serious conventional security threat to Swedish territory is to Gotland, an island located off southern Sweden's Baltic Sea coast. On a 16 March Rossiya-1 segment, Igor Korotchenko claimed that Russian fighter jets could deploy S-400s and Bastion coastal anti-ship systems to

Gotland in the event of an invasion of the Baltic states. Russia's deployments in Gotland would complement Russia's military build-up in the Suwałki Corridor between Poland and Lithuania, block NATO reinforcements and create a 400km no-fly zone in the Baltic Sea. Korotchenko concluded that if Russia successfully invaded the Baltic states, it would request a 99-year lease on Gotland and compel Sweden to agree to "perpetual neutrality." Zelensky highlighted the Russian threat to Gotland in his 24 March address to Swedish lawmakers, which was greeted with mixed reactions. Danielsson did not see Russia's occupation of Gotland as plausible even in a "worst-case scenario," as NATO would swiftly take control of Gotland to protect the Baltic states.[71] Nevertheless, Sweden increased the frequency of its patrols around Gotland in mid-January 2022, as tensions rose over Ukraine, and announced the expansion of its military presence in Gotland on 29 April.[72]

Russia's Growing Isolation in the Black Sea Littoral Region

Although Russia invaded Ukraine to secure hegemony over the Black Sea, Moscow's relationships with its littoral countries experienced severe strains. The escalation of tensions between Russia and Bulgaria, which traditionally had close ties with Moscow, was especially striking. In March 2022, Bulgaria expelled ten Russian diplomats for espionage and summoned Russian ambassador to Bulgaria Eleonora Mitrofanova for claiming that Sofia's anti-Russian policies defied public opinion.[73] Bulgaria's expulsion of seventy remaining Russian diplomats on espionage charges in June 2022, which more than halved the size of the embassy, caused Peskov to threaten a complete suspension of diplomatic relations with Sofia.[74] Although Bulgaria imported 3 billion cubic metres of gas per year from Russia, which amounted to 90% of its natural gas needs, Bulgarian deputy prime minister

Assen Vassilev declared on 19 March that Sofia would not renew its contracts with Gazprom.[75] Bulgaria compensated for Russia's subsequent suspension of Russian gas exports by inaugurating a 182km Greece–Bulgaria pipeline in July 2022 that transported Azerbaijani gas. Bulgarian MEP Radan Kanev believed that Bulgarian industry's robust performance left it in a stronger position to weather higher gas prices than Hungary or the Czech Republic.[76] However, Russia's weaponisation of gas could have major economic repercussions, as U.S. LNG is unlikely to compensate for Bulgaria's energy shortfalls, and rising gas prices could leave over 25% of Bulgarians unable to heat their homes and result in 250,000 job losses.[77] Bulgaria also faced a challenge securing non-Russian nuclear fuel for the Kozloduy plant's two Soviet-generation reactors. While Bulgaria officially opposed arming Ukraine until 3 November, it supplied one billion euros worth of weapons to Kyiv via third party brokers.[78] Bulgaria's extensive Soviet-standard ammunition stocks ensured that it was a vital security partner for Ukraine, even though it refrained from exporting Mi-29 jets to Kyiv.

Despite the escalation of tensions between Bulgaria and Russia, there were some silver linings for Moscow. The Kremlin could capitalise on substantial pro-Russian popular sentiments in Bulgaria and had political surrogates which could advance its interests. Around 70% of Bulgarians consistently opposed arming Ukraine, as they feared it would make Bulgaria a party to the conflict, while 30% of Bulgarians typically supported the war and 50% had sympathies with Moscow.[79] Kanev attributed these sentiments to Russia's historical image as Bulgaria's liberator from the Ottoman Empire and the saturation of local Bulgarian newspapers with pro-Russian disinformation.[80] Bulgarian television host Martin Karbovski, who has 530,000 Facebook followers, amplified Russian conspiracies about Azovstal, and was proposed as a possible media regulator in April 2022. These pro-Russian sentiments permeated into Bulgaria's political establishment, as oligarchs and former state security agents promoted Kremlin narratives. The Bulgarian Socialist Party claimed that Russia's recognitions of DNR and LNR were "maybe violations of international law" and threatened to leave the coalition on 14 April if Sofia armed Ukraine.[81] Bulgarian defence minister Stefan Yanev resigned on 28 February after he supported Putin's description of the Ukraine War as an "operation" and insisted that Bulgaria should not adopt a "pro-Russian, pro-American or pro-European position."[82] Bulgarian energy minister Rosen Hristov's reconsideration of talks with Gazprom in August 2022 underscored the potential for Moscow's elite-level links to moderate Sofia's support for EU sanctions.

Romania's consistent support for Ukraine, which transcended historical boundary disputes, escalated tensions with Russia. Romania's announcement of planned reforms to its security policy on 19 April, which allowed it to provide arms to Ukraine as well as NATO countries, caused particular angst in Moscow. In late April, Killnet launched a series of cyberattacks against Romania over its pledge to provide lethal arms to Ukraine, which came on the heels of Zelensky's address to the Romanian parliament.[83] Russian media outlets promoted conspiracy theories about Romania's alleged plans to invade Moldova and Transnistria. After the April 2022 Tiraspol explosions, Sergei Markov claimed that Romania wanted to carry out an "Anschluss of Moldova," accused Moldovan president Maia Sandu of being a Romanian agent and claimed that Romanian forces dressed as Moldovan troops planned to invade Transnistria.[84] Due to Russia's confidence that it would swiftly annex Odesa and create a land bridge to Transnistria, Regnum columnist Vladimir Vasiliev warned that Romania only had a narrow window of time to unite with Moldova and limit Russia's influence on its borders.[85] Russian media outlets also highlighted alleged Romanian irredentism towards Ukraine and Tsargrad claimed that once Ukraine was de-nazified, it would divide its western regions between Hungary, Romania and Poland.[86] The U.S. Army's 101st Airborne Division's October 2022 deployment to Romania, which was its first in Europe since the Second World War, further increased tensions with Russia. Peskov warned that Romania's hosting of U.S. troops was destabilising, while Solovyov publicly mused about Russia carrying out a nuclear strike on U.S. bases in Romania.

These deteriorating relationships coincided with Russia's continued efforts to promote instability in Moldova and Georgia. On 28 February, Moldovan foreign minister Nicu Popescu declined to sanction Russia, as Moldova was a neutral country and economically "too integrated and dependent on Russia."[87] Moldova's pursuit of EU membership, which resulted in a formal application in March 2022, was followed by rising instability in Transnistria. On 25 April, explosions hit the Ministry of State Security in Tiraspol and a drone strike was fired on Tiraspol airport. These attacks were followed by explosions at the Grigoriopol transmitter on 26 April, which knocked out two radio antennae that broadcast Russian stations. On 27 April, drones flew over the Cobasna ammunition depot, one of Eastern Europe's largest caches. The use of RPG-18 and RPG-27 launchers pointed to Russian or Transnistrian culpability in the Ministry of State Security explosion, while Transnistria accused Ukraine of threatening the Cobasna depot, which was guarded by 1,500 Russian troops. Russian defence expert Sergey Ishchenko claimed that Ukraine had instigated sabotage attempts in Tiraspol and Mayak and would invade Transnistria in order to strengthen its defence of Odesa.[88] Alarmism about a potential Ukrainian invasion spread across the Russian information space and encouraged Transnistria to mobilise all men between 18 and 55 and allegedly provided contract soldiers to the Russian military. Russia's alleged missile strike on a Black Sea estuary bridge near Bilhorod-Dnistrovsky caused Arestovych to warn that Russia could launch a paratrooper operation in Transnistria.[89] Ukraine's concerns about a Russian escalation in Transnistria stemmed from its fears that it could use the enclave as an additional invasion axis in southern Ukraine.

While a major escalation in Transnistria was ultimately averted, Moldova's security situation remained tense and Chișinău–Moscow relations exhibited extreme volatility. As Moldova possessed just 6,000 troops and Transnistria had a 10,000-man standing army, Sandu called for a sweeping military modernisation to prevent Russia from violating its neutrality.[90] German defence minister Christine Lambrecht's 1 October pledge to provide Moldova with military training and drones underscored NATO's willingness to help Moldova defend itself against Russian aggression.[91] The Russian foreign ministry responded to these developments by warning that NATO military involvement in Transnistria "would have the most serious negative consequences for the country and the region."[92] Russian deputy foreign minister Sergei Rudenko also warned Moldova against accepting Western military assistance as a neutral state, as it would not increase its security.[93] Russia paired these veiled threats with incendiary rhetoric that threatened Moldova's sovereignty. Slutsky's 7 September proclamation that "Transnistria is our territory" underscored Russia's willingness to threaten annexation to counter Moldova's pro-Western tilt.[94] Lavrov emphasised Russia's desire to defend Russian-language speakers in Moldova and railed against Moldova's Ukraine-style cancellation of Russian culture. In addition to warning that Moldova was pursuing a military solution in Transnistria, which could threaten Russian peacekeepers and place it in direct conflict with Russia, Lavrov incensed the Moldovan authorities by highlighting Gagauzia's goal of special recognition.[95]

Although Russia's defeat in Kherson will likely prevent its military from creating a Transnistria land bridge, it can still credibly threaten Moldova's security and stability. On 31 October, Ukrainian air defences intercepted a Russian fussilade, which caused missile debris to land in northern Moldova's Naslavcea village.[96] Popescu described Russia's attacks on Ukrainian civilian infrastructure as a threat to Moldova's "energy and human security" and declared a Russian diplomat persona non grata in protest.[97] Due to interconnections between Moldova and Ukraine's energy systems, Russian strikes on Ukrainian electrical grids caused mass power outages in Moldova. Much like with Nord Stream, Russia has also been accused of weaponising gas against Moldova under the guise of "technical problems." Despite renewing Gazprom's supply deal with Moldovagaz in November 2021, Alexei Pushkov claimed that Russia was too accommodating of Moldova's financial issues on 21 January after Sandu condemned Russian conduct in Transnistria.[98] Moldova's offer to pay for Russian gas in both roubles and euros from 1 May and clearance of its $35.9 million outstanding debt in late September did not allay this dispute. Gazprom's decision to cut 30% of its exports to Moldova on 1 October increased Chișinău's energy dependence on Romania, which now supplies 90% of its electricity.[99] Russian state media outlets expressed solidarity with pro-Kremlin former president Igor Dodon after his May 2022 arrest for treason and amplified protests by activists from his Party of Socialists. *RIA Novosti*'s 26 October headline "People in Despair. Parallel Government Created in Moldova" exemplified Russia's concerted framing of Moldova as an authoritarian state.[100]

Georgia's initial response to Russia's invasion of Ukraine mirrored Moldova's cautious reaction. On 25 February, Georgian prime minister Irakli Garibashvili insisted that Georgia would not participate in sanctions against Russia, as "this would only damage our country and populace more," and insisted that Russia posed no threat to Georgia. Garibashvili accused opposition parties of trying to recreate the provocations that had led to the 2008 Georgian War and resisted domestic pressure to visit Ukraine.[101] Kakhaber Kemoklidze, who served as head of Georgia's National Security Council, believed that Garibashvili feared that Russia would blockade grain, wine and food if it joined the sanctions regime.[102] Garibashvili's stance triggered intense domestic backlash and criticisms from Ukraine. Mass pro-Ukraine protests erupted in Georgia immediately after the invasion, which condemned Russia's aggression and Garibashvili's response. On 1 March, Droa Party leader Elene Khoshtaria told cheering demonstrators that "Irakli Garibashvili must leave" so Georgia could help Ukraine and join the EU.[103] Kemoklidze believed that political opposition to Gharibashvili's policies stemmed from the belief that Georgia could have rallied the West to sanction Russia for its occupations of Abkhazia and South Ossetia, which previously were unpunished.[104] Garibashvili's implicit promotion of the view that Zelensky goaded Russia to war and concerns from senior Ukrainian officials such as Iryna Vereshchuk that Georgia was acting as a conduit for sanctioned Russian goods strained Tblisi's relations with Kyiv.[105] Zelensky accused Georgia of "immoral behaviour" while Ukraine's prime minister Denys Shmyhal urged Garibashvili to lift his ban on Georgian foreign fighters for Ukraine.[106] Danilov accused Georgia of behaving unethically, as it had resisted Ukraine's efforts to create a second front for Russia in the South Caucasus, Kaliningrad or the Kuril Islands.[107]

Over time, Georgia's policy towards the Ukraine War drifted closer to the Western line. Georgia swiftly complied with Western financial sanctions against Russia, stripping VTB of its local operations, and Georgian president Salome Zourabichvili pledged to support Ukraine in all international resolutions.[108] The Georgian Legion, which was formed in 2014, trained newly mobilised Ukrainian forces and persisted in military operations to defend Kyiv, such as the battles of Antonov Airport and Hostomel. These policies were greeted with scepticism in Kyiv, as Georgian officials had previously operated on the assumption that Russia would defeat Ukraine in a matter of days and released statements on the war that were enthusiastically promoted by Russian state media outlets.[109] On 3 March, Georgia expressed interest in becoming an EU member, but its application stalled, as the European Commission announced in June 2022 that it would need to implement reforms before being granted candidate status. Georgia's delicate balancing act did not deter Russia from infringing on its sovereignty. On 31 March, South Ossetia's president Anatoly Bibilov announced plans to hold a referendum on joining Russia on 17 July. However, his successor Alan Gagloev shelved this proposal after his May 2022 electoral triumph over Bibilov.[110] On 28 March, Ukraine's General Staff claimed that 150 South Ossetian troops were fighting alongside the Russian military.[111] Abkhazia supported Russia's invasion but refrained from deploying troops to Ukraine or requesting an annexation referendum.

Looking ahead, Russia's principal security threats to Georgia pertain to their ongoing border dispute and the influx of asylum seekers. Khurvateli, a village located 60km from Tblisi that is almost entirely encircled by South Ossetia, is the latest theatre of Russia's "creeping occupation" of Georgian territory. This policy began after the 2008 Georgian War and caused Russia to incrementally expand the de facto borders of Georgia's occupied regions by constructing ditches and barbed wire fences.[112] At the time of writing, Georgia has experienced two waves of Russian asylum seekers since the Ukraine War began. In March 2022, 30,000 Russians fled to Georgia, which caused an influx of anti-war liberals and economic migrants to settle in Tbilisi. Georgia's flexible visa policies, which allow Russians to stay for one year, the proliferation of Russian-language media, and an established community of dissidents, such as Navalny-aligned Siberian journalist Leo Jimmer, enhanced its appeal as an asylum destination.[113] The second wave of anti-mobilisation asylum seekers, who arrived in September 2022, received a frostier reception in Georgia. On the Russia–Georgia border, banners reading "Putin is Russia. While Putin rules the country and people obey him" and "In surveys, most of you support the war. So why now are you leaving?" greeted Russian asylum seekers.[114] Despite this hostile welcome, a 3,000-vehicle queue formed on the Russia–Georgia border after mobilisation began and the estimated wait time for border crossing was 48 hours. From 27 September to 21 October, Russia operated a screening checkpoint to vet young men fleeing to Georgia and South Ossetia, as 78,000 Russians fled to Georgia during the first two weeks after mobilisation was announced.[115] Former Georgian diplomat Ekaterina Meiering believed this asylum wave reflected Garibashvili's appeasement of Russia, as RT and Russian education resurfaced, while dissidents affiliated with *Dozhd* and Navalny were struggling to enter Georgia.[116]

Russia's Destabilising Conduct in the Western Balkans

Since the beginning of the Ukraine War, Western officials have expressed concern that Russia could create a second front of instability in the western Balkans to distract NATO. Liz Truss addressed this risk during her May 2022 visit to Sarajevo, as she highlighted Russia's "malign" influence in former Yugoslavia and accused Russia of trying to reignite a conflict in the western Balkans.[117] Maria Zakharova responded by condemning NATO's "unscrupulously destructive" influence in the western Balkans, reviving memories of NATO bombings of Belgrade and highlighting Britain's failure to help Yugoslavia against Nazi Germany during the Second World War.[118] While Truss's alarmist rhetoric did not come to pass, Russia's strategy in the western Balkans pivoted from a multi-vector policy to a Serbia-centric approach. This pivot was driven by practical necessity, as Russia's relations with other states in the western Balkans sharply deteriorated. Despite Croatian president Zoran Milanovic's pre-invasion condemnations of Britain's provocative policies towards Russia and threat to not send troops to NATO's force contingent in Eastern Europe, Croatia–Russia relations markedly deteriorated over the course of 2022. On 26 May, Russia commemorated the thirtieth anniversary of its diplomatic relationship with Croatia by condemning Zagreb's hostile actions, which included the expulsion of eighteen Russian diplomats in April 2022.[119] Milanovic's pro-Russian tone also softened, as he confined his comments to criticisms of the efficacy of sanctions against Russia.[120] Albania co-sponsored a UNSC resolution with the U.S. condemning Russia's annexation referenda and encouraged Russians fleeing mobilisation to consider settlement in Tirana. Montenegro used sanctions enforcement to shed its reputation as a "Russian VIP resort," as 40% of its real estate is owned by Russians, but Russian buyers still led the way from February to July.[121] Montenegro's 30 September expulsion of six Russian diplomats for espionage was followed by Russia's closure of its embassy in Podgorica.[122]

Although Serbia opposed the invasion of Ukraine, it refused to impose sanctions on Russia. On 25 February, Serbian president Alexander Vučić reiterated Putin's description of Russians and Ukrainians as fraternal nations and attributed its position to "national interests" and "traditional friendships."[123] Air Serbia expanded travel links between Moscow and Belgrade, even as Russian airlines were excluded from European airspace. Despite countervailing EU pressure, Vučić announced an "extremely favourable" natural gas deal with Russia on 29 May and prepared to welcome Lavrov to Belgrade in early June.[124] While Lavrov did not ultimately visit Belgrade, Serbia and Russia signed a "Consultation Plan" to upgrade cooperation in 2023–4 on the sidelines of the UNGA on 24 September. Serbia downplayed this agreement as "technical" rather than security-related and claimed that it had signed similar agreements with Russia every year since 1996.[125]

Vučić's efforts to strengthen Serbia–Russia relations during the Ukraine War received enthusiastic support from his political allies and the Serbian public. Serbian interior minister Alexander Vulin railed against the West's cancellation of Russian culture, engaged with Patrushev on security threats and questioned the merits of Serbia's EU candidacy. Serbian academic Orhan Dragaš's highlighting of Russia's pervasive influence in the security and intelligence sectors, which was evidenced by GRU infiltration of the Serbian army and organisation of anti-government riots in Belgrade, built on Vučić's overarching pro-Russian agenda.[126]

These elite-level relationships have spilt over into pro-Russian activism. Serbian media outlet *Objektiv* gleefully predicted that Russia would overrun Ukraine in one day while *Večernje Novosti* framed Russia's invasion as a response to NATO threats.[127] Ahead of the April 2022 elections, Dragaš proclaimed that Putin would win 70% of the vote if he was a candidate in Serbia.[128] Pro-Russian demonstrations featuring thousands of people brandishing the Z logo were a recurrent feature of Serbian political life, and posters commemorating Darya Dugina and the Wagner Group popped up on the streets of Belgrade. Alexander Dugin's proclamation that "Serbia is my love," which aligned with his belief that Serbia fit into an Orthodox Russian South, revealed linkages between far-right movements in the two countries.

Yevgeny Prigozhin's efforts to capitalise on these links by ensconcing a place for the Wagner Group in Serbia have received greater attention. On 8 December, the Wagner Group announced that it established a "friendship and cooperation" centre in Belgrade that would use soft power to strengthen Russia–Serbia relations.[129] Following a trip by the Serbian nationalist People Patrol organisation to the Wagner Group's corporate headquarters in St. Petersburg, U.S. State Department Counsellor Derek Chollet alleged that the Wagner Group was trying to recruit Serbian mercenaries to fight in Ukraine.[130] RT's newly minted Serbian channel has played a crucial role in aiding the Wagner Group's recruitment of mercenaries. After initially staying silent, Vucic lashed out angrily at the Wagner Group on Serbian national TV, stating "Why do you, from Wagner, call anyone from Serbia when you know that it is against our rules?"[131] Prigozhin subsequently denied recruiting Serbian fighters to Ukraine but it is clear that Russia–Serbia security cooperation is at its highest level since Slobodan Milo ševic's overthrow.

The endurance of Russia–Serbia cooperation was intriguing, as Vučić did not completely align his country with the Kremlin's conduct in Ukraine. Except for its abstention in the 14 November UNGA on reparations, Serbia repeatedly voted to condemn Russian conduct. Vučić attributed Serbia's vote to suspend Russia from the UNHRC to the threat of Western sanctions, as he feared the EU would restrict Belgrade's ability to purchase Russian oil after 15 May.[132] Vučić's opposition to Russia's territorial annexations likely stemmed from frustrations with Putin's comparison of the DNR and LNR's secession with Kosovo, which saw Serbia's *Republika* outlet claim that Russia had stabbed it in the back.[133] Despite Vučić's justifications, Serbia's deviations from a rigid pro-Russian line received far-right backlash. On 15 April, far-right activists staged protests in Belgrade against Russia's UNHRC suspension, which featured the slogans "Serbs and Russians—Brothers Forever" and "Crimea is Russia, Kosovo is Serbia."[134] Serbian Radical Party founder Vojislav Šešelj claimed that referenda in Donetsk, Luhansk, Kherson and

Zaporizhzhia aligned with the UN Charter, as they had the right to secession and faced the "threat of destruction by the neo-Nazi regime in Kyiv."[135] Despite these far-right demonstrations, Serbia accepted 45,000 Russians fleeing the Ukraine War and mobilisation. Although Hungary and Serbia agreed to construct a pipeline on 10 October that would facilitate Russian oil exports, Vučić took tentative steps towards divesting from Russian energy. On 14 July, Serbia mulled undoing its sale of a 51% stake in its NIS oil company to Gazprom, while Vučić stated on 29 August that Serbia's finances were robust enough to purchase energy from alternative sources.[136] As just 26% of Serbs blame Russia for the war, Vučić's solidarity with Moscow was driven primarily by domestic political considerations rather than Serbia's long-term strategic outlook, which favoured continued economic integration with the EU and a multi-vector security policy.[137]

Despite Vučić's balancing strategy, concerns persisted about Russia's support for Serbian revanchism in the western Balkans. As tensions between Serbia and Kosovo escalated in August 2022, the Russian foreign ministry accused Kosovo of "taking another step towards the expulsion of the Serbian population from Kosovo and the ouster of Kosovo Serbian institutions" and described the Kosovar authorities as "radicals."[138] Zakharova described Kosovo as a "terrible black hole" which saw people get "dissected alive" for the sale of their internal organs.[139] Dzhabarov accused the West of trying to drag Russia into a Ukraine-style intervention in Serbia and boasted of Moscow's ability to supply energy or arms to Belgrade if tensions with Kosovo boiled over.[140] Dragaš linked these statements to a "massive hybrid operation" to instigate violence between Serbs and Albanians in northern Kosovo, and a potential clash between Serbia and the NATO mission in Kosovo (KFOR). Dragaš noted that Russia's disinformation campaign consisted of falsified statements from Vučić, who was trying to restrict the escalation, rumours that

Serbia was imminently planning to invade Kosovo and conspiracies about dead bodies on the Serbia–Kosovo border.[141] Russia's operation of a humanitarian aid centre close to the Serbia–Kosovo border and weak rule of law in Serb-minority areas of Kosovo provided openings for the Kremlin's active measures.[142] As the locus of Serbia–Kosovo negotiations shifted from the UN to EU format, which excluded Russia, Kosovo's foreign minister Meliza Haradinaj believed that Moscow could be trying to derail EU talks and revive the UN's dominance.[143]

Russia posed a similar if less immediate threat to the stability of Bosnia-Herzegovina. When asked about the possibility of Bosnia-Herzegovina joining NATO in March 2022, Russian ambassador to Bosnia-Herzegovina Igor Kalabukhov declared that "Should there be any threat, we will respond" and warned that "Ukraine's example shows what we expect."[144] Republika Srpska president Milorad Dodik endorsed Russia's invasion of Ukraine, as he stated that 15 million Russian-language speakers were deprived of rights by Kyiv, and compared their alleged desire to unite with Russia to the wishes of Bosnian Serbs to be part of Serbia.[145] On 20 September, Dodik met with Putin and subsequently declared "We have the best possible relations with Russia."[146] The Bosnian Serb Assembly tried to thwart Bosnia-Herzegovina from imposing sanctions on Russia but Dodik ally president Branislav Borenovic stated that these efforts did not succeed.[147] Despite its destabilising ambitions, it is unclear whether Russia will be able to leverage its partnership with Serbia to destabilise Bosnia-Herzegovina. Although Vučić would likely arm the Bosnian Serbs in the event of a civil war, Bosnian analyst Harun Karčić argued that Vučić wants to avoid an outright conflict, as the status quo allows Serbia to deniably project influence.[148] Given Serbia's calculus, Russia is likely to confine its destabilisation of Bosnia-Herzegovina to provocative actions such as thwarting financing of the High Representative post.

Belarus: A Restrained Co-Aggressor in the Ukraine War

Due to Belarus's extensive logistical support for the Ukraine invasion, Alexander Lukashenko has been a resolute supporter of Russia's war effort. Lukashenko endorsed Putin's stated goals of demilitarisation and denazification, as he warned of the threat of NATO deploying weapons with nuclear warheads to Ukraine and decried "sprouts of fascism" appearing in Ukraine.[149] During a 12 April meeting with Putin, Lukashenko decried the Bucha Massacre as a British-organised "psychological special operation," and claimed that the FSB and Belarusian security services could provide addresses, car numbers and car brands that arrived in Bucha. Lukashenko handed over documents to Putin on the Bucha Massacre, which Peskov claimed "would be examined by the special services."[150] In addition to showing fealty to the Kremlin, Lukashenko tried to justify his support for Russia's military interventions by highlighting security threats to Belarus. On 10 October, he warned that the military-political leadership of NATO and European countries were "already openly considering options for possible aggression against our country, up to a nuclear strike."[151] Belarusian officials claim that this threat had first surfaced in 2010, as tight sanctions were imposed against Lukashenko's government, and intensified after the 2020 protests, which fuelled concerns of an imminent attack by external forces.[152] Lukashenko warned that 25,000 NATO forces were stationed near Belarus's borders. This reflected the creation of new brigades in northern and eastern Poland, as well as training exercises at Pabradė, Lithuania, which is 15km from the Belarusian border.[153] Lukashenko also sounded the alarm about a potential Ukrainian strike against Belarus and spread conspiracies about Poland's movement of nuclear weapons near Belarusian territory.[154]

Despite these threat narratives, Belarus refrained from intervening militarily in Ukraine. This restraint surprised Ukrainian officials, who incorrectly warned on 1 March that columns of Belarusian troops had entered Chernihiv. According to GUR, this decision contravened the Kremlin's wishes, as Putin's regular meetings with Lukashenko were aimed at soliciting Belarusian military support.[155] Lukashenko's refusal to deploy troops to Ukraine can be explained by intense domestic opposition. In the event of direct Belarusian military intervention in Ukraine, Tsikhanouskaya urged Belarusian soldiers to "lay down their arms, join the guerrillas, change sides, join the Ukrainian military."[156] During the Kyiv offensive, Belarusian partisans carried out eighty acts of sabotage on railways that hindered Russia's invasion of Ukraine and threats of execution did not deter them from disrupting Russia's war effort. A regiment of Belarusian dissidents formed in Poland and named after nineteenth century revolutionary Kastus Kalinouski vowed to "liberate Belarus through the liberation of Ukraine."[157] Andrei Sannikov averred that Belarusian conscripts would mobilise 2020 election protesters, who could turn their weapons against Lukashenko's regime, and although the Belarusian military is very loyal to Lukashenko's regime, it is unclear how the internal security services would respond in such a situation.[158] The Belarusian military's poor combat effectiveness also contributed to Lukashenko's non-intervention decision. Valery Kavaleuski believes that Belarus's military would merely be "cannon-fodder" as it has not served in open combat since independence, and Belarus has just 10,000 contract soldiers at its disposal.[159] While Belarus has not deployed troops to Ukraine, it has assisted Russia's military campaign in other ways. Since Russia's defeat in Kyiv, the Russian military has launched sporadic missile strikes from Belarusian territory and Belarus has used its air defence systems to guard the Union State's Western flank.[160] Belarus's mobilisation of "people's militias," which began in late May, advance this cause. On 21 September, Belarusian Security Council State Secretary

Alexander Volfovich described these militias as a bulwark against NATO aggression towards Russia from the western axis.[161] Belarus also plans to move 12,000 tons of ammunition to Russian territory, which will partially alleviate shortages caused by Russia's rapid depletion of ammunition stocks.[162]

The combined impact of the Ukraine War and Western sanctions has caused Belarus to deepen its integration with Russia. On 3 October, Belarusian prime minister Roman Golovchenko predicted that trade with Russia would increase to $45 billion in 2022, a 12.5% increase from 2021, and exports would rise by 30%.[163] In August 2022, Russia and Belarus expanded their list of joint import substitution projects to twenty. Lukashenko predicted that these projects were valued at $2 billion and described the construction of Belarusian ports in St. Petersburg and Murmansk as especially promising.[164] Despite this expanded cooperation, Russia's unwillingness to facilitate the global expansion of Belarusian potash exports and the collapse of Belarus's trade links with Ukraine were significant economic blows.[165] Although Belarus's raw material-centric trade links with Europe were not completely derailed by sanctions, its economic isolation drifted it further into Moscow's orbit. The expansion of Belarus's security cooperation with Russia was equally noteworthy. On 28 February, Belarus held a referendum which saw 65.16% of its citizens vote to allow Russia to deploy nuclear weapons and establish a permanent military presence on its territory. After meeting with Lukashenko on 25 June, Putin vowed to supply Iskander-M tactical missile systems, which can use ballistic missiles, cruise missiles and nuclear weapons, to Belarus. These deliveries were paired with Russia's promises to modernise Belarusian fighter jets. On 26 August, Lukashenko boasted that Belarus's Su-24 jets could be refitted to carry nuclear weapons and stated that "The West must understand, that if they opt for escalation, no helicopters or planes will save them."[166] These arms deliveries were followed by the creation of a Russia–Belarus regional grouping on 10 October, which resulted in 9,000 additional Russian troops, equipment and MiG-31 jets being stationed on Belarusian territory.[167] This regional grouping, which adds heft to previously unused terms of early 2000s Union Treaty negotiations, will likely be followed by the construction of joint military training centres for Russian and Belarusian forces.

While Belarus is unambiguously supportive of Russia's war against Ukraine, it still tries to frame itself as a voice of de-escalation. Belarusian diplomats routinely highlight their mediation efforts during the initial stages of the war but concede that Belarus could only act as a host venue and not influence the intransigent positions of conflicting parties. Nevertheless, Belarusian officials claim to want to end the war and prevent a conflict of this kind from erupting again. Historical memory drives Belarus's purported commitment to pacifism, as Belarus's population is lower than it was during the Second World War and its territory has been historically trespassed during inter-state conflicts.[168] Despite the breakdown of Minsk II and Turkey's emergence as the mediator of choice, Belarus still retains hope of reviving a mediation role. On 5 May, Lukashenko snapped that Russia's "operation has dragged on" and claimed that "Thanks to yours truly, me that is, negotiations between Ukraine and Russia have begun."[169] Mirroring official Kremlin statements on diplomacy, Lukashenko accused Ukraine of being disinterested in negotiations, even though the war was being fought on its territory. On 14 October, Lukashenko urged Western countries not to push Russia into a corner, as it could lead to nuclear weapons use if its territory was threatened.[170] Given Belarus's standing as a co-aggressor that had consistently defended Russian aggression in the UNGA, Lukashenko was likely framing himself as a de-escalation voice in a gambit to alleviate Western sanctions and appear less like a Russian client.

Russia's Eroding Soft Power in the South Caucasus and Central Asia

The marked decline of Russian soft power in the post-Soviet space was laid bare by its dearth of support in the South Caucasus and Central Asia. The events that unfolded at the 23 November CSTO Summit in Yerevan underscored Russia's diminished stature in its sphere of influence. During the summit, Putin and Lukashenko went to great lengths to highlight the existential importance of CSTO solidarity. Putin's address emphasised "the common history" of CSTO states which predictably hinged on the Great Patriotic War. Lukashenko's speech included more strident language, as he warned about the "wild" nuclear rhetoric of NATO's countries and raged against Poland's pledge to host U.S. nuclear weapons. Lukashenko also urged recalcitrant CSTO members to rally behind Russia, stating "If Russia wins, the CSTO will live. If God forbid, it does not win, the CSTO will not exist."[171] These calls for CSTO unity did not translate to the summit proceedings. Kazakhstan emphasised the need for peace negotiations in Ukraine. In a rebuke of Russia's inconsistent efforts to negotiate peace in Nagorno-Karabakh, Nikol Pashinyan refused to sign a CSTO declaration on assistance measures to Armenia as it was not "sufficiently finalized." Due to Pashinyan's dissent, Putin was forced to admit to "problems" amongst CSTO members that needed to be discussed without cameras.[172] These backchannel negotiations have not eased tensions with Russia's treaty allies. On 30 December, the Russian Foreign Ministry denounced Pashinyan's "public attacks" on its peacekeepers and warned that they could tangibly harm the Armenia-Azerbaijan normalisation process.[173] While Kazakhstan deported a FSB major who fled Russia over the Ukraine War on 29 December, it has also tried to supplant Russian oil shipments to Germany and purchased discounted Russian bonds from investors seeking to free their assets from sanctions.

In spite of its long-standing position as a loyal Russian treaty ally, Armenia has refrained from backing Russian policy in Ukraine. On 23 February Armenia's foreign ministry stated that "There is no such issue on the agenda" when asked about recognising the DNR and LNR, and Yerevan maintained a policy of neutrality towards the Ukraine War. Armenia's tepid expressions of solidarity with Moscow, such as its opposition to Russia's expulsion from the Council of Europe, and decision to sidestep Ukraine-related issues in Pashinyan's call with Putin on 26 February, reflected its delicate balancing act.[174] Armenia's imposition of sanctions on Zatulin and Simonyan on 26 October underscored its desire to distance itself from Russian propagandists. Armenia allegedly helped Russia circumvent sanctions, while also experiencing considerable economic dislocations from the conflict. The U.S. worked with Armenian banks on sanctions compliance, as it was feared that local banks would aid Russian citizens.[175] The U.S. Treasury Department sanctioned Taco LLC, an Armenian partner of Radioatomivka, for aiding Russia's military campaign in Ukraine. The 49% increase in Russia–Armenia trade observed in August 2022 prompted concerns about third country exports.[176] Armenia became a haven for Russian anti-war liberals, and in March, an estimated 6,000 Russians and Ukrainians were arriving in Armenia each day.[177] This influx of migrants coincided with the erosion of Armenia's economic competitiveness, as the declining rouble relative to the dram during the early stages of the war reduced Russia's imports of Armenian goods.[178] While a resurgent rouble eased Armenia's export woes, World Bank GDP 2022 growth prospects for Armenia slid from 5.3% to 1.2% after the war began.

Azerbaijan's position towards the Ukraine War mirrored the ambiguities witnessed in Armenia's stance. Farid Shafiyev, the chairman of Baku's AIR Center, claimed that experts tended to overemphasise the 21 February Russia–Azerbaijan agreement, while ignoring president Ilham Aliyev's 15 January meeting with Zelensky which upgraded Azerbaijan–Ukraine cooperation.[179] Azerbaijan's provisions of humanitarian aid to Ukraine and 20% increase in trade with Russia, which was noted in an 18 November Russia–Azerbaijan meeting on economic cooperation, underscored this balancing act.[180] Shafiyev averred that the Ukraine War was not universally negative for Azerbaijan's geopolitical interests, as it reduced Russia's ability to provide military support for Armenia and increased its dependency on Turkey, which would restrict its desire to destabilise the South Caucasus.[181] Azerbaijan's decision to ban protests outside the Russian Embassy in Baku underscored the primacy of these elite-level interests over popular anti-Russian sentiments.

As Azerbaijan's expansion of energy exports to Europe from 8.2 billion to 11 billion cubic metres had a limited impact, the Nagorno-Karabakh conflict was its principal source of friction with Russia. On 26 March, the Russian defence ministry accused Azerbaijan of using Bayraktar TB-2 drones in Nagorno-Karabakh, which prompted Putin to hold two trouble-shooting calls with Pashinyan. The Kremlin issued a direct appeal for Azerbaijan to withdraw its troops.[182] Mikhail Delyagin's subsequent denunciation of Azerbaijan as a proxy of the U.S. and Turkey, which included calls for a Russian nuclear strike on Azerbaijan's oil and gas industry, escalated tensions between Moscow and Baku.[183] While Peskov walked back Delyagin's comments by urging Russian lawmakers to avoid "emotional statements" on Nagorno-Karabakh, concerns about Azerbaijani aggression lingered in Moscow. The failure of Russia's signature 3+3 format in the South Caucasus, which was marred by Georgia's non-participation, underscores the Kremlin's limited influence over the frozen conflict.

Russia's influence in Central Asia was marred by the weaknesses of regional institutions and the dissonant policies of its treaty allies. On 25 February, Russia's economic development ministry praised the EAEU's "huge potential that is fully untapped" and predicted that sanctions would lead to a drastic expansion of intra-regional trade.[184] Russia's restrictions on grain exports to the EAEU and currency and remittance-related economic growth declines in Kazakhstan and Kyrgyzstan derailed this vision.[185] On 3 October, Kazakhstan's foreign ministry released a statement confirming that the CSTO would not be a party in the Ukraine War, as it favoured "territorial integrity, sovereign equality and peaceful coexistence of states" under the UN Charter.[186] The CSTO's implicit rebuke of Russia's invasion of Ukraine earned it derision on state media. On a 13 November episode of Solovyov's show, Simonyan declared that the CSTO would not help Russia counter attacks on annexed Ukrainian territory, as Russia's boundaries were different when it joined the bloc. On a 15 November *Soloviev Live* episode, Solovyov proclaimed, "Our territory is actively shelled. There are enemy Nazi troops on our territory. And so? Did CSTO say anything? Did CSTO speak up?" and lambasted dependent countries for abstaining on a UN resolution calling for Russian reparations. The Grey Zone Telegram channel similarly expressed frustration with abstentions from Central Asian countries that only existed due to Russia.[187] These positions reflected the Ukraine War's unpopularity in Central Asia due to its contribution to inflation and remittance revenue cuts. A May–June 2022 Central Asian Barometer Survey showed that 70% of people in Kyrgyzstan believed the war would adversely impact their country, while 55% concurred in Kazakhstan.[188]

Kazakhstan's unwillingness to toe Russia's line on Ukraine caused particular angst in the Kremlin. This did not absolve Kazakhstan from the threat of Western sanctions, as Liz Truss vowed to "look into the issues around Kazakhstan" after being asked by Labour MP Margaret Hodge about that possibility.

While Kazakhstan's foreign ministry received assurances from Britain that no sanctions would be imposed, this near-miss encouraged Tokayev to vigorously defy Russia. On 6 March, 5,000 demonstrators gathered in Almaty with pro-peace slogans and insults against Putin, and these protests were not repressed by the Kazakh authorities.[189] On 28 March, Kazakhstan dispatched 17.5 tons of humanitarian aid to Ukraine, and citing budgetary constraints, cancelled its 9 May Victory Day parade. Kazakhstan's Victory Day cancellation received domestic backlash, as 600,000 Kazakh troops perished in the Second World War, but reflected Tokayev's desire to distance himself from Russia.[190] At the St. Petersburg Economic Forum on 17 June, Tokayev called the DNR and LNR "quasi-state entities" that Kazakhstan would not recognise and compared them to Abkhazia, South Ossetia, Taiwan and Kosovo. Tokayev warned that recognising states based on self-determination would produce 500–600 countries, which would lead to chaos.[191] Kazakhstan's growing assertiveness earned strident criticism from Zatulin and Simonyan's husband Tigran Keosayan, who threatened Ukraine-style Russian retaliations. These tensions persisted, as Russia announced the temporary closure of Novorossiyk oil terminal, which facilitated the export of Kazakh oil to EU countries, on 6 July. Although Kazakhstan pledged to extradite "wanted" Russians escaping mobilisation, it nonetheless granted asylum to 200,000 Russians fleeing the draft.

Kazakhstan's cautious defiance of Russia's aggression towards Ukraine was mirrored by other Central Asian countries, albeit to a less pronounced degree. Tajikistan's president Emomali Rahmon's 15 October CIS Summit proclamation that "We have always respected the interests of our main strategic partner. We want respect, too" underscored rising discontent with Russia amongst its Central Asian allies. Although Kyrgyz president Sadyr Zhaparov appeared to endorse the invasion on a 26 February call with Putin, which caused Ukraine to recall its ambassador from Bishkek, Zhaparov subsequently emphasised Kyrgyzstan's neutrality and inability to impact the war.[192] Kyrgyz MediaHub investigative media outlet's July 2020 discovery that the Wagner Group was recruiting Kyrgyz and Uzbek nationals to fight in Ukraine further soured relations.[193] Although the Wagner Group was willing to offer Kyrgyz nationals $4,383 a month and Russian citizenship after around six months of service, Central Asian mercenaries risked criminal charges if they ever attempted to return home. On 22 September, Uzbekistan's state prosecutors overtly warned its citizens against joining foreign armies after Russia reiterated these citizenship offers, and Ukraine captured Uzbek POWs fighting for the Russian military.[194] Uzbekistan's overt support for Ukraine's territorial integrity and calls for an end to the war, paired with its efforts to divest from Russia through the establishment of economic corridors with Azerbaijan and Turkey, undermined another critical Russian regional partnership. Thus has Russia's neo-imperial pursuit of territorial expansion in Ukraine ironically destroyed its sphere of influence.

9

RUSSIA PIVOTS TO THE EAST

On 15 September 2022, SCO leaders arrived in Samarkand, Uzbekistan for two days of bilateral and multilateral consultations. The stakes were especially high for Vladimir Putin, as he wanted to convince the international community that Russia was not isolated on the world stage. The SCO summit's ambiguous outcomes reinforced Russia's "virtual great power" status, as Putin engaged his counterparts in a business-as-usual fashion, but achieved few substantive breakthroughs. Xi Jinping highlighted Sino-Russian cooperation against the common threat of "colour revolutions" and built on Russia's advocacy for local currency trade.[1] Iranian president Ebrahim Raisi's meeting with Vladimir Putin included discussions of a new treaty, which would elevate Russia–Iran cooperation to a strategic partnership, and preparations for the arrival of eighty Russian companies in Iran for trade links.[2] This meeting reinforced the SCO's potential to act as a Russian economic forum that could quell the impact of Russian sanctions. Nevertheless, Russia's increasingly limited appeal as a partner for SCO countries was also on display. Narendra Modi's "now is not the time for war" invective to Putin received particular scrutiny, even though Russia's ambassador to India, Denis Alipov, accused the Western media of "cherry-picking" and Indian media outlets framed the comment as in keeping with Modi's past rhetoric.[3] Videos of Putin being kept waiting by the leaders of Turkey, Azerbaijan, India and Kyrgyzstan were a source of widespread mockery of the Russian president.

These public embarrassments came on the heels of the underwhelming Eastern Economic Forum in Vladivostok, which was only attended by two heads of state: Nikol Pashinyan, and Myanmar's junta leader, Min Aung Hlaing. While the SCO summit exposed the limitations of Moscow's clout in the collective non-West, Russia views the Indo-Pacific region as its most important foreign policy vector in an era of sanctions. Russia's eastward pivot primarily targeted China, India and Iran, but Moscow's relationships with middle powers such as Pakistan, Vietnam and Indonesia, and isolated regimes such as North Korea, Myanmar and the Taliban, have also strengthened. Russia's hopes of balancing between West and East in the Indo-Pacific region have been dashed, however, as Japan, South Korea, Taiwan and Australia have joined the Western sanctions regime. This chapter will outline the various dimensions of Russia's eastward pivot during the Ukraine War, and highlight the strengths and limitations of its major partnerships in the Indo-Pacific region.

Russia's Partnership with China: Growing Dependence, Cautious Support

As it was swiftly apparent that Russia's invasion of Ukraine would lead to its near-complete isolation from the West, Moscow closely monitored China's response. China's official reaction to the Ukraine War largely aligned with the Kremlin's hopes. On 24 February, China refused to describe Russia's actions as an "invasion" and its assistant foreign minister, Hua Chunying, snapped: "The U.S. has been fuelling the flame, fanning up the blame, how do they want to put out the fire?"[4] When asked by CBS's Margaret Brennan on 20 March why China refused to describe Russia's actions as an invasion, China's ambassador to the U.S., Qin Gang, said, "Don't be naïve. It doesn't solve the problem. I will be surprised if Russia backs down by condemnation."[5] China's UN Ambassador Zhang Jun also asserted that "bloc confrontation, political isolation, sanctions and pressurisation" would only lead to a dead end.[6] This position has endured in spite of mounting Western pressure. On 25 December, Wang Yi resolutely defended China's adhesion to "objectivity and impartiality," and pledged to further strengthen Sino–Russian relations.[7] This statement followed joint naval drills between Russia and China in the East China Sea, and presaged plans for combined exercises off South Africa's coast in February 2023. It also coincided with China's rare purchase of three ships of Arctic crude, which underscores Beijing's desire to capitalise on EU–Russia energy trade disruptions.[8]

Despite China's solidarity with Russia against U.S. condemnations and sanctions, the September 2022 SCO summit exposed the partnership's limits. Putin was forced to acknowledge Xi Jinping's "concerns" about Russia's actions in Ukraine, failed to secure major export or technological cooperation deals and got no assurance that a coveted bilateral meeting with Xi would occur in the near future.[9] Putin's trademark "no-limits" slogan to describe the Russia–China partnership was also notably absent from post-summit official statements. China's refusal to recognise any of Russia's territorial claims in Ukraine, which contrasted with Russia's consistent backing of Chinese actions in Hong Kong and Taiwan, also disappointed the Kremlin. This mixed picture was apparent in Russia's assessments of its relationship with China. In September 2022, Dmitry Suslov contended that the escalation of tensions between the U.S. and

China under Trump contributed to Beijing's level of support but noted that Moscow wanted "much more drastic escalations" with the West than China, and Iran was a more reliable commercial partner in an era of sanctions.[10]

As Russia's trade with the West nosedived, China expanded its role as an economic partner. During the first eight months of 2022, bilateral trade between Russia and China increased 31.4% to $117.2 billion and total commercial interactions between the two countries was expected to reach $200 billion by year end.[11] In August 2022, China's imports from Russia increased by 60% to $11.2 billion, which reflected surging demand for Russian coal, and exports to Russia increased by 26% to $8 billion.[12] China's purchases of discounted natural gas from Russia gained particular attention. On 6 February, China and Russia signed a thirty-year gas supply contract, which saw Gazprom pledge to supply China National Petroleum Company (CNPC) 10bcm of gas a year. These additional gas exports would occur via Sakhalin-2, which transports gas from the Russian Far East Sakhalin Island across the Sea of Japan to China's Heilongjiang province.[13] In September 2022, the Sakhalin-2 LNG export plant sold several shipments to China for a December delivery date at nearly half the contemporary market price.[14] Although the initial plan was for transactions to take place in euros, the post-war climate meant that these payments would be transacted in yuan and roubles. Gazprom CEO Alexei Miller's 6 September negotiations with CNPC chief Dai Houliang also touched upon an expansion of the Power of Siberia pipeline project, which exported 16.5bcm from Russia to China in 2021. However, China's economy remained heavily dependent on coal and oil, which even at a discount was 40% higher than 2019 rates, and Russia's ability to capitalise on its gas pipeline network with China was limited.

In stark contrast to the expansion of Chinese raw material imports from Russia, the investment picture was murkier.

Chinese investment in Russia had been in terminal decline from $2.96 billion in 2015 to $570 million in 2020, which belied the growing strength of bilateral relations between the two countries. Although China signed $2 billion in Belt and Road Initiative (BRI)-related deals in 2021, new BRI-related investments in Russia fell to zero during the first half of 2022.[15] This freeze, which was a unique low point in the BRI's history, reflected a broader downturn in Chinese BRI investments, which extended to partners like Egypt and Pakistan, and the impact of secondary sanctions. The BRI's pivot to rail cargo transfers across Central Asia, the Caucasus and Turkey to Europe reflects the impact of EU road transit sanctions on China's presence in the Russian economy. Despite this disappointing picture, the Russian Far East has been a noteworthy beneficiary of Chinese investment, as China streamlines its imports of oil, gas and agricultural goods from Russia. In June, the Heihe–Blagoveshchensk Bridge over the Amur River was inaugurated and in mid-September, the Quanzhou–Far East shipping line made its maiden voyage. A 2,200-metre Tongjiang–Nizhneleninskoye railway bridge was also expected to be constructed in the coming months.[16] Despite numerous false starts, substantive de-dollarisation was also taking shape. On the Moscow stock exchange, yuan/ruble settlements ranged between 30 to 70 billion rubles a day, ten times pre-war figures.[17] At the Eastern Economic Forum, the deputy chairman of Sberbank's board, Alexander Vedyakhin, announced plans to provide yuan-denominated loans later in 2022. This built on the decision by one-third of Russian banks to allow yuan accounts and the Russian finance ministry's ambitious push to issue bonds in yuan, which was then being reviewed by Chinese regulatory bodies.[18]

China's security cooperation with Russia also steadily advanced. As Patrushev travelled to China for consultations, Russia's Security Council released a statement on 19 September claiming that it had agreed to "further military cooperation" with China, which included exercises and senior contacts.[19] The August 2022 Vostok military drills were historic in nature, as they were the first exercises that involved all three of China's forces and included joint naval drills on the Sea of Japan right as tensions were escalating over Taiwan. Rear-Admiral Vladimir Kazakov of Russia's Pacific Fleet hailed a "new level" of integration between the Russian and Chinese navies, which countered the U.S.'s Exercise Pitch Black drills.[20] China also engaged in cyberattacks against 600 Ukrainian websites on 23 February but this disruptive action was likely aimed at surveillance rather than aiding Russia.[21] Although China relied heavily on Russian arms prior to its mid-2000s pivot to domestic production, the Ukraine War is unlikely to intensify the bilateral arms trade. Vassily Kashin admits that China could provide a great deal of useful hardware for Russia's war effort in Ukraine but conceded that the Russian military's aversion to importing hardware would prevent cooperation in this sphere.[22] Russia is also fiercely protective of technological innovations, which was evidenced by a Novosibirsk court's 30 June arrest of a scientist with Stage IV cancer, Dmitry Kolker, for collaborating with China on hypersonic weapons.[23] China's April 2022 pause in cooperation with the Russian Academy of Sciences will likely sharpen technological competition in the defence sphere. China could capitalise on the 26% decline in Russian arms exports in 2022 and sell lower-cost arms to Russian clients where it has an established presence, such as Angola, Nigeria, Myanmar and Bangladesh.

China's coordination with Russia in the information war against the West also expanded. This disinformation nexus was on display in domestic and international media coverage. For instance, a 4 April *People's Daily* article accused the U.S. of instigating the Ukraine War, using the conflict to "loot and profit" its defence companies and forcing Europe to swap Russian gas for

U.S. LNG to get a "double income."[24] On 21 April, Chinese commentator Li Zhiwei argued that "The U.S. has been fanning the flames over Ukraine, not just for the past few months, but for the past eight years, fuelling escalating tensions."[25] *Global Times* contributor Song Zhongping told Phoenix TV that Ukraine had faked the Bucha Massacre, as Russia had no motivation to kill civilians and Zelensky was an actor.[26] Russian media outlets have reciprocated China's solidarity to rally pro-Chinese sentiments at home. To highlight the inappropriateness of Western challenges to Chinese sovereignty over Taiwan, Tibet and Xinjiang, Timofey Bordachev compared it to not recognising Russia's control over Siberia.[27] The Tsargrad Telegram channel mocked Taiwan's deterrence efforts against China by stating that "The Taiwanese army almost burned the island while trying to start their own exercises."[28] During a 17 April segment on Vladimir Solovyov's Rossiya-1 show, Margarita Simonyan praised Chinese censorship policies, stating, "I very much want us to be like China. I dream about us being like China."

These synergies have permeated into China and Russia's international messaging. On 8 March, Chinese foreign ministry spokesman Zhao Lijian endorsed Russia's conspiracies about U.S. biological laboratories in Ukraine and accused the U.S. of obstructing the Biological Weapons Convention under the pretext of strengthening global public health.[29] On 18 April, Hua Chunying emphasised that only a minority of the international community wanted to sanction Russia, as "sanctions cannot bring peace but disaster to the world economy and people's living."[30] On 1 July, Zhao quipped, "NATO is a defensive alliance? Joke of the Century" and highlighted NATO's bombings of Yugoslavia, Afghanistan, Iraq and Libya as proof.[31] The Russian foreign ministry reciprocally backed China's narrative that Pelosi's Taiwan visit was a "provocation," and accused the U.S. of deliberately escalating China–Taiwan tensions.[32] Vladimir Putin also sounded the alarm about NATO's expanded activities in the Indo-Pacific region and auxiliary security agreements such as AUKUS between Australia, Britain and the U.S.[33] As Russian media outlets are censored in the West and expand their presence in the Global South, China could act as a surrogate for Kremlin narratives in Western countries and benefit from Russian propaganda in Africa, the Middle East and Latin America.

China's ability to support Russia during the Ukraine War is restricted by two principal factors. The first factor is China's desire to avoid becoming a party to the conflict, which would expose it to Western sanctions. Even in the absence of overt support for Russia, China's position on the Ukraine War has exposed it to Western condemnations and the tangible threat of economic sanctions. On 2 March, U.S. officials revealed that China had advance knowledge about the war and urged Russia to delay its invasion of Ukraine until the 2022 Beijing Winter Olympics were complete.[34] Chinese foreign ministry spokesperson Wang Wenbin called these allegations "utterly despicable" but speculation along these lines has endured. On 6 April, Jens Stoltenberg asserted that China's position questions "the right of nations to pursue their own path."[35] This hostile rhetoric compounds the escalation of China–U.S. tensions over Taiwan, which peaked following Nancy Pelosi's August 2022 visit and resulted in a suspension of dialogue on intra-military cooperation and climate change. Due to these tensions, Beihang University legal expert Tian Feilong quipped that "today's Russia could be tomorrow's China," and China University of Political Science and Law Professor Huo Zhengxin warned of the high risk of U.S. and EU secondary sanctions.[36] This view was not universally shared, as Taihe analytical centre expert Jia Jiashing highlighted established yuan/ruble trade mechanisms and China's lack of foreign exchange reserves in Russia as mitigating factors, but it has permeated widely in Chinese analytical circles.[37] China's decision to hold a "stress test" in late February and early March, which called upon banking regulation and international trade bodies to devise potential responses to Russia-style sanctions, underscored Beijing's fears about Western economic coercion.[38]

China's concerns about prospective secondary sanctions to punish its cooperation with Russia have empirical grounding. On 29 June, the U.S. imposed sanctions on five Chinese companies—Connec Electronic, Hong Kong-based World Jetta, Logistics Ltd., King Pai Technology and Winninc Electronic—for providing military assistance to Russia. On 30 September, the U.S. treasury department slapped sanctions on Sinno Electronics for providing support for Radioatomivka. These sanctions passed, even though China reportedly rejected Russian requests for military aid in March 2022 and the U.S. admitted on 3 May that China had abided by Lloyd Austin's request to his counterpart Wei Fenghe not to assist Russia.[39] To prevent sanctions in civilian economic sectors, China's credit card processor UnionPay refused to work with Russian banks after Visa and Mastercard stopped serving them, and China blocked Russian airlines from flying foreign-owned planes into its airspace.[40] On 28 March, China's state-owned oil company Sinopec suspended talks for a $500 million petrochemical investment and gas marketing venture in Russia, as it feared secondary sanctions for conducting business with Sibur minority stakeholder Gennady Timchenko.[41] Huawei was initially expected to be a beneficiary of the Ukraine War, as it replaced European companies in Russia's telecommunications market and earned Putin's trust following the Crimea annexation sanctions.[42] On 12 April, however, Huawei began furloughing employees in Russia over sanctions concerns and by late summer, Huawei had relocated its business activities in the post-Soviet space to Kazakhstan and Uzbekistan.[43]

The second factor is China's desire to position itself as a voice of de-escalation in the Ukraine conflict. In June 2022, the

Chinese embassy in the U.S. stated that "China's position on the Ukrainian issue has been consistent and clear. We have been playing a constructive role in promoting peace talks and have not provided military assistance to conflicting parties."[44] This statement reflected China's official policies from the early stages of the conflict. Chinese state media highlighted the 25 February Xi–Putin phone call, which saw Putin agree to hold talks with Ukraine, and the frequency of Chinese engagement with Western, Russian and Ukrainian officials, only rivalled in recent times by COVID-19.[45] On 7 March, Wang Yi expressed China's interest in mediation for the first time, following the high-profile shooting of a Chinese national escaping Ukraine. In keeping with its proxy war narrative, China urged the EU and U.S. to participate directly as diplomatic parties. This position was clearly articulated by Hua Chunying on 18 March, who quipped, "It takes two hands to clap. He who tied the bell to the tiger must take it off."[46] China's diplomatic efforts have received some positive feedback in the West and amongst anti-war Russian experts. On 5 March, Josep Borrell praised China's potential to serve as a mediator but distanced himself from Beijing's claims that the West could play a de-escalation role as dialogue parties.[47] Victor Mizin contended that China would try to preclude Russia from using a tactical nuclear weapon in Ukraine, as it would create chaos right as Xi Jinping was seeking stability after the 20th Chinese Communist Party Conference on 16 October.[48]

In Ukraine, China's role as an enabler of Russian aggression was viewed harshly. Ukrainian Rada Deputy Mykola Kniazhytskyi stated that "China must understand that signing the declaration on the establishment of a new world order on 4 February this year, perceived by Putin as Beijing's permission for a full-scale invasion of Ukraine, was a tremendous mistake."[49] Volodymyr Omelyan contended that China was "morally responsible" for the Ukraine War, and given its superpower aspirations, it had acted irresponsibly through a policy of neutrality.[50] China's refusal to be a security guarantor for Ukraine, in spite of repeated outreaches from Ukrainian officials and its pledges to serve in this role in 2013, added to the mood of disappointment in Kyiv. These mistrusts diluted the strength of China–Ukraine economic cooperation. On 23 September, Zelensky acknowledged that a call with Xi Jinping "would be difficult" and expressed frustration that pre-war communications channels with China, which had consisted of extensive economic and trade cooperation, had been destroyed.[51] Although China regularly provided humanitarian aid to Ukraine since 9 March, its prospects for investment in Ukraine's reconstruction were less certain. Alexey Maslov contended that although China viewed Belarus and Ukraine as key entry points into Europe, its investment prospects depended on the nature of the regime in Kyiv, as China was dissatisfied with Ukraine's decision to thwart its investment in its Motor Sich aerospace company.[52] Omelyan cites the negative precedent of China pledging investment in Black Sea port infrastructure in Mykolaiv or roads in Berdyansk and reneging as signs of what to expect in a post-war reconstruction scenario.[53]

Due to this mixed picture of progress and constraints, there was heated debate around whether China would benefit from a Russian victory or defeat in Ukraine. Sergei Karaganov contended that China was invested in Russia's success in Ukraine due to self-interest, as "the defeat of Russia will result in a qualitative deterioration in the position of the PRC."[54] This contention aligned with the belief in China that confrontation with the West was inevitable. Tsinghua University Professor Yan Xuetong stated, "the war in Ukraine has intensified the confrontation between the U.S. and China," and created a bipolar order that was not necessarily favourable, as Beijing had strained relations with Germany, France, Britain and Japan.[55] Hu Wei, vice-chairman of the Public Policy Research Center of the Counselor's Office of the State

Council in Beijing, declared, "China cannot only not stand with Putin but also should take concrete action to prevent Putin's adventures," representing a view that has been banished from Chinese foreign policy discourse. The dominance of Chinese hardliners pushed it closer to Russia, and Moscow pandered to this trend. Hu Xijin contended that Russia was China's most crucial partner against U.S. "maximum strategic coercion," as it could supply energy, food and raw materials to China, help stabilise Central Asia, deter the U.S. from nuclear blackmail, aid in containing Japan and facilitate ties with India.[56] Mirroring Xijin's warnings about U.S. coercion, Dmitry Medvedev opined on 23 March that after humiliating Russia, the U.S. would turn towards the "total weakening of China," which would facilitate a global crisis, breakdown of energy and food supplies, the collapse of collective security and a "big nuclear explosion."[57]

The case for China lobbying for a weakened Russia hinged on Beijing's desire to subjugate Moscow into a vassal state. Plekhanov Russian University of Economics Professor Oleg Glazunov asserted that Western sanctions on Russia "play into the hands of China, because Russia is eliminated as a competitor."[58] The potential for China to subordinate Russia's sovereignty was acutely felt in Moscow, even if Moscow's isolation from the West precluded an easy solution. Vladimir Inozemtsev believed that "Russians fear China even more than the West," as it was misunderstood and anti-Chinese sentiments would rise as Russia's desire for an independent course precluded "exchanging a pro-Western way for a pro-Chinese way."[59] Suslov contended that no-one in Russia wanted dependency on the West to be replaced by dependency on China, as it was not "strategically beneficial", but conceded that Moscow's immediate thoughts were about surviving its hybrid war with the West.[60] While it appeared as if China was rooting tacitly for Russia's success in Ukraine, Russia's movement towards the precipice of defeat could cause Beijing to see the benefits of a weakened Russia.

Russia and India: An Enduring but Limited Partnership

In keeping with its neutrality during the Crimea annexation, India refused to condemn Russia after its invasion of Ukraine. On 24 February, India called for an "immediate de-escalation" of the Ukraine War and focused on the evacuation of 20,000 Indian nationals residing in Ukraine. Despite Western entreaties to condemn Russian aggression, Denmark's claims that India could help de-escalate the war and Zelensky's outreach to India on security guarantees, Modi has remained unflinchingly committed to neutrality. India's policy towards Ukraine, which has been often described as "strategic ambivalence," can be explained by three factors. The first is historical precedent: the Soviet-era partnership with New Delhi, which crystallised with Khrushchev's 1955 support for India's claims to Jammu and Kashmir, and New Delhi's past reluctance to call out Soviet aggression towards Hungary, Czechoslovakia and Afghanistan, conditioned Modi's restraint.[61] Anti-Ukrainian sentiments, which spiked after social media videos showing racist actions from Ukrainian officials towards Indian students surfaced, helped perpetuate the enduring pro-Russia lean in Indian society.[62]

Anuradha Chenoy, a Professor at Jawaharlal Nehru University, also noted India's long tradition of opposing unilateral sanctions, apparent from its policies towards Iraq and Iran.[63] India's refusal to condemn Saddam Hussein's 1990 invasion of Kuwait, inspired by Iraq's support for India in Kashmir, is another relevant parallel.[64] The alignment between India's position on the Ukraine War and foreign policy traditions was challenged by Modi's critics. Former UN Under-Secretary General Shashi Tharoor expressed disapproval with Modi's refusal to condemn Russia's "regime change operation" in Ukraine when it "had consistently opposed such interventions," and urged Modi to look past Russia's "legitimate security concerns" and call for an end to war.[65] While Tharoor's case that "resort to war is impossible to accept or justify"[66] mirrors Modi's SCO summit comments, New Delhi is unwilling to break with its historical solidarity with Russia or aversion to sanctions.

The second factor is India's scepticism of the prevailing Western narrative that Putin is a unilateral aggressor in Ukraine, and desire to avoid taking sides in the Russia–West narrative war. Chenoy notes that Putin is not regarded as an "irrational madman" in India, as he has proven to be credible when he stated that he would not retaliate against NATO membership for Sweden and Finland, and insisted that NATO was a party in the conflict, as it was creating a Cuban Missile Crisis scenario for Russia.[67] India's unwillingness to dismiss Russian conspiracies was evident in its response to the Bucha Massacre. On 6 April, India condemned the killings but called for an "independent investigation" of who was culpable.[68] Former Indian ambassador to Russia Kanwal Sibal stated that it was not in India's interests to "endorse the U.S.'s anti-Russian policy or speak the anti-Western language of Russia."[69] This led India to highlight double standards, as it perceived the West as overreacting to events in Ukraine and downplaying similar crises elsewhere. India's external affairs minister, S. Jaishankar, presented this argument to Liz Truss on 1 April, as he noted that Europe was much more apathetic than India to events in Afghanistan, which were much less proximate to Europe.[70] In response to Britain's military aid deliveries to Ukraine, former Indian diplomat Anil Trigunayat stated, "Perhaps they should consider helping out the dire situation in Sri Lanka rather than stoking the flames."[71]

The third factor is India's continued reliance on Russia for raw materials and defensive equipment. India steadfastly resisted Western pressure to impose a price cap on Russian oil and expanded its imports from Russia from 2% in February to an estimated 12–13% by September 2022.[72] India claimed that the expansion of its oil imports from Russia was linked to its inflation management efforts. Nevertheless, India scaled back its reliance on Russian oil from an 18% peak in June 2022, which saw Russia surpass Iraq as its second largest supplier, and it is unclear at the time of writing whether Russia's offers of discounts in exchange for rejecting the G7 cap will reverse that trend.[73] Despite India's April 2022 decision to suspend purchases of 48 Mi-17V5 helicopters in favour of locally produced alternatives and concerns about secondary sanctions, New Delhi remains a reliable purchaser of Russian military equipment. The head of Russia's Federal Service for Military-Technical Cooperation, Dmitry Shugaev, confirmed in August 2022 that Russia would deliver all five S-400 air defence systems to India by the end of 2023.[74] The Russian military's underwhelming performance in the Ukraine War has not shaken India's confidence in Russian weaponry. Major General Harsha Kakar said that "confidence in Russian weapons is not reduced," as tactical shortfalls and extensive Western assistance were crucial mitigating factors.[75] The notions that Russia was preserving its most advanced weaponry for a potential conflict with the U.S. and had never wanted to annex Kyiv were also widely accepted in the Indian defence community.[76] Therefore, India's purchases of arms from France and the U.S., as well as domestic weapons development, would not end its reliance on Russia for equipment and spare parts.

Despite India's stringent non-aligned stance in Ukraine, New Delhi was not entirely passive in the crisis. With the exception of India's reliance on Russian fertiliser, agricultural export uncertainties had a limited impact on India's economy, and New Delhi's attention to this issue reflected its desire to elevate its prestige as a world power. Sneha Dubey, the First Secretary in India's UN Mission, stated that a swift diplomatic resolution of the Ukraine conflict was necessary to ensure that hunger could be eradicated in the Global South by 2030.[77] Despite imposing a ban on wheat exports on 13 May to prevent food price inflation, India had supplied 1.8 million tons of wheat to the Global South by late June, which countered the supply disruptions caused by the Black Sea grain export impasse. While India presented itself as an apolitical contributor to alleviating the humanitarian crisis in Ukraine, Russia's narratives about food insecurity were widely accepted in New Delhi. Sibal argued that Western sanctions were a critical cause of food supply disruptions, as Russian ships that supplied grain were blockaded in European ports, and the erroneous conspiracy that the Black Sea grain deal had not benefited the Global South was uncritically accepted.[78] Russia was often framed as a responsible actor which refrained from an indefinite blockade of grain supplies to protect its influence in the Global South and allowed Ukraine to profit from grain exports even as Western sanctions sought to destroy the Russian economy.[79] Due to its propensity to align with Russian narratives, Lavrov proposed India as a potential mediator on 1 April, but this request was largely ignored in New Delhi.

Looking ahead, the Ukraine War will likely facilitate greater Russia–India cooperation on constructing a multipolar world order, but this collaboration is partially offset by sharpening frictions in other spheres. The primary way in which Russia and India are advancing multipolarity in the economic sphere is through de-dollarisation. Sergey Uyanaev, deputy director of the Institute of the Far East, highlighted Modi's creation of working groups to mitigate the impact of anti-Russian sanctions and create alternatives to the U.S. dollar. These working groups were a throwback to the Cold War, when the Soviet Union conducted fixed rate trade with India in domestic currencies to circumvent the U.S. dollar. As a fixed rate would not account for geopolitical volatilities, there were different interpretations of how de-dollarisation would be implemented. Uyanaev concluded that a rupee–rouble trade format pegged to the yuan would be effective and that Russia–India bilateral trade could circumvent the U.S. dollar without creating an alternative to SWIFT.[80] India's desire to avoid a repeat of the 1999–2003 experience when a fixed rate that was detached from market prices gave it unfavourable loan and arms deals ensured that it backed a market-determined rupee-to-rouble exchange rate.[81] This rupee-to-rouble scheme allowed India to purchase Russian oil at discounted prices and provided an opening for Indian small and medium-sized businesses to invest in the Russian economy. India's participation in the September 2022 Vostok military drills, in spite of U.S. warnings about further exercises with Russia, reflected its desire to contribute to Moscow's vision of a multipolar collective security order.[82]

Despite the positive spirit of Russia–India cooperation, the bilateral partnership's substantive development is uncertain. Chenoy contended that deeper scientific and technological linkages, service-sector cooperation, free trade agreements and the expansion of the North–South Transit Corridor would be crucial next steps for Russia–India economic cooperation.[83] At the 2022 St. Petersburg Economic Forum, Oleg Deripaska called for a bilateral investment treaty, expanded cryptocurrency cooperation and Caspian Sea transport corridor via Iran to India.[84] Deripaska viewed Russia's development of trade networks with Europe from 1991 to 2003 as a role model that could be applied to India. These ambitious plans could prove illusory, as negotiations on a bilateral investment treaty have stalled, talks on an EAEU–India free trade agreement have stagnated since 2017 and the JCPOA impasse limits Iran–India trade prospects. Russia's courtship of Indian investment in the oil and gas sector, publicly announced on 12 March, has produced few tangible results.[85] Sibal attributed these failings to the "westward trajectory" of Indian economic policy.[86] JNU academic Happymon Jacob concurred, asserting that India's older elites are nostalgic for the Russia partnership but its young elites see Russia as a partner in "terminal decline."[87]

Russia's growing dependence on China is also problematic for New Delhi, as a Russia–China–India strategic triangle is unlikely to take shape. Russia's freedom to defy Beijing in a 2020 Ladakh-style China–India border dispute could be limited. JNU academic Rajesh Rajagopalan says that he does not expect Russia to support China in a Sino-Indian War but Moscow "won't provide India with diplomatic support, especially on issues where China has a different position."[88] Jacob believes that Russia might be less reliable than France or the U.S. in advancing India's interests in the UNSC and China could pressure Russia to stop selling arms to India if Beijing–New Delhi tensions escalate.[89] While India resisted pressure from Japan to take an anti-Russian position at the Quadrilateral Security Dialogue format, New Delhi's growing reliance on this format to combat China could create a conflict of interest. The indigenisation of India's defence industry will likely accelerate after the Ukraine War, which means it will eventually diminish its reliance on sophisticated Russian technology like fifth-generation fighter jets. These weaknesses suggest that Russia might not be able to rely on India as a cornerstone of its post-Western foreign policy, as sanctions erode its economic potential and U.S.–India relations continue to strengthen.

The Multidimensional Expansion of Russia–Iran Cooperation

Since the war began, Iran balanced expressions of sympathy for the rationales behind Russia's invasion of Ukraine with calls for a de-escalation of the conflict. Iranian president Ebrahim Raisi spoke with Putin hours after the Ukraine invasion, and warned that NATO expansion was a "serious threat" to European security.[90] In an hour-long 1 March speech, Ayatollah Ali Khamenei expressed support for a cessation of hostilities but claimed that the U.S. "mafia regime" had instigated the war in Ukraine and ignored Russia. Khamenei's condemnations of a "colour revolution" in Ukraine and claims that the Ukrainian people disapproved of Zelensky's government mirrored Russian propaganda.[91] The Iranian foreign ministry stated that "the Eurasia region is on the verge of entering a pervasive crisis" because of NATO's actions but rejected war as a solution to the problem.[92] This expression of support for diplomacy became an increasingly prominent feature of Iran's response as the war progressed. On 14 March, Kuleba stated that "Iran is against the war in Ukraine, supports a peaceful solution," and asked Iranian foreign minister Hossein Amirabdhollahian to convey his demands for a Russian withdrawal from Ukraine to Moscow.[93] On 31 August, Mohammad Jamshidi, director of the presidential office for political affairs, stated that a "senior leader of Western Europe" had asked Iran to mediate in the Ukraine War and the ISNA News Agency confirmed that Emmanuel Macron had made this request.[94] This balancing act continued until Iran's supply of UAVs to Russia soured its relationship with Ukraine. Mykhailo Podolyak stated that "Iran's elite still has not realised how to rise from the bottom of civilisation," and Ukraine cut its diplomatic presence in Tehran.[95] This escalation in Ukraine–Iran tensions caused former Iranian ambassador to China Hossein Malaek to remark, "Iran is fully with Russia in this conflict. Good or Bad."[96]

The evolution of Iran's approach to the Ukraine War aligned with its past responses to Russian military interventions and reflected broader geopolitical trends. During the 2008 Georgian War and the 2014–15 Russian invasion of Ukraine, Iran blamed Western provocations for Moscow's actions but refused to recognise the outcomes of Russian aggression, such as the independence of Abkhazia and South Ossetia or the Crimea annexation. This delicate balancing act reflected concerns about separatism and polarisations in Iranian public opinion towards Russia, which resurfaced during the current Ukraine War. A 13 March article in hardline newspaper *Kayhan* stated that "if Putin is talking about deterrence, or if he is talking about a serious security threat to his people, there is evidence."[97] University of Tehran Professor Elahe Kolaei accused Zelensky of stoking Russian aggression much like Saakashvili did in Georgia in 2008 but also stated that the 1979 revolution's values would support the Ukrainian people.[98] Opposition to Russia's conduct in Ukraine transcended ideological divides: reformist University of Tehran Professor Sadegh Zibakalam apologised to the people of Ukraine for Iran's support for Russian aggression, while hardline former president Mahmoud Ahmadinejad praised Zelensky's "heroic resistance."[99] Iran's efforts to position itself as a de-escalating force in Ukraine built on its participation in the Astana Peace Process in Syria, intra-Afghan dialogue efforts and four-point plan to end the Yemeni Civil War. The sharpening of Iran's pivot towards Russia could be explained by the impasse in the JCPOA negotiations, which had been triggered by Iranian uranium enrichment and clashes over inspections, and hostilities towards the U.S., such as the 2 September seizure of two American drones in the Red Sea.

Despite the fluctuations in Iranian policy towards the Ukraine War, cooperation between Russia and Iran strengthened against Western sanctions, and in the military sphere due to Tehran's UAV transfers to Russia. On 30 March, Lavrov pledged to work with Iran on combatting "unilateral sanctions," which reflected Russian efforts to connect Iranian banks to SPFS and discussions about Iran's recognition of the Mir card system.[100] On 1 April, Mohsen Karimi, the deputy head of the Iranian Central Bank for International Affairs, offered to share Iran's experience circumventing U.S. sanctions with Russia.[101] Due to Iran's significant strides towards import substitution and development of indigenous weapons programmes, Russia viewed Iran as a positive model to emulate. Iran's interest in barter deals of metallurgy for auto parts and gas turbines, the 80% increase in bilateral trade in

2021 and Russia–Iran trade in the Caspian Sea without third country participation added substantive weight to cooperation against sanctions.[102] On 17 July, Iran's Bank Melli and Sberbank signed cooperation agreements, which were swiftly followed by rial-to-rouble trading on the Tehran stock exchange and Peskov's pledge to eliminate U.S. dollar trade between Russia and Iran.[103] Raisi's SCO summit vow that Iran "does not and never will recognise sanctions against Russia" suggested that this collaboration would grow.[104]

Russia's support for the JCPOA's reinstatement further boosted the prospects of sanctions-free trade with Iran. The Kremlin's commitment to the JCPOA was briefly questioned in early March, as the prospective return of Iranian oil to world markets would deprive Russia of valuable revenues and instability in the Middle East was deemed to be in Moscow's interest.[105] The Russian foreign ministry denied these claims, stating that "at no point did Russia stand in the way of concluding the deal, despite some speculations in this regard," and insisted that it merely "wanted to make sure that this avalanche of illegitimate sanctions against us by the collective West over Ukraine doesn't do any damage to the agreement and our commitments."[106] Since Lavrov received reassurances on 15 March that Russia–Iran trade under the JCPOA's regulations would not be impeded by sanctions, Moscow became a steadfast supporter of the nuclear deal's restoration.[107] Despite the escalation of Russia–West tensions over Ukraine, the Russian foreign ministry claimed that "Vienna talks are probably the most crisis-proof negotiations ever," and that the talks narrowly averted collapse on four occasions.[108] Beyond participating in multilateral diplomacy, Russia's primary objectives were to convince Iran to abide by uranium enrichment criteria and to ensure that the modernisation of the enrichment plant in Fordow returned to its focus on producing medical isotopes.[109] A return to the JCPOA had numerous advantages for

Russia, as it could eventually use Iran as a back-door market to sell oil to Europe once the EU-wide oil embargo took effect in December 2022.[110]

Throughout the Ukraine War, Iran allegedly provided military assistance to Russia. On 12 April, *The Guardian* reported that Iran-aligned militias in Iraq had supplied Russia with RPGs, anti-tank missiles and Brazilian-designed rocket launcher systems, while an Iranian-made Bavar-373 missile system and S-300 were also returned to Moscow.[111] Putin's July 2022 meeting with Erdogan in Tehran revived speculation about Russia–Iran military cooperation in Ukraine. On 12 July, U.S. national security advisor Jake Sullivan stated that Iran was planning to provide Russia with "up to several hundred UAVs, on an expedited timeline" and warned that Tehran would swiftly begin training the Russian military to use these UAVs.[112] Sullivan's claims were shrouded in ambiguity in the weeks that followed. Russian defence expert Kirill Semenov contended that training, the translation of vast amounts of documentation, shortages of Iranian UAVs and Russia's focus on domestic production of drones rendered a deal with Iran unlikely.[113] While Iran officially denied selling UAVs to Russia, it offered circumstantial evidence of a deal. On 15 August, the IRGC confirmed that it was holding joint drone exercises with Russia at the Kashan airbase alongside Belarus and Armenia. Hamidreza Azizi, a Berlin-based former professor at Shahid Beheshti University in Tehran, stated there was "no real evidence yet that the drone deal has taken place" but asserted that the IRGC's desire to showcase Iranian military power "outweighs any diplomatic consideration" and could facilitate a UAV deal with Russia.[114]

On 13 September, Ukraine shot down an Iranian-made Shahed-136 drone, which confirmed the entry of Iran's UAVs into the conflict. These drones, which were shipped alongside the Mohajer-6 model, likely arrived in Russia on 19 August but did not immediately enter the battlefield due to testing malfunctions.[115] Despite strenuous denials from Iranian officials, *Kayhan* reported that Iran had supplied drones to Russia as part of its $5.6 billion UAV export target and highlighted the Ukrainian army's struggles to intercept the UAVs and urgent requests for U.S. assistance against Iran's drones.[116] There were conflicting reports of the battlefield efficacy of Iranian drones. Odesa regional military administration spokesman Serhiy Bratchuk acknowledged that Russia could cluster drone strikes as they were inexpensive and could replicate the impact of missile strikes that terrorised the local population.[117] Russian Telegram channels warned that Ukraine would need to spend billions more on air defence and hundreds of millions on maintenance in Odesa, and expressed hope that these drones could destroy anti-aircraft batteries and help Russia achieve its elusive goal of air superiority.[118] A 22 September *Voyenni Osvedomitel* post boasted that Ukraine had not taken down a single Shahed-136 drone and that they could operate in pairs.[119] Despite this bombastic rhetoric, Ukraine claimed it had shot down twenty UAVs by early October, and Taras Berezovets contended that "Iranian UAVs are still outdated and can easily be targeted by Ukrainian aircraft."[120] Nikolay Kozhanov contended that Iran had likely supplied Russia with less sophisticated drones, and the state-owned nature of IRGC drone production could prioritise quantity over quality more than Turkey's Baykar.[121]

While the efficacy of Iranian UAVs on the battlefield is mixed, Russia remains increasingly reliant on Tehran for military hardware. After a brief supply pause in late November, Iranian UAV shipments resumed in early December and have featured prominently in civilian infrastructure strikes.[122] Ukrainian intelligence reports, which provided evidence for post-invasion manufacturing dates for Russia-bound Mohajer-6 UAVs, have played a crucial role in strengthening the case for war-related sanctions on

Iran.[123] U.S. and British intelligence officials have also expressed concern about the imminent construction of joint Russian-Iranian drone production lines. Alexander Fomin's 3 December visit to Tehran prompted renewed fears that Iran would supply ballistic missiles to Russia. Four Israeli intelligence officials warned that Iran could supply modified Fateh-110 missile systems, which have a range of 300km, but had abandoned plans to send Russia Zolfaghar missile systems, which have a 700km radius, as they breach UNSC resolutions.[124] In recent months, U.S. and EU sanctions have targeted key actors in Iran's military-industrial complex, such as UAV producer Qods Aviation Industries and the director of Iran's Aerospace Industrial Organization, which oversees ballistic missile production.[125] These sanctions are unlikely to deter Iran's military cooperation from Russia but could impede Tehran's procurement of Western-made components that are vital for UAV production.

Looking ahead, the Russia–Iran partnership will likely develop at a faster pace than Moscow's relationships with China and India and possess fewer sources of friction. The persistence of popular unrest in Iran will likely trigger stronger cooperation with Russia, as Moscow has consistently supported the Iranian authorities since the 2009 Green Movement. Sergei Markov's assertion that Iranians believe that the U.S. is instigating these protests because of Iran's supply of UAVs to Russia reflects Moscow and Tehran's common cause.[126] At the time of writing, despite power asymmetries and uncertain cohesion, a Russia–China–Iran axis has gained strength in recent months, and the autumn 2022 military drills point to its growing momentum. As secondary sanctions limit the marketability of Russian weapons, Iran's much-discussed negotiations with Russia on the purchase of 24 Su-35E fighter jets could finally produce a breakthrough. The revival of the JCPOA could result in the shift in tone from Iran towards the conflict, as it could try to overcome the UAV controversy and return to its prior support for de-escalation. An IRNA commentator told me: "Iran can make peace in Ukraine, if the EU and U.S. de-escalate with Iran, and open up trade and business with Iran. We are worried about the humanitarian situation in Ukraine. Iranian intellectuals want friendly ties with the EU and U.S."[127] Despite this rhetoric, Russia views a partnership with Iran as an integral component of its anti-hegemonic ambitions, and Moscow–Tehran cooperation in Syria will ensure that the partnership is not disrupted by the JCPOA's reinstatement.

Russia's Middle Power Partnerships in South and Southeast Asia

Russia's post-Ukraine invasion courtship of new partners in South and Southeast Asia has achieved some noteworthy successes but the strategic depth of its influence in both regions remains limited. Russia's relationship with Pakistan was thrust into the spotlight at the start of the war, as prime minister Imran Khan met with Putin hours after his fateful "special military operation" speech. Khan expressed "regret" that the war in Ukraine had not been averted, and proceeded to engage with Putin on Afghanistan, Islamophobia and the Pakistan–Stream gas pipeline.[128] In an *RT* interview ahead of the invasion, Khan defended his trip, stating that "the Ukraine crisis does not concern us" and emphasised Pakistan's desire to avoid becoming part of any bloc. On 28 February, Khan announced plans to purchase 2 million tons of Russian wheat and purchase Russian natural gas, which shielded the Pakistani economy against rising LNG prices and the redirection of LNG contracts towards more lucrative European markets.[129] Khan also announced cuts in fuel and electricity prices to prevent domestic unrest, but faced criticism as the Kremlin contradicted his claims that he had secured discounts on Russian wheat and gas. Despite Khan's emphasis on engaging with Russia, army chief Qamar Javed Bajwa condemned

Russia's invasion as a "huge tragedy" and compared Ukraine's resistance to what Pakistan would do if attacked by India.[130] This reflected intra-agency frictions, which culminated in Khan's 10 April ouster, but also aligned with Pakistan's calls for a de-escalation, which were apparent at the Organisation of Islamic Cooperation (OIC) summit in March 2022.

Bangladesh's response mirrored Pakistan's, as it decried the war's impact on the Global South without condemning Putin. Bangladeshi prime minister Sheikh Hasina called the Ukraine War "meaningless" as "only the arms producers are making profits," but also decried Western sanctions on Russia as a "violation of human rights" for creating food shortages.[131] Bangladesh's response reflected both its enduring gratitude for the Soviet Union's recognition of its independence from Pakistan in 1971, and desire to mitigate record-breaking food inflation in March 2022, which threatened to undo two decades of progress against malnutrition. Sri Lanka was also forced to strengthen ties with Russia, as its president, Ranil Wickremesinghe, asked Vladimir Putin to help alleviate its economic crisis in July 2022. The Russia–Sri Lanka partnership is likely to continue strengthening, as peaceful protests against food and fuel shortages erupted in March 2022, and Wickremesinghe mirrored Moscow's narratives about popular unrest by calling some protesters "fascists."

Russia has also assiduously courted new commercial opportunities and diplomatic partnerships in Southeast Asia, with mixed results. During the August 2022 ASEAN summit, Lavrov quipped that he had engaged with "everyone who was not hiding." Russia's relationships with Vietnam, Thailand, Indonesia, Malaysia and Laos have made considerable progress, while its partnerships with Cambodia and the Philippines have experienced strains. Despite Vietnam's critical importance to the U.S.'s Indo-Pacific strategy, its historical security links with Russia have endured despite the Ukraine War. On 19 April, Russia announced that the Eastern Military District and Vietnam's armed forces had reached an agreement on military drills, which was followed by a clarification from Hanoi that only army games were on the cards.[132] Lavrov's 6 July visit to Hanoi underscored Vietnam's continued appreciation for the Soviet Union's role in its struggle for independence and reunification, and Hanoi's continuing dependence on Russian energy as China steps up its assertiveness in the South China Sea. Due to historical links between the Thai royal family and Russia, which date back to the era of Tsar Alexander III, and the historical memory of Russian support for Siam against European colonialism, Bangkok has broken with the majority of fellow major non-NATO allies by refusing to condemn Russia in the UNGA.[133] These nostalgic sentiments are paired with shared commercial interests. In May 2022, Thailand discussed expanding its trade with Russia from $2.7 billion to $10 billion and pursued an FTA with the EAEU.

Due to the pervasiveness of Russian disinformation in social media and anti-American sentiments, Indonesia has refused to condemn Russian aggression. In July 2022, Indonesian president Joko Widodo offered to mediate between Russia and Ukraine ahead of the G20 summit in Jakarta and travelled to both Kyiv and Moscow to advance this agenda. Malaysia condemned the invasion of Ukraine in the UNGA but domestic opinion towards Russia remains highly polarised. In keeping with former prime minister Mahathir Mohamad's claims that Russia was "scapegoated" for the MH-17 shoot-down, Malaysia possesses a vocal bloc that depicts Russia as an anti-colonial superpower.[134] The prevailing narrative amongst Malaysian netizens was that Ukraine had provoked Russia to war and Russian soft power in Malaysia has remained resilient in spite of the Ukraine War. According to a June 2022 Pew Research survey, a 47% plurality of Malaysians have a favourable view of Russia, while 59% of Malaysians believed that Vladimir Putin would do the "right thing" in world affairs.[135] Laos has pivoted towards Russia to counter-balance an exclusive reliance on China, and as inflation surged to 23%, it pushed to purchase oil from Russia at a 70% discount in early May.[136] Despite Patrushev's December 2021 consultation with Cambodia's top military intelligence official Hun Manith about the "colour revolution" threat, president Hun Sen has broken with many fellow Southeast Asian leaders by condemning Russian aggression.[137] Cambodia framed its position as being categorically against invasions and subsequently engaged with Russia on national currency trade. Despite cordial ties with Russia under Rodrigo Duterte, his successor as president of the Philippines Ferdinand Marcos cancelled a $244 million deal for 16 Mi-17 helicopters over secondary sanctions fears.

Russia's Allies in Isolation: North Korea, Myanmar and the Taliban

In a poignant symbol of its dearth of international allies, Russia has made concerted outreaches to North Korea, Myanmar's junta and the still-unrecognised Taliban-led Islamic Emirate of Afghanistan. On 28 February, North Korea blamed the U.S.'s "hegemonic policy" for the Ukraine War, which included NATO's eastward expansion and "attempts to deploy attack weapons systems."[138] North Korea's endorsement of Russia's narratives on the Ukraine War was followed by a 22 March meeting on "developing bilateral relations." On 26 May, Russia rewarded North Korea for its loyalty by joining China in blocking new UN sanctions over Pyongyang's ballistic missile launches.[139] Russia's vote was the first breach in the UN sanctions regime on North Korea's ballistic missile programme since sanctions were first imposed in 2006. This solidarity has extended to potential collaboration in Donbas and Russia's alleged arms purchases from North Korea. After North Korea recognised the DNR and LNR's independence on 14 July, Russian Ambassador to Pyongyang Alexander Matsegora claimed that "highly skilled and hardworking workers" in North Korea could help rebuild civilian and industrial infrastructure in Donbas.[140] Matsegora's proposal, which included offers of spare parts and manufactured goods from Donbas to North Korea, caused international controversy, as it signalled Russia's willingness to violate sanctions against Pyongyang. Nevertheless, Pushilin called for tighter DNR–North Korea cooperation in August 2022, and the DNR's ambassador to Russia, Olga Makeeva, mused about North Korean participation in their tribunals against alleged Ukrainian war criminals.[141] On 4 October, North Korea became the first country in the world to recognise Russia's illegal annexations of Donetsk, Luhansk, Kherson and Zaporizhzhia.

As Russia's stocks of military hardware began to diminish, Moscow allegedly turned to North Korea for weapons in September 2022. The U.S.'s assertions that Russia planned to purchase millions of rockets and artillery shells from North Korea were unconfirmed. Nevertheless, these accusations became fodder for the digital information war. Ukraine's defence ministry taunted Russia by stating that while Kyiv replaced Soviet-era weapons with NATO-class arms, Moscow was heading towards "North Korean standards" in weapons, politics and standard of living.[142] Chizhov stated that Russia's purchases of arms from North Korea were "made up by Western media," while Pyongyang denied ever exporting weaponry to Russia and accused the U.S. of spreading false rumours to discredit North Korea.[143] Despite these denials, U.S. intelligence believes that North Korea is covertly supplying artillery to Russia under the guise of shipments to the Middle East and Africa.[144] Satellite imagery reveals that five train cars with weapons caches left North Korea on 18 November and the destination of these arms shipments was the Wagner Group.[145] Beyond securing hard currency, North Korea's military assistance reflects its growing economic dependence on Russia, as grain shipments from Primorsky Krai arrived to ameliorate its malnutrition crisis.[146] Speculation has also grown about direct North Korean military assistance to Russia's war in Ukraine. Igor Korotchenko claimed that Russia and North Korea should establish "normal trade," as it could lead to North Korea sending 100,000 troops to Ukraine, while Solovyov asserted that North Korea could be part of a Russian-led international coalition in Ukraine. The Russian foreign ministry has denied these reports, and despite North Korea's historical participation in the Vietnam War, the risk of high casualties, lack of joint training and language barriers make direct Moscow–Pyongyang cooperation unlikely.[147] Therefore, the Russia–North Korea partnership in Ukraine is more likely to be symbolic than substantive in the months ahead.

Much like North Korea, Myanmar's military regime rushed to defend Russia's aggression in Ukraine. In a 25 February interview, General Zaw Min Tun, a spokesperson for Myanmar's military council, stated that Putin's war with Ukraine helped "consolidate its sovereignty" and showed that "Russia is a world power."[148] The pro-junta *Myanmar Alin* newspaper similarly described Putin as a "visionary leader" who had strengthened Russia's military and economy, and decried Zelensky as a "puppet of the West."[149] Myanmar also expressed its intention to purchase Russian arms, as only Russia, Serbia and China supplied arms to the junta, and Yangon relies on Russian air force technology and surface-to-air missile parts. Russian military technology is especially valuable for the junta, as it has used MiG-29 fighter jets and Yak-130 ground attack aircraft to strike resistance fighters in southern and central Myanmar. Russia could also supply the junta with anti-drone systems and naval upgrades, which build on the kilo class submarines it received in 2020.[150] In March 2022, Rostec joined a delegation of EAEU companies to discuss defence exports to Myanmar and Russian deputy defence minister Alexander Fomin attended the Armed Forces Day parade.[151] These gatherings were followed by Shoigu's 17 July meeting with Min Aung Hlaing in Moscow, Lavrov's 3 August visit to Yangon and Putin's trade negotiations with the junta chief at the Eastern Economic Forum. Despite the plethora of bilateral interactions, it remains unclear whether Russia and Myanmar can develop an economic partnership that withstands Western sanctions. While Russia and Myanmar struck a nuclear energy cooperation roadmap on 6 September, SWIFT sanctions act as a potential deterrent for arms transfers. Myanmar's de-dollarisation measures, which bar ownership of foreign currency, and interest in Russia's SPFS could alleviate these challenges. Nevertheless, Myanmar regards Russia as a useful partner as it seeks to alleviate its long-standing dependence on China and counter its isolation from ASEAN.

Due to its refusal to recognise the Islamic Emirate and terrorism designation against the Taliban, Russia–Taliban cooperation is shallower than with North Korea and Myanmar. The Taliban highlighted its "foreign policy of neutrality" after the Ukraine War began and called for "restraint on both sides."[152] Despite these ambiguities, Russia joined China, Pakistan and Turkmenistan in accrediting Taliban-appointed diplomats on 9 April, and the Taliban attended the St. Petersburg Economic Forum in June 2022. On 28 September, the Taliban announced plans to purchase 1 million tons of petroleum, 1 million tons of diesel, 500,000 tons of cooking gas and 2 million tons of wheat from Russia as it sought to alleviate Afghanistan's humanitarian crisis.[153] Beyond humanitarian aid, which plays into Russia's aversion to Western sanctions and U.S. regime change missions, Moscow also eyes access to Afghanistan's vast rare earth metal reserves. Going forward, Russia is also likely to view the Taliban as a security partner rather than a potential threat. Putin's Special

Envoy to Afghanistan Zamir Kabulov insists that the Taliban poses no threat to Central Asia, using the Islamic Emirate's diplomacy with Uzbekistan and Turkmenistan to illustrate this point.[154] Former Afghan ambassador to Pakistan Omar Zakhilwal contends that Russia sees ISIS as the largest threat to Central Asia, and sees the Taliban as an "effective force to combat the threat of ISIS on Afghan soil."[155] Therefore, Russia's policy with "engagement without recognition" of the Taliban will likely continue for the foreseeable future.

The Escalation of Russia's Tensions with U.S. Allies in the Indo-Pacific Region

Despite Russia's years-long attempts to court U.S. partners in the Indo-Pacific region, Washington's allies stood firmly with Ukraine and against Russian aggression. Japanese prime minister Fumio Kishida's condemnation of Russia for pursuing "unilateral change to the status quo by force" marked an end to a quarter-century of efforts to thaw relations with Moscow.[156] Japan courted Russia after a post-Cold War foreign policy once prime minister Ryutaro Hashimoto's late 1990s "Eurasia diplomacy" doctrine was unveiled. Former prime minister Shinzo Abe met with Vladimir Putin twenty-seven times from 2013 to 2020, which resulted in the expansion of Japanese economic relations with Siberia and tentative steps towards shelving Second World War-era territorial disputes with Russia.[157] However, Japan's initial sanctions on the Russian economy were milder than those of its Western counterparts. Japan's visa bans on DNR and LNR officials were symbolic, as Tokyo had stopped issuing visas to foreigners over COVID-19, and it was unclear whether Russia issued meaningful amounts of sovereign debt in Japan. Atsuko Higashino, an academic at the University of Tsukuba in Ibakari, stated that although Japan aligned with the G7 consensus on sanctions, its "actions are really slow and small, and trying to limit the influence as much as possible."[158] Kuleba indirectly criticised Japan's incrementalism, stating that Ukraine expected a "stronger reaction", and appealed to Tokyo's concerns about sovereignty violations, which extended to Taiwan and the Kuril Islands.[159] After mounting pressure from the West and Kyiv, Japan expanded its sanctions regime against Russia, and announced a ban on semiconductor exports.[160] Japan also pledged to divert a larger amount of LNG to Europe in March 2022, which implemented the U.S. and EU's 9 February requests.[161]

Japan's imposition of sanctions on Russia was predictably followed by an escalation of tensions over the Kuril Islands. On 28 February, Japanese foreign ministry Europe department director Hideki Uyama called the Southern Kurils illegally "occupied by Russia," which contrasted markedly with Tokyo's traditionally milder claim that the Southern Kurils were "covered by Japanese sovereignty."[162] The Russian foreign ministry chastised the "absence of Japan's own foreign policy line in international affairs," and stated that Japan had rejected an "excellent programme of interaction and cooperation" with Russia to appease Washington.[163] This statement followed Japan's suspension of most-favoured nations trade status to Russia on 16 March, which dashed Moscow's strategy of capitalising on U.S.–Japan technological competition and promoting Japanese goods to EAEU countries.[164] On 21 March, Russia unilaterally suspended peace treaty negotiations with Japan over its "unfriendly" actions. Russia also terminated 1991 and 1999 visa-free travel agreements allowing Japanese citizens to visit the Southern Kurils, quit dialogue on Kuril Islands economic cooperation and blocked the extension of Japan's status as a sectoral dialogue partner of the Organization of Black Sea Economic Cooperation.[165] Dmitri Medvedev, who was already an unpopular figure in Japan for his controversial 2019 visit to Etorofu Island, facetiously called Japan

"proud independent samurai" and supported Russia's development of the Kuril Islands, which included road and airport construction.[166] Japan's reinstatement of the word "illegal" in reference to Russia's occupation of the Kuril Islands, which was the
first use of this phrase in its official diplomatic report since 2003,
intensified frictions with Moscow. On 23 May, Dmitry Rogozin
supported renaming the Kuril Islands "Varyag," "Korean" and
"Vsevolod Rudnev," which referred to famous ships and events of
the 1905 Russo–Japanese War.[167]

As the Kuril Islands dispute reheated, energy became a new
front line in Russia's confrontation with Japan. On 8 May,
Kishida agreed in principle to a G7 ban on Russian oil imports
but conceded that Japan would take time to phase it out.[168]
Kishida also insisted that Japan would maintain its investments
in the Sakhalin-1 and Sakhalin-2 LNG projects. Kishida's cautious approach to Russia's energy divestment reflected Japan's
economic realities, which were distinct from those of its G7
counterparts. Japan imported only 3.6% of its oil from Russia
but had only 11% energy self-sufficiency, which meant that an
LNG ban would hurt the Japanese economy more than the
Russian economy.[169] Sensing that Japan's reliance on Russian
energy was a point of leverage, Russian lawmakers and media
outlets called for counter-sanctions against Tokyo. In a May 2022
Duma debate, Vyacheslav Volodin told Alexei Kudrin that Japan's
presence in Sakhalin-1 and 2 was problematic and called for the
seizure of Mitsui's 12.5% and Mitsubishi's 10% stake by Russian
state-owned companies.[170] Volodin's call to seize Japanese investments, which mirrored his threats to seize Shell Oil's 27.5%
share in the Sakhalin projects, was enthusiastically supported by
nationalist media outlets. A 7 June Tsargrad article highlighted
how Japan's "samurai gentlemen" had frozen $33 billion in
Russian Central Bank assets and warned that a "heavily militarised" Japan had designs of an invasion of the Kuril Islands.[171]

Russia ultimately did not retaliate against Japan, however, aside from occasional pressure on rouble payments.

While a major escalation of Japan–Russia tensions over energy was averted, bilateral relations continued to deteriorate. Despite their close relationship, Putin did not attend Abe's funeral in September 2022. Prior to his assassination, Abe had described Putin as an "extreme pragmatist" akin to sixteenth-century Japanese warlord Oda Nobunaga and stated that the Ukraine War was the result of "badly mistaken judgment."[172] Russia's detention of Japan's consul in Vladivostok Tatsunori Motoki on espionage allegations was followed by Tokyo's reciprocal expulsion of the Russian consul in Sapporo on 4 October. Japan also imposed sanctions on twenty-one Russian defence organisations, which were especially geared at preventing Russia from replenishing its chemical weapons stocks.[173] This strident reaction was triggered by revelations that the FSB had subjected Motoki to coercive interrogation, which saw him blindfolded and restrained for several hours, over accusations that he had paid for classified information.[174] Beyond these tit-for-tat retaliations, Japan has emerged as an increasingly vocal opponent of Russia's obstructionist activities in the UN. Kishida's September 2022 UNGA address emphasised why Russia's actions should lead to UNSC reforms, which built on themes from Zelensky's March 2022 address to Japan.[175] As Japan tries to reform a UNSC, which it sees as unfairly punishing the losers of the Second World War, it could carve out an independent niche in the containment of Russian diplomatic influence.

Although president Moon Jae-in was the first South Korean leader to visit Russia since 1999 and engaged actively with Putin on North Korea's nuclear threat, South Korea supported the Western sanctions regime against Russia. Nevertheless, South Korea refused to impose unilateral sanctions against Russia and Moon-aligned Democratic Party of Korea candidate Lee Jaemyung caused controversy by blaming Zelensky's NATO membership ambitions for Putin's invasion.[176] South Korea's restraint was attributed to possible Russian leverage over North Korea and Russia's importance as a market for South Korea's electronics. Russia was also South Korea's second largest supplier of gas and coal, and fourth largest supplier of oil. Despite these reservations, South Korea banned semiconductor, automobile and electronic exports to Russia, and cut major Russian banks from SWIFT. BKF bank analytical department head Maxim Osadchiy warned that Seoul's actions could disrupt Russia's energy supply to South Korea, but the Russian economy suffered from major disruptions in trade with its twelfth largest partner.[177] Under president Yoon Suk-yeol's leadership, South Korea has deepened its security cooperation with NATO, supplied forty-eight light combat aircraft to Poland and transferred Chiron MANPADS to Ukraine via the Czech Republic. This muscular foreign policy poses risks, especially to South Korea's balancing act between the U.S. and China, but has revitalised South Korea's defence sector and will be a critical component of Washington–Seoul cooperation in the years ahead.

As the Russian military marched on Kyiv, pro-Ukrainian protests erupted in Taipei and Taiwan joined the sanctions regime against Russia. Despite their solidarity with Ukraine, Taiwanese officials dismissed concerns that "today's Ukraine is tomorrow's Taiwan"—Taiwanese president Tsai Ing-wen insisted that the Taiwan Strait acted as a natural barrier against Chinese aggression.[178] This rhetoric resonated at a popular level, as 63% of Taiwanese did not expect China to capitalise on the Ukraine War by invading Taiwan.[179] Even if the Ukraine War will not invite Chinese aggression, it has significantly strained Taiwan–Russia relations. Alexey Maslov describes Taiwan's reaction as a significant break in its past relations with Russia, which cultivated educational and economic ties in spite of Russia's belief that

Taiwan was part of China. Maslov warned that Taiwan's semiconductor sanctions were especially devastating, as Russia cannot domestically produce the semiconductors it needs for computers and negotiations with China have not led to Beijing supplying them.[180] Although Taiwan, Japan and South Korea collectively purchased $5.5 billion in Russian fuel, Taiwan announced its complete divestment from Russian coal on 24 August.[181] Taiwan had already suspended Russian oil purchases in 2016 and begun to draw down from LNG purchases in March 2022, underscoring its leadership role in divesting from Russian energy in the Indo-Pacific region.

Australia's response to the Ukraine War was the most hawkish of the U.S.'s core allies in the Indo-Pacific region. On 1 March, Australian prime minister Scott Morrison called Russia a "pariah state," supported Russia's potential expulsion from the G20 and pledged $70 million in missiles and ammunition to Ukraine.[182] Morrison subsequently authorised the imposition of targeted sanctions on Russian oligarchs with substantial business interests in Australia. On 18 March, Australia imposed sanctions on Oleg Deripaska, who possessed a 20% share in the Queensland Alumina Limited (QAL) alumina refinery in Gladstone via Rusal, and Viktor Vekselberg, who works with Origin Energy on fracking the Beetaloo Basin in Northern Territory.[183] On 20 March, Australia announced a ban on alumina exports to Russia, which cut off 20% of the Russian economy's supply. In April 2022, Australia began delivering Bushmaster armoured vehicles, which Ukraine used effectively in its Kharkiv counteroffensive; by 15 September, it had delivered 40 of the 60 it had pledged to Kyiv.[184] Due to the efficacy of Australian equipment, Ukraine has requested an additional order of Bushmasters and expressed interest in 30 Hawkei armoured vehicles, a lighter seven-ton armoured vehicle. Beyond further sanctions and supplies of military equipment, Australia is likely to supply humanitarian aid to Ukraine modelled after the March 2022 thermal coal donation that powered up to one million homes. The Ukraine War has, therefore, practically eviscerated Russia's hopes of expanding its commercial presence and influence amongst U.S. allies in the Indo-Pacific.

10

THE RESILIENCE OF RUSSIA'S INFLUENCE
IN THE GLOBAL SOUTH

During the summer of 2022, Sergei Lavrov showcased Russia's partnerships in the Global South through a series of high-profile diplomatic visits. Lavrov's trips emphasised the West's inability to isolate Russia on the world stage and whitewashed Moscow's responsibility for food shortages across the Global South. On 25 July, Lavrov addressed the Arab League summit in Cairo, which saw him present Russia's case for war with Ukraine and reassure Arab leaders of Russia's commitment to the Black Sea grain export deal. Immediately after this speech, Lavrov travelled to Ethiopia, Uganda and the Republic of Congo. During this trip, he hailed the Russia–Africa partnership as a bulwark against the U.S.–Europe unipolar order and claimed that the COVID-19 pandemic created a pernicious cycle of Western sanctions that created food insecurity in Africa.[1] In an op-ed before the trip, he emphasised the Soviet Union's commitment to decolonisation and the construction of hundreds of African companies, and highlighted Russia's track record of helping African countries overcome their problems while allowing them to live the way they wanted.[2] During the 3 August 2022 ASEAN summit, he quipped that he engaged with "everyone who was not hiding," and paired his bloc-level engagement with bilateral trips to Vietnam and Myanmar. While Lavrov did not embark on a full-fledged Latin American tour, he held talks with Brazilian officials on the sidelines of the UNGA and vowed to strengthen relations with Caracas after welcoming Venezuelan foreign minister Carlos Faria to Moscow on 4 July.

While Lavrov's trips did not produce major commercial deals, they underscored the resilience of Russia's presence in the Global South and ability to carry out business-as-usual relationships with the collective non-West. Russia paired these bilateral and summit-level outreaches with the empowerment of BRICS and the G20, cardinal institutions of the multipolar world order. On 15 June, Nikolay Patrushev urged BRICS to play a leading role in solving the world's most urgent problems and hailed the organisation's planned expansion, which had been announced in May.[3] Russian experts believe that BRICS could serve as a cohesive bloc against unilateral sanctions, as even Brazil regards NATO's linkage of environmental policy to security as a potential gateway for Amazon-related sanctions, and describe BRICS as a bulwark against Western Russophobia.[4] Although Joe Biden publicly supports Russia's removal from the G20, Russia has been able to maintain a seat at the table at this multilateral institution due to disagreements amongst its member states. At the St. Petersburg Economic Forum, Russia sought to bridge the BRICS and G20 together to cultivate cooperation on Arctic security.[5]

This chapter examines Russia's power projection in the Middle East, with a focus on Turkey, Israel, Syria and the Gulf monarchies; Africa and Latin America, and assesses the sustainability of Moscow's "virtual great power" status in the Global South.

Turkey's Balancing Act Between NATO and Russia

Turkey's policy of "strategic autonomy," requiring a delicate balance between NATO and Russia, caused it to carve out a unique role in the Ukraine conflict. It consistently condemned Russia's invasion of Ukraine and accompanying human rights abuses, while periodically expressing sympathy with Moscow's anti-Western grievances and refusing to impose sanctions on Russia. Erdogan spoke with Zelensky on the first day of the invasion and stated that "We reject Russia's military operation."[6] This position aligned with Turkey's steadfast support for Ukrainian sovereignty. Due to their Turkic origin, Erdogan has regularly expressed concern about the plight of Crimean Tatars and demanded the release of the Crimean Tatar Mejlis deputy chairman Nariman Dzhelyal at the 23 August Crimea Platform summit.[7] Despite Erdogan's consistent pro-Ukraine stance, Mevlüt Çavuşoğlu stated that some NATO allies want a longer war to "weaken Russia" and hinted that some European countries were seeking to sabotage the Black Sea grain agreement.[8] Erdogan ruled out imposing sanctions on Russia due to Turkey's dependence on Russia for half of its gas supply and construction of the Akkuyu nuclear power plant with Russia. Erdogan's spokesman Ibrahim Kalin defended Turkey's refusal to sanction Russia on 26 June by asking, "If everyone ruins the bridges, who will be speaking with Russia then?"[9]

Turkey's policies towards the Ukraine War reflect the balance set by its official rhetoric. After heavy pressure from Ukraine, Çavuşoğlu announced on 28 February that no warships would pass through the Bosporus or Dardanelles and invoked Article 19 of the 1936 Montreux Convention to enforce this policy. On 2 March, Çavuşoğlu announced that he had denied a Russian request to allow several ships to sail through the Turkish Straits.[10] The Turkish Straits blockade was expected to greatly

345

increase the logistical costs of Russia's Mediterranean Sea presence, which is closely intertwined with the activities of the Black Sea Fleet, and complicate Moscow's ability to supply its military forces in Syria.[11] Turkey also provided military and humanitarian assistance to Ukraine. On 28 June, Oleksiy Reznikov stated that Ukraine had received fifty Turkish Bayraktar TB-2 drones since Russia's invasion began, and Poland had aided Turkey in the transit of these drones.[12] Baykar Technologies, which produces the Bayraktar TB-2 drones, categorically ruled out supplying these drones to Russia but had entrusted engine production for its equipment to Ukrainian companies.[13] By 21 April, Turkey had supplied eighty-two trucks of humanitarian aid to Ukraine, and authorised the shipment of two trucks specifically for Crimean Tatars to showcase its commitment to their cause.[14] Despite these gestures and the uptick in Turkey's popularity in Ukraine after the Bayraktar TB-2 deliveries, Ankara's refusal to side firmly against Russia sullied its image amongst the Ukrainian public in the autumn of 2022.[15]

As Russia's totalitarian tilt accelerated, Turkey emerged as a critical haven for anti-war liberals. Much like how hundreds of thousands of White Russian aristocrats and military officers fled the 1917 Bolshevik Revolution, a "Little Russia" emerged in Istanbul.[16] One notable dissident who arrived in Istanbul was Yabloko Party St. Petersburg municipal council member Irina Gaisina, who participated in Navalny rallies and supported anti-war petitions after the Ukraine invasion began.[17] More than 50,000 Russians resided in Turkey before the war and this figure increased in October 2022 due to an influx of anti-mobilisation protesters. On the day Putin announced partial mobilisation, flights to Istanbul sold out even though prices reached 80,000 roubles for a one-way ticket.

Despite Turkey's attractiveness as an emigration spot, difficulties finding employment have complicated integration for Russian liberals and scepticism about Ankara's too-close-for-comfort relationship with Moscow abound. Speaking with me in September 2022, Ilya Matveev, a political scientist from St. Petersburg who fled to Istanbul after the war began, contended that Turkey did not have a "scary view" of Russian activities, as it was an imperial power with special operations in its own sphere of influence. Matveev believed that Erdogan was motivated by ameliorating Turkey's economic instability ahead of the 2023 elections and was willing to support the Russian economy to achieve this goal.[18] In October, Andrei Soldatov contended that Russian intelligence services continue to operate networks inside Turkey which could ultimately target dissidents and stated that he was "strongly advised against going to Turkey" as he plotted his escape.[19] Turkey's informal restrictions on Russian migrants in several cities, which have gained attention since December 26, is likely to further heighten mistrust.[20]

Despite these gestures of solidarity with Ukraine and the Russian opposition, Turkey deepened its commercial and security links with Russia. Turkey's purchases of Russian oil, such as Urals and Siberian Light grade crude, doubled to over 200,000 barrels per day in 2022, and trade between Russia and Turkey increased by 50% between May and July.[21] Through a $9.1 billion loan brokered by Rosatom and Gazprombank, the Akkuyu nuclear plant's construction continued apace and Putin announced on 13 October its first phase would be complete by Turkey's centenary in May 2023. On 16 September, Turkey announced that 25% of its purchases of Russian gas would be conducted in roubles, building on Erdogan's de-dollarisation measures aimed at strengthening the Turkish lira.[22] Turkey also withstood U.S. pressure to abandon its Russian S-400s. On 23 February, Erdogan stated that Turkey would be willing to use S-400s if it was attacked with missiles.[23] On 16 August, Dmitry Shugaev stated that Russia had signed a contract with Turkey at the

Army-2022 International Forum to deliver a second regiment of the S-400 and allow for local production of S-400 components.[24] On 6 September, Andrei Klimov confirmed that the S-400 deal was proceeding according to plan, even though the talks "require silence" and contrasted Russia's supply of defensive weapons to Turkey with the U.S. supplying offensive fighter jets to Greece.[25]

Turkey has sought to capitalise on sanctions against Russia and Turkish finance minister Nureddin Nebati reportedly told Western investors that "we are going to benefit from sanctions on Russia as we did in Iraq."[26] During the first month of the war, Turkey courted 450 international brands that had left the Russian economy and encouraged legally accrued oligarch assets to enter Turkey.[27] Lukoil's $1 billion investments in the Turkish economy, which included 600 fuel stations, provided a sanctions-proof base for Vagit Alekperov to park his assets,[28] and eleven yachts belonging to Russian oligarchs docked in Turkish ports after the war began, including four superyachts owned by Roman Abramovich, worth more than $1 billion.[29] However, Turkey's non-compliance with Western sanctions had a darker side. The influx of "black money" from Azerbaijan, Russia, Kazakhstan and Ukraine since the 2016 Turkish coup attempt helped land Turkey on the Financial Action Task Force (FATF) Grey List. The Russian Central Bank views the lira as a "friendly country" currency and has supported shadowy transactions to prop up its value. In July, Rosatom reportedly supplied $5 billion to its Turkish subsidiary, which provided Erdogan with vital foreign currency as Turkey's inflation rate soared to 80%.[30] Until 29 September, Turkish state lenders VakifBank, Ziraat and İşbank used Russia's MIR system for electronic fund transfers.

Turkey's potential complicity in the illicit smuggling of Ukrainian agricultural produce and Russian energy is especially concerning. On 3 June, Ukraine's ambassador to Turkey, Vasily Bodnar, asserted that Russia had smuggled Ukrainian grain onto

Turkish territory. Although Turkey cited the risky precedent of detaining Russian commercial vessels without sufficient evidence, Kyiv believed that Turkey was trying to recoup its agricultural investments from occupied Ukrainian territories and succumbing to Russia's efforts to dilute Ankara's 2017 directive against accepting ships from Crimea.[31] On 5 July, Turkey seized a Russian-flagged ship, the Zhibek Zholy, in Karasu that allegedly carried 7,000 tons of smuggled grain from Berdyansk.[32] Turkey's release of the ship, which accorded with Lavrov's protestations that the ship was from Kazakhstan and implementing an Estonia–Turkey export contract, caused Ukraine to summon the Turkish ambassador in Kyiv. Russian Telegram channels have speculated about Turkey's potential role as an intermediary in trade between the EU and Russia, as it has established warehouses and logistical hubs that performed this role for Iran.[33] Despite U.S. warnings of secondary sanctions over its aid to the Russian economy, Nebati asserted that U.S. threats "should not cause concern in business circles" and hailed Turkey's standing as a commercial centre.[34] This intransigence suggests that Turkey is likely to remain a spoiler of Western sanctions against Russia and an essential backchannel between conflicting parties in Ukraine for the foreseeable future.

Israel's Cautious Opposition to the Ukraine War

Despite its prior reluctance to condemn Russian aggression against Georgia and Ukraine, Israel unequivocally criticised Putin's invasion of Ukraine. Israeli then-foreign minister Yair Lapid called Russia's actions a "grave violation of international law," pledged humanitarian assistance to Ukraine and stated that Israel's history showed that "war is not the way to resolve conflicts."[35] Lapid's response contrasted markedly with Israel's silence after Russia's DNR and LNR recognitions and reportedly occurred without prior consultation with the Kremlin. Notwithstanding Lapid's condemnation, Israel's approach to containing Russia has been much more cautious than Washington or Kyiv desired. Israel's then prime minister Naftali Bennett immediately steered Israel's discourse on Ukraine back to its pre-war neutrality, as his first statement on the invasion stated ambiguously "our hearts are with the civilians of eastern Ukraine" but did not mention Russia by name.[36] Israel's restraint on Ukraine extended to war crimes and military assistance—it voted to suspend Russia's membership from the UNHRC but condemned the Bucha Massacre without explicitly labelling Russia.[37] Zelensky expressed "shock" about Israel's refusal to supply Ukraine with air defences and Israel has blocked Estonia, Latvia and Lithuania from sending German–Israeli Spike anti-tank missiles to Ukraine.[38] On 12 July, Israeli defence minister Benny Gantz authorised the supply of defensive military equipment, including 1,500 helmets and 1,000 gas masks, to Ukraine. Despite Andriy Yermak's claim that Ukraine and Israel's intelligence services cooperated closely,[39] Israel did not supply Ukraine with Iron Dome air defence technology or Pegasus NSO spyware, and did not respond to Ukraine's intelligence-sharing request relating to Iran's military assistance to Russia.

Israel's refusal to impose sanctions on Russia was an especially sore point for the U.S. and Ukraine. In a 12 March interview on Israel's Channel 12, U.S. Undersecretary of State for Political Affairs Victoria Nuland urged Israel to sanction Russia.[40] During his 1 September call with Lapid, Zelensky stated that he expected Israel to accede to sanctions against Russia, but his appeal was also ignored.[41] To assuage Western concerns, Israel vowed strict compliance with secondary sanctions. On 14 March, Lapid pledged that "Israel will not be a route to bypass sanctions imposed on Russia by the United States and other Western countries."[42] Lapid's pledge had an immediate impact, as Roman

Abramovich withdrew assets from Israel and Russian businesses searched out destinations less affected by sanctions, but the Russian diaspora and appeal of Israeli technology prevented an iron-clad secondary sanctions regime.[43] Five Israeli companies exploited a loophole in the U.S. sanctions regime, which allowed Israel to act as an intermediary between Alrosa Diamond and the U.S. market.[44] In 2021, Russia exported $413 million in diamonds to Israel, so this sanctions evasion provided noteworthy revenues for Russia's mining sector.

Israel's passive approach to the Ukraine invasion can be explained by three potential factors. The first was Israel's national security imperative of engaging with Russia on Syria. On 26 February, the Russian Embassy in Israel released a statement confirming that the "deconfliction mechanism," established in 2015 to prevent Russia from obstructing Israeli strikes on Iranian targets, remained intact.[45] While the Russian ministry of defence had periodically expressed open disdain for Israeli unilateralism, especially following the September 2018 Il-20 jet shoot-down, Putin had absolved Israel from responsibility on unilateral strikes and played a personal role in upholding this backchannel.[46] While Israel was hesitant to comment publicly on coordination with Russia in Syria, Gantz stated on 2 May that, "As we do on all fronts, we are coordinating with the Russians in this region."[47] As military cooperation between Russia and Iran tightened, Moscow's hostility towards Israel's airstrikes in Syria deepened. On 26 July, Gantz revealed that Russian forces had opened fire on Israeli jets using S-300s after Israel had attacked Masyaf in northern Syria. Gantz described this as a "one-off incident," but it followed Alexander Lavrentiyev's warnings on 15 June that Israeli strikes on Syria were "unacceptable."[48] On 23 August, Lavrov condemned Israel's strikes on Damascus International Airport and the Tartus port as a "dangerous practice" in front of Syrian foreign minister Faisal Mekdad.[49] Eran Etzion, former deputy head of Israel's

National Security Council, stated in October 2022 that the GPS blockage Russia used to impede Israeli strikes in Syria was a warning for Lapid not to go too far in backing Ukraine. Nevertheless, Etzion believes that Russia–Israel coordination on Syria is unchanged and says that Iran's drone shipments to Russia will allow Israel to learn how Iranian drones function and help Israel to rally Western support against Iran.[50]

The second factor in Israel's passive response to the Ukraine invasion can be explained by domestic polarisations within Israel. The Russian invasion of Ukraine faced extensive grassroots resistance in Israel. On 26 February, thousands of Israelis took part in demonstrations in Jerusalem and Tel Aviv, which included slogans like "Putin Murders People: He is Violent and Dangerous" and featured the spray-painting of "Stop Russian Fascism" on the Russian Embassy.[51] The diaspora community was another source of anti-war sentiments, as it consisted largely of Soviet Jews who fled oppression and Russians who had left over their disquiet with Putin's regime.[52] The anti-Semitic undertones of Russia's denazification campaign in Ukraine also received widespread Israeli media criticism, as it trivialised and distorted Holocaust history.[53] The Likud Party was the primary supporter of a more conciliatory Israeli position towards Russia. Former Israeli prime minister Benjamin Netanyahu urged "utmost caution" on Ukraine as Israel's primary focus was on containing Iran.[54] Likud MK Yariv Levin rejected a Knesset proposal to create a committee on Ukrainian refugee resettlement, even though Israeli internal affairs minister Ayelet Shaked predicted an influx of 100,000 to 200,000 Jews from Moscow, Kyiv and Odesa. There was also a vocal pro-Kremlin minority within Israel's diaspora community—which saw Ukraine as anti-Semitic due to Stepan Bandera's enduring popularity and recalled the Russian role in liberating Second World War concentration camps—and a faction of younger Russian Israelis who supported

Netanyahu's approach.[55] Israel's Ukraine policy, which paid fealty to the "Netanyahu rule" of not enraging Russia while seeking to placate the U.S. and EU wherever possible, reflected the irreconcilable nature of domestic polarisations.[56] This policy also reflected public opinion: 67% of Israelis believed Russia was the aggressor but 60% opposed sanctions on Russia and just 22% supported arming Ukraine.[57]

The third factor was Israel's potential to serve as a mediator in the Ukraine War. Hours after the war had erupted, Zelensky asked Bennett to serve as a mediator between Russia and Ukraine, and proposed Jerusalem as a site for peace talks.[58] Bennett seized the opportunity to become an interlocutor between Russia and Ukraine, as Israel was in the rare position of having positive relations with both warring parties and Bennett wished to bolster his marginal international profile. On 5 March, Bennett discussed the Ukraine War with Putin in Moscow on the Jewish Sabbath, which highlighted his moral case for mediation, and relayed their discussion to Zelensky. In the initial weeks of the war, Bennett called Putin on two occasions and Zelensky on six occasions and vowed that "Israel will continue to prevent bloodshed and bring the aides from the battlefield to the conference table."[59] Yermak praised Bennett's mediation efforts and on 5 April, Zelensky stated that he wanted post-war Ukraine to be a "big Israel" and follow Israel's balance between democracy and national security preservation.[60] Despite this optimism, Israel's ambassador to the U.S., Michael Herzog, revealed that communications between Bennett and Putin had stopped on 12 April.

As Lapid has not revived Bennett's mediation ambitions, the prospect for heightened tensions between Russia and Israel has increased. Sergei Lavrov's anti-Semitic comments about Adolf Hitler's alleged Jewish roots and Zakharova's allegations that Israeli "mercenaries" fight alongside Ukrainian neo-Nazis caused severe backlash in Israel. Lapid demanded an apology for Lavrov's comments, which occurred during Putin's 5 May phone call with Bennett.[61] Despite Russia's long-held arbitration ambitions in the Arab–Israeli conflict, Moscow sharpened its pro-Palestinian stance. After Israel's UNHRC vote, the Russian foreign ministry stated that "It is also noteworthy that the longest occupation in the post-war world history is carried out with the tacit connivance of leading Western countries and the actual support of the United States."[62] On 15 April, Russia accused Israel of trying to "exploit the situation around Ukraine" and divert international attention from the Israeli–Palestinian conflict.[63] Capitalising on these statements and the controversy surrounding Lavrov's comments, a Hamas delegation held talks with senior Russian officials from 4–5 May. Alexander Fomin also met with Palestinian Authority-aligned Major General Nidal Abu Dukhan at the Army-2022 forum and Lavrov feted Hamas leader Ismail Haniyeh in Moscow on 13 September. Israel's condemnations of the 10 October strikes on Kyiv and Russia's retort that Israel had remained silent during eight years of Ukrainian terrorism in Donbas will likely continue this negative trend.[64]

Netayanhu's return as Israel's Prime Minister will likely prevent an escalation of tensions with Russia, even if a full return to the pre-February 2022 spirit of cooperation is unlikely. After Netanyahu returned to power on 29 December, Putin praised his personal role in strengthening Russia–Israel relations and expressed optimism about an expansion of bilateral cooperation.[65] Israeli Foreign Minister Eli Cohen's decision to speak with Lavrov before calling Kuleba and claims that he would be less public about Israel's position on the war caused further angst in Kyiv.[66] Despite Ukraine's concerns about Netanyahu's cordiality towards Putin, Podolyak endorsed Netanyahu as a potential conflict mediator. Netanyahu confirmed that he received a mediation overture during his tenure as opposition leader but preferred to defer Ukraine-related diplomacy to the sitting government.[67] Zelensky's decision to miss a UNGA vote on referring Israeli conduct in Palestine to the International Court of Justice, which departed from Kyiv's previous support for the motion, followed consultations with Netanyahu.[68] Despite these olive branches, Netanyahu's refusal to authorise Israeli military assistance to Ukraine, which would help intercept Iranian UAVs, remains a sore point in the bilateral relationship.

Russia Attempts to Consolidate its Influence in the Arab World

In stark contrast to the fluctuations in Russia's relationships with Turkey and Israel, Moscow's bilateral relationships with Arab countries have remained remarkably stable. The Arab League has framed itself as a potential mediator in the Ukraine War, which reflects the non-aligned positions of the majority of its members. On 27 February, the Arab League convened an emergency meeting and subsequently established a contact group on the Ukraine War, which addressed conflict resolution, food insecurity and energy security.[69] From 5–6 April, a delegation consisting of Arab League secretary Ahmed Aboul Gheit and the foreign ministers of Iraq, Jordan, Egypt, Algeria and Sudan met with Lavrov, Rau and Kuleba to discuss a political settlement in Ukraine. To counter what Lavrov described as a "balanced, fair, responsible" Arab League position during his speech, Ukraine's special envoy to the Middle East Maksym Subkh addressed the Arab League on 11 August and urged Arab countries to pay attention to Russia's weaponisation of food.[70] However, Ukraine's entreaties have not shifted the Arab world's neutral position on the conflict or resulted in a reversal of Russia's rising presence in the Middle East. In keeping with the region's neutrality, Russia has not made Arab countries parties of the Ukraine War, as its drive to recruit 17,000 foreign fighters from the Middle East did not gain traction. Russia's strategy towards the Arab world has focused on three crucial pillars: preventing disruption to Russia's military intervention in Syria; strengthening relations with the Gulf monarchies; and mitigating the negative impacts of the war's spill-over effects to other regional actors.

Russia Maintains its Geopolitical Foothold in Syria

On the surface, Russia's invasion of Ukraine had a negligible impact on its influence in Syria. On 25 February, Bashar al-Assad denounced Western "hysteria" about the Ukraine War and praised Putin's actions as a "correction of history and restoration of balance in the world which was lost after the breakup of the Soviet Union."[71] As the Syrian opposition expressed solidarity with Ukraine, Assad's government encouraged a pro-Russian rally with the Z symbol at Damascus University on 12 March. This propaganda rallied volunteers for Russia's attempt to recruit Syrians with experience in urban combat for the Ukraine War.[72] Despite the presence of Russian-language speakers in Syria's officer corps and a logistical path to Ukraine via Khmeimim airbase, Russia ultimately decided to keep Syria's forces focused on combatting domestic threats.[73] On 22 May, at least fifty Syrian technicians with experience building barrel bombs were working with the Russian military, which prompted fears that Russia would use chemical weapons in Ukraine.[74] On 29 June, Syria formally recognised the DNR and LNR's independence, which suspended its diplomatic relations with Ukraine. Russia rewarded Assad for his solidarity by consistently transferring smuggled Ukrainian grain to Syria, which was confirmed by Kyiv on 2 June and fulfilled Moscow's pledge to supply 1 million tons of grain to Syria in 2021.[75] On 12 July, Russia vetoed a UNSC resolution that would have allowed the supply of humanitarian aid to rebel-held Idlib, which denied the UN its only route to transfer supplies to north-west Syria.[76] This veto, which followed years of Russia's reluctant extensions of this aid provision, aimed to showcase Moscow's support for Assad's possession of total sovereignty in Syria.

Russia's military and diplomatic involvement in Syria has been largely unaffected by the Ukraine War. On 15 February, Shoigu met with Assad in Damascus to reaffirm Russia–Syria "counter-terrorism cooperation," visited Khmeimim airbase and observed Russia's drills in the eastern Mediterranean which featured hypersonic weapons. Russia's joint patrols with the Syrian armed forces, which began in January 2022, and patrols with Turkey in Idlib continued at a reduced frequency. In June 2022, Russia carried out aerial reconnaissance in northern Syria's Tal Rifat region and tried to establish a defence system in Kurdish-controlled Qamishli airport. In July 2022, Russian warplanes struck villages south of Idlib like Balshon and Marian, Russian and Syrian forces carried out joint shelling of the region and Russia transferred advanced sniper rifles to Syria for the first time.[77] On 18 July, Russia, Iran and Turkey held trilateral talks on a peace settlement in Syria, which built on the Astana Peace Process that was established in 2017. Former Syrian diplomat Bassam Barabandi contended that Russia wanted to show that its operations in Ukraine would not dilute its presence in Syria, and as the Ukraine War stagnated, Moscow could step up efforts to legitimise Assad in the Arab world and weaken U.S. influence in Syria.[78] Kirill Semenov contended that Syria's strategic importance for Russia had risen due to its rapprochement with Turkey and remained Moscow's main outpost to directly influence Middle Eastern affairs.[79]

Despite these apparent continuities, Russia's long-term influence in Syria was threatened by the erosion of its military capabilities in Ukraine and Turkey's growing belligerence towards northern Syria. The resource strains caused by the Ukraine conflict reluctantly forced Russia to scale back its military operations in Syria. Its drawdown from Syria began with the redeployment of small groups of Wagner Group PMCs to Ukraine at the start of 2022.[80] In early May, Russia reportedly scaled back its military presence in Syria further and handed over bases to the IRGC and Hezbollah.[81] In mid-August, Israeli satellite imagery revealed that Russia had redeployed a S-300 anti-aircraft battery from Masyaf, Syria to Novorossiyk via Turkey's Dardanelles Strait.[82] On 30 September, the Syrian Observatory for Human Rights reported that Russia's airstrikes in the Syrian desert had declined steeply and the annual death toll from Russian actions in Syria had fallen to its lowest level since 2015.[83] Notwithstanding the positive tone of Moscow–Tehran relations, Russia's vulnerabilities could exacerbate its latent rivalry with Iran in Syria. Russian reconnaissance operations in Tal Rifat were reportedly aimed at restricting Iranian influence in northern Syria and Russia blocked Iran from attending a summit with the Assad regime and Kurdish officials on 30 May.[84] In response to Israeli strikes on central and western Syria, Russia reportedly urged Iran to remove its long-range missile stockpiles from Hama.[85]

On 23 April, Mevlüt Çavuşoğlu announced the closure of Turkey's airspace for Russian military and civilian jets bound for Syria. This move was greeted with displeasure in Moscow. Alexander Perendzhiev, professor at the Plekhanov Russian University of Economics, attributed Turkey's actions to its frustrations with Damascus's growing regional profile and desire "to tie up Russia's actions in various theatres of military-political actions and support Zelensky."[86] Russian experts were divided on its impact on Russia's military operations in Syria. Kirill Semenov anticipated little disruption from Turkey's actions, as Russia could use Iranian and Iraqi airspace to supply its forces in Syria and move cargo via the Black Sea, but Konstantin Sivkov called it a "hidden form of imposing sanctions on Russia" that posed a "serious threat to Russia's security" and forced it to rely on a single Iranian air route.[87] Russia's concerns about Turkey's intentions in Syria were further amplified by Erdogan's warnings about a potential offensive on Tal Rifat and Manbij. Lavrov responded to this threat by expressing his "understanding" of Turkey's security concerns on the Syrian border, which included alleged U.S. support for the People's Protection Units (YPG) but called for Ankara to comply with the Astana Peace Process's diktats.[88]

On 20 July, Erdogan requested Russia and Iran's support for Turkey's fight against "terrorist organisations" in northern Syria, which Moscow cautiously opposed, and Tehran explicitly rejected. Russia has combined intra-Syrian diplomacy and bilateral engagement with Turkey to defuse the threat of an offensive. The North Thunderbolt joint operations room, which is located at a Russian base in Hardatnin in the northern countryside of Aleppo, hosted an anti-Turkish coalition of Hezbollah, Iran-aligned Fatemiyoun militias and the YPG.[89] Lieutenant General Alexander Chalko, the chief of Russian forces in Syria, met with SDF commander Mazoum Abdi in north-eastern Syria on 28 November to discuss the impact of Turkish airstrikes.[90] Syrian analyst Ammar Waqqaf contended that Russia had created a "new breed of Syrian opposition" that could pave the way for a political settlement and had facilitated talks between Damascus and Ankara to defuse the risk of a Turkish offensive.[91] This prediction came to pass, as Russia brokered talks between Turkey and Syria's Defence Ministers in Moscow on 29 December. These negotiations pointed to a possible Erdogan–Assad normalisation if Damascus, which was supported by Russia and the UAE. The cordial nature of Putin and Erdogan's 5 August meeting in Sochi about Syria, which emphasised the close nature of Russia–Turkey counterterrorism cooperation, suggested that an imminent crisis between the two countries over the Kurdish issue had been temporarily forestalled.

Russia Courts the Gulf Monarchies and Preserves its Regional Influence

Despite their deep security partnerships with the U.S., the Gulf monarchies were cautious in regard to Russia's invasion of Ukraine. The United Arab Emirates (UAE) held talks with Russia on 23 February about strengthening their strategic partnership, abstained from a UNSC Resolution condemning the invasion and suspended visa-free travel for Ukrainians on 1 March.[92] Anwar Gargash, a diplomatic advisor to the UAE's president, stated that Abu Dhabi supported a political solution in Ukraine and that "taking sides would only encourage more violence."[93] Saudi Arabia's neutrality was underscored by the presence of competing Russian and Ukrainian weapons at the 6 March World Defence Show in Riyadh, and desire to mediate in the Ukraine War. Saudi Arabia's arbitration ambitions were articulated by Crown Prince Mohammed bin Salman during his 3 March phone call with Putin and put into action over the September 2022 Azov Regiment–Viktor Medvedchuk prisoner exchange. Saudi Arabia and the UAE also coordinated on the December 2022 prisoner exchange between arms dealer Viktor Bout and U.S. basketball star Brittney Griner. These efforts complemented the UAE's brokering of backchannel meetings between Russian and Ukrainian officials to discuss prisoner swaps and facilitated Russian ammonia exports.[94] While Bahrain and Oman mirrored Riyadh and Abu Dhabi's approaches, Qatar's support for Ukraine's territorial integrity and Kuwait's criticisms of the violence resulting from the Ukraine War could be interpreted as indirect criticisms of Russia. Nevertheless, all six GCC countries refused to support Russia's suspension from the UN Human Rights Council, which reflected authoritarian solidarity and an aversion to isolating Russia.

The GCC's collective neutrality on Ukraine has placed its member states on a collision course with the U.S. and EU.

Brazen actions, such as Mohammed bin Salman and Abu Dhabi Crown Prince Mohammed bin Zayed's initial refusal to speak with Biden on Ukraine, and OPEC+'s 5 October decision to cut 2 million barrels of oil production, were viewed in Washington as unacceptable displays of solidarity with Moscow. To convince the Gulf monarchies to change course, Western countries and Ukraine have combined co-option with moral suasion. On 21 March, the U.S. transferred Patriot anti-missile receptors to Saudi Arabia to assuage its concerns about strikes from Yemen's Houthis. In late March, Boris Johnson pressured Mohammed bin Salman to condemn Russian aggression and Robert Habeck warned that OPEC countries were profiteering from the Ukraine War.[95] Kuleba held talks with Kuwait, which compared Russia's invasion of Ukraine to Iraq's 1990–1 occupation of Kuwait, and with the UAE on food security. Despite these outreaches, Ukraine received little tangible political support from the Gulf monarchies and was forced to settle for humanitarian aid and the promise of a potential free trade agreement with the UAE.

The Gulf Cooperation Council (GCC)'s break with U.S. policy towards Ukraine can be explained by collective indifference to the conflict, the Arabian Peninsula's sharpened pivot to a multipolar world order and the potential benefits of economic cooperation with Russia. The UAE's abstention can be explained by its representation of the Asian and Arab blocs within the UNSC, as well as its belief that Russia's invasion of Ukraine is unjustified but a "European issue."[96] Saudi Arabia's media debates on the Ukraine War reveal the stark contrast between its moral disapproval of Russia's actions and reticence about a harsh response. An 8 March *Okaz* article called Russia's invasion of Ukraine a destabilising action akin to the 1990 Iraqi invasion of Kuwait and claimed that Russia had "put its international reputation, prestige and even its national dignity to a severe test."[97] This reticence about the illegality of Russia's actions reflected itself in

GCC votes to condemn Russia on 2 March and the UAE's 30 September vote to condemn Russia's annexation referenda. Nevertheless, Saudi commentaries framed the Ukraine conflict as a proxy war which did not necessitate GCC solidarity with the West. *Al-Jazirah* columnist Ahmad al-Farraj warned that the U.S. had put Europe and Ukraine into a confrontation with Russia because it "does not need Russia's oil and gas like you do."[98] Mohammed Alyahya, the former editor of *Al-Arabiya*, asked, "Why should America's regional allies help Washington contain Russia in Europe when Washington is strengthening Russia and Iran in the Middle East?"[99]

The GCC's unwillingness to contain Russia underscores a bloc-wide commitment to balancing between West and East. Reflecting on the UAE experience, Dubai-based political scientist Abdulkhaleq Abdulla described the 1980s as a "turning point for UAE foreign policy" which saw it court global partners and normalise with the Soviet Union after informal consultations with Saudi Arabia.[100] This decades-long transition to multipolarity accelerated over the past decade, as inadequate U.S. support for the Syrian rebels and the JCPOA reduced the GCC's confidence in U.S. global leadership. The Biden administration's human rights criticisms of GCC partners, weak response to Houthi drone strikes, chaotic withdrawal from Afghanistan and revival of the JCPOA negotiations caused GCC countries to look towards the collective non-West. Russia's courtship of Saudi Arabia and the UAE reflected this trend. RIA Novosti commentator Sergey Savchuk published an article on 21 March entitled "Arab Oilmen are Ready to Destroy the USA," which warned that GCC countries were willing to join Russia and China's axis against U.S. diktats.[101] Russian Senator Viktor Bondarev praised Saudi Arabia and the UAE as "reactionary," while Sergei Naryshkin extolled Mohammed bin Salman's undisguised disrespect for Joe Biden.[102] Qatar's simultaneous decision to fete Zelensky at the Doha Forum and increase the Russian embassy's diplomatic presence in Doha mirrors this trend.[103] Russia's 28 February support for an arms embargo against the Houthis, which followed criticisms of their drone strikes on the UAE, reinforced Moscow's reliability as an alternative partner.

The GCC's relatively accommodating attitude towards Russia was also motivated by economic opportunities. The UAE is a major beneficiary from Western sanctions on Russia, as Dubai has emerged as a critical alternative investment hub for Russia's wealthiest citizens. The percentage of global private jet flights to Dubai stood at 3% on 24 February but Ukraine War-related sanctions caused this figure to soar to 14% by May. Dubai-based property firm Mira Estate recorded a 100% increase in real estate sales to Russian buyers and Roman Abramovich moved his $350 million Boeing-787 jet to Dubai while exploring real estate in Palm Jumeirah.[104] The UAE's golden visa scheme, which allows applicants to secure long-term residency by investing 10 million dirhams, has added to its 60,000-strong Russian expatriate population. The UAE's lax financial transparency regulations has allowed Russian businesspeople to use Coinsfera to conduct cryptocurrency deals and Russia has pursued intra-bank agreements in the UAE to secure access to the Emirati stock exchange.[105] In June, the Moscow Exchange announced plans to start trading the dirham at an unspecified time, which could allow the dirham to become an intermediary currency in Russian deals with India and Bangladesh.[106] The UAE's potential entry into de-dollarisation ensures that it does not cede ground on this sphere to Iran, Turkey and Egypt, and helps ensure that the post-24 February rise in the dirham's value continues.

As the UAE has already been added to the FATF Grey List, its sanctions-evasion assistance to Russia has resulted in further pressure from Western countries. Despite deputy prime minister Sheikh Mansour bin Zayed's alleged personal involvement in facilitating Russian investment in the UAE, Abu Dhabi insists that it complies with Western sanctions against Russian oligarchs.[107] On 2 March, Dubai's Mashreqbank stopped lending to Russian banks and announced that it was reviewing its exposure to Russia due to Ukraine War-related risks.[108] These concessions did not preclude secondary sanctions on the UAE. Abdulla stated that the UAE was taking a "case by case" approach to secondary sanctions but insisted that "most of the Russians in the UAE are doing legitimate business. They should not be a target."[109] Qatar and Saudi Arabia mirrored the UAE's approach to secondary sanctions, albeit on a smaller scale. On 25 May, the Qatar Investment Authority (QIA) conceded that "We can't do much in Russia" but insisted it would not leave key projects, such as the 19% stake it possesses in Rosneft.[110] In February and March 2022, Saudi Arabia's Kingdom Holding, which is controlled by billionaire Alwaleed Bin Talal, invested $365 million in Gazprom, $109 million in Lukoil and $52 million in Rosneft.[111] Talal al-Faisal, a Saudi businessman from the Al-Saud family, insisted that this deal was independent of state policy, as "a Saudi-based public company made those investments, not the state, months before the PIF acquired a minority stake in it."[112] Nevertheless, the risk of Western backlash abounds for GCC investors who try to maintain a foothold in Russia.

Elsewhere in the Arab world, Russia has managed to maintain its foothold in spite of countervailing Western and economic pressures. Despite its close partnership with the U.S., Jordan refused to condemn Russia and focused its response to the conflict on humanitarian issues, such as the evacuation of 1,700 Jordanian students stranded in Ukraine.[113] On 18 May, King Abdullah II stated that Russia's presence in southern Syria provided "tranquillity," which underscored Amman's enduring belief that Moscow could counter Iranian influence in Syria.[114] Iraq's neutrality can be explained by internal polarisations, as pro-Iran

Popular Mobilisation Forces (PMF) militias and Tehran-aligned former Iraqi prime minister Nouri al-Maliki sympathise with Russia, while cleric Moqtada al-Sadr and Iraqi Kurdistan's president Nechirvan Barzani are non-aligned.[115] Despite calls from the Iraqi Central and Trade Bank to avoid commercial dealings with Russia, Moscow believes that its $14 billion investment portfolio in Iraq will stay intact and that the dearth of alternative investors will keep Rosneft's post-2017 presence in Iraqi Kurdistan afloat.[116] Lebanon's position on the Ukraine War was defined by similar divisions, as Hezbollah blamed U.S. aggression for the conflict while then Lebanese president Michel Aoun condemned the war. While Iraq's food price increases do not stem from a reliance on Russian and Ukrainian wheat, Lebanon faced a wheat crisis due to the combined impact of the 2020 Beirut port explosion and the Ukraine War.[117] Russia's compliance with the Black Sea grain export deal will play a crucial role in upholding this partnership.

Africa Becomes a Lynchpin of Russia's Post-Western Foreign Policy

After the Ukraine War began, Africa was polarised between rare supporters of Putin's invasion, adherents to neutrality and critics of the war's negative implications, such as food insecurity and neo-colonialism. Until its abstention during the UNGA annexation referendum vote, Eritrea was the only African country that consistently voted to defend Russian aggression in the United Nations. Amongst African officials, president Yoweri Museveni's son Lieutenant General Muhoozi Kainerugaba, who serves as Uganda People's Defence Forces chief, was a rare supporter of the Russian invasion. In a much-publicised tweet, Kainerugaba stated that "The majority of mankind that are non-white support Russia's stand in Ukraine. Putin is absolutely right!" and compared NATO's alleged provocations against Russia to the Cuban Missile Crisis.[118] Supporters of neutrality either expressed sympathy with Russian narratives or insisted that the conflict was irrelevant to Africa. While Museveni called his son's pro-Putin stance a personal view, he chastised Western double standards, repeated Kremlin narratives about the destruction of Libya in 2011 and implicitly recognised Russia's right to a sphere of influence by calling it a "centre of gravity" in Eastern Europe.[119] Although South Africa indirectly criticised Russia's use of force and violations of international law, Cyril Ramaphosa stated on 18 March that the Ukraine War could have been avoided if NATO had refrained from eastward expansion.[120] Guinea's prime minister Mohamed Béavogui was one of the few African leaders to express this position publicly. At the 30 March Dubai Forum, Béavogui said, "For years people said don't worry about war, 'it's only in Africa.' Now it is in the middle of Europe, and we are suddenly asked to choose."[121]

Amongst the twenty-eight African countries that voted to condemn Russia in the UNGA on 2 March, solidarity with Ukraine was sparse, as the pernicious secondary implications of the conflict for Africa were much more significant. During their 24 May joint statement in Accra, the presidents of Ghana and Mozambique condemned the Russian invasion's devastating impact on Africa and global security. In a 25 May statement commemorating the anniversary of the Organization of African Unity's formation, African Union Commission chairperson Moussa Faki Mahamat described Africa as a "collateral victim" of the Ukraine War and warned that the conflict would increase the structural fragility of African economies.[122] Cyril Ramaphosa similarly warned that Western sanctions on Russia hurt "countries that are either bystanders or not part of the conflict."[123] Kenyan UN Ambassador Martin Kimani's powerful 22 February speech was widely interpreted in the West as a display of solidarity with Ukraine but could be more accurately depicted as an emphatic defence of international law.[124] Kimani accused Vladimir Putin's pursuit of military solutions as putting multilateralism on its "deathbed" and stated his opposition to "irredentism and expansionism on any basis". Zelensky's much-anticipated 21 June address to the AU, which occurred ten weeks after his initial speaking request, poignantly warned that Africa was a "hostage" of the Ukraine War but was received by only four African heads of state, with the remaining countries sending lower level representatives. Despite his passionate plea against African neutrality, Kuleba's decision to cut short his African tour due to the 10 October strikes epitomised Kyiv's limited ability to influence elite and public opinion on the continent.

Due to its apparent indifference to its war crimes in Ukraine and Kyiv's limited diplomatic profile, Russia views Africa as an increasingly important vector of its multipolar foreign policy. On the economic front, Russia wishes to ensure that sanctions do not derail its traditional spheres of cooperation with Africa, such as nuclear energy, oil and gas and mining, as well as its standing as the continent's leading arms vendor. Empirical evidence presents a mixed picture of Russia's ability to sanctions-proof its trade links with Africa. During the first five months of 2022, Russia's trade with Africa increased by 34% from 2021 levels. Rosatom's flagship El Dabaa nuclear reactor in Egypt has continued to progress, while Gazprombank could take part in South Africa's Eastern Cape Coega special economic zone LNG gas-to-power project and Russia is trying to construct a Morocco to Nigeria pipeline. Despite intense secondary sanctions pressure from the U.S., Egyptian pilots continued training in Russia for use of Su-35 jets and Russia upgraded its military cooperation with Cameroon in April 2022. Notwithstanding these successes, Russia has not secured new mega-projects in Africa and has seen flagship projects disintegrate. Even though Nigerian president

Muhammadu Buhari has released $2 billion in funds to Russia since 2020, the Nigerian government reportedly negotiated a new contract with a British company to oversee the Ajaokuta steel factory project.[125]

The Kremlin advanced a series of sanctions-proofing tactics to preserve its economic interests. On 25 May, deputy foreign minister Mikhail Bogdanov announced that many of Russia's key partners in Africa would switch to trading in national currencies, which would counter the impact of SWIFT sanctions.[126] Louis Gouend, the president of the Cameroonian Diaspora Association in Africa, called for the establishment of a Russian bank in Africa which would circumvent SWIFT sanctions.[127] As it is unclear whether these plans will come to fruition, Russia has also relied on illicit tactics to secure additional revenues. Russia's smuggling of 30 tons of illicit Sudanese gold per year via Dubai has helped counter punitive measures against the Russian Central Bank. This smuggling network is undergirded by Russia's growing partnership with Lieutenant General Mohamed Hamdan "Hemedti" Dagalo, who visited Moscow immediately before the invasion, and Prigozhin's shell company Meroe Gold.[128] Russia's transport of smuggled Ukrainian grain to Africa is another economic lifeline which has been praised or ignored in African countries. Hassan Khannenje, the director of HORN International Institute for Strategic Studies in Nairobi, said that "Africans don't care where they get their food from, and if someone is going to moralise about that, they are mistaken."[129] In keeping with his promotion of the narrative that SWIFT sanctions are the main cause of food insecurity, African Union Chairman and Senegalese president Macky Sall praised Russia's willingness to constructively address the grain export impasse during his meeting with Putin on 3 June.

Russia's military interventions in Africa continued with minimal disruptions from the Ukraine War. There have been no signs of a clandestine Russian military withdrawal from Libya, where

Moscow backs Libya National Army (LNA) chief Khalifa Haftar against the Tripoli authorities, and the Wagner Group's control over key facilities in eastern Libya is so pervasive that LNA forces need to ask permission for entry.[130] Russia's deployment of 2,000 Wagner Group PMCs in Libya is complemented by grain exports and provocative actions, such as the alleged shooting down of a U.S. drone over Benghazi.[131] Ukraine's defence ministry alleges that Russia has recruited Libyan foreign fighters for its war effort. LNA Major General Khaled Mahjoub has denied these reports, stating that the army "has nothing to do whatsoever with the Ukrainian War."[132] In Sudan, Russia's Port Sudan Red Sea naval base negotiations have progressed and the Wagner Group defends gold mining assets. A 5 June *New York Times* report revealed the existence of "The Russian Company," a tightly guarded gold processing plant 200 miles north of Khartoum operated by the Wagner Group.[133] The Wagner Group has also used force to protect Prigozhin's gold mining interests on the Sudan–CAR border. A March 2022 report revealed that Wagner Group PMCs and aligned CAR forces used automatic weapons to create a mass grave of at least 20 Sudanese miners and up to 70 miners could have perished in these assaults.[134] The Wagner Group's military support for CAR president Faustin-Archange Touadéra's struggle against ex-Seleka rebels continues. These operations have resulted in large numbers of civilian casualties—on 11–12 April, the Wagner Group and the CAR armed forces killed between 10 and 15 civilians in Gordile and Ndah villages, which precipitated the inception of a UN investigation on 15 April.[135]

As France's Operation Barkhane winds down, Russia views the Sahel as an increasingly important theatre of military power projection. Since late 2021, the Wagner Group has been on the frontlines of the Assimi Goïta-led Malian junta's counterterrorism operations. While the Wagner Group has achieved few military successes, its operations have continued during the Ukraine War. On 30 March, Russia transferred two Mi-35M attack helicopters and an advanced radar system to Mali, and the Kremlin claims that 200 Malian service members and nine police officers are already being trained in Moscow.[136] Much like in CAR, the humanitarian consequences of Russia's military involvement in Mali has faced international criticism. Between 27 and 31 March, the Malian armed forces and Wagner Group PMCs killed 300 civilian men in the central Malian town of Moura. The Federal News Agency rebutted these allegations as manifestations of France's insecurity about losing its influence in Mali,[137] and through the alleged movement of corpses, Russia falsely accused France of carrying out a Moura-style massacre in Gossi. These deflections belie the growing human costs of the Wagner Group's counter-insurgency operations in Mali. On 30 October, Malian officials and "white soldiers," who were presumably Russian PMCs, murdered at least thirteen civilians in Mopti, and Victoria Nuland warned that terrorism in Mali has increased since Wagner's arrival.[138]

The 30 September coup in Burkina Faso, which propelled Ibrahim Traoré to power, could provide Russia with another partner in the Sahel. Sergei Markov claimed that "our people" had helped Traoré take power.[139] Prigozhin praised Traoré for taking necessary actions to satisfy the demands of young officers, while acknowledging his predecessor Paul-Henri Sandaogo Damiba's liberation of Burkina Faso from colonial-era plunder and gang violence.[140] Although Traore denied that Burkina Faso wanted to hire Wagner Group PMCs, concerns were heightened after Prime Minister Kyélem Apollinaire de Tambèla visited Moscow in December. At the subsequent U.S.–Africa Summit, Ghana's President Nana Akufo-Addo told Blinken that Burkina Faso acquiesced to the Wagner Group's entry in exchange for selling a mine in southern Burkina Faso to Russia.[141] While the veracity of these allegations is unclear, Burkina Faso's moves to expel France's ambassador and crackdowns on French media outlets portend closer ties with Russia.

As the July 2023 Russia–Africa summit in St. Petersburg draws nearer, there is optimism in Moscow about the trajectory of Russian influence in Africa. Andrey Maslov and Dmitry Suslov predict breakthroughs for Russian policy in Africa as "none of the African countries perceives Russia as an enemy, a former colonialist or a potential hegemon."[142] There are calls for a more proactive Russian approach to Africa and Moscow's expanded engagement with middle powers that resist Western or Chinese hegemony. Russian commentator Yuri Sigov warns that Russian officials are not doing enough to facilitate a full-scale "turn towards Africa," as military ties progress unevenly, Russian language instruction lags and education is focused on training professionals instead of future leaders.[143] A 4 June *Vzglyad* article argued that Russia could capitalise on opposition to Chinese neo-colonialism and leverage ties with countries, such as Turkey, which acted as conduits for Russian products in African markets.[144] Russia's ability to achieve these ambitious goals, as its economic resources dwindle and its prestige in Africa is eroded by military setbacks in Ukraine, remains an open question heading into 2023.

Latin America's Non-Aligned Position Towards the Ukraine War

Although the foundations of Russian influence in Latin America are shallower than in the Middle East or Africa, Russia has preserved its partnerships with the region's leading powers and shored up its ties with traditional anti-Western regimes. The resilience of Russia's relationships with Latin American countries appeared improbable during the early stages of the war. On 24 February, Colombia, Argentina and Chile led a coalition of

Latin American countries calling for Russia's swift withdrawal from Ukraine.[145] On 2 March, Brazil voted to condemn Russian aggression in Ukraine, while Cuba and Nicaragua abstained in the UNGA. In late March, Mexico and France jointly pushed for a UN Security Council resolution on Ukraine's humanitarian crisis, which implicated Russia's invasion. On 9 April, Colombian president Iván Duque stated that there was "no relationship" between Colombia and Russia because of Russia's atrocities in Ukraine.[146] The Organization of American States (OAS) suspended Russia's observer status on 22 April. As the war progressed, Latin American countries were less willing to side against Russia. Brazil abstained from a 30 September UNSC resolution on the annexation referenda, while Mexico, Brazil and Argentina refused to call for Russia's immediate exit from Ukraine in the OAS on 7 October.[147] The Mercosur bloc denied Zelensky's speaking request on 20 July, while U.S. pressure has not resulted in Latin American countries sanctioning Russia.

This changing tide caused Russia to elevate Latin America's previously peripheral strategic importance. On 25 February, the Russian foreign ministry extolled Latin America as a "region of political goodwill, economic opportunity, cultural closeness and a similar mentality."[148] On 8 October, Lavrov claimed that trade between Russia and Latin America had increased by 27% from 2021–2 to $11 billion, including $3.7 billion in fertiliser exports, and hailed Moscow's "pragmatic, de-ideologised" approach to diplomacy with Latin American countries.[149] The mantra of Lavrov's engagement with the region was "for building bridges, not erecting walls," referring to the region's refusal to sanction Russia.[150] Russia had reasons to be confident about its short-term prospects for influence in Latin America; the June 2022 election of left-wing president Gustavo Petro in Colombia converted one of Russia's main regional foes into a prospective ally. Putin praised Petro as a "promising partner," which reflected

Petro's criticisms of Western involvement in Latin America and the alleged involvement of veteran political technologist Colonel Dmitry Tarantsov in election interference campaigns in Colombia.[151] Ukraine's limited diplomatic footprint in Latin America, which saw it focus its cooperation on Guatemala and the Caribbean, also allowed Russian disinformation about the war to spread with impunity.

Despite these prospects, Russia's potential to expand its influence in Latin America is stymied by two factors. First, Latin America's refusal to sanction Russia is not generally indicative of solidarity with Moscow's actions in Ukraine. Dmitry Razumovsky, the director of the Institute of Latin American Studies at the Russian Academy of Sciences, noted that countries such as Argentina have legal restrictions on unilateral sanctions and claimed that Russia's understanding of a multipolar world order clashes with Latin American perceptions. Razumovsky contended that Latin America rejects Russia's view that the post-Soviet space is its sphere of influence, as it suffered due to the U.S.'s Monroe Doctrine.[152] This view was broadly shared by Western and Ukrainian diplomats. Gérard Araud contended that Latin American countries "don't want to be associated with the West and to be involved in any way in this war" but "their links to Russia are quite limited."[153] Latin American leaders were alarmed by Russia's weaponisation of energy towards Europe, and in Argentina, Chile and Uruguay the view that NATO had instigated the war was confined to the margins of political discourse.[154] Sergiy Kyslytsya noted that, unlike India, Brazil had criticised Russia's annexation of Ukrainian territory even when it abstained from UN resolutions.[155] Due to extensive social media access, public opinion about the Ukraine War was detached from pro-Russian state media discourse, even in Moscow-aligned countries such as Cuba.

Second, Russia has struggled to diversify its commercial interactions with Latin American countries. Its trade links there have typically been concentrated in agriculture, energy and defence. The Ukraine War has tested the established parameters of Russia–Latin America trade relations and constrained opportunities for future growth. Although Ecuador exported $3 billion worth of fruits and $311 million worth of flowers to Russia from 2019–21, sanctions-imposed delivery issues and the complete shutdown of the Ukrainian market caused Quito's agricultural exports in the post-Soviet space to dry up.[156] There are also concerns in Moscow that Russian trade statistics conceal the extent of the impact of secondary sanctions, which has caused Russian investors to focus their attention on partner country trade figures, and risks span from the railway to the communications sectors.[157] Due to the risk of Western secondary sanctions, Russia's prospective forays outside its narrow range of established spheres are small-scale, such as an entry into Peru's textile markets or investment in Nicaragua's Augusto Sandino International Airport in Managua and the Bluefields sea port.[158] Given these obstacles, Russian academic Petr Yakovlev warned that Russia–Latin America economic relations had entered a "zone of uncertainty" but asserted that Latin America could be a lucrative market for essential goods that Russia would have previously sold to Europe.[159]

Despite these constraints, Russia strengthened relations with Argentina, Brazil and Mexico with mixed results, and preserved its traditional anti-American partnerships with Cuba, Nicaragua and Venezuela. On 3 February, Argentina's president, Alberto Fernández, signalled his desire to strengthen relations with Russia, as he called for an abandonment of his country's dependence on the U.S. and IMF in Moscow. Argentina's statements on the Ukraine War emphasised the collateral impact of Western sanctions on Russia for Latin America and urged the international media to pay more attention to non-European emergencies such as the humanitarian crisis in Haiti.[160] Secondary sanctions had an adverse impact on Argentina's economy, as the removal of Vnesheconombank from SWIFT risked derailing a January 2022 $864 million Argentine railway contract with TMH International.[161] Yury Ushakov, an aide to Putin, also expressed tentative support for Argentina's accession to BRICS.[162] Razumovsky believed that Russia theoretically supported Argentina's inclusion in BRICS as it showed that it was not isolated but might not actively lobby for its membership due to strenuous Brazilian opposition.[163]

Despite fierce polarisations on domestic and foreign policy issues, the Brazilian political establishment was relatively united in supporting a conciliatory stance towards Russia. On 16 February, Brazilian president Jair Bolsonaro visited Moscow, in spite of intense U.S. pressure, and expressed "solidarity" with Russia. Bolsonaro's cordial stance towards Russia, which included pledges to collaborate in the defence, gas and agriculture sectors, broke with his pro-U.S. stance during the Trump administration.[164] On 27 February, Bolsonaro did not condemn Russia and repeated Putin's mantra that Russia and Ukraine were "brother nations," as many Ukrainians speak Russian.[165] Bolsonaro also expressed interest in helping to de-escalate the Ukraine conflict. After his February 2022 meeting with Putin, former Brazilian environment minister Ricardo Salles falsely claimed that Biden and the Western world had thanked Bolsonaro for preventing Putin from invading Ukraine, and urged for Bolsonaro to be awarded the Nobel Peace Prize for preventing World War III.[166] Bolsonaro alluded to a 1982 Falklands War-style solution to the Ukraine War, pitched his peace plan to Zelensky and offered Brazil as a mediator in the conflict. Former president Lula da Silva, Bolsonaro's main rival, claimed that Zelensky was as responsible for the Ukraine War's outbreak as Putin and stated that the U.S. and EU were "also guilty" for not negotiating intensely enough with Russia before the invasion.[167]

In keeping with this rhetoric, Brazil expanded diesel purchases from Russia and lobbied the U.S. for sanctions loopholes on fertiliser, as it imported 25% of its requirement from Russia. Despite this cooperation, secondary sanctions likely explained Petrobas's April 2022 abrogation of a deal to sell nitrogen fertiliser to Russia's Acron PJSC and could confine bilateral trade to the commodity sphere.

Mexican president Andrés Manuel López Obrador distanced himself from U.S. policies on Ukraine and emphasised Mexico's neutrality in relation to the Ukraine War. Although Mexico abstained on the UNHRC vote, Obrador condemned the vote as jeopardising the UN's ability to act as an intermediary between Russia and Ukraine.[168] On 22 September, Mexico converted its neutrality and calls for dialogue into action by proposing a backchannel format that would include Pope Francis, Narendra Modi and Antonio Guterres.[169] Mexico's diplomatic efforts received little traction, aside from an endorsement from Venezuela and Colombia, which linked their backing of Obrador's campaign to humanity's inability to survive a world war.[170] The U.S. expressed alarm at overt displays of solidarity between Mexico and Russia. The creation of a Mexico–Russia friendship caucus by six Obrador-aligned lawmakers in March 2022, which hosted a disinformation-riddled address by the Russian ambassador to Mexico Viktor Koronelli, caused particular angst in Washington. Ken Salazar, the U.S. ambassador to Mexico, rebuked Koronelli for his address; the U.S. warned that Russia had stationed more GRU agents in Mexico than any other country, and mulled revoking visa access for Mexico–Russia Friendship Committee members.[171] Mexico's enforcement of a September 2021 space cooperation agreement with Russia, which allowed GLONASS systems to be installed on its territory, augmented tensions due to Moscow's potential use of satellite technology to threaten the U.S.[172]

Before invading Ukraine, Russia strengthened ties with its anti-American allies in Latin America. In January 2022, Putin called Cuban president Miguel Díaz-Canel, Nicaraguan president Daniel Ortega and Venezuelan president Nicolás Maduro, and pledged to deepen Russia's "strategic partnerships in each and every field."[173] On 16 February, Russia's deputy foreign minister Yury Borisov signed a series of strategic cooperation agreements with Venezuela, which extended to the military sphere, and subsequently visited Cuba and Nicaragua. Sergei Rybakov's 13 January comments that Russia could "neither confirm or exclude" military-technical measures in Cuba and Venezuela if NATO continued its provocations caused particular controversy. Russian defence expert Yury Lyamin contended that Russian ships and strategic missile carriers could pressure the U.S. through frequent visits to Cuba and Venezuela. Lyamin concluded this would lead to the construction of bases within a few months but could trigger U.S. sanctions and require Russia to provide greater economic support for Cuba.[174] Mikhail Khodaryonok contended that Cuba and Venezuela could host submarines, Iskander-M systems could arrive in Cuba and Venezuelan airfields could host Tu-160s.[175] Razumovsky believed that Russia had refrained from such actions because it would be viewed by Mexico and Brazil as breaking Latin America's "fragile equilibrium" as a peaceful region, and support for the implementation of Rybakov's proposal was confined to hardliners such as Alexander Dugin.[176]

Russia capitalised on Cuba and Nicaragua's shared aversion to unilateral sanctions to strengthen bilateral relations. Cuba's 23 February statement, which decried NATO's "progressive expansion" towards Russia's borders, aligned with its long-standing policy of defending Russian military interventions.[177] Cuban state media repeated Russia's claims that it was carrying out a "special military operation" in Ukraine and warnings about Ukrainian Nazism, while RT's Spanish language channel had extensive reach in Cuba.[178] Russia returned the favour by helping Cuba divest from its traditional reliance on Venezuelan oil;

from July to September, Russia sent three oil tankers containing 700,000 barrels of oil each to Cuba. Nevertheless, the scope of the Russia–Cuba economic partnership fell short of Borisov's expansive pledges in February, and sanctions pose risks to Russian tourism and automobile part supplies. On 10 June, Ortega authorised the deployment of Russian military personnel to combat drug trafficking, which would also lead to an "exchange of experiences and training."[179] On 16 September, Ortega signed a media agreement with Sputnik, which would make Russian state media available to 6.6 million people on twenty state channels. Ortega's son Daniel Edmundo Ortega Murillo personally spearheaded this initiative to strengthen Russia–Nicaragua relations, while Sputnik International Cooperation Directorate head Vasily Pushkov claimed that the deal would get rid of "informational garbage."[180]

On 1 March, Nicolás Maduro condemned the "destabilising actions of the United States and NATO" in a call with Vladimir Putin and spoke out against "Western lies and disinformation." In addition to offering Russia "strong support," Maduro posted a Twitter post with Putin and pledged to pursue dialogue as a path to peace.[181] Venezuela's solidarity with Russia derailed negotiations between Maduro and the opposition, which were co-convened by the U.S. and Colombia in Mexico City, but the U.S. saw a glimmer of hope in Caracas's non-recognition of DNR and LNR.[182] As Russia replaced Venezuela's market share in the U.S. energy sector, which amounted to 650,000 barrels a day before 2019, U.S. officials hoped that they could revive this historical partnership.[183] Although Maduro hailed his "respectful, cordial and very diplomatic" talks with U.S. officials and released two U.S. citizens on 9 March, he remained loyal to Russia even as Venezuela's state-owned PDVSA oil company's exposure to Russian banks generated U.S. sanctions. Despite subsequent U.S. overtures, Venezuela continued to strengthen its partnership with Russia, and openly courted Russian tourists with an offer to use the rouble currency in its resorts. Venezuelan media outlet Telesur's partnership with RT Spanish ensures that Russian propaganda about the Ukraine War spreads across Latin American television screens. As Maduro's political rival U.S.-recognised president Juan Guaidó has expressed solidarity with Ukraine, the Moscow–Caracas partnership is likely to persist despite U.S. appeals.

CONCLUSION

Russia in 2023: A Year of Implosion?

In 2022, Vladimir Putin saw his efforts to subjugate Ukraine through force unravel in spectacular fashion. Volodymyr Zelensky's government survived Russia's regime change campaign and Ukrainian civic nationalism reached historic highs. Russia's humiliating withdrawal from Kyiv, failed offensive on Odesa and ignominious surrenders to Ukraine in Kharkiv and Kherson exposed the chimeric nature of Russia's post-2008 military modernisation. Russia's homeland security was threatened by long-range Ukrainian strikes on border regions and military assets deeper in Russian territory. While the Russian economy temporarily staved off economic collapse due to high energy prices and an unexpectedly resilient rouble, the domestic agenda that propelled Putin to a fourth term is in tatters. The unity of Western countries in providing military support for Ukraine and sanctioning Russia derailed the Kremlin's hopes of stoking divisions in the collective West. Russia's must-discussed embrace of a multipolar world order proved to be largely symbolic. Non-Western countries refused to impose sanctions on the Russian economy but also warily responded to Moscow's commercial and security overtures. With the exception of Belarus, Russia's prestige in the post-Soviet space plunged to post-Cold War lows. In short, 2022 was an annus horribilis for Russia, which exposed the shallowness of Putin's claims to have rebuilt Russia's global influence, military might and economic foundations.

Heading into 2023, Putin's prospects to transform the military situation in Ukraine remain dim, as steady supplies of NATO-class weaponry to Kyiv and the diminishing returns of mobilisation leave Russia with a dwindling array of options. Russia's battlefield setbacks, which have resulted in mounting casualties and rising frustration from nationalists at home, will encourage it to continue its undeclared war on Ukrainian civilians. While the threat of popular unrest from anti-war liberals has been temporarily defused, the risk of an intra-elite schism between war hawks and the Russian Defence Ministry remains high. Russia's economic outlook is set to deteriorate as European countries continue divesting from Russian energy and the corrosive impact of sanctions becomes apparent. This toxic combination of military weakness, internal discord and economic decline might push Russia towards the bargaining table, but Ukraine is unlikely to voluntarily surrender a historical opportunity to liberate its territory. As paths to a military victory or an honourable peace in Ukraine are remote, Putin faces the uncomfortable prospect of watching his legacy be eviscerated on the battlefield, compromising with internal factions to maintain his totalitarian grip on power and accepting Russia's inexorable decline as a global power.

Russia's Post-Kherson Withdrawal Military Strategy in Ukraine

Since completing its exit from Kherson, Russia has combined offensive operations in Donetsk with the construction of fortifications to prevent a Kharkiv-style Ukrainian counter-offensive. The primary focus of Russia's offensive operations in Donetsk remains Bakhmut. In tandem with its withdrawal from Kherson,

CONCLUSION

Russia intensified its military campaign against Bakhmut, which resulted in the near-complete destruction of power plants that serve the city and Soledar.[1] Zelensky acknowledged the resilience of Ukrainian forces defending Bakhmut and attempted to boost the morale of local residents by visiting the city on December 20. Zelensky's trip received mixed reactions in Bakhmut, as the absence of Internet service made some residents unaware of his trip and support for a negotiated settlement with Russia persists, but it nonetheless reflected Ukraine's belief that Russia's Donetsk offensive is destined to fail.[2] This confident assessment is borne by the military situation on the ground. Russia's intensified assault in Bakhmut resulted in heavy casualties, as its reservists have dug trench systems under heavy artillery fire and engaged in frontal assaults against fortified Ukrainian positions.[3] Russia's recent tactical recalibration, which has seen Wagner Group PMCs act as "shock troops" in frontal assaults and conscripts take the lead in defensive operations, have been undermined by equipment shortages. A December 26 video showed Wagner Group PMCs calling Valery Gerasimov "a piece of shit," and complaining about shell shortages."[4] Yevgeny Prigozhin has conceded that Wagner Group PMCs in Bakhmut have taken weeks to seize control of houses and contends that Ukrainian forces have erected five hundred lines of defence in Bakhmut. To highlight the offensive's costs, Prigozhin released a video in January 2023 next to the bagged bodies of convict mercenaries in a basement with the grim message "Their contract has finished, they will go home next week."[5]

Due to heavy casualties and Bakhmut's declining logistical value after the Lyman surrender, Russia's decision to sustain its offensive is hard to explain. On 25 November, Prigozhin claimed that Russia wished to create a meatgrinder in Bakhmut that would weaken the Ukrainian Armed Forces and deliberately trying to slow down its occupation of the city.[6] Ukraine's deployment of Special Forces and lesser trained Territorial Defence Forces fighters to Bakhmut in late November lends some credibility to Prigozhin's assertions.[7] As Russia's offensive persists, Ukrainian forces are likely trying to mitigate casualties amongst their elite units in Bakhmut, as the rotation of the 93rd Kholodny Yar brigade in late December indicates.[8] The extensive salt and gypsum mines located on Bakhmut's outskirts provide an economic rationale for Russia's focus on the city. Prigozhin's desire to seize these assets and use them to finance Wagner Group operations, which is confirmed by U.S. intelligence assessments, mirrors Russia's efforts to capture mineral resources in Sub-Saharan Africa.[9] If the Wagner Group were to seize these mines, it would likely use the pretext of Ukraine storing ammunition alongside gypsum reserves.[10] Prigozhin has not publicly acknowledged these economic motivations but views Bakhmut's network of "underground cities," which house people, tanks and infantry fighting vehicles at a depth of 80–100 metres, as a major asset.[11] Prigozhin claims that this strategic value has been apparent since World War I, which suggests that the Wagner Group could convert an occupied Bakhmut into an arms depot. Russia could also view its operations in Bakhmut as a face-saving measure, which counter the narrative that it is exclusively on the defensive against an emboldened Ukrainian military. Despite Prigozhin's entreaties against optimistic reporting about Bakhmut and contrary evidence, pro-war Telegram channels have regularly claimed that Russia entered central Bakhmut. A 7 January *Voenkor Kotenok Z* post described Ukraine's position in Bakhmut as "close to critical," as it was redeploying resources from Zaporizhzhia to Bakhmut.[12]

While Russia is unlikely to redeploy large numbers of forces from Bakhmut in the near future, the ISW's December 2022 assessment that its forces have "culminated" suggests that tactical shifts might be insufficient to save Moscow's faltering offensive.

CONCLUSION

The most plausible trajectory for Russian forces in Bakhmut is the increased use of squad-sized assault groups, which have limited combat firepower, instead of more effective BTGs.[13] If Russia opts to scale back its offensive operations in Bakhmut, its parallel offensive in nearby Soledar could be a beneficiary. In early January, the eastern group of Ukraine's Armed Forces admitted to "heavy bloody fighting" in Soledar, which coincided with Ukrainian and British intelligence estimates showing that Russia had diverted resources from Bakhmut to Soledar.[14] Boris Rozhin claimed that Russia's intense focus on Soledar could ultimately help it achieve a final victory in Bakhmut, as it would allow Russian forces to circle their Ukrainian counterparts in northern Bakhmut, and potentially advance on Seversk.[15] This strategy appeared to produce results in early January 2023 but the extent of Russia's progress was initially disputed. On 7 January, LNR police colonel Vitaly Kiselyov told *RIA Novosti* that Ukrainian forces had been ordered to leave Soledar even though the Kyiv authorities had requested no such withdrawal.[16] On 10 January, Prigozhin declared that the Wagner Group had occupied Soledar, even though he claimed that urban battles persisted and stated earlier in the day that fighting on its western outskirts was ongoing.[17] While Russia is still unable to completely encircle Bakhmut, this victory could give it control over the 200km salt mine tunnels and allow Wagner Group PMCs to more effectively infiltrate Ukrainian lines. Boris Rozhin pushed back against Ukrainian claims that Soledar had little strategic value by stating that Russia was able to seize a major Ukrainian small arms stash in Paraskoveevka and taunted Zelensky's decision to strip Medvedchuk's citizenship as a distraction.[18]

Elsewhere on the frontlines, Russia's military operations are almost exclusively defensive in nature. A 14 December *New York Times* satellite imagery investigation revealed that Russia erected a vast network of dragon's teeth pyramids and tank trap deep ditches to bolster its preparations for the winter war.[19] These fortifications will allow Russia to slow the movement of Ukrainian armoured vehicles and facilitate orderly retreats if necessary. This model of warfare aligns closely with historical Russian military doctrine, as Soviet forces constructed trenches during the World War II Battle of Kursk to fend off Nazi Germany's offensive. In a striking display of Russia's concern about Luhansk's vulnerability to a Ukrainian counter-offensive, a large network of trenches has been constructed in Popasna. Russia is also strengthening its network of fortifications in Zaporizhzhia to complement its military base in Melitopol, and is recruiting local residents with a 80,000 roubles per month salary to construct them.[20] While Russia's fortification network might reduce the risk of a chaotic Kharkiv-style withdrawal, which resulted in immense losses of equipment, its approach to defence has potential drawbacks. The British Ministry of Defence's 25 November intelligence update revealed that reservists were tasked with constructing trenches in Svatove and suffered heavy casualties from Ukrainian artillery fire.[21] Igor Girkin has accused the Russian military of constructing fortifications "on a whim," and warns that it will lead to a "protracted positional war" that will be suicidal for Russia.[22] Girkin has been especially vocal in his criticism of what Prigozhin describes as the impregnable Wagner Lines and warned that a single Ur-77 shot could eviscerate the fortifications.

Despite the apparent vulnerabilities of its occupations of Ukrainian territories, Russia continues to take decisive steps towards integrating annexed regions with its de jure borders. Dmitry Peskov's insistence that Ukraine needs to recognise Russia's control over the four annexed regions or negotiations will not occur reflects Moscow's maximalist ambitions. In Less than seventy-two hours after Surovikin announced Russia's retreat from Kherson, the Russian occupation authorities relocated their capital to Henichesk. The Kremlin chose Henichesk as Kherson's new capital because it was outside the range of Ukrainian artillery fire, which had devastated previous Russian command posts; was an easy resting stop from mobilised troops from Crimea; and could help coordinate resistance to a Ukrainian counter-offensive on Kherson or Melitopol.[23] Russia has transformed Mariupol into a "garrison city" which consists of Russian soldiers, builders, administrators and doctors, and has whitewashed its Ukrainian identity and evidence of Russian war crimes.[24] While Russia has largely avoided partisan unrest in its occupied territories, its policies are likely to continue provoking angst amongst their local populations. Russia used populist measures, such as lower utility tariffs in Luhansk, to earn the acquiescence of older residents to their occupation. However, the announcement of a 10% price increase for utilities in Luhansk and conscription of almost all men under age 60 in Donbas villages suggests a sharp turn away from populism.[25] This shift could allow Ukrainian forces to receive increased collaboration for locals resisting occupation and erode Russia's ability to withstand future counter-offensives.

In addition to clinging to its increasingly illusory annexations of Ukrainian territory, the Russian military has been forced to grapple with Kyiv's growing long-range strike capabilities. Ukraine's 1 January attack on Russian forces in Makiivka, Donetsk underscored the vulnerability of Russia's occupied territories to long-range strikes. The Russian Defence Ministry acknowledged 89 casualties as a result of 4 HIMARS strikes on the conscript base, which was lower than Ukraine's estimates of 400, but strikingly higher than previous admissions of fatalities.[26] The scale of fatalities renewed criticisms of Russian military incompetence, as ammunition had been hazardously stored near the conscript base and mass use of cellular data alerted Ukrainian forces to the base's existence. Boris Rozhin explicitly called out the Russian military as "incompetent," while Alexander Kots asked: "Why do we keep putting up mobilised personnel in hotels, hostels and professional schools?"[27] Commentator Semyon Pegov refuted the Ministry of Defence's cellular phone claims and warned that concentrations of conscripts would inevitably be discovered due to SBU infiltration and UAVs.[28] The scale of fatalities in Makiivka also prompted a rare vigil to commemorate the dead conscripts in Samara's central square, which included calls for revenge against Ukraine.[29] Censorship pressure from the Kremlin ultimately reined in these displays of discontent. In stark contrast to his earlier statements, Rozhin lambasted the circulation of rumours about 500 fatalities in the Russian information space and fired a warning of 15 years in prison for discrediting the Russian Armed Forces.[30] Russia's retaliatory attack on Kramatorsk on 8 January, which resulted in no casualties instead of the 600 that the Russian Defence Ministry claimed, underscored the Kremlin's desire to respond to pressure from hardliners about the growing vulnerability of its conscript forces.

This sense of vulnerability grew even more acute due to Ukraine's long-range strikes on Russian territory. In Belgorod and Bryansk, Ukraine has reportedly retaliated for Russian infrastructure strikes with electrical supply attacks that have caused significant disruption. Russia's claims that it shot down 4 HARM anti-radiation missiles over Belgorod in mid-December and predictions of a barrage of Ukrainian attacks heading into 2023 revealed these feelings of weakness.[31] The 5 December attacks on the Engels-2 airbase in Saratov, which includes Tu-95 and Tu-160 jets used in infrastructure strikes on Ukraine, and Dyagilevo airbase near Ryazan, which houses the 121st heavy bomber aviation regiment and Il-78 tankers, caused alarmism about Kyiv's strike capabilities to reach new heights. The causes of this attack were hotly debated by defence analysts. As

Ukrainian UAVs were typically geared for short-range attacks, it was initially postulated that the strike was launched by Ukrainian forces within Russia's territory.[32] Alexander Kots contended that Ukraine had used a Tu-141 Strizh UAV, which could fly across Russian territory for 600km, and was in service by the Ukrainian army as a late 1970s to early 1980s technology.[33] Yuri Knutov warned that the U.S. modernised Strizh UAVs into kamikaze drones and expressed fears that the Engels attack foreshadowed Ukrainian strikes on Russian nuclear or chemical plants.[34]

Despite the Russian Defence Ministry's claims that Ukraine's strike caused minor damage, the Engels attack stoked familiar criticism of the war effort from Russian hardliners. Oleg Tsaryov shared a photo of aircraft lying outside their hangars at Engels airbase and lamented that the cost of two destroyed war planes was more than equipping its airfields with hangars.[35] On a 7 December episode of Skabeeva's Rossiya-1 show, Knutov highlighted how the absence of Buk-M3 or Vityaz-353 surface-to-air missile systems allowed Ukraine's UAVs to fly over Russia's territory undetected. Knutov noted that these vulnerabilities meant that Moscow could eventually be at risk and to compensate for the movement of air defence systems to Ukraine, he proposed shifting systems from western Siberia. The 25 December Engels attack, which caused the Russian Defence Ministry to admit to the deaths of 3 Russian servicemen, amplified this sense of vulnerability. In a 4 January interview, State Duma Deputy Yevgeny Fedorov blamed the U.S. for carrying out the Engels attack and warned that a U.S.-instigated "demonstrative attack" on Moscow was on the immediate horizon.[36] Kyrylo Budanov's 4 January warning that attacks could be carried out "deeper and deeper" into Russian territory underscores Kyiv's growing willingness to strike Russian targets and the U.S.'s unwillingness to recognise these attacks as an escalation risk.[37]

The Winter War: A Regrouping Phase for Ukraine and Russia

While Russia's long-term ability to withstand a Ukrainian counter-offensive is unclear, the winter war has slowed the pace of
Ukraine's territorial advances. In a December BBC interview,
Budanov conceded that "the situation is just stuck. It doesn't
move" and claimed that Ukraine currently lacked the resources
to defeat Russia through a multidirectional counter-offensive.[38]
This contrasted with Ukraine's prior pledge to escalate offensive
operations once the ground on the frontlines was frozen. The
slow pace of Ukraine's counter-offensive in Luhansk is especially
striking, as Kyiv's 2km per week advance on Kreminna in late
December is the main example of progress. Ukraine's hopes for
a breakthrough in Luhansk likely rest on the seizure of the P66
highway near of Kreminna, which allows Russia to resupply
forces in northern Donbas from Belgorod.[39] Ukraine's hopes for
a decisive breakthrough in Zaporizhzhia likely hinge on gradually
eroding the strength of Russia's military infrastructure in
Melitopol. The 10 December strike with HIMARS rockets on a
former resort sheltering Wagner Group PMCs and Ukraine's 13
December strike on a critical bridge on the Molochna River
exemplified the attacks that Ukraine would need to undertake to
prevail in Melitopol. Zelensky's admission that Ukraine prefers
to liberate Crimea through non-military means if possible is less
hawkish than Arestovych's claims that Kyiv could swiftly liberate
Crimea after the Kherson withdrawal.[40]

As Ukraine remains firmly against freezing the conflict, it is
trying to secure the military hardware it needs to achieve new
offensive breakthroughs. Ukraine's pitches for military assistance
have been largely successful, even if they lag behind its ultimate
objectives. On 15 November, Dmytro Kuleba called for expanded
NATO assistance to protect Ukraine's skies, which included air
defence systems and modern aircraft like F-15s and F-16s. While

Ukraine's request for fighter jets were rebuffed again, Washington heeded Kuleba's entreaties. The U.S. House of Representatives approved $45 billion in aid to Ukraine on 23 December, which coincided with the pledged delivery of Patriot missile defence batteries. These arms deliveries were paired with Zelensky's address to Congress, which claimed that U.S. support for Ukraine was "not charity" but an investment in "global security and democracy."[41] Emmanuel Macron pledged to send Ukraine AMX-10RC armoured tanks on 4 January, which made France the first country to transfer Western tanks to Ukraine since the war began. France's tank transfer decision was followed by Germany's pledge to transfer Marder APCs to Ukraine and the U.S.'s agreement to send 50 Bradley fighting vehicles to Ukraine. Due to escalation risks and supply considerations, Ukraine's requests for ATACMS and sophisticated tanks, such as U.S. Abrams or German Leopards, remain unanswered, but it is clear that the Ukrainian military is using the winter months to prepare for a spring counter-offensive. On 4 January, Budanov declared that Ukraine will deal a "final defeat" to Russia in the spring, which will result in the liberation of Crimea and Donbas and predicted that fighting will be "hottest" in March.[42]

Beyond constructing fortifications, Russia is also using the winter war to enhance its offensive firepower. Speculation that Russia will formally announce a second mobilisation drive intensified in early January, even though Putin stated on 7 December that 150,000 conscripts are still in training centres. On 6 January, Estonia's intelligence chief Margo Grosberg claimed that Russia's partial mobilisation campaign never ended and that a new contingent of conscripts would arrive in Ukraine in March or April.[43] Vadym Skybitsky concurred with this assessment, as he stated that Russia could conscript an additional 500,000 troops for offensives in eastern and southern Ukraine. Skybitsky predicted that an official mobilisation drive would be announced on

15 January and that its efficacy over the coming six to eight months will determine the war's outcome.[44] Oleksii Reznikov made a direct appeal to Russian conscripts to not participate in the Ukraine War and warned that Russia imminently planned to close its borders to men of conscription age.[45] The scale of Russia's covert mobilisation efforts and the steady expansion of its military presence in Belarus has revived fears of a second Kyiv offensive. Valery Zaluzhny made these concerns public in a 15 December interview with *The Economist*, stating "The Russians are preparing some 200,000 fresh troops. I have no doubts they will have another go at Kyiv."[46] Zaluzhny's prediction polarised the Ukrainian political establishment, as some viewed it as alarmist. Arestovych stated that he was merely voicing a worst-case scenario so the Ukrainian Armed Forces could be prepared for all possible options.[47] The White House has pushed back against Zaluzhny's warnings and Russia's artillery ammunition constraints caused these claims to be greeted with scepticism in the U.S. national security community.[48]

Russia's ultimate course of action depends on its ability to procure military hardware and on Gerasimov's assessment of the Russian military's preparedness for a large-scale offensive. Russia's missile shortages were encapsulated by its the replacement of nuclear warheads with ballasts on 1980s era AS-15 Kent air-launched cruise missiles.[49] These equipment modifications were unlikely to compensate for the depletion of precision weaponry stocks, as they rely on kinetic energy and unspent fuel to inflict damage but illustrate Russia's willingness to sustain the war effort at any cost. Moreover, British Armed Forces chief Sir Tony Radakin warned in December that Russia suffers a critical shortage of artillery shells, as it planned for a 30-day offensive but already fought for 300 days.[50] These shortages have forced Russia to lean more heavily on foreign suppliers, ramp up production where possible and reconsider the weapons that it uses in attacks. China is unlikely to convert its cautious solidarity with Russia into an overt military alliance, Moscow's quest for military hardware hinges on its partnerships with Iran, North Korea and Belarus. As these partners are hesitant about supplying missiles to Russia and Belarus remains unlikely to join the war on Russia's behalf, the Kremlin is also seeking to bolster domestic weapons production. On 3 December, Skybitsky declared that Russia was using missiles "directly from the assembly line" in its recent strikes on Ukrainian cities and these missiles were manufactured as recently as in late August.[51] This suggests that Mykhailo Podolyak's prognostication that Russia could only carry out 2 to 3 further missile barrages against Ukrainian cities is overly optimistic. While Russia's stocks of Iskanders, Kalibrs and hypersonic missiles dwindle, it still possesses 6,980 S-300 missiles, 347 3M-55 Onyx missiles and 801 air-launched missiles that can be used on Ukrainian targets.

While it is unclear how Russia will make use of its finite resources, signals point to a greater degree of caution and long-term planning than during the war's initial stages. Russia's traditionally jingoistic community of military analysts has expressed greater candour about military vulnerabilities and urged Putin not to authorise a second blitz offensive on Kyiv. Russian defence analyst Mikhail Onufrienko warned that Russia should prepare for a Ukrainian surprise offensive in Luhansk along the Svatovo-Kreminna axis as early as February.[52] The regular barrage of Ukrainian drone attacks on Crimea has resulted in open discussions about the peninsula's vulnerability to occupation. On 20 November, Andrei Gurulyov urged Russia to calculate the risk of Ukraine and NATO launching a massive attack on Crimea that triggers a "fire defeat."[53] On a 28 November episode of Solovyov's *Rossiya-1* show, Simonyan warned "They're getting ready to take our Crimea." By early December, these warnings had died down. On 5 December, Gurulyov hailed Russia's restoration of the Crimea bridge and claimed that Ukraine's reservist shortages precluded an attack on Melitopol, but pro-Kremlin commentators continued to push for a restrained offensive.[54] Konstantin Sivkov urged the Russian military to concentrate its forces in Kharkiv and Zaporizhzhia, as this would encircle Ukrainian forces in Donbas, and potentially lead to a decisive breakthrough over a few-month time horizon.[55] Oleg Tsaryov praised the relocation of war materiel from Berdyansk to Melitopol, and called for restructuring of the military-industrial complex, replenishment of precision weaponry stocks and proper fortifications on Zaproizhzhia.[56] Tsaryov's insistence that Russia avoid the Soviet-era Shturmovshchina trap, which would entail carrying out an offensive to meet an arbitrary deadline, clashes markedly with his enthusiastic support for occupying Kyiv in March 2022.

The Russian defence establishment's recent policy manoeuvres concur with this incremental approach to rebuilding Russia's combat capabilities. On 23 December, Sergei Shoigu announced that Russia would expand its military by 30% to 1.5 million troops, which would be aged 21–30 instead of 18–27 and include 695,000 contract soldiers.[57] The timetable for this increase is indeterminate, as Shoigu wants to ensure that Russia's preoccupation with victory in Ukraine does not undermine its standing as a global military power. Although Western intelligence officials believed that Russia withdrew up to 75% of its forces in the Arctic to bolster its manpower in Ukraine, Russia has recently expanded its military infrastructure on its northern frontier.[58] Russia's radar capabilities have expanded in Olenegorsk on the Kola Peninsula and progress is being made towards the completion of one of five Rezonans-N radar systems in Ostrovnoy near Norway and Finland. These developments caused Jens Stoltenberg to warn that there is a "significant Russian military build-up in the high north" and that NATO will double its presence in response. Shoigu's rebuke of the Serdyukov reforms has coincided with new combat techniques. Ukrainian Army's Ground Forces commander Oleksandr Syrskyi noted that Sergei Surovikin is changing Russia's battlefield tactics by relying on smaller well-coordinated detachments.[59] Syrskyi believes that this transition is causing increased casualties, but the orderly Kherson withdrawal suggests that Surovikin is creating a more effective command structure.

With the exception of criticisms from Igor Girkin, who condemned his surrender of Kherson and stated that he will not comment on him as "he has not entered the field of history," Surovkin maintains broad-based backing from the Kremlin and war hawks.[60] As Surovikin views the Ukraine War as a multi-year operation, he could advocate a more cautious short-term approach to offensives in Ukraine and focus on achieving Russia's goals in Donbas. These expectations were called into question by Surovikin's surprising demotion on 11 January and Gerasimov's centralisation of control over Russia's military operations in Ukraine. These abrupt personnel changes did not immediately change Russia's battlefield tactics but were viewed in Ukraine as proof of internal discord. Oleksii Danilov declared that "Internal tensions in the Russian Federation will only intensify. There will be a war for power in Russia, since Putin is very sick and getting weaker by the day."[61] Alexander Lapin's re-emergence as chief of Russia's ground forces and the dismissal of Colonel Mikhail Teplinsky, who criticised Gerasimov's unwillingness to rely on paratroopers in offensive operations, further intensified backlash from hardliners.[62] The streamlining of Russia's command structure could improve its short-term tactical cohesion but risks reinforcing the rigid power vertical that has left it woefully unprepared to adapt to changing battlefield conditions.

Russia's Undeclared War on Ukrainian Civilians: A High-Risk, Low-Reward Gambit

As the balance of territorial control in Ukraine remains stagnant, Russia regards its capacity to destroy Ukrainian critical infrastructure as a benchmark of its success. On 15 November, the Russian military fired 100 rockets on Ukrainian critical infrastructure, which was its largest single-day barrage since the invasion and followed two days later with attacks on Ukrainian gas production facilities. Despite reports of dwindling missile stocks and an interruption in Iran's supply of Shahed-136 drones in late November, Russia's infrastructure strikes continued to escalate throughout the month of December. On 12 December, Zelensky told Biden that Russia's strikes had destroyed approximately 50% of Ukraine's power supply infrastructure.[63] Rotating blackouts and water supply shortages became a way of life in major cities that had been largely untouched by the conflict in the summer and early autumn, such as Kyiv, Odesa and Lviv. Russia's electrical infrastructure strikes also caused the Ukraine War to spill over into neighbouring countries to an unprecedented degree. The 15 November infrastructure strikes resulted in the disconnection of a power line in Moldova, which led to large-scale nationwide power outages and a new supply deal with Romania.[64] The deaths of two Polish civilians that same day also briefly prompted fears of a NATO-Russia conflict. A U.S. official erroneously told *The Associated Press* that a Russian missile had crossed the Polish border, which mirrored allegations from Ukraine and Latvia's Foreign Ministries. Even though the Russian Defence Ministry dismissed these assertions as a "deliberate provocation," war hawks enthusiastically stoked tensions between Russia and NATO.[65] The Rybar Telegram channel did not rule out a Kh-101 or Kalibr attack on Poland,[66] and Margarita Simonyan taunted NATO for not protecting its borders.[67] While a fragment of Ukraine's S-300 system was ultimately determined to have crossed the Polish border, Kyiv's need to intercept Russian missiles so close to NATO's boundaries underscored the escalation risks inherent in Russia's infrastructure bombardments.

While Russia's infrastructure attacks inflicted severe harm to the wellbeing of Ukrainian civilians, their military value have been called into question. Russian officials and state media commentators have advanced both military and political rationales for these infrastructure strikes. On 1 December, Sergei Lavrov tied Russia's infrastructure attacks to Putin's initial goal of demilitarising Ukraine, stating "The infrastructure that is now under attack is crucial to the combat potential of Ukraine's armed forces and nationalist battalions."[68] The Russian Defence Ministry has repeatedly insisted that strikes are carried out with long-range precision weapons and are aimed at destroying energy facilities that supply Ukraine's military-industrial complex.[69] As Russia faced war crimes allegations over its infrastructure strikes and Jens Stoltenberg accused Russia of weaponising winter against Ukrainians, the Kremlin emphasised that its attacks were undergirded by similar military rationales to prior NATO actions. On 30 November, Maria Zakharova quoted a May 1999 statement from NATO spokesperson Jamie Shea, which claimed that the U.S. struck water and electricity in Yugoslavia to push Slobodan Milosevic towards peace in Kosovo.[70] After Victoria Nuland claimed that Russia swapped nuclear brinkmanship for electrical infrastructure strikes, Zakharova turned the tables on the U.S. by highlighting how attacking civilian infrastructure is enshrined in U.S. military doctrine. Zakharova's reference to Major Thomas Griffith's 1994 dissertation entitled "Strategic Strikes on National Power Supply Systems," which was published after attacks on Iraqi electricity supplies during the 1991 Gulf War, was cited as evidence for her claims.[71]

Despite Russia's strenuous insistence that its civilian infrastructure attacks were grounded in sound military logic, they have proven to be largely ineffective. During a 28 November interview, Gurulyov called for a three-step process to eviscerate Ukraine's industrial capacity through missile strikes: destroying its electrical grid, bombing the centre of Ukrainian banking operations and targeting railway control centres.[72] This expansive vision has been thwarted by Ukraine's increased ability to shoot down missiles and UAVs. On 14 December, Zelensky claimed that Ukraine shot down every drone that Russia fired over Kyiv, and even during the high intensity 23 November missile barrage, Ukraine shot down 51 out of 70 missiles. The low altitude and slow speed of Iranian UAVs has allowed them to be easily shot down by NATO-class air defences, which has forced Russia to use swarms of UAVs to overpower Ukraine's air defences. Zelensky's ability to procure 1.05 billion euros in financial aid for Ukraine at an emergency 13 December conference in Paris provided it with crucial support for its electrical infrastructure.[73] The limited efficacy of civilian infrastructure strikes was acknowledged during a November 28 episode of Andrey Norkin's NTV show. Andrey Fedorov opined that the arrival of generators from Germany and Poland would allow Ukraine to survive winter, while Victor Olevich highlighted how Bosnia survived four years of electricity outages in the 1990s. Russia's goal of evacuating Ukrainian cities and weaponising refugee outflows to Europe has also been derailed. During a 28 November episode of Solovyov's show, Sergei Mikheyev declared: "We really need to make sure Ukraine is forced to send another 10–15 million refugees to Europe. And let Europe tackle these problems." By 30 December, Klitschko reported that 3.6 million people lived in Kyiv, which marked a return to its pre-war population, and 300,000 Ukrainians from other regions migrated to the capital in spite of regular infrastructure strikes.[74]

The political goals of Russia's civilian infrastructure strikes have also not been achieved. During a 17 November press conference, Peskov claimed that Ukraine's electricity and heating shortages were triggered by its failure to negotiate with Russia.[75] Instead of pushing Ukraine towards negotiations, these infrastructure strikes have sharpened Zelensky's commitment to making Russia a pariah state. On 23 November, Zelensky urged the

UNSC to take action against Russia's infrastructure strikes and declared "We cannot be hostage to one international terrorist."[76] After 120 missiles were fired on Ukrainian cities on 29 December, Podolyak facetiously declared "We're waiting for further proposals from "peacekeepers" about "peaceful settlement," "security guarantees for RF" & "undesirability of provocations."[77] Russia's expectations that infrastructure strikes would stoke social unrest in Ukraine were similarly unrealistic. In a 23 November Telegram post, Igor Korotchenko urged Ukrainians to protest against Zelensky's government and pressure Kyiv to sue for peace with Russia so normal life could be restored.[78] On NTV, State Duma Deputy Boris Chernyshov declared that "Ordinary people should take to the streets and finally put an end to Zelensky's Nazi regime." Although Russian state media figures highlighted sporadic displays of discontent, such as a Ukrainian refugee girl rebuking First Lady Olena Zelenska for "telling us about patience while we sit without heat and light," infrastructure strikes have not resulted in an uptick of Ukrainian support for peace negotiations with Russia.[79] A December 2022 Razumkov Center poll revealed that 60% of Ukrainians oppose negotiations with Russia even for the sake of saving lives and 93% of Ukrainians believe in a complete victory.[80]

As Russia's civilian infrastructure strikes serve few practical purposes, they are more effective in rallying discontented hardliners around Putin's faltering war effort. During a 9 January episode of his Rossiya-1 show, Solovyov stated "We have to fight so that our boys don't die. I don't care how many Nazis die" and bemoaned the Russian military's supposed earlier restraint about striking "peaceful infrastructure." Sergei Markov frames Russia's strikes on Ukrainian cities as retribution for Kyiv's eight years of attacks on Donbas.[81] Markov's contention invoked Putin's Donbas genocide conspiracy, which was a crucial component of his domestic case for invading Ukraine. Russia's regular strikes on Kherson, which required the Ukrainian authorities to carry out targeted evacuations of civilians in late November, also send a signal that the Kremlin has not given up on eventually recapturing all of its annexed territory. Misleading content about the efficacy of civilian infrastructure strikes in combatting NATO arms transfers has also contributed to their popularity amongst war hawks. A 29 November Rybar Telegram post falsely asserted that Russia's infrastructure strikes were causing severe disruptions to military cargo transfers to Ukraine and predicted that Ukraine will be unable to resupply its military as it relied on diesel locomotives.[82] To support these dubious claims, Rybar noted that Ukraine freed up some civilian diesel locomotives for military use after it lost them to Russian attacks on Mykolaiv and Popasna. Therefore, Russia's civilian infrastructure strikes fuel its counter-revolutionary propaganda, neo-imperial fantasies and Western hybrid warfare narratives, and will likely persist as a feature of the war even as missile stocks continue to dwindle.

Russia's Future: Economic Decline and Political Strife

While Russia has temporarily been able to freeze the frontlines in Ukraine at an immense human cost, it is veering on the precipice of an economic and political crisis heading into 2023. To assuage concerns about the state of Russia's economy, Putin announced an expected 2.5% GDP decline in 2022, which was milder than the 2.9% anticipated by his own economic team, and Russia's federal statistics agency revised GDP growth upward from 4.7% to 5.6% in 2021.[83] The Russian Central Bank claimed 12–13% inflation would be reined in by 2024 and the 1–4% GDP contraction predicted in the first half of 2023 would transform into positive growth by the second half of the year.[84] These projections reflect Russia's extensive preparations for sanctions, which included balancing the budget under the assumption that oil would be $45 per barrel and repeated stress tests, but the longer-term outlook is bleaker. Non-oil and gas budget revenues fell 20% year-on-year due to lower VAT and non-tax fees in October 2022, which caused energy-related inflows to constitute the majority of Russia's budget for the first time since April 2022.[85] The marginal 0.1% decline in industrial production that was recorded in 2022 was exclusively due to increased military expenditures, as it masked precipitous declines in automobile manufacturing, timber processing and machine-building.[86] The collapse of technology imports, with the exception of Russia's purchases from Turkey, and the ongoing IT and semiconductor embargo will also erode Russia's long-term growth potential.

The EU's decision to implement a $60/barrel price cap on Russian oil, which was followed by a gas price cap to contain the energy crisis, threatens to further erode Russia's budgetary conditions. Alexander Novak retaliated against the EU's move by threatening to cut gas production by 5–7% in early 2023 and halt sales to countries that supported the cap.[87] While these threats caused angst in global energy markets, Russia's revenue from oil and gas stood at $15.8 billion per month in November 2022, even as its exports increased to 8.1 million barrels a day.[88] Russia has been forced to expand its exports of Arctic oil to China and India at steeper discounts to compensate for revenue shortfalls from Europe.[89] A rare silver lining has been the partial recovery of Russia's automobile imports. Although light vehicle production collapsed by 97% immediately after the Ukraine invasion and car sales slid by more than 80% when the economic crisis peaked in May–June 2022, the car market recovered somewhat in late 2022. While only 14 of the 60 major car brands in Russia remain available for purchase, Chinese automobiles now make up over 30% of the total car market share.[90] A former BMW AG factory in Kaliningrad and Nissan Motor Corporation's plant in St. Petersburg have either started or will imminently begin producing Chinese automobiles.[91] Despite this ray of optimism, there are few signs of large-scale investment from Russia's partners in the collective non-West that will forestall a lost decade for the Russian economy.

While Russia's dire economic outlook is unlikely to trigger mass protests that threaten political stability, Putin's hold on power could eventually be imperilled by the growing assertiveness of hardliners. Yevgeny Prigozhin's growing influence is an especially alarming trend. On 22 December, John Kirby claimed that Russian military officials were often subordinated to the Wagner Group's command and warned that Wagner was emerging as a "rival power centre to the Russian military and other Russian ministries."[92] Kirby backed up his contentions by highlighting the Wagner Group's expansion to a 50,000-troop army, which had 10,000 PMCs and 40,000 prisoners, and Prigozhin's $100 million monthly budget for Wagner Group operations. Prigozhin's continued attacks on Russia's political institutions and regional governors also reflect his growing political ambitions. Aside from his well-documented feud with St. Petersburg Governor Alexander Beglov, Prigozhin previously relied on aligned Telegram channels and surrogates to vent his frustrations with the Russian elite. Since he unmasked himself as the head of the Wagner Group, Prigozhin has become increasingly outspoken. On 31 October, Prigozhin railed against the failure of elites to give their fair share of sacrifices for the war effort, stating "The oligarchs and other representatives of the elite, have always lived in boundless comfort, and continue to do so. Until their children go to war, the country will not be fully mobilised."[93] On 11 November, Prigozhin unflatteringly compared Russian elites to prisoners that he recruited for the Wagner Group, quipping "The inmates have the highest level of consciousness—much higher than the Russian elites."[94] On 18 November, Prigozhin accused oligarchs of receiving assets through redistribution and accused them of smuggling assets out of Russia to get Israeli and Uzbek citizenship. Prigozhin paired his attacks on Russian elites with criticisms of the Russian Defence Ministry's authorisation of territorial withdrawals, as he warned that a World War II-style march by Russian enemies on the Urals was possible.[95]

Prigozhin has also elevated his profile in the Russian public consciousness through outlandish statements, high-profile security initiatives and anti-Western diatribes. Following the sledgehammer execution of former Wagner Group PMC Evgeny Nuzhin on 13 November, Prigozhin praised the execution video for its "excellent directorial work" and lambasted Nuzhin as a traitor.[96] The unveiling of the Wagner Centre on 4 November, which saw nationalist speakers pledge to "make our great country even better," and courtship of cooperation with IT start-ups further enhanced his profile. While Prigozhin was not present at the unveiling ceremony, volunteer Alexey Savinsky claimed that he had been planning the centre's opening since early 2021.[97] The European Parliament's 23 November decision to include the Wagner Group in its resolution labelling Russia as a state sponsor of terrorism sharpened Prigozhin's wrath against the West. Prigozhin declared the European Parliament "dissolved," pledged to file an information case against the EU and allegedly authorised the delivery of a bloody sledgehammer to European lawmakers.[98] Prigozhin's calls for France to be recognised as a state sponsor of terrorism after an assassination attempt against his ally Dmitry Sytii in the Central African Republic further underscored his vitriolic anti-Western rhetoric.[99] Although Prigozhin denies that he has plans to establish a political party or join any established party, his elevated profile could point to the creation of a conservative movement based on "patriotism and statism."[100] Prigozhin's anti-elite rhetoric and focus on anti-corruption curiously draws inspiration from his erstwhile foe Alexei Navalny.[101]

While Prigozhin remains a loyal surrogate of Putin and has not formed an alternative power vertical, his custom brand of populist ultranationalism has a growing legion of supporters. Tsaryov shared Prigozhin's disdain for the disengagement of the Russian elites, which contrasted markedly with their attitudes during World War I and has aggressively pushed the narrative that elites are more interested in sanctions relief than in winning the war.[102] Prigozhin's shadow campaign against Roman Abramovich has resonated especially strongly amongst hardliners. On 5 December, the Wagner Group-aligned Grey Zone Telegram channel disparagingly called Abramovich a liaison who represents Russia's interests in Britain and blamed him for the Kherson withdrawal, Black Sea grain export deal renewal and release of Azov Battalion fighters in exchange for Viktor Medvedchuk.[103] These comments tapped into nationalist disdain for Abramovich's provision of gifts to released Azov Battalion fighters and participation in the perceived unequal prisoner exchange. Prigozhin's strident support for Surovikin and rebuke of the Russian Defence Ministry reflects growing support for less civilian oversight of the military's prosecution of the war. On 29 December, Konstantin Sivkov claimed that 90–95% of war planning was conducted by politicians and just 5–10% was carried out by the military. Sivkov alleged that civilian restraints on the military explained why Russia carried out only one major air operation in the Ukraine War and responded inadequately to the Engels airbase attacks.[104]

Vladimir Putin's regular personnel shuffles, civilian infrastructure strikes, use of ultranationalist rhetoric and resistance to diplomacy with Ukraine have thus-far appeased hardliners. Prigozhin's influence depends on maintaining his decades-long friendship with Putin and displays of derision towards him from fellow ultra-nationalists, such as Leonid Slutsky and Igor Girkin, could prevent him from leading a hawkish coalition against the status quo. Patriarch Kirill also remains a crucial surrogate, who provides religious legitimacy to Putin's propaganda on the

CONCLUSION

Ukraine War. During the January 2023 Orthodox Christmas celebrations, Patriarch Kirill claimed that Russians and Ukrainians were one people, predicted cataclysms in the West and vowed that Ukrainian Orthodoxy would survive the "moral relativism" that infiltrated Western culture.[105] The Kremlin's depiction of the Ukraine War as a struggle of good against evil, which has been enthusiastically reiterated by Putin, complements Patriarch Kirill's rhetoric. On 25 October, Assistant Secretary of Russia's Security Council Aleksey Pavlov called for the urgent "desatanisation" of Ukraine and converted Ramzan Kadyrov's statements on jihad into official policy.[106] Putin has also distanced himself from out-of-touch oligarchs through choreographed displays of solidarity with the sacrifices of Russian soldiers. Putin's 25 November appearance next to a handpicked delegation of mothers of soldiers, which included a personal friend of Kadyrov, was used to highlight his empathy for conscripts and included warnings about Internet disinformation on the war.[107] This meeting was meant to assuage criticisms from veteran rights activists, such as Valentina Melnikova, that Putin was hiding from his critics and not taking decisive action to curb mobilisation's excesses.

The primary threat to Putin's delicate balancing act between hardliners and parochial supporters of the war stems from the ongoing debate on further rounds of mobilisation. Despite the uncertain effectiveness and high costs associated with conscription, a camp of state media hardliners views mobilisation as the best hope for Russia's war effort. After Surovikin's Kherson withdrawal, Sergei Markov called for general mobilisation and a war economy in Russia, and lamented Putin's refusal to mobilise in the spring and summer.[108] On 29 December, Kadyrov called for total mobilisation of Chechens against Satanism, including schoolchildren and students.[109] On a 9 January episode of his Rossiya-1 show, Solovyov claimed that young conscripts who accrued six months of training wished to join their fathers on the frontlines.[110] Andrei Gurulyov has been the leading voice amongst hardliners against launching another round of mobilisation in the first six months of 2023.[111] Gurulyov also believes that a war economy has already emerged, as old factories are working three shifts and new factories are being built.[112] Gurulyov also argues that Western sanctions have led to the nationalisation of assets, which reversed the 1990s runaway privatisations.[113] Similar polarisations can be observed over the issue of imposing martial law in Russia. Dmitry Medvedev has championed the possibility of special wartime rules modelled after World War II-era measures, stating "During wars, there are always such special rules. And quiet groups of impeccably inconspicuous people who effectively execute them."[114] Andrei Klishas and political scientist Alexey Martynov opposed this measure, as they feared it would lead to the suspension of the constitution and the authority of legislative bodies.[115] To straddle both sides of these debates, Putin is likely to stealthily expand Russia's ranks of conscripts without declaring a general mobilisation and intensify his repression of alleged fifth columns, especially at the elite level.

Prospects for the Resolution of the Ukraine War in 2023

Despite the increasingly stagnant battlefield situation, the prospects for a diplomatic resolution of the Ukraine War in 2023 are remote. Beyond the vastly divergent bargaining positions of both sides, NATO countries have reaffirmed their willingness to support Ukraine's push for total victory and war hawks have pushed Putin towards resisting serious negotiations. After the Kherson victory, concerns grew in Kyiv about the West's willingness to provide long-term military assistance. The Republican Party's narrow victory in the House of Representatives in November

CONCLUSION

2022 was expected to lead to greater oversight of arms shipments to Ukraine, while Josep Borrell's repeated warnings of depleted EU weapons stocks sat uneasily in Kyiv. In early November, U.S. officials led by Jake Sullivan urged Ukraine to publicly present itself as amenable to negotiations with Russia.[116] This pushed back against Zelensky's policy of refraining from talks with Russia while Putin is in power. On November 16, Mark Milley claimed that Ukraine may not be able to achieve a military victory and the winter would provide Kyiv with an opportunity for negotiations. This statement sparked fierce polarisations within the Biden administration. In response to criticisms, Milley revised his position to mirror the official view in Ukraine, stating "There may be a political solution where politically the Russians withdraw. You want to negotiate at a time when you're at your strength and your opponent is at weakness. And it's possible that maybe, there will be a political solution. All I'm saying is that there is a possibility for it."[117] Aside from Blinken's 6 December comment that the U.S. was focused on helping Ukraine expel Russia from territory occupied after 24 February, which raised questions about its support for liberating Donbas and Crimea, Western countries have resolutely supported Ukraine with rhetorical solidarity, economic assistance and heavy weaponry.[118]

Russia has defiantly responded to NATO's reaffirmation of support for Ukraine, even as its prospects for victory continue to recede. On 26 December, Lavrov reiterated Putin's initial goals of demilitarisation and denazification of Ukraine with a warning shot for Kyiv to accept Russia's terms: "The point is simple: Fulfil them for your own good. Otherwise, the issue will be decided by the Russian army."[119] This hard-line stance reflects how war hawks have restrained Russia's capacity to negotiate a diplomatic off-ramp from the Ukraine War. Post-facto commentaries from Angela Merkel and Francois Hollande about how Minsk II was a stalling measure to prevent Ukraine from being overrun by Russia have fuelled lengthy diatribes about the follies of negotiating with Western countries. Despite Ukraine's autumn counter-offensive, Russian hardliners have continued to express support for the complete subjugation of Ukraine. During a 7 December episode of Solovyov's Rossiya-1 show, commentator Yevgeny Satanovsky waxed lyrically about a proposed Russian annexation of Lviv. Satanovsky claimed that Lviv was an integral part of a Russian Empire from Dublin to Vladivostok, as it was the western edge of the Soviet Union.[120] During a 14 December episode of Skabeeva's Rossiya-1 show, Gurulyov asserted that negotiations were only possible when the Russian army reached Ukraine's borders with Poland, Slovakia, Hungary and Romania.[121] High-profile Russian fertiliser shipments to Africa, such as the 29 November export of 20,000 metric tons of Russian fertiliser from The Netherlands to Malawi, have not eviscerated criticisms of the Black Sea grain export deal. Rumours of a handover of the Zaporizhzhia nuclear plant to Ukraine prompted fears that Putin was sacrificing Russia's interests to forestall mobilisation.[122] These criticisms could explain Russia's unwillingness to fully implement IAEA measures to safeguard the plant.

As Russia and Ukraine are unlikely to reach a negotiated settlement, prisoner exchanges remain a rare area of consistent dialogue. Despite the escalation of Russia's infrastructure strikes in Ukrainian cities, both sides agreed to a swap of 50 POWs on 1 December and 64 POWs on December 15. After escalations of nuclear brinkmanship in the spring and early autumn, the prospects of a spill-over of the Ukraine War into a Russia-NATO conflict have receded. Strident denunciations of the U.S. over Patriot deliveries to Ukraine, such as Medvedev's description of NATO as a "criminal entity" that delivers arms to "extremist regimes" and threats to deploy a hypersonic weapons-carrying frigate on the U.S.'s Eastern Seaboard, have not resulted in meaningful escalations.[123] The controversial 8 December Viktor Bout-Brittney Griner prisoner exchange reflected the enduring possibility of narrowly defined diplomacy between the U.S. and Russia. Bout's subsequent expressions of fervent support for the Ukraine War and entry into political activism in the LDPR did not cause the Biden administration to change its position on the deal's merits. While Russia's postponement of arms control negotiations in Cairo, which could have led to a resumption of New START inspections, is a significant setback, the U.S. is likely to prod Russia to resume arms limitations talks in 2023. Therefore, Russia will likely continue to engage in sabre-rattling and NATO will persist in arming Ukraine without crossing established thresholds for escalation.

Nearly one year after Putin's decision to invade Ukraine, it is apparent that Russia cannot win and cannot afford to lose the war. Ukraine regards the full liberation of its territory as an existential need, even if a complete victory is a multi-year process and seizing Crimea risks a nuclear escalation. Polarisations between the collective West and non-West, and the striking inefficacies of multilateral institutions ensure the impasse in Ukraine will linger. It remains to be seen whether the Ukrainian people can fulfil their aspirations of living in a free sovereign country or if Putin's neo-imperial designs will achieve a sufficient degree of success to keep his totalitarian regime in power. Whatever the outcome, the future of European security and the rules-based international order hang in the balance.

NOTES

1. PUTIN'S WAR ON UKRAINE: AN OPPORTUNISTIC COUNTER-REV-OLUTIONARY GAMBIT

1. Andrew Osborn and Polina Nikolskaya, Russia's Putin Authorises "Special Military Operation" Against Ukraine, Reuters, 24 February 2022, https://www.reuters.com/world/europe/russias-putin-authorises-military-operations-donbass-domestic-media-2022–02–24/
2. Neil MacFarlane and Albert Schnabel, Russia's Approach to Peacekeeping, *International Journal*, Volume 50, Number 2, Spring 1995.
3. Russia will Help Ukrainians "Get Rid of Regime," Lavrov Says, Al Jazeera, 25 July 2022, https://www.aljazeera.com/news/2022/7/25/in-pivot-russia-says-goal-in-ukraine-is-to-oust-zelenskyy
4. Address by the President of the Russian Federation, President of Russia, 24 February 2022, http://en.kremlin.ru/events/president/news/67843
5. Julian Borger, UN International Court of Justice Orders Russia to Halt Invasion of Ukraine, *The Guardian*, 16 March 2022, https://www.theguardian.com/world/2022/mar/16/un-international-court-of-justice-orders-russia-to-halt-invasion-of-ukraine
6. John Mearsheimer on Why the West is Principally Responsible for the Ukrainian Crisis, *The Economist*, 19 March 2022, https://www.economist.com/by-invitation/2022/03/11/john-mearsheimer-on-why-the-west-is-principally-responsible-for-the-ukrainian-crisis
7. John Mearsheimer, Why the Ukraine Crisis is the West's Fault, *Foreign Affairs*, September/October 2014, https://www.foreignaffairs.com/articles/russia-fsu/2014–08–18/why-ukraine-crisis-west-s-fault
8. NATO's Military Presence in Ukraine Poses Threat to Russia—Putin, TASS, 21 October 2021, https://tass.com/politics/1352611

9. Pulling Ukraine into NATO Creates Risks of Large-Scale Conflict in Europe—Lavrov, TASS, 24 December 2021, https://tass.com/world/1380355

10. Anita Kumar, Ukrainian Tweet Scrambles Biden's Press Conference, *Politico*, 14 June 2021, https://www.politico.com/news/2021/06/14/ukraine-biden-nato-press-conference-494460

11. German Chancellor Says Ukraine's NATO Membership not on the Agenda, TASS, 15 February 2022, https://tass.com/world/1404013

12. Press Statement and Answers to Questions at a Joint News Conference with Ukrainian President Leonid Kuchma, President of Russia, 17 May 2002, http://en.kremlin.ru/events/president/transcripts/21598

13. Nick Paton-Walsh, Russia Tells Ukraine to Stay out of NATO, *The Guardian*, 8 June 2006, https://www.theguardian.com/world/2006/jun/08/russia.nickpatonwalsh

14. Ukraine President Claims Win for Pro-West Parties, *The New York Times*, 27 October 2014, https://www.nytimes.com/2014/10/27/world/europe/ukrainian-parliamentary-elections.html

15. CIA Director: Putin Too Healthy, *Politico*, 20 July 2022, https://www.politico.com/news/2022/07/20/cia-putin-health-00047046

16. Robert Person, Balance of Threat: The Domestic Insecurity of Vladimir Putin, *Journal of Eurasian Studies*, Volume 8, Issue 1, January 2017, p. 45

17. Timothy Frye, *Weak Strongman: The Limits of Power in Putin's Russia*, Princeton: Princeton University Press, 2021.

18. Frye, p. 147.

19. Henry Mance, Mikhail Khodorkovsky: "Putin has Embarked on a Route that is Going to Lead to his Demise," *Financial Times*, 19 June 2022, https://www.ft.com/content/8b58a54e-6b0b-49c7-bfff-6189affa4449

20. Peter Duncan, Contemporary Russian Identity Between East and West, *The Historical Journal*, Volume 48, Number 1, March 2005, p. 277.

21. Anne Clunan, *The Social Construction of Russia's Resurgence: Aspirations, Identity and Security Interests*, Baltimore: Johns Hopkins University, June 2009, pp. 66–70.

22. Andrei Tsygankov, *Russia's Foreign Policy: Change and Continuity in National Identity*, Lanham: Rowman and Littefield, 2013, p. 170.

23. Hope Harrison, *Driving the Soviets Up the Wall: Soviet–East German Relations, 1953–61*, Princeton: Princeton University Press, 2003.

24. Frederick Barghoon, *Soviet Foreign Propaganda*, Princeton: Princeton University Press, 1964.

25. Ibid.

26. Mark Kramer, "The Prague Spring and the Soviet Invasion in Historical Perspective" in Gunter Bischof et al, *The Prague Spring and Warsaw Pact Invasion of Czechoslovakia*, in 1968, Lanham: Rowman and Littlefield, 2010.

27. Theodore Karasik, *Russia and Eurasia Military Review Annual, Volume 16, 1992–93*, Gulf Breeze, Florida: Academic International Press, 2004.

28. How to Oppose Russia's Weaponization of Corruption, USIP, 9 June 2022, https://www.usip.org/publications/2022/06/ukraine-how-oppose-russias-weaponization-corruption

29. Roman Solchanyk, *Ukraine and Russia: The Post-Soviet Transition*, Lanham: Rowman and Littlefield, 1997, p. 129.

30. Andrew Wilson, *Ukraine's Orange Revolution*, New Haven: Yale University Press, 2006.

31. Steven Pifer, How Ukraine Views Russia and the West, Brookings Institution, 18 October 2017, https://www.brookings.edu/blog/order-from-chaos/2017/10/18/how-ukraine-views-russia-and-the-west/

32. Rob Lee, Moscow's Compellence Strategy, Foreign Policy Research Institute, 18 January 2022, https://www.fpri.org/article/2022/01/moscows-compellence-strategy/

33. Poll: For Third Year Running, Russians Take Pride in Military, *The Moscow Times*, 4 May 2017, https://www.themoscowtimes.com/2017/05/04/for-third-year-in-a-row-military-replaces-culture-in-the-short-list-of-what-russians-are-proud-of-a57902

34. Stalo izvestno o razvortyvanii na Donbasse «superoruzhiya» protiv ukrainskikh tankov (It Became Known about the Deployment of a "Superweapon" Against Ukrainian Tanks in Donbas), Avia.pro, 18 March 2021, https://avia.pro/news/sily-dnr-razvernuli-na-donbasse-ubiyc-ukrainskih-tankov-poteri-tankov-vsu-za-chas-mogut

35. Bolgariya dayet Ukraine shest' chasov do porazheniya v sluchaye voyny s Rossiyey (Bulgaria Gives Six Hours Before Defeat in Case of War with Russia), *Izvestia*, 4 September 2021, https://iz.ru/1217134/2021-09-04/v-bolgarii-otveli-ukraine-shest-chasov-do-porazheniia-v-sluchae-voiny-s-rossiei

36. Eksperty nazvali varianty razvitiya operatsii v Ukraine (Experts Called the Options for the Development of the Operation in Ukraine), RBC, 24 February 2022, https://www.rbc.ru/politics/24/02/2022/62173c379a79476f7a338d3d

37. Mikhail Khodaryonok, Prognozy krovozhadnykh politologov (Predictions of Bloodthirsty Political Scientists), *Nezavisimaya Gazeta*, 3 February 2022, https://nvo.ng.ru/realty/2022–02-03/3_1175_donbass.html

38. Gwendolyn Sasse, Most People in Separatist-Held Areas of Donbas Prefer Reintegration with Ukraine—New Survey, The Conversation, 14 October 2019, https://theconversation.com/most-people-in-separatist-held-areas-of-donbas-prefer-reintegration-with-ukraine-new-survey-124849

39. Ekspert ozhidayet «dekorativnykh» sanktsiy Zapada iz-za priznaniya DNR i LNR (The expert expects "decorative" sanctions of the West due to the recog-

nition of DPR and LPR), RIA Novosti, 22 February 2022, https://ria.ru/20220222/sanktsii-1774394271.html

40. Zapad v lyubom sluchaye vvedet sanktsii protiv Rossii, zayavil Lavrov (West Will Impose Sanctions on Russia in Any Case, Lavrov Said), RIA Novosti, 22 February 2022, https://ria.ru/20220222/sanktsii-1774299562.html

41. Rossiya gotova otvetit' na yevropeyskiye sanktsii kontrsanktsiyami, zayavil Chizhov (Russia is Ready to Respond to European Sanctions with Counter-Sanctions, Chizhov Said), RIA Novosti, 5 February 2022, https://ria.ru/20220205/sanktsii-1771222117.html

42. "Russia Cannot Afford to Lose so we Need a Kind of Victory": Sergey Karaganov on What Putin Wants, *New Statesman*, 2 April 2022, https://www.newstatesman.com/world/europe/ukraine/2022/04/russia-cannot-afford-to-lose-so-we-need-a-kind-of-a-victory-sergey-karaganov-on-what-putin-wants

43. Alexei Levinson, Putin May Have High Ratings—But Russians Are Terrified Too, *The Guardian*, 9 May 2022, https://www.theguardian.com/commentisfree/2022/may/09/putin-may-have-high-ratings-but-russians-are-terrified-too

44. Approval of Institutions, State of Affairs in the Country, Trust in Politicians, Levada Center, 4 February 2022, https://www.levada.ru/2022/02/04/odobrenie-institutov-polozhenie-del-v-strane-doverie-politikam/

45. Conflict with Ukraine: July 2022, Levada Center, 1 August 2022, https://www.levada.ru/2022/08/01/konflikt-s-ukrainoj-iyul-2022-goda/

46. Ibid.

47. David Rothkopf, Ukraine Invasion by Russia is the Beginning of the End for Putin and his Friends, The Daily Beast, 24 February 2022, https://www.thedailybeast.com/ukraine-invasion-by-russia-is-the-beginning-of-the-end-for-putin-and-his-friends?ref=author

48. William Courtney, If Regime Change Were to Come to Moscow, The RAND Blog, 18 March 2022, https://www.rand.org/blog/2022/03/if-regime-change-were-to-come-to-moscow.html

49. Thousands Detained at Anti-War Protests Across Russia, RFE/RL, 6 March 2022, https://www.rferl.org/a/russia-1000-protesters-arrested-ukraine-invasion/31738786.html

50. US has no Strategy of "Regime Change" in Russia, Blinken Says, Al Jazeera, 27 March 2022, https://www.aljazeera.com/news/2022/3/27/the-us-has-no-plan-for-regime-change-in-russia-blinken

51. Sarantis Michalopoulos, Brussels Says it is Not After a Regime Change in Russia, Euractiv, 27 March 2022, https://www.euractiv.com/section/politics/short_news/brussels-says-it-is-not-after-a-regime-change-in-russia/

52. Timothy Frye, Why Regime Change in Russia Might not be a Good Idea,

Politico, 12 April 2022, https://www.politico.com/news/magazine/2022/04/12/regime-change-russia-putin-00023953

53. Russia: Repression Escalates, Human Rights Watch, 13 January 2022, https://www.hrw.org/news/2022/01/13/russia-repression-escalates

54. Rachel Denber, In Closing Memorial, Russia Heralds a New, Grimmer Era of Repression, *The Moscow Times*, 29 December 2021, https://www.themoscow-times.com/2021/12/29/in-closing-memorial-russia-heralds-a-new-grimmer-era-of-repression-a75951

55. "Russians and Ukrainians are One People"—Putin, Interfax, 3 March 2022, https://interfax.com/newsroom/top-stories/75337/

56. Half of Russians Say it Would Be Right to Use Military Force to Keep Ukraine Out of NATO, CNN, 23 February 2022, https://edition.cnn.com/interactive/2022/02/europe/russia-ukraine-crisis-poll-intl/index.html

57. Alexander Dugin, *Osnovy geopolitiki: Geopoliticheskoe budushchee Rossii (Foundations of Geopolitics: The Geopolitical Future of Russia)*, Moscow: Arktogeya, 1997.

58. Anna Dolgov, Navalny Wouldn't Return Crimea, Considers Immigration Bigger Issue than Ukraine, *The Moscow Times*, 16 October 2014, https://www.the-moscowtimes.com/2014/10/16/navalny-wouldnt-return-crimea-considers-immigration-bigger-issue-than-ukraine-a40477

59. Escalation in Southern Ukraine, Levada Center, 19 May 2021, https://www.levada.ru/en/2021/05/19/escalation-in-southeast-ukraine/

60. Ukraine and Donbas, Levada Center, 4 March 2022, https://www.levada.ru/en/2022/03/04/ukraine-and-donbass/

61. Levada Center, 19 May 2021.

62. Andrew Roth and Pjotr Sauer, Who has Putin's Ear? Inside the President's Inner Circle, *The Guardian*, 2 April 2022, https://www.theguardian.com/world/2022/apr/02/who-has-putins-ear-inside-the-presidents-inner-circle

63. Andrew Monaghan, Putin's Removal of Ivanov as Chief of Staff is More About Rejuvenation, Chatham House, 15 August 2016, https://www.chathamhouse.org/2016/08/putins-removal-ivanov-chief-staff-more-about-rejuvenation

64. Michael McFaul, Russia's Road to Autocracy, *Journal of Democracy*, Volume 32, Issue 4, October 2021, pp. 11–26, https://www.journalofdemocracy.org/articles/russias-road-to-autocracy/

65. Ibid.

66. M. Steven Fish, *Democracy Derailed in Russia: The Failure of Open Politics*, Cambridge: Cambridge University Press, 2005.

67. Michael McFaul and Kathryn Stoner-Weiss, The Myth of the Authoritarian Model: How Putin's Crackdown Holds Russia Back, *Foreign Affairs*, 1 January

2008, https://carnegieendowment.org/2008/01/01/myth-of-authoritarian-model-how-putin-s-crackdown-holds-russia-back-pub-19808

68. Democracy in Today's Russia, Levada Center, 20 January 2016, https://www.levada.ru/en/2016/01/20/democracy-in-todays-russia/

69. David Lewis, *Russia's New Authoritarianism: Putin and the Politics of Order*, Edinburgh: Edinburgh University Press, 2020.

70. Vladimir Shlapentokh, How Putin's Russia Embraces Authoritarianism: The Case of Yegor Gaidar, *Communist and Post-Communist Studies*, Volume 40, Number 4, December 2007.

71. *The Guardian* View on Russian Dissent: A Slide to Totalitarianism, *The Guardian*, 2 March 2022, https://www.theguardian.com/commentisfree/2022/mar/02/the-guardian-view-on-russian-dissent-a-slide-to-totalitarianism

72. Andrei Kolesnikov, Putin's War Has Moved Russia from Authoritarianism to Hybrid Totalitarianism, Carnegie Endowment for International Peace, 19 April 2022, https://carnegiemoscow.org/2022/04/19/putin-s-war-has-moved-russia-from-authoritarianism-to-hybrid-totalitarianism-pub-86921

73. Masha Gessen, *The Future is History: How Totalitarianism Reclaimed Russia*, London: Granta Publications, 2017.

74. Putin is Profoundly Anti-Modern. Masha Gessen Explains what that Means for the World, *The New York Times*, 11 March 2022, https://www.nytimes.com/2022/03/11/opinion/ezra-klein-podcast-masha-gessen.html

75. Kolesnikov, 19 April 2022.

76. Alexander Motyl, Is Putin's Russia Fascist?, The Atlantic Council, 23 April 2015, https://www.atlanticcouncil.org/blogs/ukrainealert/is-putin-s-russia-fascist/

77. Timothy Snyder, We Should Say it. Russia is Fascist, *The New York Times*, 19 May 2022, https://www.nytimes.com/2022/05/19/opinion/russia-fascism-ukraine-putin.html

78. Francis Fukuyama: Russia Now Resembles Nazi Germany, DW, 20 July 2022, https://www.dw.com/en/francis-fukuyama-russia-now-resembles-nazi-germany/av-62538492

79. Robert Coalson, Nasty, Repressive, Aggressive—Yes. But is Russia Fascist? Experts Say No, RFE/RL, 9 April 2022, https://www.rferl.org/a/russia-repressive-aggressive-not-fascist/31794918.html

80. Marlene Laruelle, In Search of Putin's Philosopher, Riddle, 19 April 2018, https://ridl.io/in-search-of-putins-philosopher/

81. Lavrov: Russia–West Relations are Worse than in the Cold War Era, TASS, 16 April 2018, https://tass.com/politics/1000039

82. Mark Trevelyan, Russia Forges New Partnerships in Face of West's "Total Hybrid War," Lavrov Says, Reuters, 14 May 2022, https://www.reuters.com/world/

lavrov-says-hard-predict-how-long-wests-total-hybrid-war-russia-will-last-2022–05–14/

83. Pepe Escobar, Exclusive: Russia's Sergey Glazyev Introduces the New Global Financial System, *The Cradle*, 14 April 2022, https://thecradle.co/Article/interviews/9135

84. Zongyuan Liu and Mihaela Papa, The Anti-Dollar Axis, *Foreign Affairs*, 7 March 2022, https://www.foreignaffairs.com/articles/russian-federation/2022–03–07/anti-dollar-axis

2. RUSSIA TRIES TO OVERTURN THE EURO-MAIDAN REVOLUTION

1. Vladimir Putin Describes Secret Meeting When Russia Decided to Seize Crimea, *The Guardian*, 9 March 2015, https://www.theguardian.com/world/2015/mar/09/vladimir-putin-describes-secret-meeting-when-russia-decided-to-seize-crimea

2. Putin: deystviya v Kiyeve podgotovleny izvne, eto ne revolyutsiya, a pogrom (Putin: Actions in Kyiv Prepared from Outside, This is Not a Revolution, but a Pogrom), RIA Novosti, 2 December 2013, https://ria.ru/20131202/981344124.html

3. Ukraine PM Mykola Azarov Warns of Force to End Protests, BBC, 22 January 2014, https://www.bbc.co.uk/news/world-europe-25838682

4. Ukraine Crisis: Putin Advisor Accuses Ukraine of Meddling, BBC, 6 February 2014, https://www.bbc.co.uk/news/world-europe-26068994

5. Howard Amos, Shaun Walker and Haroon Siddique, Ukraine's New Government is Not Legitimate—Dmitry Medvdev, *The Guardian*, 24 February 2014, https://www.theguardian.com/world/2014/feb/24/ukraine-viktor-yanukovych-arrest-warrant

6. Comment by the Information and Press Department of the Russian Ministry of Foreign Affairs Regarding the Situation in Ukraine, The Ministry of Foreign Affairs of the Russian Federation, 7 March 2014.

7. Understanding Ukraine's Presidential Shift, Council on Foreign Relations, 8 February 2010, https://www.cfr.org/interview/understanding-ukraines-presidential-shift

8. Paul D'Anieri, *Ukraine and Russia: From Cultural Divorce to Uncivil War*, Cambridge: Cambridge University Press, 2019, p. 175.

9. Yanukovych Says Kyiv Will Wait for Better Deal, RFE/RL, 26 November 2013, https://www.rferl.org/a/ukraine-protests-eu-yanukovych/25180413.html

10. Luke Harding, Viktor Yanukovych Promises Ukraine will Embrace Russia, *The*

Guardian, 5 March 2010, https://www.theguardian.com/world/2010/mar/05/ukraine-russia-relations-viktor-yanukovych

11. Oleg Bondarenko, Viktor Yanukovych, Crush the Reptille!, *Izvestia*, 20 January 2014, https://iz.ru/news/564295

12. Sergei Petukhov, Za chto Rossiya i Ukraina skhlestnulis' na tamozhne (Why Russia and Ukraine Clashed at Customs), RIA Novosti, 16 August 2013, https://ria.ru/20130816/956721953.html

13. Shaun Walker, Ukraine's EU Trade Deal will be Catastrophic, Says Russia, *The Guardian*, 22 September 2013, https://www.theguardian.com/world/2013/sep/22/ukraine-european-union-trade-russia

14. Interview with author, July 2015.

15. Ibid.

16. Interview with author, November 2018.

17. Russia Finds Unlikely Ally in Ukraine's Tymoshenko, Reuters, 5 October 2008, https://www.reuters.com/article/us-russia-ukraine-tymoshenko-analysis-idUS-TRE4940GP20081005

18. Interview with Kyiv-based expert Oleksiy Haran, November 2018.

19. Miriam Elder, Vladimir Putin Accuses Hillary Clinton of Encouraging Russia Protests, *The Guardian*, 8 December 2011, https://www.theguardian.com/world/2011/dec/08/vladimir-putin-hillary-clinton-russia

20. Sergey Podosenov, Tret rossiyan schitayut soglasheniye mezhdu Ukrainoy i YES predatelstvom (A Third of Russians Consider the Agreement Between Ukraine and the EU a Betrayal), *Izvestia*, 23 November 2013, https://iz.ru/news/561190

21. Leonid Ragozin, Ukraine Protests: The View from Moscow, Al Jazeera, 23 December 2013, https://www.aljazeera.com/opinions/2013/12/23/ukraine-protests-the-view-from-moscow

22. Patriarkh Kirill: My vidim revolyutsionnuyu situatsiyu v Ukraine (Patriarch Kirill: We See a Revolutionary Situation in Ukraine), Pravmir, 7 January 2014, https://www.pravmir.ru/patriarx-kirill-na-ukraine-my-vidim-revolyucionnuyu-situaciyu/

23. Natalia Narochnitskaya, «Ne boytes' slova «russkiye»—vsya eta zemlya polita nashey krov'yu» (Don't be Afraid of the word "Russians"—All this Land has been Watered with our Blood), Vzglyad, 16 January 2014, https://www.pravmir.ru/nataliya-narochnickaya-ne-nado-boyatsya-slova-russkie-nashej-krovyu-polita-vsya-eta-zemlya/

24. Vadym Dubnov, Ukraina bez Vilnyusa, ili Yanukovich pridet na maydan (Ukraine Without Vilnius or will Yanukovych Come to Maidan), RIA Novosti, 28 November 2013, https://ria.ru/20131128/980363944.html?in=t

25. Sergei Petukhov, Nasolko Vgodnya Yevropeyskaya Integratsiya Dlya Protsykh

Ukraintsev? (How Beneficial is European Integration to Ordinary Ukrainians), RIA Novosti, 28 November 2013.

26. Dubnov, 28 November 2013.

27. Mikhail Rostovsky, Gosudarstvennyy perevorot na Ukraine: yest' li amerikanskiy sled? (Coup in Ukraine: Is there an American Trace?), RIA Novosti, 26 February 2014, https://ria.ru/20140226/997047114.html

28. Crimea Referendum: 34%, Not 97%, Says Former Russian Government Advisor, Liberty Voice, 25 March 2014, https://guardianlv.com/2014/03/crimea-referendum-34-percent-not-97-percent-says-former-russian-government-adviser/

29. Putin Reclaims Crimea for Russia and Bitterly Denounces the West, *The New York Times*, 19 March 2014, https://www.nytimes.com/2014/03/19/world/europe/ukraine.html

30. Okolo 600 tysyach chelovek vyshli na mitingi v podderzhku Kryma v gorodakh RF (About 600 Thousand People Came to Rallies in Support of Crimea in the Cities of the Russian Federation), RIA Novosti, 18 March 2014, https://ria.ru/20140318/1000101736.html

31. Rogozin zayavil o kontse odnopolyarnogo mira (Rogozin Announced the End of the Unipolar World), RIA Novosti, 18 March 2014, https://ria.ru/20140318/1000069137.html

32. Yuri Teper, Official Russian Identity Discourse in Light of the Annexation of Crimea: National or Imperial?, Post-Soviet Affairs, 18 August 2015.

33. Crimea, Levada Center, 12 November 2014, https://www.levada.ru/en/2014/11/12/crimea/

34. Russia: Ousted Ukrainian President Requested Military Help, Voice of America, 3 March 2014, https://www.voanews.com/a/russia-ousted-ukrainian-president-requested-military-help/1863514.html

35. Ibid.

36. Kathy Lally and Will Englund, Putin Says he Reserves Right to Protect Russians in Ukraine, *The Washington Post*, 4 March 2014, https://www.washingtonpost.com/world/putin-reserves-the-right-to-use-force-in-ukraine/2014/03/04/92d4ca70-a389–11e3-a5fa-55f0c77bf39c_story.html

37. Vladimir Putin Submitted Appeal to the Federation Council, TASS, 1 March 2014, http://en.kremlin.ru/events/president/news/page/535

38. "Krym pochemu-to stal russkoy zemley" (Crimea for Some Reason Became Russian Land), Lenta.ru, 2 March 2014, https://lenta.ru/articles/2014/03/02/simferopol/

39. Olena Goncharova, Debunking the Kremlin Myth About the "Korsun Pogrom," *Kyiv Post*, 18 March 2015, https://www.kyivpost.com/article/content/war-against-ukraine/debunking-the-kremlin-myth-about-the-korsun-pogrom-video-383832.html

40. Interview with author, September 2018.

41. Ibid.

42. Levada Center, 12 November 2014.

43. Statement by the President on Ukraine, The White House, 20 March 2014, https://obamawhitehouse.archives.gov/the-press-office/2014/03/20/statement-president-ukraine

44. Russia Criticizes UN Resolution Condemning Crimea's Secession, Reuters, 28 March 2014, https://www.reuters.com/article/us-ukraine-crisis-un-russia-idUSBREA2R0DA20140328

45. Antikonstitutsionnyy perevorot i zakhvat vlasti—Prezident RF dal otsenku tomu, chto proizoshlo v Kiyeve (Anti-Constitutional Coup and Seizure of Power: The President of the Russian Federation Assessed what Happened in Kyiv), Channel One, 4 March 2014, https://www.1tv.ru/news/2014-03-04/45181-antikonstitutsionnyy_perevorot_i_zahvat_vlasti_prezident_rf_dal_otsenku_tomu_chto_proizoshlo_v_kieve

46. Luke Harding, Ukraine Nationalist Attacks on Russian Supporters—Fact or Kremlin Fairytale?, *The Guardian*, 20 March 2014, https://www.theguardian.com/world/2014/mar/20/ukraine-nationalist-attacks-russia-supporters-kremlin-deaths

47. Dmitri Simes, An Interview with Sergey Glazyev, The National Interest, 24 March 2014, https://nationalinterest.org/commentary/interview-sergey-glazyev-10106

48. Lidia Kelly, Russian Politician Proposes New Division of Ukraine, Reuters, 24 March 2014, https://www.reuters.com/article/ukraine-crisis-partition-letter-idUSL5N0ML1LO20140324

49. Roy Allison, Russia's Deniable Intervention in Ukraine: How and Why Russia Broke the Rules, International Affairs, Volume 90, Issue 6, 2014, p. 1280.

50. Ibid.

51. Interview with author, November 2018.

52. Ibid.

53. Ibid.

54. Ibid.

55. Interview with author, June 2016.

56. Ibid.

57. Andrew Wilson, *The Ukraine Crisis and What it Means for the West*, New Haven: Yale University Press, 2014.

58. Wojciech Kononczuk, Russia's Real Aims in Crimea, Carnegie Endowment for International Peace, 13 March 2014, https://carnegieendowment.org/2014/03/13/russia-s-real-aims-in-crimea-pub-54914

59. Roy Allison, Russian Revisionism, Legal Discourse and the "Rules Based" International Order, *Europe-Asia Studies*, Volume 72, 2020, p. 976.

60. Sergei Karaganov, Yevropa: konets kholodnoy voyne (Europe: End the Cold War), *Izvestia*, 8 April 2014, https://iz.ru/news/568861

61. Interview by the Russian Foreign Minister Sergei Lavrov, Given to the programme "Voskresnoye Vremya," 28 March 2014, https://www.rusemb.org.uk/article/307

62. Interview with author, September 2015.

63. Interview with Moscow-based security expert, September 2022.

64. Interviews with Moscow-based academics, September 2015.

65. Zapad ne budet vvodit' «nastoyashchiye sanktsii» protiv Rossii, schitayet Rogozin (West will not impose "real sanctions" against Russia, Rogozin believes), RIA Novosti, 18 March 2014, https://ria.ru/20140318/1000068212.html

66. Channel One, 4 March 2014.

67. Eksperty: otkaz ot kontrakta po "Mistralyam" stanet udarom po Frantsii (Experts: Refusal of the Mistral Contract will be a Blow to France), RIA Novosti, 18 March 2014, https://ria.ru/20140318/999983198.html

68. Sechin o sanktsiyakh: rossiyskomu biznesu yest' kuda perebazirovat' svoyu deyatel'nost (Sechin on Sanctions: Russian Business has a Place to Relocate its Activities), RIA Novosti, 18 March 2014, https://ria.ru/20140318/1000014478.html

69. Vladimir Radyukhin, Putin Thanks India for its Stand on Ukraine, *The Hindu*, 18 March 2014, https://www.thehindu.com/news/international/world/putin-thanks-india-for-its-stand-on-ukraine/article5800989.ece

70. Russia Seeks Several Military Bases Abroad—Defence Minister, Sputnik, 26 February 2014, https://sputniknews.com/military_news/20140226/187917901/Russia-Seeks-Several-Military-Bases-Abroad—Defense-Minister.html

71. Elena Minina and Maria Repnikova, Sochi 2014: Celebrating Authoritarianism, Al Jazeera, 8 February 2014, https://www.aljazeera.com/opinions/2014/2/8/sochi-2014-celebrating-authoritarianism

72. Paul Sonne, At Home Even Putin Critics Welcome Crimea Takeover, *Wall Street Journal*, 6 March 2014, https://www.wsj.com/articles/SB10001424052702304554004579423502634166782

73. Andreas Umland, Alexei Navalny is a Russian Nationalist but he may still be Good News for Ukraine, The Atlantic Council, 18 February 2021, https://www.atlanticcouncil.org/blogs/ukrainealert/alexei-navalny-is-a-russian-nationalist-but-he-may-still-be-good-news-for-ukraine/

74. Ukraine Crisis: Russians Opposed to Putin, BBC, 12 March 2014, https://www.bbc.co.uk/news/magazine-26531310

75. Separatysty v luhans'komu SBU vyrishyly staty "parlamentom" (Separatists in

the Luhansk SBU Decided to Become a "Parliament"), *Ukrainskaya Pravda*, 8 April 2014, https://www.pravda.com.ua/news/2014/04/8/7021757/

76. Ukraine Crisis: Protesters Declare Donetsk "Republic," BBC, 7 April 2014, https://www.bbc.co.uk/news/world-europe-26919928

77. MID Rossii: YES dolzhen uvazhat' rezul'taty referenduma (Russian Foreign Ministry: EU Should Respect Referendum Results), RIA Novosti, 12 May 2014, https://ria.ru/20140512/1007527118.htm

78. Ukraine Leader Says "Huge Loads of Arms" Pour in From Russia, *The New York Times*, 29 August 2014, https://www.nytimes.com/2014/08/29/world/europe/ukraine-conflict.html

79. Gabrielle Tetrault-Farber, Kremlin Says Russia Respects Poroshenko's Election, *The Moscow Times*, 26 May 2014, https://www.themoscowtimes.com/2014/05/26/kremlin-says-russia-respects-poroshenkos-election-a35836

80. Ibid.

81. Lidia Kelly and Richard Balmforth, Poroshenko's Ukraine Peace Plan Gets Limited Support from Putin, Reuters, 22 June 2014, https://www.reuters.com/article/uk-ukraine-crisis-idUKKBN0EW0EJ20140622

82. Luke Harding, Ukraine Says Most Russian Troops Have Moved Back Across Border, *The Guardian*, 10 September 2014, https://www.theguardian.com/world/2014/sep/10/ukraine-russia-troops-border-east-poroshenko

83. Ian Bateson, Poroshenko Calls on Lawmakers to Revoke Special Status for East, Sends More Troops to Key Cities, *Kyiv Post*, 4 November 2014, https://www.kyivpost.com/article/content/war-against-ukraine/poroshenko-calls-on-lawmakers-to-revoke-special-status-for-east-sends-more-troops-to-key-cities-370640.html

84. Ukraine Crisis: Leaders Agree on a Roadmap, BBC, 12 February 2015, https://www.bbc.co.uk/news/world-europe-31435812

85. Ministers Agree to Extend Heavy Weapons Withdrawal in Ukraine, Reuters, 14 April 2015, https://www.reuters.com/article/uk-ukraine-crisis-ministers-agreement-idUKKBN0N42CF20150413

86. Ian Traynor and Alec Luhn, Poroshenko: Ukraine Conflict Risks Spiralling Out of Control, *The Guardian*, 11 February 2015.

87. Interview with author, September 2022.

88. Ukraine's Nationalist Right Sector Rejects Minsk Deals, TASS, 13 February 2015.

89. Interview with author, September 2022.

90. Amelia Gentleman, Putin Asserts Right to Use Force in Eastern Ukraine, *The Guardian*, 17 April 2014, https://www.theguardian.com/world/2014/apr/17/vladimir-putin-denies-russian-forces-eastern-ukraine-kiev

91. Adrian Basora and Aleksandr Fisher, Putin's Greater Novorossiya: The

Dismemberment of Ukraine, Foreign Policy Research Institute, 2 May 2014, https://www.fpri.org/article/2014/05/putins-greater-novorossiya-the-dismemberment-of-ukraine/

92. Shaun Walker, Vladimir Putin's Advisor Calls Ukrainian President a "Nazi" as EU Deal Signed, *The Guardian*, 27 June 2014, https://www.theguardian.com/world/2014/jun/27/vladimir-putin-adviser-ukrainian-president-nazi-eu-deal-signed

93. Irina Yarovaya, Maydan Yavlyayetsya Zakaznym Ubiystvom Ukrainy (Maidan is the Contract Killing of Ukraine), *Izvestia*, 12 September 2014.

94. Michael Kofman and Matt Rojansky, A Closer Look at Russia's "Hybrid War," Wilson Center April 2015.

95. Alexander Motyl, A Stalemate Ukraine Can Win, *Foreign Policy*, 4 March 2015, https://foreignpolicy.com/2015/03/04/a-stalemate-ukraine-can-win-russia-war-donetsk-donbass/

96. Interview with Ukrainian military analyst, September 2022.

97. Interview with author, September 2022.

98. Interviews with Ukrainian officials, 2022.

99. Interview: Ex-President Kuchma Says Only West Can Resolve Ukraine Crisis, RFE/RL, 13 April 2014, https://www.rferl.org/a/ukraine-kuchma-west-can-resolve-crisis/25331611.html

100. Dmitry Kosyrev, Minsk-2 kak proyavleniye iskusstva dvigat'sya shag za shagom (Minsk II as the Manifestation of the Art of Moving Step by Step), 12 February 2015, https://ria.ru/20150212/1047357961.html

101. Tomila Lankina and Kohei Watanabe, "Russian Spring" or "Spring Betrayal"? The Media as a Mirror of Putin's Evolving Strategy in Ukraine, *Europe-Asia Studies*, pp. 1526–1556.

102. "K vesne Ukraina razvalitsya" (By Spring, Ukraine will Fall Apart), 30 September 2014, https://www.ng.ru/politics/2014–09–30/4_ukraina.html

103. Kurginyan: Strelkov ne vypolnil klyatvu umeret' v Slavyanske (Kurginyan: Strelkov did not Fulfill his Oath to Due in Slavyansk), Rosbalt, 7 July 2014, https://www.rosbalt.ru/ukraina/2014/07/07/1289266.html

104. Michael Weiss, All is Not Well in Novorossiya, *Foreign Policy*, 12 July 2014, https://foreignpolicy.com/2014/07/12/all-is-not-well-in-novorossiya/

105. The Crisis in Ukraine, Levada Center, 3 March 2015, https://www.levada.ru/en/2015/03/03/the-crisis-in-ukraine/

106. VP Miletsky, Reintegratsiya Kryma v sotsial'no-ekonomicheskoye prostranstvo Rossii v kontekste sovremennykh politicheskikh megatrendov (Reintegration of Crimea into the Socio-Economic Space of Russia in the Context of Modern Political Megatrends), *Russia: Trends and Development Prospects*, 2015.

107. Kreml' po "Minsku-2": vse resheniya nado vypolnyat', gotov vystupit' garan-

tom (The Kremlin on Minsk II: All Decisions Must be Implemented, Ready to be a Guarantor), RIA Novosti, 13 February 2015, https://ria.ru/201502 13/1047567488.html

108. Natalya Bashlykova, Minskiye soglasheniya spotknulis' o Debal'tsevskiy kotel (The Minsk Agreements Stumbled over the Debaltseve Cauldron), *Izvestia*, 18 February 2015, https://iz.ru/news/583206

109. Ibid.

110. Luke Harding, Russian Delegation Suspended from Council of Europe Over Crimea, *The Guardian*, 10 April 2014, https://www.theguardian.com/ world/2014/apr/10/russia-suspended-council-europe-crimea-ukraine

111. Sanctions will cost Russia More than $100 Billion, CNN, 21 April 2015, https://money.cnn.com/2015/04/21/news/economy/russia-ukraine-sanc- tions-price/

112. Blocking Russian Access to SWIFT Network May Cause 5% GDP Fall— Kudrin, TASS, 16 September 2014, https://tass.com/economy/749754

113. Andrey Movchan, Glazyev's Economic Policy of the Absurd, Carnegie Moscow Center, 15 September 2015, https://carnegiemoscow.org/commentary/61271

114. Interview with author, September 2022.

115. Ibid.

116. France's Cash-Strapped Far-right Turns to Russian Lender, France 24, 23 November 2014, https://www.france24.com/en/20141123-france-far-right- turns-russian-lender-national-front-marine-le-pen

117. Nicole Sagener, Russia-Ukraine Conflict Divides Germany's Eurosceptics, Euractiv, 22 August 2014, https://www.euractiv.com/section/global-europe/ news/russia-ukraine-conflict-divides-germany-s-eurosceptics/

118. Ivan Egorov, Nikolay Patrushev: "Vytrezvleniye» ukraintsev budet zhestkim i boleznennym" (Nikolay Patrushev: "Sobering Up" of Ukrainians will be Tough and Painful), *Rossiyskaya Gazeta*, 15 October 2014, https://rg.ru/2014/10/15/ patrushev.html

119. Nikolay Surkov, Yevgeny Primakov on Ukraine: "We Somewhat Overdid Our Coverage of Events," *RBTH*, 4 July 2014, https://www.rbth.com/interna- tional/2014/07/03/yevgeny_primakov_on_ukraine_we_somewhat_overdid_ our_coverage_of_37911.html

120. Karaganov, 8 April 2014.

121. Yuriy Kasyuk, Igor Manokhin and Igor Kharichkin, Globalizatsiya i novyy mirovoy poryadok (Globalization and the new World Order), Bulletin of Moscow State Linguistic University, 2016.

122. Roman Goncharenko, Belarus Hosts Ukraine Talks, Strikes Neutral Position Between Moscow and Kyiv, DW, 26 August 2014, https://www.dw.com/en/

belarus-hosts-ukraine-talks-strikes-neutral-position-between-moscow-and-kyiv/a-17878883

123. Andrew Wilson, Belarus Wants Out, *Foreign Affairs*, 20 March 2014, https://www.foreignaffairs.com/articles/belarus/2014–03–20/belarus-wants-out

124. Richard Weitz, Kazakhstan Responds to the Ukraine Crisis, Jamestown Foundation, 24 March 2014, https://jamestown.org/program/kazakhstan-responds-to-ukraine-crisis/

125. Giorgi Lomsadze, Azerbaijan Condemns Crimea Takeover in UN Show of Hands, Eurasianet, 27 March 2014, https://eurasianet.org/azerbaijan-condemns-crimea-takeover-in-un-show-of-hands

126. Umida Hashimova, Defending Uzbekistan's Sovereignty in the Face of the Ukraine Crisis—A Net Assessment of Developments in Uzbekistan Since the Start of 2014, Jamestown Foundation, 17 October 2014, https://jamestown.org/program/defending-uzbekistans-sovereignty-in-face-of-the-ukraine-crisis-a-net-assessment-of-developments-in-uzbekistan-since-the-start-of-2014/

127. Interview with former Armenian Prime Minister Tigran Sargsyan, October 2017.

128. Ibid.

129. Interview with Alexei Malashenko, September 2015.

130. Casey Michel, A Common Currency for the EEU?, *The Diplomat*, 11 December 2014, https://thediplomat.com/2014/12/a-common-currency-for-the-eeu/

131. Steven Pifer, Pay Attention, America: Russia is Upgrading its Military, Brookings Institution, 5 February 2016, https://www.brookings.edu/opinions/pay-attention-america-russia-is-upgrading-its-military/

132. Dmitry Gorenburg, Russia's Naval Strategy in the Mediterranean, July 2019, https://www.marshallcenter.org/en/publications/security-insights/russias-naval-strategy-mediterranean-0

133. Etot god dlya VMF Rossii budet urozhaynym na korabli i podvodnyye lodki (This year for the Russian Navy will be Fruitful for Ships and Submarines), RIA Novosti, 25 July 2014, https://ria.ru/20140725/1017460532.html

134. Thomas Fedysyn, Russian Navy "Rebalances" to the Mediterranean, Atlantic Council, 19 March 2014, https://www.atlanticcouncil.org/blogs/natosource/the-russian-navy-rebalances-to-the-mediterranean/

135. Hans Kristensen, Russian Nuclear Weapons Modernization: Status, Trends and Implications, FAS, 19 September 2014, https://uploads.fas.org/2014/05/Brief2014-Paris-RussiaNukes.pdf

136. Alexei Anishchuk, As Putin Looks East, China and Russia Sign $400 Billion Gas Deal, Reuters, 21 May 2014, https://www.reuters.com/article/us-china-russia-gas-idUSBREA4K07K20140521

137. Allison Quinn, Russia-China Gas Deal Signed to Applause and Skepticism,

The Moscow Times, 21 May 2014, https://www.themoscowtimes.com/2014/05/21/russia-china-gas-deal-signed-to-applause-and-skepticism-a35653

138. Jason Burke and Shaun Walker, Putin and Modi have Much in Common, Say Aides Ahead of Summit, *The Guardian*, 9 December 2014, https://www.theguardian.com/world/2014/dec/09/vladimir-putin-narendra-modi-summit-delhi-russia-india

139. Putin and Modi Reaffirm Joint Bond Between Russia and India, *The New York Times*, 12 December 2014, https://www.nytimes.com/2014/12/12/world/asia/putin-and-modi-reaffirm-bond-between-russia-and-india.html

140. Anton Tsvetov, Russia Still Seeking a Role in ASEAN, Carnegie Moscow Center, 19 May 2016, https://carnegiemoscow.org/commentary/63628

141. Russia to Fly Bombers Over Gulf of Mexico, DW, 12 November 2014, https://www.dw.com/en/russia-to-fly-bombers-over-gulf-of-mexico/a-18059643

3. BRINKMANSHIP AND THE UNFREEZING OF THE UKRAINE WAR

1. Address by the President of the Russian Federation, President of Russia, 21 February 2022, http://en.kremlin.ru/events/president/news/67828

2. Putin Orders Russian Forces to "Perform Peacekeeping Functions" in Eastern Ukraine's Breakaway Regions, Reuters, 22 February 2022, https://www.reuters.com/world/europe/putin-orders-russian-peacekeepers-eastern-ukraines-two-breakaway-regions-2022-02-21/

3. Ukraine Conflict: Daily Reality of the East's "Frozen War," BBC, 15 April 2016, https://www.bbc.co.uk/news/world-europe-35990401

4. Mansur Mirovalev, Donetsk and Luhansk: What You Should Know About the Republics, Al Jazeera, 22 February 2014, https://www.aljazeera.com/news/2022/2/22/what-are-donetsk-and-luhansk-ukraines-separatist-statelets

5. Kyiv Says There Are About 6,000 Russian Soldiers, 40,000 Separatists in Donbas, Interfax, 11 September 2017.

6. Kremlevskiye eksperty prognoziruyut zamorozku Minskikh soglasheniy (Kremlin Experts Predict Freeze of Minsk Agreements), RBC, 5 September 2016, https://amp.rbc.ru/rbcnews/politics/05/09/2016/57cc3e699a79472d827ae986

7. John Herbst, Now is Not the Time to Scrap the Minsk Agreement, Atlantic Council, 29 June 2016, https://www.atlanticcouncil.org/blogs/ukrainealert/now-is-not-the-time-to-scrap-the-minsk-agreement/

8. John Herbst, Russia, Not Ukraine, is Serial Violator of Ceasefire Agreement, Atlantic Council, 21 June 2016, https://www.atlanticcouncil.org/blogs/ukrainealert/russia-not-ukraine-is-serial-violator-of-ceasefire-agreement/

9. Eduard Solovyov, Minskiye soglasheniya: problemy implementatsii (Minsk Agreements: Problems of Implementation), IMEMO RAS, *Russia and the New*

States of Eurasia, Number 4, pp. 11–23, https://www.imemo.ru/publications/periodical/RNSE/archive/2017/4/ukraine-today/minsk-agreements-problems-of-implementation

10. State Duma Speaker Suggests EU Sanction Kiev Over Minsk Violations, *The Moscow Times*, 19 January 2016, https://www.themoscowtimes.com/2016/01/19/state-duma-speaker-suggests-eu-sanction-kiev-over-minsk-violations-a51495

11. Slutskiy: Kiyev prodolzhayet sabotirovat' «Minsk-2», otkazyvayas' ot predlozheniya Rossii po mirotvortsam (Slutsky: Kyiv Continues to Sabotage "Minsk-2", Refusing Russia's Proposal for Peacekeepers), TASS, 20 September 2017.

12. Zakharova: Rossiya ne narushayet Minskiye soglasheniya, tak kak ne yavlyayetsya ikh predmetom (Zakharova: Russia Does not Violate the Minsk Agreements, as it is not Their Subject), Gazeta.ru, 27 March 2016, https://www.gazeta.ru/politics/news/2016/03/27/n_8423555.shtml?updated

13. Andrei Kortunov, Will Donbass Live to See UN Peacekeepers, Russian International Affairs Council, 11 December 2017, https://russiancouncil.ru/en/analytics-and-comments/analytics/will-donbass-live-to-see-the-un-peacekeepers/

14. Ukraine's Interior Minister Deems Minsk Deal Dead, No Longer Worth Talking About, Censor.net, 28 November 2017, https://censor.net/en/news/464283/ukraines_interior_minister_deems_minsk_deal_dead_no_longer_worth_talking_about

15. Interview with author, November 2018.

16. Zakonom o reintegratsii Donbassa legalizuyem Minskiye soglasheniya v pravovom pole Ukrainy (By the Law on the Reintegration of Donbass, we Legalize the Minsk Agreements within the Legal Framework of Ukraine), Gordonua, 3 October 2017, https://gordonua.com/blogs/nayem/zakonom-o-reintegracii-donbassa-my-legalizuem-minskie-soglasheniya-v-ramkah-pravovogo-polya-ukrainy-210281.html

17. Peacekeeping In Ukraine's Donbas: Opportunities and Risks, International Crisis Group, 6 March 2018, https://www.crisisgroup.org/europe-central-asia/eastern-europe/ukraine/donbas-peacekeeping-opportunities-and-risks

18. Medvedchuk: De-yure Krym—tse Ukrayina, ale de-fakto Rosiya (Medvedchuk: De Jure, Crimea is Ukraine, but De Facto Russia), *Ukrainskaya Pravda*, 24 August 2016, http://pda.pravda.com.ua/news/id_7118613/

19. Interview with author, March 2017.

20. Ibid.

21. Interview with author, February 2017.

22. Interview with Dmytro Kuleba, November 2018.

23. Interview with author, September 2017.

24. Most Ukrainians Would Vote for Joining NATO in Referendum—Poll, Interfax-Ukraine, 15 August 2015, https://www.kyivpost.com/article/content/ukraine-

politics/most-ukrainians-would-vote-for-joining-nato-in-referendum-poll-395809.html

25. Interview with Olexiy Haran, November 2018.

26. MID: Rossiya ne namerena zhertvovat' interesami radi vygody dlya Kiyeva ot Zony svobodnoy torgovli (Foreign Ministry: Russia Does not Intend to Sacrifice Interests for the Sake of Benefits for Kyiv from the Free Trade Zone), RIA Novosti, 22 December 2015, https://ria.ru/20151222/1346773194.html

27. Russian Lawmaker: Revolution of Dignity in Ukraine has Turned into Nationalist Coup, TASS, 22 February 2016, https://tass.com/politics/858369

28. "More than 90%" of Russian Airstrikes in Syria Have not Targeted ISIS, US Says, *The Guardian*, 7 October 2015, https://www.theguardian.com/world/2015/oct/07/russia-airstrikes-syria-not-targetting-isis

29. Zakharova zayavila, chto SSHA prikryvayut boyevikov v Sirii (Zakharova Said that the United States Shielded Militants in Syria), RIA Novosti, 24 November 2016, https://ria.ru/20161124/1482102299.html?in=t

30. Artyom Lukin, The Russia-China Entente and its Future, *International Politics*, Volume 58, Issue 3, 2021, pp. 363–380.

31. Russian Orthodox Church a "national security threat" to Ukraine, says President, *Politico*, 28 July 2018, https://www.politico.eu/article/petro-poroshenko-ukraine-russian-orthodox-church-a-national-security-threat-to-ukraine-says-president/

32. Poroshenko potreboval ot predstaviteley RPTS pokinut' Ukrainu (Poroshenko Demanded that the Representatives of the Russian Orthodox Church leave Ukraine), RIA Novosti, 8 November 2018, https://ria.ru/20181108/1532327607.html

33. Tserkovnyy blef: zachem Poroshenko nuzhna pravoslavnaya karta v politicheskoy igre (Church Bluff: Why Poroshenko Needs an Orthodox Card in a Political Game), RIA Novosti, 28 May 2017, https://ria.ru/20170528/1495251455.html?in=t

34. Ukraine Complains Russia is Using New Crimea Bridge to Disrupt Shipping, Bloomberg, 25 July 2018, https://www.bloomberg.com/news/articles/2018-07-25/ukraine-complains-russia-uses-crimea-bridge-to-disrupt-shipping?leadSource=uverify%20wall

35. Matthew Bodner and Patrick Greenfield, Ukraine President Proposes Martial Law After Russia Seizes Ships, *The Guardian*, 26 November 2018, https://www.theguardian.com/world/2018/nov/25/russia-border-guards-ram-tugboat-ukraine-navy-crimea

36. Russia Reopens Kerch Strait to Shipping After Ukraine Standoff—Ria, Reuters, 26 November 2018, https://www.reuters.com/article/ukraine-crisis-russia-strait-idINKCN1NV0GT

37. Andrew Roth, Ukraine President Warns Russia Tensions Could Lead to "Full Scale War," *The Guardian*, 28 November 2018, https://www.theguardian.com/world/2018/nov/27/russia-to-charge-ukrainian-sailors-as-kerch-crisis-deepens

38. Poroshenko: Over 80,000 Troops in and Around Ukraine, Al Jazeera, 1 December 2018, https://www.aljazeera.com/news/2018/12/1/poroshenko-over-80000-russian-troops-in-and-around-ukraine

39. Patrick Wintour, Ukraine President Calls for NATO Warships in Sea of Azov, *The Guardian*, 29 November 2018, https://www.theguardian.com/world/2018/nov/29/russia-blocked-ukrainian-azov-sea-ports-minister

40. V Gosdume nazvali zayavleniye Poroshenko o narashchivanii voysk vozle Rossii farsom (The State Duma Called Poroshenko's Statement About the Build-up of Troops near Russia a Farce), *Izvestia*, 6 December 2018, https://iz.ru/820834/2018-1206/v-gosdume-nazvali-farsom-zaiavlenie-poroshenko-o-narashchivanii-voisk-vblizi-rossii

41. Rossiya prizvala Ukrainu vozderzhat'sya ot avantyur v Azovskom more (Russia Called on Ukraine to Refrain from Adventures in the Sea of Azov), Lenta.ru, 21 November 2018, https://lenta.ru/news/2018/11/21/avantura/

42. Alina Polyakova, Want to Know What's Next in Russian Election Interference? Pay Attention to Ukraine's Elections, 28 March 2019, https://www.brookings.edu/blog/order-from-chaos/2019/03/28/want-to-know-whats-next-in-russian-election-interference-pay-attention-to-ukraines-elections/

43. Russia Seeks to Thwart Ukraine Elections by Disinformation, Cyberattacks—Poroshenko, UNIAN, 8 October 2018, https://www.unian.info/politics/10290567-russia-seeks-to-thwart-ukraine-elections-by-disinformation-cyber-attacks-poroshenko.html

44. Nikolas Kozloff, Ukraine's 2019 Elections; Preparing for More Russian Cyberattacks, The Wilson Center, 7 December 2018, https://www.wilsoncenter.org/blog-post/ukraines-2019-elections-preparing-for-more-russian-cyber-attacks

45. Polyakova, 28 March 2019.

46. Mansur Mirovalev, How Ukraine's Donbas has "Evolved" Under Pro-Russian Separatists, Al Jazeera, 22 April 2022, https://www.aljazeera.com/news/2022/4/22/reporters-notebook-how-donbas-evolved-under-separatists

47. Interview with UNIAN Director General Misha Gannytskyi, September 2022.

48. Alexander Motyl, Ukraine's TV President is Dangerously Pro-Russian, *Foreign Policy*, 1 April 2019, https://foreignpolicy.com/2019/04/01/ukraines-tv-president-is-dangerously-pro-russian/

49. Dmitri Medvedev, Facebook, 22 April 2019, https://www.facebook.com/Dmitry.Medvedev/posts/10155914578871851

50. Pobeda Zelenskogo na vyborakh—chto prineset Ukraine novyy shoumen-pre-

zident (Zelensky's Victory in the New Elections—What New Showman President will Bring to Ukraine), Sputnik, 22 April 2019, https://ru.sputnik.kz/20190422/pobeda-zelenskij-ukraine-mnenie-9918091.html

51. Ukraine's Zelenskyy Proposes New Peace Talks with Russia's Putin, Al Jazeera, 9 July 2019, https://www.aljazeera.com/news/2019/7/9/ukraines-zelenskyy-proposes-new-peace-talks-with-russias-putin

52. Angelina Krechetova, Putin vpervyye pogovoril po telefonu s Zelenskim (Putin Spoke with Zelensky on the Phone for the First Time), *Vedomosti*, 11 July 2019, https://www.vedomosti.ru/politics/articles/2019/07/11/806402-zelenskim

53. Igor Karmazin, Original'naya kopiya: kak Zelenskiy prevrashchayetsya v podobiye Poroshenko (Original Copy: How Zelensky Turns into a Poroshenko Likeness), *Izvestia*, 11 June 2019, https://iz.ru/887599/igor-karmazin/originalnaia-kopiia-kak-zelenskii-prevrashchaetsia-v-podobie-poroshenko

54. Ivan Apuleev, Ustupka i kompromiss": komu ne nravitsya" formula Shtaynmayyera" ("Concession and Compromise": Who Does not like the "Steinmeier Formula"), Gazeta.ru, 3 October 2019, https://www.gazeta.ru/politics/2019/1 0/03_a_12726607.shtml

55. Russia's "Passportization" of the Donbas, SWP Berlin, 3 August 2020, https://www.swp-berlin.org/10.18449/2020C41/

56. George Barros and Joseph Kyle, Putin will Likely Punish Kyiv for not Holding Elections in Russian-Controlled Eastern Ukraine, ISW, 30 November 2020, https://www.understandingwar.org/backgrounder/putin-will-likely-punish-kyiv-not-holding-elections-russian-controlled-eastern-ukraine

57. Olena Roshchina, Zelensky's Team has Been Preparing for War Since 2019—Danilov, *Ukrainska Pravda*, 24 August 2022, https://www.pravda.com.ua/eng/news/2022/08/24/7364606/

58. Philip Pangalos, Ukraine's President Zelensky Meets Senior EU, NATO Officials in Brussels, Euronews, 24 October 2019, https://www.euronews.com/2019/06/04/ukraine-s-president-zelensky-meets-senior-eu-nato-officials-in-brussels

59. Novi ambitsiyi ta pandemiya koruptsiyi: pro shcho my hovoryly v Bryusseli (New Ambitions and the Corruption Pandemic: What We Talked about in Brussels), *Ukrainskaya Pravda*, 7 October 2020, https://www.eurointegration.com.ua/experts/2020/10/7/7115104/

60. V Rossii prokommentirovali polucheniye Ukrainoy statusa partnera NATO (Russia Commented on Ukraine Obtaining NATO Partnership Status), RIA Novosti, 12 June 2020, https://ria.ru/20200612/1572867453.html

61. Sergei Prudnikov, Bazovyy nabor: pochemu Donbassu ne strashny novyye ob"yekty VSU po obraztsu NATO (Basic Set; Why Donbas is Not Afraid of New Facilities of the Armed Forces of Ukraine on the Model of NATO), *Izvestia*,

18 February 2020, https://iz.ru/977592/sergei-prudnikov/bazovyi-nabor-pochemu-donbass-ne-pugaiut-novye-obekty-vsu-po-obraztcu-nato

62. Roman Olearchyk, Ukraine Shuts TV Channels it Accuses of Spreading "Russian Disinformation," *Financial Times*, 3 February 2021, https://www.ft.com/content/176c0332-b927–465d-9eac-3b2d7eb9706a

63. Brian Milakovsky, Banning Pro-Russian Media: Fighting Disinformation, Silencing Dissonant Opinions or Both?, The Wilson Center, 18 February 2021, https://www.wilsoncenter.org/blog-post/banning-pro-russian-media-fighting-disinformation-silencing-dissonant-opinions-or-both

64. Masur Mirovalev, In Risky Move, Ukraine's President Bans Pro-Russian Media, Al Jazeera, 5 February 2021, https://www.aljazeera.com/news/2021/2/5/ukraines-president-bans-pro-russian-networks-risking-support

65. Milakovksy, 2021.

66. Oleachryk, 2021.

67. Irina Alksnis, Ukraina dobilas' svoyego i vstala na put' SSHA (Ukraine has Achieved its Goal and Embarked on the Path of the United States), 4 February 2021, https://ria.ru/20210204/ukraina-1595906917.html?in=t

68. Ukrainian President Signs Decree Imposing Sanctions Against Medvedchuk, Others with Ties to Kremlin, RFE/RL, 20 February 2021, https://www.rferl.org/a/ukraine-sanctions-putin-friendly-politician-and-tycoon-medvedchuk/31112119.html

69. Kreml' uvidel risk voyennogo resheniya v Donbasse posle sanktsiy Zelenskogo (The Kremlin Saw the Risk of a Military Solution in Donbas after Zelensky's Sanctions), RBC, 20 February 2021, https://www.rbc.ru/politics/20/02/2021/6030ecc69a79475dff18e185

70. Kurylev Petrovich, Belarus' kak ob"yekt «tsvetnoy revolyutsii» (Belarus as an Object of Colour Revolution), *Post-Soviet Studies*, 2018.

71. Ivan Nechepurenko, In Belarus, Russian Mercenaries Turned from Saboteurs to Friends, *The New York Times*, 20 September 2020, https://www.nytimes.com/2020/09/20/world/europe/belarus-russian-mercenaries-wagner.html

72. Tom Balmforth, Russia Accuses U.S. of Promoting Revolution in Belarus, Toughens Stance, Reuters, 16 September 2020, https://www.reuters.com/article/us-belarus-election-idCAKBN2672NC

73. Shaun Walker, Belarus's Leader Pleads for Putin's Help as Post-Election Protests Grow, *The Guardian*, 15 August 2020, https://www.theguardian.com/world/2020/aug/15/belarus-leader-pleads-for-putins-help-as-post-election-protests-grow-lukashenko

74. Shaun Walker, Belarus Protests: Putin Ready to Send Lukashenko Military Support, *The Guardian*, 27 August 2020, https://www.theguardian.com/

world/2020/aug/27/belarus-protests-putin-ready-to-send-lukashenko-military-support

75. Russia's SVR Informs Belarus About West's Destabilization Plans, Belta, 6 November 2020, https://eng.belta.by/society/view/russias-svr-informs-belarus-about-wests-destabilization-plans-134814-2020/

76. Brian Whitmore, Ukraine Reveals Military Plans for "Full-Scale Invasion of Belarus," Atlantic Council, 20 April 2022, https://www.atlanticcouncil.org/blogs/belarusalert/ukraine-reveals-russian-military-plans-for-full-scale-invasion-of-belarus/

77. Interview with author, September 2022.

78. Interview with author, September 2022.

79. Whitmore, 2022.

80. Irina Alksnis, Belarus' khoronit «tsvetnuyu revolyutsiyu» (Belarus Buries the Colour Revolution), RIA Novosti, 23 October 2020, https://ria.ru/20201023/belorussiya-1581045582.html

81. Belarus' stala tret'yey stranoy, gde provalilas' tsvetnaya revolyutsiya—rossiys-kiy politolog (Belarus Became the Third Country Where the Colour Revolution Failed—Russian Political Scientist), Belta.by, 11 August 2021, https://www.belta.by/politics/view/belarus-stala-tretjej-stranoj-gde-tsvetnaja-revoljutsija-ne-udalas-rossijskij-politolog-454949-2021/

82. C. Todd Lopez, U.S. Withdraws from Intermediate-Range Nuclear Forces Treaty, U.S. Department of Defense, 2 August 2019, https://www.defense.gov/News/News-Stories/Article/Article/1924779/us-withdraws-from-intermediate-range-nuclear-forces-treaty/

83. Interview with author, September 2022.

84. Theo Merz, EU Imposes Sanctions on Kremlin Chiefs over Alexei Navalny Poisoning, *The Guardian*, 15 October 2020, https://www.theguardian.com/world/2020/oct/15/eu-announces-sanctions-against-kremlin-chiefs-over-alexei-navalny-poisoning

85. Lavrov prigrozil YES zerkal'nym otvetom na sanktsii po «delu Naval'nogo» (Lavrov Threatened the EU with a Mirror Response to the Sanctions on the "Navalny Case"), RBC, 14 October 2020, https://www.rbc.ru/politics/14/10/2020/5f86c7e49a794707b56501b0?

86. Interview with Dmitry Suslov, September 2018.

87. Interview with author, September 2022.

88. Rosiya styahuye viys'ka do kordonu z Ukrayinoyu—Khomchak (Russia Pulls Troops to the Border with Ukraine—Khomchak), *Ukrainskaya Pravda*, 30 March 2021, https://www.pravda.com.ua/news/2021/03/30/7288381/

89. Matthew Funaiole and Joseph Bermudez, Unpacking the Russian Troop Buildup

Along the Ukrainian Border, CSIS, 22 April 2021, https://www.csis.org/analysis/unpacking-russian-troop-buildup-along-ukraines-border

90. Dumitru Minanzari, The Russian Military Escalation Around Ukraine's Donbas, SWP Berlin, 27 April 2021, https://www.swp-berlin.org/publications/products/comments/2021C27_DonbasEscalation.pdf

91. Anton Stepura, Boyovyky "DNR" zayavyly pro dozvil na vedennya "poperedzhuval'noho vohnyu na znyshchennya" (Militants of the "DNR" Announced Permission to Conduct "Warning Fire" for Destruction), Suspilne, 3 March 2021, https://suspilne.media/110005-bojoviki-dnr-zaavili-pro-dozvil-vesti-uperedzuvalnij-vogon-na-znisenna/?

92. Vlada traktuye zahostrennya na Donbasi yak porushennya peremyr'ya, a ne yoho prypynennya—Arestovych (Authorities Interpret Aggravation in Donbas as Violation of Truce, not its Termination—Arestovych), Zn.ua, 26 March 2021, https://zn.ua/POLITICS/vlasti-traktujut-obostrenie-v-donbasse-kak-narushenie-peremirija-a-ne-eho-prekrashchenie-arestovich.html

93. Volodin prokommentiroval ul'timatum Kravchuka na peregovorakh po Donbassu (Volodin Commented on Kravchuk's Ultimatum at the Talks on Donbas), RIA Novosti, 4 April 2021, https://ria.ru/20210404/donbass-1604171769.html

94. Zelenskiy odobril strategiyu «deokkupatsii i reintegratsii» Kryma (Zelensky Approved the Strategy of "Deoccupation and Reintegration" of Crimea), *Izvestia*, 24 March 2021, https://iz.ru/1141747/2021–03–24/zelenskii-utverdil-strategiiu-deokkupatcii-i-reintegratcii-kryma

95. Patrushev predupredil ob ugroze teraktov v Krymu (Patrushev Warned about the Threat of Terrorist Attacks in Crimea), TASS, 14 April 2021, https://tass.ru/politika/11145871

96. Kakaya Ukraina nam ne nuzhna (What Kind of Ukraine do we not Need), RIA Novosti, 10 April 2021, https://ria.ru/20210410/ukraina-1727604795.html

97. Shoygu otreagiroval na voyennyye ucheniya NATO v Yevrope (Shoigu Responded to NATO Military Exercises in Europe), *Izvestia*, 27 April 2021, https://iz.ru/1157461/2021-04-27/shoigu-otreagiroval-na-voennye-ucheniia-nato-v-evrope

98. Germany Says Russia Seeking to "Provoke" with Troop Buildup at Ukraine Border, RFE/RL, 14 April 2021, https://www.rferl.org/a/russia-ukraine-military-germany-nato/31203229.html

99. Vladimir Isachenkov, Russia Orders Troop Pullback but Keeps Weapons near Ukraine, Associated Press, 22 April 2022, https://apnews.com/article/world-news-russia-government-and-politics-crimea-ukraine-e6e8d6c0792517f753fc774713d1fe44

100. Interview with Ukrainian defence ministry official, October 2022.

101. Vladimir Isachenkov, Kremlin Denies Plans to Invade Ukraine, Alleges NATO Threats, Associated Press, 12 November 2021, https://apnews.com/article/ukraine-europe-russia-moscow-83ed7632b8a544ff733cdfbfbca56e77

102. Steven Pifer, U.S.-Russia Relations, One Year after Geneva, Brookings Institution, 16 June 2022, https://www.brookings.edu/blog/order-from-chaos/2022/06/16/u-s-russia-relations-one-year-after-geneva/

103. Bayden i Putin nachali igru. Vpolne vozmozhno, bol'shaya igra (Biden and Putin Started the Game. Quite Possibly a Big Game), *Nezavisimaya Gazeta*, 17 June 2021, https://www.ng.ru/editorial/202106-17/2_8176_editorial.html

104. Interview with author, October 2022.

105. Mansur Mirovalev, What's Putin's Gain in the Belarus Migrant Crisis?, Al Jazeera, 15 November 2021, https://www.aljazeera.com/news/2021/11/15/whats-putins-gain-in-the-belarus-migrant-crisis

106. Interview with author, September 2022.

107. Ibid.

108. Valery Mikhailov, Delo Medvedchuka reshayet sud'bu Ukrainy (The Medvedchuk Case Decides the Fate of Ukraine), RIA Novosti, 14 May 2021, https://ria.ru/20210514/medvedchuk-1732305462.html

109. V Krymu otsenili obvineniya Medvedchuka v razgrablenii poluostrova (In Crimea, Assessed the Accusations Against Medvedchuk in Plundering the Peninsula), RIA Novosti, 14 May 2021, https://ria.ru/20210514/krym-1732283279.html?in=t

110. Peter Dickinson, Putin's Key Ukraine Ally Charged with Treason, Atlantic Council, 13 May 2021, https://www.atlanticcouncil.org/blogs/ukrainealert/putins-key-ukraine-ally-charged-with-treason/

111. Interview with Ukrainian official, September 2022.

112. Ibid.

113. Poroshenko Denies Allegations of Ties with Medvedchuk, *Kyiv Post*, 8 October 2021, https://www.kyivpost.com/ukraine-politics/poroshenko-denies-allegations-of-ties-with-medvedchuk.html

114. Poroshenko Might Become Ukrainian President Again in Early Election—Poll, TASS, 29 December 2021, https://tass.com/world/1382315

115. Peter Dickinson, What Could the Prosecution of Petro Poroshenko Mean for Ukrainian Democracy, Atlantic Council, 22 June 2020, https://www.atlanticcouncil.org/blogs/ukrainealert/what-could-the-prosecution-of-petro-poroshenko-mean-for-ukrainian-democracy/

116. Audio Intercepts Suggest Energy Mogul Akhmetov Being Drawn into Coup Plot—Zelensky, Ukrinform, 26 November 2021, https://www.ukrinform.net/rubric-polytics/3357981-audio-intercepts-suggest-energy-mogul-akhmetov-being-drawn-into-coup-plot-zelensky.html

117. Patrick Wintour, Ukraine has Uncovered a Russian-Linked Coup Plot, says President, *The Guardian*, 26 November 2021, https://www.theguardian.com/world/2021/nov/26/ukrainian-intelligence-warns-russia-backed-december-coup

118. Slawomir Matuszak and Tadeusz Iwanski, Zelensky vs. Akhmetov—A Test of Strength, Center for Eastern Studies, 22 December 2021, https://www.osw.waw.pl/en/publikacje/osw-commentary/2021-12-22/zelensky-vs-akhmetov-a-test-strength

119. «Prezident zhalkiy»: Rada zayavila o «neuspekhe i pozore» Zelenskogo ("The President is Pathetic:" The Rada Announced the "Failure and Shame" of Zelensky), RIA Novosti, 2 December 2021, https://ria.ru/20211202/pozor-1761741500.html?in=t

120. Vladimir Putin, On the Historical Unity of Russians and Ukrainians, President of Russia, 12 July 2021, http://en.kremlin.ru/events/president/news/page/110

121. Liza Semko, Zelensky Reacts to Putin's Article: Russian President Must Have Lots of Free Time, *Kyiv Post*, 13 July 2021, https://www.kyivpost.com/ukraine-politics/zelensky-reacts-to-putins-article-russian-president-must-have-lots-of-free-time.html

122. Vladimir Putin Accuses Lenin of Placing a "Time Bomb" under Russia, *The Guardian*, 25 January 2016, https://www.theguardian.com/world/2016/jan/25/vladmir-putin-accuses-lenin-of-placing-a-time-bomb-under-russia

123. Pochemu bessmyslenny kontakty s nyneshnim rukovodstvom Ukrainy (Why Contacts with the Current Ukrainian Leadership are Meaningless), *Kommersant*, 11 October 2021, https://www.kommersant.ru/doc/5028300

124. Interv'yu Ministra inostrannykh del Rossiyskoy Federatsii Sergeya Lavrova telekanalu «Rossiya 24», Moskva, 1 noyabrya 2021 (Interview of the Minister of Foreign Affairs of the Russian Federation Sergey Lavrov to the Rossiya 24 TV Channel, Moscow, 1 November 2021), Ministry of Foreign Affairs of the Russian Federation, 1 November 2021.

125. Gustav Gressel, Russia's Military Movements: What they could Mean for Ukraine, Europe and NATO, European Council on Foreign Relations, 17 November 2021, https://ecfr.eu/article/russias-military-movements-what-they-could-mean-for-ukraine-europe-and-nato/

126. Sandrine Amiel, Russia's Military Build-up Near Ukraine is Different this Time, say Experts, Euronews, 6 December 2021, https://www.euronews.com/my-europe/2021/11/24/russia-s-military-build-up-near-ukraine-is-different-this-time-say-experts

127. Michael Kofman, Putin's Wager in Russia's Standoff with the West, War on the Rocks, 24 January 2022, https://warontherocks.com/2022/01/putins-wager-in-russias-standoff-with-the-west/

128. Gressel, 2021.

129. Guy Falconbridge, Russian Mercenaries with Spy Links Increasing Presence in Ukraine, Reuters, 14 February 2022, https://www.reuters.com/world/europe/exclusive-russian-mercenaries-with-spy-links-increasing-presence-ukraine-western-2022-02-14/

130. Phil Stewart, Russia Moves Blood Supplies Near Ukraine, Adding to U.S. Concern, Officials Say, Reuters, 29 January 2022, https://www.reuters.com/world/europe/exclusive-russia-moves-blood-supplies-near-ukraine-adding-us-concern-officials-2022-01-28/

131. Kofman, 2022.

132. Ibid.

133. Medvedev Slams Kazakhstan Unrest as Attempted Colour Revolution, TASS, 28 January 2022, https://tass.com/world/1394385

134. Kak i otkuda terror prishel v Kazakhstan (How and Where did Terror Come to Kazakhstan), *Rossiyskaya Gazeta*, 9 January 2022, https://rg.ru/2022/01/09/kak-i-otkuda-v-kazahstan-prishel-terror.html

135. Bruce Pannier, How the Intervention in Kazakhstan Revitalized the Russian-led CSTO, Foreign Policy Research Institute, 7 March 2022, https://www.fpri.org/article/2022/03/how-the-intervention-in-kazakhstan-revitalized-the-russian-led-csto/

136. Protests in Kazakhstan, Levada Center, 18 February 2022, https://www.levada.ru/en/2022/02/18/protests-in-kazakhstan/

137. Steven Pifer, Russia's Draft Agreement with NATO and the United States: Intended for Rejection, Brookings Institution, 21 December 2021, https://www.brookings.edu/blog/order-from-chaos/2021/12/21/russias-draft-agreements-with-nato-and-the-united-states-intended-for-rejection/

138. U.S. Suggests Russia Pull Troops out of Crimea, Transnistria, Abkhazia—El Pais, TASS, 2 February 2022, https://tass.com/world/1396411

139. Patrick Wintour, Emmanuel Macron's Remarks on Russia Set Alarm Bells Ringing, *The Guardian*, 8 February 2022, https://www.theguardian.com/world/2022/feb/08/emmanuel-macron-remark-russia-set-alarm-bell-ringing-ukraine-crisis-talk-vladimir-putin

140. Interview with author, October 2022.

141. Ukraine Crisis: Russia Does not Want War, Putin Says After Meeting Scholz, Euronews, 15 February 2022, https://www.euronews.com/2022/02/15/ukraine-crisis-germany-s-scholz-meets-putin-in-moscow-to-address-burning-issues

142. Interview with Christian Democratic Union MEP Dennis Radtke, October 2022.

143. Twitter, 13 January 2022, https://twitter.com/M_Simonyan/status/1481645 341917126657?s=20&t=bpl61—HNqIZQ4f730CQfA

144. Ukraine-Russia Crisis: Ceasefire Violations Rise at Contact Line, Al Jazeera, 1 February 2022, https://www.aljazeera.com/news/2022/2/1/ukraine-russia-crisis-ceasefire-violations-rise-at-contact-line

145. Secretary Antony J Blinken on Russia's Threat to Peace and Security at the UN Security Council, U.S. Department of State, 17 February 2022, https://www.state.gov/secretary-antony-j-blinken-on-russias-threat-to-peace-and-security-at-the-un-security-council/

146. Interview with author, September 2022.

147. Russia Claims US Mercenaries Plan Chemical Attack in Ukraine, *Politico*, 21 December 2021, https://www.politico.eu/article/russia-us-mercenaries-plan-chemical-attack-ukraine/

148. Donetsk Leader Urges Global Community to Prevent Use of Chemical Weapons in Donbas, TASS, 22 December 2021, https://tass.comworld/1378991

149. Shelling by Russian-Backed Separatists Raises Tensions in East Ukraine, *The Guardian*, 17 February 2022, https://www.theguardian.com/world/2022/feb/17/shelling-by-russian-backed-separatists-hits-school-in-east-ukraine

150. Russia and Belarus Begin Military Drills near Belarusian Border with Ukraine, *The Guardian*, 10 February 2022, https://www.theguardian.com/world/2022/feb/10/russia-belarus-military-drills-near-belarusian-border-ukraine

151. Russia and Belarus Extend Military Drills Amid Ukraine Tensions, Al Jazeera, 20 February 2022, https://www.aljazeera.com/news/2022/2/20/russia-and-belarus-extend-military-drills-amid-ukraine-tensions

152. Julia Davis, Kremlin TV Asks Where's the Champagne? As Ukraine's Kids are Prepped for War, *The Daily Beast*, 22 February 2022, https://www.the-dailybeast.com/margarita-simonyan-asks-wheres-the-champagne-on-russian-state-tv-as-ukraines-children-are-prepped-for-war

153. V Gosdumu vnesen proyekt obrashcheniya k Putinu o priznanii DNR i LNR (A Draft Appeal to Putin on Recognition of DNR and LNR Submitted to State Duma), *Kommersant*, 19 January 2022, https://www.kommersant.ru/doc/5172792

154. Deputat otvetil na vopros o vozmozhnosti priznaniya DNR i LNR (The MP Answered the Question about the Possibility of Recognizing DNR and LNR), RIA Novosti, 19 January 2022, https://ria.ru/20220119/priznanie-1768624929.html

155. Treaties with Lugansk, Donetsk Let Putin Use Army Without Upper House Decisions—Source, TASS, 24 February 2022, https://tass.com/world/1407907

156. Elena Mukhametshina and Ekaterina Grobman, Vladimir Putin postavil tochku v voprose prinadlezhnosti Donbassa Ukraine (Vladimir Putin Puts an

End to the Issue of Donbas Belonging to Ukraine), *Vedomosti*, 21 February 2022, https://www.vedomosti.ru/politics/articles/2022/02/21/910355-putin-obyavil-o-priznanii

157. Mukhametshina and Grobman, 2022.

158. Ibid.

159. U.S. Treasury Imposes Immediate Economic Costs in Response to Actions in the Donetsk and Luhansk Regions, U.S. Department of the Treasury, 22 February 2022, https://home.treasury.gov/news/press-releases/jy0602

160. Politolog dopustil priznaniye DNR i LNR ocherednym sopernikom SSHA (The Political Scientist Allowed the Recognition of DNR and LNR as Another Rival of the United States), *Izvestia*, 22 February 2022, https://iz.ru/1295199/2022–02–22/politolog-dopustil-priznanie-dnr-i-lnr-eshche-odnim-sopernikom-ssha

4. THE "SPECIAL MILITARY OPERATION" BEGINS

1. «Demilitarizatsiya» Ukrainy: kakiye tseli u rossiyskoy armii i chto budet dal'she? ("Demilitarization" of Ukraine: What are the Goals of the Russian Army and What will Happen Next?), BBC Russian, 25 February 2022, https://www.bbc.com/russian/features-60524014

2. Ibid.

3. Elizabeth Wilmshurst, Ukraine: Debunking Russia's Legal Justifications, Chatham House, 24 February 2022, https://www.chathamhouse.org/2022/02/ukraine-debunking-russias-legal-justifications

4. Interview with author, October 2022.

5. Russia to Check Reports About Ukrainian Military's Plans to Attack Crimea, Donbas, TASS, 6 March 2022, https://tass.com/emergencies/1418035

6. Veronika Krasheninnikova, Razoruzhit' i obezvredit': demilitarizatsiya Ukrainy (Disarm and Defuse: The Demilitarization of Ukraine), RIA Novosti, 27 February 2022, https://ria.ru/20220227/ukraina-1775299142.html

7. Telegram, 1 March 2022, https://t.me/strelkovii/2204

8. Rossiyskiye voyennyye unichtozhili 74 ob"yekta nazemnoy infrastruktury VSU (The Russian Military Destroyed 74 Ground Infrastructure Facilities of the Armed Forces of Ukraine), Interfax, 24 February 2022, https://www.interfax.ru/world/824246

9. Russian Troops Destroy 2,396 Ukrainian Military Facilities—Top Brass, TASS, 7 March 2022, https://tass.com/defense/1418143

10. Ukraine's Demilitarization in Full Swing, Military Infrastructure Destroyed—Spokesman, TASS, 2 April 2022, https://tass.com/russia/1431561

11. Rossiya vystupayet za demilitarizatsiyu segodnyashney Ukrainy (Russia Stands

for the Demilitarization of Today's Ukraine), TASS, 22 February 2022, https://tass.ru/politika/13811449?utm_source=google.com&utm_medium=organic&utm_campaign=google.com&utm_referrer=google.com

12. The Weapons and Military Aid the World Is Giving Ukraine, *Politico*, 22 March 2022, https://www.politico.com/news/2022/03/22/ukraine-weapons-military-aid-00019104

13. Ibid.

14. Putin osudil postavki oruzhiya zapadnymi stranami v Ukrainu (Putin Condemned the Supply of Weapons by Western Countries to Ukraine), *Izvestia*, 16 March 2022, https://iz.ru/1306001/2022-03-16/putin-osudil-postavki-stranami-zapada-oruzhiia-na-ukrainu

15. Putin rasporyadilsya perevesti sily sderzhivaniya na osobyy rezhim boyevogo dezhurstva (Putin Ordered to Transfer the Deterrent Forces to a Special Mode of Combat Duty), RIA Novosti, 27 February 2022, https://ria.ru/20220227/putin-1775389742.html

16. Would Putin Strike NATO Supply Lines to Ukraine? History Says No, *The New York Times*, 28 March 2022, https://www.nytimes.com/2022/03/28/us/politics/russia-ukraine-nato-weapons.html

17. Postavki zapadnogo oruzhiya v Ukrainu ne izmenyat situatsiyu na fronte—ekspert (Deliveries of Western Weapons to Ukraine Will Not Change the Situation at the Front—Expert), RIA Novosti, 25 March 2022, https://crimea.ria.ru/20220325/postavki-zapadnogo-oruzhiya-ukraine-ne-izmenyat-situatsiyu-na-fronte—ekspert-1122762560.html

18. Zelensky Denies Weapons of Mass Destruction Projects in Ukraine, TASS, 11 March 2022, https://tass.com/world/1420309

19. V LNR zayavili, chto Ukraina gotovitsya primenit' khimoruzhiye (The LNR Said that Ukraine was Preparing to Use Chemical Weapons), RIA Novosti, 20 March 2022, https://ria.ru/20220320/lnr-1779122784.html

20. Ukrainians Told to Shelter after "Leak" at Ammonia Plant, AFP, 21 March 2022, https://www.themoscowtimes.com/2022/03/20/ukraine-says-russia-bombs-mariupol-school-sheltering-400-a77006

21. Zelensky's Full Speech at the Munich Security Conference, *Kyiv Independent*, 19 February 2022, https://kyivindependent.com/national/zelenskys-full-speech-at-munich-security-conference

22. Interview with author, March 2017.

23. Ukraina khotela poluchit' kompensatsiyu oboronitel'nym vooruzheniyem za svoy yadernyy arsenal (Ukraine Wanted to be Compensated with Defensive Weapons for its Nuclear Arsenal), Lenta.ru, 18 December 2021, https://lenta.ru/news/2021/12/18/arsenal/

24. Zelenskiy dopustil peresmotr otkaza Ukrainy ot yadernogo oruzhiya (Zelensky

Allowed a Review of the Refusal of Ukraine from Nuclear Weapons), Lenta. ru, 20 February 2022, https://lenta.ru/news/2022/02/20/budapest/

25. Interview with author, September 2022.

26. Rossiyskaya armiya likvidiruyet ugrozu poyavleniya yadernogo oruzhiya v Ukraine (The Russian Army Eliminates the Threat of the Emergence of Nuclear Weapons in Ukraine), RIA Novosti, 3 March 2022, https://ria.ru/20220302/minoborony-1776131480.html

27. «Mir dlya nikh—dzhungli». Ekspert po razrabotke yadernogo oruzhiya Ukrainoy (The World for Them is a Jungle: Expert on the Development of Nuclear Weapons by Ukraine), Sputnik Radio, 3 March 2022, https://radiosputnik.ria.ru/20220303/ukraina-1776357533.html?in=t

28. Rossiya trebuyet ot SSHA raz yasneniy po povodu deyatel'nosti biolaboratoriy v Ukraine (Russia Demands Clarification from the United States on the Activities of Biological Laboratories in Ukraine), Channel One, 9 March 2022, https://www.1tv.ru/news/2022–03–09/422991-rossiya_trebuet_ot_ssha_raz_yasneniy_o_deyatelnosti_biologicheskih_laboratoriy_na_ukraine

29. Ibid.

30. Biological Threat Reduction Program, U.S. Embassy in Ukraine, mbassy/kyiv/sections-offices/defense-threat-reduction-office/biological-threat-reduction-program/

31. Mikrobiolog zayavil o prevrashchenii Ukrainy v «superpoligon» SSHA po bio-logicheskomu oruzhiyu (The Microbiologist Announced the Transformation of Ukraine into a "Super-range" of the United States for Bioweapons), Lenta. ru, 12 March 2022, https://lenta.ru/news/2022/03/12/microbiologist/

32. Statement by Permanent Representative Vasily Nebenzia at UNSC Briefing on Biological Laboratories in Ukraine, Permanent Mission of the Russian Federation in the United Nations, 11 March 2022, https://russiaun.ru/en/news/110322n_u

33. Russian Envoy Points to Proof of Germany's Military Biological Activity in Ukraine, TASS, 31 March 2022, https://tass.com/politics/1430637

34. Telegram, 22 March 2022, https://t.me/slutsky_l/915

35. Sergei Karaganov, We are at War with the West. The European Security Order is Illegitimate, Russian International Affairs Council, 15 April 2022, https://russiancouncil.ru/en/analytics-and-comments/comments/we-are-at-war-with-the-west-the-european-security-order-is-illegitimate/

36. Interview with author, September 2022.

37. Aksenov sravnil kiyevskiy rezhim s satanistami (Akysonov Compared the Kyiv Regime with Satanists), RIA Novosti, 18 April 2022, https://ria.ru/20220418/ukraina-1784122526.html

38. Gennadiy Zyuganov: Ukraina dolzhna byt' ochishchena ot natsizma i banderovt-

sev (Gennady Zuganov: Ukraine must be Cleansed of Nazism and Bandera), The State Duma, 5 April 2022, http://duma.gov.ru/news/53962/

39. Patrushev zayavil, chto natsizm v Ukraine neobkhodimo iskorenit (Patrushev Said that Nazism in Ukraine Must be Eradicated), Regnum, 24 March 2022, https://regnum.ru/news/polit/3599491.html

40. Senator Tsekov: Ukrainoy rukovodyat voyennyye, a ne Zelenskiy (Senator Tsekov: Ukraine is Run by the Military, not Zelensky), First Sevastopol, 29 March 2022, https://sev.tv/news/65166.html

41. State Duma Speaker Volodin Says Zelensky Left Ukraine, Interfax, 4 March 2022, https://interfax.com/newsroom/top-stories/75499/

42. Narkolog Shurov otsenil povedeniye Zelenskogo vo vremya vystupleniya na Buche (Narcologist Shurov Appreciated Zelensky's Behaviour During a Speech on Bucha), *Izvestia*, 5 April 2022, https://iz.ru/1315571/2022-04-05/narkolog-shurov-otcenil-povedenie-zelenskogo-vo-vremia-vystupleniia-po-buche

43. V Gosdume zayavili, chto Zelenskiy poteryal kontrol' nad natsbatami (The State Duma Said that Zelensky Had Lost Control over the Nationalist Battalions), RIA Novosti, 28 March 2022, https://ria.ru/20220328/zelenskiy-1780391733.html

44. Response to author, April 2022.

45. Andrey Medvedev, Ukrainskiy natsizm—gremuchaya smes' yazychestva i satanizma (Ukrainian Nazism is an Explosive Mixture of Paganism and Satanism), Vesti, 1 May 2022, https://www.vesti.ru/article/2720706

46. Ibid.

47. Polyanskiy rasskazal zamestitelyu gossekretarya SSHA o natsizme v Ukraine (Polyanskiy Told the US Deputy Secretary of State About Nazism in Ukraine), *Izvestia*, 30 March 2022, https://iz.ru/1312650/2022-03-30/polianskii-rasskazal-zamgossekretariu-ssha-o-natcizme-na-ukraine

48. Zapadnyye SMI: boyeviki «Azova»—ne natsisty. Potomu chto oni ne nemtsy (Western Media: Azov Militants are not Nazis. Because they are not German), RIA Novosti, 25 March 2022, https://ria.ru/20220325/natsisty-1779936761.html

49. Nikolai Dolgachev, Kamery i zastenki: strashnyye svidetel'stva zverstv ukrainskikh natsistov (Chambers and Torture Chambers: Terrible Evidence of Atrocities of Ukrainian Nazis), *Vesti*, 10 March 2022, https://www.vesti.ru/article/2687511

50. Telegram, 27 February 2022, https://t.me/NeoficialniyBeZsonoV/7288

51. Minoborony obvinilo Ukrainu v tom, chto ona derzhit «zhivoy shchit» dlya natsistov v Mariupole (The Ministry of Defence Accused Ukraine of holding a "Human Shield" for the Nazis in Mariupol), Lenta.ru, 16 March 2022, https://lenta.ru/news/2022/03/16/mariup/

52. Slutskiy: sobytiya v Odesse napominayut prestupleniya natsistov na voyne (The

Events in Odesa Resemble the Crimes of Nazis in the War), RIA Novosti, 3 May 2014, https://ria.ru/20140503/1006370447.html

53. Right-Wing Azov Battalion Emerges as a Controversial Defender of Ukraine, *The Washington Post*, 6 April 2022, https://www.washingtonpost.com/world/2022/04/06/ukraine-military-right-wing-militias/

54. Sergei Karaganov, My voyuyem s Zapadom. Poryadok yevropeyskoy bezopasnosti nelegitimen (We are at War with the West. The European Security Order is Illegitimate), Russian International Affairs Council, 15 April 2022, https://russiancouncil.ru/en/analytics-and-comments/comments/we-are-at-war-with-the-west-the-european-security-order-is-illegitimate/

55. Sergey Mirkin, Zachem Ukraine nuzhna denatsifikatsiya (Why Ukraine needs Denazification), *Vzglyad*, 3 March 2022, https://vz.ru/opinions/2022/3/3/1146639.html

56. Vladimir Skachko, Denatsifikatsiya—eto i yest' osvobozhdeniye Ukrainy (Denazification is the Liberation of Ukraine), Sputnik, 25 February 2022.

57. Ibid.

58. Interview with author, September 2022.

59. Interview with Russian opposition political scientist Ilya Matveev, September 2022.

60. Problem of Glorifying Nazism Emerged in Ukraine Long Before 2014—Russian Diplomat, 1 April 2022, https://tass.com/politics/1431235

61. Elena Novoselova, Kak v Ukraine prorosli rusofobiya i natsizm (How Russophobia and Nazism Sprouted in Ukraine), *Rossiyskaya Gazeta*, 30 April 2022, https://rg.ru/2022/04/27/kak-na-ukraine-prorastali-rusofobiia-s-nacizmom.html

62. Pochemu natsizm vozrodilsya v Ukraine, a Ne v Germanii (Why Nazism Revived in Ukraine and not in Germany), *Rossiyskaya Gazeta*, 9 April 2022, https://rg.ru/2022/04/06/pochemu-nacizm-vozrodilsia-na-ukraine-a-ne-v-germanii.html

63. Konstantin Dolgov: narod Ukrainy dolzhen ochistit'sya ot natsizma (Konstantin Dolgov: The People of Ukraine Must Cleanse itself of Nazism), RIA Novosti, 4 March 2022, https://ria.ru/20220304/dolgov-1776326702.html

64. Glava krymskogo parlamenta rasskazal, kogda nachalas' «natsifikatsiya» Ukrainy (The Head of the Crimean Parliament told when the "Nazification" of Ukraine Began), RIA Novosti, 13 April 2022, https://ria.ru/20220413/natsifikatsiya-1783237656.html

65. Novoselova, 2022.

66. Istoki i znacheniye amerikanskogo totalitarizma (The Origins and Meanings of American Totalitarianism), Ukraina.ru, 30 April 2022, https://ukraina.ru/20220430/1033895596.html

67. *Vesti*, 1 May 2022.

68. Rossiya smenit natsistskiy rezhim v Kiyeve, kak by ni opravdyvalsya posol Meshkov (Russia Will Change the Nazi Regime in Kyiv, No Matter How Much Ambassador Meshkov Justifies), Regnum, 15 March 2022, https://regnum.ru/news/polit/3533965.html

69. Ekspert: Natsionalisty na zapade Ukrainy tozhe budut ispol'zovat' naseleniye kak «zhivoy shchit» (Expert: Nationalists in Western Ukraine will also Use the Population as a "Human Shield"), *Vzglyad*, 11 March 2022, https://vz.ru/news/2022/3/11/1148121.html

70. Denazifikatsiya Ukrainy: chto nuzhno postavit' vne zakona (Denazification of Ukraine: What Should be Outlawed), *Vesti*, 6 March 2022, https://www.vesti.ru/article/2685717

71. Ibid.

72. Pushilin zayavil, chto raboty po denatsifikatsii zaymut ne odin god (Work on Denazification will Take More than One Year, Pushilin Said), RIA Novosti, 29 March 2022, https://ria.ru/20220329/denatsifikatsiya-1780740228.html

73. Chairman of the State Duma; Zelensky and his Henchmen Must Answer for Their Actions, State Duma, 25 March 2022, http://duma.gov.ru/en/news/53834/

74. Ekspert predskazal vozrozhdeniye natsizma v Yevrope (Expert Predicts the Revival of Nazism in Europe), *Vesti*, 21 May 2022, https://www.vesti.ru/article/2756041

75. Justin Bronk, Is the Russian Air Force Actually Incapable of Complex Air Operations, RUSI, 4 March 2022, https://rusi.org/explore-our-research/publications/rusi-defence-systems/russian-air-force-actually-incapable-complex-air-operations

76. Ibid.

77. Ibid.

78. Interview with Ukrainian defence ministry official, September 2022.

79. Russian Aircraft Losses in Ukraine "Unsustainable for More than a Fortnight," *The Telegraph*, 7 March 2022, https://www.telegraph.co.uk/world-news/2022/03/07/russian-aircraft-losses-ukraine-unsustainable-fortnight/

80. Interview with Ukrainian defence ministry official, October 2022.

81. Interview with Moscow-based expert, September 2022.

82. Bonnie Berkowitz and Artur Galocha, Why the Russian Military is Bogged Down by Logistics in Ukraine, *The Washington Post*, 30 March 2022.

83. Ibid.

84. Luke Harding, Demoralised Russian Soldiers Tell of Anger at Being "Duped" into War, *The Guardian*, 4 March 2022, https://www.theguardian.com/world/2022/mar/04/russian-soldiers-ukraine-anger-duped-into-war

85. Furvah Shah, Russian Mothers Accuse Kremlin of "Using our Sons as Cannon Fodder" Amid Mounting Casualties, *The Independent*, 7 March 2022, https://www.independent.co.uk/news/world/europe/russian-mothers-putin-as-cannon-fodder-b2030066.html

86. Russia Admits Conscripts "Take Part" in Ukraine Operation, *The Moscow Times*, 9 March 2022, https://www.themoscowtimes.com/2022/03/09/russia-admits-conscripts-take-part-in-ukraine-operation-a76846

87. Anonymous hacks Russian TV and News Agencies to Broadcast "Truth from the Frontlines," LBC, 28 February 2022, https://www.lbc.co.uk/news/anonymous-hacks-russian-tv-news-ukraine-war/

88. Interview with Evgeny Minchenko, September 2022.

89. Interview with Ukrainian defence analyst Viktor Kovalenko, September 2022.

90. Interview with author, October 2022.

91. Interview with Kyiv-based defence expert Mykola Bieliskov, September 2022.

92. Munifa Mustaffa, The Kadyrovtsy: Putin's Force Multiplier or Propaganda Tool?, Newlines Institute, 4 March 2022, https://newlinesinstitute.org/russia/the-kadyrovtsy-putins-force-multiplier-or-propaganda-tool/

93. Mansur Mirovalev, The Real Role of pro-Russian Chechens in Ukraine, Al Jazeera, 18 August 2022, https://www.aljazeera.com/news/2022/8/18/the-real-role-of-pro-russian-chechens-in-ukraine

94. Rossiya planirovala gosudarstvennyy perevorot i sozdaniye «narodnykh respublik» v zapadnykh oblastyakh Ukrainy (Russia Planned a Coup and the Creation of "People's Republics" in the Western Regions of Ukraine), Delo.ua, 12 April 2022, https://delo.ua/ru/politics/rossiya-planirovala-perevorot-i-sozdanie-narodnyx-respublik-v-zapadnyx-oblastyax-ukrainy-395491/

95. Aleksandra Klitina, Lawmakers from Opposition Platform—For Life Have Fled or Regrouped, *Kyiv Post*, 25 April 2022, https://www.kyivpost.com/ukraine-politics/lawmakers-from-opposition-platform-for-life-have-led-or-regrouped.html

96. Russian Offensive Campaign Assessment, Critical Threats, 1 March 2022, https://www.criticalthreats.org/analysis/russian-offensive-campaign-assessment-march-1

97. David Axe, Ukraine's Best Tank Brigade Has Won the Battle for Chernihiv, Forbes, 31 March 2022, https://www.forbes.com/sites/davidaxe/2022/03/31/ukraines-best-tank-brigade-has-won-the-battle-for-chernihiv/?sh=5a10177db9af

98. Bucha ta Hostomel' pid kontrolem RF. Pered ZSU postavleno zavdannya ne dopustyty voroha cherez Irpin' i vyyty na Kyyiv (Bucha and Hostomel under the Control of the Russian Federation. The Armed Forces of Ukraine were Given the Task of Preventing the Enemy from Crossing the Irpin River and

Going to Kyiv), Strana, 22 March 2022, https://strana.today/news/382846-bucha-i-hostomel-nakhodjatsja-pod-kontrolem-rossijan.html

99. Luke McGee, Here's What we Know About the 40-mile-long Russian Convoy Outside Ukraine's Capital, CNN, 3 March 2022, https://edition.cnn.com/2022/03/03/europe/russian-convoy-stalled-outside-kyiv-intl/index.html

100. David Vergun, Russian Troops Bogged Down in Face of Stiff Ukraine Resistance, Says DOD Official, U.S. Department of Defense, 16 March 2022, https://www.defense.gov/News/News-Stories/Article/Article/2969010/russian-troops-bogged-down-in-face-of-stiff-ukraine-resistance-says-dod-official/

101. Russian Troops Advance within 20 miles of Ukraine Capital, Pentagon Says, NBC News, 24 February 2022, https://www.nbcnews.com/news/world/russia-launches-attacks-key-ukrainian-cities-rcna17482

102. ZSU znyshchyly kadyrivtsiv, yaki planuvaly vbyty Zelens'koho—rozvidka (The Armed Forces Destroyed the Kadyrovtsy who were Planning to Kill Zelensky—Intelligence), *Ukrainskaya Pravda*, 1 March 2022, https://www.pravda.com.ua/news/2022/03/1/7327224/

103. Putin Calls for Ukraine Army to Overthrow Zelensky, *The Moscow Times*, 25 February 2022, https://www.themoscowtimes.com/2022/02/25/putin-calls-for-ukraine-army-to-overthrow-zelensky-a76598

104. Telegram, 22 September 2022, https://t.me/ghost_of_novorossia/3978

105. Eks-deputat Verkhovnoy Rady Murayev oproverg zayavleniye MID Velikobritanii (Ex-Deputy of Verkhovna Rada Murayev Rejected the Statement of the British Foreign Office), Interfax, 23 January 2022, https://www.interfax.ru/world/817872

106. Interviews with Ukrainian officials, September 2022.

107. Sergei Glazyev, Chto proiskhodit? Rossiya i Ukraina ugodili v obshchuyu lovushku (What's Happening? Russia and Ukraine Fell into a Common Trap), Tsargrad, 14 October 2022, https://amp.tsargrad.tv/articles/chto-proishodit-rossija-i-ukraina-ugodili-v-obshhuju-lovushku_644121

108. Interview with Dmytro Natalukha, September 2022.

109. Bogdan Stepovoy and Alexey Ramm, Korabli yest: Chernomorskiy flot zhdet usileniya (Ships There: The Black Sea Fleet is Waiting for Strengthening), *Izvestia*, 15 December 2021, https://iz.ru/1264466/bogdan-stepovoi-aleksei-ramm/tuda-suda-chernomorskii-flot-zhdet-usilenie

110. Tayfun Ozberk, Russia-Ukraine Conflict: What has Happened in the Black Sea so Far?, Naval News, 27 February 2022, https://www.navalnews.com/naval-news/2022/02/russia-ukraine-conflict-what-happened-in-the-black-sea-so-far/

111. Interview with author, September 2022.

112. Ibid.

113. So vzyatiyem Odessy Rossiya reshit problemu blokady Pridnestrov'ya (With the Capture of Odesa, Russia will Solve the Problem of the Blockade of Transnistria), Topcor.ru, 25 February 2022, https://topcor.ru/24214-so-vzja-tiem-odessy-rossija-reshit-problemu-blokady-pridnestrovja.html

114. Telegram, 2 March 2022, https://t.me/anna_news/22896

115. Telegram, 29 March 2022, https://t.me/denazi_UA/4711

116. Interview with Volodymyr Dubovyk, September 2022.

117. Ekspert: feyk o roddome v Mariupole, sdelannyy po tekhnologii «Belykh kasok» (Expert: Fake About Maternity Hospital in Mariupol Made Using White Helmets Technology), RIA Novosti, 10 March 2022, https://ria.ru/20220310/roddom-1777559653.html

118. Bezhenets iz Mariupolya rasskazal o deystviyakh «Azova» pered vzryvom v teatre (A Refugee from Mariupol Spoke about the Actions of "Azov" Before the Explosion in the Theatre), RIA Novosti, 1 April 2022, https://ria.ru/20220401/mariupol-1781242294.html

119. U.S., EU Unlikely to Cut Russia off SWIFT for Now—Biden, Reuters, 24 February 2022, https://www.reuters.com/business/finance/eu-unlikely-cut-russia-off-swift-now-sources-say-2022-02-24/

120. "They're Capable of Anything Stupid:" Kremlin Slams Western Sanctions Against Putin, TASS, 3 April 2022, https://tass.com/politics/1431703

121. Russia's GDP to Fall 15% this year on Ukraine-Linked Sanctions—IIF, Reuters, 10 March 2022, https://www.reuters.com/markets/rates-bonds/rus-sias-gdp-fall-15-this-year-ukraine-linked-sanctions-iif-2022-03-10/

122. Russia's Stocks Crash 44%, Central Bank Unveils Emergency Support, *The Moscow Times*, 24 February 2022, https://www.themoscowtimes.com/2022/02/24/russias-stocks-crash-44-central-bank-unveils-emergency-support-a76554

123. Russian Central Bank Hikes Rate to 20% in Emergency Move, Tells Firms to Sell FX, Reuters, 28 February 2022, https://www.reuters.com/business/finance/russia-hikes-key-rate-20-tells-companies-sell-fx-2022-02-28/

124. Russia; Capital Controls were Tit-for-Tat Move After Central Bank Reserves were Frozen, Reuters, 25 March 2022, https://www.reuters.com/world/europe/russia-says-capital-controls-were-tit-for-tat-move-after-reserves-were-frozen-2022-03-25/

125. TSB podgotovil zakonoproyekt o zaprete kriptovalyuty i predlozhil shtrafy (The Central Bank has Prepared a Draft to Ban Cryptocurrency and Proposed Fines), RBC, 18 February 2022, https://www.rbc.ru/finances/18/02/2022/620f75b69a7947762be3a633

126. Medvedev ob'yavil o natsionalizatsii aktivov ukhodyashchikh iz Rossii kompaniy (Medvedev Announced the Nationalisation of the Assets of Companies

Leaving Russia), Lenta.ru, 10 March 2022, https://lenta.ru/news/2022/03/10/bankrot/

127. Medvedev ne isklyuchil natsionalizatsiyu imushchestva lits, zaregistrirovan-nykh v SSHA i stranakh YES (Medvedev did not Rule Out the Nationalisation of the Property of Persons Registered in the US and EU Countries), Interfax, 26 February 2022, https://www.interfax.ru/russia/824761

128. Konstantin Dvinsky, Nam Nuzhna Chistka v Pravitelstve. Voyna v Ukraine Podnimayet Vopros Ostavki Liberalov (We Need a Cleanup in the Government. The War in Ukraine Raises the Question of the Dismissal of Liberals), Tsargrad, 3 March 2022, https://tsargrad.tv/articles/nuzhna-zachistka-v-pravi-telstve-vojna-na-ukraine-stavit-vopros-ob-uvolnenii-liberalov_505240

129. Russian Central Banker Wanted Out over Ukraine, Putin Said No, Bloomberg, 23 March 2022, https://www.bloomberg.com/news/articles/2022–03–23/rus-sia-central-banker-wanted-out-over-ukraine-but-putin-said-no

130. Sofia Sachivko, Kuda propal Kudrin? Glava Schetnoy palaty nedelyu molchit (Where did Kudrin Disappear To? The Head of the Accounts Chamber is Silent for a Week), Svoboda Press, 17 March 2022, https://svpressa.ru/econ-omy/article/328329/

131. Russia Privately Warns of Deep and Prolonged Economic Damage, Bloomberg, 5 September 2022, https://www.bloomberg.com/news/articles/2022–09–05/russia-risks-bigger-longer-sanctions-hit-internal-report-warns?leadSource=uverify%20wall

132. Silicon Lifeline: Western Electronics at the Heart of Russia's War Machine, RUSI, 8 August 2022, https://rusi.org/explore-our-research/publications/special-resources/silicon-lifeline-western-electronics-heart-russias-war-ma-chine

133. Interview with author, September 2022.

134. Ibid.

135. Neadekvatnost' Zapada rabotayet na Rossiyu (The Inadequacy of the West Works for Russia), RIA Novosti, 5 March 2022, https://ria.ru/20220305/neadekvatnost-1776607876.html

136. Dan Milmo, Russia Blocks Access to Facebook and Twitter, *The Guardian*, 4 March 2022, https://www.theguardian.com/world/2022/mar/04/russia-completely-blocks-access-to-facebook-and-twitter

137. Interview with Russian opposition figure Andrei Soldatov, October 2022.

138. "Scum and Traitors:" Vladimir Putin Threatens Anti-War Russians, Al Jazeera, 17 March 2022, https://www.aljazeera.com/news/2022/3/17/scum-and-trai-tors-vladimir-putin-threatens-anti-war-russians

139. Pjotr Sauer, Putin Praises Russian "Unity" at Rally as Glitch Cuts State TV Broadcast, *The Guardian*, 18 March 2022, https://www.theguardian.com/

world/2022/mar/18/putin-praises-russian-unity-at-rally-but-state-tv-broad-cast-is-cut-off

140. Telegram, 25 February 2022, https://t.me/kremlinprachka/17347

141. Ramzan Kadyrov Vozmetsil Zavaleniye Peskova o Patrtitoizme Ivana Urganta (Ramzan Kadyrov Angered by Peskov's Statement about Ivan Urgant's Patriotism), Tsargrad, 3 April 2022, https://am.tsargrad.tv/news/ramzana-kadyrova-razozlilo-zajavlenie-peskova-naschjot-patriotizma-ivana-urganta_523334

142. Dmitry Rodionov, Chubays uyekhal iz Rossii: zapishut li yego v "natsional-predateli"? (Chubais Left Russia: Will They Write him Down as National Traitor?), Svoboda Press, 24 March 2022, https://svpressa.ru/politic/article/329100/

143. Ukraine says talks with Russia agreed on humanitarian corridors, Reuters, 3 March 2022, https://www.reuters.com/world/europe/ukraine-says-talks-with-russia-agreed-humanitarian-corridors-2022-03-03/

144. Ukraine Blasts Russian Plan for "Humanitarian Corridors," Al Jazeera, 7 March 2022, https://www.aljazeera.com/news/2022/3/7/ukraine-blasts-russia-plan-corridor

145. Russian Official Sees Progress with Ukraine on Neutrality, not with "Denazification," Reuters, 18 March 2022, https://www.reuters.com/world/russian-official-sees-progress-with-ukraine-neutrality-not-denazification-2022-03-18/

146. Zelensky Says Ukraine Prepared to Discuss Neutrality in Peace Talks, BBC, 28 March 2022, https://www.bbc.co.uk/news/world-europe-60901024

147. Russia no Longer Requesting Ukraine be Denazified as Part of Ceasefire Talks, *Financial Times*, 28 March 2022, https://www.ft.com/content/7f14efe8-2f4c-47a2-aa6b-9a755a39b626

148. Interview with author, September 2022.

149. Togi peregovorov v Stambule ne oznachayut okonchaniya voyennoy operatsii (The results of the talks in Istanbul Do Not Mean the End of the Military Operation), *Vedomosti*, 30 March 2022, https://www.vedomosti.ru/politics/articles/2022/03/29/915784-itogi-stambule

150. Ibid.

151. Oleg Sukhov, Ukraine Seeks Security Guarantees "Stronger than NATO's," Outlines Other Terms for Peace Deal with Russia, *Kyiv Independent*, 29 March 2022, https://kyivindependent.com/national/ukraine-seeks-security-guarantees-stronger-than-natos-outlines-other-terms-for-peace-deal-with-russia

152. Peskov zayavil o prodolzhenii denatsifikatsii Ukrainy (Peskov Announced the Continuation of Denazification of Ukraine), *Vzglyad*, 29 March 2022, https://vz.ru/news/2022/3/29/1151011.html

153. Daniel Boffey and Shaun Walker, Russia Bombards Chernihiv Hours After Pledging to Halt Shelling, *The Guardian*, 30 March 2022, https://www.theguardian.com/world/2022/mar/30/ukraine-russia-bombards-chernihiv-hours-after-pledging-to-halt-shelling

154. Vladimir Medinsky, К 300-летию Российской империи (To the 300th Anniversary of the Russian Empire), Istoria.ru, 4 February 2022.

155. Medinskiy nazval nyneshnyuyu Ukrainu «istoricheskim fantomom» (Medinsky Called the Current Ukraine a "Historical Phantom"), TASS, 22 February 2022, https://tass.ru/politika/13803945?utm_source=google.com&utm_medium=organic&utm_campaign=google.com&utm_referrer=google.com

156. Gerrard Kaonga, Russia Being Pushed to "Collapse" by West, Vladimir Putin Aide Fears, *Newsweek*, 24 March 2022, https://www.newsweek.com/vladimir-putin-russia-ukraine-invasion-war-west-vladimir-medinsky-1691366

157. Slutskiy: Rossiya i Ukraina opredelyat mekhanizm organizatsii gumanitarnykh koridorov (Slutsky: Russia and Ukraine will Determine the Mechanism for Organising Humanitarian Corridors), *Rossiyskaya Gazeta*, 3 March 2022, https://rg.ru/2022/03/03/sluckij-rossiia-i-ukraina-opredeliat-mehanizm-organizacii-gumanitarnyh-koridorov.html

158. Kadyrov o peregovorakh Rossii i Ukrainy v Turtsii: «Tolku ne budet» (Kadyrov About the Talks between Russia and Ukraine in Turkey: There will be No Sense), *Business Gazeta*, 29 March 2022, https://m.business-gazeta.ru/news/544979

159. Sergei Aksenov, Zamenit li Putin Medinskogo Kadyrovym? (Will Putin Replace Medinsky with Kadyrov?), *Svobodnaya Pressa*, 30 March 2022, https://svpressa.ru/war21/article/329784/

160. Peregovory v Stambule: Rossiya gotovit novyy Khasavyurt? (Negotiations in Istanbul: Russia is Preparing a New Khasavyurt), Regnum, 30 March 2022, https://regnum.ru/news/3548990.html

161. V Gosdume posle peregovorov v Stambule ukazali na zatyagivaniye Kiyevom srokov (In the State Duma, after the talks in Istanbul, they pointed to the dragging out of time by Kyiv), *Izvestia*, 30 March 2022, https://iz.ru/1313023/202203-30/v-gd-posle-peregovorov-v-stambule-ukazali-na-zatiagivanie-vremeni-kievom

5. RUSSIA DOWNSIZES ITS GOALS IN UKRAINE

1. Andrew Roth, Putin Ties Ukraine Invasion to Second World War in Victory Day Speech, *The Guardian*, 9 May 2022, https://www.theguardian.com/world/2022/may/09/putin-ties-ukraine-invasion-second-world-war-victory-day-speech-russia

2. Interview with author, September 2022.

3. Interview with author, September 2022.

4. Nazvany osnovnyye tseli vtorogo etapa spetsoperatsii v Ukraine (Named the Main Goals of the Second Phase of the Special Military Operation in Ukraine), RIA Novosti, 22 April 2022, https://crimea.ria.ru/20220422/nazvany-glavnye-tseli-vtoroy-fazy-spetsoperatsii-na-ukraine-1123022439.html

5. Telegram, 19 April 2022, https://t.me/rybar/31427

6. Ksenia Smirnova, Prilepin otsenil, skol'ko yeshche mozhet prodlit'sya operatsiya na Ukraine (Prilepin Estimated how Long the Operation in Ukraine can Last), OCH, 27 March 2022, https://www.osnmedia.ru/world/prilepin-otsenil-skolko-eshhe-mozhet-prodlitsya-operatsiya-na-ukraine/?utm_source=smi2&utm_medium=partner&utm_campaign=72247&utm_content=11860659

7. Kadyrov predlozhil provesti vtoroy etap spetsoperatsii po vsey Ukraine (Kadyrov Proposed to Conduct the Second Stage of the Special Operation Throughout Ukraine), RIA Novosti, 3 May 2022, https://ria.ru/20220503/kadyrov-1786700429.html

8. Karoun Demirlian and Rachel Pannett, Russia learns from Failure to Take Kyiv as New Offensive Begins, U.S. Says, *The Washington Post*, 19 April 2022, https://www.washingtonpost.com/world/2022/04/19/russia-invasion-eastern-ukraine-donbas-war/

9. Ukraine Says Russia's Offensive in Donbas has Begun. Here's what we know, NPR, 19 April 2022, https://www.npr.org/2022/04/19/1093501394/ukraine-russia-donbas-offensive

10. Victor Biryukov, Vtoroy etap voyennoy operatsii v Ukraine: Vse idet po planu (The Second Stage of the Military Operation in Ukraine: Everything is Going to Plan), Topwar.ru, 11 May 2022.

11. Ibid.

12. Putin Calls off Plan to Storm Mariupol Plant, Opts for Blockade Instead, Reuters, 21 April 2022, https://www.reuters.com/world/europe/putin-cancels-russian-plans-storm-mariupol-steel-plant-opts-blockade-instead-2022-04-21/

13. Posle resheniya Putina otmenit' shturm «Azovstali» nachnetsya tonnel'naya «voyna» (After Putin's Decision to Cancel the Assault on Azovstal, a tunnel war Began), Mk.ru, 21 April 2022, https://www.mk.ru/politics/2022/04/21/posle-resheniya-putina-ob-otmene-shturma-azovstali-nachnetsya-tunnelnaya-voyna.html

14. Russia-held Popasna in Ukraine is a Ghost Town After End of Siege, Reuters, 15 July 2022, https://www.reuters.com/world/europe/russian-held-popasna-ukraine-is-ghost-town-after-end-siege-2022-07-14/

15. Ukraine Pushes Back Russian Troops in Counter-Offensive Near Kharkiv,

Reuters, 11 May 2022, https://www.reuters.com/world/europe/missiles-pound-ukraines-odesa-after-russia-marks-ww2-victory-2022–05–10/

16. Russian Warship Sinks in the Black Sea After Ukraine Claims it was Hit by a Missile, CNN, 14 April 2022, https://edition.cnn.com/2022/04/14/europe/russia-navy-cruiser-moskva-fire-abandoned-intl-hnk-ml/index.html

17. Daniel Boffey, "It was like a Movie:" Recaptured Bucha Recounts Violence of Russian Invasion, *The Guardian*, 3 April 2022, https://www.theguardian.com/world/2022/apr/03/bucha-violence-invasion-russia-ukraine

18. Bodies of Mutilated Children Among Horrors the Russians Left Behind, *The Times*, 2 April 2022, https://www.thetimes.co.uk/article/bodies-of-mutilated-children-among-horrors-the-russians-left-behind-5ddnkkwp2

19. Jennifer Rankin and Daniel Boffey, Killing of Civilians in Bucha and Kyiv Condemned as "Terrible War Crime", *The Guardian*, 3 April 2022, https://www.theguardian.com/world/2022/apr/03/eu-leaders-condemn-killing-of-unarmed-civilians-in-bucha-and-kyiv

20. Paul Niland, Putin's Mariupol Massacre is One of the 21st Century's Worst War Crimes, Atlantic Council, 24 May 2022, https://www.atlanticcouncil.org/blogs/ukrainealert/putins-mariupol-massacre-is-one-the-worst-war-crimes-of-the-21st-century/

21. Daniel Boffey and Lorenzo Tondo, Russia Accused of Shelling Mariupol Humanitarian Corridor, *The Guardian*, 26 April 2022, https://www.theguardian.com/world/2022/apr/26/russia-accused-of-shelling-mariupol-humanitarian-corridor

22. Aleksandra Klitina, Russian Military Executes Ukrainians Surrendering in Donbas, *Kyiv Post*, 28 April 2022, https://www.kyivpost.com/ukraine-politics/russian-military-executes-ukrainians-surrendering-in-donbas.html

23. Emman Graham-Harrison, Men and Boys Among Alleged Rape Victims of Russian Soldiers in Ukraine, *The Guardian*, 3 May 2022, https://www.theguardian.com/world/2022/may/03/men-and-boys-among-alleged-victims-by-russian-soldiers-in-ukraine

24. Volodymyr Zelensky, Speech by the President of Ukraine at a meeting of the UN Security Council, 5 April 2022, https://www.president.gov.ua/en/news/vistup-prezidenta-ukrayini-na-zasidanni-radi-bezpeki-oon-74121

25. Halya Coynash, Horrific Conditions and Torture in Russian Filtration Camp "Ghetto" for Mariupol Residents, Kharkiv Human Rights Protection Group, 11 May 2022, https://khpg.org/en/1608810538

26. One Ukrainian Family's Perilous Journey Through Russia's "Filtration Camps", *Politico*, 26 May 2022, https://www.politico.com/news/2022/05/26/ukraine-filtration-camps-00034862

27. Joyce Sohyun Lee, Video Shows Russian "Filtration Camp," Mariupol Mayor's

Office Says, *The Washington Post*, 6 May 2022, https://www.washingtonpost.com/world/2022/05/06/ukraine-mariupol-russian-filtration-camp-video/

28. Pavlo Krivosheyev, Ukrainian Teachers Balk as Moscow Seeks to Impose "Russian Standards" in Occupied Territories, RFE/RL, 22 May 2022, https://www.rferl.org/a/ukraine-kherson-education-russian-occupation/31862426.html

29. Ibid.

30. Michael Wasiura, Russian TV says Mariupol Almost "Normal," Schools to Use Russian Textbooks, *Newsweek*, 29 April 2022, https://www.newsweek.com/russian-tv-says-mariupol-almost-normal-schools-use-russian-textbooks-1702255

31. Amanda Seitz and Arijeta Lajka, Russian Media Campaign Falsely Claims Bucha Deaths are Fakes, Associated Press, 6 April 2022, https://apnews.com/article/russia-ukraine-kyiv-business-media-facebook-21d36ea4370bab98b1c-c93baa0815dd8

32. Satellite Images Show Bodies Lay in Bucha for Weeks, Despite Russian Claims, *The New York Times*, 4 April 2022, https://www.nytimes.com/2022/04/04/world/europe/bucha-ukraine-bodies.html

33. Satellite Images show Long trench at Ukrainian Mass Grave Site, Maxar Says, Reuters, 3 April 2022, https://www.reuters.com/world/europe/satellite-images-show-45-foot-long-trench-grave-site-bucha-maxar-2022-04-03/

34. German Intelligence Intercepts Radio Traffic Discussing the Murder of Civilians, Spiegel International, 7 April 2022.

35. Michal Kranz, Brutal Sect of Putin's Army Accused of Murdering their Own Comrades, *Daily Beast*, 30 April 2022, https://www.thedailybeast.com/chechen-soldiers-in-bucha-civilian-massacre-accused-of-killing-russian-comrades

36. New Evidence Shows how Russian Soldiers Executed Men in Bucha, *The New York Times*, 19 May 2022, https://www.nytimes.com/2022/05/19/world/europe/russia-bucha-ukraine-executions.html

37. Spiegel International, 7 April 2022.

38. Kuleba Calls on ICC Mission to Come to Bucha to Collect Evidence of Russian War Crimes, Interfax, 3 April 2022, https://en.interfax.com.ua/news/general/820649.html

39. Rory Sullivan, Chief ICC Prosecutor Declares Ukraine a "Crime Scene" after Visiting Bucha to Investigate Russia's War, *The Independent*, 14 April 2022, https://www.independent.co.uk/news/world/europe/icc-investigation-bucha-war-crimes-b2057997.html

40. Russian War Crimes in Ukraine: EU Supports the International Criminal Court Investigation with 7.25 Million Euros, European Commission, 8 June 2022, https://ec.europa.eu/commission/presscorner/detail/en/IP_22_3543

41. Marc Bennetts, Interpol is "Useless" on Russian War Crimes, *The Times*, 13 October 2022, https://www.thetimes.co.uk/article/interpol-is-useless-on-russian-war-crimes-gp2jdnhpm

42. Lidia Kelly, Ukraine Asks Red Cross not to Open Office in Russia's Rostov-on-Don, Reuters, 27 March 2022, https://www.reuters.com/world/europe/ukraine-asks-red-cross-not-open-office-russias-rostov-on-don-2022-03-27/

43. Aaron Clements-Hunt, Supping with the Kremlin Devil: The Red Cross Dilemma, CEPA, 5 April 2022, https://cepa.org/article/supping-with-the-kremlin-devil-the-red-cross-dilemma/

44. Kuleba Calls for Setting up Procedure to Suspend Russia from OSCE, Ukrinform, 8 April 2022, https://www.ukrinform.net/rubric-ato/3452657-kuleba-calls-for-setting-up-procedure-to-suspend-russia-from-osce.html

45. Andrey Zagorski, The OSCE, Ukraine and Peace Process, Russian International Affairs Council, 12 August 2022, https://russiancouncil.ru/en/analytics-and-comments/comments/the-osce-ukraine-and-peace-process/

46. Rachel Treisman, Zelensky Urges UN Security Council to Boot Russia or Dissolve for World's Sake, NPR, 5 April 2022, https://www.npr.org/2022/04/05/1091050554/zelenskyy-un-security-council-speech

47. Kyslytsya Slams UN Security Council for its Impotence over Crisis Caused by Russian Invasion, Ukrinform, 20 April 2022, https://www.ukrinform.net/rubric-polytics/3462200-kyslytsya-slams-un-security-council-for-its-impotence-over-crisis-caused-by-russian-invasion.html

48. Dan Maurer, A U.N. Security Council Permanent Member's De Facto Immunity from Article 6 Expulsion: Russia's Fact or Fiction, Lawfare, 15 April 2022, https://www.lawfareblog.com/un-security-council-permanent-members-de-facto-immunity-article-6-expulsion-russias-fact-or-fiction

49. Stephen McGrath and Jamey Keaten, US to Seek Russia's Suspension from Human Rights Council, Associated Press, 5 April 2022, https://apnews.com/article/russia-ukraine-united-nations-general-assembly-kyiv-linda-thomas-greenfield-europe-aa1a1c7c6609873f0495c4bfb2ea257e

50. Interview with author, October 2022.

51. UN Approves Czech Republic to Replace Russia on Human Rights Council, RFE/RL, 10 May 2022, https://www.rferl.org/a/un-human-rights-council-russia-czech-republic/31843431.html

52. Ukraine Parliament has Recognized the Actions of the Russian Federation as Genocide against Ukrainians, *Ukrainskaya Pravda*, 14 April 2022, https://www.pravda.com.ua/eng/news/2022/04/14/7339618/

53. Ibid.

54. Interview with author, September 2022.

55. Interview with author, September 2022.

56. Julian Borger, Russia is Guilty of Inciting Genocide in Ukraine, Expert Report Concludes, *The Guardian*, 27 May 2022, https://www.theguardian.com/world/2022/may/27/russia-guilty-inciting-genocide-ukraine-expert-report

57. Victor Jack, Bucha Killings "Not Far Short of Genocide," Boris Johnson Says, *Politico*, 6 April 2022, https://www.politico.eu/article/boris-johnson-bucha-killings-ukraine-genocide-russia/

58. Joe Biden Accuses Vladimir Putin of Committing Genocide in Ukraine, *The Guardian*, 13 April 2022, https://www.theguardian.com/world/2022/apr/13/joe-biden-accuses-vladimir-putin-of-committing-genocide-in-ukraine

59. Peter Dickinson, Memo to Macron: Putin's Ukraine Genocide is not the Act of a Brother, Atlantic Council, 13 April 2022, https://www.atlanticcouncil.org/blogs/ukrainealert/memo-to-macron-putins-ukraine-genocide-is-not-the-act-of-a-brother/

60. Waitman Wade Beorn, No, Russia Isn't Committing "Genocide" in Ukraine, *The Washington Post*, 15 March 2022, https://www.washingtonpost.com/outlook/2022/03/15/genocide-ukraine-russia-zelensky/

61. Minoborony nazvalo kadry iz Buchi postanovkoy Kiyeva dlya zapadnykh SMI (The Ministry of Defence called the Footage from Bucha a Production of Kyiv for Western Media), RIA Novosti, 3 April 2022, https://ria.ru/20220403/minoborony-1781557525.html

62. Russia to Insist on UN Security Council Meeting on Bucha Situation on April 4—Envoy, TASS, 4 April 2022, https://tass.com/politics/1432217

63. Ibid.

64. Telegram, 3 April 2022, https://t.me/SolovievLive/98367

65. Rossiya sozyvayet Sovbez OON posle provokatsii v ukrainskoy Buche (Russia Convenes UN Security Council after Provocation in Ukrainian Bucha), Channel One, 4 April 2022, https://www.1tv.ru/news/2022–04–04/425506-rossiya_sozyvaet_sovet_bezopasnosti_oon_posle_provokatsii_v_ukrainskoy_buche

66. Zapad khochet sdelat' iz Buchi novuyu Srebrenitsu, govorit veteran «Al'fy» (West Wants to Make a New Srebrenica out of Bucha, says Alfa Veteran), RIA Novosti, 3 April 2022, https://ria.ru/20220403/ukraina-1781566047.html?in=t

67. Bucha Massacre: The Guardian Fails the Fake, *Pravda*, 25 April 2022, https://english.pravda.ru/news/hotspots/151417-bucha_massacre/

68. Minoborony: Ukrainskiy raketnyy divizion nanes udar po Kramatorsku (Defence Ministry: Ukrainian Missile Battalion Struck Kramatorsk), RIA Novosti, 8 April 2022, https://ria.ru/20220408/kramatorsk-1782524882.html

69. «Vooruzhennyye sily Rossii ne imeli ognevykh zadach v Kramatorske» (The Russian Armed Forces had no Fire Missions in Kramatorsk), *Kommersant*, 8 April 2022, https://www.kommersant.ru/doc/5303560

70. Yuri Nechaev, Zapadnyye SMI priznali, chto za obstrelom vokzala v Kramatorske stoit Kiyev (Western Media Acknowledged that Kyiv is Behind the Shelling of the Station in Kramatorsk), *Rossiyskaya Gazeta*, 13 April 2022, https://rg.ru/2022/04/13/zapadnye-smi-priznali-za-obstrelom-vokzala-v-kramatorske-stoit-kiev.html

71. Mason Clark and Kateryna Stepanenko, Russian Offensive Campaign Assessment, Understanding War, 8 April 2022, https://www.understanding-war.org/backgrounder/russian-offensive-campaign-assessment-april-8

72. Scott Lucas, Updated: More Russian Attacks on Oil Refineries in North Syria, EA Worldview, 15 March 2021, https://eaworldview.com/2021/03/pro-assad-attack-syria-oil-refineries/

73. Clark and Stepanenko, 2022.

74. Russians Published Evidence of Tochka-U Missile System Use in Ukraine by Their Troops, Mil.in.ua, 10 July 2022, https://mil.in.ua/en/news/russians-published-evidence-of-tochka-u-missile-system-use-in-ukraine-by-their-troops/#:~:text=As%20previously%20reported%2C%20Russia%20has,village%20of%20Desnianka%2C%20Chernihiv%20region

75. Adam Schreck and Cara Anna, Missile Kills at Least 52 at Crowded Ukrainian Train Station, Associated Press, 9 April 2022, https://apnews.com/article/russia-ukraine-europe-ap-top-news-migration-united-nations-ee2fa37bb0ace7b-4714c084998765f65

76. Rossiya reshila dosrochno vyyti iz Soveta OON po pravam cheloveka (Russia Decided to Withdraw Early from the UN Human Rights Council), RBC, 7 April 2022, https://www.rbc.ru/politics/07/04/2022/624f1a179a7947e70a2fac7d

77. Ekaterina Postnikova, Otbroshennyy sovet: chto oznachayet priostanovka chlenstva Rossii v SPCH OON? (Discarded Advice: What Does the Suspension of Russia's Membership in the UNHRC Mean?), *Izvestia*, 7 April 2022, https://iz.ru/1317269/ekaterina-postnikova/otbroshennyi-sovet-chto-znachit-priostanovka-chlenstva-rossii-v-spch-oon

78. Interview with author, October 2022.

79. Ibid.

80. V ofise OBSE v Luganske nashli server dlya peredachi sekretnykh dannykh (In the OSCE Office Luhansk Found a Server for the Transmission of Classified Data), *Izvestia*, 16 April 2022, https://iz.ru/1321721/2022–04-16/v-ofise-obse-v-luganske-nashli-server-dlia-peredachi-zasekrechennykh-dannykh

81. Rossiya vyshla iz SE, no yest' smysl v OON i OBSE (Russia Left the CE but the UN and the OSCE Make Sense), RIA Novosti, 6 April 2022, https://ria.ru/20220406/kosachev-1782019581.html

82. Vyacheslav Volodin: yesli s Viktorom Medvedchukom chto-to sluchitsya, otve-chat' pridetsya Zelenskomu (Vyacheslav Volodin: If Something Happens to Viktor Medvedchuk, Zelensky will Have to Answer), The State Duma, 13 April 2022, http://duma.gov.ru/news/54061/

83. Verkhovnyy sud rassmotrit vopros o priznanii terroristicheskogo batal'ona «Azov» (The Supreme Court will Consider the Recognition of the Terrorist Battalion "Azov"), RBC, 17 May 2022, https://www.rbc.ru/politics/17/05/20 22/6283a7a39a794704b0c988c7

84. Slutskiy prizval primenit' smertnuyu kazn' k plennym boyevikam «Azova» (Slutsky Urged to Apply the Death Penalty to Captured Azov Fighters), Mk.ru, 17 May 2022, https://www.mk.ru/politics/2022/05/17/sluckiy-prizval-prime-nyat-k-plennym-boycam-azova-smertnuyu-kazn.html

85. Resheniye Prinyato. Zelensky I Natsisty Kiyeva Zhdot Tribunala (The Decision is Made. Zelensky and the Nazis of Kyiv are Waiting for the Tribunal), Tsargrad, 3 April 2022, https://tsargrad.tv/news/reshenie-prinjato-zelenskogo-i-nacis-tov-kieva-zhdjot-tribunal_523337

86. Ekaterina Lazareva, Deputat Gosdumy: Rossiya imeyet pravo ustroit' sud nad Zelenskim i natsistami (State Duma Deputy: Russia has a Right to Arrange a Trial of Zelensky and the Nazis), Ura.ru, 7 April 2022, https://ura.news/arti-cles/1036284315

87. Lyudi s «Azovstali»: chto rasskazali evakuirovannyye s territorii zavoda v Mariupole (People from Azovstal: What the Evacuees from the Territory of the Plant in Mariupol Said), *Izvestia*, 2 May 2022, https://iz.ru/1329079/anton-lavrov-roman-kretcul-bogdan-stepovoi/liudi-iz-azovstali-chto-rasskazali-evakuirovannye-s-territorii-zavoda-v-mariupole

88. Zhiteli Mariupolya rasskazali o prestupleniyakh ukrainskikh natsbatov (Residents of Mariupol Spoke About the Crimes of Ukrainian National Battalions), RIA Novosti, 6 April 2022, https://ria.ru/20220406/mariupol-1782024512.html

89. Timofey Sergeytsev, Что России делать с Украиной? (What Should Russia do with Ukraine?), RIA Novosti, 3 April 2022, https://ria.ru/20220403/ukraina-1781469605.html

90. Anton Shekhovstov, The Shocking Inspiration for Putin's Atrocities in Ukraine, *Haaretz*, 13 April 2022, https://www.haaretz.com/israel-news/2022-04-13/ty-article-opinion/the-shocking-inspiration-for-russias-atrocities-in-ukraine/00000180–5bd0-d718-afd9-dffc6b210000

91. Patrushev: Zapad sozdal imperiyu lzhi, predpolagayushchuyu unichtozheniye Rossii (Patrushev: West has created an Empire of Lies, Involving the Destruction of Russia), *Rossiyskaya Gazeta*, 26 April 2022, https://rg.ru/2022/04/26/patru-shev-zapad-sozdal-imperiiu-lzhi-predpolagaiushchuiu-unichtozhenie-rossii.html

92. Karaganov, 15 April 2022.

93. Advokat obrisoval budushcheye sdannogo «Azova» (The Lawyer Outlined the Future of the Surrendered "Azov"), Mk.ru, 17 May 2022, https://www.mk.ru/politics/2022/05/17/yurist-obrisoval-budushhee-sdavshikhsya-v-plen-azovcev.html

94. Telegram, 17 May 2022, https://t.me/voenkorKotenok/36464

95. Edward Fishman, Why the US has Hit Some Russian Oligarchs with Sanctions but not Others, *Financial Times*, 13 April 2022, https://www.ft.com/content/238aba34-7a4d-45f2-9488-3c28e8dbc73a

96. US Carves out Mechanism for Insulating Russian Fertilizer Exports from Sanctions, *The Economic Times*, 1 April 2022, https://economictimes.indiatimes.com/news/international/world-news/us-carves-out-mechanism-for-insulating-russian-fertilizer-exports-from-sanctions/articleshow/90577961.cms?from=mdr

97. EU Adopts Fifth Round of Sanctions Against Russia over its Military Aggression Against Ukraine, European Council, 8 April 2022, https://www.consilium.europa.eu/en/press/press-releases/2022/04/08/eu-adopts-fifth-round-of-sanctions-against-russia-over-its-military-aggression-against-ukraine/

98. Mateusz Morawiecki, Poland's 10-Point Plan to Save Ukraine, *Politico*, 25 March 2022, https://www.politico.eu/article/poland-10-point-plan-save-ukraine/

99. Russia Sees 38% Rise in Energy Export Earnings this Year: Report, Al Jazeera, 17 August 2022, https://www.aljazeera.com/economy/2022/8/17/russia-sees-38-rise-in-energy-export-earnings-this-year-reuters

100. Putin Says Russia will Enforce Rouble Payment for Gas from Friday, Reuters, 31 March 2022, https://www.reuters.com/business/energy/putin-says-russian-gas-must-be-paid-roubles-friday-2022-03-31/

101. Kremlin Warns West: Rouble-for-Gas Scheme is the Prototype, Euractiv, 4 April 2022, https://www.euractiv.com/section/economy-jobs/news/kremlin-warns-west-rouble-for-gas-scheme-is-the-prototype/

102. Sam Meredith and Natasha Turak, EU Struggles to Reach an Agreement on Russian Oil Embargo as Hungary Holds Firm, CNBC, 30 May 2022, https://www.cnbc.com/2022/05/30/eu-to-discuss-watered-down-oil-embargo-on-russia-as-hungary-holds-firm.html

103. Jennifer Rankin, Hopes for EU ban on Russian oil despite Hungary Comparing Plan to "Nuclear Bomb," *The Guardian*, 10 May 2022, https://www.theguardian.com/world/2022/may/10/hopes-raised-for-eu-oil-ban-on-russia-despite-hungary-comparing-plan-to-nuclear-bomb

104. After Orban Pipes up, Hungary Skips Russian Oil Ban, *Politico*, 31 May 2022, https://www.politico.eu/article/orban-hungary-eu-oil-ban-exempt-euco/

105. Denmark, U.S. Sending Kyiv Harpoon Missiles and Howitzers, Says Ukrainian Defence Minister, RFE/RL, 28 May 2022, https://www.rferl.org/a/ukraine-harpoon-missiles-howitzers-denmark-united-states/31872812.html

106. Cristina Gallardo, UK and Germany Won't Send Tanks to Ukraine, *Politico*, 8 April 2022, https://www.politico.eu/article/uk-germany-rule-out-send-tanks-ukraine/

107. Swiss Veto German Request to Re-Export Tank Ammunition to Ukraine, Reuters, 26 April 2022, https://www.reuters.com/business/aerospace-defense/swiss-veto-german-request-re-export-tank-ammunitionukraine-2022-04-26/

108. Putin says West Treating Russian Culture like "Cancelled" JK Rowling, *The Guardian*, 25 March 2022.

109. Lavrov Hits out at "Absurd" Level of Racism Against Russians in Western Countries, TASS, 6 May 2022, https://tass.com/world/1447767

110. Bucha i kontsentrirovannoye zlo: posledniy argument protiv russkikh (Bucha and Concentrated Evil: The Last Argument Against the Russians), RIA Novosti, 5 April 2022, https://ria.ru/20220405/rusofobiya-1781778401.html

111. Telegram, 15 April 2022, https://t.me/margaritasimonyan/11082

112. Maksim Shugaley privez neobkhodimyye kantstovary detyam iz Pervomayska dlya ucheby v shkolakh (Maxim Shugaley Brought the Necessary Stationery for Children from Pervomaisk to Study in Schools), RIAFAN, 16 April 2022, https://riafan.ru/23076635-maksim_shugalei_privez_detyam_iz_pervomaiska_neobhodimie_kantstovari_dlya_obucheniya_v_shkolah

113. Interview with St. Petersburg-based academic Alexei Miller, September 2022.

114. Putin Agrees that US is Ready to Resist Russia "to the last Ukrainian," TASS, 12 April 2022, https://tass.com/politics/1436579

115. Russian Church Leader Appears to Blame Gay Pride Parades for Ukraine War, *The Moscow Times*, 7 March 2022, https://www.themoscowtimes.com/2022/03/07/russian-church-leader-appears-to-blame-gay-pride-parades-for-ukraine-war-a76803

116. Katherine Kelaidis, The Russian Patriarch Just Gave his Most Dangerous Speech Yet—And Almost No One in the West has Noticed, Religion Dispatches, 4 April 2022, https://religiondispatches.org/the-russian-patriarch-just-gave-his-most-dangerous-speech-yet-and-almost-no-one-in-the-west-has-noticed/

117. Patriarkh Kirill zayavil, chto Rossiya ni na kogo ne napadala (Patriarch Kirill Says Russia has Never Attacked Anyone), RIA Novosti, 3 May 2022, https://ria.ru/20220503/patriarkh-1786640294.html?in=t

118. Liam James, Ukraine War: Russian state TV claims NATO has Started "World War 3," *The Independent*, 31 May 2022, https://www.independent.co.uk/news/world/europe/russia-ukraine-world-war-3-b2091224.html

119. Simon Childs, "It is What it Is:" Russian State TV in Normal Discussion About Nuclear War, VICE, 28 April 2022, https://www.vice.com/en/article/g5q73m/it-is-what-it-is-russian-state-tv-in-normal-discussion-about-nuclear-war

120. Julia Davis, Russian Citizens are Now Being Prepared for Nuclear War, *The Daily Beast*, 21 December 2021, https://www.thedailybeast.com/russian-citizens-are-now-being-prepped-for-nuclear-war

121. Russia-Ukraine War: Lavrov Warns of Risk of Nuclear Conflict, Al Jazeera, 26 April 2022, https://www.aljazeera.com/news/2022/4/26/russia-ukraine-war-lavrov-warns-of-risk-of-nuclear-conflict

122. Vyacheslav Volodin: Rossiya mozhet primenit' yadernoye oruzhiye tol'ko v otvet na yadernyy udar (Vyacheslav Volodin: Russia Can Use Nuclear Weapons Only as Response to Nuclear Strike), The State Duma, 5 May 2022, http://duma.gov.ru/news/54237/

123. Russia's "Satan-2" Missile Changes Little for U.S., Scholars Say, *The Washington Post*, 20 April 2022, https://www.washingtonpost.com/world/2022/04/20/satan-2-icbm/&cd=2&hl=en&ct=clnk&gl=uk/

124. S Plesetska osushchestvlen uspeshnyy pusk mezhkontinental'noy ballisticheskoy rakety «Sarmat» (A Successful Launch of the Intercontinental Ballistic Missile "Sarmat" was Carried out from Plesetsk), *Izvestia*, 20 April 2022, https://iz.ru/1323849/2022-04-20/s-plesetcka-proveden-uspeshnyi-pusk-mezhkontinentalnoi-ballisticheskoi-rakety-sarmat

125. Oksana Belkina, Effekt bumeranga: kak sanktsii udaryat po yevropeyskim bankam (Boomerang Effect: How Sanctions will Hit European Banks), *Izvestia*, 12 March 2022, https://iz.ru/1303914/oksana-belkina/effekt-bumeranga-kak-sanktcii-udariat-po-evropeiskim-bankam

126. Sergey Savchuk, Gazovyy ul'timatum Putina. U Yevropy net variantov (Putin's Gas Ultimatum. Europe has No Options), RIA Novosti, 24 March 2022, https://ria.ru/20220324/gaz-1779749576.html?in=t

127. Viktoria Nikiforova, Velikobritaniya tshchatel'no okhranyayet svoyu glavnuyu taynu (Britain Carefully Guards its Main Secret), RIA Novosti, 16 May 2022, https://ria.ru/20220516/tseny-1788677778.html

128. Delyagin prizval vyyti iz MVF (Delyagin Urged Withdrawal from the IMF), If24.ru, 2 March 2022, https://www.if24.ru/delyagin-prizval-vyjti-iz-mvf/

129. Matviyenko otsenila veroyatnost' vvedeniya embargo YES na postavki gaza iz Rossii (Matviyenko Assessed the Likelihood of an EU Embargo on Gas Supplies from Russia), *Parlamentskaya Gazeta*, 14 April 2022, https://www.

pnp.ru/economics/matvienko-ocenila-veroyatnost-embargo-es-na-post-avki-gaza-iz-rossii.html

130. Andrey Sushentsov, There is Still Room for Compromise Between Russia and the West, RT, 15 April 2022, https://www.rt.com/russia/553913-ukrai-nian-crisis-stress-test-globalisation/

131. Andrew Roth and Pjotr Sauer, "Our Voices are Louder if We Stay", *The Guardian*, 27 March 2022, https://www.theguardian.com/world/2022/mar/27/our-voices-are-louder-if-we-stay-russian-anti-war-activists-refuse-to-flee

132. As Families Seek Truth, Kremlin Refuses to Discuss Moskva Sinking, Al Jazeera, 19 April 2022, https://www.aljazeera.com/news/2022/4/19/as-fami-lies-seek-truth-kremlin-refuses-to-discuss-moskva-sinking

133. Interview with author, September 2022.

134. Russian Tycoon Oleg Tinkov Denounces "Insane War" in Ukraine, *The Guardian*, 20 April 2022, https://www.theguardian.com/world/2022/apr/20/russian-tycoon-oleg-tinkov-denounces-insane-war-in-ukraine

135. Russian Tycoon Tinkov Claims he was Forced to Sell Bank Stake after Denouncing "Crazy War," *Financial Times*, 2 May 2022, https://www.ft.com/content/41b887c4-ed52–4cf0–8a6f-394d578ea6a2

136. Shaun Walker and Andrew Roth, "I'm Never Going Back": The High-Profile Russian Defectors Rejecting War, *The Guardian*, 25 May 2022, https://www.theguardian.com/world/2022/may/25/im-never-going-back-the-high-pro-file-russian-defectors-rejecting-war

137. «Kadyrov, kak i lyuboy drugoy grazhdanin Rossii, imeyet pravo na sobstven-nuyu tochku zreniya» (Kadyrov like any other citizen of Russia, has the right to his own point of view), Fontanka.ru, 31 March 2022, https://www.fon-tanka.ru/2022/03/31/70732877/

138. Telegram, 20 April 2022, https://t.me/strelkovii/2455

139. Dugin: novyy miroporyadok slozhitsya po rezul'tatam spetsoperatsii na Ukraine (Dugin: The New World Order will be Formed as a Result of Special Military Operation in Ukraine), RIA Novosti, 11 April 2022, https://ria.ru/20220411/miroporyadok-1782934426.html

140. Telegram, 6 April 2022, https://t.me/SolovievLive/99168

141. Andrei Kortunov, Search for Compromise or a Demand for Surrender, Russian International Affairs Council, 14 April 2022, https://russiancouncil.ru/en/analytics-and-comments/analytics/search-for-a-compromise-or-demand-for-surrender/

142. Ivan Timofeev, No Time for Fatalism, Russian International Affairs Council, 27 April 2022, https://russiancouncil.ru/en/analytics-and-comments/analyt-ics/no-time-for-fatalism/

6. RUSSIA'S SUMMER WAR: MINOR VICTORIES AND MANUFAC-
TURED CRISES

1. Putin poruchil obespechit' otdykh boytsam, osvobozhdavshim LNR (Putin
Instructed to Provide Rest for Soldiers who Liberated the LNR), *Izvestia*, 4 July
2022, https://iz.ru/1359352/2022-07-04/putin-poruchil-predostavit-otdykh-
osvobozhdavshim-lnr-voennosluzhashchim

2. Zhiteli Lisichanska vstrechali armii Rossii i LNR (Residents of Lysychansk
Met the Armies of Russia and LNR), RIA Novosti, 4 July 2022, https://ria.
ru/20220704/lisichansk-1800079926.html

3. Luganskaya Narodnaya Respublika Polnostyu Osvobozhdena Ofitsalnoye
Zayavleniye (The Luhansk People's Republic has Been Completely Liberated,
Official Statement), Tsargrad, 3 July 2022, https://tsargrad.tv/news/lugans-
kaja-narodnaja-respublika-osvobozhdena-polnostju-oficialnoe-zajavle-
nie_577895

4. Lisa Haseldine, Chechen Warlord Kadyrov Mocks Zelensky in Spoof Video,
The Spectator, 4 July 2022, https://www.spectator.co.uk/article/chechen-war-
lord-kadyrov-mocks-zelensky-in-spoof-video

5. Sam Jones, Putin Declares Victory in Luhansk after Fall of Lysychansk, *The
Guardian*, 4 July 2022, https://www.theguardian.com/world/2022/jul/04/
ukraine-donetsk-next-russian-target-after-capture-of-luhansk-says-governor

6. Russian Offensive Campaign Assessment, ISW, 21 May 2022, https://www.
understandingwar.org/backgrounder/russian-offensive-campaign-assessment-
may-21

7. Telegram, 21 May 2022, https://t.me/epoddubny/10778

8. Russian Offensive Campaign Assessment, ISW, 28 May 2022, https://www.
understandingwar.org/backgrounder/russian-offensive-campaign-assessment-
may-28

9. Some 70% of Severodonetsk Controlled by Russian Occupiers, Part of Ukrainian
Defenders Retreat to More Advantageous Pre-Prepared Positions, Interfax,
1 June 2022, https://en.interfax.com.ua/news/general/836273.html

10. Ukrainian Troops Beat Back Russians in Battle for Severodonetsk, RFI, 6 June
2022, https://www.rfi.fr/en/international/20220606-ukrainian-troops-beat-
back-russians-in-battle-for-severodonetsk

11. Kremlin Orders Army Commander Dvornikov to Take Severodonetsk by
June 10—Regional Governor, New Voice of Ukraine, 5 June 2022, https://eng-
lish.nv.ua/nation/kremlin-orders-commander-dvornikov-to-take-severodo-
netsk-by-june-10–50247754.html

12. Pjotr Sauer, Fighting in Eastern Ukraine Rages as Severodonetsk Chemical
Plant Hit, *The Guardian*, 12 June 2022, https://www.theguardian.com/

world/2022/jun/12/fighting-eastern-ukraine-rages-sievierodonetsk-chemical-plant-hit

13. Ibid.

14. Pjotr Sauer, Ukraine Ignores Russian Ultimatum to Surrender Severodonetsk, *The Guardian*, 15 June 2022, https://www.theguardian.com/world/2022/jun/15/ukraine-ignores-russian-ultimatum-to-surrender-sievierodonetsk

15. Fall of Severodonetsk Russia's Biggest Victory Since Mariupol, Al Jazeera, 25 June 2022, https://www.aljazeera.com/news/2022/6/25/fall-of-severodo-netsk-is-russias-biggest-victory-since-mariupol

16. Russian Offensive Campaign Assessment, ISW, 17 June 2022, https://www.understandingwar.org/backgrounder/russian-offensive-campaign-assessment-june-17

17. James Kilner, "Butcher of Aleppo" Sacked as Vladimir Putin Shakes up Russian Top Command Again, *The Telegraph*, 25 June 2022, https://www.telegraph.co.uk/world-news/2022/06/25/russia-shakes-up-top-command-ex-syria-war-general-sacked/

18. Telegram, 27 June 2022, https://t.me/agurulev/1694

19. Aidar Battalion Command, Staff Surrender Near Severodonetsk—Source, TASS, 18 June 2022, https://tass.com/defense/1468091

20. Telegram, 27 June 2022, https://t.me/strelkovii/2805

21. «Izbavilis' ot stereotipa Krasnoy Armii»: Arestovich nazval otstupleniye ot Lisichanska dostizheniyem dlya Ukrainy (We Got Rid of the Red Army Stereotype: Arestovycvh Called the Retreat from Lysychansk an Achievemnet for Ukraine), Top War, 4 July 2022, https://topwar.ru/198585-izbavilis-ot-krasnoarmejskogo-stereotipa-arestovich-nazval-otstuplenie-iz-lisichanska-dostizheniem-dlja-ukrainy.html

22. Russian Offensive Campaign Assessment, ISW, 25 July 2022, https://understandingwar.org/backgrounder/russian-offensive-campaign-assessment-july-25

23. Russian Advance Struggling in Donbas, Unlikely to Hit Deadline: UK, *Newsweek*, 5 September 2022, https://www.newsweek.com/russian-advance-struggling-donbas-u-k-1739786

24. Russia has "Strategically Lost" War, Says UK Defence Chief, as Lavrov Says Moscow Unashamed, *The Guardian*, 17 June 2022, https://www.theguardian.com/world/2022/jun/17/russia-has-strategically-lost-war-declares-uk-admiral-as-lavrov-says-no-shame-in-war-crimes

25. Telegram, 9 August 2022, https://t.me/strelkovii/3064

26. Steve Holland, Russia's Military Suffering Manpower Shortages—U.S. Intelligence, Reuters, 31 August 2022, https://www.reuters.com/world/europe/russias-military-suffering-manpower-shortages-us-intelligence-2022–08–31/

27. Russian Offensive Campaign Assessment, Critical Threats, 16 July 2022, https://

www.criticalthreats.org/analysis/russian-offensive-campaign-assessment-july-16

28. Russian War Report: Ukraine Uses HIMARS Effectively to Hit Russian Ammo Dumps, Atlantic Council, 8 July 2022, https://www.atlanticcouncil.org/blogs/new-atlanticist/russian-war-report-ukraine-himars-russian-ammo-dumps/

29. Historic Wooden Orthodox Church Burns Down in Donetsk Monastic Complex, Euronews, 5 June 2022, https://www.euronews.com/2022/06/05/historic-wooden-orthodox-church-burns-down-in-donetsk-monastic-complex

30. Response to author, 9 June 2022.

31. Response to author, 9 June 2022.

32. Telegram, 29 July 2022, https://t.me/V_Zelenskiy_official/2724

33. No International Missions Allowed to Olenivka Following Russian Terrorist Attack—Podolyak, Ukrinform, 5 September 2022, https://www.ukrinform.net/rubric-ato/3565886-no-international-missions-allowed-to-olenivka-following-russian-terrorist-attack-polodyak.html

34. Opublikovany spiski pogibshikh pri nalete na SIZO v Yelenovke (Published Lists of those Killed in the Strike on the Pre-Trial Detention Center in Yelenovka), RIA Novosti, 30 July 2022, https://crimea.ria.ru/20220730/opublikovany-spiski-pogibshikh-pri-udare-po-sizo-v-elenovke-1124005749.html

35. Russia Claims Ukraine Used U.S. Arms to Kill Jailed POWs. Evidence Tells a Different Story, CNN, 11 August 2022, https://edition.cnn.com/interactive/2022/08/europe/olenivka-donetsk-prison-attack/

36. Ukraine Denounces Russian Embassy Tweet Calling for "Humiliating Death" of Azov Regiment Members, RFE/RL, 30 July 2022, https://www.rferl.org/a/ukraine-russian-embassy-tweet-azov/31966871.html

37. Russia Designates Azov Regiment a "Terrorist Group," Euractiv, 3 August 2022, https://www.euractiv.com/section/global-europe/news/russia-designates-ukraines-azov-regiment-a-terrorist-group/

38. Ekspert: Rossiya smozhet unichtozhit' terroristov «Azova» po vsemu miru (Expert: Russia will be able to destroy the terrorists of "Azov" Around the World), Vzglyad, 2 August 2022, https://vz.ru/news/2022/8/2/1170605.html

39. Russia Outlines Plans to Rebuild Ukraine's Devastated Mariupol—Official, The Moscow Times, 1 August 2022, https://www.themoscowtimes.com/2022/08/01/russia-outlines-plans-to-rebuild-ukraines-devastated-mariupol-official-a78461

40. Mariupol Reconstruction Will Cost More than $14B, Take Up to 10 Years—City Council, Ukrinform, 6 July 2022, https://www.ukrinform.net/rubric-ato/3523163-mariupol-reconstruction-will-cost-more-than-14b-take-up-to-10-years-city-council.html

41. The Occupiers Want to Demolish Azovstal, Ukrainskaya Pravda, 18 May 2022, https://www.pravda.com.ua/eng/news/2022/05/18/7346969/

42. V DNR nadeyutsya, chto Kadyrov pomozhet vosstanovit' mechet' v Mariupole (The DNR Hopes that Kadyrov Will Help Restore the Mosque in Mariupol), RIA Novosti, 27 July 2022, https://ria.ru/20220727/mariupol-1805317174.html?in=t

43. Luc Lacroix and Alexandra Dalsbaek, A First Look Inside Occupied Mariupol, a City Rebuilding Itself Yet Surrounded by Death, *The Telegraph*, 21 June 2022, https://www.telegraph.co.uk/world-news/2022/06/21/first-look-inside-occupied-mariupol-city-rebuilding-yet-surrounded/

44. Ukraine to Launch Counter-Offensive by Mid-June: Zelensky Aide, Nikkei, 2 May 2022, https://asia.nikkei.com/Editor-s-Picks/Interview/Ukraine-to-launch-counteroffensive-by-mid-June–Zelenskyy-aide

45. John Psaropoulos, Ukraine Plans on Summer Counter-Offensive to Oust Russian Forces, Al Jazeera, 30 June 2022, https://www.aljazeera.com/news/2022/6/30/ukraine-says-summer-counteroffensive-will-oust-russia

46. Ukraine Has One Million Ready for Fightback to Recapture South, *The Times*, 10 July 2022, https://www.thetimes.co.uk/article/ukraine-has-one-million-ready-for-fightback-to-recapture-south-3rhkrhstf

47. Dan Sabbagh, Ukraine Needs Many More Rocket Launchers from West, Says Advisor, *The Guardian*, 6 June 2022, https://www.theguardian.com/world/2022/jun/06/ukraine-needs-many-more-rocket-launchers-from-west-says-adviser

48. Dan Sabbagh and Luke Harding, Ukraine Aiming to Create Chaos Within Russian Forces, Zelensky Advisor Says, *The Guardian*, 16 August 2022, https://www.theguardian.com/world/2022/aug/16/creating-chaos-zelenskiys-adviser-outlines-ukraines-military-strategy

49. Ibid.

50. Paraic O'Brien, Russia About to "Run Out of Steam" in Ukraine, Says MI6 Chief, Channel 4, 21 July 2022, https://www.channel4.com/news/russia-about-to-run-out-of-steam-in-ukraine-says-mi6-chief

51. Ukraine Tries to Make the Case that it Can Win Citing Recent Strikes, *The New York Times*, 21 July 2022, https://www.nytimes.com/2022/07/21/world/europe/ukraine-russia-weapons-war.html

52. Ofis Zelenskogo priznalsya v feyke kontrnastupleniya na Khersone (Zelensky's Office Admits to Fake Counteroffensive in Kherson), Lenta.ru, 9 August 2022, https://lenta.ru/news/2022/08/09/counteradvance/

53. Telegram, 26 May 2022, https://t.me/russ_orientalist/10964

54. Telegram, 1 June 2022, https://t.me/strelkovii/2631

55. Telegram, 26 May 2022, https://t.me/m0sc0wcalling/6200

56. Vadym Skibits'kyy, HUR Minoborony: Vysokotochna zbroya v Rosiyi uzhe na mezhi (Vadym Skibitsky, Head of Ministry of Defence: High-Precision

Weapons in Russia are Already on the Verge), RBC.ua, 27 August 2022, https://www.rbc.ua/ukr/news/vadim-skibitskiy-gur-minoborony-vysokotoch-noe-1661514783.html

57. Ibid.

58. Russia May be Using Unguided "Dumb" Bombs in Ukraine War—U.S. Official, Reuters, 9 March 2022, https://www.reuters.com/world/russia-may-be-using-unguided-dumb-bombs-ukraine-war-us-official-2022-03-09/

59. Dana Hordiichuk, Russia Fired $200 Million Worth of Missiles at Ukraine Over the Weekend—Forbes, *Ukrainskaya Pravda*, 27 June 2022, https://www.pravda.com.ua/eng/news/2022/06/27/7355046/

60. Russian Federation Will Run out of Shells, Artillery and Armoured Vehicles by Year End, *Ukrainskaya Pravda*, 31 August 2022, https://www.pravda.com.ua/eng/news/2022/08/31/7365546/#:~:text=Russia%20will%20face%20an%20acute,and%20military%20equipment%20for%20Russia

61. Tim Lister, Snake Island: The Tiny Speck of Land Playing an Outsized Role in Russia's War on Ukraine, CNN, 13 May 2022, https://edition.cnn.com/2022/05/13/europe/snake-island-ukraine-strategic-war-cmd-intl/index.html

62. Ibid.

63. Ukraine Battles Russia in Black Sea Over Strategic Island, Swiss Info, 11 May 2022, https://www.swissinfo.ch/eng/ukraine-battles-russia-in-black-sea-over-strategic-snake-island/47585550

64. Ibid.

65. Ukraine Lines Up Russia's Vsevolod Bobrov Ship Off Coast of Snake Island, Ukrinform, 12 May 2022, https://www.ukrinform.net/rubric-ato/3481792-ukraine-lines-up-russias-vsevolod-bobrov-ship-off-coast-of-snake-island.html

66. Ukraine Military Shoot Down Russia's Ka-52 Approaching Snake Island, Ukrinform, 30 June 2022, https://www.ukrinform.net/rubric-ato/3519074-ukrainian-military-shoot-down-russias-ka52-approaching-snake-island.html

67. Telegram, 30 June 2022, https://t.me/rian_ru/169290

68. Telegram, 7 July 2022, https://t.me/tsargradtv/19429

69. Voyennyy ekspert predskazal Zmeinomu ostrovu novyye boi (Military Expert Predicted New Battles for Snake Island), *Izvestia*, 22 June 2022, https://iz.ru/1353420/2022-06-22/voennyi-ekspert-sprognoziroval-novye-boi-za-ostrov-zmeinyi

70. Telegram, 26 June 2022, https://t.me/rybar/34418

71. Telegram, 28 June 2022, https://t.me/agurulev/1705

72. Interview with Volodymyr Dubovyk, September 2022.

73. Russian Forces Strike Ukrainian Weapons Hangars in Kremechug, Top Brass Reports, TASS, 28 June 2022, https://tass.com/defense/1472531

74. Russian Offensive Campaign, ISW, 1 June 2022, https://www.understanding-war.org/backgrounder/russian-offensive-campaign-assessment-june-1

75. Eyeing a City Captured by Russia, Ukraine Prepares an Ambitious Counterattack, *The New York Times*, 25 July 2022, https://www.nytimes.com/2022/07/25/world/europe/ukraine-kherson-russia-counterattack.html

76. Resupply for Russians in Kherson Reliant on Two Pontoon Crossings—British Intelligence, Ukrinform, 13 August 2022, https://www.ukrinform.net/rubric-ato/3549814-resupply-for-russians-in-kherson-reliant-on-two-pontoon-cross-ings-british-intelligence.html

77. Russia Leaves 20,000 Soldiers Stranded in Tactical Withdrawal to the East, *The Telegraph*, 14 August 2022, https://www.telegraph.co.uk/worldnews/2022/08/14/russia-leaves-10000-soldiers-stranded-tactical-withdrawal-west/

78. George Allison, Russian Forces Preparing for Ukrainian Counterattack, 6 August 2022, https://ukdefencejournal.org.uk/russian-forces-preparing-for-ukrainian-counterattack/

79. Aleksandra Klitina, Kherson Partisans Kill Russia-Installed Local Official, *Kyiv Post*, 24 June 2022, https://www.kyivpost.com/russias-war/kherson-partisans-kill-russia-installed-local-official.html

80. Tim Lister and Sanyo Fylppov, Traitor or Hero? Ukraine Finds it Tough to Identify Russian Collaborators, CNN, 9 June 2022, https://edition.cnn.com/2022/06/08/europe/ukraine-hunt-for-collaborators-intl/index.html

81. Olena Mukhina, Growing Partisan Movement of Kherson Oblast Now Bombs Collaborators, Euromaidan Press, 25 June 2022, https://euromaidanpress.com/2022/06/25/growing-partisan-movement-of-kherson-oblast-now-bombs-collaborators/

82. Over 10,000 Kherson Residents Receive Russian Passports in One Month, TASS, 12 July 2022, https://tass.com/world/1478567

83. Iryna Romaliyska, Kherson Clampdown: Russian Authorities Going Door-to-Door, Mandating Russian Passports, Official Says, RFE/RL, 15 August 2022, https://www.rferl.org/a/kherson-clampdown-russia-passports-ukraine/31989546.html

84. Ruble Zone will be Introduced in Kherson Region from May 1, TASS, 28 April 2022, https://tass.com/economy/1444801

85. Russia has Blocked 20-Million Tons of Grain from Being Exported from Ukraine, NPR, 3 June 2022, https://www.npr.org/2022/06/03/1102990029/russia-has-blocked-20-million-tons-of-grain-from-being-exported-from-ukraine

86. Ibid.

87. Tony Wesolowsky, Can Grain Trains Save Ukrainian Farmers and Avert a Global

Food Crisis?, RFE/RL, 5 June 2022, https://www.rferl.org/a/ukriane-grain-trains-strain/31884299.html

88. Euractiv, Silos on the Ukraine Border Would Keep Grain out of Russian Hands, 17 June 2022, https://www.euractiv.com/section/global-europe/news/silos-on-ukraine-border-would-keep-grain-out-of-russian-hands-says-us/

89. Servet Gungerigok, Russia's War in Ukraine Exacerbating Global Food Crisis: U.S. Diplomat, Anadolu Agency, 30 March 2022, https://www.aa.com.tr/en/americas/russias-war-in-ukraine-exacerbating-global-food-crisis-us-diplo-mat/2549742

90. Eddy Wax, Poland Says Biden's Plan to Export Ukrainian Grain "Interesting" but Will Take Months, *Politico*, 15 June 2022, https://www.politico.eu/article/poland-biden-ukraine-grain-plan-interesting-take-months/

91. Lizzy Davies, Aid Agencies Race to Get Food Supplies to Ukrainian Cities at Risk of Siege, *The Guardian*, 17 March 2022, https://www.theguardian.com/global-development/2022/mar/17/aid-agencies-race-food-to-ukraine-cit-ies-kyiv-kharkiv-dnipro

92. Wesolowsky, 2022.

93. UN Warns of Hunger Risk as Talks Stall over Ukraine Grain Blockade, *Financial Times*, 8 June 2022, https://www.ft.com/content/5946a436-b27c-49b2–8ced-470442a03e86

94. Edith Lederer, UN Food Chief: Ukraine's War Food Crisis is Worst Since World War II, Associated Press, 30 March 2022, https://apnews.com/article/russia-ukraine-business-africa-europe-united-nations-c0aa09215a99cb625c57f-cb40f7df8bf

95. Ibid.

96. Gungerigok, 2022.

97. Ukraine and the Food and Fuel Crisis, 4 Things to Know, UN Women, 22 September 2022, https://www.unwomen.org/en/news-stories/feature-story/2022/09/ukraine-and-the-food-and-fuel-crisis-4-things-to-know#:-:text=As%20the%20war%20in%2Ukraine, 19%2C%20climate%20change%20and%20conflict

98. War in Ukraine Threatens to Unleash "Unprecedented Wave" of Global Hunger and Destitution, UN Chief, Sustainable Development Goals, 8 June 2022, https://www.un.org/sustainabledevelopment/blog/2022/06/war-in-ukraine-threatens-to-unleash-unprecedented-wave-of-global-hunger-and-destitution-warns-un-chief/#:-:text=World%20Food%20Programme%20estimates%20show,to%20323%20million%20in%202022

99. Alena Uzbekova, Dayte ukho (Give an Ear), *Rossiyskaya Gazeta*, 15 June 2022, https://rg.ru/2022/06/14/podajte-kolos.html

100. Rossiya zapodozrila YES v nakoplenii ukrainskogo zerna vmesto eksporta nuzhdayushchimsya (Russia Suspected the EU of Accumulating Ukrainian Grain Instead of Exporting to the Needy), Lenta.ru, 19 May 2022, https://lenta.ru/news/2022/05/19/zerna/

101. Russia Offers Safe Passage for Ukraine Grain, Not Responsible for Corridors, Reuters, 15 June 2022, https://www.reuters.com/world/europe/russia-offers-safe-passage-ukraine-grain-not-responsible-corridors-2022-06-15/

102. Minoborony pokazalo, kak rossiyskiye sapery pomogayut ukrainskim agrariyam (The Ministry of Defence Showed How Russian Sappers Help Ukrainian Farmers), RIA Novosti, 13 April 2022, https://ria.ru/20220413/sapery-1783253025.html?in=t

103. Ukraina dumayet ob eksporte zerna: a chto zhrat' budet sama (Ukraine Thinks About Grain Export, What Will it Eat Itself), Mk.ru, 11 May 2022, https://www.mk.ru/economics/2022/05/11/ukraina-zadumalas-ob-eksporte-zerna-no-chto-budet-est-sama.html

104. Araz Salekhov, «Nasha yeda protiv ikh sanktsiy»: Medvedev oboznachil punkty prodovol'stvennoy bezopasnosti RF ("Our Food is Against their Sanctions:" Medvedev Outlined the Points of Food Security of the Russian Federation), Vm.ru, 1 April 2022, https://vm.ru/news/957378-medvedev-oboznachil-punkty-prodovolstvennoj-bezopasnosti-rf

105. Sergei Savchuk, Protiv Zapada u Rossii yest' oruzhiye gorazdo strashneye raket (Against the West, Russia has Much More Terrible Weapons than Missiles), RIA Novosti, 22 April 2022, https://ria.ru/20220422/eda-1784835298.html

106. Ibid.

107. Putin Ties Ukraine Grain Flow to Sanctions Relief; Macron and Scholz Urge Serious Peace Effort, RFE/RL, 28 May 2022, https://www.rferl.org/a/putin-ukrainian-grain-exports-sanctions/31872896.html

108. Russian Agri Commodities not Subject to Sanctions, US Says, as Food Insecurity Fears Grow, GTR, 18 July 2022, https://www.gtreview.com/news/global/russian-agri-commodities-not-subject-to-sanctions-us-says-as-food-insecurity-fears-grow/

109. Leonie Kijewski, EU Slaps More Sanctions on Russia, Introduces Food Exceptions, *Politico*, 20 July 2022, https://www.politico.eu/article/eu-slap-sanction-russia-introduce-food-exception/

110. How Russian Ships are Laundering Grain Stolen from Occupied Ukraine, Bloomberg, 17 October 2022, https://www.bloomberg.com/graphics/2022-russian-stolen-grains/

111. Crimea Harvests Record Grain Crop—Regional Ministry, Reuters, 1 August 2022, https://www.reuters.com/article/ukraine-crisis-grains-crimeaidAFL1N-2ZD0SS

112. Orysia Hrudka, Threatening Kherson Farmers, Russian Troops Steal Grain from Ukraine, Euromaidan Press, 29 April 2022, https://euromaidanpress. com/2022/04/29/threatening-kherson-farmers-russian-troops-steal-grain-from-ukraine/

113. Ibid.

114. Tim Lister, Russians Steal Vast Amounts of Ukrainian Grain and Equipment, Threatening this Year's Harvest, CNN, 5 May 2022, https://edition.cnn. com/2022/05/05/europe/russia-ukraine-grain-theft-cmd-intl/index.html

115. SBU identifies Collaborators Behind Large-Scale Theft of Ukrainian Grain, *Kyiv Independent*, 4 August 2022, https://kyivindependent.com/uncategorized/ sbu-identifies-collaborators-behind-large-scale-theft-of-ukrainian-grain

116. Tatyana Karabut, Khersonshchina nachala eksport zerna v Rossiyu (Kherson Region Began Exporting Grain to Russia), *Rossiyskaya Gazeta*, 30 May 2022, https://rg.ru/2022/05/30/hersonskaia-oblast-nachala-eksport-zerna-v-rossiiu.html

117. Kherson Region Seeks Ways to Sidestep Ukraine's Sea Blockade to Export Grain, 16 June 2022, https://tass.com/economy/1465929

118. Twitter, Julia Davis, 2 May 2022, https://twitter.com/JuliaDavisNews/status/1521155508626984960

119. Patrick Wintour, UK Backs Lithuania's Plan to Lift Russian Blockade of Ukrainian Grain, *The Guardian*, 23 May 2022, https://www.theguardian. com/world/2022/may/23/lithuania-calls-for-joint-effort-on-russia-black-sea-blockade

120. Voyennyy ekspert otsenil zhelaniye Velikobritanii napravit' voyennyye korabli v Odessu (Military Expert Appreciated Britain's Desire to Send Warships to Odesa), *Vzglyad*, 24 May 2022, https://vz.ru/news/2022/5/24/1159879.html

121. Turkey Announces Deal with Ukraine, Russia and UN Aimed at Resuming Grain Exports, *The Guardian*, 14 July 2022, https://www.theguardian.com/ world/2022/jul/14/turkey-announces-deal-with-ukraine-russia-and-un-aimed-at-resuming-grain-exports

122. Telegram, 12 March 2022, https://t.me/energoatom_ua/2852

123. Drew Hinshaw and Joe Parkinson, Russian Army Turns Ukraine's Largest Nuclear Plant into a Military Base, *Wall Street Journal*, 5 July 2022, https:// www.wsj.com/articles/russian-army-turns-ukraines-largest-nuclear-plant-into-a-military-base-11657035694

124. Russian Vehicles Seen Inside Turbine Hall at Ukraine Nuclear Plant, CNN, 19 August 2022, https://edition.cnn.com/2022/08/19/europe/ukraine-zaporizhzhia-nuclear-plant-russian-vehicles-intl-hnk/index.html

125. Hinshaw and Parkinson, 2022.

126. Interview with Ukrainian defence ministry official, September 2022.

127. Update 89—IAEA Director General Statement on Situation in Ukraine, IAEA, 9 August 2022, https://www.iaea.org/newscenter/pressreleases/update-89-iaea-director-general-statement-on-situation-in-ukraine

128. Russians, Ukrainians Again Trade Blame for New Shelling Near Nuclear Plant, France 24, 15 August 2022, https://www.france24.com/en/europe/20220815-russians-ukrainians-again-trade-blame-for-new-shelling-near-nuclear-plant

129. Zaporizhzhia NPP: Europe Now Facing Nuclear Disaster as Russia Opts for New Plot, Ukrinform, 6 August 2022, https://www.ukrinform.net/rubric-ato/3545058-russians-shelling-zaporizhia-npp-to-disconnect-it-from-ukraines-energy-system-energoatom.html

130. Telegram, 23 August 2022, https://t.me/DIUkraine/1177

131. Russia Doesn't Acknowledge Radiological Risk at Ukraine Nuclear Power Plant, U.S. Says, Reuters, 28 August 2022, https://www.reuters.com/world/europe/russia-doesnt-acknowledge-radiological-risk-ukraine-nuclear-power-plant-us-says-2022-08-28/

132. Accident at ZNPP Would Send Radiation Cloud Towards Southern Ukraine, Certain Russian Regions—Report, Ukrinform, 28 August 2022, https://www.ukrinform.net/rubric-ato/3559824-accident-at-znpp-would-send-radiation-cloud-toward-southern-ukraine-certain-russian-regions-forecast.html

133. Hanna Arihova, Ukraine Nuclear Workers Recount Abuse, Threats from Russians, Associated Press, 5 October 2022, https://apnews.com/article/russia-ukraine-kyiv-business-153cc4ffe3a9eede8f852d22abd5ed01

134. Elektropostachannya Zaporiz′koyi oblasti zdiysnyuyet′sya cherez Krym (Electricity is Supplied to Zaporizhzhia Region Through Crimea), RIA Novosti, 12 September 2022, https://ria.ru/20220912/elektroenergiya-1816228646.html

135. Mykola Topalov, Rosiyany khochut′ vidklyuchyty vid Ukrayiny Zaporiz′ku AES. Chy mozhlyvo tse i yaki mozhut′ buty naslidky? (The Russians Want to Disconnect Zaporizhzhia NPP from Ukraine. Is it Possible and What Could be the Consequences?), *Ekonomichna Pravda*, 8 August 2022, https://www.epravda.com.ua/publications/2022/08/8/690123/

136. UN Nuclear Agency Again Asks to Visit Ukraine Nuclear Plant, *Korea Times*, 24 August 2022, https://www.koreatimes.co.kr/www/nation/2022/08/501_334922.html

137. Russia Calls UN Idea to Demilitarize Ukraine's Zaporizhzhia Nuclear Plant Unacceptable, Reuters, 18 August 2022, https://www.reuters.com/world/europe/russian-foreign-ministry-says-un-proposal-demilitarise-zaporizhzhia-nuclear-2022-08-18/

138. Interview with author, September 2022.

139. Ibid.

140. Ibid.

141. Response to author, October 2022.

142. Interview with Russian foreign ministry official, September 2022.

143. Ibid.

144. Interview with author, October 2022.

145. Sergey Savchuk, Kiyev nanosit udary po Zaporozhskoy AES dal'nim pritse-lom (Kyiv Strikes at the Zaporizhzhia Nuclear Plant with a Long-Range Sight), RIA Novosti, 21 July 2022, https://ria.ru/20220721/zaes-1803914730.html?in=t

146. Andrey Grigoriev, Atomnuyu bombu pytayutsya sdelat' iz Zaporozhskoy AES (They are Trying to Make an Atomic Bomb from the Zaporizhzhia Nuclear Plant), Smotrim, 25 August 2022, https://smotrim.ru/article/2909725

147. Ukraine Says Any IAEA Visit to Occupied Zaporizhzhia "Unacceptable," World Nuclear News, 27 May 2022, https://www.world-nuclear-news.org/Articles/Ukraine-says-any-IAEA-visit-to-occupied-Zaporizhyz

148. Ukraine: Support Grows for IAEA Visit to Zaporizhzhia, Energy Intelligence, 12 August 2022, https://www.energyintel.com/000001828ef1-ddd5-affe-bef3426a0000

149. Russia Opposes Demilitarization of Zaporizhzhia Nuclear Power Plant, *Ukrainskaya Pravda*, 12 August 2022, https://www.pravda.com.ua/eng/news/2022/08/12/7362924/

150. So-Called Demilitarization of ZNPP to Put it in Ukrainian Army's Hands—Local Official, TASS, 6 September 2022, https://tass.com/world/1503601

151. Interview with author, September 2022.

152. Russia says Thwarted Ukrainian Attempt to Capture Zaporizhzhia Nuclear Plant, Reuters, 1 September 2022, https://www.reuters.com/world/europe/fighting-erupts-ukrainian-troops-deploy-near-enerhodar-reports-2022-09-01/

153. Russia says it Foiled Ukrainian Attempt to Seize Nuclear Plant, Reuters, 3 September 2022, https://www.reuters.com/world/europe/russia-says-it-foiled-ukrainian-attempt-seize-nuclear-plant-2022-09-03/

154. Isabel van Brugen, Ukraine Soldiers Pretend to be Dead to Trick Russians in Video, Newsweek, 3 September 2022, https://www.newsweek.com/ukraine-soldiers-dead-trick-russians-video-1740532

155. Russia "Regrets" IAEA Report did not Blame Ukraine: UN Envoy, France 24, 6 September 2022, https://www.france24.com/en/live-news/20220906-russia-regrets-iaea-report-did-not-blame-ukraine-un-envoy

156. Interview with senior Zaporizhzhia official, September 2022.

157. Ibid.

158. Russia is Not Interested in Completely Stopping Gas Deliveries to Europe—Kremlin, TASS, 25 July 2022, https://tass.com/economy/1484405

159. Ibid.

160. Putin Warns of Nord Stream 1 Gas Capacity Cuts over Turbine Repairs, Euractiv, 20 July 2022, https://www.euractiv.com/section/energy/news/putin-warns-of-nord-stream-1-gas-capacity-cuts-over-turbine-repairs/

161. Russia Slashes Nord Stream Gas Supply to Europe, *Politico*, 25 July 2022, https://www.politico.eu/article/gazprom-nord-stream-flows-to-halve-beginning-wednesday/

162. Wilhelmine Preussen, Canada to Return 5 Remaining Nord Stream Turbines to Germany, *Politico*, 25 August 2022, https://www.politico.eu/article/canada-to-return-five-more-turbines-to-germany/

163. EU Allows Get-Out Clause in Russian Gas Cut Deal, BBC, 26 July 2022, https://www.bbc.co.uk/news/business-62305094

164. Kate Connolly, Germany to Reactivate Coal Power Plants as Russia Curbs Gas Flow, *The Guardian*, 8 July 2022, https://www.theguardian.com/world/2022/jul/08/germany-reactivate-coal-power-plants-russia-curbs-gas-flow

165. Russia's Aggression Against Ukraine: the EU Targets Additional 54 Individuals and 10 Entities, European Council, 22 July 2022, https://www.consilium.europa.eu/en/press/press-releases/2022/07/22/russia-s-aggression-against-ukraine-the-eu-targets-additional-54-individuals-and-10-entities/

166. David Vergun, Defence Official Says Sanctions Nearly Stall Russian Offensive in Ukraine, U.S. Department of Defense, 29 July 2022, https://www.defense.gov/News/News-Stories/Article/Article/3110809/defense-official-says-sanctions-nearly-stall-russian-offensive-in-ukraine/

167. Irina Slay, Why the Russian Oil Price Cap Won't Work, OilPrice, 5 September 2022, https://oilprice.com/Energy/Crude-Oil/Why-The-Russian-Oil-Price-Cap-Wont-Work.html

168. Rossiya ne budet postavlyat' neft' v strany, podderzhivayushchiye tsenovoy limit (Russia will not Supply Oil to Countries that Support the Price Limit), RIA Novosti, 1 September 2022, https://ria.ru/20220901/neft-1813791825.html

169. Sergei Savchuk, Zapad reshil, chto tseny na neft' nedostatochno vysoki, i gotovit ikh rost (The West has Decided that Oil Prices are not High Enough, and is Preparing their Growth), RIA Novosti, 2 September 2022, https://ria.ru/20220902/neft-1813897394.html

170. German Chancellor Scholz Publicly Brands Russia an Unreliable Gas Supplier, Yahoo, 24 July 2022, https://news.yahoo.com/german-chancellor-scholz-publicly-brands-070200923.html

171. Response to author, September 2022.

172. Telegram, 4 September 2022, https://t.me/medvedev_telegram/173

173. Russia Alleges Ukrainian Helicopters Struck Belgorod Fuel Depot, Al Jazeera, 1 April 2022, https://www.aljazeera.com/news/2022/4/1/russia-alleges-ukrainian-helicopters-struck-belgorod-fuel-depot

174. Pjotr Sauer, Large Fires Break Out at Russian Oil Depots, *The Guardian*, 25 April 2022, https://www.theguardian.com/world/2022/apr/25/large-fires-break-out-russian-oil-depots-bryansk-near-ukraine-border

175. Jessica Elgot, Minister Backs Ukraine Carrying Out Russia Strikes with British Weapons, *The Guardian*, 26 April 2022, https://www.theguardian.com/politics/2022/apr/26/britain-backs-ukraine-carrying-out-strikes-in-russia-says-minister

176. Prestupnyy udar VSU po Belgorodu trebuyet reshitel'nogo vozmezdiya (The Criminal Strike of the Armed Forces of Ukraine on Belgorod Requires Decisive Retribution), *Vzglyad*, 3 July 2022, https://vz.ru/society/2022/7/3/1165927.html

177. Satellite Pictures Show Devastation at Russian Air Base in Crimea, Voice of America, 11 August 2022, https://www.voanews.com/a/satellite-pictures-show-devastation-at-russian-air-base-in-crimea/6697179.html

178. Dan Sabbagh and Samantha Lock, Russian Warplanes Destroyed in Crimea Airbase Attack, Satellite Images Show, *The Guardian*, 11 August 2022, https://www.theguardian.com/world/2022/aug/11/russian-warplanes-destroyed-in-crimea-saky-airbase-attack-satellite-images-show

179. Interview with author, September 2022.

180. Telegram, 17 July 2022, https://t.me/Bratchuk_Sergey/15707

181. Andrew Roth, Russian Security Service Accuses Ukraine of Darya Dugina's Murder, *The Guardian*, 22 August 2022, https://www.theguardian.com/world/2022/aug/22/russian-security-service-accuses-ukraine-over-darya-dugina-killing

182. Russia Names 2nd Suspect in Killing of Daria Dugina, Daughter of "Putin's Brain," Associated Press, 29 August 2022, https://apnews.com/article/russia-ukraine-estonia-moscow-1cf26a2e2b7667b8e687ef95b047427a

183. Rabia Iclal Turan, Ukraine Denies Accusations it Killed Russian Journalist Dugina, Anadolu Agency, 23 August 2022, https://www.aa.com.tr/en/russia-ukraine-war/ukraine-denies-accusations-it-killed-russian-journalist-dugina/2667885

184. U.S. Believes Ukrainians were Behind an Assassination in Russia, *The New York Times*, 5 October 2022, https://www.nytimes.com/2022/10/05/us/politics/ukraine-russia-dugina-assassination.html

185. Diplomat on Dugina Murder: Traces Pointing to Kiev Would Confirm Policy of State Terror, TASS, 22 August 2022, https://tass.com/politics/1496409

186. Mironov: voyennaya operatsiya na Ukraine mozhet pererasti v kontrterrorizm

(Mironov: Military Operation in Ukraine May Develop into Counterterrorism Operation), RTVI, 25 August 2022, https://rtvi.com/news/mironov-voen-naya-operaciya-na-ukraine-mozhet-pererasti-v-kontrterroristicheskuyu/

187. Senator Vows Estonia to Face Rightful Clampdown if it Refuses to Extradite Dugina's Killer, TASS, 22 August 2022, https://tass.com/politics/1496821

188. Pjotr Sauer, Putin Claims FSB Foiled Western Plot to Kill Pro-Western Journalist, *The Guardian*, 25 April 2022, https://www.theguardian.com/world/2022/apr/25/putin-claims-fsb-foiled-western-plot-to-kill-pro-krem-lin-journalist

189. Telegram, 24 August 2022, https://t.me/voenkorKotenok/39569

190. Telegram, 22 August 2022, https://t.me/glazieview/2168

191. Milonov o smerti Gorbacheva: yego nasledie mozhno sravnit' s katastrofoy (Milonov on the Death of Gorbachev: His Legacy Can be Compared to Disaster), RIAFAN, 30 August 2022, https://riafan.ru/23618639-milonov_o_smerti_gorbacheva_ego_nasledie_mozhno_sravnit_s_katastrofoi

192. Telegram, 3 September 2022, https://t.me/medvedev_telegram/172

7. COUNTER-OFFENSIVE AND MOBILISATION

1. Zelensky Visits Liberated Izyum as Ukraine Aims to Keep Russia on the Run, *The Washington Post*, 14 September 2022, https://www.washingtonpost.com/world/2022/09/14/izyum-zelensky-ukraine-russia-liberated/

2. Twitter, 14 September 2022, https://twitter.com/Podolyak_M/status/1570101480039776256?s=20&t=oc6AK7XtfJco5UU1gnAecQ

3. Interview with author, September 2022.

4. Ukraine Claims Early Success in Counteroffensive as Zelensky Vows to "Chase" Russians to the Border, CNN, 30 August 2022, https://edition.cnn.com/2022/08/30/europe/ukraine-kherson-counteroffensive-intl/index.html

5. Ibid.

6. Isobel Koshiw and Pjotr Sauer, Ukrainian Adviser Warns Progress will be Slow as Southern Counterattack Begins, *The Guardian*, 20 August 2022, https://www.theguardian.com/world/2022/aug/30/zelenskiy-tells-russian-forces-to-flee-as-ukraine-counteroffensive-begins-in-kherson

7. Ibid.

8. Yaroslav Trofimov, Ukraine Braces for Brutal Fight for Occupied Southern Regions as Referendum Looms, *The Wall Street Journal*, 4 August 2022, https://www.wsj.com/articles/ukraine-braces-for-brutal-fight-for-occupied-southern-regions-as-referendum-looms-11659519001

9. Perspektyvy zabezpechennya viys'kovoyi kampaniyi 2023 roku: ukrayins'kyy pohlyad (Prospects for Securing the Military Campaign of 2023: The Ukrainian

View), Ukrinform, 7 September 2022, https://www.ukrinform.ua/rubric-ato/3566162-ak-zabezpeciti-voennu-kampaniu-u-2023-roci-ukrainskij-poglad.html

10. Jim Garamone, Russian Efforts to Raise Numbers of Troops "Unlikely to Succeed," U.S. Official Says, U.S. Department of Defense, 29 August 2022, https://www.defense.gov/News/News-Stories/Article/Article/3143381/russian-efforts-to-raise-numbers-of-troops-unlikely-to-succeed-us-official-says/

11. Jim Sciutto and Tim Lister, Ukrainian Forces Aim to Retake Kherson by Year's End as Gains Made in South, US and Ukrainian Officials Say, CNN, 7 September 2022, https://edition.cnn.com/2022/09/07/politics/ukraine-russia-war-kherson/index.html

12. Jim Sciutto, Ukrainian Forces Begin "Shaping" Battlefield for Counteroffensive, Senior US Officials Say, CNN, 29 August 2022, https://edition.cnn.com/2022/08/29/politics/ukraine-shaping-counteroffensive/index.html

13. Minoborony Rossii zayavilo o neudavsheysya popytke napadeniya na VSU (The Russian ministry of defence announced a failed attack attempt by the Armed Forces of Ukraine), RIA Novosti, 29 August 2022, https://ria.ru/20220829/nastuplenie-1813011342.html

14. Telegram, 31 August 2022, https://t.me/Stremousov_Kirill/268

15. Kherson Says Ukrainian Counter-Offensive Failed, TASS, 5 September 2022, https://tass.com/politics/1502487

16. Interviews with Moscow-based defence analysts, September 2022.

17. Interview with author, August 2022.

18. Telegram, 4 September 2022, https://t.me/strelkovii/3168

19. Sciutto and Lister, 2022.

20. Interview with Ukrainian special forces officer, September 2022.

21. Telegram, 31 August 2022, https://t.me/csources/109626

22. Marc Champion, Ukraine's Military Breakthrough in North Threatens Russian Grip, Bloomberg, 9 September 2022, https://www.bloomberg.com/news/articles/2022-09-09/ukraine-military-breakthrough-in-north-threatens-russian-grip?leadSource=uverify%20wall

23. Ukraine's Southern Offensive "Was Designed to Trick Russia," *The Guardian*, 10 September 2022, https://www.theguardian.com/world/2022/sep/10/ukraines-publicised-southern-offensive-was-disinformation-campaign

24. Samuel Oakford and Alex Horton, Here's What Russian Soldiers Left Behind when They Withdrew from Izyum, *The Washington Post*, 13 September 2022, https://www.washingtonpost.com/investigations/2022/09/13/russia-retreat-abandoned-weapons-izyum/

25. Iryna Balachuk, V Izyumi zavershyly eks humatsiyu—pidnyaly 447 til, sered nykh bahato zhinok i ditey (Exhumation was Completed in Izyum—447 Bodies

were Raised, Among Them Many Women and Children), *Ukrainskaya Pravda*, 23 September 2022, https://www.pravda.com.ua/news/2022/09/23/7368817/

26. Alena Vargina, Na Khar'kovshchine SBU arestovala uchiteley, prepodayush-chikh russkiy yazyk (In the Kharkiv Region, the SBU Arrested Teachers Speaking Russian), Ura, 13 September 2022, https://ura.news/news/1052586405

27. Voyska soyuznikov uderzhivayut Kupyansk, nesmotrya na slozhnuyu obstanovku v etom rayone (Allied Forces Hold Kupiansk Despite the Difficult Situation in the Area), RIA Novosti, 9 September 2022, https://ria.ru/20220909/kupy-ansk-1815632361.html

28. Telegram, 30 August 2022, https://t.me/rsotmdivision/620

29. Telegram, 10 September 2022, https://t.me/Postovo/16610

30. Kadyrov poobeshchal vernut' vse goroda na khar'kovskom napravlenii (Kadyrov Promised to Return All Cities in the Kharkiv Direction), RIA Novosti, 11 September 2022, https://ria.ru/20220911/svo-1815944003.html?in=t

31. Pjotr Sauer, "We Have Already Lost": Far-Right Bloggers Slam Military Failures, *The Guardian*, 8 September 2022, https://www.theguardian.com/world/2022/sep/08/we-have-already-lost-far-right-russian-bloggers-slam-kremlin-over-army-response

32. Telegram, 11 September 2022, https://t.me/holmogortalks/24243

33. Telegram, 17 September 2022, https://t.me/olegtsarov/3446

34. Telegram, 7 September 2022, https://t.me/sashakots/35397

35. As Russian Losses Mount in Ukraine, Putin Gets More Involved in War Strategy, *The New York Times*, 23 September 2022, https://www.nytimes.com/2022/09/23/us/politics/putin-ukraine.html

36. Dan Sabbagh, Putin Involved in War "At Level of Colonel or Brigadier," say Western Sources, *The Guardian*, 16 May 2022, https://www.theguardian.com/world/2022/may/16/putin-involved-russia-ukraine-war-western-sources

37. Luke Harding, Russia No Longer has Full Control of Luhansk Region After Ukraine Captures Village, *The Guardian*, 19 September 2022, https://www.theguardian.com/world/2022/sep/19/russia-no-longer-has-full-control-of-luhansk-as-ukraine-recaptures-village

38. Ukrainian Forces Attempting to Advance to Donetsk Airport Neutralized—DPR Head, TASS, 12 September 2022, https://tass.com/world/1506511

39. Telegram, 13 September 2022, https://t.me/strelkovii/3232

40. Zyuganov: Rossii neobkhodimo mobilizovat' sily i resursy (Zuganov: Russia Needs to Mobilize Forces and Resources), *Kommersant*, 13 September 2022, https://www.kommersant.ru/doc/5559253

41. Interview with author, August 2022.

42. Interview with author, September 2022.

43. Interview with author, October 2022.

44. Telegram, 10 September 2022, https://t.me/talipovonline/7104
45. Russian Duma Mulls Scrapping Upper Age Limit of 40 For Military Enrolment, RFE/RL, 20 May 2022, https://www.rferl.org/a/russia-age-limit-removed-military-draft-bill/31859884.html
46. David Axe, To Replenish its Army in Ukraine, Russia Plans to Strip its Training Units. It can only do this Once, Forbes, 28 May 2022, https://www.forbes.com/sites/davidaxe/2022/05/28/to-replenish-its-army-in-ukraine-russia-plans-to-strip-its-training-units-it-can-only-do-this-once/?sh=42f0c74da98f
47. Russia Turns to Trucks and Big Wages to Woo Volunteer Soldiers, Al Jazeera, 18 September 2022, https://www.aljazeera.com/news/2022/9/18/russia-turns-to-trucks-and-big-wages-to-woo-volunteer-soldiers
48. Tim Lister and John Pennington, Russia is Recruiting Thousands of Volunteers to Replenish its Ranks in Ukraine. Prior Experience Isn't Always Required, CNN, 29 July 2022, https://edition.cnn.com/2022/07/29/europe/russia-recruits-volunteer-battalions-ukraine-war-cmd-intl/index.html
49. Russia Forming Third Army Corps for War in Ukraine—ISW, Ukrinform, August 2022, https://www.ukrinform.net/rubric-ato/3544612-russia-forming-3rd-army-corps-for-war-in-ukraine-isw.html
50. Occupiers Mobilized Many Drug Addicts and Alcoholics for War—General Staff, Ukranews, 14 September 2022, https://ukranews.com/en/news/882086-occupiers-mobilized-many-drug-addicts-and-alcoholics-for-war-general-staff
51. The W Orchestra Awaits You, Meduza, 21 July 2022, https://meduza.io/en/feature/2022/07/21/the-w-orchestra-awaits-you
52. Pjotr Sauer, "We Thieves and Killers are Now Fighting Russia's War": How Moscow Recruits from its Prisons, The Guardian, 20 September 2022, https://www.theguardian.com/world/2022/sep/20/russia-recruits-inmates-ukraine-war-wagner-prigozhin
53. Ibid.
54. Ibid.
55. "Oni ne zhdut, chto kto-to ottuda vernetsya" ("They Don't Expect Anyone to Return from There"), Meduza, 17 August 2022, https://meduza.io/feature/2022/08/17/oni-ne-rasschityvayut-chto-ottuda-kto-to-vernetsya
56. Navalny's Team Posts Video of a Man Allegedly Recruiting Russian Inmates to Fight in Ukraine, RFE/RL, 15 September 2022, https://www.rferl.org/a/russia-prigozhin-prisoners-vagner/32035035.html
57. Telegram, 14 September 2022, https://t.me/vchkogpu/32947
58. Putin to Look at Revising "Cheating" Ukrainian Grain Export Deal, Reuters, 7 September 2022, https://www.reuters.com/markets/commodities/putin-says-developing-world-being-cheated-by-ukraine-grain-deal-2022-09-07/
59. Ships with Ukrainian Grain Going to Countries not Facing Famine- Russian Envoy, TASS, 17 August 2022, https://tass.com/world/1494887

60. Cara Anna and Vladimir Isachenkov, Ukraine Says Grain Coming to Somalia, But Russia Skeptical, Associated Press, 7 September 2022, https://apnews.com/article/russia-ukraine-zelenskyy-putin-kenya-somalia-8bc64e0cc29713d3cb-43d6a8e386bedc

61. Dmytro Kuleba: 2/3 of Ukrainian Grain Under the Grain Initiative was Directed to Countries of Africa, Asia and the Middle East, Ministry of Foreign Affairs of Ukraine, 7 September 2022, https://mfa.gov.ua/en/news/dmytro-kuleba-23-ukrainian-grain-under-grain-initiative-was-directed-countries-africa-asia-and-middle-east

62. Anna and Isachenkov, 7 September 2022.

63. Betul Yuruk, Russia "Not Optimistic" about Ukraine Grain Deal's Extension: Official, Anadolu Agency, 20 October 2022, https://www.aa.com.tr/en/russia-ukraine-war/russia-not-optimistic-about-ukraine-grain-deals-extension-official/2715898

64. Zayavleniye MID Rossii o "Chernomorskoy initsiative" po eksportu ukrainskikh produktov pitaniya (Statement by the Russian Foreign Ministry on the "Black Sea Initiative" for the export of Ukrainian Grain), Ministry of Foreign Affairs, 29 October 2022, https://www.mid.ru/ru/foreign_policy/news/1835797/

65. Myatezh na korable: sdelka s zernom prodolzhayetsya. Kak Otvechayet Rossiya?, Tsargrad, 31 October 2022, https://tsargrad.tv/news/bunt-na-korable-zernovaja-sdelka-otmenena-no-prodolzhaetsja-chem-otvetit-rossija_655757

66. Razorvat' soglasheniye—pravil'no: Chesnokov podderzhal resheniye Rossii vyyti iz zernovoy sdelki (Breaking the Agreement is the Right Thing: Chesnokov Supported Russia's Decision to Withdraw from the Grain Deal), RIAFAN, 30 October 2022, https://riafan.ru/23723792-razriv_soglasheniya_vesch_pravil_naya_chesnokov_podderzhal_reshenie_rossii_viiti_iz_zernovoi_sdelki

67. UN, NATO, EU and US Call on Russia to Resume Ukrainian Grain Deal, *The Guardian*, 30 October 2022, https://www.theguardian.com/world/2022/oct/30/un-nato-eu-and-us-demand-russia-resumes-ukrainian-grain-deal

68. Posol Antonov vozmushchen reaktsiyey SSHA na priostanovku sdelki s Rossiyey po zernu (Ambassador Antonov Angered by US Reaction to Russia's Suspension of Grain Deal), RIAFAN, 30 October 2022, https://riafan.ru/23724867-posla_antonova_vozmutila_reaktsiya_ssha_na_priostanovku_uchastiya_rossii_v_zernovoi_sdelke

69. Konets «peremiriya na more»: politolog Suzdal'tsev ob"yasnil, pochemu Rossiya priostanovila zernovuyu sdelku (The End of the Truce at Sea: Political Scientist Suzdaltsev Explained Why Russia Suspended the Grain Deal), RIAFAN, 30 October 2022, https://riafan.ru/23724887-konets_peremiriyu_na_more_politolog_suzdal_tsev_ob_yasnil_pochemu_rossiya_priostanovila_zernovuyu_sdelku

70. Politolog Kornilov otsenil dal'neyshiye perspektivy zernovoy sdelki posle vykhoda RF (Political Analyst Kornilov Assessed the Future Prospects of the Grain Deal after the Withdrawal of the Russian Federation), RIAFAN, 31 October 2022, https://riafan.ru/23727091-politolog_kornilov_otsenil_dal_neishie_perspektivi_zernovoi_sdelki_posle_vihoda_iz_nee_rf

71. Russia Agrees to Rejoin Ukraine Export Deal, Al Jazeera, 2 November 2022, https://www.aljazeera.com/news/2022/11/2/ukraine-grain-shipments-resume-as-russia-rejoins-deal

72. Putin: We Could Quit Grain Deal Again, but Would not Block Grain for Turkey, Reuters, 2 November 2022, https://www.reuters.com/world/russia-resume-participation-black-sea-grain-deal-defence-ministry-2022-11-02/

73. Erdogan, Putin Agreed to Send Russian Grains to Poor African Countries for Free, Reuters, 4 November 2022, https://www.reuters.com/world/erdogan-says-agreed-with-putin-grains-should-go-poor-african-countries-free-2022-11-04/

74. Russia's December Wheat Exports Close to Record, Experts Say, Reuters, 7 December 2022, https://www.reuters.com/markets/commodities/russias-december-wheat-exports-close-record-experts-say-2022-12-07/

75. Ukraine Says Russia Delaying Inspections of Ships, World Grain, 27 December 2022, https://www.world-grain.com/articles/17903-ukraine-says-russia-delaying-inspections-of-ships

76. Chto zhdet Severnyy potok (What's Next for Nord Stream), RIA Novosti, 1 October 2022, https://crimea.ria.ru/20221001/chto-budet-dalshe-s-severnym-potokom-1124683888.html

77. Ibid.

78. Twitter, 27 September 2022, https://twitter.com/dpol_un/status/1574840289419792384

78. Kiev Carried out Terrorist Attack on Black Sea Fleet in Sevastopol—Ministry, TASS, 29 October 2022, https://tass.com/russia/1529537

80. Russia Ready to Resume Gas Supplies to Europe Via Yamal–Europe Pipeline—Novak, Reuters, 26 December 2022, https://www.reuters.com/business/energy/russia-ready-resume-gas-supplies-europe-via-yamal-europe-pipeline-novak-2022-12-25/

81. Joe Parkinson and Drew Hinshaw, "The Hole": Gruesome Accounts of Russian Occupation Emerge from Ukrainian Nuclear Plant, *Wall Street Journal*>, 18 November 2022, https://www.wsj.com/articles/russian-occupation-of-nuclear-plant-turns-brutal-with-accusations-of-torture-and-beatings-11668786893

82. Ibid.

83. Putin Issues Decree to Put Zaporozhye NPP on List of Russia's Federal Assets, TASS, 5 October 2022, https://tass.com/politics/1518309

84. Activist says Ukraine Plans Attack on ZNPP from Several Sides, TASS, 16 October 2022, https://tass.com/defense/1523495

85. Putin Warns US, NATO Against Nuclear Threats, TASS, 21 September 2022, https://tass.com/politics/1511081

86. Kadyrov says Russia Should use Low-Yield Nuclear Weapon, Reuters, 1 October 2022, https://www.reuters.com/world/europe/russia-says-its-troops-left-lyman-avoid-encirclement-2022-10-01/

87. Russian Military Leaders Discussed Use of Nuclear Weapons, *The New York Times*, 2 November 2022, https://www.nytimes.com/2022/11/02/us/politics/russia-ukraine-nuclear-weapons.html

88. Russia's Defence Chief Warns of "Dirty Bomb" Provocation, CNBC, 22 October 2022, https://www.cnbc.com/2022/10/23/russias-defense-chief-warns-of-dirty-bomb-provocation.html

89. (Konkord otreagiroval na video s muzhchinoy, pokhozhim na Prigozhina, v kolonii) Concord Responded to a Video with a Man Similar to Prigozhin in a Colony, RBC, 15 September 2022, https://www.rbc.ru/politics/15/09/2022/63230f279a79476cbb5ddeca?from=article_body

90. Prigozhin rasskazal ob istokakh gruppy Vagnera (Prigozhin Spoke About the Origins of the Wagner Group), RBC, 26 September 2022, https://www.rbc.ru/politics/26/09/2022/63314cef9a7947bf65368f6c

91. "We Were Nothing to Them:" Russian Volunteer Reservists Return from War Against Ukraine Feeling Deceived, RFE/RL, 12 August 2022, https://www.rferl.org/a/russia-volunteers-ukraine-treatment-minimal-training-war/31985377.html

92. Telegram, 15 September 2022, https://t.me/RKadyrov_95/2822

93. Telegram, 16 September 2022, https://t.me/readovkanews/41860

94. Telegram, 16 September 2022, https://t.me/strelkovii/3253

95. Telegram, 20 September 2022, https://t.me/rybar/39071

96. Shoygu: 300 tysyach rezervistov budut prizvany v ramkakh mobilizatsii (Shoigu: 300,000 Reservists will be Called Up as Part of Mobilisation), *Rossiyskaya Gazeta*, 21 September 2022, https://rg.ru/2022/09/21/shojgu-v-ramkah-mobilizacii-budut-prizvany-300-tysiach-rezervistov.html

97. Studentov ne berem": kogo otpravyat na Donbass ("We Do Not Take Students:" Who Will be Sent to Donbas), RIA Novosti, 21 September 2022, https://ria.ru/20220921/mobilizatsiya-1818389189.html

98. Kadyrov prokommentiroval ob"yavleniye o chastichnoy mobilizatsii (Kadyrov Commented on the Announcement of Partial Mobilisation), RIA Novosti, 21 September 2022, https://ria.ru/20220921/mobilizatsiya-1818439827.html

99. Zelensky: Mobilization of Russian Reservists Won't Change Ukraine's Plans, *Kyiv Independent*, 21 September 2022, https://kyivindependent.com/news-feed/zelensky-mobilization-of-russian-reservists-wont-change-ukraines-plans

100. Russia's Plans to Mobilize 300,000 People Indicate Real Loss of 150,000—
     Arestovych, Ukranews, 21 September 2022, https://ukranews.com/en/news/
     883353-russia-s-plans-to-mobilize-300-000-people-indicate-real-loss-of-150-
     000-arestovych

101. Russia to Conscript 1.2 Million People, Meduza, 23 September 2022, https://
     meduza.io/en/feature/2022/09/23/russia-to-conscript-up-to-1-2-million-peo-
     ple

102. Andrew Roth, "It's a 100% Mobilization": Day One of Russia's Drive to Build
     its Army, *The Guardian*, 22 September 2022, https://www.theguardian.com/
     world/2022/sep/22/russia-mobilisation-ukraine-war-army-drive

103. Pjotr Sauer, Coffins in Buryatia: Ukraine Invasion Takes Toll on Russia's
     Remote Regions, *The Guardian*, 30 March 2022, https://www.theguardian.
     com/world/2022/mar/30/coffins-in-buryatia-ukraine-invasion-takes-toll-on-
     russias-remote-regions

104. Interview with author, October 2022.

105. Mariia Shynarenko, Putin's Mobilization and Crimean Tatars: What Can We
     Expect?, NYU Jordan Center, 4 October 2022, https://jordanrussiacenter.org/
     news/mobilization-of-the-crimean-tatars-for-russias-war-against-ukraine-
     what-can-we-expect/#.Y2pZquzP10s

106. Interview with author, October 2022.

107. Lily Hyde, "A Kind of Murder:" Putin's Draft Targets Crimean Tatars, *Politico*,
     4 October 2022, https://www.politico.eu/article/murder-putin-draft-target-
     crimea-tatars/

108. Elena Gorshkova, Simon'yan vyzvalas' pomoch' tem, kogo mobilizovali pro-
     tiv pravil (Simonyan Volunteered to Help Those who are Mobilised Against
     the Rules), Ura.ru, 24 September 2022, https://ura.news/news/1052589468

109. Protests, Drafting Mistakes and an Exodus: Putin's Mobilization Off to a
     Chaotic Start, CNN, 25 September 2022, https://edition.cnn.com/2022/09/25/
     europe/russian-mobilization-putin-exodus-chaos-new-laws-intl-hnk/index.
     html

110. Pjotr Sauer, "The Army has Nothing:" New Russian Conscripts Bemoan Lack
     of Supplies, *The Guardian*, 20 October 2022, https://www.theguardian.com/
     world/2022/oct/20/the-army-has-nothing-new-russian-conscripts-bemoan-
     lack-of-supplies

111. Peskov prokommentiroval nekhvatku sredstv v regionakh dlya mobilizovan-
     nykh (Peskov Commented on the Lack of Funds in the Regions for Mobilised),
     RIA Novosti, 5 October 2022, https://ria.ru/20221005/mobilizovannye-182167
     6818.html?in=t

112. Interview with Andrei Soldatov, October 2022.

113. Navalny Slams Putin's Mobilization Order as Opposition Calls for Protests,

RFE/RL, 21 September 2022, https://www.rferl.org/a/russia-ukraine-mobilization-navalny-protests/32044653.html

114. Anti-War Protest Held in Grozny, OC Media, 22 September 2022, https://oc-media.org/anti-war-protest-held-in-grozny/

115. Tearful Scenes and Protest as Mobilization Gets Underway in Russia, CNN, 23 September 2022, https://edition.cnn.com/2022/09/22/europe/russia-protests-partial-mobilization-ukraine-intl-hnk/index.html

116. Russia Protests: More than 1,300 Arrested in Anti-War Demonstrations, *The Guardian*, 22 September 2022, https://www.theguardian.com/world/2022/sep/22/russia-protests-more-than-1300-arrested-at-anti-war-demonstrations-ukraine

117. Telegram, 21 September 2022, https://t.me/O_Arestovich_official/2638

118. Isabel van Brugen, Putin's Top Priest Tells Russians Not to Fear Death Amid Mobilization, Newsweek, 23 September 2022, https://www.newsweek.com/russia-priest-patriarch-kirill-mobilization-putin-death-ukraine-1745616

119. "Inevitable Conflict:" In Dagestan, Kremlin's Mobilization Inflames Ethnic Tensions, RFE/RL, 2 October 2022, https://www.rferl.org/a/russia-daghestan-mobilization-pushback/32061760.html

120. Telegram, 25 September 2022, https://t.me/utro_dagestan/2877

121. «Goryachiy narod u nas»: kogo raskachivayut protesty na Kavkaze ("We Have a Hot People:" Who is Rocking the Protests in the Caucasus), RIA Novosti, 5 October 2022, https://ria.ru/20221005/dagestan-1821422494.html

122. Alexander Yeo, Quelling Anti-Mobilization Unrest in Dagestan, The Central Asia-Caucasus Analyst, 27 October 2022, http://www.cacianalyst.org/publications/analytical-articles/item/13736-quelling-anti-mobilization-unrest-in-dagestan.html

123. Henry Ridgwell, Thousands of Russians Flee Military Mobilization as Anti-War Protests Erupt, Voice of America, 23 September 2022, https://www.voanews.com/a/thousands-of-russians-flee-military-mobilization-as-anti-war-protests-erupt/6760669.html

124. Telegram, 27 September 2022, https://t.me/logikamarkova/3581

125. Andrey Perla, Mobilisatsiya Dachnikov. Glavnaya Oshibka Rossii (Mobilisation of Summer Children. The Main Mistake of Russia), Tsargrad, 24 September 2022, https://tsargrad.tv/articles/mobilizacija-letnih-detej-glavnaja-oshibka-rossii_631263

126. Telegram, 28 September 2022, https://t.me/strelkovii/3388

127. Sovet Federatsii predlozhil zapretit' lyudyam prizyvnogo vozrasta vyyezzhat' za granitsu (The Federation Council Proposed to Ban People of Military Age from Travelling Abroad), RIA Novosti, 26 September 2022, https://ria.ru/20220926/mobilizatsiya-1819450931.html

128. V Gosdume otsenili vozmozhnost' provedeniya v DNR i LNR referendumov o prisoyedinenii k Rossii (The State Duma Assessed the Possibility of Referendums in DNR and LNR on Joining Russia), RIA Novosti, 10 April 2022, https://ria.ru/20220410/referendum-1782736262.html

129. Russia Ruling Party Proposes Nov. 4 Annexation Votes for Occupied Ukraine, *The Moscow Times*, 7 September 2022, https://www.themoscowtimes.com/2022/09/07/russia-ruling-party-proposes-nov-4-annexation-votes-for-occupied-ukraine-a78738

130. Andrew Roth, Kherson's Military Administrators to Call for Russian Annexation, *The Guardian*, 11 May 2022, https://www.theguardian.com/world/2022/may/11/kherson-military-administrators-to-call-for-russian-annexation-ukraine

131. Glava DNR zayavil o planakh rassmotret' vopros o prisoyedinenii respubliki k Rossii (The Head of the DNR Announced Plans to Consider the Issue of Joining the Republic to Russia), Meduza, 29 March 2022, https://meduza.io/news/2022/03/29/glava-dnr-zayavil-o-planah-rassmotret-vopros-o-vhozhdenii-respubliki-v-sostav-rossii

132. Istochniki «Meduzy» utverzhdayut, chto v seredine maya LNR i DNR sobirayutsya provesti referendum o prisoyedinenii k Rossii. (Meduza's Sources Claim that in mid-May, the LNR and DNR are Going to Hold a Referendum on Joining Russia), Meduza, 27 April 2022, https://meduza.io/feature/2022/04/27/istochniki-meduzy-utverzhdayut-v-seredine-maya-v-lnr-i-dnr-sobirayutsya-provesti-referendum-o-prisoedinenii-k-rossii

133. Telegram, 7 June 2022, https://t.me/kastyukevich_live/1534

134. Vitse-korol' Donbassa (Viceroy of Donbas), Meduza, 8 June 2022, https://meduza.io/feature/2022/06/08/vitse-korol-donbassa

135. Ibid.

136. Rossiyskiye lidery byli by polezny Donbassu (Russian Leaders Would be Useful for Donbas), *Kommersant*, 29 May 2022, https://www.kommersant.ru/doc/5379618

137. Meduza, 8 June 2022.

138. Po dannym «Meduzy», Kreml' khochet ob"yedinit' okkupirovannyye territorii Ukrainy v novyy federal'nyy okrug v sostave RF (According to Meduza's Sources, the Kremlin Wants to Unite the Occupied Territories of Ukraine into a New Federal District within the Russian Federation), Meduza, 9 June 2022, https://meduza.io/feature/2022/06/09/kak-utverzhdayut-istochniki-meduzy-kreml-hochet-ob-edinit-okkupirovannye-territorii-ukrainy-v-novyy-federalnyy-okrug-v-sostave-rf

139. Ibid.

140. Ibid.

141. Interview with author, September 2022.

142. Ibid.

143. У Кам'янці-Дніпровській знищили склад бюлетенів псевдореферендуму та базу ФСБ (In Kamianets-Dniprovska Storage of Pseudo-Referendum Ballots and FSB Bases were Destroyed), GUR, 5 September 2022, https://gur.gov.ua/en/content/v-kam-iantsidniprovskii-znyshcheno-sklad-biuletenivpsevdoreferendumu-ta-bazu-fsb.html

144. Interview with Zaporizhzhia-based official, September 2022.

145. Ibid.

146. Yuliya Talmazan, Russian Occupied Regions in Ukraine Begin Staged Votes as the Kremlin Denies Reports of Men Fleeing Partial Mobilization, NBC, 23 September 2022, https://www.nbcnews.com/news/world/russian-ukraine-referendums-regions-fleeing-military-service-rcna49099

147. Yulia Gorbunova, Fictitious Annexation Follows "Voting" at Gunpoint, Human Rights Watch, 30 September 2022, https://www.hrw.org/news/2022/09/30/fictitious-annexation-follows-voting-gunpoint

148. Talmazan, 23 September 2022.

149. Russia Says Annexed Zones' Borders not Set as Ukraine Gains, Bloomberg, 3 October 2022, https://www.bloomberg.com/news/articles/2022–10–03/russia-says-annexed-zones-borders-not-set-as-ukraine-army-gains?leadSource=uverify%20wall

150. Telegram, 3 October 2022, https://t.me/olegtsarov/3611

151. Golosuyushchiye zhiteli Donbassa zayavili, chto zhdali referenduma vosem' let (Voting Residents of Donbas Said they had Been Waiting for a Referendum for Eight Years), RIA Novosti, 24 September 2022, https://ria.ru/20220924/referendum-1819197448.html?in=t

152. Putin's Speech on Annexation: What Exactly Did he Say?, Al Jazeera, 30 September 2022, https://www.aljazeera.com/news/2022/9/30/russia-ukraine-war-putins-annexation-speech-what-did-he-say

153. Ibid.

154. Kremlin Says Any Attack on Annexed Territory will be an Attack on Russia, Reuters, 30 September 2022, https://www.reuters.com/world/europe/kremlin-says-any-attack-annexed-territory-will-be-an-attack-russia-2022–09–30/

155. «Nam nuzhna bezopasnost'». Donbass poprosilsya v Rossiyu ("We Need Security:" Donbas Asked to Go to Russia), RIA Novosti, 19 September 2022, https://ria.ru/20220919/politika-1817971803.html?in=t

156. Ibid.

157. U.S. Cracks Down on Top Russian Officials with New Sanctions, Politico, 30 September 2022, https://www.politico.com/news/2022/09/30/u-s-russia-financial-sanctions-00059744

158. Zelensky About Pseudo-Referendums: Anyone Involved in this Farce will be held Accountable, Ukrinform, 30 September 2022, https://www.ukrinform.net/rubric-ato/3583400-zelensky-about-pseudoreferendums-anyone-involved-in-this-farce-will-be-held-accountable.html

159. Luke Harding and Isobel Koshiw, Ukraine Applies for NATO Membership after Russia Annexes Territory, *The Guardian*, 30 September 2022, https://www.theguardian.com/world/2022/sep/30/ukraine-applies-for-nato-membership-after-russia-annexes-territory

160. U.S. Official: Ukraine's NATO Bid "Should be Taken up at a Different Time," *Kyiv Independent*, 1 October 2022, https://kyivindependent.com/news-feed/us-official-ukraines-nato-application-should-be-taken-up-at-a-different-time

161. Telegram, 27 September 2022, https://t.me/rybar/39465

162. Telegram, 30 September 2022, https://t.me/rybar/39568

163. Telegram, 1 October 2022, https://t.me/sashakots/36146

164. V LNR soobshchili o tyazhelom boyu v Krasnom Limane (The LNR Reported a Difficult Battle in Krasny Liman), Mk.ru, 30 September 2022, https://www.m24.ru/news/politika/30092022/506966

165. Minoborony Rossii ob"yavilo o vyvode voysk iz Krasnogo Limana (Russian Defence Ministry Announces Withdrawal of Forces from Krasny Liman), Lenta.ru, 1 October 2022, https://lenta.ru/news/2022/10/01/limaannnn/

166. Sergei Kuznetsov, Kyiv Vows Russian Troops will "Simply be Exterminated" after Putin Annexes Ukrainian Territory, *Politico*, 30 September 2022, https://www.politico.eu/article/ukraine-reject-russia-annexation-territory-putin-zelenskyy-crimea-war/

167. Interview with author, October 2022.

168. Police: 146 Bodies Found at Mass Burial Site in Liberated Lyman, *Kyiv Independent*, 20 October 2022, https://kyivindependent.com/news-feed/police-146-bodies-found-at-mass-burial-site-in-liberated-lyman

169. Telegram, 1 October 2022, https://t.me/RKadyrov_95/2911

170. Telegram, 1 October 2022, https://t.me/agurulev/2077

171. Telegram, 2 October 2022, https://t.me/strelkovii/3405

172. Telegram, 30 September 2022, https://t.me/strelkovii/3401

173. Putin Accuses Ukraine of "Terrorist Act" in Kerch Bridge Blast, *Politico*, 10 October 2022, https://www.politico.eu/article/putin-accuses-ukraine-of-terrorist-act-in-kerch-bridge-blast/

174. Podolyak: Crimean Bridge Explosion Result of Conflict Between Russian Military and Law Enforcement, *Kyiv Independent*, 8 October 2022, https://kyivindependent.com/news-feed/podolyak-crimean-bridge-explosion-result-of-inner-conflict-among-russian-law-enforcement

175. Security Service of Ukraine Behind Explosion on Crimea Bridge, *Ukrainskaya*

Pravda, 8 October, 2022, https://www.pravda.com.ua/eng/news/2022/10/8/7370891/

176. Telegram, 8 October 2022, https://t.me/SolovievLive/132592
177. Telegram, 8 October 2022, https://t.me/rybar/39915
178. Raketni udary po ukrayins'kiy stolytsi ta infrastrukturi rosiyany planuvaly z pochatku zhovtnya (The Russians have been Planning Missile Strikes on the Ukrainian Capital and Infrastructure since the Beginning of October), GUR, 10 October 2022, https://gur.gov.ua/content/raketni-udary-po-ukrainskii-stolytsi-ta-infrastrukturi-rosiiany-planuvaly-shche-z-pochatku-zhovtnia.html
179. Telegram, 10 October 2022, https://t.me/Prigozhin_hat/1793
180. Telegram, 11 October 2022, https://t.me/RKadyrov_95/2967
181. Telegram, 10 October 2022, https://t.me/medvedev_telegram/191
182. Russian War Commander Admits Kherson Situation "Very Difficult," Al Jazeera, 19 October 2022, https://www.aljazeera.com/news/2022/10/19/russia-war-commander-admits-kherson-situation-very-difficult
183. Dan Sabbagh and Artem Mazhulin, Zelenskiy Accuses Russia of Plotting to Blow Up Ukrainian Dam, *The Guardian*, 21 October 2022, https://www.the-guardian.com/world/2022/oct/21/zelenskiy-accuses-russia-plot-blow-up-nova-kakhovka-dam-ukraine
184. Luke Harding, Russian Troops Loot Kherson as Lines Redrawn Ahead of Final Battle for City, *The Guardian*, 5 November 2022, https://www.the-guardian.com/world/2022/nov/05/ukraine-russian-troops-loot-kherson-as-lines-redrawn-ahead-of-final-battle-for-city
185. Ibid.
186. Ibid.
187. Russian Authorities Urge Residents to Leave Kherson "Immediately," Al Jazeera, 22 October 2022, https://www.aljazeera.com/news/2022/10/22/russian-authorities-urge-residents-to-leave-kherson-immediately
188. Invaders Deport 34 More Children from Kherson Region to Russia, Ukrinform, 5 November 2022, https://www.ukrinform.net/rubric-society/3608531-invaders-deport-34-more-children-from-kherson-region-to-russia.html
189. Governor Haidai Officially Announces Beginning of De-Occupation of Luhansk Region, Ukrinform, 5 October 2022, https://www.ukrinform.net/rubric-ato/3586362-governor-haidai-officially-announces-beginning-of-deoccupation-of-luhansk-region.html
190. Wagner Group Says Fortifying Defensive Line in Eastern Ukraine, Ukranews, 19 October 2022, https://www.thedefensepost.com/2022/10/19/wagner-defense-eastern-ukraine/
191. Russians Instructed to Break Ukraine Army's Defence in Luhansk Region—Haidai, Ukrinform, 6 November 2022, https://www.ukrinform.net/rubric-

ato/3608721-russians-instructed-to-break-ukraine-armys-defense-in-luhansk-region-haidai.html

192. Russian Military Leaders Discussed Use of Nuclear Weapons, *The New York Times*, 2 November 2022, https://www.nytimes.com/2022/11/02/us/politics/russia-ukraine-nuclear-weapons.html

193. Russia's Defence Chief Warns of "Dirty Bomb" Provocation, CNBC, 22 October 2022, https://www.cnbc.com/2022/10/23/russias-defense-chief-warns-of-dirty-bomb-provocation.html

8. RUSSIA'S ISOLATION FROM THE WEST AND THE POST-SOVIET SPACE

1. Playing to Western Discord, Putin Says Russia is Battling "Strange" Elites, *The New York Times*, 27 October 2022, https://www.nytimes.com/2022/10/27/world/europe/ukraine-russia-war-putin.html

2. Elena Teslova, Russia Proposes Common Energy Market in the Eurasian Economic Union, Anadolu Agency, 21 October 2022, https://www.aa.com.tr/en/economy/russia-proposes-common-energy-market-in-eurasian-economic-union/2717620

3. Maia de la Baume, European Parliament Presses EU to Sanction Figures like Gerhard Schroder over Russia Ties, *Politico*, 19 May 2022, https://www.politico.eu/article/european-parliament-presses-eu-to-sanction-figures-like-gerhard-schroeder-over-russia-ties/

4. Kate Connolly, Ex-German Chancellor Gerhard Schroder Under Fire for Meeting Putin, *The Guardian*, 3 August 2022, https://www.theguardian.com/world/2022/aug/03/ex-german-chancellor-gerhard-schroder-under-fire-for-meeting-putin

5. ks-glava MID Avstrii rasskazala, pochemu pereyekhala v Livan, a ne v Rossiyu (Ex-Austrian Foreign Minister Told Why She Moved to Lebanon and Not to Russia), RIA Novosti, 5 September 2022, https://ria.ru/20220905/knaysl-1814433352.html

6. Sarah Wheaton, EU Moves Toward Russian Lobbyist Ban, *Politico*, 21 June 2022, https://www.politico.eu/article/eu-russia-lobbyist-ban/

7. German President Steinmeier Admits Mistakes Over Russia, DW, 4 May 2022, https://www.dw.com/en/german-president-steinmeier-admits-mistakes-over-russia-policy/a-61362153

8. Tristian Fiedler, German President Steinemier Arrives in Kyiv (at Last), *Politico*, 25 October 2022, https://www.politico.eu/article/frank-walter-steinmeier-ukraine-war-kyiv-visit-german-president/

9. Zeman: Russia has Lost Everything, Euractiv, 24 August 2022, https://www.euractiv.com/section/politics/short_news/zeman-russia-lost-everything/

10. Berlusconi, Caught on Tape Gushing About Putin, Heightens Anxiety About Italy, *The New York Times*, 20 October 2022, https://www.nytimes.com/2022/10/20/world/europe/silvio-berlusconi-vladimir-putin-russia-italy.html

11. Nicole Winfield, Italy's Meloni Issues Warning to Berlusconi over Putin Ties, Associated Press, 19 October 2022, https://apnews.com/article/russia-ukraine-putin-italy-wine-silvio-berlusconi-5ae5079575f1b38fbae9f129cb7d6881

12. In Greece, Russian Sympathies Die Hard Despite Ukraine War, France 24, 12 March 2022, https://www.france24.com/en/live-news/20220312-in-greece-russia-sympathies-die-hard-despite-ukraine-war

13. Greece Vows to Rebuild Bombed Maternity Clinic in Mariupol, Voice of America, 21 March 2022, https://www.voanews.com/a/greece-vows-to-rebuild-bombed-maternity-clinic-in-mariupol-/6494016.html

14. Nick Theodoulou, Cyprus is the Only EU State where Majority Disagrees Russia is to Blame for Ukraine War, *Cyprus Mail*, 5 May 2022, https://cyprus-mail.com/2022/05/05/cyprus-the-only-eu-state-where-majority-disagrees-that-russia-is-to-blame-for-ukraine-war/

15. Cyprus Tourism Rebounds Despite Sanctions-Hit Russia Plunge, France 24, 31 July 2022, https://www.france24.com/en/live-news/20220731-cyprus-tourism-rebounds-despite-sanctions-hit-russia-plunge

16. Julia Davis, Inside the Bizarre Conspiracy Theory that Halted Putin's Bombing Plans, *The Daily Beast*, 24 April 2022, https://www.thedailybeast.com/russian-state-media-commentators-tell-60-minutes-senior-nato-officials-are-inside-azovstal-steel-plant

17. Etienne Soula, Interference in the 2022 French Presidential Elections: Where Things Stand Ahead of the First Round, Alliance for Securing Democracy, 8 April 2022, https://securingdemocracy.gmfus.org/interference-in-the-2022-french-presidential-elections-where-things-stand-ahead-of-the-first-round/

18. Telegram, 7 November 2022, https://t.me/Prigozhin_hat/1978

19. Heather Stewart, Jeremy Corbyn Urges West to Stop Arming Ukraine, *The Guardian*, 2 August 2022, https://www.theguardian.com/politics/2022/aug/02/jeremy-corbyn-urges-west-to-stop-arming-ukraine

20. Seoirse Mulgrew, MEP Clare Daly Criticises EU Sanctions Against Russia and Claims it is a "Tool" of NATO, Independent.ie, 6 April 2022, https://www.independent.ie/news/mep-clare-daly-criticises-eu-sanctions-against-russia-and-claims-it-is-a-tool-of-nato-41527697.html

21. Angela Giuffrida, Cracks Show Over Russia as Italy's Far-Right Alliance Heads for Election Win, *The Guardian*, 9 September 2022, https://www.theguardian.com/world/2022/sep/09/cracks-show-in-meloni-salvini-alliance-over-russia-sanctions-italy

22. Marine Le Pen Warns EU Banning Russian Oil Tantamount to "Harakiri," TASS, 9 March 2022, https://tass.com/politics/1419095

23. Germany: Far Right Demo Slams Russia Sanctions, Coalition, DW, 8 October 2022, https://www.dw.com/en/germany-far-right-demo-protests-russia-sanctions-energy-policy/a-63380291

24. Italian Rally Calls for Country to Stop Sending Weapons to Ukraine, Euronews, 5 November 2022, https://www.euronews.com/2022/11/05/italian-rally-calls-for-country-to-stop-sending-weapons-to-ukraine

25. Charlie Parker, Kremlin is Behind Pro-Russian Protests in Europe, *The Times*, 16 April 2022, https://www.thetimes.co.uk/article/kremlin-is-behind-pro-russian-protests-in-europe-9gj27s8g5

26. Jon Henley, Westerners in No Mood for Concessions to Russia in Ukraine, Poll Finds, *The Guardian*, 14 October 2022, https://www.theguardian.com/world/2022/oct/14/westerners-in-no-mood-for-concessions-to-russia-in-ukraine-poll-finds

27. Nearly Half of Germans Believe Sanctions Harm Germany More than Russia—Poll, TASS, 17 July 2022, https://tass.com/world/1481015

28. Ola Cichowlas, Orban Pledges Cooperation with Putin in Storm of Ukraine Crisis, *The Moscow Times*, 1 February 2022, https://www.themoscowtimes.com/2022/02/01/orban-pledges-cooperation-with-putin-in-storm-of-ukraine-crisis-a76225

29. Zalan Zubor, "Respect and Gratitude to Putin"—Blatant Kremlin Propaganda on Pro-Government Media Channels in Hungary, 24 February 2022, https://english.atlatszo.hu/2022/02/24/respect-and-gratitude-to-putin-blatant-kremlin-propaganda-on-pro-government-media-channels-in-hungary/

30. Hungary Refuses to Allow Weapons Transit to Ukraine, *Politico*, 28 February 2022, https://www.politico.eu/article/hungary-foreign-minister-peter-szijjarto-weapon-transit-ukraine/

31. Victor Jack, Poland's Kaczynski Slams Orban for Refusing to Condemn Bucha Killings, *Politico*, 8 April 2022, https://www.politico.eu/article/poland-kaczynski-slams-hungary-orban-for-refusing-to-condemn-bucha-killings/

32. Jennifer Rankin, "Decide Who you are With," Ukrainian Leader Tells Viktor Orban, *The Guardian*, 25 March 2022, https://www.theguardian.com/world/2022/mar/25/ukraine-leader-volodymyr-zelenskiy-hungary-viktor-orban

33. Hungary Says EU Should Not Consider New Sanctions Against Russia, Reuters, 20 September 2022, https://www.reuters.com/world/europe/hungary-says-eu-should-not-consider-new-sanctions-against-russia-2022-09-20/

34. Philip Oltermann, Gazprom has Increased Gas Supply to Hungary, Says Official, *The Guardian*, 14 August 2022, https://www.theguardian.com/world/2022/aug/14/gazprom-increase-gas-supply-hungary-turkstream-pipeline

35. Interview with author, April 2022.

36. Henley, 2022.

37. Orban Calls for U.S.–Russia Talks on Ukraine War, Says Kyiv Can't Win, RFE/RL, 23 July 2022, https://www.rferl.org/a/orban-ukraine-war-us-russia-talks/31956804.html

38. Interview with Zoltan Kovacs, April 2022.

39. Liudas Dapkus, US Defence Chief: Russia "Uncoiling and Poised to Strike," Associated Press, 19 February 2022, https://apnews.com/article/russia-ukraine-russia-vladimir-putin-moscow-europe-db70f99704ed821ef6735b23a6149555

40. Estonia Urges NATO to Send More Troops to Eastern Europe to Send "Strong Message to Russia," *The Telegraph*, 21 February 2022, https://www.telegraph.co.uk/news/2022/02/21/estonia-urges-nato-send-troops-eastern-europe-send-strong-message/

41. Germany Blocks NATO Ally from Transferring Weapons to Ukraine, *Wall Street Journal*, 21 January 2022, https://www.wsj.com/articles/germany-blocks-nato-ally-from-transferring-weapons-to-ukraine-11642790772

42. Interview with author, September 2022.

43. Ibid.

44. Zygintas Abromaitis, Lithuania Running Dry on Weapons to Hand Over to Ukraine, LRT, 25 April 2022, https://www.lrt.lt/en/news-in-english/19/1680463/lithuania-running-dry-on-weapons-to-hand-over-to-ukraine

45. Zakharova ukazala na natsizm v slovakh latviyskogo deputata (Zakharova Pointed to Nazism in the Words of the Latvian Deputy), *Vzglyad*, 13 May 2022, https://vz.ru/news/2022/5/13/1158252.html

46. Daniel Boffey, Russia Threatens Retaliation as Lithuania Bans Goods Transit to Kaliningrad, *The Guardian*, 20 June 2022, https://www.theguardian.com/world/2022/jun/20/russia-condemns-lithuania-transit-ban-some-goods-kaliningrad

47. Daniel Boffey, Russia Threatens Serious Consequences as Lithuania Blocks Rail Goods, *The Guardian*, 21 June 2022, https://www.theguardian.com/world/2022/jun/21/kaliningrad-russia-threatens-serious-consequences-as-lithuania-blocks-rail-goods

48. Ekspert rasskazal, chem Rossiya mozhet otvetit' Litve na blokadu Kaliningrada (The Expert Told How Russia Can Respond to Lithuania on the Blockade of Kaliningrad), RIA Novosti, 20 June 2022, https://ria.ru/20220620/blokada-1796782439.html

49. Germany's Scholz Urges Free Transit for Russian Goods to Kaliningrad, *Politico*, 30 June 2022, https://www.politico.eu/article/olaf-scholz-urges-free-transit-for-russian-goods-to-kaliningrad/

50. Interview with author, October 2022.

51. Prime Minister Mateusz Morawiecki: Our Solidarity Can Resist Russia's Destructive Economic Policy, The Chancellery of the Prime Minister, 23 April

2022, https://www.gov.pl/web/primeminister/prime-minister-mateusz-mora-wiecki-our-solidarity-can-resist-russias-destructive-economic-policy

52. Interview with author, October 2022.

53. Interview with author, October 2022.

54. Medvedev Blasts Poland's "Talentless Politicians Puppeteered by the US" Who Fuel Russophobia, TASS, 21 March 2022, https://tass.com/politics/1425035

55. Naryshkin: Pol'sha planiruyet okkupirovat' svoi «istoricheskiye vladeniya» v Ukraine (Naryshkin: Poland Plans to Occupy its "Historical Possession" in Ukraine), RIA Novosti, 28 April 2022, https://ria.ru/20220428/polsha-1785 925942.html

56. Andrey Suzdal'tsev: ekonomiki v Ukraine seychas prosto net (Andrey Suzdaltsev: There is Simply No Economy in Ukraine Right Now), RIA Novosti, 30 August 2022, https://ria.ru/20220830/suzdaltsev-1812885903.html

57. Medvedev rasskazal o podderzhke Ukrainy so storony Pol'shi (Medvedev Spoke About the Support of Ukraine by Poland), Krasnaya Vesna, 31 March 2022, https://rossaprimavera.ru/news/6ce5afcb

58. Telegram, 13 May 2022, https://t.me/olegmorozov0511/585

59. Telegram, 25 September 2022, https://t.me/agurulev/2033

60. Russia Spreads Disinfo to Undermine Poles' Refugee Support, Euractiv, 3 March 2022, https://www.euractiv.com/section/politics/short_news/russia-spreads-disinfo-to-undermine-poles-refugee-support/

61. Interview with author, October 2022.

62. Finland's PM Says NATO Membership is "Very Unlikely" in her Current Term, Reuters, 20 January 2022, https://www.reuters.com/world/europe/finlands-pm-says-nato-membership-is-very-unlikely-her-watch-2022-01-19/

63. Interview with author, October 2022.

64. Interview with author, October 2022.

65. Patrick Wintour, Sweden's Ruling Social Democrats Divided on Decision to Join NATO, *The Guardian*, 4 May 2022, https://www.theguardian.com/world/2022/may/04/sweden-ruling-social-democrats-divided-on-decision-to-join-nato

66. V Gosdume nazvali prikhod NATO v Finlyandiyu signalom rasshireniya al'yansa (The State Duma Called the Arrival of NATO in Finland a Signal of the Expansion of the Alliance), RIA Novosti, 26 October 2022, https://ria.ru/20221026/signal-1827034735.html

67. My ochen' natovskiye. Chto budet, yesli shvedy i finny vstupyat v soyuz (We are very NATO. What will happen if Sweden and Finland Join the Alliance), RIA Novosti, 9 May 2022, https://ria.ru/20220509/nato-1787501825.html?in=t

68. Vopros dnya: smozhet li NATO sdelat' Baltiku svoim «vnutrennim morem»? (Question of the Day: Will NATO be able to Make the Baltic their "Inland Sea?"), *New Izvestia*, 14 August 2022, https://newizv.ru/article/general/14-08-2022/vopros-dnya-smozhet-li-nato-sdelat-baltiku-svoim-vnutrennim-morem

69. Russia Threatens Military Build Up if Finland or Sweden Join NATO, Euronews, 14 April 2022, https://www.euronews.com/2022/04/14/russia-threatens-military-build-up-if-finland-or-sweden-join-nato

70. Andrew Roth, Putin Issues Fresh Warning to Finland and Sweden on Installing NATO Infrastructure, *The Guardian*, 29 June 2022, https://www.theguardian.com/world/2022/jun/29/russia-condemns-nato-invitation-finland-sweden

71. Interview with author, October 2022.

72. Sweden to Boost Military on Gotland Amidst Russia Fears, Reuters, 29 April 2022, https://www.reuters.com/world/europe/sweden-boost-military-gotland-amid-russia-fears-2022-04-29/

73. Bulgaria to Summon its Ambassador from Moscow for Consultations—Prime Minister, TASS, 24 March 2022, https://tass.com/world/1426865

74. Russian Foreign Ministry to Consider Closure of Embassy to Bulgaria—Peskov, Interfax, 1 July 2022, https://interfax.com/newsroom/top-stories/80873/

75. Bulgaria will not Hold Talks to Renew Gas Deal with Gazprom, Reuters, 19 March 2022, https://www.reuters.com/business/energy/bulgaria-will-not-hold-talks-renew-gas-deal-with-gazprom-2022-03-19/

76. Interview with author, September 2022.

77. Bulgaria Struggles with Gas Supply after Denying Ruble Payment for Russian Gas, Al-Arabiya, 16 September 2022, https://english.alarabiya.net/News/world/2022/09/16/Bulgaria-struggles-with-gas-supply-after-denying-ruble-payment-for-Russian-gas

78. Antonia Kotseva and Krassen Nikolov, Bulgaria Doesn't Send Weapons to Ukraine but Arms Industry Flourishes, Euractiv, 31 October 2022, https://www.euractiv.com/section/all/short_news/bulgaria-doesnt-send-weapons-to-ukraine-but-arms-industry-flourishes/

79. Kotseva and Nikolov, 2022.

80. Interview with author, September 2022.

81. Krassen Nikolov, Bulgarian Government May Fall if it Sends Weapons to Ukraine, Euractiv, 14 April 2022, https://www.euractiv.com/section/politics/short_news/bulgarian-government-may-fall-if-it-sends-weapons-to-ukraine/

82. Christian Oliver, Bulgarian PM Fires Defence Minister for Promoting Putin's Spin, *Politico*, 28 February 2022, https://www.politico.eu/article/bulgaria-pm-fires-defense-minister-stefan-yanev-promote-vladimir-putin-spin/

83. Andrei Chirileasa, Romania Under Cyberattack Coming from Russia's Killnet, Romania Insider, 2 May 2022, https://www.romania-insider.com/romania-cyberattack-russia-killnet-2022

84. «Vtorzheniye v Pridnestrov'ye mozhet byt' uzhe segodnya» ("Invasion of Transnistria can be Already Today"), Mk.ru, 26 April 2022, https://www.mk.ru/politics/2022/04/26/vtorzhenie-v-pridnestrove-mozhet-byt-uzhe-segodnya.html

85. Vladimir Vasiliev, Rumyniya natselilas' na Moldovu, a Ukraina na Pridnestrov'ye (Romania Sets its Sights on Moldova, and Ukraine on Transnistria), Regnum, 27 April 2022, https://regnum.ru/news/polit/3577039.html

86. Sergey Latyshev, Sovsem Ne To, Chto vy Dumali: Glavnaya Prichina Ne Toropitsya S Osvobzhdeniyem Ukrainy (Not at all What You Thought: The Main Reason not to Hurry with the Liberation of Ukraine), Tsargrad, 16 May 2022, https://tsargrad.tv/articles/sovsem-ne-to-chto-vy-dumali-glavnaja-prichina-ne-speshit-s-osvobozhdeniem-ukrainy_547089

87. Moldova Stays Neutral, Won't Join Sanctions Against Russia—FM, Interfax, 28 February 2022, https://interfax.com/newsroom/top-stories/74843/

88. Ukraina Nachnet Bitvu za Odessu Vtorzheniyem v Pridnestyovye—Ekspert (Ukraine will Start the Battle for Odesa with the Invasion of Transnistria— Expert), Tsargrad, 29 April 2022, https://herson.tsargrad.tv/news/ukraina-nachtjot-srazhenie-za-odessu-s-vtorzhenija-v-pridnestrove-jekspert_539275

89. Mansur Mirovalev, Will Vladimir Putin Succeed in Occupying Southwestern Ukraine, Al Jazeera, 27 April 2022, https://www.aljazeera.com/news/2022/4/27/will-putin-succeed-in-seizing-southwestern-ukraine

90. Moldova Must Boost Defences, Given Presence of Russia Troops—President, Reuters, 28 September 2022, https://www.reuters.com/markets/europe/moldova-must-boost-defences-given-presence-russia-troops-president-2022-09-28/

91. In Visit to Moldova, German Defence Chief Promises Further Military, Energy Aid, RFE/RL, 1 October 2022, https://www.rferl.org/a/moldova-germany-visit-lambrecht-/32060898.html

92. MID predostereg NATO ot popytok vmeshatel'stva v pridnestrovskiy vopros (The Foreign Ministry Warned NATO Against Trying to Intervene in the Transnistrian Issue), RIA Novosti, 6 September 2022, https://ria.ru/20220906/pridnestrove-1814748473.html?in=t

93. V MID prokommentirovali plany YES po postavkam bespilotnikov v Moldovu (The Foreign Ministry Commented on EU Plans to Supply Drones to Moldova), RIA Novosti, 6 September 2022, https://ria.ru/20220906/bespilotniki-1814723388.html?in=t

94. Slutskiy prizval usilit' podderzhku Pridnestrov'ya (Slutsky Urged to Increase Support for Pridnestrovie), RIA Novosti, 7 September 2022, https://ria.ru/20220907/pridnestrove-1815263492.html

95. Vitalie Calugareanu, Russia Warns Moldova over Transnistria Troops, DW, 3 September 2022, https://www.dw.com/en/russia-warns-moldova-over-transnistria-troops/a-63013005

96. Debris of Russian Missile Downed by Ukraine Lands in Moldovan Village, Reuters, 31 October 2022, https://www.reuters.com/world/europe/russian-

missile-downed-by-ukraine-lands-moldovan-village-interior-ministry-2022-10-31/

97. Moldova Expels Russian Diplomat Over Ukraine Missile Debris, *The Moscow Times*, 1 November 2022, https://www.themoscowtimes.com/2022/11/01/moldova-expels-russian-diplomat-over-ukraine-missile-debris-a79255

98. Telegram, 21 January 2022, https://t.me/alexey_pushkov/6097

99. How Russian Strikes on Ukraine Heighten Moldova's Energy Crisis, Euronews, 17 November 2022, https://www.euronews.com/2022/11/17/how-russian-strikes-on-ukraine-heighten-moldovas-energy-crisis

100. «Lyudi v otchayanii». V Moldove sozdano parallel'noye pravitel'stvo ("People in Despair." Parallel Government Created in Moldova), RIA Novosti, 26 October 2022, https://ria.ru/20221026/moldaviya-1826709136.html?in=t

101. Georgia Won't Join Russia Sanctions, PM Says, Civil.ge, 25 February 2022, https://civil.ge/archives/475153

102. Interview with author, September 2022.

103. Protesters in Tbilisi Decry Georgian Government's Inadequate Support for Ukraine, RFE/RL, 1 March 2022, https://www.rferl.org/a/ukraine-invasion-tbilisi-protest-georgia/31731006.html

104. Interview with author, September 2022.

105. Interview with former Georgian diplomat Ekaterina Meiering, October 2022.

106. Giorgi Lomsadze, Ukraine Recalls Ambassador from Georgia, Eurasianet, 1 March 2022, https://eurasianet.org/ukraine-recalls-ambassador-from-georgia

107. Danilov on Karabakh, Kuril Islands and Kaliningrad: Opening New Fronts Against Russia Would Help Us, *Ukrainskaya Pravda*, 26 March 2022, https://www.pravda.com.ua/eng/news/2022/03/26/7334816/

108. Georgia Joins Ukraine-Related Financial Sanctions on Russia—President, TASS, 31 March 2022, https://tass.com/world/1430685

109. Interview with Ekaterina Meiering, October 2022.

110. Georgia's South Ossetia Cancels Referendum on Joining Russia, Al Jazeera, 31 May 2022, https://www.aljazeera.com/news/2022/5/31/georgias-south-ossetia-cancels-referendum-on-joining-russia

111. Tornike Mandaria, South Ossetian Troops Fighting for Russia in Ukraine, Eurasianet, 29 March 2022, https://eurasianet.org/south-ossetian-troops-fighting-for-russia-in-ukraine

112. Clement Giradot, The Georgian Village Facing Russian "Creeping Occupation," Al Jazeera, 3 July 2022, https://www.aljazeera.com/features/2022/7/3/the-georgian-village-facing-russian-creeping-occupation

113. Conor Sheils, In Georgian Capital, a Sanctuary for Russians Opposed to Putin's War, *Christian Science Monitor*, 20 March 2022, https://www.csmonitor.com/

World/Europe/2022/0330/In-Georgian-capital-a-sanctuary-for-Russians-opposed-to-Putin-s-war

114. Emma Burrows, "Most of you Support the War:" Georgians Slam Russia Fleeing Mobilization, ITV, 28 September 2022, https://www.itv.com/news/2022-09-28/most-of-you-support-the-war-georgians-slam-russians-fleeing-army-mobilisation

115. Russia Closes Mobilization Screening Checkpoint at Georgia Border, *The Moscow Times*, 21 October 2022, https://www.themoscowtimes.com/2022/10/21/russia-closes-mobilization-screening-checkpoint-at-georgia-border-a79160

116. Interview with author, October 2022.

117. James Crisp and Dominic Nicholls, Liz Truss Warns Russian Meddling Could Reignite Conflict in the Western Balkans, *The Telegraph*, 26 May 2022, https://www.telegraph.co.uk/world-news/2022/05/26/liz-truss-warns-russian-meddling-could-reignite-conflict-western/

118. Russian Diplomat Slams UK Foreign Secretary's Comments on Russia's Balkan Influence, TASS, 30 May 2022, https://tass.com/politics/1458023

119. Zoran Radosavljevic, Russia Complains to Croatia over "Hostile Behaviour," Euractiv, 26 May 2022, https://www.euractiv.com/section/politics/short_news/russia-complains-to-croatia-over-hostile-behaviour/

120. New EU Sanctions to Make Putin Smile, Croatian President Says, TASS, 31 May 2022, https://tass.com/world/1458621

121. Samir Kajosevic, Montenegro Freezes Property of Two Russians on EU Sanctions List, Balkan Insight, 27 July 2022, https://balkaninsight.com/2022/07/27/montenegro-freezes-property-of-two-russians-on-eu-sanctions-list/

122. Montenegro Expels Russian Diplomats Amid Spying Suspicions, DW, 30 September 2022, https://www.dw.com/en/montenegro-russian-diplomats-expelled-amid-spying-suspicions/a-63290933

123. Serbia Supports Ukraine's Sovereignty but Opposes Sanctions on Russia, Vučić Says, Balkan Insight, 25 February 2022, https://balkaninsight.com/2022/02/25/serbia-supports-ukraines-sovereignty-but-opposes-sanctions-on-russia-vucic-says/

124. Dusan Stojanovic, Serbia Ignores EU Sanctions, Secures Gas Deal with Putin, 29 May 2022, https://apnews.com/article/russia-ukraine-putin-european-union-aleksandar-vucic-5a6bbab20373ef26829378c6a0eb6065

125. Serbian Foreign Minister Plays Down Deal with Lavrov after Flak from Brussels, Euronews, 25 September 2022, https://www.euronews.com/2022/09/25/serbian-foreign-minister-plays-down-agreement-with-lavrov-amid-criticism

126. Interview with author, September 2022.

127. Milica Stojanovic, Serbian Pro-Regime Media Praise Russia "Overrunning" Ukraine, Balkan Insight, 25 February 2022, https://balkaninsight.com/2022/02/25/serbian-pro-regime-media-praise-russia-overrunning-ukraine/

128. Georgi Gotev, Analyst Says if Putin was a Candidate in Serbia, he would get over 70% of the Vote, Euractiv, 18 March 2022, https://www.euractiv.com/section/enlargement/interview/analyst-says-if-putin-was-a-candidate-in-serbia-he-would-get-over-70-of-the-vote/

129. Russian Mercenary Group Wagner Opens "Cultural Center" in Serbia, Anadolu Agency, 8 December 2022, https://www.aa.com.tr/en/europe/russian-mercenary-group-wagner-opens-cultural-center-in-serbia/2758885

130. James Kilner, Russia's Wagner Group Recruits "Serbian Nationalists" to Fight in Ukraine, *The Telegraph*, 13 January 2023, https://www.telegraph.co.uk/world-news/2023/01/13/russias-wagner-group-recruits-serbian-nationalists-fight-ukraine/

131. Guy Delauney, Ukraine War: Serbia Uproar over Wagner Mercenaries Recruiting for Russia, BBC, 19 January 2023, https://www.bbc.co.uk/news/world-europe-64329371

132. Vuchich ob'yasnil, pochemu Serbiya podderzhala zamorozku uchastiya Rossii v SPCH OON (Vučić Explained why Serbia Supported the Freeze of Russia's Participation in the UNHRC), RIA Novosti, 8 April 2022, https://ria.ru/20220408/serbiya-1782413495.html

133. Putin Zabio Noz U Leda Srbij! Trampio Kosovo za Donjeck I Lugansk (Putin Stabbed Serbia in the Back! Trampled Kosovo for Donetsk and Luhansk), *Republika*, 26 April 2022, https://www.republika.rs/svet/svet/356699/vladimir-putin-kosovo-nezavisnost-donjeck-lugansk

134. Pro-Russian Right-Wing Serbs Hold Another Demonstration in Belgrade, RFE/RL, 15 April 2022, https://www.rferl.org/a/serbia-ukraine-russia-right-wing-un-human-rights-council/31805557.html

135. Seselj: referendumy v DNR, LNR, Zaporozhskoy i Khersonskoy oblastyakh polnost'yu sootvetstvuyut Khartii OON (Seselj: Referendums in the DNR, LNR, Zaporizhzhia and Kherson Regions are Fully Consistent with the UN Charter), TASS, 20 September 2022, https://tass.ru/mezhdunarodnaya-panorama/15813647

136. President Says Serbia Can Afford Alternatives to Russian Fuel, Reuters, 29 August 2022, https://www.reuters.com/world/europe/president-says-serbia-can-afford-alternatives-russian-fuel-2022-08-29/

137. Maxim Samorukov, Last Friend in Europe: How Far will Russia Go to Preserve its Alliance with Serbia? Carnegie Endowment for International Peace, 16 June 2022, https://carnegieendowment.org/politika/87303

138. Russia Accuses "Radical" Kosovo of Displacing Serbs in Border Row, *The Moscow Times*, 1 August 2022, https://www.themoscowtimes.com/2022/08/01/russia-accuses-radical-kosovo-of-displacing-serbs-in-border-row-a78454

139. Zakharova nazvala Kosovo territoriyey eksperimentov «chernykh» transplantologov (Zakharova Called Kosovo the Territory of Experiments of "Black" Transplants), RIA Novosti, 3 August 2022, https://ria.ru/20220803/kosovo-1806876324.html?in=t

140. Russia Can Aid Serbia with Energy or Arms Supplies, if Necessary—Senator, TASS, 1 August 2022, https://tass.com/world/1487519

141. Interview with author, September 2022.

142. Interview with senior Kosovar official, October 2022.

143. Interview with author, October 2022.

144. Russian Ambassador says BiH Can Join NATO, but Moscow will React, Euractiv, 17 March 2022, https://www.euractiv.com/section/politics/short_news/russian-ambassador-says-bih-can-join-nato-but-moscow-will-react/

145. Zoran Radosavljevic, Russia's Invasion Fully Justified, says Bosnian Serb Leader, Euractiv, 20 September 2022, https://www.euractiv.com/section/politics/short_news/russias-invasion-fully-justified-says-bosnian-serb-leader/

146. Eldar Emric, Bosnian Serb Separatist Leader Blasts West, Praises Russia, Associated Press, 28 September 2022, https://apnews.com/article/russia-ukraine-putin-elections-presidential-moscow-6eb1a7e1526d7d58082cd-a15b496b85d

147. RS Opposition: Putin Confirmed that BiH had Imposed Sanctions on Russia, *Sarajevo Times*, 19 June 2022, https://sarajevotimes.com/rs-opposition-putin-confirmed-that-bih-had-imposed-sanctions-on-russia/

148. Interview with author, October 2022.

149. Lukashenko zayavil, chto v Ukraine poyavilis' rostki fashizma (Lukashenko said that Sprouts of Fascism Appeared in Ukraine), RIA Novosti, 1 September 2022, https://ria.ru/20220901/ukraina-1813740607.html

150. Lukashenko Apparently Gave Putin New Files on Staged Events in Bucha—Kremlin, TASS, 12 April 2022, https://tass.com/politics/1436757

151. Lukashenko: NATO i ryad yevropeyskikh stran rassmatrivayut varianty vozmozhnoy agressii protiv Belarusi (Lukashenko: NATO and a Number of European Countries are Considering Options for Possible Aggression Against Belarus), Belta, 10 October 2022, https://www.belta.by/president/view/lukashenko-nato-i-rjad-stran-evropy-rassmatrivajut-varianty-vozmozhnoj-agressii-protiv-belarusi-528288-2022/

152. Interview with Belarusian diplomat, October 2022.

153. Lukashenko zayavil, chto Pol'sha narashchivayet voyennyye sily u belorusskikh granits (Lukashenko said that Poland is Building up Military Forces Near the

Belarusian Borders), RIA Novosti, 4 October 2022, https://ria.ru/20221004/polsha-1821376135.html

154. Ukraina gotovitsya nanesti udar po Belarusi—Lukashenko (Ukraine is Preparing to Strike at Belarus—Lukashenko), RIA Novosti, 10 October 2022, https://crimea.ria.ru/20221010/ukraina-gotovitsya-k-udaru-po-belorussii—lukashenko-1124800187.html

155. Rosiya namahayet´sya vtyahnuty Bilorus´ u vidkrytu viynu proty Ukrayiny (Russia Trying to Draw Belarus into Open War Against Ukraine), GUR, 8 October 2022, https://gur.gov.ua/en/content/rosiia-namahaietsia-vtiahn-uty-bilorus-u-vidkrytu-viinu-z-ukrainoiu.html

156. Opposition Leader says Belarus Shouldn't Fight for Russia, Associated Press, 25 October 2022, https://apnews.com/article/russia-ukraine-business-esto-nia-moscow-belarus-be7f0377a563702e9cf85645c4ddfa9f

157. Belarusians Fight for Ukraine with an Eye on Ousting Lukashenko, Euronews, 17 October 2022, https://www.euronews.com/2022/10/17/belarusians-fight-for-ukraine-with-an-eye-on-ousting-lukashenko

158. Interview with author, October 2022.

159. Interview with author, October 2022.

160. Yauheni Preiherman, Belarusian-Russian Cooperation Against the Backdrop of the Ukraine War, Jamestown Foundation, 27 September 2022, https://jamestown.org/program/belarusian-russian-cooperation-against-the-back-drop-of-the-ukraine-war/

161. Volfovich: Belarus is No Threat to Anyone; People's Militia is Meant to Protect the Country, Belta, 21 September 2022, https://eng.belta.by/politics/view/volfovich-belarus-is-no-threat-to-anyone-peoples-militia-is-meant-to-pro-tect-country-153261–2022/

162. Telegram, 4 August 2022, https://t.me/AFUStratCom/4892

163. Trade Between Russia and Belarus Expected to Grow to a Record $45 Billion in 2022—PM Golovchenko, Interfax, 3 October 2022, https://interfax.com/newsroom/top-stories/83475/

164. Lukashenko: Belarus has a Myriad of Joint Projects with Russia, Belta, 1 September 2022, https://eng.belta.by/president/view/lukashenko-belarus-has-a-myriad-of-joint-projects-with-russia-152856–2022/

165. Interview with Valery Kavaleuski, October 2022.

166. Belarus Fighter "Ready to Carry Russian Nukes," *The Telegraph*, 26 August 2022, https://www.telegraph.co.uk/world-news/2022/08/26/russia-ukraine-war-putin-nuclear-power-plant-live-news/

167. Artyom Shraibman, What's Behind Russia's New Deployment of Troops to Belarus, Carnegie Endowment for International Peace, 25 October 2022, https://carnegieendowment.org/politika/88249

168. Interviews with Belarusian diplomats, October 2022.

169. Belarus Doing "Everything" to End Ukraine War: Lukashenko, Al Jazeera, 5 May 2022, https://www.aljazeera.com/news/2022/5/5/belarus-doing-every-thing-to-end-ukraine-war-lukashenko

170. Belarus Warns Against Pushing Nuclear-Armed Russia "Into Corner," Al Jazeera, 14 October 2022, https://www.aljazeera.com/news/2022/10/14/belarus-warns-ukraine-on-pushing-nuclear-armed-russia-into-corner

171 Mikhail Kotlyar, «Lyubaya voyna zakanchivayetsya mirnymi peregovorami». O chem govorili na sammite ODKB ("Any War Ends with Peace Negotiations: What was Discussed at the CSTO Summit"), Gazeta.ru, 23 November 2022, https://www.gazeta.ru/politics/2022/11/23/15831649.shtml

172 We Will Talk About CSTO Problems without Cameras, News.am, 23 November 2022, https://news.am/eng/news/731686.html

173 Russia Denounces Criticism of Nagorno-Karabakh Peacekeepers, Al Jazeera, 30 December 2022, https://www.aljazeera.com/news/2022/12/30/russia-denounces-criticism-of-nagorno-karabakh-peacekeepers

174. Lilian Avedian, Armenia Silent on Russian Invasion of Ukraine, *Armenian Weekly*, 2 March 2022, https://armenianweekly.com/2022/03/02/armenia-silent-on-russian-invasion-of-ukraine/

175. SSHA rabotayut s armyanskimi bankami nad sanktsiyami protiv Rossii, soob-shchayut SMI (US Working with Armenian Banks on Sanctions Against Russia, Media Report), Radio Sputnik, 16 April 2022, https://radiosputnik.ria.ru/20220416/sanktsii-1783872686.html

176. Ani Mejlumyan, Armenian Trade with Russia Raises Questions About Re-Exports, Eurasianet, 31 August 2022, https://eurasianet.org/armenian-trade-with-russia-raises-questions-about-re-exports

177. Fearing Arrest, Russian Critics of Ukraine War Find Refuge in Armenia, France 24, 18 March 2022, https://www.france24.com/en/europe/20220318-fearing-arrest-russian-critics-of-ukraine-war-find-refuge-in-armenia

178. kak povliyaet vozmozhnoe otklyuchenie rossii ot swift na armeniyu kommen-tariy eks ministra (How the Possible Disconnection of Russia from SWIFT will Affect Armenia, Comment of Ex-Minister), Sputnik, 28 February 2022, https://ru.armeniasputnik.am/20220228/kak-povliyaet-vozmozhnoe-otkly-uchenie-rossii-ot-swift-na-armeniyu-kommentariy-eks-ministra-39170186.html

179. Interview with author, October 2022.

180. Elena Teslova, Azerbaijan, Russia Eye Further Development of Economic Cooperation, 18 November 2022, https://www.aa.com.tr/en/europe/azerbaijan-russia-eye-further-development-of-economic-cooperation/2742289

181. Ibid.

182. Russia Accuses Azerbaijan of Violating Nagorno-Karabakh Ceasefire, France 24, 26 March 2022, https://www.france24.com/en/europe/20220326-russia-accuses-azerbaijan-of-violating-nagorno-karabakh-ceasefire

183. Heydar Isayev, Russian MP Threatens to Nuke Azerbaijan, Eurasianet, 30 March 2022, https://eurasianet.org/russian-mp-threatens-to-nuke-azer-baijan

184. Russia to Boost Trade, Economic Ties with Asian Countries Amid Sanctions Says Ministry, TASS, 25 February 2022, https://tass.com/economy/1411085

185. Kataryna Wolczuk and Rilka Dragneva, Putin's Eurasian Dream May Soon Become a Nightmare, Chatham House, 3 May 2022, https://www.chatham-house.org/2022/05/putins-eurasian-dream-may-soon-become-nightmare

186. Meiramgul Kussainova, Russia-Led Military Alliance Won't be Party to Ongoing War in Ukraine: Kazakhstan, Anadolu Agency, 3 October 2022, https://www.aa.com.tr/en/world/russian-led-military-alliance-wont-be-party-to-ongoing-war-in-ukraine-kazakhstan/2701736

187. Telegram, 17 November 2022, https://t.me/grey_zone/15844

188. Russia's War in Ukraine and its Impact on Central Asia, *The Diplomat*, 24 October 2022, https://thediplomat.com/2022/10/russias-war-in-ukraine-and-its-impact-on-central-asia/

189. Russia Ally Kazakhstan Permits Large Pro-Ukraine Rally Amid Sanctions Fears, France 24, 6 March 2022, https://www.france24.com/en/live-news/20220306-russia-ally-kazakhstan-permits-large-pro-ukraine-rally-amid-sanc-tions-fears

190. Wilder Sanchez and Kamila Auyezova, Kazakhstan Cancels Victory Day in Protest Over Putin's Ukraine War, Atlantic Council, 11 May 2022, https://www.atlanticcouncil.org/blogs/ukrainealert/kazakhstan-cancels-victory-day-in-protest-over-putins-ukraine-war/

191. Joanna Lillis, Kazakhstan–Russia Frictions Over Ukraine War Go Public, Eurasianet, 20 June 2022, https://eurasianet.org/kazakhstan-russia-frictions-over-ukraine-war-go-public

192. Telefonnyy razgovor s Prezidentom Kyrgyzstana Sadyrom Zhaparovym (Telephone Conversation with President of Kyrgyzstan Sadyr Zhaparov), President of Russia, 26 February 2022, http://www.kremlin.ru/events/presi-dent/news/67869

193. Wagner Recruiting Kyrgyz, Uzbek Citizens to Fight in Ukraine—Reports, *The Moscow Times*, 20 July 2022, https://www.themoscowtimes.com/2022/07/20/wagner-recruiting-kyrgyz-uzbek-citizens-to-fight-in-ukraine-reports-a78353

194. Uzbekistan warns Citizens not to Join Foreign Armies Amid Ukraine Conflict, Reuters, 22 September 2022, https://www.reuters.com/world/europe/uzbeki-

stan-warns-citizens-not-join-foreign-armies-amid-ukraine-conflict-2022-09-22/

9. RUSSIA PIVOTS TO THE EAST

1. China's Xi Urges Russia and Other Countries to Work at Preventing "Color Revolutions," Reuters, 16 September 2022, https://www.reuters.com/world/asia-pacific/chinas-xi-says-china-will-help-train-law-enforcement-personnel-sco-countries-2022–09–16/

2. Vladimir Putin Says 80 Large Russian Companies to Visit Iran Next Week, The National, 15 September 2022, https://www.thenationalnews.com/mena/iran/2022/09/15/vladimir-putin-says-80-large-russian-companies-to-visit-iran-next-week/

3. West's "Cherry-Picking" PM Modi's "Not the Time for War" Comment, No Change in Indo-Russian Ties: Envoy, *Tribune India*, 24 September 2022, https://www.tribuneindia.com/news/nation/west-cherry-picking-pm-modis-not-the-time-for-war-comment-no-change-in-indo-russia-ties-envoy-434626

4. Evelyn Chang, China Refuses to Call Russian Attack on Ukraine an "Invasion," Deflects Blame to U.S., CNBC, 24 February 2022, https://www.cnbc.com/2022/02/24/china-refuses-to-call-attack-on-ukraine-an-invasion-blames-us.html

5. Transcript: Chinese Ambassador to the U.S. Qing Gang on "Face the Nation," CBS, 20 March 2022, https://www.cbsnews.com/news/qin-gang-chinese-ambassador-face-the-nation-03-20-2022/

6. Remarks by Ambassador Zhang Jun at the UN Security Council Briefing on Ukraine, Permanent Mission of the People's Republic of China to the UN, 27 September 2022, http://un.china-mission.gov.cn/eng/hyyfy/202209/t202 20928_10772816.htm

7. China Defends Ukraine War Stance, Aims to Deepen Ties with Russia, Al Jazeera, 25 December 2022, https://www.aljazeera.com/news/2022/12/25/china-defends-ukraine-stance-to-deepen-ties-with-russia

8. China Scoops up Rare Russian Oil as Top Buyer Boosts Imports, Bloomberg, 10 January 2023, https://www.bloomberg.com/news/articles/2023-01-10/china-scoops-up-rare-russian-oil-as-top-buyer-boosts-imports?leadSource=uverify%20wall

9. Clara Ferreira Marques, Putin Discovers the Limits of Comrade Xi's Friendship, Bloomberg, 16 September 2022, https://www.bloomberg.com/opinion/articles/2022-09-15/putin-discovers-the-limits-of-xi-s-limitless-friendship-in-samarkand

10. Interview with author, September 2022.

11. China's Trade with Russia Picks Up Speed in August, Reuters, 7 September 2022, https://www.reuters.com/markets/europe/chinas-trade-with-russia-picks-up-speed-august-2022-09-07/

12. China's Imports of Russian Coal Hit 5-Year High as Ties Deepen, Al Jazeera, 20 September 2022, https://www.aljazeera.com/economy/2022/9/20/chinas-imports-of-russian-coal-hit-5-year-high-as-ties-deepen

13. Russia, China Agree 30-Year Gas Deal via New Pipeline, to settle in euros, Euractiv, 6 February 2022, https://www.euractiv.com/section/global-europe/news/russia-china-agree-30-year-gas-deal-via-new-pipeline-to-settle-in-euros/

14. Stephen Stapczynski, China Snaps Up Half-Price Russian LNG as Europe Shuns Supplies, Bloomberg, 8 September 2022, https://www.bloomberg.com/news/articles/2022-09-08/china-snaps-up-half-price-russian-lng-as-europe-shuns-supplies

15. Christoph Nedopil Wang, Brief: China Belt and Road Initiative (BRI) Investment Report H1 2022, Green Finance and Development Center, 24 July 2022, https://greenfdc.org/china-belt-and-road-initiative-bri-investment-report-h1–2022/

16. Frank Tang and Orange Wang, Chinese Investment in Russia's Resource-Rich Far East is Growing, but Western Sanctions are Clouding the Outlook, *South China Morning Post*, 6 October 2022, https://www.scmp.com/economy/global-economy/article/3194913/chinese-investment-russias-resource-rich-far-east-growing

17. Anastasia Bashtakova, Dollar strelyayet vpustuyu (The Dollar Shoots Empty), *Nezavisimaya Gazeta*, 6 September 2022, https://www.ng.ru/economics/2022-09-06/1_8532_dollar.html

18. Ibid.

19. Russian Security Council Touts "Further Military Cooperation" with China, RFE/RL, 19 September 2022, https://www.rferl.org/a/russia-security-council-military-cooperation-china/32040797.html

20. Henry Ridgwell, China-Russia Military Ties Boosted by Invasion of Ukraine, VOA, 6 September 2022, https://www.voanews.com/a/china-russia-military-ties-boosted-by-invasion-of-ukraine-/6732055.html

21. Dan Milmo, China Accused of Cyberattacks on Ukraine Before Russian Invasion, *The Guardian*, 2 April 2022, https://www.theguardian.com/technology/2022/apr/01/china-accused-of-launching-cyber-attacks-on-ukraine-before-russian-invasion

22. UK Intelligence: Russia Started Using Iranian Drones from New Batch, Ukrinform, 19 December 2022, https://www.ukrinform.net/rubric-ato/3630916-uk-intelligence-russia-started-using-iranian-drones-from-new-batch.html

23. Isobel Koshiw, Drone Analysis in Ukraine Suggests Iran has Supplied Russia

since War Began, <I>The Guardian</I>, 10 November 2022, https://www.the-guardian.com/world/2022/nov/10/iranian-made-drones-supplied-to-russia-after-february-invasion-says-ukraine

24. Barak Ravid, Scoop: Iran Plans to Limit the Range of Missiles Sent to Russia, Israeli Officials Say, Axios, 12 December 2022, https://www.axios.com/2022/12/12/ukraine-war-russia-missiles-iran-limit

25. Amanda Macias, U.S. Slaps Iran with Another Round of Sanctions over Drones used in Russia's War on Ukraine, CNBC, 6 January 2023, https://www.cnbc.com/2023/01/06/us-sanctions-iran-over-drones-used-in-russias-war-on-ukraine.html

26. Interview with author, September 2022.

27. Vedushchiy rossiyskiy razrabotchik giperzvukovykh raket zaderzhan po obvineniyu v gosudarstvennoy ismene (Leading Russian Developer of Hypersonic Missiles Detained for Treason), UNIAN, 6 August 2022, https://www.unian.net/world/vedushchiy-rossiyskiy-razrabotchik-giperzvukovyh-raket-zaderzhan-za-gosizmenu-novosti-mira-11931210.html

28. Měiguó jiè é wū chōngtú lüèduó shìjiè (rè yì) (The U.S. is Looting the World with the Help of Russia-Ukraine Conflict), *People's Daily*, 4 April 2022, http://world.people.com.cn/n1/2022/0404/c1002-32391419.html

29. "Li Zhiwei, Měiguó duì wūkèlán wéijī fù zhǔyào zérèn"(shēndù guānchá) (U.S. Bears Primary Responsibility for the Ukraine Crisis), 21 April 2022, http://world.people.com.cn/n1/2022/0421/c1002-32404329.html

30. John Feng, Chinese TV Pundit Says Bucha Killings Were Staged, Newsweek, 5 April 2022, https://www.newsweek.com/bucha-ukraine-killing-russia-warchina-song-zhongping-china-1695059

31. Timofey Bordachev, Nachnetsya li voyna za kitayskiy «ostrov Krym»? (Will the War for the Chinese Island of Crimea Begin?), *Vzglyad*, 21 July 2022, https://vz.ru/opinions/2022/7/21/1168743.html

32. Telegram, 6 August 2022, https://t.me/tsargradtv/21262

33. Foreign Ministry Spokesperson Zhao Lijian's Regular Press Conference, Ministry of Foreign Affairs of the People's Republic of China, 8 March 2022, https://www.fmprc.gov.cn/mfa_eng/xwfw_665399/s2510_665401/2511_665403/202203/t20220309_10649938.html

34. Twitter, 19 April 2022, https://twitter.com/SpokespersonCHN/status/1516425929525972995

35. Twitter, 1 July 2022, https://twitter.com/zlj517/status/1542774878184427520?lang=en

36. Russia Condemns Potential Pelosi Visit to Taiwan as "Provocation," *The Moscow Times*, 2 August 2022, https://www.themoscowtimes.com/2022/08/02/russia-condemns-potential-pelosi-visit-to-taiwan-as-provocation-a78481

37. Putin Accuses U.S. of Fanning Asia Tension with Taiwan Visit, AUKUS Pact, Reuters, 16 August 2022, https://www.reuters.com/world/putin-western-countries-want-extend-nato-like-system-asia-pacific-region-2022-08-16/

38. China Asked Russia to Delay Ukraine Until After Olympics, U.S. Officials Say, *The New York Times*, 2 March 2022, https://www.nytimes.com/2022/03/02/us/politics/russia-ukraine-china.html

39. Press Conference, NATO, 5 April 2022, https://www.nato.int/cps/eb/natohq/opinions_194325.htm

40. Chen Qingqing, China Vows Legislation Focus on Tackling Foreign Interference, *Global Times*, 8 March 2022, https://www.globaltimes.cn/page/202203/1254350.shtml

41. Sanktsii ne povliyayut na sotrudnichestvo Rossii i Kitaya, schitayet ekspert (Sanctions Won't Effect Cooperation Between Russia and China, Expert Says), RIA Novosti, 2 March 2022, https://ria.ru/20220302/sanktsii-1775979395.html

42. Vincent Ni, Beijing Orders "Stress Test" as Fear of Russia-Style Sanctions Mount, *The Guardian*, 4 May 2022, https://www.theguardian.com/world/2022/may/04/beijing-orders-stress-test-as-fears-of-russia-style-sanctions-mount

43. Steve Holland, Trevor Hunnitcut and David Brunnstorm, U.S. Relieved as China Appears to Heed Warnings on Russia, Reuters, 3 May 2022, https://www.reuters.com/world/us-relieved-china-appears-heed-warnings-russia-2022-05-03/

44. Kylie Atwood and Katie Lillis, First on CNN: US Accuses North Korea of Trying to Hide Shipments of Ammunition to Russia, CNN, 2 November 2022, https://edition.cnn.com/2022/11/02/politics/north-korea-russia-ammunition/index.html

45. Ethan Jewell, New Photos Show North Korea Sent Weapons to Russian Paramilitary Group: US, NK News, 21 January 2023, https://www.nknews.org/2023/01/new-photos-show-north-korea-sent-weapons-to-russian-paramilitary-group-pentagon/

46. Ifang Bremer, Russia Says it Shipped Grain to North Korea, but Doesn't Say How Much, NK News, 23 January 2023, https://www.nknews.org/2023/01/russia-says-it-shipped-grain-to-north-korea-but-doesnt-say-how-much/

47. Joe McDonald, China's Russia Dealings Irk U.S., but don't Breach Sanctions, Associated Press, 1 June 2022, https://apnews.com/article/russia-ukraine-putin-china-united-states-8c2466d549f6d082d0295cf0efb635d9

48. China's Sinopec Pauses Russia Projects, Beijing Wary of Sanctions—Sources, Reuters, 28 March 2022, https://www.reuters.com/business/energy/exclusive-chinas-sinopec-pauses-russia-projects-beijing-wary-sanctions-sources-2022-03-25/

49. Huawei Faces Dilemma Over Russia Links that Risk Further U.S. Sanctions, *Financial Times*, 30 March 2022, https://www.ft.com/content/3c3c1db5–21d5–45e7–85a8-d5d25cc9ad7b

50. Marina Tyunaeva and Anastasia Kurasheva, Huawei vynuzhdena perevodit' sotrudnikov iz Rossii v Kazakhstan (Huawei is Forced to Transfer Employees from Russia to Kazakhstan), *Vedomosti*, 4 September 2022, https://www.vedomosti.ru/technology/articles/2022/09/04/939126-huawei-perevodit-sotrudnikov

51. No Military Assistance Provided to Parties Involved in Russia-Ukraine Conflict: Chinese Embassy in US, *Global Times*, 29 June 2022, https://www.globaltimes.cn/page/202206/1269299.shtml

52. Zhōngguó wòxuán wūkèlán wéijī bèi shòu zhǔmù (China's Efforts to Mediate Ukraine Crisis High Profile), CCTV, 20 March 2022, https://news.cctv.com/2022/03/20/ARTIo9m4ixqI1ED0lPwxlmjt220320.shtml

53. Ibid.

54. Russia's War on Ukraine: "It has to be China" as Mediator, EU Foreign Policy Chief Says, *South China Morning Post*, 5 March 2022, https://www.scmp.com/news/china/diplomacy/article/3169407/russias-war-ukraine-it-has-be-china-mediator-eu-foreign-policy

55. Interview with author, September 2022.

56. Interview with author, September 2022.

57. Interview with author, September 2022.

58. Zelensky: I Would Like China to Help Ukraine, Interfax, 23 September 2022, https://en.interfax.com.ua/news/general/860788.html

59. Interview with author, September 2022.

60. Interview with author, September 2022.

61. Karaganov: Eto nado pryamo nazyvat' chetvertoy otechestvennoy voynoy (Karaganov: This Should be Directly Called for the Fourth Patriotic War), Vybor Naroda, 26 September 2022, http://vybor-naroda.org/lentanovostey/227331-karaganov-jeto-nado-prjamo-nazvat-chetvertoj-otechestvennoj-vojnoj.html

62. Vincent Ni, Ukraine War Deepens China's Mistrust of the West, *The Guardian*, 6 June 2022, https://www.theguardian.com/world/2022/jun/06/ukraine-war-deepens-chinas-mistrust-of-the-west

63. Hu Xijjin, Russia a Crucial Partner in Deterring U.S., *Global Times*, 22 March 2022, https://www.globaltimes.cn/page/202203/1256525.shtml

64. Medvedev: Posle razvala Rossii SSHA zaymutsya oslableniyem Kitaya (Medvedev: After the Collapse of Russia, the United States would be Engaged in the Weakening of China), *Kommersant*, 23 March 2022, https://www.kommersant.ru/doc/5271168

65. Sanktsii protiv Rossii igrayut na ruku Kitayu? Mneniye eksperta (Sanctions Against Russia Play into the Hands of China? Expert Opinion), Sputnik Radio, 6 March 2022, https://radiosputnik.ria.ru/20220306/1776912127.html?in=t

66. Interview with author, September 2022.

67. Interview with author, September 2022.

68. Ashley Tellis, "What is in Our Interest": India and the Ukraine War, Carnegie Endowment for International Peace, 25 April 2022, https://carnegieendowment.org/2022/04/25/what-is-in-our-interest-india-and-ukraine-war-pub-86961

69. Amrit Dhillon, Why India has Not Spoken Out Against Invasion, *The Times*, 3 March 2022, https://www.thetimes.co.uk/article/why-india-has-not-spoken-out-against-invasion-pgrrx3fsr

70. Interview with author, September 2022.

71. Katrik Bommakanti, No Retreat from Russia: Strategic Autonomy and Interests are Synonymous, ORF, 9 March 2022, https://www.orfonline.org/expert-speak/no-retreat-from-russia/

72. Response to author, 24 February 2022.

73. Ibid.

74. Interview with author, September 2022.

75. Ukraine: India Strongly Condemns Bucha Killings, BBC, 6 April 2022, https://www.bbc.co.uk/news/world-asia-india-61006169

76. Interview with author, September 2022.

77. Jaishankar Refers to Afghan Situation Even as Truss Pushes India on Ukraine, *Economic Times*, 1 April 2022, https://economictimes.indiatimes.com/news/defence/jaishankar-refers-to-afghan-situation-even-as-truss-pushes-india-on-ukraine/articleshow/90581252.cms?from=mdr

78. Response to author, 8 May 2022.

79. Aftab Ahmed, India Says it is Importing Russian Oil to Manage Inflation, Reuters, 8 September 2022, https://www.reuters.com/business/energy/india-finmin-says-importing-russian-oil-part-inflation-management-2022-09-08/

80. Countering G7 Price Cap Proposal, Russia Offers Discounted Oil to India, Business Standard, 11 September 2022, https://www.business-standard.com/article/economy-policy/countering-g7-price-cap-proposal-russia-offers-discounted-oil-to-india-122091100265_1.html

81. Russia Delivers S-400 Air Defence Systems to India Pursuant to Schedule—Official Says, TASS, 16 August 2022, https://tass.com/defense/1494191

82. Interview with author, September 2022.

83. Interviews with New Delhi-based experts, September 2022.

84. Ukraine War can Hit Food Security Bid: India at the UN, *The Times of India*, 20 July 2022, https://timesofindia.indiatimes.com/india/ukraine-war-can-hit-food-security-bid-india-at-un/articleshow/92992115.cms

85. Interview with author, September 2022.
86. Ibid.
87. Rossiya-Kitay-Indiya-SSHA: slozhnoye perepleteniye «treugol'nikov Kissindzhera» (Russia-China-India-USA: The Complex Interweaving of "Kissinger Triangles"), Interfax, 17 April 2022, https://www.interfax.ru/russia/835350
88. India-Russia Explore a rupee-rouble Payment Scheme to Bypass War, Al Jazeera, 31 March 2022, https://www.aljazeera.com/economy/2022/3/31/india-russia-explore-a-rupee-rouble-payment-scheme-to-bypass-war
89. Indian Troops Join Russian Military Exercise Despite U.S. Concerns, Reuters, 1 September 2022, https://www.reuters.com/world/indian-troops-join-russian-military-exercise-despite-us-concerns-2022-09-01/
90. Anuradha Chenoy, Russia-India Relations in a Transformative World Order, Valdai Discussion Club, 20 July 2022, https://valdaiclub.com/a/highlights/russia-india-relations-in-a-transformative-world/
91. Ksenia Kondratieva, India, Russia Should Have Direct Trade and Investment Agreements, *The Hindu*, 22 June 2022, https://www.thehindu.com/news/international/sanctions-have-a-lifespan-of-2-years-says-russian-tycoon-oleg-deripaska/article65554296.ece
92. Russia Seeks Indian Investment in the Oil and Gas Sector, Reuters, 12 March 2022, https://www.reuters.com/business/energy/russia-seeks-indian-investment-its-oil-gas-sector-2022-03-12/
93. Interview with author, September 2022.
94. Happymon Jacob, Russia is Losing India, Foreign Affairs, 22 September 2022, https://www.foreignaffairs.com/india/russia-losing-india
95. Interview with author, September 2022.
96. Jacob, 2022.
97. Iranian President Tells Putin that NATO's Expansion is "Serious Threat" to Region's Stability and Security, Reuters, 24 February 2022, https://www.reuters.com/world/iranian-president-tells-putin-that-natos-expansion-is-serious-threat-regions-2022-02-24/
98. Khamenei Backs Putin in First Public Reaction to Ukraine Invasion, IranWire, 1 March 2022, https://iranwire.com/en/iran/71387/
99. "Rooted in NATO:" Iran Responds to Russia's Ukraine Attack, Al Jazeera, 24 February 2022, https://www.aljazeera.com/news/2022/2/24/rooted-in-nato-inside-irans-response-to-the-ukraine-crisis-2
100. After Phone Call with Tehran, Ukraine Foreign Minister says Iran is "Against the War," Reuters, 14 March 2022, https://www.reuters.com/world/after-phone-call-with-tehran-ukraine-foreign-minister-says-iran-is-against-war-2022-03-14/
101. Macron Reportedly Asks Iran to Mediate in Ukraine War, Mehr News,

31 August 2022, https://en.mehrnews.com/news/190878/Macron-reportedly-asks-Iran-to-mediate-in-Ukraine-war

102. President's Office Reacts to Iran's Supply of Kamikaze Drones to Russia, Kyiv Post, 24 September 2022, https://www.kyivpost.com/ukraine-politics/presidents-office-reacts-to-irans-supply-of-kamikaze-drones-to-russia.html

103. Interview with author, September 2022.

104. awekeraan: neguaha bh rashh haa jengu (Ukraine: A Look at the Roots of War), Kayhan, 13 March 2022, https://kayhan.irfa/news/237835/ اوکراین-نگاهی- به-ریشه-های-جنگ-یادداشت-روز%E2%80%8C

105. aaran baad ba terfa khewd ra der qebal jengu aberaz kened (Iran Should Express Its Neutrality Towards the War), Ensaf, 8 March 2022, http://www.ensaf-news.com/332107/ایران-باید-بی-طرفی-خود-را-نسبت-به-جنگ-اب/

106. Samuel Ramani, Russo-Iranian Alignment will Continue Despite Differences, Gulf International Forum, 23 March 2022, https://gulfif.org/russo-iranian-alignment-will-continue-despite-differences/

107. Lavrov zayavil o planakh Rossii i Irana vmeste nayti sposoby obkhoda sanktsiy (Lavrov Announced the Plans of Russia and Iran to Work Together to Find Ways to Circumvent Sanctions), Kommersant, 30 March 2022, https://www.kommersant.ru/doc/5283025

108. Dmitry Saveliev, Iran predlagayet Rossii sposob izbezhat' sanktsiy SSHA (Iran Offers Russia a Way to Avoid US Sanctions), Ura, 1 April 2022, https://ura.news/news/1052542829

109. Iran—yestestvennyy soyuznik Rossii v obkhode sanktsiy—ekspert (Iran is Russia's Natural Ally in Circumventing Sanctions), Regnum, 27 May 2022, https://regnum.ru/news/economy/3603426.html

110. Tehran Exchange Launches Trading in Iranian Rial/Rouble, Mehr News, 19 July 2022, https://en.mehrnews.com/news/189247/Tehran-exchange-launches-trading-in-Iranian-rial-ruble

111. Iran Reaffirms Opposition to Sanctions on Russia, Tasnim News Agency, 15 September 2022, https://www.tasnimnews.com/en/news/2022/09/15/2774900/iran-reaffirms-opposition-to-sanctions-on-russia

112. Golnaz Esfandiari, Will Russia's Invasion of Ukraine Derail the Iran Nuclear Deal?, RFE/RL, 10 March 2022, https://www.rferl.org/a/russia-iran-nuclear-deal-demands-invasion/31746877.html

113. Interview with senior Russian foreign ministry official, September 2022.

114. Russia Says it has Received US Guarantees over Iran Nuclear Deal, Al Jazeera, 15 March 2022, https://www.aljazeera.com/news/2022/3/15/russia-says-it-has-received-us-guarantees-over-iran-nuclear-deal

115. Interview with senior Russian foreign ministry official, September 2022.

116. Ibid.

117. Russia Eyes Iran as Sanctions-Busting Backdoor for Oil Sales, *Politico*, 23 August 2022, https://www.politico.eu/article/russia-eyes-iran-as-sanctions-busting-backdoor-for-oil-sales/

118. Bethan McKernan and Vera Mironova, Russia "Using Weapons Smuggled by Iran from Iraq Against Ukraine," *The Guardian*, 12 April 2022, https://www.theguardian.com/world/2022/apr/12/russia-using-weapons-smuggled-by-iran-from-iraq-against-ukraine

119. Pjotr Sauer, Putin Due in Tehran as U.S. Says Iran to Supply Drones to Russia, *The Guardian*, 12 July 2022, https://www.theguardian.com/world/2022/jul/12/iran-drones-russia-uav-combat-ukraine

120. Interview with author, September 2022.

121. Interview with author, September 2022.

122. Iran Sends First Shipment of Drones to Russia for Use in Ukraine, *The Washington Post*, 29 August 2022, https://www.washingtonpost.com/national-security/2022/08/29/iran-drones-russia-ukraine-war/

123. Mebarezh Ken Kheda ma Dhed (Fight God Delivers), Kayhan, 23 September 2022, https://kayhan.ir/fa/news/250148/می-خدا-بجنگید%C8%80%E2روز-رساندیادداشت

124. Marc Champion, Iranian Drones, Cheap and Plentiful, Help Russia Terrorize the port of Odesa, Bloomberg, 3 October 2022.

125. Ibid.

126. Telegram, 22 September 2022, https://t.me/milinfolive/90859

127. Interview with author, September 2022.

128. Interview with author, September 2022.

129. Telegram, 21 September 2022, https://t.me/logikamarkova/3457

130. Interview with author, September 2022.

131. Pakistani PM Khan Meets Putin Amid Ukraine Invasion, Al Jazeera, 25 February 2022, https://www.aljazeera.com/news/2022/2/25/pakistan-imran-putin-russia-ukraine-invasion

132. Ayaz Gul, Khan After Putin Visit: Pakistan to Import Wheat, Gas from Russia, Voice of America, 28 February 2022, https://www.voanews.com/a/khan-after-putin-visit-pakistan-to-import-wheat-gas-from-russia-/6463734.html

133. Ayaz Gul, Pakistan Army Chief Blasts Russia's Aggression Against Ukraine, Voice of America, 2 April 2022, https://www.voanews.com/a/pakistan-army-chief-blasts-russia-aggression-against-ukraine/6512372.html

134. Hasina Urges US to Withdraw Sanctions Imposed on Russia, *Telegraph India*, 8 July 2022, https://www.telegraphindia.com/world/sheikh-hasina-urged-the-us-to-withdraw-sanctions-imposed-on-russia/cid/1873684

135. Joshua Kurlantcizk, Vietnam Caught Between the U.S. and Russia on Ukraine, Council on Foreign Relations, 21 April 2022, https://www.cfr.org/blog/vietnam-caught-between-us-and-russia-ukraine

136. Richard Ehrlich, Russia-Thailand Ties Remain Strong Despite Ukraine, *Asia Times*, 11 April 2022, https://asiatimes.com/2022/04/russia-thailand-ties-remain-strong-despite-ukraine/

137. Benjamin Low and Munira Mustaffa, Why Some Malaysian Netizens are Pro-Russian and Support Putin, ThinkChina, 5 May 2022, https://www.thinkchina.sg/why-some-malaysian-netizens-are-pro-russia-and-support-putin

138. A.R. Zurairi, Pew Survey: Half of Malaysians View Russia Positively, with Six in 10 Feeling Putin "Doing the Right Thing" in World Affairs, Yahoo, 27 June 2022, https://malaysia.news.yahoo.com/pew-survey-half-malaysians-view-23 0000166.html

139. David Hutt, Will Laos be Sanctioned for Embracing Russia?, *Asia Times*, 27 July 2022, https://asiatimes.com/2022/07/will-laos-be-sanctioned-for-embracing-russia/

140. Chhengpor Aun, How is Cambodia Navigating the Impacts of Russia's War with Ukraine?, *The Diplomat*, 30 March 2022, https://thediplomat.com/2022/03/how-is-cambodia-navigating-the-impacts-of-russias-invasion-of-ukraine/

141. Answer of Spokesperson for Ministry of Foreign Affairs of DPRK, KCNA, 28 February 2022, http://kcna.kp/en/article/q/b18477ffa6e6e3d1152f1d-891cf105e3.kcmsf

142. Michelle Nichols, China, Russia Veto U.S. Push for More UN Sanctions on North Korea, Reuters, 26 May 2022, https://www.reuters.com/world/china-russia-veto-us-push-more-un-sanctions-north-korea-2022-05-26/

143. Severnaya Koreya pomozhet vosstanovit' Donbass (North Korea will Help Restore Donbas), Lenta.ru, 19 July 2022, https://lenta.ru/news/2022/07/19/koreya/

144. V DNR predlozhili Severnoy Koreye uchastvovat' v tribunale nad ukrainskimi voyennymi (In DNR North Korea Offered to *Participant* in the Tribunal Over the Ukrainian Military), Lenta.ru, 29 July 2022, https://lenta.ru/news/2022/07/29/severkoreya/

145. Matt Murphy, Ukraine War: North Korea Supplying Russia with Weapons, Says US, BBC, 6 September 2022, https://www.bbc.co.uk/news/world-europe-62804825

146. N Korea Denies Sending Weapons to Russia, Tells US to "Shut Up," Al Jazeera, 22 September 2022, https://www.aljazeera.com/news/2022/9/22/n-korea-denies-sending-weapons-to-russia-tells-us-to-shut-up

147. Artyom Lukin, Russia and North Korea: Moving Toward Alliance 2.0?, 38 North, 27 September 2022, https://www.38north.org/2022/09/russia-and-north-korea-moving-toward-alliance-2-0/

148. Myanmar's Military Council Supports Russia's Invasion of Ukraine, VOA,

25 February 2022, https://www.voanews.com/a/myanmar-s-military-coun-cil-supports-russia-s-invasion-0f-ukraine/6458527.html

149. Bertil Lintner, Russia's War Means Fewer Arms for Myanmar, *Asia Times*, 22 March 2022, https://asiatimes.com/2022/03/russias-war-means-fewer-arms-for-myanmar/

150. James Crabtree and Amara Thiha, Myanmar's Twin Objectives in Drawing Closer to Russia, IISS, 15 September 2022, https://www.iiss.org/blogs/analysis/2022/09/myanmars-twin-objectives-in-drawing-closer-to-russia

151. "Stronger Together:" Myanmar, Russia Parade Military Relationship, Al Jazeera, 27 March 2022, https://www.aljazeera.com/news/2022/3/27/hold-stronger-togethermyanmarrussiaparademilitary-relationship

152. Anuj Pant, Taliban Calls for Calm in Ukraine, *The Independent*, 25 February 2022, https://www.independent.co.uk/news/world/europe/ukraine-russia-tal-iban-casualties-concern-b2023250.html

153. Taliban Signs "Preliminary" Deal with Russia for Oil, Gas, Wheat, Al Jazeera, 28 September 2022, https://www.aljazeera.com/news/2022/9/28/taliban-signs-preliminary-deal-with-russia-to-buy-gas-wheat

154. Sergey Savchuk, Rossiya gotovit bol'shiye peremeny dlya Afganistana (Russia is Preparing for Big Changes in Afghanistan), RIA Novosti, 16 June 2022, https://ria.ru/20220616/afganistan-1795617516.html

155. Interview with author, September 2021.

156. Japan Condemns Russian Attack on Ukraine as Shaking Int'l Order, Kyodo News, 24 February 2022, https://english.kyodonews.net/news/2022/02/9cf5c8f99a31-japan-to-consider-natl-interest-in-shaping-ukraine-response-kishida.html

157. Joshua Walker and Hidetoshi Azuma, Shinzo Abe's Unfinished Deal with Russia, War on the Rocks, 11 September 2020, https://warontherocks.com/2020/09/shinzo-abes-unfinished-deal-with-russia/

158. Michelle Ye Hee Lee, Japan Cautiously Moves Towards Stern Response to Russia After Years of Trying to Improve Relations, *The Washington Post*, 24 February 2022, https://www.washingtonpost.com/world/2022/02/24/japan-russia-sanctions/

159. Ukraine Foreign Chief Hopeful for Further Actions by Japan, Nippon, 24 February 2022, https://www.nippon.com/en/news/yjj2022022400143/

160. Japan to Sanction Chip Exports to Russia Over Ukraine, AFP, 25 February 2022, https://www.voanews.com/a/japan-to-sanction-chip-exports-to-rus-sia-over-ukraine-/6458848.html

161. Yuka Obayashi and Marwa Rashad, Japan to Divert LNG to Europe Amid Russia-Ukraine Tension, Reuters, 10 February 2022, https://www.reuters.com/business/energy/japan-diverting-lng-europe-some-already-route-indus-try-minister-2022-02-09/

162. Southern Kurils Occupied by Russia, Japanese Foreign Ministry Official Claims, TASS, 28 February 2022, https://tass.com/politics/1412893

163. MID svyazal novyye zayavleniya Yaponii po Kurilam s politikoy SSHA (The Foreign Ministry Linked Japan's New Statements on the Kurils with U.S. Policy), RIA Novosti, 16 March 2022, https://ria.ru/20220316/mid-1778376195.html

164. Alexander Matveev, Rossiya i Yaponiya otkazyvayutsya ot mirnogo soglasheniya (Russia and Japan Reject Peace Agreement), Russian International Affairs, 23 March 2022, https://russiancouncil.ru/blogs/a-matveev/rossiya-i-yaponiya-otkazalis-ot-mirnogo-soglasheniya/

165. Russia Terminates Peace Treaty Talks with Japan—Foreign Ministry, TASS, 21 March 2022, https://tass.com/politics/1425283

166. Telegram, 22 March 2022, https://t.me/medvedev_telegram/14

167. Rogozin predlozhil pereimenovat' Kurily (Rogozin Proposed to Rename Kuril Islands), RIA Novosti, 23 May 2022, https://ria.ru/20220523/rogozin-1790267153.html

168. Japan to Take Time Phasing Out Russian Oil Imports, Says PM Kishida, Reuters, 9 May 2022, https://www.reuters.com/world/asia-pacific/japan-ban-russian-oil-imports-in-principle-pm-kishida-2022-05-08/

169. Japan Should Maintain Investments in Russian Oil and Gas Projects, CSIS, 15 June 2022, https://www.csis.org/analysis/resolved-japan-should-maintain-investments-russian-oil-and-gas-projects

170. Konstantin Dvinsky, Dostali Iz-Zemli: Zapadnym Kompaniyam Ukazali Vykhod (They Got it Out of the Ground: Western Companies Were Shown the Way Out), Tsargrad, 26 May 2022, https://tsargrad.tv/articles/iz-pod-zemli-dostali-zapadnym-kompanijam-ukazali-na-vyhod_555104

171. Konstantin Dvinsky, Yaponiya Gotovitsya K Voyne Za Kurily—Za Nash Schet (Japan is Preparing for a War for the Kurils—At Our Expense), Tsargrad, 7 June 2022, https://kemerovo.tsargrad.tv/articles/japonija-gotovitsja-k-vojne-za-kurily-za-nash-schjot_562086

172. Ex-PM Abe Compares Russia's Putin to 16th Century Japanese Warlord Oda Nobunaga, The Mainchi, 23 April 2022, https://mainichi.jp/english/articles/20220423/p2a/00m/0na/005000c

173. Japan Expands Sanctions on Russia, Bans Export of Chemical Weapons-Related Goods, TASS, 26 September 2022, https://tass.com/world/1513217

174. Justin McCurry, Japan Consul "Blindfolded and Restrained" during FSB Interrogation in Russia, *The Guardian*, 27 September 2022, https://www.theguardian.com/world/2022/sep/27/japan-consul-blindfolded-and-restrained-during-fsb-interrogation-in-russia

175. Russia's Invasion of Ukraine "Tramples" UN Charter: Japan PM, Al Jazeera,

21 September 2022, https://www.aljazeera.com/news/2022/9/21/russias-inva-sion-of-ukraine-tramples-un-charter-japan-pm

176. Terrible Logic, *Korea Herald*, 2 March 2022, http://www.koreaherald.com/view.php?ud=20220301000260

177. Ekspert prokommentiroval novyye sanktsii Yuzhnoy Korei protiv Rossii (The Expert Commented on South Korea's New Sanctions Against Russia), RIA Novosti, 7 March 2020, https://ria.ru/20220307/sanktsii-1777029950.html

178. Taiwan Dismisses Concern Ukraine Crisis Could Spill over to Asia, Bloomberg, 25 February 2022, https://www.bloomberg.com/news/articles/2022-02-25/taiwan-throws-its-weight-behind-u-s-led-sanctions-on-russia

179. Helen Davidson, "Of Course I Worry:" Shock Waves from Ukraine Reach Taiwan, *The Guardian*, 25 February 2022, https://www.theguardian.com/world/2022/feb/25/of-course-i-worry-shockwaves-from-ukraine-reach-taiwan

180. Interview with author, September 2022.

181. Taiwan's Power Utility Says Has Made Last Payment to Russia for Coal, Reuters, 24 August 2022, https://www.reuters.com/markets/commodities/taiwans-power-utility-says-has-made-last-payment-russia-coal-2022-08-24/

182. Daniel Hurst, "Pariah State": Australia Gives $70m to Ukraine Weapons Fund and Calls for Diplomatic Isolation of Russia, *The Guardian*, 1 March 2022, https://www.theguardian.com/australia-news/2022/mar/01/pariah-state-aus-tralia-gives-70m-to-ukraine-weapons-fund-and-calls-for-diplomatic-isola-tion-of-russia

183. Henry Belot, Russian Oligarchs with Business Interests in Australia Sanctioned Amid Ukraine War, ABC, 17 March 2022, https://www.abc.net.au/news/2022-03-18/oleg-deripaska-gladstone-alumina-refinery-australia-sanction/1009 20488

184. Tyrone Dalton, Ukraine Calls for More Bushmasters, Hawkeis as war with Russia Rages on, ABC, 15 September 2022, https://www.abc.net.au/news/2022–09–15/ukranian-ambassador-calls-for-more-bushmas-ters/101442472

10. THE RESILIENCE OF RUSSIA'S INFLUENCE IN THE GLOBAL SOUTH

1. Robert Plummer, Ukraine War: Russia Denies Causing Food Crisis, BBC, 25 July 2022, https://www.bbc.co.uk/news/world-middle-east-62284377

2. Kester Kenn Klomeagh, Sergey Lavrov's Working Visit to Africa, Modern Diplomacy, 24 July 2022.

3. Rasshireniye BRIKS ukrepit pozitsii organizatsii v mire, schitayet Patrushev (BRICS Expansion will Strengthen the Organisation's Position in the World,

Patrushev Believes), RIA Novosti, 15 June 2022, https://ria.ru/20220615/briks-1795510945.html

4. Interviews by author with Moscow-based experts, October 2022.

5. BRIKS i G20 khotyat sotrudnichat' s Rossiyey v Arktike, zayavili v MID (BRICS and G20 Want to Cooperate with Russia in the Arctic, Foreign Ministry Says), RIA Novosti, 15 June 2022, https://ria.ru/20220615/arktika-1795371435.html?in=t

6. Erdogan: Russia Attack on Ukraine "Heavy Blow" to Regional Peace, Al Jazeera, 24 February 2022, https://www.aljazeera.com/news/2022/2/24/erdogan-russia-attack-ukraine-heavy-blow-regional-peace

7. Diyar Guldogan, Return of Crimea to Ukraine a Requirement of International Law: Turkish President, Anadolu Agency, 23 August 2022, https://www.aa.com.tr/en/russia-ukraine-war/return-of-crimea-to-ukraine-a-requirement-of-international-law-turkish-president/2667680

8. Several NATO States Want Ukrainian Conflict to Continue—Turkish Top Diplomat, TASS, 23 August 2022, https://tass.com/world/1497045

9. Turkey not to Join Anti-Russian Sanctions—Presidential Spokesman, TASS, 26 June 2022, https://tass.com/economy/1471595

10. Sinan Tavsan, Turkey Rejects Russia's Request for Navy Ships to Pass Bosporous, Nikkei, 2 March 2022, https://asia.nikkei.com/Politics/Ukraine-war/Turkey-rejects-Russia-s-request-for-navy-ships-to-pass-Bosporus

11. Nicholas Myers, The Significance of the Turkish Straits to the Russian Navy, FPRI, 4 March 2022, https://www.fpri.org/article/2022/03/the-significance-of-the-turkish-straits-to-the-russian-navy/

12. Ragip Soylu, Ukraine Received 50 Turkish Bayraktar TB-2 Drones Since Russian Invasion, Middle East Eye, 28 June 2022, https://www.middleeasteye.net/news/russia-ukraine-war-tb2-bayraktar-drones-fifty-received

13. Turkey's Baykar Drone Company "Will Never" Supply Russia: CEO, Al Jazeera, 19 July 2022, https://www.aljazeera.com/news/2022/7/19/turkish-firm-wont-supply-uavs-widely-used-by-ukraine-to-russia

14. Turkey Sends More Humanitarian Aid to Ukraine Amid Russian Invasion, *Daily Sabah*, 21 April 2022, https://www.dailysabah.com/politics/diplomacy/turkey-sends-more-humanitarian-aid-to-ukraine-amid-russian-invasion

15. Amberin Zaman, Ukraine's Turkey Ambassador: Strategic Ties Intact but Public Unhappy Over Turkish Stance on Russia, Al-Monitor, 7 July 2022, https://www.al-monitor.com/originals/2022/07/ukraines-turkey-ambassador-strategic-ties-intact-public-unhappy-over-turkish

16. Liberal Young Flee to Turkey's "Little Russia," France 24, 18 March 2022, https://www.france24.com/en/live-news/20220318-liberal-young-flee-to-turkey-s-little-russia

17. Russians Fleeing War and Repression Seek Solace in Istanbul, DW, 2 July 2022, https://www.dw.com/en/russians-fleeing-war-and-repression-seek-solace-in-istanbul/a-62325191

18. Interview with author, September 2022.

19. Interview with author, October 2022.

20. Turkey Stops Granting Residence Permits to New Russian Arrivals—Report, The Moscow Times, 23 January 2023, https://www.themoscowtimes.com/2023/01/23/turkey-stops-granting-residence-permits-to-new-russian-arrivals-report-a80018

21. Turkey Doubles Russian Oil Imports, Filling EU Void, Reuters, 21 August 2022, https://www.reuters.com/business/energy/turkey-doubles-russian-oil-imports-filling-eu-void-2022-08-22/

22. Putin: 25% of Russian Gas Supplies to Turkey Will be Paid for in Roubles, Reuters, 16 September 2022, https://www.reuters.com/world/putin-25-russian-gas-supplies-turkey-will-be-paid-roubles-2022-09-16/

23. Erdogan Says Turkey Ready to Use S-400 Missile Systems if Need Be, TASS, 23 February 2022, https://tass.com/world/1408995

24. Contract for Delivery of 2nd Regiment of S-400 System Signed with Turkey—Russian Agency, TASS, 16 August 2022, https://tass.com/defense/1494285

25. Russia, Turkey Have no Problems Regarding Shipment of S-400 Air Defence Systems—Senator, TASS, 6 September 2022, https://tass.com/defense/1503451

26. Zaman, 7 July 2022.

27. Karen Gilchrist, Turkey May Become the New Playground for Russian Oligarchs—But it's a Risky Strategy, CNBC, 30 March 2022, https://www.cnbc.com/2022/03/30/turkey-welcomes-russian-oligarch-money-but-its-risky-for-its-economy.html

28. Amberin Zaman, Why Russia's Vladimir Putin is Rooting for Turkey's Erdogan, Al-Monitor, 13 September 2022, https://www.al-monitor.com/originals/2022/09/why-russias-vladimir-putin-rooting-turkeys-erdogan

29. Oligarch Super Yachts Avoid International Sanctions in Neutral Turkey, *Times of Israel*, 28 August 2022, https://www.timesofisrael.com/oligarch-super-yachts-avoid-international-sanctions-in-neutral-turkey/

30. Zaman, 13 September 2022.

31. Yevgeniya Gaber, Grain Drain: Why Turkey Can't Afford to Ignore Russian Grain Smuggling from Ukraine, Atlantic Council, 25 June 2022, https://www.atlanticcouncil.org/blogs/turkeysource/grain-drain-why-turkey-cant-afford-to-ignore-russian-grain-smuggling-from-ukraine/

32. Daniel Boffey, Turkey Seizes Russian Ship Carrying "Stolen" Ukrainian Grain, *The Guardian*, 5 July 2022, https://www.theguardian.com/world/2022/jul/05/ukraine-russia-turkey-ship-grain-stolen

33. Telegram, 8 September 2022, https://t.me/vladivostok1978/10665

34. Turkey Plays Down US Sanctions Threat Over Russia Ties, Euractiv, 26 August 2022, https://www.euractiv.com/section/global-europe/news/turkey-plays-down-us-sanctions-threat-over-russia-ties/

35. Lazar Berman, Jerusalem Pans Russian Attack on Ukraine: "A Grave Violation of International Order," *Times of Israel*, 24 February 2022, https://www.timesofisrael.com/jerusalem-pans-russian-attack-on-ukraine-a-grave-violation-of-international-order/

36. Lazar Berman, Bennett Refrains from Condemning Russia in First Remarks since Invasion of Ukraine, *Times of Israel*, 24 February 2022, https://www.timesofisrael.com/bennett-refrains-from-condemning-russia-in-first-remarks-since-invasion-of-ukraine/

37. Israel Envoy to Ukraine Says Killing of Civilians in Bucha Unjustifiable "War Crime," *Times of Israel*, 3 April 2022, https://www.timesofisrael.com/israel-envoy-to-ukraine-says-killing-of-civilians-in-bucha-unjustifiable-war-crime/

38. Zelensky "Shocked" by Israel's Refusal to Give Ukraine Air Defence Systems, Ukrinform, 24 September 2022, https://www.ukrinform.net/rubric-polytics/3578889-zelensky-shocked-by-israels-refusal-to-provide-ukraine-with-air-defense-systems.html

39. Israeli Intelligence "Cooperating Very Closely" With Ukraine, Top Zelensky Aide Says, *Haaretz*, 24 March 2022, https://www.haaretz.com/israel-news/2022-03-24/ty-article/top-zelenskyy-aide-israeli-intelligence-cooperating-very-closely-with-ukraine/00000180–5bba-de8c-a1aa-dbbae1f70000

40. US Calls on Israel to Join Sanctions Against Russia, Anadolu Agency, 12 March 2022, https://www.aa.com.tr/en/americas/us-calls-on-israel-to-join-sanctions-against-russia/2533070

41. Sara Serfaty, After First Call with Lapid, Zelensky Says Expects Israel to Join Russia Sanctions, *Times of Israel*, 3 September 2022, https://www.timesofisrael.com/after-first-call-with-lapid-zelensky-says-expects-israel-to-join-russia-sanctions/

42. Lapid Vows Israel Won't be a "Route to Bypass" Sanctions on Russia, *Times of Israel*, 14 March 2022, https://www.timesofisrael.com/lapid-vows-israel-wont-be-a-route-to-bypass-sanctions-on-russia/

43. Interview with Israeli expert, September 2022.

44. Daniel Schwartz, Dirty Diamonds: How Israel Helps Russia Fund its War on Ukraine, *Haaretz*, 2 October 2022, https://www.haaretz.com/israel-news/2022-10-02/ty-article-opinion/.highlight/dirty-diamonds-how-israel-helps-russia-fund-its-war-on-ukraine/00000183–8947-d91b-a7c7-af6766730000

45. Russia Sees Military Coordination with Israel on Syria Continuing Amid Ukraine Crisis, Reuters, 26 February 2022, https://www.reuters.com/world/

middle-east/russia-sees-military-coordination-with-israel-syria-continuing-2022–02–26/

46. Interview with former Soviet diplomat Viacheslav Matuzov, September 2018.

47. Gantz Says Israel Still Coordinates with Russia on Syria, Al-Monitor, 2 May 2022, https://www.al-monitor.com/originals/2022/05/gantz-says-israel-still-coordinates-russia-syria

48. Emmanuel Fabian, Russia Fired S-300 at Israeli Jets over Syria in "One-Off" Incident, Gantz Confirms, *Times of Israel*, 26 July 2022, https://www.timesofisrael.com/russia-fired-s-300-at-israeli-jets-over-syria-in-one-off-incident-gantz-confirms/

49. MID Rossii osudil udary Izrailya po Sirii (Russian Foreign Ministry Condemned Israeli Strikes on Syria), *Izvestia*, 23 August 2022, https://iz.ru/1383899/2022–08–23/mid-rf-osudil-udary-izrailia-po-sirii

50. Interview with author, October 2022.

51. Mazal Mualem, Ukraine War Pits Netanyahu Fans, Foes Against Each Other, Al-Monitor, 3 March 2022, https://www.al-monitor.com/originals/2022/03/ukraine-war-pits-netanyahu-fans-foes-against-each-other

52. Interview with Israeli security expert, September 2022.

53. Allison Sommer, Israel's Top Holocaust Institution Slams Putin's Ukraine "Denazification" Campaign, *Haaretz*, 27 February 2022, https://www.haaretz.com/israel-news/2022–02–27/ty-article/.premium/israels-top-holocaust-institution-slams-putins-ukraine-denazification-campaign/0000017f-f500-d318-afff-f763d1bf0000

54. Carrie Keller-Lynn, Netanyahu Tells Government to be Quiet on Russia and Focus on Iran, *Times of Israel*, 28 February 2022, https://www.timesofisrael.com/netanyahu-tells-government-to-be-quiet-on-russia-and-focus-on-iran/

55. Interview with Israeli security analyst, September 2022.

56. Interview with Eran Etzion, October 2022.

57. 60% of Israelis Back the Government Policy on the Russia-Ukraine Conflict—Special Survey, The Israel Democracy Institute, 25 March 2022, https://en.idi.org.il/articles/38624

58. Zelensky Asks Israel's Bennett to Play Ukraine-Russia Mediator, *Times of Israel*, 25 February 2022, https://www.timesofisrael.com/liveblog_entry/we-want-jerusalem-to-host-talks-zelensky-asks-bennett-to-play-ukraine-russia-mediator/

59. Josef Federman, Israel's Bennnett Emerges as Mediator in Russia-Ukraine War, Associated Press, 16 March 2022, https://apnews.com/article/russia-ukraine-putin-jerusalem-israel-europe-80971697a5bf5f09ec17aea4e6a9a69b

60. Daniel Shapiro, Zelensky Wants Ukraine to be "a big Israel." Here's a Roadmap, Atlantic Council, 6 April 2022, https://www.atlanticcouncil.org/blogs/new-atlanticist/zelenskyy-wants-ukraine-to-be-a-big-israel-heres-a-road-map/

61. Putin Apologizes to Israel for Lavrov's Anti-Semitic Remarks, Voice of America, 5 May 2022, https://www.voanews.com/a/putin-apologizes-to-israel-for-lav-rov-s-anti-semitic-remarks/6559586.html

62. Stasa Salacanin, Moscow's Overtures to Hamas: A Message to Israel and the US, The New Arab, 8 June 2022, https://english.alaraby.co.uk/analysis/mos-cows-overtures-hamas-message-israel-and-us

63. Rasha Abou Jalal, Hamas Appeals to Russia for Support in Confrontation with Israel, Al-Monitor, 12 April 2022, https://www.al-monitor.com/originals/2022/05/hamas-appeals-russia-support-confrontation-israel

64. Russia in Retort to Lapid: Israel Stood Silent in Face of Kyiv's "Terrorism," *Times of Israel*, 10 October 2022, https://www.timesofisrael.com/russia-in-retort-to-lapid-israel-stood-silent-in-face-of-kyivs-terrorism/?utm_source=article_hpsidebar&utm_medium=desktop_site&utm_campaign=russias-lavrov-meets-with-hamas-politburo-chief-haniyeh-in-moscow

65. Russia's Putin Welcomes Netanyahu Back to Power in Israel, Al Jazeera, 30 December 2022, https://www.aljazeera.com/news/2022/12/30/russias-putin-welcomes-netanyahu-back-to-power-in-israel

66. Cohen Passed US Messages to Russia's Lavrov During Phone Call- Israeli Diplomat, *Times of Israel*, 3 January 2023, https://www.timesofisrael.com/cohen-passed-us-messages-to-russias-lavrov-during-phone-call-israeli-diplo-mat/

67. Zelensky Advisor: Netanyahu Could be an "Effective Mediator" Between Kyiv, Moscow, *Times of Israel*, 5 January 2023, https://www.timesofisrael.com/zel-ensky-adviser-netanyahu-could-be-an-effective-mediator-between-kyiv-mos-cow/

68. Netanyahu, Zelensky Spoke Before Ukraine Skipped UN Vote on Anti-Israel Resolution, *Times of Israel*, 31 December 2022, https://www.timesofisrael.com/netanyahu-zelensky-spoke-before-ukraine-skipped-vote-on-israel-resolution/

69. Sami Hegazi, Arab League Seeks to Contribute to International Diplomatic Efforts to End Ukraine Crisis, *Daily News Egypt*, 6 June 2022, https://daily-newsegypt.com/2022/06/06/arab-league-seeks-to-contribute-to-international-diplomatic-efforts-to-end-ukraine-crisis/

70. Kamal Tabikha, Ukraine Special Envoy to Middle East Warns Arab League Against Russian Intervention, The National, 11 August 2022, https://www.thenationalnews.com/mena/2022/08/11/ukraine-special-envoy-to-middle-east-warns-arab-league-against-russian-intervention/

71. "Correction of History:" Syria President Praises Ukraine Invasion, Al Jazeera, 25 February 2022, https://www.aljazeera.com/news/2022/2/25/syrias-assad-praises-russias-ukraine-invasion-as-correction

72. Russia Recruiting Syrians for Urban Combat in Ukraine, U.S. Officials Say,

Wall Street Journal, 6 March 2022, https://www.wsj.com/articles/russia-recruiting-syrians-for-urban-combat-in-ukraine-u-s-officials-say-11646606234

73. Danny Makki, Russia-Ukraine War: Pro-Assad Syrian Soldiers Prepare to Fight for Kremlin, Middle East Eye, 16 March 2022.

74. Syria's Barrel Bomb Experts in Russia to Help with Potential Ukraine Campaign, *The Guardian*, 22 May 2022, https://www.theguardian.com/world/2022/may/22/syrias-barrel-bomb-experts-in-russia-to-help-with-potential-ukraine-campaign

75. Ukrainian Embassy Says Russia Ships "Stolen" Wheat to Syria, Reuters, 2 June 2022, https://www.reuters.com/world/europe/ukrainian-embassy-says-russia-ships-stolen-wheat-syria-2022-06-02/

76. UN Yields to Russia's Limits on Aid Mission to Syria, *The New York Times*, 12 July 2022, https://www.nytimes.com/2022/07/12/us/politics/syria-refugees-russia-un.html

77. Khaled al-Kateb, Syrian Government, Russia Escalate Attacks in Idlib Amid Looming Turkish Operation, Al-Monitor, 17 July 2022, https://www.al-monitor.com/originals/2022/07/syrian-government-russia-escalate-attacks-idlib-amid-looming-turkish-operation

78. Interview with author, October 2022.

79. Interview with author, September 2022.

80. More Russian Mercenaries Deploying to Ukraine to Take On Greater Role in War, *The New York Times*, 25 March 2022, https://www.nytimes.com/2022/03/25/us/politics/russian-mercenaries-ukraine-wagner-group.html

81. Russia Said to Pull Troops from Syria to Bolster Forces in Ukraine, *Times of Israel*, 8 May 2022, https://www.timesofisrael.com/russia-said-to-pull-troops-from-syria-to-bolster-forces-in-ukraine/

82. Russia Ships S-300 Air Defence Missiles Out of Syria—Satellite Images, Reuters, 29 August 2022, https://www.reuters.com/world/russia-ships-s-300-air-defence-missiles-out-syria-satellite-images-2022-08-29/

83. Russian Airstrikes in Syria Reported to Have Decreased Since Ukraine War, Middle East Eye, 30 September 2022, https://www.middleeasteye.net/news/syria-russia-air-strikes-decreased-ukraine-war

84. Omer Koparan, Russian Forces Conducting Air Patrol in Northern Syria, Anadolu Agency, 4 June 2022, https://www.aa.com.tr/en/europe/russian-forces-conducting-air-patrol-in-northern-syria/2605693

85. Russia Tells Iranians to Evacuate Syrian Posts After Strikes Attributed to Israel, Report Says, *Haaretz*, 2 September 2022, https://www.haaretz.com/middle-east-news/syria/2022-09-02/ty-article/russia-tells-iranians-to-evacuate-syrian-posts-after-strikes-attributed-to-israel-report/00000182-fde7-d824-a7aa-fdef0bb50000

86. Turtsiya vvodit skrytyye sanktsii protiv Rossii iz-za Ukrainy (Turkey Imposes Covert Sanctions Against Russia over Ukraine), *Vzgylad*, 24 April 2022, https://vz.ru/world/2022/4/24/1155355.html

87. Ibid.

88. Nazian Ertan, Russia Expresses "Understanding" for Turkey's Security Concerns in Northern Syria, Al-Monitor, 8 June 2022, https://www.al-monitor.com/originals/2022/06/russia-expresses-understanding-turkeys-security-concerns-north-syria

89. Mohammed Hardan, Kurdish, Syrian, Iranian Forces Coordinate Ahead of Turkish Operation, Al-Monitor, 17 June 2022, https://www.al-monitor.com/originals/2022/06/kurdish-syrian-iranian-forces-coordinate-ahead-turkish-operation

90. Russian Army Chief Meets Kurds over Turkey Tensions, Associated Press, 28 November 2022, https://apnews.com/article/russia-ukraine-middle-east-business-syria-europe-73079d87bc57d43bfa08d7b9ffde11ed

91. Interview with author, October 2022.

92. James Jeffrey and Merissa Khurma, Reactions from MENA to the Russian Invasion of Ukraine, Wilson Center, 25 February 2022, https://www.wilsoncenter.org/article/reactions-mena-russian-invasion-ukraine

93. UAE Not Taking Sides in Ukraine Conflict, Senior Official Says, Reuters, 27 February 2022, https://www.reuters.com/world/uae-not-taking-sides-ukraine-conflict-favours-negotiations-official-2022-02-27/

94. Aziz El Yaakoubi, Pavel Polityuk and Jonathan Saul, Exclusive: Russians, Ukrainians Met in UAE to Discuss Prisoner Swap, Ammonia, Sources Say, Associated Press, 24 November 2022, https://www.reuters.com/world/europe/exclusive-russians-ukrainians-met-uae-discuss-prisoner-swap-ammonia-sources-say-2022-11-24/

95. Samuel Ramani, A Middle Path for Saudi Arabia: How Does the War in Ukraine Affect Saudi Foreign Policy?, Gulf International Forum, 15 April 2022, https://gulfif.org/a-middle-path-for-saudi-arabia-how-does-the-war-in-ukraine-affect-saudi-foreign-policy/

96. The Ukraine Crisis and the Gulf: An Emirati Perspective, Institut Montaigne, 1 September 2022, http://www.institutmontaigne.org/en/analysis/ukraine-crisis-and-gulf-emirati-perspective

97. mueadalat alharb alruwsiat al'uwkrania (The Russo-Ukrainian Equation), Okaz, 8 March 2022, https://www.okaz.com.sa/articles/authors/2099237

98. Response to author, 30 September 2022.

99. Mohammed Al-Yahya, America is Dismantling the Pillars of its Own Empire—Saudi Editor to the Post, *Jerusalem Post*, 29 March 2022, https://www.jpost.com/opinion/article-702499

100. Interview with author, November 2020.

101. Arabskiye neftyaniki gotovy unichtozhit' SSHA (Arab Oilmen are Ready to Destroy the USA), RIA Novosti, 21 March 2022, https://ria.ru/20220321/neft-1779158083.html

102. V Sovfede nazvali prichiny obostreniya otnosheniy SSHA s Blizhnim Vostokom (The Federation Council Called the Reasons for the Aggravation of US Relations with the Middle East), *Izvestia*, 2 April 2022, https://iz.ru/1314552/2022-04-02/v-sovfede-nazvali-prichiny-obostreniia-otnoshenii-ssha-s-blizhnim-vostokom

103. Interview with Nikolay Kozhanov, September 2022.

104. Natasha Turak, Villas by the Sea: Rich Russians Fleeing Sanctions are Pumping up Dubai's Property Sector, CNBC, 7 July 2022, https://www.cnbc.com/2022/07/07/rich-russians-fleeing-sanctions-are-pumping-up-dubais-property-sector.html

105. Ahmed Alqarout, How the UAE Became Russia's Safe Haven for Evading Sanctions, The New Arab, 25 August 2022, https://english.alaraby.co.uk/analysis/how-uae-became-russias-safe-haven-evading-sanctions

106. Moscow Exchange to Start Trading Uzbek Sum, Armenian Dram, S African Rand June 27, Interfax, 21 June 2022, https://interfax.com/newsroom/top-stories/80455/

107. Alqarout, 2022.

108. Saeed Azhar and Yousef Saba, UAE's Mashreqbank Halts Russian Bank Loans over Credit Concerns—Sources, Reuters, 2 March 2022, https://www.reuters.com/markets/europe/exclusive-uaes-mashreqbank-halts-lending-russian-banks-sources-2022-03-02/

109. Interview with author, October 2022.

110. Qatar Investment Authority "Cannot" Abandon Russian Market, Doha News, 25 May 2022, https://dohanews.co/qatar-investment-authority-cannot-abandon-russian-market/

111. Saudi Oil Fund Invested $500 Million in Russian Oil as Ukraine Invasion Began, CNN, 15 August 2022, https://edition.cnn.com/2022/08/15/energy/saudi-arabia-russian-oil-investments/index.html

112. Response to author, August 2022.

113. Jordan is Walking a Diplomatic Tightrope on Russia's Invasion of Ukraine, Middle East Institute, 5 April 2022, https://www.mei.edu/publications/jordan-walking-diplomatic-tightrope-russias-invasion-ukraine

114. Mohammed Ersan, Syria: Why Jordan Sees Trouble in Russia's Retreat, Middle East Eye, 18 May 2022, https://www.middleeasteye.net/news/syria-jordan-russia-retreat-sees-trouble-why

115. Samuel Ramani, What Does Russia's War in Ukraine Mean for Iraq?, Middle

East Institute, 4 April 2022, https://www.mei.edu/publications/what-does-russias-war-ukraine-mean-iraq

116. Rebaz Ali, Russia Reaffirms Interest in Iraq and Kurdistan Region, Rudaw, 1 March 2022, https://www.rudaw.net/english/world/010320221

117. Lebanon Facing Wheat Crisis Amid Russia-Ukraine Conflict: President Aoun, Business Standard, 22 March 2022, https://www.business-standard.com/article/international/lebanon-facing-wheat-crisis-amid-russia-ukraine-conflict-president-aoun-122032200113_1.html

118. Hilary Kumuyu, Museveni Son Backs Russia Assault on Ukraine, Nairobi News, 2 March 2022, https://nairobinews.nation.africa/museveni-son-backs-russia-assault-on-ukraine/

119. Uganda Leader Says China-Style Diplomacy "Better than" the West's, Nikkei, 17 March 2022, https://asia.nikkei.com/Editor-s-Picks/Interview/Uganda-leader-says-China-style-diplomacy-better-than-the-West-s

120. S Africa's Ramaphosa: NATO to Blame for Russia's War in Ukraine, Al Jazeera, 18 March 2022, https://www.aljazeera.com/news/2022/3/18/update-1-s-africas-ramaphosa-blames-nato-for-russias-war-in-ukraine

121. Patrick Ryan, African Leaders Tell Forum in Dubai Why they did not Condemn Russian Invasion of Ukraine, The National, 30 March 2022, https://www.thenationalnews.com/uae/government/2022/03/30/african-leaders-tell-forum-in-dubai-why-they-did-not-condemn-russian-invasion-of-ukraine/

122. AU Chairperson Says Africa a "Collateral Victim" of Ukraine War, Al Jazeera, 25 May 2022, https://www.aljazeera.com/economy/2022/5/25/au-chairperson-says-africa-a-collateral-victim-of-ukraine-war

123. S Africa's Ramaphosa: Russia Sanctions Hurting "Bystander" States, Al Jazeera, 24 May 2022, https://www.aljazeera.com/economy/2022/5/24/update-2-s-africas-ramaphosa-russia-sanctions-hurt-bystander-countries

124. Kenyan UN Ambassador Compares Ukraine's Plight to Colonial Legacy in Africa, NPR, 22 February 2022, https://www.npr.org/2022/02/22/1082334172/kenya-security-council-russia

125. Williams Anuku, Russia Forfeited $2'bn Ajaokuta Steel Renovation Contract over war with Ukraine—Adegbite, Daily Post, 31 March 2022, https://dailypost.ng/2022/03/31/russia-forfeited-2bn-ajaokuta-steel-renovation-contract-over-war-with-ukraine-adegbite/

126. Strany Afriki i Blizhnego Vostoka pereydut na torgovlyu s RF v natsional'noy valyute (The Countries of Africa and the Middle East will Switch to Trade with the Russian Federation in National Currency), Izvestia, 25 May 2022, https://iz.ru/1340014/2022–05–25/strany-afriki-i-blizhnego-vostoka-pere-idut-na-torgovliu-s-rf-v-natcvaliute

127. Abbey Makoe, Africa Mulls How to Circumvent Western Sanctions and Leans

More to Russia, *The Sunday Independent*, 17 July 2022, https://www.iol.co. za/sundayindependent/analysis/africa-mulls-how-to-circumvent-western-sanctions-and-leans-more-to-russia-3da604bc-a6c8-4c2b-8e1e-daa5251824cd

128. Russia is Plundering Gold in Sudan to Boost Putin's War Effort in Ukraine, CNN, 29 July 2022, https://edition.cnn.com/2022/07/29/africa/sudan-russia-gold-investigation-cmd-intl/index.html

129. Declan Walsh and Valerie Hopkins, Russia Seeks Buyers for Plundered Ukrainian Grain, U.S. Warns, *The New York Times*, 5 June 2022, https://www.nytimes.com/2022/06/05/world/africa/ukraine-grain-russia-sales.html

130. Giorgio Cafiero and Emily Miliken, Russians Unlikely to Leave Libya Despite Ukraine War, Al Jazeera, 15 April 2022, https://www.aljazeera.com/news/2022/4/15/russians-unlikely-leave-libya-despite-ukraine-war

131. Interview with Libya expert Jalel Harchaoui, October 2022.

132. LNA Denies Kyiv's Allegation of Sending Mercenaries to Ukraine, The Libya Update, 21 March 2022, https://libyaupdate.com/lna-denies-kyivs-allegation-of-sending-mercenaries-to-ukraine/

133. Declan Walsh, From Russia with Love: A Putin Ally Mines Gold and Plays Favorites in Sudan, *The New York Times*, 5 June 2022, https://www.nytimes.com/2022/06/05/world/africa/wagner-russia-sudan-gold-putin.html

134. Ibid.

135. Central African Republic: Abuses by Russia-Linked Forces, Human Rights Watch, 3 May 2022, https://www.hrw.org/news/2022/05/03/central-african-republic-abuses-russia-linked-forces

136. Colum Lynch, Amy Mackinnon and Robbie Gramer, Russia Flounders in Ukraine but Doubles Down in Mali, *Foreign Policy*, 14 April 2022, https://foreignpolicy.com/2022/04/14/russia-ukraine-mali-wagner-group-mercenaries/

137. Frantsiya opravdyvayet zverstva boyevikov, chtoby diskreditirovat' maliyskiye vlasti (France Justifies Militant Atrocities to Discredit Malian Authorities), Federal News Agency, 13 April 2022, https://riafan.ru/23016992-frantsiya_opravdivaet_zverstva_boevikov_dlya_diskreditatsii_vlastei_mali

138. Jason Burke, Russian Mercenaries Accused of Civilian Massacre in Mali, *The Guardian*, 1 November 2022, https://www.theguardian.com/world/2022/nov/01/russian-mercenaries-accused-of-civilian-massacre-in-mali

139. Telegram, 1 October 2022, https://t.me/logikamarkova/3659

140. Telegram, 1 October 2022, https://t.me/Prigozhin_hat/1736

141. Kent Mensah, Ghana Says Burkina Faso Paid Russian Mercenaries with Mine, Voice of America, 15 December 2022, https://www.voanews.com/a/ghana-says-burkina-faso-paid-russian-mercenaries-with-mine-/6878119.html

142. Andrey Maslov and Dmitry Suslov, Vozvrashcheniye v Afriku: kak sdelat' eto prioritetom dlya Rossii (Return to Africa: How to Make it a Russian Priority),

Russia in Global Affairs, 10 January 2022, https://globalaffairs.ru/articles/voz-vrashhenie-v-afriku-prioritet/

143. Yuri Sigov, Afrikanskaya povestka Moskvy (Moscow's African Agenda), *Nezavisimaya Gazeta*, 15 May 2022, https://www.ng.ru/dipkurer/2022-05-15/9_8435_africa.html

144. Kak Rossiya vyvedet Afriku iz-pod vliyaniya Zapada (How Russia will Take Africa out of the Influence of the West), *Vzglyad*, 4 June 2022, https://vz.ru/politics/2022/6/4/1161521.html

145. Some Latin American Nations Call for Russian Withdrawal from Ukraine, Reuters, 24 February 2022, https://www.reuters.com/world/americas/some-latin-american-nations-call-russian-withdrawal-ukraine-2022–02–25/

146. Ivan Duque says Colombia has no Relationship with Russia After its Invasion of Ukraine, Infobae, 9 April 2022, https://www.infobae.com/en/2022/04/09/ivan-duque-says-colombia-has-no-relationship-with-russia-after-its-invasion-of-ukraine/

147. Argentina, Brazil, Mexico not Siding with OAS on Russia Statement, Mercopress, 7 October 2022, https://en.mercopress.com/2022/10/07/argentina-brazil-mexico-not-siding-with-oas-on-russia-statement

148. Jalen Small, As U.S. Popularity Declines, Putin Gains Foothold in Latin America, *Newsweek*, 25 February 2022, https://www.newsweek.com/us-popularity-declines-putin-gains-foothold-latin-america-1682702

149. Rossiya pomogayet Latinskoy Amerike v voprosakh bezopasnosti, zayavil Lavrov (Russia Helps Latin America in Security Matters, Lavrov Says), RIA Novosti, 8 October 2022, https://ria.ru/20221008/lavrov-1822446582.html

150. Ibid.

151. Putin elogia al presidente colombiano Gustavo Petro: 'Es un socio promete-dor' (Putin Praises Colombian President Gustavo Petro: "He is a Promising Partner"), El American, 21 September 2022, https://elamerican.com/putin-praises-colombian-president-gustavo-petro-he-is-a-promising-partner/

152. Interview with author, October 2022.

153. Response to author, October 2022.

154. Interview with EU diplomat, October 2022.

155. Interview with author, September 2022.

156. Petr Yakovlev, Vzaimodeystviye Rossii s Latinoamerikanshimi Stranami v Usloviyakh Geopoliticheskogo Pereloma (Russia's Interactions with Latin American Countries in Conditions of a Geopolitical Turn), Actual Problems of Europe, 2022.

157. Interview with Moscow-based academic, October 2022.

158. Xavier Medina, Kakiye strany Latinskoy Ameriki gotovy sotrudnichat' s Rossiyey v usloviyakh ekonomicheskikh sanktsiy? (Which Latin American Countries Are Ready to Cooperate with Russia Under Economic Sanctions?),

Russian International Affairs Council, 14 April 2022, https://russiancouncil.
ru/analytics-and-comments/analytics/kakie-strany-latinskoy-ameriki-gotovy-
sotrudnichat-s-rossiey-v-usloviyakh-ekonomicheskikh-sanktsiy/

159. Yakovlev, 2022.

160. Argentina Won't Impose Sanctions on Russia, says Country's Prime Minister, TASS, 24 April 2022, https://tass.com/world/1442159

161. Sanctions Against Russia Complicate Argentina's Rail Agenda, Bnamericas, 9 March 2022, https://www.bnamericas.com/en/features/sanctions-against-russia-complicate-argentinas-rail-agenda

162. V Kremle privetstvovali zhelaniye Argentiny prisoyedinit'sya k BRIKS (The Kremlin Welcomed the Desire of Argentina to Join BRICS), RIA Novosti, 27 June 2022, https://ria.ru/20220627/briks-1798508277.html

163. Interview with author, October 2022.

164. Terrence McCoy, Brazil's Bolsonaro Embraced the U.S. Under Trump. Now he's in "Solidarity" with Russia, *The Washington Post*, 16 February 2022, https://www.washingtonpost.com/world/2022/02/16/bolsonaro-putin-brazil-russia-ukraine/

165. Bolsonaro won't Condemn Putin, says Brazil will Neutral Over Invasion, Reuters, 27 February 2022, https://www.reuters.com/world/bolsonaro-wont-condemn-putin-says-brazil-will-remain-neutral-over-invasion-2022–02–27/

166. Bolsonaro Supporters Claim President Stopped war in Ukraine. He Obviously Didn't, The Brazilian Report, 15 February 2022, https://brazilian.report/live-blog/2022/02/15/bolsonaro-war-ukraine/

167. Brazil's Ex-President Lula Claims Zelensky Equally to Blame for War, *The Guardian*, 4 March 2022, https://www.theguardian.com/world/2022/may/04/brazil-lula-zelenskiy-blame-war

168. Fabiola Martinez and Roberto Garduno, México se abstendrá en votación para suspender a Rusia de organismo de ONU (Mexico Will Abstain in Vote to Suspend Russia from UN Body), *La Jornada*, 7 April 2022, https://www.jornada.com.mx/notas/2022/04/07/politica/mexico-se-abstendra-en-votacion-de-onu-para-expulsar-a-rusia-amlo/

169. At UN, Mexico Proposes a High-Level Diplomatic Delegation to Mediate Between Russia and Ukraine, United Nations, 22 September 2022, https://news.un.org/en/story/2022/09/1127731

170. Venezuela Joins Mexico's Initiative for Ceasefire in Ukraine, Telesur, 25 September 2022, https://www.telesurenglish.net/news/Venezuela-Joins-Mexicos-Initiative-for-Ceasefire-in-Ukraine-20220925–0012.html

171. Arturo Sarukhan, Lopez Obrador's Flirtation with Russia Risks Worsening US-Mexican Relations, Brookings Institution, 11 April 2022, https://www.brookings.edu/blog/order-from-chaos/2022/04/11/lopez-obradors-flirtation-with-russia-risks-worsening-us-mexican-relations/

172. AMLO: Mexico-Russia Space Agreement Won't be Used for Espionage, *San Diego Union Tribune*, EFE, 10 October 2022, https://www.sandiegounion-tribune.com/news/nation-world/story/2022–10–10/amlo-mexico-russia-space-agreement-wont-be-used-for-espionage

173. Putin Concurs with Cuban, Nicaraguan and Venezuelan Leaders on Boosting Cooperation—Lavrov, TASS, 26 January 2022, https://tass.com/politics/1393375

174. Eksperty nazvali preimushchestva i riski razmeshcheniya rossiyskikh voysk na Kube (Experts Called the Benefits and Risks of the Deployment of Russian Troops in Cuba), RBC, 14 January 2022.

175. Ibid.

176. Interview with author, October 2022.

177. Russia Ally Cuba Slams US over Ukraine Crisis, Urges Diplomacy, Reuters, 23 February 2022, https://www.reuters.com/markets/europe/russia-ally-cuba-slams-us-over-ukraine-crisis-urges-diplomacy-2022–02–23/

178. Claudia Patron, Cuban Gov Media Promotes Russia's Narrative about Ukraine, *Havana Times*, 31 March 2022, https://havanatimes.org/features/cuban-gov-media-promotes-russias-narrative-about-ukraine/

179. Nicaragua Authorizes Deployment of Russian Military Forces, Al Jazeera, 10 June 2022, https://www.aljazeera.com/news/2022/6/10/nicaragua-autho-rises-deployment-of-russian-military-forces

180. Houston Casillo Vado, Nicaragua Cuts Deal with Kremlin Station Sputnik to Air Content, Voice of America, 14 September 2022, https://www.voanews.com/a/nicaragua-cuts-deal-with-kremlin-station-sputnik-to-air-con-tent-/6747611.html

181. Russia Receives Venezuela's "Strong Support," France 24, 1 March 2022, https://www.france24.com/en/live-news/20220301-russia-receives-venezu-ela-s-strong-support

182. Phil Gunson, Venezuela's Crisis Could be Another Casualty of Russia's Ukraine Invasion, International Crisis Group, 1 March 2022, https://www.crisisgroup.org/latin-america-caribbean/andes/venezuela/venezuelas-crisis-could-be-another-casualty-russias-ukraine-invasion

183. Ukraine War: US Turns to Old Foe Maduro to Help Shut Off Russia's Oil Revenues, France 24, 9 March 2022, https://www.france24.com/en/europe/20220309-ukraine-war-us-turns-to-old-foe-maduro-to-help-shut-off-russia-s-oil-revenues

CONCLUSION

1. Russian Forces Pound Donetsk with "Greatest Brutality," Ukrainian Authorities

Say, Euronews, 7 November, 2022, https://www.euronews.com/2022/11/06/russian-forces-pound-donetsk-with-greatest-brutality-ukrainian-authorities-say

2. Zelensky Drop-In Barely Registers in Bakhmut, a "Hell on Earth," France-24, 21 December, 2022, https://www.france24.com/en/live-news/20221221-zelensky-drop-in-barely-registers-in-bakhmut-a-hell-on-earth

3. Russian Reservists Suffer "Heavy Casualties" Digging Trenches While Under Fire, *The Telegraph*, 25 November, 2022, https://www.telegraph.co.uk/world-news/2022/11/25/russian-reservists-suffer-heavy-casualties-digging-trenches/

4. Twitter, 26 December, 2022, https://twitter.com/christogrozev/status/1607 355691551064064

5. Peter Beaumont and Pjotr Sauer, "Every House is a Fortress:" Wagner Leader Counts Costs as Russia Stalls in Bakhmut, *The Guardian*, 3 January, 2023, https://www.theguardian.com/world/2023/jan/03/ukraine-wagner-leader-counts-cost-as-russian-offensive-stalls-in-bakhmut

6. Telegram, 25 November, 2022, https://t.me/Prigozhin_hat/2108

7. In Ukraine, Bakhmut Becomes a Bloody Vortex for Two Militaries, *The New York Times*, 28 November, 2022, https://www.nytimes.com/2022/11/27/world/europe/ukraine-war-bakhmut.html

8. Dmytro Guliichuk, U ZSU poyasnyly, chy spravdi 93 bryhada zalyshaye Bakhmut (The Armed Forces Explained Whether the 93rd Brigade is Really Leaving Bakhmut), TSN, 12 December, 2022, https://tsn.ua/ato/u-zsu-poyasnili-chi-diysno-93-ya-brigada-vihodit-z-bahmuta-2221282.html

9. Putin Ally Fighting to Control Salt and Gypsum Mines Near Ukraine City of Bakhmut, Says US, *The Guardian*, 6 January, 2023, https://www.theguardian.com/world/2023/jan/06/putin-ally-fighting-to-control-salt-and-gypsum-mines-near-ukraine-city-of-bakhmut-says-us

10. Voyenkor Simonov rasskazal ob operativnoy situatsii na Bakhmutskom napravlenii (Military Commander Simonov Spoke About the Operational Direction in the Bakhmut Direction), RIAFAN, 5 January, 2023, https://riafan.ru/23832647-voenkor_simonov_rasskazal_ob_operativnoi_situatsii_na_bahmutskom_napravlenii

11. Telegram, 7 January, 2023, https://t.me/Prigozhin_hat/2342

12. Telegram, 7 January, 2023, https://t.me/voenkorKotenok/44240

13. Isabel van Brugen, Russia Running Out of Troops in Battle for Bakhmut, Battalions Split Up-ISW, *Newsweek*, 28 December, 2022, https://www.newsweek.com/russia-troops-battle-bakhmut-battalions-isw-1769895

14. Russia Claims to have Broken Through Ukrainian Defences at Soledar, Ukraine Denies the Claims, Meduza, 7 January, 2023, https://meduza.io/en/news/2023/01/07/russia-claims-to-have-broken-through-ukrainian-defenses-at-soledar-ukraine-denies-the-claims

15. Telegram, 7 January, 2023, https://t.me/voenkorKotenok/44240
16. Ukrainskiye voyska v blizhaysheye vremya pokinut Soledar, soobshchayet LNR (Ukrainian Forces will leave Soledar in Near Future, According to the LNR), *RIA Novosti*, 7 January, 2023, https://ria.ru/20230107/soledar-1843381730.html
17. Telegram, 10 January, 2023, https://t.me/Prigozhin_hat/2364
18. Telegram, 10 January, 2023, https://t.me/boris_rozhin/74915
19. Marco Hernandez and Josh Holder, Defences Carved into the Earth, *The New York Times*, 14 December, 2022, https://www.nytimes.com/interactive/2022/12/14/world/europe/russian-trench-fortifications-in-ukraine.html#:-:text=The%20fortifications%20are%20designed%20to,vulnerable%20to%20artillery%20and%20missiles.&text=This%20is%20just%20a%20tiny,of%20satellite%20radar%20data%20shows.
20. Russian Occupiers Dismantle Roads and Canals to Build Fortifications in Melitopol, Ukrainskaya Pravda, 14 November, 2022, https://www.pravda.com.ua/eng/news/2022/11/14/7376293/
21. Twitter, 25 November, 2022, https://twitter.com/DefenceHQ/status/1596036164854902784/photo/1
22. Telegram, 6 December, 2022, https://t.me/strelkovii/3495
23. UK Intelligence: Russia Made Henichesk "Temporary Capital" of Occupied Parts of Kherson Oblast, *Kyiv Independent*, 15 November, 2022, https://kyivindependent.com/news-feed/uk-intelligence-russia-made-henichesk-temporary-capital-of-occupied-parts-of-kherson-oblast
24. In occupied Mariupol, Russia's Rebuild is Erasing Ukrainian Identity and any Evidence of War Crimes, Euronews, 22 December, 2022, https://www.euronews.com/2022/12/22/in-occupied-mariupol-russias-rebuild-is-erasing-ukrainian-identity-and-any-evidence-of-war
25. Telegram, 23 November, 2022, https://t.me/luhanskaVTSA/6999
26. Ukraine Missile Strike on Russian-held City of Makiivka Kills Scores of Troops, *The Guardian*, 2 January, 2023, https://www.theguardian.com/world/2023/jan/02/ukraine-strike-russian-held-makiivka-reportedly-kills-troops
27. Ibid.
28. Voyenkor Pegov: istoriya s mobil'nikami v Makeyevke ne ochen' ubeditel'na (Voenkor Pegyov: The Story of Mobile Phones in Makiivka is not Very Convincing), News.ru, 4 January, 2023, https://news.ru/russia/voenkor-pegov-istoriya-s-mobilkami-v-makeevke-ne-slishkom-ubeditelna/
29. Anger and Grief at Rare Public Commemoration in Russia after Makiivka Strike, *The Guardian*, 3 January, 2023, https://www.theguardian.com/world/2023/jan/04/anger-and-grief-at-rare-public-commemoration-in-russia-after-makiivka-strike

30. HIMARS Napadayet Na Mobilirizovannykh v Makeyevke? Chto Izvestno Na Nastoyashcheye Vremya (HIMARS Attacks in Makiivka. What is Known Currently?), Tsargrad, 1 January, 2023, https://tsargrad.tv/news/udar-himars-po-mobilizovannym-v-makeevke-chto-izvestno-k-jetomu-chasu_697187

31. Telegram, 31 December, 2022, https://t.me/olegtsarov/4583

32. Pjotr Sauer, Details of the Two Russian Military Airbases Hit by Explosions, *The Guardian*, 5 December, 2022, https://www.theguardian.com/world/2022/dec/05/details-of-the-two-russian-military-airbases-hit-by-explosions

33. Telegram, 5 December, 2022, https://t.me/grey_zone/16054

34. SSHA Prichastny k Atakam Po Rossiyskim Aeroplodam: Tspepochka Sobytiy Vypolnayetsya (US Involved in Attacks on Russia: Chain of Events Lined Up), Tsargrad, 7 December, 2022, https://tsargrad.tv/news/k-atakam-na-russkie-ajerodromy-prichastny-ssha-vystroilas-cep-sobytij_680354

35. Telegram, 5 December, 2022, https://t.me/olegtsarov/4305

36. Twitter, 4 January, 2023, https://twitter.com/Gerashchenko_en/status/1610606365784801282

37. Expect More Strikes "Deeper and Deeper" into Russia, Ukraine's Spy Chief Tells ABC News, ABC, 4 January, 2023, https://abcnews.go.com/International/expect-strikes-deeper-deeper-russia-ukraines-spy-chief/story?id=96127220

38. Hugo Bachega, Ukraine Fighting is Deadlocked, Spy Chief Kyrylo Budanov Tells BBC, 29 December, 2022, https://www.bbc.co.uk/news/world-europe-64109024

39. Ukraine's Control of P66 Highway Could Undermine Russia's Defence of Kreminna in Luhansk Region—UK Intel, 2 January, 2023, https://www.ukrinform.net/rubric-ato/3645074-ukraines-control-of-p66-highway-could-undermine-russias-defense-of-kreminna-in-luhansk-region-uk-intel.html

40. Zelensky: Peace Solutions not Including Liberation of Crimea are "Waste of Time," *Kyiv Independent*, 25 November, 2022, https://kyivindependent.com/news-feed/zelensky-peace-solutions-not-including-liberation-of-crimea-are-waste-of-time

41. Full Transcript of Zelensky's Speech Before Congress, *The New York Times*, 21 December, 2022, https://www.nytimes.com/2022/12/21/us/politics/zelensky-speech-transcript.html

42. Intelligence Chief: Ukraine Planning Major Counter-Offensive in Spring, *Kyiv Independent*, 4 January, 2023, https://kyivindependent.com/news-feed/intelligence-chief-ukraine-planning-major-counter-offensive-in-spring

43. Estonian Intelligence: Russia Never Stopped Mobilization Drive, *Kyiv Independent*, 6 January, 2023, https://kyivindependent.com/news-feed/estonian-intelligence-russia-never-stopped-mobilization-drive

44. Isobel Koshiw and Pjotr Sauer, Russia Preparing to Mobilize Extra 500,000

Conscripts, Claims Ukraine, *The Guardian*, 6 January, 2023, https://www.the-guardian.com/world/2023/jan/06/russia-preparing-mobilise-extra-500000-con-scripts-claims-ukraine

45. Ukrainian Defence Minister Claims Russia is Planning a New Mobilization, Urges Russia to Avoid it, RFE/RL, 31 December, 2022, https://www.rferl.org/a/russia-ukraine-defense-minister-mobilization-putin-war/32202105.html

46. A Looming Russian Offensive, *The Economist*, 15 December, 2022, https://www.economist.com/leaders/2022/12/15/a-looming-russian-offensive

47. Povtornyy nastup Rosiyi na Kyyiv ye nevyrishenym pytannyam—Arestovych (Russia's Repeated Offensive on Kyiv is an Unresolved Issue—Arestovych), NV, 19 December, 2022, https://nv.ua/world/geopolitics/nastuplenie-rossii-na-kiev-k-chemu-nuzhno-byt-gotovymi-arestovich-novosti-ukrainy-50291921.html

48. Russia's Ability to Mount Kyiv Offensive Questioned by Analysts, Al Jazeera, 17 December, 2022, https://www.aljazeera.com/news/2022/12/17/russian-abil-ity-to-mount-kyiv-offensive-questioned-by-analysts

49. Russia Firing Ageing Cruise Missiles Because Stocks are Depleted, MoD Suggests, *The Guardian*, 26 November, 2022, https://www.theguardian.com/world/2022/nov/26/russia-firing-ageing-cruise-missiles-because-stocks-are-depleted-mod-suggests

50. ?????

51. Ukrainian Intelligence: Russia Using More Newly Produced Missiles as Existing Stockpiles Run Low, *Kyiv Independent*, 3 December, 2022, https://kyivinde-pendent.com/news-feed/ukrainian-intelligence-russia-using-more-newly-pro-duced-missiles-as-existing-stockpiles-run-low

52. Ekspert Onufriyenko: VSU mogut popytat'sya pereyti v nastupleniye v fevrale (Expert Onufrienko: Armed Forces of Ukraine May Try to Launch an Offensive in February), RIAFAN, 5 January, 2023, https://riafan.ru/23832663-ekspert_onufrienko_vsu_mogut_popitat_sya_razvernut_nastuplenie_uzhe_v_fevrale

53. Telegram, November 20, 2022, https://t.me/agurulev/2285

54. Telegram, December 5, 2022, https://t.me/agurulev/2359

55. Alexandra Ganga, Vremya: Konstantin Sivkov O Reshayushchem Udare Rossii v Khode NMP (It's Time: Konstantin Sivkov on Decisive Blow of Russia During the NWO), Tsargrad, 25 December, 2022, https://tsargrad.tv/special_projects/pora-konstantin-sivkov-o-reshajushhem-udare-rossii-v-hode-svo_691739

56. Telegram, 25 December, 2022, https://t.me/olegtsarov/4521

57. Russia Proposes Major Military Reorganization, Conscription Changes, Increase in Troop Numbers, RFE/RL, 23 December, 2022, https://www.rferl.org/a/russia-military-reorganization-expansion/32190811.html

58. Nick Paton Walsh and Sarah Dean, Russia's Militarization of the Arctic Shows No Sign of Slowing Down, CNN, 22 December, 2022, https://edition.cnn.com/2022/12/21/europe/russia-arctic-military-intl/index.html

59. Russia Changing War Tactics Under Surovikin's Leadership—Commander of Ukraine's Ground Forces, Ukrinform, 15 December, 2022, https://www.ukrinform.net/rubric-ato/3634886-russia-changing-war-tactics-under-surovikins-leadership-commander-of-ukraines-ground-forces.html

60. Telegram, 7 December, 2022, https://t.me/strelkovii/3498

61. Oleksandr Kulbachnyi, Danilov on Surovikin's Demotion: The Next 2-3 Months will be Decisive in War, The Page, 12 January 2023, https://en.thepage.ua/news/danilov-commented-on-surovikins-demotion

62. Telegram, Grey Zone, 21 January 2023, https://t.me/grey_zone/16736

63. Ukraine to Take Part in G7 Summit, Expects Aid from U.S.—Zelensky, Following Phone Call with Biden, Interfax, 12 December, 2022, https://interfax.com/newsroom/top-stories/85987/

64. Cristian Jardan and Stephen McGrath, Power Outages in Moldova after Russian Strikes in Ukraine, Associated Press, 15 November, 2022, https://apnews.com/article/russia-ukraine-war-moldova-power-outages-edfd0a2990ee1a151e970755657ee73b

65. Russia's Defence Ministry Denies Russian Missiles Struck Polish Territory, Reuters, 15 November, 2022, https://www.reuters.com/world/europe/russias-defence-ministry-denies-russian-missiles-struck-polish-territory-2022-11-15/

66. Telegram, 15 November, 2022, https://t.me/rybar/41178

67. Telegram, 15 November, 2022, https://t.me/margaritasimonyan/12437

68. Russia Targets Only Ukraine's Military Potential-Related Infrastructure-Lavrov, TASS, 1 December, 2022, https://tass.com/politics/1544357

69. NASA pokazalo, kak Ukraina ostalas' bez elektrichestva posle rossiyskikh udarov (NASA Showed how Ukraine was Left Without Electricity After Russian Strikes), *RIA Novosti*, 19 December, 2022, https://ria.ru/20221219/nasa-1839628741.html?in=t

70. Zakharova napomnila ob obstrelakh ob"yektov infrastruktury v Yugoslavii silami NATO (Zakharova Recalled the Shelling of Infrastructure Facilities in Yugoslavia by NATO Forces), *Izvestia*, 30 November, 2022, https://iz.ru/1433393/2022-11-30/zakharova-napomnila-ob-obstrelakh-obektov-infrastruktury-iugoslavii-silami-nato

71. Telegram, 3 December, 2022, https://t.me/MariaVladimirovnaZakharova/4255

72. Twitter, 28 November, 2022, https://twitter.com/Gerashchenko_en/status/1597254844028706816?s=20&t=H0OwMZLgNvQ80ZuvDK8lgw

73. Patrick Wintour, Generators "as Important as Armour" to Ukraine Surviving Winter, says Zelensky, *The Guardian*, 13 December, 2022, https://www.theguardian.com/world/2022/dec/13/ukraine-winter-zelenskiy-generators

74. Klitschko: Kyiv's Population Returns to Pre-War Level, *Kyiv Independent*, 30 December, 2022, https://kyivindependent.com/news-feed/klitschko-kyivs-population-returns-to-pre-war-level

75. Peskov Said that the Russian Federation Strikes at Ukraine's Infrastructure Facilities with Military Potential, Interfax, 17 November, 2022, https://www.interfax.ru/russia/872938

76. Zelensky Appeals to UN Security Council Over Russian Strikes on Infrastructure, Reuters, 23 November, 2022, https://www.reuters.com/world/europe/zelenskiy-expected-address-un-security-council-meeting-russian-missiles-strikes-2022-11-23/

77. Twitter, 29 December, 2022, https://twitter.com/Podolyak_M/status/1608362511501344771

78. Telegram, 23 November, 2022, https://t.me/igor_korotchenko/11701

79. Telegram, 30 November, 2022, https://t.me/skabeeva/14803

80. Most Ukrainians Think Peace Talks with Russia Impossible, Ukrinform, 29 December, 2022, https://www.ukrinform.net/rubric-society/3643258-most-ukrainians-think-peace-talks-with-russia-impossible-poll.html

81. Telegram, 30 November, 2022, https://t.me/logikamarkova/4433

82. Telegram, 28 November, 2022, https://t.me/rybar/41555

83. Russia Revises up 2021 GDP Growth Estimate from 4.7% to 5.6%, Euronews, 30 December, 2022, https://www.euronews.com/next/2022/12/30/russia-economy-gdp

84. Sderzhannyy spros na fone neopredelennosti (Restrained Demand Amid Uncertainty), Russian Bank, 8 November, 2022, https://www.cbr.ru/about_br/publ/ddkp/longread_4_40/

85. Neft' i gaz vnov' stali osnovnymi istochnikami dokhodov byudzheta (Oil and Gas Again Became the Main Sources of Budget Revenues), RBC, 11 November, 2022, https://www.rbc.ru/economics/11/11/2022/636e39d39a794707800ae207

86. Alexandra Prokopenko, The Cost of War: Russian Economy Faces a Decade of Regress, Carnegie Moscow Center, 19 December, 2022, https://carnegieendowment.org/politika/88664

87. Olzhas Auyezov and Vladimir Soldatkin, Russia Says it May Cut Oil Output up to 7% over Price Cap, Reuters, 23 December, 2022, https://www.reuters.com/business/energy/russia-may-cut-oil-output-response-price-caps-report-2022-12-23/

88. Alex Lawson, Russian Oil Revenues Fall in November Despite Production Boost, *The Guardian*, 14 December, 2022, https://www.theguardian.com/business/2022/dec/14/russian-oil-revenues-fall-in-november-despite-production-boost

89. Florence Tan and Nidhi Verma, Russia Sends more Arctic Oil to China, India After Sanctions, Reuters, 5 January, 2023, https://www.reuters.com/business/energy/russia-sends-more-arctic-oil-china-india-after-sanctions-2023-01-05/

90. Paul Abelsky, Car Market's Turn East May Signal Russia's Economic Future,

Bloomberg, 14 December, 2022, https://www.bloomberg.com/news/articles/2022-12-14/car-market-s-turn-east-may-be-a-sign-of-russia-s-economic-future?leadSource=uverify%20wall

91. Ibid.

92. Kevin Liptak, US Believes Wagner Mercenary Group is Expanding Influence and Took Delivery of North Korean Arms, CNN, 22 December, 2022, https://edition.cnn.com/2022/12/22/politics/russia-wagner-group/index.html

93. VK, 31 October, 2022, https://vk.com/concordgroup_official?w=wall-17742 7428_1361

94. VK, 11 November, 2022, https://vk.com/concordgroup_official?w=wall-177427 428_1431

95. Telegram, 18 November, 2022, https://t.me/Prigozhin_hat/2069

96. Guy Falconbridge, Video Shows Sledgehammer Execution of Russian Mercenary, 13 November, 2022, https://www.reuters.com/world/europe/sledgehammer-execution-russian-mercenary-who-defected-ukraine-shown-video-2022-11-13/

97. Russia's Wagner Group Opens Defence Tech Center in St. Petersburg, *The Guardian*, 4 November, 2022, https://www.theguardian.com/world/2022/nov/04/russias-wagner-group-opens-defence-tech-centre-in-st-petersburg

98. Telegram, 23 November, 2022, https://t.me/Prigozhin_hat/2093

99. Telegram, 16 December, 2022, https://t.me/Prigozhin_hat/2228

100. Andrey Pertsev, He Grasps Things Very Quickly, Meduza, 15 November, 2022, https://meduza.io/en/feature/2022/11/15/he-grasps-things-very-quickly

101. Ibid

102. Telegram, 15 October, 2022, https://t.me/olegtsarov/3802

103. Telegram, 5 December, 2022, https://t.me/grey_zone/16049

104. Konstantin Sivkov: Vmesto Pobedy Nas Gotovyat k Porazheniyu Rossii? (Konstantin Sivkov: Instead of Victory, Are we Prepared for Defeat of Russia?), Tsargrad, 29 December, 2022, https://tsargrad.tv/articles/konstantin-sivkov-vmesto-pobedy-nas-gotovjat-k-porazheniju-rossii_694967

105. Patriarkh Kirill rasskazal, chto nuzhno dlya sokhraneniya pravoslaviya v Ukraine (Patriarch Kirill Told What is Needed to Preserve Orthodoxy in Ukraine), *RIA Novosti*, 7 January, 2023, https://ria.ru/20230107/ukraina-1843365727.html

106. Apparat Sovbeza RF schitayet vse boleye aktual'nym provedeniye «desatanizatsii» Ukrainy (The Apparatus of the Security Council of the Russian Federation Considers it Increasingly Urgent to Carry out the "Desatanization" of Ukraine), TASS, 25 October, 2022, https://tass.ru/politika/16150577

107. Andrew Roth and Pjotr Sauer, Putin Talks to Mothers of Soldiers Fighting in Ukraine in Staged Meeting, 25 November, 2022, https://www.theguard-

ian.com/world/2022/nov/25/putin-talks-to-mothers-of-soldiers-fighting-in-ukraine-in-staged-meeting

108. Telegram, 9 November, 2022, https://t.me/logikamarkova/4190

109. Twitter, 29 December, 2022, https://twitter.com/Gerashchenko_en/status/1608469848434311168?s=20&t=rHhT27JzhNfKgI_Vklq9Dg

110. Twitter, 10 January, 2023, https://twitter.com/Gerashchenko_en/status/1612748092364976130

111. Koshiw and Sauer, 2023

112. Telegram, 26 November, 2022, https://t.me/agurulev/2313

113. Telegram, 14 December, 2022, https://t.me/agurulev/2388

114. Medvedev napomnil o pravilakh voyennogo vremeni protiv predateley (Medvedev Recalls Wartime Rules Against Traitors), *RIA Novosti*, 8 January, 2023, https://ria.ru/20230108/zakony-1843545106.html

115. Telegram, 8 January, 2023, https://t.me/andreyklishas/1881

116. Natasha Bertrand, Kylie Atwood and Oren Liebermann, US Officials Urge Ukraine to Signal it is Still Open to Diplomatic Discussions with Russia, CNN, 7 November, 2022, https://edition.cnn.com/2022/11/07/politics/us-ukraine-diplomacy/index.html

117. Oren Liebermann, Top US General Argues Ukraine May be in a Position of Strength to Negotiate Russian Withdrawal, CNN, 16 November, 2022, https://edition.cnn.com/2022/11/16/politics/milley-ukraine-strength-russia/index.html

118. U.S. Goal in Ukraine: Drive Russians Back to Pre-Invasion Lines, Blinken Says, *The Wall Street Journal*, 6 December, 2022, https://www.wsj.com/articles/u-s-goal-in-ukraine-drive-russians-back-to-pre-invasion-lines-blinken-says-11670351786

119. Russia's Lavrov Issues Ultimatum to Ukraine: "For Your Own Good," Al Jazeera, 27 December, 2022, https://www.aljazeera.com/news/2022/12/27/russias-lavrov-issues-ultimatum-to-ukraine-for-your-own-good

120. Twitter, 8 December, 2022, https://twitter.com/Gerashchenko_en/status/1600852293309517824

121. Telegram, 14 December, 2022, https://t.me/agurulev/2388

122. Telegram, 21 November, 2022, https://t.me/obrazbuduschego2/12011

123. Russia's Medvedev warns NATO over Supplying Ukraine with Patriot Systems, Reuters, 29 November, 2022, https://www.reuters.com/world/europe/russias-medvedev-warns-nato-over-supplying-ukraine-with-patriot-systems-2022-11-29/

INDEX

INDEX

INDEX

INDEX

INDEX

INDEX

INDEX

INDEX

INDEX

INDEX

INDEX

INDEX

INDEX

INDEX

INDEX

INDEX

INDEX

INDEX

INDEX

INDEX

evacuation of civilians (2022), 147

filtration camps, 158

as 'garrison city', 387

humanitarian corridors, 146

indiscriminate violence in, 166

Kerch Strait crisis (2018), 82

Nazi occupation (1941–3), 158

maternity clinic bombing (2022), 268–9

occupation administration (2022–), 160, 195–6

reconstruction (2022), 195–6, 245, 268–9

Russian offensive (2014–22), 15, 54, 55, 56, 84

Russian offensive (2022), 2, 31, 124, 139–40, 146, 153, 155, 158, 172, 190, 256, 272

Ukrainian counter-offensive (2022), 202

theatre airstrike (2022), 124, 140

Markov, Sergei, 244, 256–7, 283, 328, 370, 399, 405

Marran, Mikk, 273

martial law, 406

Martynov, Alexey, 406

Martynov, Danylo, 135

Marzhetsky, Sergey, 139

Mashreqbank, 364

Maslov, Alexey, 340

Maslov, Andrey, 371

Maslovka, Ukraine, 105

Mastercard, 313

Masyaf, Syria, 358

Matsegora, Alexander, 333

Matveev, Ilya, 183, 347

Matviyenko, Valentina, 182, 241

Maxar satellite, 160

maximalism, 23, 58, 147, 386

May, Theresa, 85

Mayak, Transnistria, 284

McDonald's, 142

Mearsheimer, John, 5

measles, 120

Medinsky, Vladimir, 147–50

Mediterranean Sea, 80, 346, 357

Meduza, 239

Medvedchuk, Viktor, 46, 49, 56, 78, 84–5, 89, 136

arrest (2021), 100–101, 136, 170–71

citizenship, stripping of (2022), 385

prisoner exchange (2022), 360, 404

Medvedev, Dmitry

China, relations with, 316

denazification, views on, 104, 173

Donbas Republics, recognition of (2022), 111

Eurasianism, 173

Euro-Maidan revolution (2013–14), 35

Finland, relations with, 280

food, weaponisation of, 206

Georgian War (2008), 39, 111

Germany, views on, 219

Gorbachev's death (2022), 223

historical revisionism, 104

Japan, relations with, 337–8

Kazakh protests (2022), 106

martial law, views on, 406

nationalisation, views on, 142

NATO, views on, 408–9

nuclear threats, 181

Poland, relations with, 277

sanctions, views on, 63

sovereign democracy, views on, 24

Sweden, relations with, 280

Ukraine invasion (2022), 130

World War III warnings, 220

Zelensky, relationship with, 85, 104

Meeting Place, 252

Meiering, Ekaterina, 289

Mekdad, Faisal, 351

Melikov, Sergei, 243

Melitopol, Zaporizhzhia, 130, 138–9, 169, 202, 207, 245, 386, 387, 394

Melnychuk, Serhiy, 78–9

INDEX

INDEX

nationalisation, 142, 406
nationalism, 26, 143–5, 174, 404
NATO (North Atlantic Treaty
  Organization), 2, 4–6, 14, 21–2, 31,
  32, 117, 273
  Article Five, 17
  Belarus, relations with, 295
  Brinkmanship Crisis, First (2021),
    94, 96
  Brinkmanship Crisis, Second
    (2022), 105, 107–8
  Bucharest Summit (2008), 4
  China, relations with, 311–12
  Cuba, relations with, 377
  Eastern Ukraine annexations
    (2022), 249
  Finland and, 278–80, 318
  grain exports deal (2022), 209, 259
  hot peace period (2021), 98
  hybrid war, 179–80
  Kosovo mission, 293
  Latin America, relations with, 373
  Sea Breeze exercises, 36
  South Africa, relations with, 366
  South Korea, relations with, 340
  Sweden and, 278–81, 318
  Ukraine, relations with, *see*
    NATO–Ukraine relations
  Warsaw Summit (2016), 274
  weaponry, supply of, 1, 154, 176,
    191–2, 254, 333, 382, 400
NATO–Ukraine relations, 4–6, 35–6,
  73–4, 78–9, 87–8, 147, 148
  command-and-control architecture,
    73
  counterterrorism, 78
  Enhanced Opportunities Partner
    status, 87–8
  formal application (2022), 249–50
  joint exercises, 5, 73–4
  Membership Action Plan (MAP),
    35, 87
  membership prospects, 4–6, 14,
    22, 35–6, 48, 58, 87–8, 119,
    147–8, 340

public opinion and, 6, 148
  weaponry, supply of, 1, 154, 176,
    191–2, 196
  Yanukovych and, 35–6
  Zelensky and, 87–8, 119
natural gas, 64, 175, 216–19, 267,
  274, 276, 401
  Bulgaria and, 281–2
  China and, 68, 308
  crisis (2005–6), 13, 39
  Germany and, 176, 182, 274
  Japan and, 337, 338
  Moldova and, 286
  Morocco and, 367
  Naftogaz decision (2013), 37
  Nigeria and, 367
  Nord Stream 1 pipeline, 216–19,
    261, 286
  Nord Stream 2 pipeline, 17, 64,
    98–9, 112, 261, 267, 274, 286
  Pakistan and, 329
  rouble payment demand (2022), 175
  Russian–Ukrainian Action Plan
    (2013), 38
  sanctions and, 64, 98–9, 175,
    216–19, 267
  Saudi Arabia and, 364
  South Africa and, 367
  Taiwan and, 341
  Turkey and, 345, 347
Navalny, Alexei, 19, 20, 21, 39,
  40–41, 52, 93, 183, 236, 242, 289,
  346, 403
Nayyem, Mustafa, 38, 77
Nazarbayev, Nursultan, 106
Nazi Germany (1933–45), 26, 49, 83,
  121–2, 123
  Anschluss (1938), 53, 283
  Battle of Kursk (1943), 185, 386
  Battle of Kyiv (1943), 154
  collaborators, 42, 103, 125–6
  Holocaust (1941–5), 122, 125, 144
  Jewish intelligentsia in, 104
  Mariupol occupation (1941–3), 158

INDEX

INDEX

INDEX

INDEX

INDEX

569

INDEX

INDEX

INDEX

INDEX

INDEX

INDEX

Cuban Missile Crisis (1962), 318, 366

Czechoslovakia invasion (1968), 3, 11–12, 317

death penalty decree (1947), 126

decolonisation, support for, 343

dissolution (1991), 9, 23, 223, 248

East Germany protests (1953), 11

Holodomor (1932–3), 159

Hungarian Revolution (1956), 11, 317

India, relations with, 317

Molotov–Ribbentrop Pact (1939), 47

nostalgia for, 25, 145

post-war reconstruction, 173–4, 185

Shturmovshchina trap, 394

UAE, relations with, 362

Ukrainian Insurgent Army conflict (1942–56), 15, 42

Vietnam War (1955–75), 331, 334

World War II (1939–45), *see* World War II

weaponry from, 1, 73, 177, 282, 333

Sovsun, Inna, 164, 165

space, 376

Spain, 133, 271

Sparta Battalion, 233

Spasatel Vasily Bekh, 200

special military operation, 1, 3, 31, 151, 170, 178

Spetsnaz, 278

SPFS, 29, 324, 335

Spike anti-tank missiles, 350

Sputnik, 85, 144, 269, 378

Srebrenica massacre (1995), 168

Sri Lanka, 318, 330

St. George Ribbon, 125, 145

St. Petersburg, Russia, 240, 242, 245, 297, 401

St. Petersburg Economic Forum, 303, 321, 335, 344

Stalin, Joseph, 24, 25, 73, 103, 185

Starovoit, Roman, 237

Starstreak anti-aircraft missiles, 117, 177

statist self-image, 9

Steinmeier, Frank-Walter, 57, 267

Steinmeier formula (2019), 86

Stepanovka, Kherson, 256

Stinger anti-aircraft defence systems, 117, 129

Stoltenberg, Jens, 312, 394

Strandhäll, Annika, 279

Stremousov, Kirill, 159, 202, 208, 228, 230, 245, 255, 256

Strizh UAVs, 389

Struk, Volodymyr, 156

Stubb, Alexander, 278

Su-24 jets, 297

Su-34 jets, 129

Su-35 jets, 200, 328, 367

Subkh, Maksym, 355

Sudan, 12, 45, 70, 260, 355, 368, 369

Sufism, 243

SUGS, 145

Sukhovetsky, Andrey, 135

Sullivan, Jake, 250, 326, 407

Sumy, Ukraine, 118, 133

Sumykhimprom ammonia leak (2022), 118

Sunak, Rishi, 259

sunflowers, 204, 207, 208

surface-to-air missiles, 334, 389

surface-to-surface missiles, 227, 328

Surkov, Vladislav, 22, 24, 46, 61, 76, 153, 184

Surovikin, Sergei, 193, 253–4, 255, 256, 386, 394–5, 404, 405

Sushentsov, Andrey, 182

Sushko, Oleksandr, 48

Suslov, Dmitry, 50, 148, 233, 307, 316, 371

Suwałki corridor, 281

Suzdaltsev, Andrey, 206, 277

Svatovo, Luhansk, 190, 257, 386, 393

Sviatohirsk Lavra monastery, Donetsk, 194

INDEX

SVR (*Sluzhba vneshney razvedki*), 90,
111
Sweden, 27, 261, 271, 278–81, 318
SWIFT, 28, 29, 63, 140–41, 175, 181,
207, 321, 340, 368
Switzerland, 27, 63, 177
Sycheva, Yulia, 249
Syria, 3, 7, 12, 15, 68, 75, 76, 79–80,
129, 154, 158, 163, 190, 191, 241,
344, 356–9
Astana Peace Process (2016–), 324,
357, 359
barrel bombs in, 356
chemical weapons, use of, 79–80,
167–8, 356
cluster munitions in, 169
death corridors in, 158
disinformation on, 167–8
Donbas Republics, recognition of
(2022), 356
Eastern Ukraine annexations
(2022), 249
false flag conspiracy theories, 140
GCC, relations with, 362
Iran, relations with, 70, 324, 329,
357, 358–9, 364
Israel, relations with, 351–2
Moskva operations, 156
Orthodox Church and, 81
Revolution (2011), 40
Surovikin in, 253–4
Turkey, relations with, 70, 346, 357,
358
UNGA Resolution ES-11/1 (2022),
28
UNGA Resolution 68/262 (2014),
45
US oil seizure plan (2019), 213
VKS jets in, 129
Wagner Group in, 29, 80, 235, 237,
358
Syriza, 64, 268
Syrskyi, Oleksandr, 394
System Capital Management, 48

Sytii, Dmitry, 403
Szijjártó, Péter, 272

T-62 tanks, 234
T-72 tanks, 177
T-80 tanks, 230
T-80BV tanks, 235
T-90M tanks, 235
Taco LLC, 300
Taiwan, 32, 303, 306, 310, 311, 337,
340–41
Tajikistan, 3, 28, 67, 303
Tal Rifat region, Syria, 357, 358, 359
Taliban, 306, 332, 335–6
Talipo V, 234
de Tambèla, Apollinaire Kyélem, 370
Tambov, Russia, 236
tanks, 16, 82, 87, 94, 169, 176–7,
230, 234, 391
Taran, Sergiy, 38
Tarantsov, Dmitry, 373
Tasheva, Tamila, 240
Tatars, 45, 239–40, 345
Tchaikovsky, Pyotr, 178, 277
TCS Group, 184
teachers, 159–60
technology imports, 174, 337, 340,
341, 401
Telegram
anti-war movement and, 145
Battle of Bakhmut, 384
Battle of Severodonetsk, 189
Central Asia and, 302
civilian infrastructure attacks and,
399
Dagestani networks, 243
demilitarization, discourse on, 115
Donbas offensive, 153, 185
Dugina assassination (2022), 221,
223
genocide and, 164
Girkin on, 185, 232
Grey Zone, 302, 404
Holmogor Talks, 232

INDEX

INDEX

INDEX

INDEX